THE AMAZON JOUR

OF ROGER CASEME

To Gertrude Bannister
"Gee"

THE AMAZON JOURNAL OF ROGER CASEMENT

EDITED AND WITH AN INTRODUCTION BY

ANGUS MITCHELL

Moyra Hinds —
With best wishes
from the editor
Angus Mitchell
Cushendun
2/xi/97

LONDON
ANACONDA EDITIONS

First published by Anaconda Editions Ltd 1997
in association with The Lilliput Press, Dublin

Anaconda Editions Limited
84 St Paul's Crescent, London NW1 9XZ
web-site: http://www.anaconda.win-uk.net/
email: editions@anaconda.win-uk.net

British Library Cataloguing in Publication Data

Casement, Sir Roger
The Amazon journal of Roger Casement
1. Casement, Sir Roger – Diaries 2. Casement, Sir Roger – Journeys – Amazon River Region 3. Amazon River Region – Social conditions
I. Title II. Mitchell Angus
981.1'05'092

ISBN 1 901990 00 1 pbk
1 901990 01 X hbk

Printed and bound in Great Britain by
Redwood Books, Trowbridge, Wiltshire

CONTENTS

MAPS

PREFACE

In November 1993 I was commissioned by a London publisher to write a book about the Putumayo atrocities — an all but forgotten episode in the disastrous annals of the Amerindian tribal experience at the hands of the Western world. The events of this genocide remained in the public eye between 1909 and 1914. Besides being a well-documented aspect of the long, tragic, extermination of the Amazon Indian, what gave the telling of this story a peculiar interest were the documents that stood at the centre of the narrative, the infamous *Black Diaries of Roger Casement*. In March 1994 those diaries were finally released into the public domain under the Open Government Initiative, and it was something of a surprise to discover that three of the four *Black Diaries* dealt in the most part with Casement's voyages into the Amazon to investigate the Putumayo atrocities in 1910 and 1911. For the next two years I steadily gathered relevant documentation and puzzled over what happened long ago in the darkest forests of South America. Though I was aware of the accusations of some Irish historians claiming that the *Black Diaries* were forged, my initial belief in their authenticity rested upon the opinions expressed by official British history, Casement's recent biographers and current orthodoxy among anthropologists.

In April 1995, after returning from a three-month trip across northern Peru and down the Amazon, I signed a further publishing contract to co-edit "Casement Diaries" with Dr Roger Sawyer, whose biography *The Flawed Hero* contains the fullest bibliography on Casement and was of invaluable service to my own research. It was our intention to publish diary material that had never before been published, including the most explicit diary of all, the 1911 *Letts's Desk Diary*. Permission was obtained from the Parry family, Casement's most direct relatives, to publish the documents.

In the summer of 1995 I spent six weeks at the National Library of Ireland (N.L.I) in Dublin going through two large metal boxes containing Casement's personal papers relevant to his consular career in Brazil and his part in the Putumayo atrocities. Among them was the massive manuscript of his Putumayo Journal and a number of fragmentary diary entries describing other parts of his voyage. Perhaps because of the sheer size of this archive it had been almost wholly overlooked. During my last week of work at the N.L.I. my understanding of the Putumayo atrocities had to be seriously revised as I began to have grave doubts about the authenticity of the *Black Diaries*. There was, quite simply, too much documentation that did not add up and too much to suggest that Casement had been the victim of a brilliant, though sinister, scheme hatched by British intelligence to prevent him attaining martyrdom upon his execution for treason in 1916. It was also clear that Casement's biographers had only touched the surface of his Amazon investigations. When I returned to London I began to make my own investigations into the authenticity of the documents and was forced to investigate the rumours surrounding the *Black Diaries*. In October 1995 over one hundred and seventy closed Casement files were opened twenty years early, also under the Open Government Initiative, and after eighty controversial years the Casement affair was effectively exorcized by the British government. But an ensuing correspondence in *The Irish Times* showed that though the British press was unequivocal in its portrait of Casement as the "Gay Traitor" there was still a strong lobby of Irish opinion that was not prepared to let the matter rest.

The breakdown in the Anglo-Irish peace process in early 1996 seemed to bring a reaction to the mounting interest in what might politely be called republican elements in Irish history. The book I had originally intended to write no longer reflected my understanding of Casement's life. It was clear that if Casement's reputation was ever going to be cleared of the defamation it had undergone, it was necessary for his genuine writings to speak for themselves. What mattered was the publication of his own narrative through the reconstruction of his own chronicle built from what remains of his own genuine journals and letters. Only by printing primary material and showing how it differed from the *Black Diaries* might this deeply entrenched lie about the man be cleared up and the opinion, conjecture and straightforward lies surrounding his character be historically exposed.

My attitude to the *Black Diaries* also changed. There now seemed no need to publish them unless one wished to throw oil on the fire. They have poisoned the reputation of Casement and muddied the waters of South American history. To publish them only serves to inspire more hatred and create more public confusion over a serious issue. Perhaps least of all do they serve the gay community or merit a place in twentieth-century homosexual literature. They were manufactured in an age when acts of homosexuality were considered sexually degenerate. Whoever wrote the diaries had a desire to portray Casement and homosexuality as a sickness, perversion and crime for which a person should suffer guilt, repression, fantasy, hatred and, most of all, alienation and loneliness. These are not the confessions of a Jean Genet or Tennessee Williams, W.H. Auden or Oscar Moore. Rather than sympathizing with the struggle of the homosexual conscience, they are clearly homophobic documents.

After three years' work it also became clear that the Putumayo atrocities were a far more complicated and detailed affair than I had ever imagined. The whole "economy" of wild rubber that boomed between 1870 and 1914 gave rise to two of the worst genocides in the history of both Africa and South America — genocides that were a well-kept secret at the time and have been overshadowed by the even greater horrors wrought subsequently this century. Some of the horror the world has witnessed in the last few years in Rwanda, Burundi and Zaire (formerly the Congo Free State, renamed as the Democratic Republic of Congo), the war that continues in the frontier regions of the north-west Amazon, even the murder of Chico Mendes and the execution of Ken Saro-Wiwa are all historically rooted in the horrors committed in the Congo and Amazon in the collection of rubber a century ago. The African writer Chinua Achebe has said that "Africa is to Europe as the picture is to Dorian Gray", and though South America is a more peaceful continent than Africa, the Amazon basin remains one of the most brutalized ends of the earth where the last significant community of Amerindian people is being forced to live out its apocalypse.

It is hoped that the publishing of *The Amazon Journal of Roger Casement* will stimulate deeper awareness of the historical tragedy, as well as confirm his place as a great humanitarian. It is also hoped that those who are prone to confuse rhetoric for evidence, biography for history or official history for truth might now come to know the facts for themselves.

My work on this subject has been helped by many friends, friends of friends and librarians. In England my thanks are due to the staff at The British Library; Public Record Office at Kew; British Library of Political and Economic Science; Rhodes House Library, Oxford; the Bodleian Library, Oxford and especially to Dr Jeremy Catto at my old college, Oriel.

In South America, to the former Spanish Consul Carlos Maldonado in Lima; Alejandra Schindler and Joaquín García Sánchez at the Biblioteca Amazónica in Iquitos; to the staff at the Biblioteca Amazónica in Leticia. In Brazil to the highly co-operative staff at the Archivo Público in Belém do Pará and Manaos and at the Palacio Itamaraty, Rio de Janeiro. It should be said that Iquitos, Leticia and Belém have three of the most beautiful libraries in which I have had the pleasure to work.

At the National Library of Ireland I must extend a special thanks to Gerard Lyne of the manuscripts department, who threw so much revealing light on the whole subject; to Father Ignatius at the Franciscan Library Killiney; to Séamus Ó'Síocháin and his wife Etáin at Maynooth; to Margaret Lannin at the National Museum of Ireland, who was so helpful in tracing the various indigenous artefacts that Casement brought back from the Amazon.

Among correspondents I must thank Maura Scannell for her effusive botanical knowledge, Michael Taussig, Father James McConica, Sir John Hemming, Ronan Sheehan, Veronica Janssen, Andrew Gray, Jack Moylett, Eoin Ó Maille, Howard Karno and the antiquarian book dealer Arthur Burton-Garbett. Miriam Marcus led me through the critical labyrinth of Conrad and the heart of darkness debate and proof read the script. John Maher kept me on the historical level and did vital work in perfecting the final draft.

But my greatest debt of thanks must extend to Carla Camurati, who supported me with a loyalty and belief which was utterly Brazilian, and gave me peace of mind in the highlands of Brazil to get quietly on with my work.

My father did not live to see the publication of this book — but his own humanitarian achievement in setting up the HALO Trust (Hazardous Areas Life-Support Organization), which by the time of his death on 20 July 1996 had become the largest mine-clearing charity on earth, was a great inspiration to many besides myself. I hope that the diffusion of these papers, which I trust will reveal the real Roger Casement, will help in the historical understanding of Casement the man and of the complicated relationship between Britain and Ireland. Casement would have deplored any continuing bloodshed. Equally intolerable would have been the hypocrisy that continues to guide so much international foreign policy where "trading interest" is given priority over human interest.

ANGUS MITCHELL
Sitio Ajuara, Albuquerque
Brazil 1997

ABBREVIATIONS

A.P.S.: Aborigines Protection Society
A.S.A.P.S.: Anti-Slavery & Aborigines Protection Society
B.B.: Blue Book
B.D.P and F.: *Brewer's Dictionary of Phrase and Fable*
D.V.: *Deo volente* — By God's will
F.L.K.: Franciscan Library Killiney
FO: Foreign Office
HO: Home Office
H.S.I.: Handbook of South American Indians
LSE: London School of Economics
N.L.I.: National Library of Ireland
N.A.I.: National Archive of Ireland
O.G.I.: Open Government Initiative
P.A.Co: Peruvian Amazon Company
PRO: Public Record Office — Kew
P.P.: Puerto Peruano
R.H.: Rhodes House
S/P: Peruvian Sol

GLOSSARY

Alvarenga: Amazon river craft.
Amazindian: Collective name for the tribes of the Amazon basin.
Arroba: A measure of weight equal to 32 lb, or 14.75 kilograms.
Batalon: Small Amazon river craft.
Blancos: Hispanic whitemen.
Borracha: Rubber.
Caboclo: A person of Indian or mixed Indian and white heritage.
Cachaça: Sugar-cane alcoholic spirit.
Cacique: Tribal chief.
Caboclo: Literally "copper-coloured" applied to an Indian.
Cafuzo: Offspring of Indian and Black.
Cepo: Stocks.
Chacara: Planted land.
Cholo: A person of Indian heritage.
Chorizo: Sausage-shaped bale of rubber.
Correría: Premeditated attacks on tribal communities in order to enslave.
Cushmas: Long skirts worn by the Indian slave women.
Delegado: Delegate.
Empleados: Subservient Company employees.
Estradas: Forest pathways.
Fabrico: Rubber season normally lasting seventy-five days.
Farinha:Flour.
Maloca: Widely used Amazonian term to describe Indian thatched dwelling.
Montaña: Name for the forested eastern foothills of the Andes descending towards the Amazon basin.
Muchachos de Confianza/Muchachos: Confidence boys — armed Indian quislings used by the Chiefs of Section to kill and torture.
Pamalcari: Name given to the thatched roof that covered part of smaller Amazon river craft.

Puesta: A rubber delivery — one *fabrico* (rubber season) might be broken up into five *puestas* (deliveries).
Quebrada: Waterfall.
Racionales: Employees of the company able to read and write.
Rapaz: Colloquial Portuguese for "chap" or "bloke".
Seringueiro: Brazilian term for rubber tapper equivalent to Peruvian *cauchero*.
Sernamby: Poor quality rubber.
Tula: Large woven frame used for carrying rubber.
Veracucha: Local Huitoto word for the whiteman.
Veradero: Forest path.

PART ONE

THE DIARIES CONTROVERSY

— Well, says J.J., if they're any worse than those Belgians in the Congo Free State they must be bad. Did you read that report by a man what's this his name is?
— Casement, says the citizen. He's an Irishman.
— Yes, that's the man, says J.J. Raping the women and girls and flogging the natives on the belly to squeeze all the red rubber they can out of them.
— I know where he's gone, says Lenchan, cracking his fingers.
— Who? says I.

James Joyce, *Ulysses*

Sir Roger Casement (1864–1916), the humanitarian and Irish revolutionary, was put on trial at the end of June 1916 on a charge of High Treason against the British Crown. He had served the British state as a conscientious consul in both Africa (1895–1904) and South America (1906–13), until his resignation from the Foreign Office in the summer of 1913 when he began to devote his energies to the cause of Irish freedom. At the end of October 1914 British intelligence got wind of Casement's efforts to bring about a German–Irish alliance. Despite efforts to undermine his activities, it was not until April 1916 that he was eventually arrested on the beach at Banna Strand in County Kerry, on the south-west coast of Ireland, hours before the outbreak of the Easter Rising in Dublin.

On the fourth and last day of his trial for treason, an exchange took place in court between the Attorney-General, Sir Frederick Smith — leading the prosecution counsel — and the Chief Justice, which referred publicly for the first time to "Casement's diary".[1] It is the earliest recorded public mention of such documents. The "Casement diaries" have become the most taboo documents in Anglo–Irish relations. Casement was an indefatigable writer, and diaries and diary fragments in various forms have been preserved to this day in both England and Ireland. The question of whether

[1] Verbatim Report of trial and appeal pp. 201–202 HO 144/1636 — Chief Justice: "Mr Attorney, you mentioned a passage in the diary. Is there any mention as to whose diary it is?"
Attorney-General: "It was a diary. I will give your lordship the evidence of it. It was a diary found."
Chief Justice: "I know, but as far as my recollection goes there was no further evidence beyond the fact that it was found. Whose writing it is, or whose diary it is, there is no evidence."
Attorney-General: "I do not think I said it was the diary of any particular person. I said 'the diary'. By 'the diary' I mean the diary which was found, and it is in evidence as having been found."
Chief Justice: "I thought it right to indicate that, because it might have conveyed to the jury that it was Casement's diary. There is no evidence of it."
Attorney-General: "You have heard, gentlemen, what my lord has said. If there was any misunderstanding I am glad it should be removed. It was a diary found with three men as to whom I make the suggestion that they had all come from Germany. There is no evidence before you as to which of the three the diary belonged, but whoever kept the diary made the note that on 12 April, the day the ticket was issued from Berlin to Wilhelmshaven..."

he wrote the pornographic diaries, known as the *Black Diaries,* is a matter that still rankles over eighty years after his execution. Many Irish and others continue to believe that Casement was the victim of British Intelligence. Now that the documents are in the public domain historians should be able to make more balanced conclusions about the private character of this very extraordinary man.

When rumours about Roger Casement's "sexual degeneracy" began to percolate among newspapers, politicians, ambassadors and gentlemen's clubs in July 1916, those who had known him most closely found it hardest to believe. The coteries of intellectuals and friends who had known the man personally had never had a whiff of any kind of impropriety. But in that dark, apocalyptic summer of 1916 it was doubtless reconciled in the minds of most, that a man capable of co-operating with Germany — and who had himself admitted to treason — was capable of anything.

In the month between his trial and execution, as the battle of the Somme raged on the Western Front, no less than six petitions were raised urging the government to grant a reprieve. But on 18 July a Cabinet Memorandum made reference for the first time to the *Black Diaries*. It alleged that the documents clearly showed that Casement "had for years been addicted to the grossest sodomitical practices".[2] Material circulated at the highest government level in both Britain and the United States wholly undermined the campaign for clemency and successfully prevented[3] Casement from attaining martyrdom.[4] The intellectuals, humanitarians and those

[2] Cabinet Memorandum HO 144/1636/311643/3A — dated July 15, circulated at Cabinet meeting on July 18: "Casement's diaries and his ledger entries, covering many pages of closely typed matter, show that he has for years been addicted to the grossest sodomitical practices. Of late years he seems to have completed the full circle of sexual degeneracy, and from a pervert has become an invert — a 'woman' or pathic who derives his satisfaction from attracting men and inducing them to use him..."

[3] In March 1922 Michael Collins began a correspondence with Casement's brother, Tom, about "a matter that I cannot write about — or at least is so lengthy as to make it difficult for me to write about it." The precise nature of the "matter" was never made clear but the correspondence between the two men opens N.A.I D/Taoiseach S9606 — Roger Casement Diaries.

[4] It is not clear exactly who was shown diary material, either photographed extracts or typed copy. Copies were seen by King George V, John Redmond, a number of representatives of the British and U.S. press, the American Ambassador Sir Walter Page, the Rev. John Harris (on behalf of the Archbishop of Canterbury, Dr Randall Davidson), Sir William Wiseman [see letter HO 144/23454]. The Home Office did, however, admit in March 1994 at the time of the release of the *Black Diaries* that

of high public standing who had gathered round Casement were completely confused by the accusations. Though most did not believe it, there was little they could do. Early in the morning on 3 August 1916 Casement was hanged.

THE SECRET LIFE OF THE BLACK DIARIES

In 1921 the prosecutor in Casement's trial, the Lord Chancellor Sir F.E. Smith, later First Earl of Birkenhead, showed certain diaries, purported to be by Roger Casement, to the Sinn Fein leader Michael Collins: the first occasion on which an independent Irish witness was shown the documents. Collins claimed he recognized Casement's handwriting — a judgment that apparently satisfied Irish opinion. Nevertheless, access was closed to the diaries. Not long before his death in 1935 T. E. Lawrence tried to obtain access to the diaries, as he toyed with the idea of writing a biography of Casement, but his request was denied and without seeing them he understood the book was worthless. His view of Casement, nevertheless, is interesting:

> Casement. Yes, I still hanker after the thought of writing a short book on him. As I see it, his was a heroic nature. I should like to write upon him subtly, so that his enemies would think I was with them till they finished my book and rose from reading it to call him a hero. He has the appeal of a broken archangel. But unless the P.M. will release the 'diary' material, nobody can write of him. Do you know who the next Labour P.M. might be? In advance he might pledge himself, and I am only 46, able, probably, to wait for years: and very determined to make England ashamed of itself, if I can.[5]

In the 1930s the first two Casement biographies appeared. Denis Gwynn wrote *Traitor or Patriot: The Life and Death of Roger Casement* (1931) and G. Parmiter published *Roger Casement* (1936). Both biographers remained almost silent on the subject of the secret diaries. Parmiter's few thoughts on the matter are reflective of the darkness in which the mystery had been shrouded:

> While the appeal was pending there began to appear rumours which have persisted to the present day. These rumours took the form of imputations against Casement's moral character, although for a long time they were never openly

---

is probable that the Intelligence services began their campaign against Casement well in advance of his capture.

[5] Quoted in Malcolm Brown (ed.), *The Letters of T.E. Lawrence* (J.M.Dent 1988). The letter of mid-December 1934 to Charlotte Payne-Townshend, wife of George Bernard Shaw, is held in the British Library.

made. They made their way through the smoking rooms of clubs into ordinary conversation, and have latterly found their way into print.

The story that was put about was that Casement for many years led a life of gross moral perversion, and it was said that there was in existence a diary, in the possession of Scotland Yard, which was nothing more than a record of indecencies committed in London, Paris, Putumayo. Eventually there appeared photographic copies of pages of this diary which emanated, unofficially, from Scotland Yard. Those of Casement's friends who saw these reproductions had no doubt but that the diary was in Casement's handwriting. These photographic copies had a considerable circulation and even found their way to America. This propaganda to blacken Casement's moral character had considerable effect and alienated a large amount of sympathy from him.

While Parmiter had little doubt that the diaries were "propaganda", such accusations were more directly aimed in 1936 when an Irish-American academic, Dr William Maloney, published the daringly titled book *The Forged Casement Diaries*, in which he openly accused the ascendant nationalist faction in the coalition War Cabinet of 1916, along with high-ranking members of British intelligence, of forging the diaries. He revealed how the alliance between British Naval Intelligence led by Captain (later Admiral) 'Blinker' Hall and the Assistant Commissioner, London Metropolitan Police, Sir Basil Thomson,[6] had both the motive and the expertise to devise the forgery and how everyone including the Prime Minister, Herbert Asquith, became party to this conspiracy to expose Casement as a "degenerate". W.B. Yeats contributed his song "Roger Casement" and poem "The Ghost of Roger Casement", and a party of "forgery theorists" was born.

George Bernard Shaw, in a letter to the *Irish Press* of 11 February 1937, made an interesting comment about attitudes current in 1916:

The trial occurred at a time when the writings of Sigmund Freud had made pschopathy grotesquely fashionable. Everybody was expected to have a secret history unfit for publication except in the consulting rooms of the psychoanalysts. If it had been announced that among the papers of Queen Victoria a diary had been found

---

[6] Thomson, Sir Basil Home (1861–1938), is the man credited with discovering the *Black Diaries*. Thomson was born in Queen's College, Oxford, and brought up at Bishopthorpe, Yorkshire, after his father's appointment as Archbishop of York. Following Eton and Oxford, Thomson entered the Colonial Service and at the age of twenty-nine became Prime Minister of Tonga. In 1913 he was made Assistant Commissioner, Metropolitan Police, and Director of Intelligence (1919–21). In 1925 he was dismissed from the post after a breach of public decency laws. He wrote over thirty books of fiction and history, including a scholarly introduction and edition of Hernan Gallego's sixteenth century text under the title, *The Discovery of the Solomon Islands*. His five conflicting accounts of how he "discovered" the *Black Diaries* continue to this day to confound the matter.

revealing that her severe respectability masked the day-dreams of a Messalina it would have been received with eager credulity and without the least reprobation by the intelligentsia. It was in that atmosphere innocents like Alfred Noyes and Redmond were shocked, the rest of us were easily credulous; but we associated no general depravity with psychopathic eccentricities, and we were determined not to be put off by it in our efforts to obtain a pardon. The Putumayo explanation never occurred to us.

A few days later, on 17 February Irish President Eamon de Valera was asked if he would take the matter of the diaries up with the British government, "No Sir," he replied, "Roger Casement's reputation is safe in the affections of the Irish people." But behind the scenes an internal memorandum drafted by the Irish Department of External Affairs for de Valera showed that despite the government's non-intervention, they were clearly deeply suspicious of the diaries.

Whatever may be the view of the present generation in Ireland regarding Roger Casement, it must not be forgotten that history has often been built on statements which to the generation concerned were obvious lies but which by clear distortion, combined with persistent propaganda, have in time been accepted as historical facts.[7]

The renewal of the world war saw the controversy rest until the 1950s when the matter was raised once again in Parliament,[8] forced by the claims of a new generation of forgery theorists. The historian Dr Herbert Mackey published a number of books arguing foul play. The poet Alfred Noyes, who was attached to the British FO during the First World War and was prominent in circulating the Casement slanders, argued in *The Accusing Ghost — Justice for Casement* (1957) the most coherent case as to why he now accepted the diaries as forged. But despite their emphatic arguments, the idea that the British intelligence would have gone to such lengths to destroy Casement seemed unlikely.

In 1959 the long spell of secrecy over the contents of the *Black Diaries* was finally lifted with their lavish publication in Paris, outside the jurisdiction of the British Crown, by the Fleet Street newspaperman, Peter Singleton-Gates, and the publisher of cen-

[7] N.A.I. D/Taoiseach S9606 — Roger Casement Diaries.

[8] On 3 May 1956 questions about the "authenticity" of the diaries were raised by the Unionist MP for Belfast, Lt-Col. Montgomery Hyde, but requests that the British Government should set up an independent enquiry and investigate the matter were turned down because (a) it would once again stir up political passions and (b) it might be unfair to Casement — "There is a fundamental principle that no official disclosure should make it possible for anyone further to blacken the memory of a man who has been imprisoned and hanged."

sored material, Maurice Girodias. In his Foreword to the book, Singleton-Gates related how:

In May 1922 a person of some authority in London presented me with a bundle of documents, with the comment that if ever I had time I might find in them the basis for a book of unusual interest. The donor had no ulterior motive for wishing such a book published; his gift was no more than a kind gesture to a journalist and writer.[9]

But Singleton-Gates's efforts to publish the diaries had been prevented in 1925 by the Home Secretary, Sir William Joynson-Hicks, and his Chief Legal Adviser, Sir Ernley Blackwell, under the Official Secrets Act. The publication of the *Black Diaries,* as they were now christened, seemed to endorse the genuineness of the documents. From 10 August 1959 the Home Secretary permitted historical researchers to see manuscript material which generally corresponded with Singleton-Gates's faulty published text. Despite considerable interest in the British and Irish press the only effort at anything near a scholarly analysis was a short essay by an Irish academic, Roger McHugh, published in a small Belfast-based magazine *Threshold*[10] in 1960. McHugh cast a number of well-argued aspersions over the legitimacy of the documents. He threw doubt on the serious discrepancies between the PRO diaries and eyewitness accounts of material exhibited in 1916 as Casement's diary. He highlighted several suspicious internal discrepancies and contradictions. He demonstrated how the chronology of the diary campaign, establishing their alleged discovery was part of a wartime propagandist intelligence initiative against Casement launched well before his arrest. Finally, he analysed how official accounts of the provenance of the *Black Diaries* were mutually contradictory.

Although McHugh's arguments were never properly refuted, once access to the *Black Diaries* had been granted there followed

---

[9] In 1995 it became clear that Singleton-Gates had acted as a "front" for the Head of Special Branch, Sir Basil Thomson, and that it was Thomson who handed Singleton-Gates the typescripts of the *Black Diaries* following his dismissal from New Scotland Yard. See HO 144/23425/311643/207. Letter from Brigadier General Sir William T.F. Horwood, Commissioner of the Metropolitan Police, to the Rt Hon. Sir John Anderson, Permanent Under-Secretary at the Home Office — 21 January 1925. This revelation about Singleton-Gates raises questions about the role of the British press and publishers in authenticating the *Black Diaries*. Discussions with former friends and colleagues of Maurice Girodias suggest, however, that he was not privy to Singleton-Gates's secret.

[10] *Threshold*, "Casement — The Public Record Office Manuscripts" Summer 1960 No. 4 Vol 1.

three considered biographies of Casement. Each one accepted almost without question the "authenticity" of the *Black Diaries* — and none of the biographers made the slightest effort to make any historically based scientific analysis of the documents themselves or refute McHugh's scholarly evaluation. Instead they preferred to base their judgments on the confused, often conflicting maze of circumstantial evidence surrounding the appearance of the documents and the "official" statements that apparently backed up their authenticity. Certainly, as the social taboos about homosexuality began to break down following the sexual revolution of the sixties and the implementation in 1967 of the 1957 Wolfenden Report recommendation in favour of the legalization of homosexuality between consenting adults, Casement's "treason" and "homosexuality" were attractive characteristics for biographers and publishers looking to sell books.

Casement's life was interpreted in terms of paradoxes — he was seen as a "fragmented and elusive" character, but nevertheless as a man capable of protecting native peoples on while quietly "perverting" them to satisfy his mounting sexual libido. His sexuality mirrored his treason, and his ambivalent and contradictory character extending from "emotional deprivation, religious uncertainties, the duality of his political commitments" was bound up with his "sexual perversion" and homosexuality.

The Irishman and former editor of *The Spectator*, Brian Inglis, published *Roger Casement* (1973) and tried to place his subject within the context of other well-known homosexuals — André Gide, Marcel Proust, Oscar Wilde. His argument against the forgery theory was brief but adamant:

> Nevertheless the case against the forgery theory remains unshaken. No person or persons, in their right mind, would have gone to so much trouble and expense to damn a traitor when a single diary would have sufficed. To ask the forger to fake the other two diaries and the cash register (and if one were forged, all of them were) would have been simply to ask for detection, because a single mistake in any of them would have destroyed the whole ugly enterprise. Besides, where could the money have been found? Government servants may sometimes be unscrupulous, but they are always tight-fisted.

In *The Lives of Roger Casement* (1976) Benjamin Reid took a more psychoanalytical approach and analysed Casement in terms of Freudian personality conflicts — a man who was "at ease with his anus". He tried "to look at the character of the man behind the great events in which he was involved". Casement was seen as the "fearless hypochondriac", the "fanatic traitor" and "fanatic patriot". In two lengthy appendices, Reid tried to prove the "authenticity" of the *Black Diaries* and rightly stated that to accept the fact that Casement was a "practising homosexual" it was necessary "to accept the diaries as genuine, for it is there that nearly all the evidence lies". Roger Sawyer, the most recent biographer, accepted the results of an "ultra-violet" test carried out before Singleton-Gates and another well-known witness, that established "without any doubt" that the diaries were "entirely in Casement's own hand". The results and nature of this test have not yet been released and in the light of what is now known about Singleton-Gates's special relationship with Basil Thomson, Sawyer's emphatic argument in favour of Casement's "disease" is hard to accept.

With these three biographies the case seemed to rest. The *Black Diaries* were generally accepted as genuine and Casement's official portrait eighty years after his death was no longer that of the sufferer of "sexual degeneracy" who had been hanged for treason, but of a "gay traitor", a confused, ambivalent figure, a lonely and misguided idealist, worn out by years spent defending primitive peoples in tropical climes. Whilst his humanitarian work in Africa and South America was seen as the greatest human rights achievement of his age, his character was seen as "flawed" due to his treacherous support of Germany, his eleventh hour conversion to the Catholic Church and his sexuality, as detailed cryptically in the *Black Diaries*.

While Casement's last biographers considered that they had understood the inner character of their subject, they failed to get to the heart of the vast amount of diaries or journal material scattered between the Public Record Office (PRO) in Kew, the National Library of Ireland (N.L.I.), Rhodes House, Oxford (R.H.) and the Franciscan Library Killiney (F.L.K.). To some extent their efforts were thwarted by the fact that they were forbidden to make photocopies of the documents. It was also the case that the documentation dealing with Casement's life is immense and is scattered in archives across the world. Moreover, the *Black Diaries* dealt in the main with Casement's South American consular career, which, though certainly an important chapter of his life, was overshadowed by his two decades in Africa, his involvement in the Irish republican movement and his trial and execution.

Following the release of the material constituting the *Black Diaries* in March 1994 and over one hundred and seventy closed Casement files in October 1995 the whole matter of "Casement's diaries" was effectively deemed to be history. In anticipation of the release, and to coincide with the acceptance in Ireland of the status of homosexuality, the BBC produced a short radio programme weighted heavily in favour of the validity of the *Black Diaries*. A handwriting expert spent a day comparing material in both London and Dublin and satisfied himself that "the bulk of handwriting ... is the work of Roger Casement".[11] To its detriment, the programme failed to make any mention of a new generation of forgery theorists who had been lobbying the BBC for some time to look into the whole matter of the *Black Diaries* in the light of their own revelations.

The controversy over the *Black Diaries* persisted and the lengthy correspondence in *The Irish Times* (between October 1995 and June 1996) showed just how confused the whole subject remained. For the historian it might best be sorted out by first of all listing the different extant diaries and relevant documentation available to researchers. Let us begin with the documents whose authenticity is most in doubt.

PHYSICAL DESCRIPTION OF THE DIARIES

The *Black Diaries* consist of five hard-back books of varying size contained in a dark green security box in the Public Record Office at Kew. The first item, known as the *Army Book*[12] — a small field-service notebook — is an apparently innocuous document with the first entry referring to the death of Queen Victoria and brief entries between 6 and 13 February 1902 and a short account of Casement's movements on 20 and 21 July when he was travelling in the Belgian Congo. It holds no obvious sexual references and is filled with a few abstract notes about distances and railway times, transcriptions from foreign newspapers and two rough sketch maps.

---

[11] "Document: The Casement Diaries" — BBC Radio 4, 23 September 1993. The handwriting expert was Dr David Baxendale, who had many years' experience working for the Home Office. With regard to the 1911 *Letts's Diary*, Baxendale stated that "the bulk of the handwriting in there is the work of Roger Casement", while in the diaries in which it was alleged there had been interpolations he stated that "the handwriting of all the entries which were of that nature correspond closely with Mr Casement's handwriting". Opinion of hand-writing experts, though it may help satisfy public opinion, is not generally considered in academic circles to be reliable evidence.

[12] HO 161/1

The first sex diary, as such, is a small *Letts's Pocket Diary and Almanac*[13] — covering the months of Casement's investigation into the Congo from 14 February 1903 to 8 January 1904 with a few notes added at the beginning and end. It is written mainly in black ink with a minimum number of entries in pencil. There are two days per page except Saturday, which has a single page. The pages for January have been torn out. The diary records sexual acts in London, the Congo, Madeira, the Canary Islands and Sierra Leone, mainly with native boys.

The next diary is the *Dollard's 1910 Office Diary*,[14] interleaved with pink blotting paper. This diary appears to correlate with Casement's movements as he left his post as Consul-General at Rio de Janeiro in February 1910 and journeyed by boat back to England via Argentina. The main body of this diary, however, coincides with Casement's first voyage to the Amazon at the end of July 1910 and continues uninterrupted until the end of the year. Entries are in both pen or pencil with a few isolated words and expressions in bold blue crayon, while a number of leaves of blotting paper have been written on. There are three days per page and no space for a Sunday entry. Sex or sexual fantasies occur in Rio de Janeiro, São Paulo, Mar del Plata, London, Belfast, Dublin and, with most frequency, up the Amazon at Belém, Manaos, Iquitos and in the Putumayo. The original is extremely messy and has been corrected, written over, crossed out — a fact that is not immediately identifiable from the microfiche. There are also several variant styles of handwriting.

The *1911 Letts's Desk Diary* — the document that has never been published and is the most explicit and pornographic in its content — follows on directly from the last entry for 31 December in the *1910 Dollard's Diary* as Casement arrived in Paris for the New Year of 1911.[15] Rebound in green buckram, this document has been

[13] HO 161/2 — The complete text with minor alterations was reproduced in the Olympia Press publication of *The Black Diaries*.

[14] HO 161/3 — Also reproduced in the Singleton-Gates/Olympia Press edition of 1959.

[15] HO 161/4 — has never been published although excerpts appeared in H. Montgomery Hyde, *Famous Trials: The Trial of Sir Roger Casement* (Penguin 1964). In another publication, *A History of Pornography*, Montgomery Hyde wrote of the *Black Diaries*: " ... the descriptions of homosexual acts which they contain are undoubtedly the frankest which have ever appeared in an open English publication." Although Montgomery Hyde is best known as an author and barrister he also had a distinguished career as a British Intelligence officer and Unionist MP for North

heavily restored. Once again the majority of the diary is written in black ink and pen. The first three days of the week are on one page, the last four on another and this diary too is interleaved with blotting paper. At the beginning are four pages of notes or memoranda in a variety of handwriting styles and written in black ink and pencil, transcribing innocuous quotes from Peruvian newspapers or passages copied from works on the flora and fauna of the Amazon. They mirror the variant styles of handwriting adopted elsewhere in the diary. After day by day entries for the first eighteen days of January, as Casement spent New Year in Paris before returning to London after his first Amazon voyage, there is a rough (unidentified) sketch covering a page in February, and a very untypical signature "Sir Roger Casement CMG" opposite May, the month Casement received news of his knighthood. After that the diary is blank until 13 August when the entries resume and detail the movements that coincide with Casement's second voyage up the Amazon to Iquitos and into the Brazilian-Peruvian frontier region of the river Javari. During this journey the sexual references are almost of daily occurrence and of the most plainly explicit nature. Long, cryptic entries of fantasy mix with nights of exceptional sexual athletics and endless descriptions of cruising along the waterfronts of Pará, Manaos and Iquitos. The most explicit entry takes place on Sunday 1 October, the start of the pheasant-shooting season in England. By this account the diarist did little on this journey except fantasize and seek out willing sexual partners or seduce under-age boys at every opportunity. After a short stay in Iquitos and an expedition to try and arrest some of the fugitive slave-drivers, the document details the return down the Amazon to Pará and then north back to Barbados. At the end are a couple of pages of figures detailing expenditure during the voyage. 1911 was in a number of ways a year of great changes for Casement. The knighthood he received for his humanitarian work, and specifically for the success of his investigation into the Putumayo, turned him into an internationally respected figure and a household name throughout the empire. Behind the scenes it was the year when he began to publish his anti-British propaganda essays, and to record the reasons for turning his back on loyalty to the empire.[16]

Belfast (1950–59) — whether such a combination of public posts made him a suitable voice to "authenticate" the diaries is open to question.

[16] A number of these essays were published in Herbert O. Mackey (ed.), *The Crime Against Europe: The Writings and Poetry of Roger Casement* (C.J. Fallon Ltd. 1959).

The last diary, known as the *Cash Ledger*,[17] is a record of daily accounts written in a blank hardback cash book. It briefly records "Expenditure" for February and March 1910 and then begins a day-by-day account of financial outgoings for 1911, from 1 January to 31 October. At the end there are a few more brief entries about 1910. There is a photograph of Casement's baby godson, Roger Hicks, glued to the inside front cover. It is written almost wholly in pen, and a number of sexual references look as if they have been interpolated into the text. The portrait of Casement revealed by this document is utterly contrary to the image of Casement presented by genuine reports, letters and memoranda that have survived. In the seven months that Casement spent in Britain between his two Amazon voyages, he was certainly working on a number of different levels but rather than sexual they are better described as anti-imperial. In the first months his priority was the writing of his substantial reports on the Putumayo atrocities which he delivered on St Patrick's Day. In the subtle wording of these reports he clearly laid the blame for the outrages against the Putumayo Indians on rampant capitalism. After delivery to the FO he devoted his time to the Morel Testimonial, and the deepening rift in Anglo–Irish affairs. From what can be reconstructed of his movements, activities and views during these months, Casement was starting to see the whole problem of slavery and ethnocide in a global dimension. He began to ally his own crusade in the Putumayo with the Mexican revolution and the overthrow of Diaz and his alliance with American business. Despite his knighthood, his views were becoming actively extreme. Behind the scenes he put pressure on not only humanitarian groups but both the Anglican and Roman Catholic Churches to support his action. He lobbied several MPs to persuade the Foreign Office itself to act. He directly attacked the Monroe Doctrine and American interference in both Mexico and South America. The

---

The earliest, "The Keeper of the Seas", written in August 1911, shows that Casement's anti-British attitudes partly derived from his experiences on his 1910 voyage into the Amazon when he first began to realize the damage wrought by the "white man's civilization" and English "trading interests". Casement's propaganda writings are another aspect of his life that have been overlooked by biographers, though they clearly show him to have been both a competent historian and something of a political visionary as well as one of the most active anti-imperialists of his time.

[17] HO 161/5. This document was printed as an appendix in the first edition of Singleton-Gates's *The Black Diaries*.

ledger serves as a sinister mask obscuring Casement's emerging revolutionary character.

The physical characteristics of the *Black Diaries* vary significantly from the journal that Casement kept during his 1910 Amazon voyage and whose authenticity has never been doubted. This document is written on one hundred and twenty-eight unbound loose leaves of lined, double-sided foolscap and covers the period from 23 September to 6 December 1910, the seventy-five days that Casement spent travelling through the Putumayo and his return to and departure from Iquitos. It is the document that is variously referred to as the "white diary" or "the cleaned-up version", since it does not contain any sexual acts or fantasies. For the purposes of clear identification in this argument it is referred to as the Putumayo Journal[18] and it forms the bulk of Casement's *Amazon Journal* reproduced in this volume.

Besides the manuscript version of this document there is a typescript version, also in the possession of the National Library of Ireland,[19] bound in two volumes of green buckram. There have been a few basic corrections in pencil to some spellings in this typescript, apparently in the hand of Casement, otherwise it is a pretty accurate copy of the manuscript. Also held among the Casement Papers at the N.L.I. are a number of fragmentary diary entries[20] covering both of Casement's voyages into the Amazon during 1910 and 1911. These fragmentary entries are written on the same double-sided foolscap in pencil in the manner of his Putumayo Journal and are written in the same open and naturally fluent style. They, too, do not contain any sexual references and despite their fragmentary nature often appear to be part of a much larger document.

The other important diaries that should be described are Casement's *German Diaries*.[21] Beginning on 7 November 1914, they record Casement's efforts at the outset of the First World War to

---

[18] MS 13,087 — [25]. This is held among the Casement Papers at the N.L.I. and has uninterrupted daily entries from 23 September to 6 December 1910.

[19] MS 1622/3. This document of 408 numbered pages does in fact amount to 414 pages.

[20] There are fragmentary entries for the following days: August 24/26/27/28/30; a letter dated 5 September headed "To be part of my diary"; September 10/11/12/17; fragments of a conversation with O'Donnell at Entre Rios on 25 October 1910; December 20. Recording his 1911 voyage up the Amazon to Iquitos there are fragmentary entries for November 4/9/11/16/27/28/29/30; December 1/5/6.

[21] MS 1689 and MS 1690 — Two notebooks 21 x 16cm.

recruit an Irish Brigade from among captured Irish prisoners of war in Germany. These diaries consist of two black hardback notebooks at the N.L.I. and are not a day-to-day record but written sporadically in both pen and pencil with some German newspaper articles glued into them. A later, more complete, section of this diary can be found at the Franciscan Library Killiney. This is a photographed document of one hundred and thirty-two pages — running between 17 March and 8 April 1916 —[22] which, from the content of the document, is indisputably a copy of Casement's *propria manu*. It is unclear where the original might be found, if, indeed, it survives. It appears, however, to be photographed from loose leaves of paper.

It should also be noted that there is one "diary extract" held at Rhodes House, written in black ink in Casement's own hand.[23] These four pages have been directly copied from Casement's manuscript Putumayo Journal. These extracts were apparently copied by Casement at the end of 1912 and sent to Charles Roberts, the chairman of the Parliamentary Select Committee Enquiry set up to investigate the atrocities. They tell us little except that Casement did refer to his genuine Putumayo Journal whenever he needed. Also at Rhodes House is Casement's lengthy correspondence with Charles Roberts talking about his diary and a two-page document titled "Casement's Diary Index of Marked Passages" which collates with the (top) typescript of the Putumayo Journal held in the National Library of Ireland. The title of this document, however, indicates that it refers to another (bottom) copy of the same typescript where some relevant passages had been marked. There is no trace of this copy and it is probably lost.

The only other documents that are central to assessing the "authenticity" of the *Black Diaries* are the voluminous Foreign Office files held at the Public Record Office in London.[24] In these files are found the official narrative of events and dozens of letters and memoranda sent by Casement to the Foreign Office regarding his Putumayo investigation.

---

[22] Franciscan Library Killiney — Eamon de Valera Papers File 1335.
[23] MSS Brit Emp S22 [G 335] — *Extracts from my diary* — p. 70 Saturday 29 October 1910 at Chorrera. These deal with Casement's visits to the store at Chorrera and his conversations with the one wholly British employee of the Company, a Mr Parr.
[24] FO Putumayo Files are as follows: FO 371 / 722; 967–968; 1200–1203; 1450–1454; 1732–1734; 2081–2082.

PROVENANCE

The provenance of both the *Black Diaries* and the Putumayo Journal is often confusing to trace accurately but it is important in establishing their authenticity to try and ascertain when they were first seen or described in the form we know them now, and if they are likely to have passed through the hands of British intelligence. We know that five trunks of Casement Papers were seized by Scotland Yard at some point between late 1914 and April 1916. These trunks were later returned to Casement's cousin, Gertrude Bannister (Mrs Sidney Parry), via George Gavan Duffy, Casement's solicitor,[25] although what documentation was retained by Scotland Yard and never returned will never be known.

The *Black Diaries* are engulfed in a cloud of confusion and conflicting statements as to their origins. How or when they came into the possession of Special Branch in the form they have now has never been made clear and is only confused by the five directly contrary declarations[26] of the Assistant Commissioner of New Scotland Yard, Sir Basil Thomson, the man who claimed to have "discovered" the *Black Diaries*. Permission has never been granted to examine Scotland Yard's records of the process of search and seize — it is anyway unlikely that they would reveal much. What is clear is that there was no clear description of the five bound volumes held today in the PRO until Roger McHugh described them in 1960 and even the Cabinet Memorandum that first gave official recognition to the diaries is indirect in its description and refers to "typed matter".

Early in May 1916, Captain Reginald Hall of Naval Intelligence, "called a number of press representatives and showed them what he identified as photographic copies of portions of Casement's diaries describing homosexual episodes".[27] A little later

---

[25] PRO HO 144/1637/311643/178. This material constitues a list of Casement property which was returned to his next of kin. Although we know from this list what was returned, it does not inform us what was not kept by the authorities only to be subsequently destroyed. the large amount of missing documentation dealing with Casement's Putumayo Journal is discussed elsewhere in this study.

[26] Sir Basil Thomson's five conflicting statements as to how the *Black Diaries* came into his possession are well known and therefore not repeated. See Singleton-Gates *op. cit.*, pp. 21–25.

[27] I have stuck here to the story as told by Reid in *The Lives of Roger Casement* p.382. Henry Nevinson tells a different story in *Last Changes Last Chances*: "Early in June, a member of the Government had called various London editors together,

the diaries were shown by Hall to a representative of the Associated Press, Ben S. Allen.[28] In a statement, Allen later described the manuscript he had been shown by Hall:

It was a rolled manuscript which Hall took from a pigeon-hole in his desk ... The paper was buff in colour, with blue lines and the sheets ragged at the top as if they had been torn from what, in my school days, we called a composition book. The paper was not quite legal size.[29]

Another possible witness to the physical state of the *Black Diaries* was the secretary of the Anti-Slavery Society, the Rev. John Harris. Harris sent a petition to the Foreign Office on behalf of Casement's humanitarian colleagues the day after the 18 July Cabinet memorandum and made six clear points as to why the humanitarian lobby doubted the accusations of moral misconduct. The points of the petition are worth reiterating:

1. Casement's whole life and conduct was a perpetual and vigorous protest against the prevailing immorality.

---

and informed them that in searching among Casement's papers they had discovered a diary, alleged to be in his handwriting, though his name did not occur upon it; and this diary was held to prove that for some years he had been addicted to 'perversion' or 'unnatural vice'."

[28] "Hall showed it to me at first at the conclusion of the regular Wednesday weekly interview with the American correspondents, and told me the Associated Press could have it for exclusive publication if it wished it ... The diary was in manuscript in what I recall as finely written in the handwriting of a person of culture and originality.

I told Hall that, while the A.P. was not interested in scandal for its own sake, because of the importance of the individual and the events in which he was playing such an important role, we might use it. However, I told him it must be authenticated completely before we would use it, and I saw only one way of doing so, and that was by permitting me to show it to Sir Roger Casement then in Pentonville. If he were to acknowledge it as authentic I would then submit the document to my chief in the London Bureau of the A.P. Hall neither assented to nor denied this request, but replaced the manuscript in his desk.

For several weeks thereafter he showed me the diary repeating the offer, and on each occasion I made the same stipulation ... Late in the negotiations Hall showed me some typewritten excerpts from the diary, evidently designed to illustrate the innuendo of perversions. Nothing in the copy I read showed anything except the ravings of the victim of perversions.

I recall my horror at those revelations. I cannot recall that any vigorous effort was made to press the diary on me, but the effort was repeated several times, and it was stated that the contents were of such significance that its publication would prove of great news interest. After the execution of Sir Roger the subject was dropped and I heard of the diary only casually until several years after."

[29] Statement held in the N.L.I.

2. Habitual immorality would have been impossible without the knowledge of his associates.
3. To our knowledge Casement was scrupulously careful to do nothing which might at any time compromise his public work in this respect.
4. In all Casement's journeys and work, he had been accompanied by reputable Englishmen who would have promptly discovered any such depravity and turned from him with loathing. Not one of these men has ever suggested, so far as we know, that Casement was other than a most lofty-minded person, and, furthermore, these are, we believe, amongst those who find the allegations most incredible. This incredulity is based not merely on Casement's character but on the grounds of the impracticability of secretly living such a life in the tropics.
5. At no other time either in Africa or South America have the enemies of Casement cast the shadow of suspicion upon his moral conduct, although in the Putumayo they did not hesitate to do so with reference to a British Officer. Both in Africa and in South America conditions were such that friends and enemies would quickly have discovered any such lapse.
6. If the allegations in the "diary" are in Casement's handwriting, clearly accusing himself of these practices and are not translated extracts from the documents of third parties, then it is submitted that they constitute proof of mental disease.

(a) It is unthinkable that a man of Casement's intelligence would under normal circumstances record such grave charges in a form in which they might at any time fall into the hands of his enemies.

(b) Is it not a fact known to medical science that certain mental diseases often take the form of self accusation of those things which normally the sufferer most loathes?

Within hours of presenting his petition Harris was called to the Home Office and on 19 July, in a letter to the Archbishop of Canterbury, he described that meeting, but referred to the diaries in the vaguest of terms:[30]

---

[30] HO 144/1636/311643/3a. This is a copy of the letter sent to Sir Ernley Blackwell for HO records.

Sir Ernley Blackwell placed everything before me yesterday at the Home Office, and as a result, I must admit with the most painful reluctance that Sir Roger Casement revealed in this evidence is a very different man from the one up to whom I have looked as an ideal character for over fifteen years.

My distress of mind at this terrible revelation will I am sure be fully appreciated by your Grace. The only consolation is that there appears to be no certain evidence that these abominable things were practised in the Congo — it may be that our presence checked them.

Equally unidentifiable is the nature of the "diary" offered by the Attorney-General, Sir F.E. Smith, to Casement's defence counsel in the days before the trial so that they might plead a case of "Guilty but insane". The only person to see this diary was the most junior member of Casement's defence counsel, Mr Artemus Jones, who had been chosen by Casement's prosecutor, the Attorney-General. Jones described the document handed to him by the Attorney-General as "a number of typewritten sheets, bound with covers of smooth brown paper. The text was in the form of a diary, the entries being made on different dates, and at various places, including Paris, also towns in Africa, and South America (the names of which would be well known to those familiar with Casement's activities in the Congo and Putumayo)".[31]

To conclude from eyewitness statements made about diary material in the weeks between Casement's arrest and execution, it is not possible directly to marry the "diary material" that was photographed and circulated in 1916 or described by independent witnesses at the time of Casement's trial with the *Black Diaries* held in the PRO today. If we accept Singleton-Gates's word, then the typed copies that came into his possession in May 1922 (excluding the *1911 Letts's Desk Diary*) were copied from the diaries held in Sir Basil Thomson's safe at Scotland Yard. Singleton-Gates also

[31] Artemus Jones conveyed this in a letter to Dr Maloney (quoted in Singleton-Gates); the letter continued: "Most of the entries related to trivial personal matters, common to diaries. At intervals appeared the passages to which the Crown attached importance in the event of the defence putting in a plea of insanity. In these the diarist describes acts of sexual perversion he had committed with other men.

As the document had been handed over for the purpose of being shown to Sullivan, I deemed it my duty to keep it locked up in the chambers until he arrived in London. I did not show it, for that reason, either to Professor J.H. Morgan or to the solicitor instructing the defence, Mr Gavan Duffy.

The fact of its existence, however, was known to both. On Sullivan's arrival in chambers I gave him the verbal message from the Attorney-General, and at the same time I took out the document from the drawer. Sullivan's reply was: 'There is no question of our pleading guilty. I don't see what on earth it has to do with the case. I don't want to read it — give it them back'."

describes being shown two of the original diaries by Sir Wyndham Childs, Thomson's successor at Scotland Yard — although he was only shown one Letts's diary, presumably the *Letts's Pocket Diary* for 1903, as well as the *Dollard's 1910 Diary*.

The *1911 Letts's Desk Diary* remained something of a mystery until its release in 1994. A typescript of this diary was not handed over to Singleton-Gates along with the other papers he received from Sir Basil Thomson. Nothing was known about this document until the first published description including brief excerpts appeared in 1960 in H. Montgomery Hyde's *The Trial of Sir Roger Casement*. But the published extracts only hinted at the true nature of this document. Biographers too have seemed reluctant to scrutinize this document too closely, since it unequivocally portrays Casement as both a pederast and obsessive fantasist. Casement's 1911 Amazon voyage has been rather briefly passed over by biographers as little more than a sexual odyssey — an officially sanctioned cruise along the harbour-fronts of Amazonia. But the evidence of an American doctor, Herbert Spencer Dickey, who travelled with Casement during much of his 1911 Amazon trip, directly contradicts this view.[32]

What has recently come to light is that extensive repair work was carried out on this document by the repairs department of the Public Record Office as recently as June 1972 — who authorized the work is unclear. The diary was bound in green buckram and a number of pages were faced in silk to support the flimsiness of the paper, others were given a gelatine size and others still left alone (it appears that the diary is either unaccountably composed of paper of different weights or some pages have decayed more rapidly than others). According to a spokesman for the PRO, the restoration was standard procedure for a document in a bad state of repair and the work was overseen by a Master of the Supreme

[32] H.S. Dickey is the most important and convincing witness to Casement's behaviour on his 1911 voyage. Dickey tells his remarkable story of his years as a freelance doctor in Colombia, Peru and Brazil in *The Misadventures of a Tropical Medico* (Bodley Head 1929). Dickey was closely connected with the Peruvian Amazon Company and spent over ten years working in the north-west Amazon and never heard a single rumour about Casement's alleged "degeneracy". In the latter half of the 1930s Dickey entered into a correspondence with Dr William Maloney and was close to finishing a biography of Casement titled *Casement the Liberator* or *The Incorrigible Irishman* {F.L.K. De Valera 1334} which he hoped would put an end to the controversy over the diaries, but it was never published. Dickey's statement regarding his voyage with Casement is held in N.L.I. J. McGarrity Papers MS17601 (3).

Court of Judicature who made a comparison between the repaired document and a photographic reproduction of the diary taken before the work was carried out.[33]

THE PUTUMAYO JOURNAL

The early provenance of Casement's Putumayo Journal can be more easily traced. When Casement handed over the responsibilities of the Putumayo investigation at the end of 1912 to Charles Roberts, the Chairman of the Parliamentary Select Committee enquiry (P.S.C.), among the documents of evidence he felt might be relevant to the enquiry he offered Roberts his diary:

> I have dug up my diary of my days on the Putumayo — a very voluminous record indeed, for I wrote day and night when not tramping about interrogating — and I find I was absolutely right in the references I made to young Parr in the committee. Not perhaps to the actual word "piracy", which is immaterial in itself, but as to his opinions expressed to me at the time and recorded at the time. You see I was isolated and had to keep my mind very much alert and to record all that I noticed or heard. I did this as faithfully as a man could do for pen and pencil was never out of my hand hardly and I often wrote far into the night. The diary is a pretty complete record and were I free to publish it would be such a picture of things out there, written down red hot as would convince anyone. I have read through some of it this morning dealing with my last stay at La Chorrera and I find young Parr several times referred to and his remarks recorded at the time. As between that record then on the spot and written with only the desire to record, and his memory two years later there cannot be much doubt. I did not misrepresent him. I am thinking of having the whole diary typed. It is extensive and much of it written with pencil — I can read every word of it — so could you or another, but it could be read so much quicker if typed — and I may get it done and send it to you ...
>
> The diary makes me sick again — positively sick — when I read it over and it brings up so vividly that forest of hell and all those unhappy people suffered. Its virtue is not its language — but its date and its being a faithful transcript of my own mind at the time and of the things around me. If I can get it typed before I go away I'll send you a copy. I am chiefly deterred by the cost — it will cost several pounds to type — and I have already spent hundreds of pounds out of my private purse over the Putumayo and I feel I am not justified in spending more.[34]

On 31 December 1912 Casement, feeling exhausted and ill, left England for some badly needed rest in the warmer climes of the Canary Islands, taking the diary with him. On 24 January 1913

[33] According to a PRO spokesperson, this photographic reproduction was destroyed after the examination, at least no record exists of its whereabouts. The PRO was not prepared to state who did the repair work, although keeping such information confidential at the PRO is standard practice.

[34] R.H. Brit. Emp. S22 G.355 Casement–Roberts Correspondence December 1912.

Roberts sent Casement a telegram via the British Consulate in Tenerife asking for Casement to send his diary.[35] Casement replied on 27 January from Quiney's English Hotel in Las Palmas enclosing the diary and describing its value as evidence in the Parliamentary Select Committee enquiry.[36] On 1 February, Roberts wrote to Casement saying the diary had been received and had been sent off to be typed.[37] On 5 June, the day the P.S.C. issued its report, Roberts wrote to Casement: "What shall I do with all your documents? ... I have your diary, and the typewritten copy I have for you, and a good deal besides!" On 7 July Casement was

---

[35] N.L.I. MS 27, 842 "FOLLOWING RECEIVED HERE STOP CAN YOU SUPPLY ME WITH YOUR DIARY IMPORTANT. CHARLES ROBERTS."

[36] R.H. Brit. Emp. S22 Casement–Roberts Correspondence. "Your telegram reached me at Orotava, 110 miles away on Saturday. I came over here at once, arriving this morning or last midnight and now send you the diary. I had it with me, but have not read it for two and a half years! It is often almost unintelligible altho' I can read it all. Naturally there is in it something I should not wish anyone to see — but then it is as it stands. If you want to go through it I advise you strongly to have it typed first by an expert. It will take an expert to read it and decipher it. Remember it is less a diary than a reflection — a series of daily and weekly reflections.

As a diary it must be read in conjunction with the evidence of the Barbados men, which ran concurrently with most of it. Also I have two notebooks in which are other portions of the diary and sometimes letters are to go in when I have left blanks.

The value of the thing, if it has any value, is that it is sincere and was written with (obviously) never a thought of being shown to others but for myself alone — as a sort of aide memoire and mental justification and safety valve.

If you get it typed I should like a copy for myself — also, whatever typist does it there are bound to be many mistakes that I alone can correct, as I know always what I meant to write or did write when the text is not clear. ...

There is much, as you will see in my diary, would expose me to ridicule were it read by unkind eyes — its only value is that it is honest — an honest record of my own mind and of the things round me at the time. I was greatly overworked on the Putumayo — for I had no clerk or secretary and the mass of writing I had to do on top of the daily fights and enquiries and interrogation generally carried me far into the night to the detriment of my eyes — which gave out on the way, as you will see in the diary. I am sometimes very hard on individuals as you will see — as Gielgud and Cazes — but I wrote then with resentment strong in me and I could not forgive then those people and others who (as I thought and really still think) had tried to hide the evil. I did not then know that I should be able to convince the Foreign Office and get them to take the line I wanted and I felt very fierce and furious against the men who had connived at concealing the crimes.

But there — you have the diary, such as it is and form your own judgement. If you get it well typed I can fill up from my other notebooks any discrepancies or omissions."

[37] N.L.I. MS 13,073 [36 I–iii]. "The Diary has just arrived with your letter. It has gone to be typed by an expert. Very many thanks."

invited to lunch by Roberts when the manuscript and one copy of the typescript were presumably handed over. What then happened to the documents is a great deal less clear.

It seems probable that the manuscript version of Casement's Putumayo Journal remained at Ebury Street and was confiscated with other papers when Casement's Pimlico apartment was raided by Special Branch, probably towards the end of 1914. The manuscript was clearly not returned to the Casement family with his other papers, which we know from the statements of his loyal cousin, Gertrude Bannister, made in a correspondence in 1920 with Casement's elder sister, Nina.[38] Her view of what happened was as follows:

> The real story is this ... While he was in the Putumayo he kept a diary in which he jotted down all the foul things he heard of the doings of the beauties out there whose conduct he was investigating. He used it later for his notes and reports. As it contained his own movements, comments, etc. and was an ordinary private diary it was not sent in with his papers to the Putumayo Commission [*i.e.* the committee headed by Charles Roberts]. When he was talking things over with the head of the commission he referred to his diary and was asked to send it to them for information. He did so. Now among the papers that were handed over to me by Scotland Yard in 1916 were all the Putumayo things, but no diary.[39]

Gertrude Bannister's story might be confirmed by the list of possessions and papers returned to the family via Casement's solicitor, George Gavan Duffy, on 17 August 1916, where the list clearly states that among articles returned by Special Branch through the Home Office to Casement's solicitor were "A quantity of envelopes, reports and manuscript dealing with the Putumayo Atrocities".[40] The diary, or Putumayo Journal, eventually reached the National Library of Ireland in 1951 after the death of Gavan

---

[38] Casement's cousin Gertrude Bannister (Mrs Sidney Parry), known affectionately to Casement as Gee, and his sister Agnes Newman (Nina), were the two women closest to Casement throughout his life and more so towards the end. Gertrude Bannister began a personal campaign after the war to find out the truth about the sexual allegations — that she had no doubt were "lying propaganda". She employed a top London solicitor to lobby the Home Office on her behalf. Her efforts are detailed in a correspondence with Nina held among the De Valera Papers {F.L.K. De Valera 1334/2} and a statement she made on 10 January 1926 — N.L.I. 11488. Her main request to the Home Office was for the return of Casement's genuine Putumayo Journal.

[39] F.L.K. Eamon de Valera Papers [1334]. Letter (4 May 1920) from Gee to Nina, Rockport, Cushendun, Co. Antrim.

[40] HO 144 1637/178. The manuscript referred to in this list most likely refers to the manuscript drafts of Casement's interviews with the Barbadians also held in {N.L.I. MS 13,087}.

Duffy (1882–1951). It was part of a large bequest of Casement Papers subsequently classified as Special List A15 — Casement Papers 1889–1945.

OTHER JOTTINGS

Casement's *German Diaries* have yet another provenance worth elucidating since they throw revealing light on how conscientious Casement was about his diaries and on the form such journals or diaries took. Before leaving Munich at the end of March 1916 Casement entrusted to his German solicitor, Charles Curry, "all he possessed in this world, his personal effects and writings and left various instructions chiefly regarding his diaries and their publication upon the close of war". The contents of these note-books were eventually published in 1922.[41] The diary referred to during the trial described in the first footnote, and quite possibly the one alluded to by F.E. Smith in his book *Famous Trials* — where he noted that the things buried in the sand by Casement just before his arrest included "some weapons, some maps of Ireland of foreign origin, and three coats, one of which contained Casement's diary"[42]— is surely the diary referred to by Captain Robert Monteith in his memoir of the Easter Rising, *Casement's Last Adventure*. Monteith says of this two-page sketch beginning on 16 February and ending on 12 April:

> The diary found in Casement's bag was a series of rough notes from which he wrote his diary proper. The names were fictitious. For Dublin must be understood Berlin; for Lough Ree: Munich; Wicklow: Wilhelmshafen. ... His last entry is full of humour: "April 12th left Wicklow in Willie's Yacht."[43]

These two pages of diary notes are clearly the ones referred to by the Attorney-General during Casement's trial. They appear to correspond with the photographic diary held among the de Valera

[41] *Diaries of Sir Roger Casement — His Mission to Germany and the Findlay Affair* (Arche Publishing Co. Munich 1922).

[42] Birkenhead, The First Earl of, *Famous Trials of History* (Hutchinson 1926). An interesting article written on the subject is by Gerard Lyne, "New Light on Material Concealed by Roger Casement near Banna Strand" in *Journal of the Kerry Archaeological and Historical Society*, No.19, 1987.

[43] The two pages of this encrypted "diary" are photographically reproduced in Monteith's privately printed edition of *Casement's Last Adventure* (Chicago 1932). It does not appear in the 1953 edition. Originals are in the N.L.I. Monteith landed with Casement on Banna Strand on the morning of 21 April but escaped the hand of the law and after months of lying low finally made his way to safety in America.

Papers, which seems to be a fuller version of these rough notes. The fact that Casement kept encrypted notes which he later used in writing up his diary proper is also interesting.

From looking at the nature and provenance of the various diaries it becomes clear that Casement conscientiously kept diaries or journals during large parts of his life, and that these were most detailed during the more momentous occasions either during his humanitarian investigations or his last adventure as a leader of the Irish uprising of 1916. It also seems probable that a large number of these personal notes fell into the hands of British Intelligence. The Putumayo Journal has survived because it was typed up as evidence for Charles Roberts and the P.S.C. Other journals and jottings that Casement kept and which he refers to in writing that has survived were apparently lost.

FRAGMENTARY DIARY ENTRIES

By far the most convincing documents in helping to expose the *Black Diaries* as forgeries, which have to date been overlooked, are the fragmentary diary entries and letters that have survived in the National Library of Ireland and among the Foreign Office papers held at the PRO giving account of Casement's movements in the Amazon. These documents either talk directly of the diary he was keeping or clearly contradict the narrative as told in the *Black Diary*.

The earliest of these is the important conversation Casement had with the rubber speculator and Iquiteño trader Victor Israel on the night of 24 August just before the S.S. *Huayna* crossed the Peruvian–Brazilian frontier. As well as serving as an important insight for Casement into local attitudes among the expatriate business community, the conversation laid out the parameters of Casement's investigation. Why is there no mention of this conversation in the corresponding Black Diary entry? The probable explanation is that this fragmentary diary entry was not accessible to the author of the *Black Diaries*.

On 13 September 1910, the night before Casement and the Commission left Iquitos for the Putumayo, Casement sent Gerald Spicer, at the American desk in the FO, a letter giving brief account of his days in Iquitos and enclosing lengthy statements of interviews he had already held with some Barbadians, British subjects recruited by the Peruvian Amazon Company. The Foreign

Office received the document on 29 October and had the letter and statements printed as a Confidential Document.[44] The letter stated:

I am keeping a diary, and part of the statement of Bishop is really a leaf of my diary — the last part. It is only sent you in case I might get lost or disappear or something up there or die of fever, and my papers might be overhauled before they reached Iquitos, or they would be at the mercy of the people who are in real dread of our visit. I am viewed with grave suspicion already …

What this clearly shows is that Casement was keeping a diary before he arrived in the Putumayo and before his Putumayo Journal proper began, although only a few fragmentary entries have apparently survived from before 23 September. It also illustrates clearly the nature of the diary that he was keeping, made clearer from the fragment he sent to the Foreign Office which is referred to in the letter. It is scribbled in pencil on the same double-sided foolscap as his main journal. It seems reasonable to deduce that the fragmentary entries that have survived are genuine. It also might be argued that since they have survived they did not fall into the hands of British Intelligence. Although this cannot be proved, it is clearly possible in the light of a letter Casement sent to Mallet at the Foreign Office in 1911:

My Putumayo Papers are all locked up in Buckinghamshire. I have telegraphed for the case to be sent here and will tackle the matter as soon as it arrives. I will stay in Ireland till end of month — but will write more fully when I get my papers.[45]

Similar fragmentary entries giving account of his 1911 journey also follow the format of the 1910 fragments and are scribbled on loose double-sided sheets of foolscap and appear as if they have been extracted from a larger and more complete document.

[44] FO 371/968. Confidential 39408.

[45] FO 371/1201 — Casement to Mallet — Ardrigh, Antrim Road Belfast, 15 April 1911. One of the central arguments that tries to sustain the authenticity of the *Black Diaries* maintains that a lot of Casement's papers, also describing licentious activities, were held in a black box that was burnt by Casement's friend Francis Joseph Bigger, the owner of Ardrigh, the house where Casement normally stayed when he was in Belfast. However, the story of the black box, as related by René MacColl, depends upon a statement made by the nephew of F.J. Bigger to a "well-known resident of Cork" — a man later identified as John J. Horgan — more than forty years after Casement's execution. It should also be remembered that Casement asked Bigger to "bury" rather than "burn" the papers in the telegram intercepted by British Naval Intelligence in 1916. On close inspection the whole story of Bigger and the burning of the black box becomes untenable. For a memoir of Casement and Bigger see Cathal O'Byrne, "Roger Casement's Ceilidhe" in *The Capuchin Annual*, 1946–7.

Though they combine to give a very fragmented picture of things, they contain enough inconsistencies with the corresponding dates in the *1911 Letts's Diary* to suggest that they too somehow avoided the long arm of British Intelligence. Finally there are Casement's Foreign Office despatches, including some of the letters which he himself stated formed "part of my diary". What is interesting here is that Casement kept draft copies of many of his missives to the Foreign Office.

CONTRADICTIONS BETWEEN THE DIARIES

By constructing the narrative of Casement's voyage from undisputed documentation, whether journals, fragmentary entries or letters, it becomes possible to make a comparison of his genuine material relating to his 1910 Amazon voyage with the narrative of his trip as told in the 1910 *Black Diary*. If this is done it becomes clear that the *Black Diary* is riddled with inaccuracies and inconsistencies that describe events in a completely different way. It also becomes impossible to contend that Casement used a shortened *Black Diary* to write subsequently his Putumayo Journal since there are far too many textual inconsistencies in the *Black Diary* to support such a view.

Those who wish to continue believing in the veracity of the *Black Diaries* should ask themselves why Casement should have kept such an incriminating document about his person when he realized that his every step was being watched and he was moving through an atmosphere of fear, suspicion and death. The possession of such a document also directly contradicts the cautious (and ultimately ironic) view he has of his diary already quoted in his letter of 13 September. The figure of Roger Casement who emerges from it is so different in general attitude and moral values from the Casement portrayed by the *Black Diaries* as to be totally irreconcilable.

The Putumayo Journal, fragmentary diary entries and FO despatches are all written in Casement's clear and succinct English prose and show his grasp of language. Throughout he is lucid, emotional, direct, structured and thoughtful. It is filled with intelligent comments by a man with a highly active inquiring mind and touches on a number of different subjects including botany, ethnology, anthropology, history, politics, race and religion, while keeping its eye firmly on the matter in hand: compiling a case against perpetrators of atrocities. It is arguably the most important surviving document Casement wrote and shows what a remarkably controlled and clear mind he possessed even when he was physically suffering and in enormous danger. Moreover, it shows how his treason developed through direct experience of the corruption and degeneration of British imperial methods that rose so clearly to the surface during the Edwardian era.

The *Black Diaries*, by contrast, have been written to mystify, befuddle, confuse and conceal. More often than not they are utterly misleading in their meaning. Far from appearing as a serious-minded figure, they portray Casement as a perverter of the innocent, a corrupter and fantasist. The language is charged with innuendo and exaggeration. Casement did describe the physical prowess and beauty of native men (and women) and his comments can be interpreted as unselfconsciously erotic, but his descriptions of racial stereotypes and physical attributes are more in the mode of an anthropologist than a sexual obsessive. Genuine phrasing is distorted in order to convey ambiguous sexual connotation. Sense has been confused, truth obscured. Genuine characters have been extracted from the context of the Putumayo Journal and given new roles as sexual partners or objects of fantasy.[46]

Casement's recent biographers have explained the existence of these two parallel diaries in terms of a sex diary and a "cleaned-up version" — a "black" and a "white" diary — as if Casement were a Dr Jekyll and Mr Hyde character. The argument can appear convincing if it is put in the context of the fact that for most of this century, certainly during Casement's lifetime, homosexuality was driven underground, and homosexuals until recently were forced to lead double lives. But such an argument fails to take into account the small and hostile world in which Casement moved and

---

[46] Painstaking investigation has been carried out over the last two decades by two Irish researchers, Eoin Ó Máille and Michael Payne. Using detailed computerized analysis of key-words and expressions, they have shown that the linguistic finger-print in Casement's genuine writings is completely at odds with the linguistic finger-print of the *Black Diaries*. Their findings were recently presented at a symposium organized by The Roger Casement Foundation and are published in *The Vindication of Roger Casement — Computer Analysis and Comparisons* (privately printed 1994). Certainly such scientifically based analysis has more credence than the opinion of hand-writing experts and is increasingly gaining acceptance among scholars. It was instrumental, for example, in establishing the identity of the previously anonymous author of the *roman à clef* based on Bill Clinton's presidential campaign, *Primary Colors*. Testing by the Cusum (cumulative sum technique) is another method that might throw more revealing light on the matter.

the fact that his every move, while investigating in one of the most dangerous frontier regions of the world, was being watched by enemies who wished him dead.

Analysed as texts, once Casement's genuine narrative is compared to corresponding *Black Diary* entries it becomes impossible to believe in the authenticity of both accounts. The genuineness of the diaries has always depended upon the argument that they were factually fool-proof. But the texts are frequently inconsistent and diverge in time and place.

It has been considered best to leave the exposure of the inconsistencies and inaccuracies that emerge through a comparison of the texts to the footnotes since they are too detailed to elaborate fully here. But it is worth expounding on two important inconsistencies that have a wider significance. The first involves Casement's eyes.

From the outset of the voyage Casement began to suffer a chronic eye infection which he referred to with mounting concern in his correspondence with friends and Foreign Office colleagues as he journeyed up river. The earliest mention is in the letter sent to Spicer on 11 August. Three days later he scribbled to Tyrrell:

> my eyes have got very bad — that is why I write in pencil, they had shown signs of weakness just before I came away, but had improved at home. On arrival at Pará the bad symptoms returned and the ship's doctor says I am threatened with Chronic Opthalmia. The worst is that there is no doctor where we are going and it is not a cheerful prospect to have a complete breakdown of eyes in the wilds of the Amazon forest.

Over the next two months the problem continued until the night of Wednesday 12 October when he was forced to bandage both eyes and was rendered momentarily blind, albeit at night. In all he mentions his eye problem on more than fifteen separate occasions in his correspondence and journals — and at times at some length. By contrast, the *Black Diary* avoids any mention of the eye infection until eighty days after the outset of the journey when it is rather nonchalantly mentioned in the entry for 10 October.

Casement's eye infection had two far-reaching effects. Firstly it forced him to be as economic with his writing as possible and avoid unnecessary strain. Why then he would have bothered to keep two diaries repeating the same information is hard to explain. More significant, however, is the fact that it also forced him to write in pencil rather than pen.

On 4 September he wrote:

My eyes have got no better — rather worse I am afraid — and that is my chief reason for using pencil. I find it less strain to write with pencil than with ink — in latter case one has to look closer at the paper and form the letters more distinctly.

Yet harder to explain is why the *Black Diary* entry for 12 October, the night of Casement's blindness when his eyes were at their very worst, is written in ink. All Casement's writings either side of that date are in pencil. Pen is used with far greater frequency in the *Black Diary* than in the undisputed writings.

Another point that makes little sense in this long saga is the comment Casement made about his sexuality on 29 September, after he had witnessed his first Indian dance at the rubber station of Occidente. Surrounded by the perpetrators of atrocities, he wrote:

I swear to God, I'd hang every one of the band of wretches with my own hands if I had the power, and do it with the greatest pleasure. I have never shot game with any pleasure, have indeed abandoned all shooting for that reason, that I dislike the thought of taking life. I have never given life to anyone myself, and my celibacy makes me frugal of human life, but I'd shoot or exterminate these infamous scoundrels more gladly than I should shoot a crocodile or kill a snake.

Exactly why Casement should have made such a direct statement about his "celibacy" while keeping a parallel sex diary has yet to be satisfactorily explained. There is not a single witness to Casement's alleged sexual antics on the Amazon as detailed by the 1910 and 1911 *Black Diaries*, and certainly South America was the main theatre for his "sexual degeneracy" if the documents are to be believed. Moreover, Casement's principal enemy on the Amazon, the Peruvian rubber baron, Julio Cesar Arana, knew all about Casement's "secret" activities such as recruiting labour for the Madeira–Mamoré railway and trying to organize an anti-Aranista party during his second voyage to Iquitos in 1911. In December 1911, when Casement made a hasty exit from Iquitos, the local newspapers were accusing him of being a "British spy" and "secret agent", but all such suggestions are edited out of the *Black Diary*. Eighty years on these documents continue to confuse and confound.

WHAT ARE THE BLACK DIARIES AND WHY WERE THEY FORGED?

The question inevitably arises: what are the *Black Diaries* and why did British Intelligence go to such complicated lengths to forge them? The strategy had both short-term and long-term objectives.

The short-term aim of the *Black Diaries* was directed at Casement's execution. They were an effective way to mislead Casement's powerful lobby of supporters and officially to defame Sir Roger Casement — the humanitarian hero, knighted in 1911 for his epic journeys in defence of tribal people on behalf of the British Crown. They are an example of a type of ruthless intellectual sabotage the British excel at when it is a matter of defeating the enemy. Granted the fact that it was wartime, and given the nature of Casement's "treason", the *Black Diaries* were an exceptional means of destroying an exceptional enemy.[47] The rumours of Casement's "sexual degeneracy" that were circulated before and after his trial in 1916 confused almost everyone; Casement's powerful lobby of supporters retreated into silence, Casement's martyrdom was prevented and the clemency appeals thwarted. His Irish supporters were in retreat, devastated by the execution of the leaders of the Easter Rising. All were fearful of speaking out in defence of a man whose treason was so clear, at a time when each day tens of thousands of British volunteers (many of them Irishmen) were being slaughtered on the front-line of the Somme. For the rest of this century the *Black Diaries* became the means by which Casement's "treason" was explained and rationalized in public.[48]

There was, however, a secondary "historical" motive for forging the *Black Diaries* that becomes clear once the documents are analysed outside the confines of the Anglo-Irish conflict and the biographical sensationalism of Casement's life. Casement's investigations into atrocities in both the Congo and Amazon are unique, officially sanctioned sources in understanding the horror that underlay wild rubber extraction from tropical forests. In these investigations, Casement collected the statements and oral

---

[47] For a well-argued essay on this subject see Owen Dudley Edwards, "Divided Treasons and Divided Loyalties: Roger Casement and Others" in *Transactions of the Royal Historical Society*, 1981. In this essay Dudley Edwards argues convincingly that Casement was given an unfair trial, although the verdict of death was just given the fact that he had been wilfully employed and decorated by the British Crown. Whether Casement should have been granted a reprieve as a result of his humanitarian achievement was clearly avoided by the use of the *Black Diaries* — a fact now conceded by the British government.

[48] See Daniel Pick, *War Machine: The Rationalization of Slaughter in the Modern Age* (Yale 1995). Pick develops a number of theses that can be considered relevant to understanding the forging of the *Black Diaries*, especially on psychoanalytical theories and views of degeneracy and effeminacy current at the start of the century and during the First World War.

testimonies that helped build a factual case supporting the historical heart of darkness which lay in the shadowy soul of Euroimperialism and the White Man's vision of civilization. Although the *Black Diaries* make impressionistic references to the horror — they cleverly scale that horror down, Casement emerges as the "degenerate" rather than the imperial systems he was investigating. It is no accident that the *Black Diaries* coincide with Casement's main humanitarian investigations into rubber atrocities in both Africa and South America, and most specifically with the Putumayo atrocities where British influence was most active and direct.

BRITISH INFLUENCE IN THE AMAZON

In the latter half of the nineteenth century British influence in the Amazon far exceeded that of any other nation. As a consequence of a series of botanical voyages of discovery by the English naturalists Spruce, Wallace and Bates in the 1850s, Britain was the first nation to realize the vast economic potential of wild rubber lying within the world's largest tropical forest. In 1855, Richard Spruce published in *Hooker's Journal of Botany* the first description of how rubber was gathered by milking the tree through small incisions in the bark, collecting the latex in a cup beneath the wounds and then coagulating it by dripping the liquid onto a spit above a slow fire until it formed a black oval-shaped bale.[49] Subsequent travellers to the Amazon regions all commented on rubber and the increasing boom in the industry which helped "regenerate" the ailing state of Pará, still in decline from the social rebellions of the 1830s. By the 1880s the profits from rubber gave birth to the modern Amazon towns of Manaos and Iquitos — and the opera house in Manaos is still held high as the great symbol of the civilizing of the jungle.

---

[49] Richard Spruce, *Note on the India Rubber of the Amazon* (1855). Richard Spruce (1817–93) was a self-taught botanist. He voyaged to the Amazon in 1849 and after learning Portuguese and Tupi-Guarani at Santarém he started exploring the vast tropical waterways of both the Brazilian and Peruvian Amazon, venturing as far as the Ecuadorian Andes and Pacific coastal regions, collecting thousands of plants and making detailed scientific notes about his botanical observations. Although he published many learned articles on his botanical findings, the account of his travels was not published until after his death by his life-long friend Alfred Russel Wallace.

When the Amazon was opened up to international trade in the 1850s, British capital and navigational expertise backed the first steamboat company. Before long, boats began to travel weekly between Liverpool and Pará, and navigation extended over two thousand miles upriver to a naval yard at Iquitos, also developed with British naval expertise. As the age of sail gave way to steam, both the Brazilian and Peruvian governments were equipped and re-equipped with arms, gunboats and commercial ships and river launches made in Britain. British–South American banking alliances played an equally important role in bringing investment to the area. All the while, British Consuls were central to keeping the Foreign Office and other government departments informed of developments in the wild rubber industry.

The commercial uses for rubber made strides in pace with increased demand. From its basic waterproofing qualities, rubber was "vulcanized" by the American, Charles Goodyear. In a more stable, heat-resistant state it was used for insulating wiring and in the 1890s became the prime commodity in the reinvention of the wheel. Rubber was paramount in the production of tyres for first the bicycle and then the motor car. Throughout the period 1870–1909 British finance drove the Amazon rubber industry forward, and as the rubber frontier pushed farther west so the demand for labour grew more acute. A great part of the Brazilian industry was built upon the migration of tens of thousands of *nordestinos*, fleeing the droughts of north-east Brazil, into the rubber frontiers of Acré and elsewhere. In many of the more obscure contested frontier regions, rubber exploiters arrived with no better intentions than enslaving the native Amazon Indians and forcing them to do the work under threat of death.

While Britain realized the potential of the wild rubber industry, it also saw the impracticalities and drawbacks of extractive economy. In 1876 the Royal Botanic Gardens at Kew, in co-operation with the British Foreign Office and the legendary plant-hunter, geographer and historian, Clements R. Markham,[50] at the

[50] Markham, Sir Clements Robert (1830–1916). Geographer, historian and grandson of William Markham, Archbishop of York, after schooling at Westminster he entered the navy aged fourteen and spent four years on H.M.S. *Collingwood* sailing between South American Pacific coast ports, picking up a knowledge of Spanish. Between 1852–3, inspired by William H. Prescott, he wandered among Inca ruins of Peru and remained fascinated with Peru for the rest of his days — writing a great deal about the country. He entered the Civil Service in 1853 and in 1860 was ordered to collect Cinchona trees and seeds in the montaña of eastern Peru — helping to domesticate this extractive commodity. In 1893 he was made president

India Office, masterminded the unauthorized exportation of 70,000 seeds of rubber from the Amazon. This legendary botanical "theft" was carried out by Henry A. Wickham — a colonial adventurer living at Santarém. After many unsuccessful efforts to domesticate the plant *Hevea brasiliensis*, trees were eventually introduced to south-east Asia (Malaya, Dutch East Indies and Ceylon). But it was not until 1910 that plantation rubber became competitively productive, forcing the virtual collapse of the Amazon rubber industry. But between 1890 and 1910, as the market demand began to outstrip the means of supply, so those parts of the world from which wild rubber was extracted were turned into slavocracies at the mercy of the White Man's rule.[51] The widespread atrocities committed in the Congo Free State alerted a group of European humanitarians to the problem. Casement was the "official" sent on behalf of the British Foreign Office to investigate these atrocities. Following his 1904 report he campaigned tirelessly for reform in the Congo and his correspondence with the acting secretary of the Congo Reform Association, E.D. Morel, shows Casement to have been an original thinker over issues of slavery, human and civil rights.

In 1910 Casement was sent to investigate the activities of an Anglo-Peruvian rubber company working in the frontier regions of the north-west Amazon. Whether the British Foreign Office's motives in sending Casement were directed by humanitarian rather than commercial considerations is a question that might be investigated further. Howard Karno has suggested that the British Foreign Office used humanitarian issues for imperial and

---

of the Royal Geographical Society and was often consulted on South American boundary disputes. He was also very active in promoting the whole idea of Arctic exploration and retained close association with a group of naval officers. He is perhaps best known for his extraordinary literary output, including twenty volumes of translated texts for the Hakluyt Society, some twenty biographies and numerous historical studies, many on Peru. He burnt to death in his bed on 30 January 1916. He supported Peru's claims to the Putumayo region

[51] Of more recent accounts, Warren Dean, *Brazil and the Struggle for Rubber: A Study in Environmental History* (CUP 1987), puts forward an excellent thesis on the "theft" of the *Hevea brasiliensis* and the Brazilian rubber market before and after the boom. Barbara Weinstein, *The Amazon Rubber Boom (1850–1920)* (Stanford 1983) deals more solidly with economic aspects of it all. British economic influence in the Peruvian Amazon is well covered in G. Pennano, *La Economía del Caucho* (Iquitos 1988), the most informed Peruvian history with an important bibliography. Brazil's main historical contribution to the Amazon rubber boom is Roberto Santos, *História econômica da Amazônia, 1800–1920* (São Paulo 1980).

commercial ends.[52] The chronology of Casement's humanitarian activities in the Amazon played nicely into the hands of the rubber market, and the publication in July 1912 of the Blue Book containing his reports turned much investment away, but the British Foreign Secretary's motives for investigating the Putumayo atrocities — and it was certainly a personal campaign on the part of Sir Edward Grey — seemed genuine from the outset. The British public was outraged by the stories and Grey wished to know something of the truth.

While British capital controlled the major part of the Amazon rubber market, it is clear that few people had much of an inkling of the vast tropical slave kingdoms to which rubber extraction had given rise. What Casement found in the Amazon outdistanced the horror he had helped reveal in the Congo, and he became the singular witness to that horror. Although other explorers and travel writers such as Col. P.H. Fawcett, James Bryce and Geraldine Guinness had made fleeting revelations about the cruelties that resulted from rubber extraction, it was Casement alone who produced the historical evidence defining the genocide. While the writings of E.D. Morel are the indispensable source in the condemnation of the atrocities committed in Leopold II's Congo Free State, so Casement's official and unofficial reports and despatches are the evidence for defining the widespread tragedy that underwrote the Amazon rubber industry. Genocide only becomes meaningful if the plight of the victims is described, recorded and popularly sensed.[53]

Britain's self-proclaimed position during the Edwardian age as the country of free trade that brought about the abolition of slavery was one that would have been clearly undermined if Sir Roger Casement's "unofficial" revelations had been allowed more air to breathe. Casement's role as consul limited what he was allowed to say about the affair in the public arena and certainly encouraged his increasingly subversive character, as he witnessed for himself the moral breakdown of the British free-trading empire. By the end of 1912 his two and a half years of tireless investigations into the Amazon rubber industry ended in a six-month-long Parliamen-

---

[52] Howard Karno, "Julio Cesar Arana, frontier *cacique* in Peru" in Robert Kern, *The Cacique* (Albaquerque 1973).

[53] The genocide of the Amazon Indian is the last study in Frank Chalk and Kurt Jonassohn, *The History and Sociology of Genocide — Analyses and Case Studies* (Yale 1990). It is hoped that this text might serve their needs in helping define the genocide of the Amazon Indian.

tary Select Committee Enquiry. What that enquiry did or did not eventually prove might be argued elsewhere. But once Casement turned against the British empire, and the motivations behind his treason were analysed, it was clear that the evidence he had collected during his Amazon investigations was as potentially subversive of the historical reputation of the empire as the man himself.

The forging of the *Black Diaries*, therefore, had what might be termed an historical motive and was the means by which Casement's unofficial revelations were obscured. Ingeniously, they threw a smoke screen around the whole position of British influence in the Amazon which Casement referred to directly in his pseudonymous letter to *The Daily News* — published on 1 March 1912.[54] By focusing on Casement's personal "degeneracy", the *Black Diaries* succeeded in diverting attention from his real private revelations about Britain's role in the Amazon rubber industry.[55]

Both in the Congo and Amazon, Casement had uncovered the horrors committed by the "White Man's civilization". It turned him first into a virulent anti-imperialist and gradually into a full-blown revolutionary. By 1916 his "treason" clearly shocked and frightened the inner circle of government when it was realized just how long he had been working to undermine the system.

The process of forging the documents would have been comparatively easy although it undoubtedly required great expertise in its execution. When British Intelligence moved in on Casement at the end of 1914, among his confiscated papers they found genuine diaries and journals detailing his journeys into the Congo and Putumayo. Using this material they would have been able, without too much difficulty, to construct the *Black Diaries* with experiences, phraseology and impressions cannibalized from genuine writings. On the surface these documents appeared to be factually fool-proof and contained a host of references and indications to give the appearance of being actual documents. The forging of the handwriting was carried out with great skill, although since there is no evidence that the *Black Diaries* held in the PRO were described by anyone in 1916, it is probable that the

[54] In this letter signed D. MacCAMMOND and written on 29 Feb 1912, Casement clearly lays the blame for the Putumayo atrocities on the duplicitous intentions of British trading interests.

[55] In the recent ten-volume *Cambridge History of Latin America*, the Putumayo atrocities receive a curt footnote: an example of how history is as capable of concealing the truth as it is of throwing light on it.

forger had several years to perfect their look. Though the formation of letters and the style of the writing is often hard to distinguish from genuine material, it ultimately fails the test of authenticity by its total lack of fluency. All Casement's writings, whether notes, letters or journals, contain a fluency of script — as if Casement was working under enormous pressure and at great speed. The *Black Diaries* completely lack this. The words seem to stutter out onto the page — they are deliberate and contrived.

THE HISTORICAL VALUE OF CASEMENT'S AMAZON JOURNAL

The Amazon Journal of Roger Casement is a major primary source for the history of the Amazon, in the most decisive moment of its destruction, and deepens our knowledge of both European and U.S. foreign policy in South America. It is also a basic source for the history of the humanitarian movement — a subject that is in need of much greater historical research. As an investigation into atrocities it is perhaps unequalled and in a number of respects sets a precedent. Many of the grievances expressed by Casement are as current today as they were in 1910. The whole matter of land rights remains fundamental to the future stability of both Peru and Brazil. Brazil's *Movimento Sem-Terra* (MST) demanding agrarian reform has much in common with Casement's analysis of land rights back in 1910. Equally, as a defence of the lifeways and assertion of the counterhistory of Amerindian tribal culture in a continuing struggle for its ancestral territories the journal has tremendous value.

In terms of current debate, *The Amazon Journal* is linked most directly to the heart of darkness and the conflict between civilization and savagery. Interest in the Putumayo atrocities has found new momentum recently as a result of the work of the American anthropologist Michael Taussig. In his pioneering and far-reaching study *Shamanism, Colonialism and the Wild Man: A Study in Terror and Healing*,[56] Taussig makes a convincing connection between

[56] Michael Taussig's thesis is best summarized in the final footnote to Mary Louise Pratt, *Imperial Eyes: Travel Writing and Transculturation* (Routledge 1992), which states that "when one tries to comprehend the practices and semiotics of terror one finds that they are constructed not only out of what is Not seen, said, known, but also out of what people do see, say, and know AND what people do not see but hear others say they have seen; on what people do not hear said, but hear or read others who say they have heard it said; on what people did not do themselves but

Casement and Joseph Conrad's *Heart of Darkness*. When reading Casement's *Amazon Journal* it is hard not to draw parallels with this extraordinarily powerful metaphysical work describing a river journey in search of the darkness at the heart of the white man's civilization. Casement's Putumayo Journal, coupled with the oral testimonies he recorded during his interviews with Barbadian overseers, serve as important evidence in analysing Europe's historical heart of darkness. There is no chapter in the whole process of extermination of South America's pre-Columbian tribal life recorded in so much depth of detail, with the possible exception of the writings of the sixteenth-century Spanish monk Bartolomé de las Casas.

While Casement's voyage is of unquestioned epic proportions, it breaks with many of the traditions of the age. Instead of being the journal of an imperial adventurer it becomes the journal of an anti-imperial investigator.[57] At the outset of the voyage Casement is clearly seen defending British imperial methods against those adopted by the Spanish and Portuguese; by the time he returns downriver, commerce and international trade have become the true villain and destroyer of the tribal way of life. He had also cut through the "jingoism" that underlay the rubber industry and the concept that commerce was a means of "civilizing" primitive peoples. As Casement had worked tirelessly to reveal the genocide committed in Leopold II's Congo Free State and expose the horrors set in motion by Stanley's exploration of the African interior, so in his Putumayo investigation he set out to expose the brutal excesses wrought by four centuries of Spanish and Portuguese conquest. This journal is one of the most important indictments ever made against perpetrators of atrocities and imperial system building, and exposes the genocide of which international commerce is capable.

---

heard others say they saw done, and so on. The cultural and ideological engine of terror, argues Taussig, runs not just on the (distorted) conceptions each side holds of its enemy, but on the distorted conceptions each side holds about the distorted conceptions its enemy holds about it."

[57] The demystifying of imperialism and the assertion of a counterhistory are subjects dealt with by Mary Louise Pratt *op. cit.* Through analysis of the exploration of the interiors of Africa and Latin America and the manner in which explorers claimed territories for European empires, she reinterprets the historical force wielded by European ideologies and the legacy of white supremacy in those continents. Although she only makes a brief reference to Casement, his *Amazon Journal* might serve as an important text for supporting her view of counterhistory.

The Amazon rubber boom that breathed new life into most South American economies between 1870 and 1914 occupied a period filled with both grand adventure and widespread, unrecorded ethnocide. The legend of Fitzcarraldo and the huge fortunes amassed by the rubber barons; the building of the Madeira–Mamoré railway; the Opera House in Manaos and the Panama Canal are epic components in the narrative of interior exploration, engineering endeavour and the "civilizing of the jungle". What such ventures cost in terms of tribal life will never be known — but there can be little doubt that these four and a half decades of South American history, directly coinciding with Europe's Age of Empire, saw an extermination of tribal culture as great as the slaughter wrought when the Conquistadors first laid foot on the New World. Just as the act of killing Indians in the period of early conquest had been justified as a religious act, so in the South America which Casement described it was considered a civilizing act.

*

NOTE ON THE EDITING

One of the principal criticisms from the readers kind enough to scrutinize *The Amazon Journal of Roger Casement* in proof stage was the sheer length of the document. Although I had no doubt that the text could easily be edited down, I was ultimately convinced by the more scholarly recommendation that publication of the complete text was necessary in order to create a source that might serve other independent investigations of the diaries controversy. Curtailment of the text would have undermined the value of the the book in this respect, and although there are moments when the narrative is repetitious and sometimes little more than a sequence of detailed jottings — each scribbling has intrinsic value in understanding Casement's state of mind.

The inclusion of the parallel *Black Diary* entries was deemed unnecessary since these are already available in printed form. Those interested in cross-checking the text with the *Black Diary* should seek out the web-site of the publishers, where the text has been made available, or refer directly to the copies held in the Public Record Office at Kew.

The correspondence that Casement posted on his way out to Iquitos forms the opening section of the journal. His stay in Iquitos from 31 August to 14 September has been assembled from fragmentary diary entries and letters. It follows, as far as possible, his day-to-day activities. The main body of the book is composed of the Putumayo Journal, the document described in the introduction. The transcription was made from the autograph manuscript since the typescript version contains a significant number of errors. It begins at 2.15 p.m. on 23 September 1910 and ends with Casement's departure from Iquitos on 6 December. A few letters and one fragmentary diary entry found elsewhere have been inserted into this narrative as well as the very revealing page that appears in the autograph manuscript but was left out of the 1913 typescript. Chapter divisions and italicized headings have been used to break up the text to allow for easier reading and retrieval. It is also hoped that the detailed index will allow readers an easy means of reference to the long list of *dramatis personae*.

Silent editing of the text has been kept to a minimum and arises where the manuscript has presented difficulties in transcription. Punctuation has occasionally been amended. He used ampersands frequently instead of the word 'and'; these have been changed where appropriate. There are a number of spelling inconsistencies — most often among proper names and local words such as Chacara, Igara-paraná — again, these have been generally corrected. The local Peruvian currency *soles* has been abbreviated to S/P $: in 1910 there were roughly S/P $10.5 to £1 sterling.

The reader should bear in mind that besides keeping this journal, Casement wrote out in long-hand the statements of the Barbadians, and their evidence formed the heart and soul of the case he built defining the atrocities. These were later published in the Blue Book [PP 1912–1913 Cd 6266) LXVIII]. Anyone wishing to consult the Barbadian statements further should refer to that document or PRO FO 371/1200 or to NLI MS 13,087 (27/i–viii). Casement averaged between three thousand and four thousand words a day during the seventy-five days he spent travelling through the Putumayo — a considerable workload.

The final section, describing Casement's return journey from Iquitos, comprises a few letters, brief information obtained from passenger lists and some details Casement provided on arriving in London. His concluding essay tracing the historical background to the destruction of the Amerindian tribal world is undated but it is likely that it was written on that return voyage. It mirrors in every respect the physical nature of his journal.

In the footnotes the name of the main tribe mentioned in the narrative, the Huitotos, is occasionally spelt in the alternative form Witotos. The term Amazindian is also often used instead of the more historic word Indian.

A second volume of documents relevant to Casement's activities during 1911 and the reconstruction of his second voyage up the Amazon made during the latter half of that year will be published in 1998.

PART TWO

THE VOYAGE TO THE PUTUMAYO

They were conquerors, and for that you want only brute force — nothing to boast of, when you have it, since your strength is just an accident arising from the weakness of others. They grabbed what they could get for the sake of what was to be got. It was just robbery with violence, aggravated murder on a great scale, and men going at it blind — as is very proper for those who tackle a darkness.

Joseph Conrad, *Heart of Darkness*.

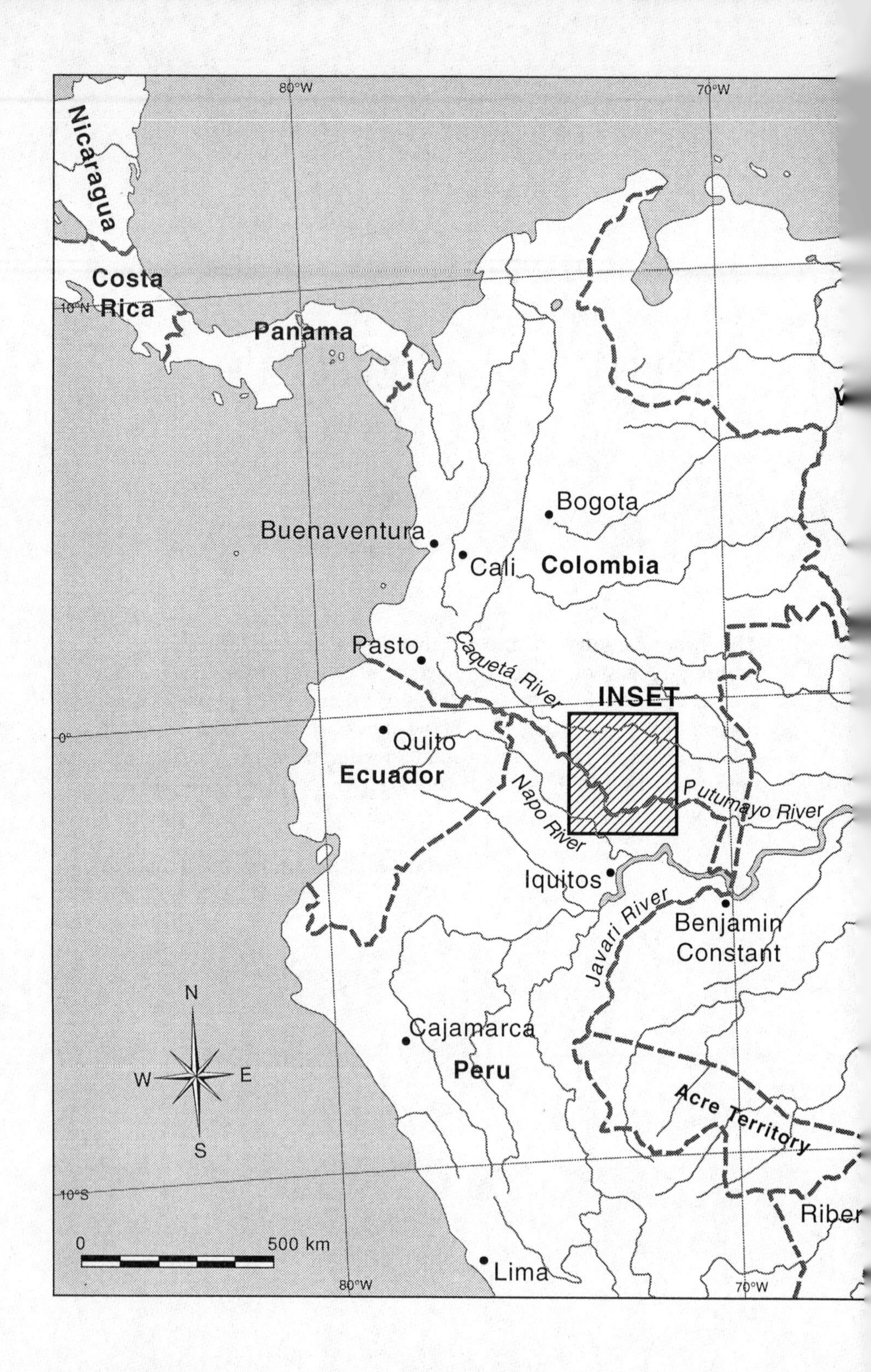

80°W
70°W
Nicaragua
Costa Rica
10°N
Panama
Bogota
Buenaventura
Cali
Colombia
Pasto
Caquetá River
INSET
0°
Quito
Ecuador
Napo River
Putumayo River
Iquitos
Javari River
Benjamin Constant
N
W
E
S
Cajamarca
Peru
Acre Territory
10°S
Riber
0
500 km
Lima
80°W
70°W

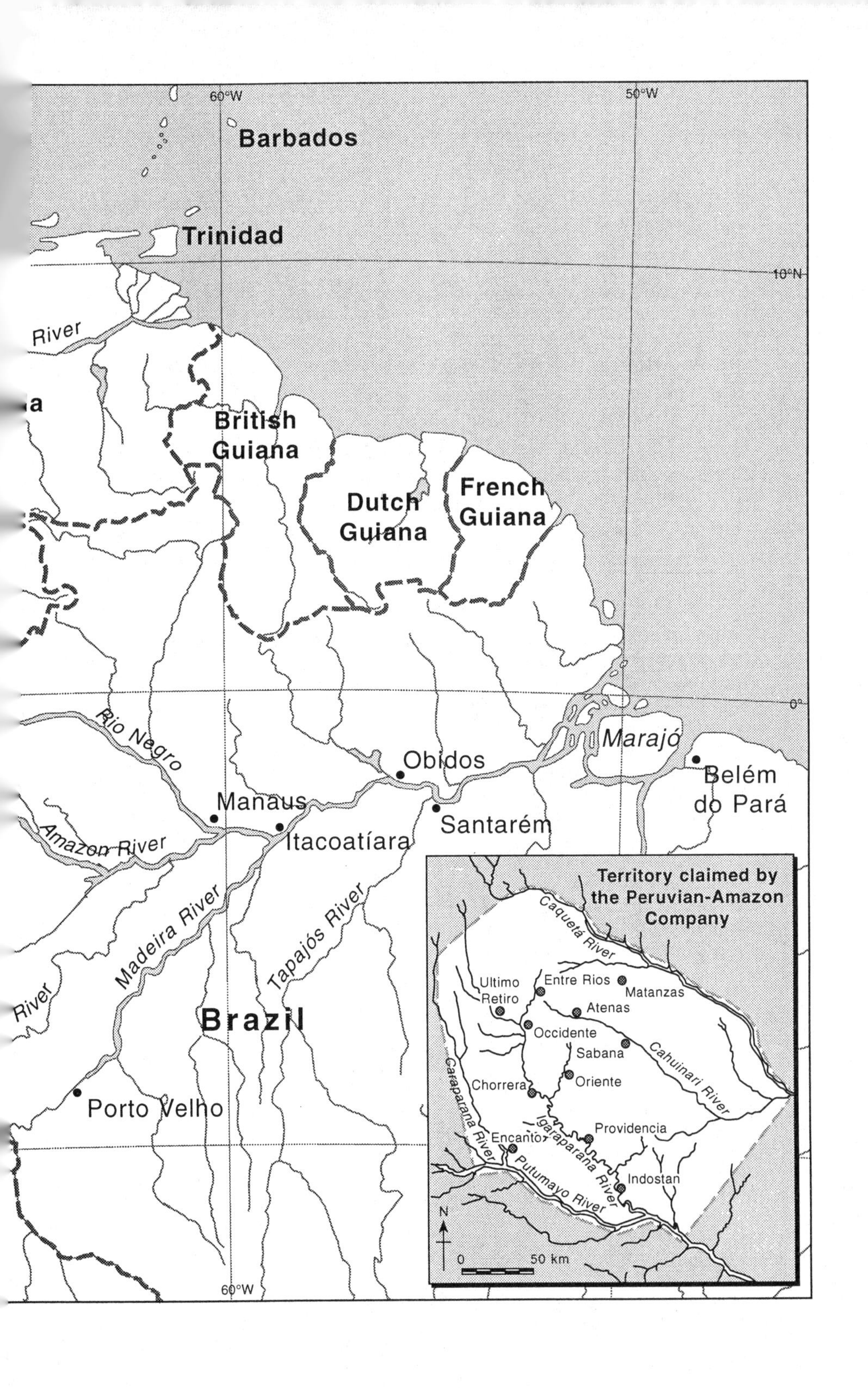

60°W
50°W
Barbados
Trinidad
10°N
River
British
Guiana
Dutch
Guiana
French
Guiana
0°
Rio Negro
Marajó
Obidos
Belém
do Pará
Manaus
Santarém
Amazon River
Itacoatíara
Madeira River
Tapajós River
River
Brazil
Porto Velho
60°W
Territory claimed by
the Peruvian-Amazon
Company
Caquetá River
Entre Rios
Matanzas
Ultimo
Retiro
Atenas
Occidente
Sabana
Cahuinari River
Caraparana River
Chorrera
Oriente
Igaraparana River
Providencia
Encanto
Putumayo River
Indostan
N
0
50 km

The British Foreign Office opened its file on the Putumayo atrocities in October 1909 as a consequence of disturbing reports published in a small London-based financial watchdog magazine called Truth. *In its 22 September issue,* Truth *told the story of a young American railroad engineer, Walt Hardenburg,*[58] *who had collected statements of atrocities by former employees of the Peruvian Amazon Company, a rubber concern operating in the frontier regions of the north-west Amazon. Pressure from the Anti-Slavery & Aborigines Protection Society, mixed with public outrage that a British-owned company could be indirectly responsible for such atrocities, helped persuade the British Foreign Secretary, Sir Edward Grey,*[59] *to act. Despite every effort to avoid the accusations, the Peruvian Amazon Company decided at the beginning of June 1910 to send a five-man commission to investigate the "commercial prospects" of the region. The Foreign Office took the opportunity to send its own representative and selected the Brazilian Consul–General, Roger Casement CMG.*

---

[58] Walter Hardenburg (1886–1942), was the American engineer responsible for bringing the Putumayo atrocities to public attention in England. In January 1908 Hardenburg and his companion, W. Perkins, while travelling down the Putumayo from Colombia, witnessed one of the final shoot-outs between the last few Colombian *caucheros* and superior Peruvian forces composed of soldiers and employees of the Peruvian Amazon Company. They were arrested and their luggage and personal belongings were stolen. Hardenburg remained in the Amazon until June 1909, compiling a case against the Company before travelling to London with a body of evidence and signed statements by ex-employees of the P.A. Co. detailing atrocities against the tribal people. On the advice of the Secretary of the Anti-Slavery Aborigines Protection Society, John Harris, Hardenburg was directed towards a weekly financial paper called *Truth*, which duly ran his story on 22 September 1909 and in subsequent issues. In this way, the story of the Putumayo atrocities was brought to public attention across the British empire. Among Casement's dossier of papers in the Amazon was a copy of the "Hardenburg Document", which he obtained from the Anti-Slavery Society and had typed at his expense. The originals of Hardenburg's statements can be found in Rhodes House Library {Brit. Emp. S22} along with the original of Hardenburg's typescript describing his pioneering journey across the Andean massifs of southern Colombia and down the Putumayo. In November 1912 Hardenburg published his story along with some of the statements he had collected and excerpts from Casement's official Putumayo Blue Book in a work suitably titled *The Putumayo, The Devil's Paradise* (Fisher and Unwin 1912). Hardenburg's Amazon adventure was later fictionalized by Richard Collier in *The River that God Forgot* (Collins 1968).

[59] Grey of Fallodon, Edward Grey, First Viscount (1862–1933), British statesman, MP for Berwick-on-Tweed (1885–1916) and British Foreign Secretary (1906–16).

Casement was in a number of respects the natural choice for the job. His investigation in 1903 into atrocities committed in the collection of wild rubber in central Africa in the Congo Free State of Leopold II gave him a good knowledge of the wild rubber industry. The "White Book" that was subsequently published, containing his report and the oral testimonies of those who had witnessed the atrocities, brought his career in Africa, spanning almost two decades, to a controversial climax.[60] *In 1906, after sa year in Ireland, he was coaxed out of early retirement by the new Liberal government's Foreign Secretary, Sir Edward Grey, and posted to the Brazilian coffee port of Santos. The following year he was transferred to Belém do Pará, the main port at the mouth of the Amazon and the centre of the Brazilian rubber trade. After a few months of service, followed by a period of illness and recuperation in Barbados, he was promoted to Consul-General in Rio de Janeiro.*

In March 1910 he returned to England on leave. In June, while staying at the family home of Magherintemple in the north of County Antrim, he was contacted by the Anti-Slavery & Aborigines Protection Society about his willingness to investigate the Putumayo atrocities. He accepted and on 13 July he was briefed at the Foreign Office by Sir Edward Grey. Casement's memorandum of that meeting describes in detail what was discussed. It was initially proposed that both a representative from Barbados and from the Colonial Office would accompany Casement and the Commissioners, because the majority of British subjects in the Company's employment were Barbadian overseers. Grey's main concern was how Casement would travel through the territory. He clearly understood that transport in that region was very difficult and passage through the Putumayo appeared to be only possible on a Company vessel if he was to reach the scene of the enquiry. But he gave Casement complete freedom as to how he wished to travel, whether alone or with the Commission, although he stressed he should watch and report on the manner in which the Commission discharged its duties.

The boundaries of Casement's investigation were defined as follows:

To investigate the charges preferred against British subjects employed by a British Company and to some extent the action of that Company itself, in so far as responsibility for its actions affected British subjects.

This would be a perfectly legitimate function for a British official to exercise in view of, among other reasons, possible claims for compensation arising out of the action of this company or its British employees.

---

[60] Correspondence and Report from His Majesty's Consul at Boma respecting the Administration of the Independent State of the Congo — PP 1904 (Cd. 1933) LXII.

No indication was furnished by Sir Edward Grey as to how an enquiry of this kind could be independently pursued in a foreign country beyond a general outline of how far it may be possible to proceed.

I pointed out that the difficulties of an investigation would be very considerable, and that independent interpretation, that is to say the presence of a person with a competent knowledge of Spanish, would be desirable. Upon this point, as upon the means of travelling and the actual methods adopted for eliciting information, it was to be understood that the Secretary of State left my judgement free exercise.

Sir Edward Grey next pointed out that in addition to the specific charges alleged against the employees of the Company in which British subjects and their interests might be involved there would arise facts connected with the general rubber regime in the country visited that it might be well to note and report on separately. It would be necessary to exercise great caution in this respect — as indeed throughout the enquiry — so as to afford no ground for possible objection being raised by the governments of the territory visited. It would be necessary from the first to treat any such information obtained as of a confidential and separate character and it would not be intended for publication nor for direct transmission to the governments or governments whose agents might be involved.

The report on the facts, in so far as these concerned a British Company and British subjects would be for publication in this country.[61]

The other Commissioners were a typical assortment of colonial Englishmen. Heading the group was Colonel Reginald Bertie. Casement had initial reservations about his suitability to lead the enquiry but soon came to respect and befriend him. After a distinguished military career in the Royal Welsh Fusiliers, Bertie had led a successful enquiry in 1898 into the massacre of soldiers and sailors during the Cretan troubles. Of the other members of the Commission the most striking was the tall, moustachioed figure of Louis Harding Barnes, a tropical agriculturist, with experience of farming in Mozambique. Walter Fox — a small and rotund pipe-smoker — was a botanist connected with the Royal Botanical Gardens and expert in planting rubber. The third independent member was Seymour Bell, an economist with a good grounding in "commercial development". Only the youngest member of the Commission, Henry Gielgud, had any first-hand experience of South America. He had visited the Amazon on behalf of the Peruvian Amazon Company's accountants the year before and, due to the favourable report and set of accounts he had presented, he had been head-hunted by the Company.

---

[61] Casement's memorandum recording his brief from Sir Edward Grey on 13 July 1910 is held in N.L.I. MS 13,080 (6/iii).

THE VOYAGE FROM LONDON TO IQUITOS

Casement and the Commission set out from Southampton aboard the R.M.S. Edinburgh Castle *of the Union-Castle line in the late afternoon of 23 July 1910. They arrived in Madeira on 27 July where they stopped over for four days. On 31 July they boarded the SS* Hilary *of the Booth Line and continued across the Atlantic to Belém do Pará, the main port at the mouth of the Amazon and centre of the Brazilian rubber industry. They arrived on 8 August but further delays prevented them from progressing up river until 13 August, when they continued aboard the SS* Hilary. *Soon after leaving Belém do Pará problems began to arise. Colonel Bertie was struck down with acute dysentery. By the time they reached Manaos, it was clear Bertie would be forced to turn back. This was a great blow to Casement since Bertie was the only Commissioner with any direct experience of investigating atrocities.*

Casement's own health was also beginning to suffer as they entered the hot and humid tropical climate and an eye infection increasingly began to trouble him. Spending just one night in Manaos, Casement left the other Commissioners and boarded another Booth steamship Huayna *on the afternoon of 17 August and continued up river at a tortuously slow pace due to the low water levels. The remaining four commissioners continued a few days later on board the* Urimaguas, *a river launch provided by the Company. Just after crossing the Brazilian border into Peruvian waters, the* Urimaguas *overtook the* Huayna *and Casement transhipped. Casement and the Commissioners arrived in Iquitos together on 31 August.*

In the months before leaving England, Casement had been actively involved in setting up a testimonial campaign for E.D. Morel[62] *in an effort*

[62] E.D. Morel, (Georges Edmond Pierre Achille Dene Morel de Ville (1873–1924) was born in Paris to a French civil servant father and English Quaker mother. Following the early death of his father he moved with his mother to England and after education at Bedford Modern entered the Elder Dempster Company in Liverpool as a shipping clerk while moonlighting as a reporter for local newspapers and specialising in west African affairs. Gradually, his work came to the attention of the humanitarians Sir Charles Dilke and Richard Fox Bourne. In 1904 Morel, under the guidance and with the encouragement of Casement and his White Book, founded the Congo Reform Association, backed by Liverpool traders such as John Holt. In 1906 he published *Red Rubber: The Story of the Rubber Slave Trade Flourishing on the Congo in the year of Grace 1906* (London 1906), just one of a series of books published between 1901 and 1911 that amassed statements and evidence regarding the widespread genocide of African tribal culture as a result of the European scramble for Africa. In 1909 Morel established the International League for the Defence of the Natives of the Conventional Basin of the Congo. During 1917 and 1918 he was imprisoned for violation of the Defence of the Realm Act. The Casement–Morel correspondence is held in the London School of

to establish some financial security for Morel and his family and to allow him to broaden his campaign in alerting public attention to the human rights plight of the African tribal world. It was also hoped that the Testimonial would serve as a suitable tribute to Morel's decade of untiring efforts to bring the horrors to an end. The Testimonial brought Casement into contact with other public figures prepared to support humanitarian issues including Sir Arthur Conan Doyle, William Cadbury and Casement's friend and confidant, the historian Alice Stopford Green. The Testimonial was launched on 11 July and the night before leaving for the Amazon Casement dashed off letters to the Liverpool Courier *and the* Daily Post & Mercury *talking about the Testimonial.*

Economics and in most of the letters Morel was referred to as "Bulldog"and Casement as "Tiger".

LSE Morel Papers F8/24 'Tiger' Casement to 'Bulldog' Morel

S.S. *Hilary* — At Sea
2 August 1910

My dear old Bulldog,

I got your letters and papers all right on getting on board on Sunday morning at Madeira. I am glad the courier, at any rate put the letter in well, altho the Post behaved in such a measly way.

All that you tell me of W.A.C.[63] is only what I thought of him! His idea that your brother-in-law should go with you is an excellent one and I do hope it may be carried out. If not, then I trust W.A.C. will send that other £300 in anonymously to the Testimonial — that would bring it up to a fine sum for the start.

I wonder what followed Thursday's Committee meeting at dear Mrs. Green's[64] house — and if the other members of the Committee have bucked up — and I hope put Gilmour on the list.

I have collected a few tiny sums en route from sympathisers — but I feel so powerless now that I can no longer do anything or know how the matter stands. I am very hopeful of old John Holt![65]

---

[63] William Cadbury was part of the great dynasty of Quaker chocolate millionaires whose factories at Bournville were held up high as examples of British industrial welfare. But in 1905 the image of the company was tarnished by evidence showing that widescale slavery underpinned the cultivation of the cocoa they bought from Portuguese Africa. The Cadburys' failure to react fast enough to the press accusations or to boycott the cocoa-producing countries led to a famous civil action, "Messrs. Cadbury Brothers *v.* the *Standard* Newspaper Company", that came up for hearing on 29 November 1909. Leading the counsel for the plaintiffs was Mr Rufus Isaacs and for the defendants, Sir Edward Carson. William Cadbury became a close friend of Casement's during 1911 and contributed to Casement's expenses during his Amazon investigation. In the years before the First World War he became one of the most active financiers supporting humanitarian causes in Britain. He never gave credence to the slanders against Casement.

[64] Alice Stopford Green (1847–1929), writer and historian, was born in County Meath in 1847, and was Casement's closest female friend. After the death of her husband, the historian John Richard Green, in 1883, she became associated with the rising tide of intellectual discontent and became increasingly anti-imperialist associating closely both the humanitarian and women's suffrage movements. Among her circle of friends she counted Florence Nightingale, Winston Churchill, John Francis Taylor, H.A.L. Fisher and Henry Levinson. Casement drew increasingly close to her after his return from Africa and maintained one of the great correspondences of his life with her {N.L.I. 10464 (2)}, at times using her as his confessor. In 1908 she published *The Making of Ireland and its Undoing*, a controversial book on early Irish history which Casement did much to promote. Casement's plan to smuggle arms into Ireland was hatched in her house in Grosvenor Road. After the events of 1916 she returned to Dublin and died on 28 May 1929. She never doubted that the *Black Diaries* were forged.

We are having a pleasant voyage — altho' I see far too much of the Peruvian Amazon Company Commission. Colonel Bertie is very anxious to rope me into his councils, and already is trying to get me to regard myself as one of his party.

I know his feelings, but I've got nothing to do with them and I intend to keep aloof as much as can be done with regard to politeness. I don't think much good can come of this journey — indirectly yes, but directly no. We shall be fairly well hoodwinked I think — the good will be in a general cleaning up and more care for the future perhaps. Bertie is not the man, I think, to find anything out, in any case. He seems very harmless and knows nothing of the country, people, traditions, ideas or anything else connected with the work in hand. His name and social standing are all that have been looked to. The chief difficulty, for me, is the seeming necessity I am under of travelling everywhere as the guest of this Commission. It is very hard, well nigh impossible to arrive at an independent judgement or to take any independent line of investigation when from start to finish I shall be doing everything "by your leave".

I wonder where I shall be in October when you start for your great Emirate — Bulldog as Emir of Kano and Sultan of Sokoto.[66] You will enjoy your journey greatly of that I am sure, and you will return to England stronger than ever and I hope with your soul strengthened for still bigger fights for the souls of Blackmen. (I like that book.)

We arrive at Pará on Monday next 8th August and I may then tranship to another vessel but I cannot say yet. From Pará about 11th this ship goes on to Manaos arriving there on 15th — and then the Commission will tranship into one of their launches for Iquitos 1300 miles higher up. They want me to accompany them, but I hope to find other means of reaching Iquitos in time — this I cannot say until reaching Pará.

I daresay I shall be far up the Putumayo when you start for Nigeria. I'll write again to you before closing this. This was to thank you for writing and for the papers. I return Ward's note.

---

[65] John Holt was Vice-President of the Liverpool Chamber of Commerce and had for many years continued a lucrative import–export business with Africa and the Congo through his fleet of cargo ships. Holt became allied to the cause of Congo reform after the truth about Belgium conduct in central Africa began to leak out and campaigned as a humanitarian supporting Morel's initiative to bring about change.

[66] Kano and Sokoto are both states of northern Nigeria.

With every kind thought of you all.
Yours ever —
Tiger

N.L.I. MS 13,087 (1) Undated fragmentary note in Casement's hand

The formation of the country — up to the Andean rise — leaves nothing to the imagination. The eye falls on unending lines of trees walling in a vast flow of discoloured waters, and behind the trees are no regions of the unknown — in the human sense — no strange tribes to be discovered, no sense of mystery, no legendary memorials of a past period of human habitation. The Indian has gone and left no trace behind him. At least this is so in Brazil — in Peru and Bolivia it is still otherwise. The rudest Brazilian settlement, 2,000 miles from Pará, will have its cheap imitation of the city life at the mouth of the Amazon: Bars, billiards and cafés, white collars and even Paris hats, while the people — those who in Africa would be indeed "the natives" — are here represented in varying degrees of imported blood mixed with aboriginal stock, by canoe-men, wood-cutters, rubber gatherers and others more idle still, who clothed in shirt and trousers, await the political news from the capital, con the provincial journals of Pará and Manaos, discuss the latest social scandal or moral delinquency of their friends, serve on juries, celebrate "festas", and vote for the deputies and senators.

All are equally citizens of a great democratic federation modelled on a French precept (Liberty, Fraternity, Equality) rather than on the American definition of it ("Blacks excluded"). In Brazil colour even counts for caste — Indian blood is prized, and I think rightly prized.

N.L.I. MS 13,074 (6ii) Postcard from Roger Casement to Gertrude Bannister

8 August 1910

I do hope you are both having a real good time of it at Cloghaneely[67] and that you find your surroundings all that I hope. The college will interest you very much I am sure. How is the lone woman of Dunfanaghy — poor old soul!

I have just sent her a card to Ballycastle and wonder where she is. It is warm here — we are just arriving at Pará where I stay for 3 days and then go on to the uttermost parts of the Earth.

Scodgie

N.L.I. MS 13158 (7) Roger Casement to Bulmer Hobson[68]

c/o H.M.Consul
Iquitos
Peru

8 August 1910

My dear Bulmer,

Here I am again at Pará! I hurried off at a moment's notice too. I am on my way right up the Amazon into Peru — some 3,000 miles of river way! Shall be about in the wilderness for fully four, perhaps six months — and I don't think I shall get letters for several months, as I am going away from posts and civilisation all the time.

I dropped you a hurried line from Madeira — and this is the sequel. I had thought often of you while in London — but did not see much outlook of hope. Now I do. If it will help and be of real good to you I think by the end of this year I could let you have, as an advance, say £150 to buy that farm, or start you on it. Do you

[67] It had been Casement's intention to spend much of his summer leave of 1910 attending the summer school at Cloghaneely in County Donegal improving his spoken Gaelic but the Putumayo investigation spoiled this plan. His cousin Gertrude Bannister visited instead. Dunfanaghy was a village a little down the coast from Cloghaneely.

[68] Bulmer Hobson (1883–1969), revolutionary and writer. Hobson was an active nationalist who started an Ulster Debating Club in 1900 with the intention of recruiting Ulster Protestants into the nationalist movement. He joined the Gaelic League and helped found *Na Fianna Éireann*, the Ulster Literary Theatre and a small broadsheet, *The Republic*. In 1907 he campaigned in the U.S. on behalf of Sinn Féin but resigned after a clash with Arthur Griffith and in 1916, along with Eóin Macneill and Casement, tried to prevent the Easter Rising. After the war he withdrew from revolutionary politics and from 1948 moved to Roundstone, County Galway, and later to Limerick.

think it would work? I mean would that sum be enough to really start you and wd. farming be for you the right, or best thing? Ask your father to advise you, as to the money, you could pay me back some day when you are more independent. I make the suggestion because I think I see my way clear to spare that sum without inconvenience — and there is no one I should wish to help more than you — for your sake and the sake of Ireland. Look on it as a loan to Ireland if you accept. You can write to me at the address given, after you have talked it over with your father. If he thinks ill of the farm perhaps the sum might help you to an independent start elsewhere — say even in the U.S.A.. It will not do you harm to go there for a time — but if the farm is the best and most permanent outlook then stay on the old soil and face destiny straight in the eyes in Ireland. Your letter cannot reach me for several months, but I did not want to go into the wilds without leaving one word of hope behind me.

Yours ever,

Roger Casement.

One of the main daily newspapers of Belém, A Província do Pará, *reported in its edition of 9 August the arrival the previous day from Le Havre of the S.S.* Hilary. *It was carrying a cargo of granite and building materials and mechanical accessories for the Pará Electric Railways Company as well as three boxes of silver one pound coins destined for Bolivia. On the long list of first-class passengers accompanying Casement were the Portuguese writer Augusto B. Lacerda and Lizardo Arana, a director of the Peruvian Amazon Company and brother of its founder, Julio C. Arana.*[69]

---

[69] Julio Cesar Arana (1864–1952) was a Peruvian rubber baron and *aviador* born in northern Peru to a family of panama hat manufacturers. In 1897 he began trading arms, liquor and goods with Colombian *caucheros*. In 1902 he became mayor of Iquitos and increased his efforts at "civilizing" the tribes of Peru's northern frontier, gradually annexing the region for himself. His business empire expanded rapidly and in 1905 he set up an office in New York. In 1907 he reorganized his business operations following the flotation of his renamed company — The Peruvian Amazon Rubber Company — on the London Stock Exchange. At about this time the first stories began to circulate downriver into Brazil that the Company was committing widespread atrocities. See Howard Karno, "Julio Cesar Arana, Frontier Cacique in Peru" in Robert Kern (ed), *The Cacique* (Albuquerque 1973). While Arana was held high in Peru as a great patriot and nationalist, his company methods led to massive tribal extermination. During the early 1920s he sat in the Peruvian senate, having won his electoral campaign in Loreto on promises of Indian protection.

PRO FO371/968 Letter from Consul–General Casement to Spicer

Pará — 11th August 1910

Dear Spicer,[70]

We got here on 8th and I found three telegrams from FO[71] — the last a long one to me from you. I entirely feel as that telegram itself indicates my line of action — and I trust all will go as it should between the Peruvian Amazon Company's Commission and myself. My wish for wishing the Iquitos Consul to be advised was mainly due to the fact that he was a "trading" man and less likely therefore to be of service should I need help. I may want money for instance, food supplies or even a steam launch — and unless the local Consul helped me I might easily be stranded. My present intention is to go with the Commission (as a "paying guest") as far as I find it useful and convenient and that may involve several months journeying on the Upper Amazon.

I have telegraphed to the Governor of Barbados to try and send Whiffen's "boy" after me.

Pará is just the same — the papers here, by the way, had a wire from London dated 6th August saying the "press of that Capital applauded the act of the Govt. in sending the British Consul at Rio" on this journey to the Putumayo — so I presume something must have been said in Parliament.

The same Brazilian papers had interesting news that bears, to some extent, on this whole question. A Rio telegram stated that the

---

[70] Gerald Sydney Spicer (1874–1942) entered the Foreign Office in 1894, serving as Permanent Under Secretary for Foreign Affairs (1903–6) and then as assistant clerk in the American Department of the Foreign Office under Sir Edward Grey. Much of Casement's official Putumayo correspondence was addressed to Spicer.

[71] N.L.I.MS 13,087 (4). Copy of telegrams received at Pará Consulate for Consul General Casement:

July 28 1910 — "Inform Consul Casement on arriving at Para per Booth Co's SS *Hilary* in a fortnight that Colonial Office has decided Barbados will not be represented separately on Putumayo Commission."

August 2 1910 — "Tell Casement that we are endeavouring to ascertain Brown's address but fear that he will be too late, late in any case for him to reach Para in time, so that he had better engage another interpreter if possible."

August 6 — "I have shown your letters to Sir Edward Grey who has sent instructions to Consul at Iquitos in the sense you desire. He quite sees that your position with the Company's representatives must be rather difficult but thinks that without letting your own work be hampered or prejudiced in any way it is important you should keep on as good terms with them as is compatible with this condition, and that you should make it your endeavour as far as possible to carry the commission with you should you be convinced of irregularities in conduct of affairs by their local representative. Spicer."

govt. had chosen Lt Colonel Rondon[72] as "Chief of the Service for the Protection of the Forest Indians". This refers to Brazilian Indian tribes — and Rondon is a very capable man I believe. It is a good thing to see that one of these republics is beginning to realise its duties and responsibilities towards the Indian tribes.

I am very good friends with Colonel Bertie and all the members of the Commission and you can rest assured of these friendly relations continuing, whatever divergence of view might arise. I fully realise that the surest hope of getting permanent good for the people of the region we are visiting is to convince the Commission and carry it with me so far as possible.

Forgive a hurried line on my knees in a dark cabin. Mosquitoes have been at us day and night — and both Bertie and I are a bit off colour.

My eyes are weakening and troubling me a bit[73]— and Bertie insists on getting a Dr for his party, wherein I think he is wise. It is not easy to find a man and the salary asked will be big — but it is not my affair.

Bertie says the Company are spending £10,000 on this Commission of theirs — they will want some results.

Thanks for all your help and believe me.

Yours,

Roger Casement

On 13 August A Província do Pará *announced the departure the day before of the S.S.* Hilary *with Casement and the Commission. The paper also contained a short item about Casement:*

O Sr. Roger Casement, que preceden neste estado como Consul Inglez, as actual Sr. G. Ambrose Pogson acaba de ser provido no lugar de Consul General, com sede no Rio de Janeiro.

---

[72] Cândido Mariano da Silva Rondon (1865–1958) was born in Mato Grosso, Brazil. As a soldier Rondon played an important part in creation of Brazilian Republic and afterwards in laying telegraph lines into remote regions of Brazil and contacting remote tribes. In 1910 he was appointed to lead the Indian Protection Service and in his long life Rondon became a great champion of the Brazilian Indians and the country's greatest twentieth-century explorer of the Brazilian interior and frontier. In 1912 the Brazilian government pledged to send Rondon to the northwest Amazon to help track down and arrest the Putumayo criminals but the promise proved empty. The Amazon state of Rondonia is named in his honour.

[73] The first mention of Casement's eye infection that grew progressively worse until the night of 12 October when he bandaged both eyes and effectively went blind in the middle of the forest. Despite frequent mention of this ailment in his correspondence with the Foreign Office during the early part of the voyage there is not a single mention of Casement's eye problems in the *Black Diaries* until 10 October.

PRO FO800/106 Consul–General Casement to Tyrrell

On S.S. *Hilary* — the Amazon River
14th August 1910

Dear Tyrrell,[74]

I am on my way to Manaos whither we hope to arrive 16th — after that everything is uncertain as to mode and means of progression. The Commission of the Peruvian Amazon Company expect to have a launch of that Company to take them 1,200 miles more to Iquitos — where they will proceed to the Putumayo in another launch of the Company. I may go on, as a "paying guest", of the Company — but I don't relish the prospect. I am good friends with Bertie and the other men of the Commission. I feel that while working with them as much as possible, I can hopefully get better results by being as detached as is possible. Col. Bertie talked of going home from Manaos the other day. He spoke to me with his mind apparently made up on the point, saying that his health was not robust enough to face the perils of the Putumayo and that on arrival at Manaos on 16th he should hand over the Commission to Mr Bell (the second member) also in this steamer. Now, however, he says he feels better and will, at any rate go on to Iquitos and see how he feels — and he may go further — but I have my doubts! The climate is a dreadful one — and the food, once we leave this mail steamer, worse. My eyes have got very bad — that is why I write in pencil, they had shown signs of weakness just before I came away, but had improved at home. On arrival at Pará the bad symptoms returned and the ship's doctor says I am threatened with chronic opthalmia. The worst is that there is no doctor where we are going and it is not a cheerful prospect to have a complete breakdown of the eyes in the wilds of the Amazon forests. However, it would never do for both Bertie and myself to come away with our work all undone and whatever the case I shall

[74] William George Tyrrell (1866–1947) was born and baptized a Roman Catholic in Naini Tal, India. Entering the Foreign Office in 1889, he was made Sir Edward Grey's Private Secretary in 1905. He was the senior Foreign Office official most closely associated with Casement's Putumayo investigation. In 1918 Tyrrell became head of the political intelligence department of the FO and in 1925 was appointed permanent under-secretary. From 1935 he held the office of the president of the British Board of Film Censors (B.B.F.C.) and was responsible for suppressing efforts to make a film of Casement. Before his death he destroyed all his personal papers and correspondence. Tyrrell has been generally considered one of Casement's allies, but his government appointments after Casement's execution suggest otherwise.

go on into the Putumayo and its tributaries — though I think it scarcely likely I shall continue with the Commission throughout all its visit. Very much of its work is purely with the economic and financial side of the Company's "properties" and seeking new fields of profit — and they talk of being around until March next. I think it highly likely I shall leave long before then. But of course all depends on what I find and how I see myself influencing it for good. From all I can gather, privately there is little doubt that Hardenburg's and Whiffen's[75] statements were not lies but mainly true. All we can hope for is to see that these devilish things are no longer occurring, and that steps can be taken to ensure they shall not recur — but this is the real difficulty. It will be enough to find things passably tolerable, even decent during the period of our sojourn on the Putumayo and to safeguard the future, where there is practically no administration save that of the Company itself and its half-caste agents — and no sense of justice at all when it comes to dealing with these poor, docile forest tribes of Indians, is another thing. As regards the Commission and its members I have every confidence in them.

By the way I see my letter to the Liverpool papers about Morel appeared on 25th July — and it reached me in Madeira. There is nothing here that anyone can take offence at I think — every word about Morel is true — for no man ever fought more unselfish and generous a fight on behalf of others than this man did.

---

[75] Captain Thomas Whiffen (1878–1922) was privately educated in England and Switzerland. A former officer in the 14th Hussars, his military career had been cut short after being badly wounded in the groin in a cavalry charge during the Boer War. In April 1908, motivated by a "weariness for civilization" and the idea of completing Alfred Wallace's unrealized journey down the Uaupes along with a desire to reveal the truth behind Eugenio Robuchon's death, he set out to explore the north-west Amazon. After crossing the Putumayo territories and a year of travel in the area he returned to England. Soon after arriving, he was contacted by the Foreign Office and asked to draft a report on his impressions of the Putumayo. This report, sent to the FO on 21 October 1909 from the United Services Club, helped to persuade Sir Edward Grey that action was necessary {FO371/722}. Whiffen's anthropological account of his journey, which borrowed much from the German anthropologist Theodor Koch-Grunberg, was eventually published as *The North-West Amazons. Notes of some months spent among Cannibal Tribes* (Constable 1915). Though the book contained much of anthropological interest it avoided any mention of atrocities or of Whiffen's close and rather shady dealings with Arana involving both extortion and blackmail. After supplying the FO with information Whiffen was referred to in all correspondence as Mr X until his identity was sensationally revealed at the P.S.C. enquiry in 1913 when his efforts to blackmail the Company were made public.

This is what Harry Johnston[76] wrote me just before I sailed after I had asked him to back up the testimonial — "Re. Morel — my whole heart goes out to the man. Of course I shall send a subscription though it will not be much for I am not affluent. I would write or would have written but have been a little put off doing so by the fact his advocate is Lord Cromer! I so dislike the tone of the latter's letter. It was far from gracious. The fact is that Morel has taught us all a lesson (which I for one have been proud to learn)" — and then he goes on to say other things of Morel's achievement which I need not quote. There is no lack of generosity in this tribute of Johnston's and I think it of value coming from such a quarter. I do hope the testimonial will be of great help to the Morel family, it is of them too I have been thinking. For Morel, the honest, dedicated champion of the African, nothing we say or give is any reward — we owe him I think our national gratitude and respect for having kept the country straight on so profound an issue. I sincerely hope Sir E. Grey's name will appear too on the ultimate list of supporters of Morel's Testimonial. It would honour Sir Edward as much as Morel — and certainly remove the cause from all questions of personalities — and make it really national in the highest sense. I hope you may be able to read this letter — my eyes are very dim. The Ship's doctor has painted them with Nitrate of Silver — they are very sore too. Adios or rather, au revoir. Please God I'll return back safe and sound inside of six months.

Yours always,

Roger Casement

<u>PRO FO 371/968 Consul-General Casement to Sir Edward Grey</u>

On Board S.S. *Hilary* at Manaos — 16th August 1910

Sir,

I have the honour to state that Colonel the Honourable R. Bertie C.B., the chief of the Commission appointed by the Peruvian Amazon Company, informs me that he is returning to Europe from this port by the S.S. *Hilary* and will hand over the leadership of the Commission to Mr Barnes.

---

[76] Harry Johnston (1858–1927) was an explorer and colonial administrator. A man well versed in African and American affairs, Johnston had provided Casement with a copy of his recent work, *The Negro in the New World*, before Casement set sail (see 23 November). Johnston was later cross-examined at the P.S.C. enquiry. He wrote the introduction to Morel's *Red Rubber* (Fisher and Unwin 1907).

Colonel Bertie's decision is due to the representations of Dr J.V. Watson the surgeon of this vessel who considers that his state of health does not justify him in proceeding further into the interior and incurring the exposure and hardship inevitable to a journey of the kind in this part of the world.

Colonel Bertie's return, and the cause of it are viewed with great regret by those who have been associated with him on the present journey.

I am proceeding to Iquitos by the Booth steamship *Huayna* tomorrow afternoon, due to arrive there 29th or 30th instant.

The members of the Peruvian Amazon Company's Commission will proceed, I understand, in a river launch placed at their disposal by the members of the firm at Manaos, and I expect to join them at Iquitos and thenceforward to share the hospitality of their vessel up to the Putumayo, and doubtless for some time after we have reached that region.

Should independent means of progression be at all available I shall not fail to secure them, but I gather it will be very hard to obtain separate means of transport at Iquitos, and in that event I propose entering into an arrangement with the representative of the Company to pay all travelling and victualling expenses that may arise.

I shall endeavour to keep the British Consul at Iquitos advised of my movements from time to time, and if it becomes necessary to telegraph to you I gather this can be done via Lima (partly by Marconigram on the Upper Ucayali) at the cost of about a day and a half from Iquitos to London.

I am told that telegraphic messages between Iquitos and Pará by this route have been exchanged within days.

I have the honour to be,

Sir,

with the highest respect,

your most obedient humble servant,

Roger Casement

N.L.I. MS 13,087 (26/i) Notes of a talk with Mr Victor Israel, a trader of Iquitos, on board SS *Huayna* when anchored off mouth of Javari, on night of August 24th 1910 — bound for Iquitos.

Mr Israel is a Maltese Jew — a British subject — about 31 years old. He came to Iquitos 11 years ago as a petty trader, but has lately launched out into larger affairs.[77]

[77] Victor Israel boarded the S.S. *Hilary* at Lisbon and travelled as a first-class passenger with Casement from Madeira. He joined the *Huayna* in Pará and their acquaintance seems to have begun after Manaos. Israel was trying to attract investment to his own rubber concern, the Pacaya Rubber Company — whose methods

Mr Israel came out with me on board the *Hilary* — about the best type of Peruvian we had aboard. He had been in London trying to float a rubber concern. He has a "river" near Iquitos, a grant from the Peruvian govt. on which he has a 100 free labourers he states — but "no Indians". He had frequently talked to Colonel Bertie and all the members of the Amazon Commission and was of all the other passengers on board the *Hilary* the one we probably saw most of. I sat at his table on the *Hilary* and on coming aboard the *Huayna* I found the steward had placed me at table beside him. He knew in a general way what we were coming out for and from time to time spoke of things at Iquitos generally favourably, although at times he criticised Peruvian methods just as one hears foreigners in Brazil criticising the methods of that country. His criticisms have however always been from the point of view of the self-interest of a trader — never from anything that could be termed a humanitarian or altruistic standpoint. This is perfectly natural. He has come here to make money by trade, or what is termed trade in these regions and he is concerned solely with this aspect of life.

We have frequently conversed on "trade" and colonisation of the Amazon as we have steamed up the dreary, tenantless wastes of the Solimões[78] — since leaving Manaos. He is the only passenger on board the *Huayna* who speaks English well, and with whom I find anything in common. I have expressed surprise at the emptiness of this vast tropical garden of all human life and have sometime wondered aloud where the former Indian inhabitants have gone to — altho' I know perfectly well. I have lent him Bates and Wallace[79] and he is now reading Lieutenant Herndon's Voyage

---

of operation would be compared to the Peruvian Amazon Company in 1911. Israel remained an important member of the Iquiteño business community well into the 1920s and was a faithful ally of Arana throughout.

[78] Solimões — the river generally known as the Amazon, draining the world's largest tropical rainforest, is in fact divided into three parts. In Peru it is called the Marañón. When the river enters Brazil at Tabatinga it is known as the Solimões until it reaches the confluence of the Rio Negro near Manaos. From there to the river delta it is known as the Amazon. In the sixteenth century it was known for a short time as Rio Orellana after Francisco de Orellana, the first European to navigate its course from the Andean *montaña*. Other maps refer to it as La Mar Dulce — the sweet sea — because its waters were fresh and not saline.

[79] Bates and Wallace were two of the great nineteenth-century English naturalists who contributed pioneering works of natural science to help elucidate Darwin's theories of evolution. The two men left Liverpool together on 26 April 1848 but after travelling for many months together went their separate ways. Henry Walter Bates (1825–92), an entomologist, eventually recorded his eleven years on the vast waterways of the Brazilian Amazon in *The*

down the Amazon in 1851[80] which deals with a region he is better acquainted with. Last night after dinner, he came round to me outside my cabin door and talked for quite a long time on the labour problem.

On this he has frequently touched, but never so fully as last night and his remarks illustrate pretty clearly what it is the Peruvian Amazon Company's commission have to deal with. I will record them while fresh in my memory. He deplored the impossibility of finding or introducing labour; a state of things which in Brazil, as I pointed out, was mainly due to the fiscal policy of the government which rendered the necessaries of life impossible luxuries. This he said did not apply to Peru whose tariff was far lower than that of Brazil. Thus at Iquitos, altho' 2,200 miles up the Amazon with a very high freight rate foodstuffs were sold far cheaper than on the sea coast of Brazil. He quoted among other commodities the following as being sold at Iquitos at reasonable prices: rice and potatoes.

I pointed out that that to my mind the barrier, greater even than the tariff or high freights, to the introduction of cheap foreign labour to the Amazon would be the opposition of the people on the spot who already had a system of exploiting the rubber zone, of long standing, which would be threatened by foreign cheap labour — and that even if the government of Brazil could be induced to permit cheap imports of food etc. etc. to meet such a new method of development, the local opposition in Peru and Manaos would inevitably upset any new method which was not in

---

Naturalist on the River Amazon (1864). Alfred Wallace (1823–1913) explored the Rio Negro and Uaupés and returned to England in July 1852, but his ship caught fire on the way home and all his notebooks, drawings, specimens and collections were lost. Before turning his attentions to Malaya he recorded his voyages from memory in *Narrative of Travels on the Amazon and Rio Negro, with an account of the Native Tribes* (1853).

[80] William Lewis Herndon (1813–1857) was a naval officer and had commanded a steamship during the US–Mexican War of 1847–8. In 1851 he was sent with fellow officer Lardner Gibbon to make an economic and strategic survey of the Amazon on behalf of the US naval department. Their resulting survey was published as *Exploration of the Valley of the Amazon made under direction of the Navy Department* (1854). Herndon had entered the Amazon through northern Peru and his book gave the most detailed account of the area Casement was himself now entering. Casement often referred to Herndon's observations about the widespread slavery of Indians he had witnessed throughout this area. See N.B. MS 13,087 (23) which gives typed extracts from Herndon's work that refer directly to oppression, exploitation and murder of Indians in northern Peru. Casement clearly admired Herndon.

accordance with the local tradition and usage. To this he agreed, and then began to talk of "Indian labour" being plentiful on many of the Peruvian rivers.

Savage tribes, still unsubdued, and barring all civilisation and development, were to be found even close to Iquitos. There were still "innumerable tribes of savages" up the various high feeders of the Amazon such as the Caquetá, the Napo, the Ucayali and the Putumayo[81] — and here at once he proceeded to explain the possibilities of profitably handling them, and instanced the case of Julio Arana as one of the happy results.

These tribes in their unconquered state were no use to anyone — they weren't any use to the white man and before anything could be got out of their rivers they had to be conquered and made to work. It required money to get out the necessary exportations to achieve these ends. The Peruvian govt. would grant a concession of the region conquered and encourage the settlement. It was the only method of subduing the Montaña — the great forest region, threaded by many rivers which stretch from the forests of the Andes to the Brazilian frontier — all the region has rubber, but no labour save its Indian tribes and the only means of starting labour is to force the Indians to work.

[The next few paragraphs are illegible, although it appears, from the few words that can be read, that Casement talks about the boundary dispute between Peru and Ecuador and the reasons that Peru was forced to colonize the area in such a brutal manner. Israel also tells Casement how Arana moved into the area — by first getting some of the rubber tappers into debt and forcing them to hand over their properties, buying some out and use of force to drive the rest into the higher regions beyond the Caquetá.]

... But these *mestizo* half breeds took their place and these latter were very sharp individuals and knew the value of money and could not be got to work at anything under two soles (4/-) per day.

---

[81] The Caquetá, Napo and Putumayo are the main tributaries draining the north-west Amazon and the Andean massifs of Ecuador and southern Colombia. The Ucayali and Huallaga are the main tributaries of the Marañón draining the Peruvian Andes. All these rivers were explored then exploited for their rubber from about 1890 onwards. The Caquetá becomes the Japura and the Putumayo the Iça on entering Brazil. On most contemporary maps the Putumayo marks the boundary between northern Peru and southern Colombia although the area is still "disputed".

"So that your system of conquering the wild Indians," I said, "instead of meeting the labour difficulty, only ends by increasing the depopulation and leaving you with expensive half-breeds."

Mr Israel continued to explain that the successful individual who was fortunate enough to possess the means of conquering a given region became a wealthy man and that was what every man wanted to become.

I asked for particulars as to how such a "conquest" was actually effected. The Indians it was clear did not abandon their forest freedom voluntarily and come gladly to collect rubber for the gentlemen who entered their untapped forest wastes. How were the preliminaries of "trading" or labour established?

"Oh!" he said, "there is fighting of course. They resist and often kill parties and burn the houses — but in the end they are reduced."

"And the Peruvian government," I asked "looks on with approval?"

"Of course — it is the only way the tribes can be civilised — how would you do it?"

I explained that in the relations of British subjects and uncivilised peoples our government did not allow private war to individual ends — and that in, say, our African colonies, native tribal and land rights were recognised by the govt. and the white settlers could not take lands from the natives — not even the govt. itself, and I instanced Southern Nigeria, where in my own official experience our government had purchased from the native chiefs the very ground upon which Government House at Old Calabra[82] stood.

This led to a somewhat long digression on British methods of colonisation and the legal safeguards that had been and were being set up by our Colonial govt. to protect natives and above all their rights over their lands. These, I pointed out, were at the bottom of all economic progress. Whether it might be Africa, Europe or America that was in case, until a people were rooted in the soil and had learned that to till the soil was the mark of all social and economic development, "getting rich" quick, and exploiting natural resources, like these of the Amazon valley we had been discussing, were all works in the wrong direction. Vegetable filibustering could never take the place of agriculture.

---

[82] Casement was given a Colonial Office appointment in the Niger Coast (Oil Rivers) Protectorate in 1891.

Mr Israel had also explained carefully that after the "conquest" of an Indian tribe and the crude forced labour which was its earliest and most lucrative product ...

[*becomes illegible once again*].

" ... He owned them as much as he owned the rubber trees on his 'territory' — they were his Indians." And all this done with the willing support of the Lima government which regard any such "conquest" of a new tribe as a patriotic act deserving of territorial rights being conferred on the conqueror. The idea of a government civil service to deal with native Indians had never entered the head of any Peruvian — and how should it? Who would go into the montaña out of curiosity or a mere desire to know the Indian or study them or for any purpose but profit? No Peruvian certainly — they like Lima and their cities too well and the few daring men who (like Arana) fitted out expeditions to acquire new territory were very fortunate in possessing the means of subduing these useless hordes of savages and turning them to useful account.

I did not seek to further point out that the dreary tale of raid and robbery and enslavement (I was careful not to so call it) could settle nothing. It was clear that Mr Israel viewed the whole question solely in the light of self-interest and that he could scarcely conceive any other point of view — and our conversation soon after came to an abrupt end, when, to clinch the argument he had been sustaining he asked me,

"What would you do, suppose the government were to offer you a large concession of forest land, up here, on which wild Indians dwelt and you could do nothing with it or with them until they had been conquered? What would you do?"

I asked him if he wanted me really to give a personal answer. He said that was what he meant — how would I deal with such a gift?

I replied that if I were a Peruvian I might probably deal with it as other Peruvians would do, but that as I was not a South American, but had been brought up in another school of thought and in accordance with a long established rule of official conduct between governing whitemen and subject peoples I could only answer his question in one way.

"And how is that?"

"I could not and would not accept any such gift of territory on any such conditions."

"Ah," he said with vehemence — "then no further discussion of the question is possible between us. There is no possibility of agreement — our points of view are too divergent."

"I think so," I said. "We view the matter from totally different perceptions of one man's relation to another."

And with that we closed a conversation of "how to develop labour on the Amazon" that I had found probably much more interesting than Mr Israel perceived at the time.

Should he ever read this conversation — supposing I were to some day publish a book on my travels in the Amazon — he will doubtless deny every statement I here attribute to him, and probably accuse me of being a drunkard because I drink Irish whiskey at table and he never takes anything stronger than Appolinaris.[83]

N.L.I. MS 13.087 (24) Notes on the Peruvian Frontier on board the *Huayna* — Friday 26th August 1910[84]

We came on from the mouth of the Javari this morning — over quite shallow bottom from 21 to 25 feet often — with swift current and did not get to Tabatinga until about 11a.m. A Brazilian military post there — although we lay within fifteen yards of the shore (in 13 fathoms of water) the military commandant had to be sent for to pay his obligatory visit. His dignity would not allow him to embark on one of the two wretched canoes that were moored on

[83] Large sections of this earliest surviving 'fragmentary entry' held in N.L.I. MS 13,087 (26/i) and written in pencil have been mysteriously rubbed out to a point of illegibility. Although Casement considered this conversation of considerable importance in establishing widely held opinions held amongst the trading community he doubtless kept the conversation secret because it clearly contravened his brief from the British Foreign Secretary, Sir Edward Grey, not to stick his nose into the affairs of other companies or countries and concentrate his investigation on the Peruvian Amazon Company. The rather general manner in which the entry is written introducing several of the broad points of his investigation such as land rights, differing methods of colonial government and a number of commercial aspects makes it the natural point of departure for his journal. It is also revealing as there is no reference whatsoever to his conversation in the corresponding "secret" entry which contains conflicting information, stating that the *Huayna* did not anchor at the mouth of the Javary until the night of 25 August.

[84] The following fragmentary entries from 26 to 30 August written in pencil on double-sided foolscap, held in N.L.I. MS 13,087 (24) deal with Casement's river journey from the Peruvian frontier at Tabatinga to the arrival of the Commission at Iquitos on 31 August.

the muddy shore. He came down in whites, with an attendant and plain clothes individual — the ship's boat, with the 2nd officer, went to bring him off.

Several (negro) soldiers in the khaki and red trousers of Brazil were on the platform above high water mark — near thirty feet rise or more here I should judge. There were three field pieces covered with tarpaulins and a brick or mud building carefully white-washed that was evidently the magazine.

The Commandant took a case of beer and two cases of wine on shore — contraband!

He was a caboclo I should say — or rather a half-caste Brazilian Indian and Portuguese.

We steamed on to Leticia about 12.30 where the Amazon SS *Esperanza* is high and dry. She ran on a submerged bank some ten or twelve days ago — and is now stranded and propped up to keep her from keeling over. She will be here till October or November. Her Iquitos cargo is being transhipped with a small Peruvian lighter and steam launch. This launch, Israel tells me, was once his when it was called the *Melita*. She is now termed *Clara* and is owned by a Brazilian rubber firm in the Javari.

The river at Tabatinga is about 1,100 yards broad I should say with a slow current of 1½ miles at outside but very deep — at present 90 feet in mid stream — but very unequal bottom I find and with a 30 foot rise there must be 120 feet of much swifter flowing water in May or June. The river is dropping 6" a day the pilots are told.

At Leticia the Comandante came off in a canoe paddled by 4 Peruvian soldiers dressed in a sort of blue dungaree. Three of them bare legged. The steersman was a brute man. All were cholos or half breed Indians and were rather fine, nice looking chaps. One was a splendid young fellow. I gave one, an Indian looking boy, cigarettes for all and he thanked me gracefully and with a good natured boyish smile. They sat down to wait for their officer who was up on the poop talking and having a good time. In an hour and a half they did not talk once, I think. A resigned, patient, docile look on all the five strong bronze faces. Captain Buston came along and said "all of them press ganged" — He then told me that when he was last in Iquitos in March 1910 the authorities were seizing all the young Indian men and cholos and sending them down to the Napo and Putumayo in drafts, crowded like sheep on their small launches. This was to meet the threat of war from Ecuador on the Napo–Putumayo boundary question — then very threatening. To escape this imprisonment, the Captain said, lots of the men of the place had fled to the forest, so much so that the *Huayna* could get no stevedore labour to discharge her cargo and this had to be done by the ship's crew.

The Captain states that seizing the Indian or native or Cholo inhabitants of Iquitos for any so called "public" need is done openly. Men were sent down, he avows, to the Putumayo in launches like the tiny *Melita* lying alongside the *Esperanza* packed 150 strong — seized in the streets of Iquitos and given one of three blue dungaree uniforms and then taken off and drilled and sent to the "frontier". The Arana launch *Liberal*[85] (of evil fame in the papers I have read of the Putumayo business) cleared from the Javari for Tabatinga at 7am yesterday morning. The Brazilian customs reported that she had many sick men, soldiers from the Putumayo on board, down with fever. The Captain says "starvation" chiefly. We hoped to possibly catch her up at Leticia today thinking that she might have stood by the *Esperanza* to try and get her off the banks, but when we saw the latter high and dry, her keel several feet above the falling river, perched on the crown of a sandbank, all hope of finding the *Liberal* in port left us. She had gone on to Iquitos at noon 25th. She is the boat, I am told, in which we shall leave Iquitos for the Putumayo. She brought 45 tons of India rubber from that river the Brazilian customs at Javari told us. That represents nearly £45,000 value at home. I wonder what actual sum or value in goods, or payment of any kind went to the Huitoto[86] and other Indians who collected this 45 tons.

If we were a proper Commission invested with authority and power to really investigate and to compel evidence on oath and had proper interpreters and guides with some local knowledge of men, places and affairs, what strange revelations of montaña "labour supply" and "rubber estates" and "Indian labour" we might bring to light. Certain things we can and no doubt shall find out, but we shall only touch the fringe of the matter I am afraid. And can we alter anything for better. It will be hard. We are up against 400 years of Latin

[85] This is the flagship of the Peruvian Amazon Company that played such a notorious part in the Peruvian Amazon Company's activities. Another telling inconsistency between the journal and the *Black Diaries* is that this information that Casement clearly heard about on 26 August is included in a margin note in the *Black Diary* entry for 25 August ... Liberal *launch reported at Guanabara as having cleared there at 7 a.m. for Iquitos from Ica with 45 tons of rubber a lot of "sick people" on board.*

[86] Huitoto (Witoto) is the name of the most numerous Indian people living in the Putumayo region. See Julian Steward, *The Witotoan Tribes*, H.S.I. Vol 3. p.749.

American dealings with the conquered. One thing we can do, by the way, and it will help a lot in showing the relations of the Peruvian Amazon Company (P.A. Co.) to the Peruvian government, is to find out what passage money is actually paid by the latter to the Company for conveyance of its "soldiers" to the Putumayo and vice versa. I would wager anything that not a cent is paid and that the local agents of the Company will assure us that it is not "customary" etc. etc. and Gielgud, or someone else will say that of course in a country like this and in face of "public need", "threatened invasion" and so on the company could do nothing less than convey the "protection of its property" free of charge. That might pass in the exceptional circumstances of the case of the late threatened war with Ecuador over this very Putumayo boundary — but we should also find out whether at any time passage rates are levied on Peruvian govt. officials and soldiers to and from the Putumayo, and if so when. The dates may be important. For instance Serrano[87] and his companions were murdered in January 1908 (six months really, after the P.A.Co. became legally responsible for the management of the Company and the P.A.Co. plead in their correspondence with the FO that "incidents" of this kind (not specifically naming the one case) were part of the frontier conflict between Peru and Colombia.

All right, but what share did the Company steamers and employees take in that public conflict? According to my information it was the Company's own agent Loayza or Flores[88] who murdered Serrano and his companions in cold blood — and it was a Peruvian soldier and officer who protested — the former being killed by Flores for the protest. We should also find out what cargo, if any, the Peruvian Government sends by the Company's steamers to and from the Putumayo and whether the freight is ever charged by the Company or paid by the government on such transactions. I fancy not. If we find that freight is not charged on government cargo or passage levied in government troops conveyed in the company's steamers it will go some way to show that Hardenburg's statement that the Peruvian "officials" and co were in the pay of the Company or received gifts from the Company is to this extent true — viz. that the Peruvian government used the Company's resources when they have need — and if this be so on the one side it is not illegitimate to surmise that the Company take advantage in

---

[87] Serrano was one of the last Colombian *caucheros* to resist Arana and was eventually murdered in 1908 by representatives of the Peruvian Amazon Co.

[88] Miguel Flores was a long-serving company chief of Section with one of the worst records for brutality and murder.

their terms of the officials and soldiers they have so benevolently conveyed and fed free of charge, to conduct their "civilising campaign" against the Indian rubber gatherers. Nous verrons tout cela.

Caoutchouc[89] was first called "india rubber" because it came from the Indies, and the earliest European use of it was to rub out or erase. It is now called India rubber because it rubs out or erases the Indians.

The soldiers on the *Liberal* are sick, Israel says with beri-beri, some of them wounded. By whom wounded? We must enquire at Iquitos. Israel states that many of the soldiers at Iquitos were brought from Cuzco and the Andes plateaux, overland and by Huallaga to Urumaguas[90] from which to Iquitos there is a mail steamer once a week. Also he states many of the Iquitos men volunteered for service against Ecuador last May and April. Captain Buston says some did volunteer and these were more respectable people. Volunteers were distinguished by a cloth band or badge across their uniforms — and one of the four soldiers on board at Leticia had this badge he says.

N.L.I. MS 13,087 (24) At anchor up Marañon on Saturday 27th August.

We have come about 30 miles this morning from Leticia which we left at 5.45. Very slow current and the S/S [steamship] came along at a great pace fully eight knots over the ground. Anchored here at 10.53 and much time wasted (1.17mts) before steam launch left at 11.10 to take soundings in the Loreto channel. She expects to be about 5 or 6 hours which will mean that we shall stay here all night. What shocking waste of time and mismanagement. Knowing this had to be done at this place the least that could have been done would have been to see that the steam launch left immediately we anchored. Then she might have been back at 3-4

[89] Caoutchouc entered European languages through France and derives from the Quechua word *Cahuchu* used by the Omagua Indians and tribes of eastern Ecuador. It was first used in Europe in 1745 in the paper offered by Charles Marie de La Condamine to the French Academy of Sciences reporting his findings regarding the uses of rubber among Amazon tribes. La Condamine is traditionally credited as the scientist who introduced rubber to Europe.

[90] Urumaguas, or, more commonly, Yurimaguas is a small settlement on the banks of the Huallaga in northern Peru and the base for Arana's earliest business operations. *Urumaguas* was also the name of the launch upon which the other commissioners were travelling on from Manaos.

— and we could have gone on until nearly 7 — four hours possibly saved or 32 miles at least. With any go or push we could have been close to Iquitos now. We shall be at anchor here possibly twenty hours until 6 am tomorrow morning — and this method of progress will be repeated daily. The vessel at this rate will take some twelve days to get to Iquitos — the Captain says "even at the best".

Israel told me at breakfast that his concession or "river" is up the Ucayali about 2½ days steaming above Iquitos. He has already 75,000 hectares of it "surveyed" and some of this cleared. The extent of the whole concession he says it is impossible to state until it is fully surveyed. He estimates it at four or five times the area already surveyed — say 300,000 to 375,000 hectares. At 2½ acres to the hectare this means 750,000 to 938,000 acres — or possibly even 1,000,000 acres. An area as large as Donegal or Galway or Mayo almost — but unfortunately so far as he has surveyed without Indians — without any inhabitants save his 100 paid workmen. The rubber trees are *Siphonia elastica*[91] he asserts — good Pará rubber trees. I doubt this very much. I wonder how he got this concession.

Captain Buston was talking about it last night after dinner and said no one knew in Iquitos how Israel had succeeded in blossoming out of late. He came here about eleven years ago, according to the Captain, and was a petty tradesman with a shop for some time — but latterly he has been spending much more money and going in for things on a bigger scale. The ship's surgeon, Dr Watson, who was out at Kumasi in the Gold Coast Service and knows Lagos, Old Calabar etc. thinks all these people, Peruvians and Brazilians, are robbers. Enslaving the Indians is the least of their crimes according to him — but then he admittedly talks from prejudice rather than actual knowledge. This is only his third voyage up to Iquitos in *Huayna*. Captain Buston has been coming for many years. He says the Indians are all enslaved — that it is forced labour from start to finish, and that the Indians and the rubber trees are equally reckoned as personal property of the estate owner.

---

[91] *Siphonia* is an alternative generic term used for the *Hevea brasiliensis* — the main rubber-producing tree of the Amazon. The term *Siphonia* was suppressed in 1865 following the publication of an article by Jean Mueller von Argau in *Linnaea*. But it is clear from this statement that it was still in wide usage over forty years later. Rubber was a complicated commodity with several different species of tree producing different grades of rubber.

He says that Indian children are stolen or brought constantly up the rivers and brought to Iquitos for sale or gifts. That he has often carried them on his ship with Peruvian families that as long as things go well with the family they are treated all right — but if they lose money these slave children are at once sacrificed. In no case do they ever, according to him, get back to their native homes — but if the family cannot maintain itself they would be cast adrift or sold possibly.

I shall ask at Iquitos to see the form of contract, if any, Arana and Co. may have made with the Barbados labourers. At least there may be some book entries. John Brown claims £30 due to him by the company and he states that over 100 Barbadians were still in the coys service and "were kept as slaves". This is probably a lie, almost certainly a lie — but there may still be some of them at back stations like Morelia or Abyssinia.

N.L.I. MS 13,087 (24) Early morning August 28th 1910 — underway from Loreto to Caballo Cocha (Horse Lake) en route for Iquitos.

We anchored last night at 6 after very trying passage up from our earlier anchorage where we had been waiting for sounding from 10 a.m. till 4. The old course of the river nearly blocked by a rising sandbank, so we took the "pre-old" course which is now becoming the modern route till in its turn it bungs up and the "old" or another opens. The one thing certain is that the water will and must get out. The rise here from present level is at least 40 feet. Depth is anything from 23 to 100 — according to current. We twice swerved onto a bank yesterday evening at 5 — and heeled over a lot — the current being stronger at that shallower spot — only 22 feet, the *Huayna* drew yesterday 20' 3" — so there was little to spare. The keel drove into the sand or mud somewhere and wheeled over a lot — the mighty shore of the forest stream of water meeting us nearly broadside on. Then the telegraph broke to the engine room in the midst of this difficulty and the poor old Captain got into a state of nervous excitement. However it was soon mended and we steamed on to the anchorage just above Loreto at 6 — could easily have gone on another half hour at least. Altogether we have wasted in lying idle when we might have been making from 7 to 8 miles an hour, since yesterday morning fully 10½ hours up to 6.30 last night — or some 70 to 80 miles.

For instance today we started from Leticia at 5.45 a.m. knowing that when we got below Loreto — some 30 miles away — the ship would have to stop for the pilots and launch to go out and sound the channel ahead up to Loreto. What happens. We reach the point in question at 9.50 and anchor. Instead of the launch and pilots being there ready and at once off to their task we all go to breakfast and they don't leave the ship until 11.20 or 1½ hours thus deliberately wasted. The launch returns at 3.30 and we don't get under way until almost 4 — or quite 4 — to go two hours more to 6 — instead of as it might have been four hours more steaming and an added half hour up to 6.30 when there is still plenty of light. Such navigation as this would have shocked any of us on the Congo with a current 2½ times as strong and furious, and where the Amazon has one sandbank the Congo has twenty. Moreover the Amazon always has plenty of water and no risk attaches to grounding here — whereas on the Congo in the innumerable shallows one might pile a ship up for months or heel her over far more easily than here.

The *Huayna*, of course, is wholly unsuited to this navigation — from every point of view — both that of manoeuvring and of passenger accommodation. The saloon is right down in the hold — and there is only one bathroom for all the male passengers. There were 23 up to Javari and then with one customs officer (Brazilian guard) and three pilots there were 27 men to have their baths (often twice daily) in a dirty little box with hardly room to turn in.

Captain Buston says lots of cases of sardines do go out to Iquitos, that he has plenty of them on board — I asked to see the ship's manifest and he promised to show it to me. I saw a summary of it made by chief officer. There are 560 packages of rifles etc. a lot of ammunition too. That is for Ecuador! But I want to see just what the Peruvian Amazon Company imports to pay its labour and its rubber. Forty-five tons of rubber in West Africa would cost (except on the Congo) in actual payment to the natives fully 2/- a pound or say some £11,000 worth of goods. In some aspects this thing is worse than the Congo — altho' it affects a very much smaller population.

We have just anchored 7.05 am after 1h 20m of steaming — say 8–9 miles. How long now I wonder will it be before the launch starts on her sounding trip? There is Caballo Cocha on right bank. I expect the *Urimaguas* will overtake us some time today or else tonight when we are at anchor.

If, as they said, she left Manaos on 19th, she could have been eight days out yesterday — say last night. At 110 miles a day that would mean 880 miles — but then she must have lost a few hours somewhere en route and certainly at Guanabarra and the mouth of Javari. From Manaos to Tabatinga is 861 miles so that I reckon she may be at Tabatinga this morning and she will be there at Leticia for a short space of time. We are now some 52 miles past Tabatinga I reckon or nearly 12 hours steaming possibly to her — except that from Tabatinga to Loreto the current is very slow so that she should do that 42 miles at fully 6 miles an hour or more — so that we ought not to be more than eight hours steaming for her now from Tabatinga. Also she is coming by a shorter "paranamiri" (channel) than we took yesterday evening — so that if she has had ordinary luck and really left on 19th, she ought surely to overtake us tonight.

The river is covered this morning with grass, weeds, scum and many tree trunks — some large ones — floating down. Yesterday it was clear and none of this. The water of one of the big tributaries above must be rising. A man who brought a canoe load of pineapples yesterday at noon when we were anchored below Loreto said it was rising. This is hopeful. I shall try and mark the effect on a log ashore near which we are now lying some 30 or 40 yards away. There is no doubt that with courage and resolution many hours might be saved each day. Up to our start this morning at 5.45 we have been at anchor 106 hours since we left Manaos at 5pm on 17th. I reckon fully 30 of these idle ones we might have been going ahead with as much safety as at any time in the twenty four hours. That would have meant from 180–200 miles on in other words we should now be close to Iquitos and getting in there by noon. This is the day we are due at Iquitos by the Company's time table. We were three days late however leaving Manaos. The Captain is far too ready to stop, and seizes at any pretext to anchor. Twice, I think, the pilots have only been able to get him to heave up and go on by overstating the depth of water they had found when sounding in the launch ahead. Our chief pilot, Noronha, is a Paraense — a typical one — half Indian, good humoured and easy tempered — always smiling — and fond of drink. He comes "of one of the best families in Pará" I am told and his sister is married to an Englishman named Jennings[92] there. He gets a conto a month — about £66 by the actual rate of Exchange

[92] T. Jennings was a representative of the Amazon Steam Navigation Company.

— none of the pilots get less than £50 a month, and a conto is the rule. This is more than twice what the Commodore Captain of the Booth line gets and about five times the pay of a chief officer! Brazilian pay and money are among the absurdities of this earth.

N.L.I. MS 13,087 (24) Tuesday 30th August on board SS *Urimaguas* (passed Pebas at 4am)

The *Urimaguas* came up at 11.20pm on Sunday night and anchored alongside. She sent over to ask if I wished to go on by her and I replied yes and begged them to remain until 5.30am.[93] All this took time and there was much excitement on the *Huayna* and all the passengers wanted to come. Four others eventually came — including Israel — and we left *Huayna* at 6.20 — but had to return as one of her passengers declared we had carried off two boxes of his. We steamed back to the urgent signals made, and went round her stern, but did not wait for the Chief Steward to come aboard to identify the boxes, as both Israel and the "advogado" declared they were not here with us — and in spite of excited whistles and cries and gestures we turned up stream again full speed and away. We remained long in sight of *Huayna* and passed her steam launch more than one hour up river.

The crew of *Urimaguas* largely Indian or *cafuzo* — one pure Huitoto boy named Ise Koroké, who is attached seemingly to Gielgud. He speaks a tiny few words of Spanish — and is a fine youngster — apparently about fifteen — sturdy, deep chested, broad and strong with an innocent face always ready to smile and those peculiar strange wild eyes that speak of a hunter (and possibly hunted) ancestry.

The *Urimaguas* brings no news. She left Manaos on 19th instant — went into Jurua river and stopped some times to fish. We shall not reach Iquitos until 1 September — my forty-sixth birthday! Is it good augury or not? I care only if I can help to right this great wrong out here — and bring some change of view. The banks of the Peruvian Amazon, or Marañon as they call it here, have certainly far more people dwelling on them than the Brazilian

[93] N.L.I. MS 13,073 [7/I} contains a card from Gielgud: "I write to enquire whether you prefer to continue the trip to Iquitos on the *Huayna* or to move over to this boat where, as I said in Manaos, we shall be very pleased to receive you. We do not anticipate leaving for Iquitos for the Putumayo before 10 September at earliest.

Excuse scrawl I am only just awake."

river can show. Moreover they are real natives. We have passed since Tabatinga some rows of palm thatched houses. Some of them quite nice — and each with its cassava and mealie patch — or sweet potatoes — and the inhabitants look almost all of them pure Indian blood. They are clothed — man, woman and children — which is stupid — for a fine bronze body in soiled raiment and draggled skirts is an error. Moreover morals go when clothes come.[94]

IQUITOS

Casement and the Commission arrived at Iquitos on 31 August and remained there two weeks. The Commission took up their quarters in a house provided by the Peruvian Amazon Company. Casement became the guest of the British Consul, Mr David Cazes.[95] *During his stay Casement sent further letters to Spicer and Tyrrell at the Foreign Office, giving account of the proceedings of his investigations.*[96] *He also began interviewing some of the Barbadian overseers, employees of the Company*

---

[94] This thought might be compared to the final comment in Montaigne's essay on cannibalism where, having expounded the doctrine of the noble savage, he sarcastically concludes: "That is all very well. But, good God, they don't wear breeches."

[95] Casement's most recent biographers Reid and Sawyer both write that on arriving at Iquitos Casement booked into the Hotel Le Cosmopolite — a statement based on their reading of the *Black Diary* entry for 31 August: *"Arrd. Iquitos at 8. All on shore. To Booth's Office and then to Consul Cazes. Lunched his wife and he. Took room 'Le Cosmopolite' Hotel dreadful* ..." Both biographers and the *Black Diary* are wrong. Casement stayed with David Cazes from the moment of his arrival, a comment supported by Casement's letter of 3 September to the FO 371/968: " ... On arrival at Iquitos the members of the Commission took up their quarters in the house of the Peruvian Amazon Company while I became the guest of Mr Cazes." When Casement returned to Iquitos in late November he stated: "took up my quarters in the very hot bedroom of before." There is also no record of Casement paying any hotel bill in Iquitos in the expense account he subsequently submitted to the FO.

[96] Besides the fragmentary entries, the following documents describe Casement's two weeks in Iquitos. The most puzzling is a typed document {N.L.I. MS 13,087 (8)} beginning at page 38. At top of page is scribbled "the proceeding 37 pages sent to Foreign Office from Belfast on 12 May 1911. R.C." — a document that implies Casement sent a typed version of his journal to the Foreign Office after he had submitted the main part of his report. Other documents include {FO371/1455 Casement to Tyrrell — Sunday, 4 September 1910; N.L.I. MS.13,087 (5) Draft of letter dated 5 September with "To be part of my diary" scribbled at the top; {FO 371/1455}; Casement to Tyrrell — 12 September1910; Casement to Spicer — 13 September 1910.

who were the British subjects he had been sent to investigate. These lengthy interviews became the evidence by which Casement was able to build his case of atrocities and eventually formed the heart of the "Blue Book" published as Miscellaneous No.8 1912 — Correspondence respecting the Treatment of British Colonial Subjects and Native Indians Employed in the Collection of Rubber in the Putumayo District. This part of the journal is constructed from diary fragments and official letters held in both the National Library of Ireland and Public Record Office, London.

... 31st August ...

I called upon the Prefect of Loreto on the day of my arrival. Mr Cazes[97] acted as my interpreter throughout. This gentleman, a Dr Paz Soldan, had not long before been appointed in succession to the Prefect Zapata more than once referred to in the Hardenburg denunciations. It is clear from Hardenburg's documents, that Zapata was openly suspected of having been in the secret pay of the Arana Brothers. No such accusation could be brought against the present official. I found Dr Soldan apparently a straightforward man, though by no means conversant with the true condition of things in the vast territory he was supposed to govern. The Department of Loreto,[98] or at any rate that region claimed by Peru of the Amazon *montaña*, is well nigh as large as France.

Dr Soldan assured me that the statements that had appeared in *Truth* were "fables" originating with blackmailers. The House of Arana, he said, had performed distinguished services to the State

---

[97] David Cazes (d.1915), of French–Gibraltarian extraction, served as Honorary Consul in Iquitos while carrying on as a local trader and running a prosperous local business: The Iquitos Trading Company. Cazes nevertheless seems to have been quite a conscientious consul and submitted commercial reports for Iquitos for 1903–1906, 1908 and 1910, although he clearly turned a blind eye to the rumours of atrocities Before arriving Casement had felt it of great importance to forge a proper friendship with Cazes (see Grey to Casement 6 August MS.13,087 (4) and Casement's reply to Spicer PRO FO 371/968). Casement's conversations with Cazes during his two weeks stay in Iquitos are recorded in {N.L.I. MS 13,087 (12) and show that Casement distrusted Cazes — and felt he was protecting trading rather than human interests. They maintained a long correspondence during 1911 and 1912 as Cazes supplied important local information to Casement his letters are held in the N.L.I. MS 13,087 (18i). Casement's letters to Cazes appear to be lost.

[98] Peru's official history regarding the conquest and foundation of the Department of Loreto, Peru's largest province (Departamento) occupying the north-east of the country is told in the eighteen volumes of Carlos Larrabure y Correa, *Colección de Leyes, Decretos, Resoluciones y otros documentos oficiales, referentes al Departamento de Loreto* (Lima, Imprenta La Opinión Nacional 1905–1909).

and stood high in the opinion of the Government. On my asking to whom I should address myself on the Putumayo in the event of my finding the condition of British subjects there one that called for intervention or protection, he gave me the names of the three principal agents of the Peruvian Amazon Company, assuring me that they were all "honourable gentlemen". I pointed out that I was already aware of the personalities of these gentlemen, but that I enquired for a Peruvian Authority not for an agent of the Company. It was only then that he suggested that the "Comisario" or magistrate who officially represented Peru in the Putumayo was a Señor Burga, the brother in law of Pablo Zumaeta.[99] As this was the individual more than once referred to in the Hardenburg documents as already in the pay of the Company, this reference to him as the principle "authority" was not encouraging.

... 1st September ... [Casement's forty-sixth birthday]

A Monsieur Vatan, a local trader who is a Frenchman and was at one time acting French Consular Agent in Iquitos, came to see me. He was recommended and introduced by Mr Cazes who speaks very well of him. While Mons. Vatan has not himself ever visited the Putumayo he has spent fourteen years in the neighbourhood and was for some time trading on the river Napo whence there is speedy land communication across to the Putumayo.

Mons. Vatan's statement, which was made in confidence, was a general one. He did not go into details, but spoke of the system, as he understood it to be applied in the Putumayo, as one in no way differing from slavery. He declared that the stories which had been told of that region were in the main true, that the treatment of the native Indians by the firm of Arana Bros. had been all that it had been described, that the whole thing was a disgrace to civilisation, but that he feared no remedy could be applied — or at any rate only a very slow one, covering a long period of years. Were the British Company to now suddenly change the method of dealing with the Indians and to treat their intercourse with them as one of even approximately honest commercial dealings, the establishments on the Putumayo would collapse, the persons with

[99] Pablo Zumaeta was the brother-in-law of Julio C. Arana and locally the most influential member of the company. Like Arana, he had been born into a local family in Rioja, where his father had been mayor. His sister Eleonora married Julio C. Arana in 1888.

money invested there would be ruined, and a "revolution" would take place which the Peruvian government would deal with by applying probably even worse measures to the Indians than those now in force.

The "payments" made to the Indians he declared were "derisory" and the whole system was one of sheer slavery. Mons. Vatan impressed me as intelligent and honest and I was assured by the Cazes' that he was one of the most trustworthy foreign residents in Iquitos. I have told Mr Barnes of what Mons. Vatan stated to me and I hope to bring these two gentlemen confidentially together before we leave Iquitos.

Bishop and Walker call on Casement

On the afternoon of the same day two Barbadians, who had just reached Iquitos from the Putumayo waited on me. They had arrived only days before by the SS *Liberal* which had brought down 23 invalided Peruvian soldiers and 45 tons of rubber from the Putumayo. Both these men had been for a long period in the company's service, having been recruited in Barbados by a Mr Brewster on behalf of Arana Hnos. in 1905[100] as will be seen on reference to the Company's despatches. They had been induced to call upon me through a Barbadian resident in Iquitos,[101] who is in frequent touch with Mr Cazes, who had informed this man of my wish to see and speak with any Barbadians in Iquitos who might have been employed on the Putumayo. When the two men actually presented themselves Mr Barnes and Mr Cazes were actually present with me and all that was stated was heard by both gentlemen who put questions to both men and were impressed as I was with the apparent truthfulness of their statements.

One of them, Nellis Walker,[102] speaks very well both of his own treatment and of the condition of things as observed by himself but his experience deals almost entirely with El Encanto, one of the

[100] In 1904 when Arana took effective control of the Putumayo region on behalf of the Peruvian Government, he despatched another brother-in-law, Abel Alarco, to Barbados to recruit a labour force through a recruiting agent named S.E. Brewster. Despite the fact that the company had no prospectus or title of deeds Alarco signed a total of 257 two-year work contracts over the next twelve months for Arana's various Amazon business activities — 196 Barbadians ended up in the Putumayo

[101] Carlton Morris also known as the "Barbadian Consul". Barbados had no official consul in Iquitos and their interests as British colonial subjects were the responsibility of the British Vice-Consul.

[102] Nellis Walker {Blue Book — Statement No.2 p.59}.

two station headquarters (La Chorrera being the other) under the management of Sr. Loayza who is generally well spoken of I find.

The other man, Frederick Bishop,[103] in a similarly simple and straightforward way told an entirely different story, amply confirming much of what Captain Whiffen had stated and revealing a most disgraceful state of things — not only in the past but continued right up to the present day. He confirmed the ill treatment of Barbadians somewhat as described by John Brown[104] in his letter to the Commissioner of Montserrat and declared that he himself had more than once flogged Indians under orders of the Company's agents for not bringing in a sufficiency of rubber. As the man spoke fearlessly and sensibly and declared he would not be afraid to say before the persons he accused all that he was telling me, I told him I should take him into my service and that he could accompany me and the members of the Commission in our journey up the Putumayo. I promised to protect him and bring him back to Iquitos with me, and my action in engaging this man is warmly approved by Mr Barnes who has heard all his statement and by the other members of the Commission.

Efforts to secure an interpreter

I have taken steps to secure an absolutely reliable interpreter of the native Indian languages. This, I think, is essential. The Commission can only get such interpreters as, at each station, the Company's agents would place at their disposal. These interpreters would be, in the very nature of the case, among the most confidential employees of those very agents and if these men had committed crimes on the Indians there is no chance of anything damaging to them coming to light.

---

[103] Frederick Bishop {Blue Book — Statement No.1 p.55–59} became Casement's trusted Barbadian guide and interpreter. He spoke some of the Huitoto language and remained a constant source of information throughout Casement's voyage into the Putumayo. Casement paid him £12/month plus food and lodging. In a letter from Casement to Sir Edward Grey written on 13 Jan 1911 Casement said of Bishop "This man I found of the greatest assistance indeed, without him my journey would have been a failure."

[104] John Brown, who had served as Whiffen's guide during his journey, had been sent by the Governor of Barbados to join Casement at Pará, but he arrived too late and only met up with Casement in November when he was preparing to leave the Company's headquarters in the Putumayo, La Chorrera. Brown was owed £30 by the Company — {Blue Book — Statement No.30 pp.137–139}. He had made a statement about what he had seen while an employee of the Company to the Governor of Barbados which was duly sent to the FO and was amongst the dossier of papers Casement had with him.

Mr Barnes tells me that he has no hope of getting an interpreter through the company and has asked me to try and obtain one. But very few persons in Iquitos, seemingly, are acquainted with the "Huitoto" or "Boras" languages — the two principal native dialects we shall encounter. Mons. Vatan — the French trader — had knowledge of a man, an Indian, who speaks Spanish well, who is said to be conversant with seven of the native languages. The man is at work some hundreds of miles from Iquitos, up the Napo river and I have sent the steam launch *Argentina* (at some expense) to try and secure him. This launch should be back in Iquitos in five or six days when I hope we shall then all proceed to the Putumayo or board the Company's steamer *Liberal*.

... 2nd September ...

We endeavoured to trace the individuals mentioned by Mr Hardenburg, but without success. Apparently none of the witnesses were in Iquitos, or if so we could not find them. The Commission interrogated the two notaries Pizarro and Guichard, before whom most of Hardenburg's witnesses had been attested. Pizarro "remembered" practically nothing and was of no assistance of any kind. The same may be said of the other Notary Public Armaldo Guichard, before whom two of the statements were signed, who was also interviewed the same day by the Commission. I was present in each case as an onlooker.

Reference to the Commission has appeared in the local press. There are actually four daily papers in Iquitos — viz. *El Loreto Comercial*; *El Oriente*; *El Heraldo*; *La Nacional*. The first two are said to be the more important; the last was described to me yesterday as in the nature of a blackmailing organ. It will be seen from these papers that prior to the arrival of the Commission it was assumed to be officially organised and sent out by His Majesty's Government; but the rectification in *El Oriente* of 1st instant goes to quite the other extreme. I drew the attention of the members of the Commission to this categoric assertion of their duties as being "exclusively mercantile and industrial" when we were gathered together to collectively discuss the most useful mode of procedure to be followed during our stay in Iquitos and our forthcoming visit to the Putumayo. They assured me that it had not been inserted by any of themselves or with their knowledge and that it misrepresented and quite unduly limited the scope of their enquiry as based on the detailed instructions issued to them by the Peruvian Amazon Company in London. They showed me a copy of these instructions which are sufficiently clear and general to cover the ground of a full and fair enquiry into the actual state of things in the Putumayo.

N.L.I. MS 13,087 (18/i) Consul Cazes to Consul–General Casement

Iquitos, 3 September (Rec'd 3 Sept.)

Dear Mr Casement,

Will you kindly let me know what instructions I should give the launch owners in the event of his not finding the man Santiago Vargas at Copal Urco. As often happens he may be away on some service in the interior. The man with whom he is working may say that the *Argentina* will have to wait 3 or 4 days while they search for him.[105]

What limit of time shall I give the launch to wait for him in this event?

Yours truly,

David Cazes

P.S. Your servant has not turned up.

Another note from Cazes to Casement on 3 September stated:

Have just met a man who can give important information respecting the Putumayo. He has promised to call again this afternoon.

Would there be any inconvenience in making an appointment for 10 a.m. tomorrow or would you prefer this afternoon. Kindly give your own time and let me know.

Yours truly,

D.Cazes

[105] Casement's determination to find the best interpreter available demanded the chartering of a river launch, the *Argentina*, to set out in search of a guide called Santiago Vargas at a place called Copal Urco. The necessary arrangements, including stocking the boat with food and kerosene for the trip, were done on 3 September and the launch left late in the afternoon and returned 9 days later. Despite the fact that Casement was the initiator of this plan and its organization took up most of the day there is no reference to it in the *Black Diary*. For the narrative inconsistencies regarding the return of the *Argentina* see below.

... 4th September ...

Guerrido called on me (at Mr Cazes suggestion) and was examined by Mr Barnes and the members of the Commission in my presence. I took no active part in this examination. When the man presented himself, on the completion of our examination of Bishop, I asked Mr Barnes to undertake his examination as I was only authorised to investigate the statements of British subjects and their relation with the Company's agents.[106]

Snr Guerrido's statement corroborates the charges bought against the past administration of the firm of Arana Bros. but does not deal with the actual state of affairs on the Putumayo. This man, Mr Cazes says he believes to be honest and trustworthy, and his resignation of a lucrative post rather than serve the persons responsible for the cruel and barbarous acts he saw committed, is surely in his favour as a witness. The man's demeanour impressed us favourably and I believe, and I think the members of the Commission believe, that he spoke with sincerity and truth.

The evidence — if such it may be termed — of Bishop and Juan Guerrido has left a painful impression on our minds. It is evident that if the true state of things on the Putumayo and its affluents is to be brought to light a very searching enquiry is needed, and under the circumstances in which our journey is being made it would seem likely that we shall not be able to do more than lay bare a small part only of what actually takes place.

Every preparation has been made for the arrival of the Commission and great courtesy and kindness have been and no doubt will be shown to the Commissioners and myself.

The Barbadian, Frederick Bishop informed Mr Cazes and myself that when Captain Whiffen was in the Putumayo all his movements were known and wherever he was going things were "cleared up" before he arrived. In the case of Mr H.L. Gielgud, who it will be remembered visited the Putumayo on behalf of the firm of auditors Deloitte, Plender and Griffiths and Co. and to whom Sr. Arana referred in his statement to the shareholders of the Peruvian Amazon Coy (26397 — 21 July 1910) (a statement that practically constitutes the Company's defence of their attitude), Bishop declares that the same procedure was followed. Mr Gielgud's name was not mentioned by me to him. He saw him

---

[106] This should be compared to the conflicting statement in the *Black Diary*: "*Interviewed F. Bishop and Juan Guerrido on Putumayo. Dreadful story — all Commission present,*" which clearly indicates that Casement did the interviewing.

at the meeting when his evidence was being taken before the united Commission and subsequently said to Mr Cazes and myself that "he knew that young gentleman and had seen him up the Putumayo" — He then said that before Mr Gielgud came to the station the prisoners were all marched off to the forest under armed guard of *muchachos de confianza* — (young Indian men in the local agents' pay and confidence) and kept out of sight until the visitor had gone.[107]

N.L.I. MS 5463 Casement to Bertie — Iquitos — Sunday September 4, 1910 *written in pencil on writing paper stamped with R.M.S.* Hilary — *Booth Line — Liverpool*

Dear Colonel Bertie,

The *Urimaguas* overtook me in Huayna last Sunday night — at midnight when we were in anchor and I came on to Iquitos by her. We arrived on Wednesday 31st August. The others took up their quarters in the house of the P.A.Co. I as the guest of Mr Cazes, the British Consul here, who, with his wife, has a very pleasant home life. We all regret your absence very much — I perhaps most of all. You could have helped enormously here — however, things will go their appointed course, I hope.

We are staying on for another 7 or 8 days I think — really for an interpreter I am trying to get from far away — the only one who can be heard of who knows the Indian dialects — unless a specially provided interpreter at one of the stations of the Coy. is considered good enough.

Iquitos is very hot and full of mosquitoes — often by day as well as by night. I was 13 days on the *Huayna* getting within 200 miles of Iquitos when the *Urimaguas* overtook me. We had anchored every night from the 2 August and often during the day for hours sounding for a channel. You will be getting near Madeira today — due there about tomorrow I expect. I used the revolver once on alligators coming up — but without effect. We saw heaps of the beastly things.

My eyes have got no better — rather worse I am afraid — and that is my chief reason for using pencil. I find it less strain to write

[107] This entry beginning on 1 September with Casement's conversation with Monsieur Vatan is taken from the draft of a letter sent apparently to Sir Edward Grey. The letter is to be found among Casement's Papers at the N.L.I. MS 13,087 (5) although there is no trace of the document amongst the FO Papers. At the top of the letter scribbled in Casement's hand is "To be part of my diary".

with pencil than with ink — in latter case one has to look closer at the paper and form the letters more distinctly.[108]

This will go down to you or to Manaos I mean by *Urimaguas* on which Lizardo Arana goes back. I like him — he was very civil me to, I must say, on the way up.

All the others are well and flourishing. The bon mot of the voyage has been awarded to Fox — one evg. at dinner he said to one of the *Urimaguas* party (a Spaniard),

"Well if the inhabitants of Iquitos are anything like the mosquitoes they are a fine warlike people." — and from the daily battles I've fought since coming up I'm convinced of it.

I expect I'll get out of the Putumayo long before the others altho' I already know of a fair number of Barbadians said to be there (possibly 20) scattered over many sections. I've got two here already. I wish you were here very much even if to go no further than Iquitos. I do hope that you are better and that you will soon pick up your health at home again — and I'll write you when I "come out" and please God we'll meet when I return and I'll tell you all.

Yours sincerely,

Roger Casement

On 7 September Casement sent a letter to Sir John Harris at the Anti-Slavery & Aborigines Protection Society reporting the progress of his investigation. This letter would subsequently cause problems for Casement and bring a sharp reprimand from the Foreign Office, who felt Casement should have behaved with greater discretion. The matter is dealt with in the footnote for Tuesday 29 November.

In the evening of 7 September Casement held a dinner party for the main representatives of the Peruvian Amazon Company, the Commissioners and David Cazes. It was a pure public relations exercise on Casement's part, intended to create a sense of goodwill with the Company and Commissioners.

... 9th September ...

On the 9th of September I interrogated four more Barbados men Walcot, Ford, Jones and Labadie.[109] First three say little but

[108] Here is the most revealing comment Casement makes about his eye problem and the effects it has on the implement he uses to write with. While all Casement's jottings of these days are in pencil, the *Black Diary* alternates between pen and pencil and there is no noticeable difference in the formation of the letters as described here.

[109] Augustus Walcott, Preston Ford, Artemus Jones, Joseph Labadie {Blue Book Statement Nos. 3–6 p.60–62}

Labadie tells story about Carlos Miranda at Sur decapitating an old woman ... "Miranda had then seized the head and holding it up by the hair to the assembled Indians, compulsory witnesses of this tragedy, had told them to look well at it for that was what would happen to all bad Indians."

I heard that three other men were at work on the steamship *Liberal*, the Company's vessel then in port, and which was being got ready to convey us all round to the Putumayo.[110]

N.L.I. MS 13,074 7/I Postcard from Casement to Gertrude Bannister

[*The posed photograph shows four women being driven in an ox-cart in Madeira. It is addressed to Miss Bannister — Queen Anne's School, Caversham, Oxford.*]

I remembered the 2nd. This is 9th September. Hope the visit to Donegal was a success and that neither rain nor any other accessories spoiled it and that Cloghaneely and Dunfannahy proved up to their hopes. Got here to Iquitos on 31st August after a voyage from 23rd July. The way is long but alas! The wind not cold.

Thine Scodgie

...10th September ... [111]

F. Bishop reports that another Barbadian named Gibb or Gibbs is here in Iquitos, a man who has been employed by the Peruvian Amazon Coy up the Putumayo, and asked if he should tell Gibbs to come to see me. I told him to bring Gibbs.

The *Liberal* returned from discharging the *Huayna* this morning and the Barbadian Stanley S. Lewis is on board of her, a member of her crew. This is the man that Jose [?] stated last night could tell us "plenty of things" as to what was done on the Putumayo and the way the Indians were treated. Lewis, he said, when in Iquitos lived

---

[110] This excerpt for 9 September is taken from the typed document N.L.I. MS 13,087 (8). It is this document that looks as if it is a fragment of a more complete diary typed up by Casement and sent to Foreign Office sometime in May 1911

[111] The only fragmentary entries for the two weeks Casement spent in Iquitos run consecutively for 10/11/12 September and can be found in MS 13,087 (24). Close comparison of these three days show clear narrative discrepancies with parallel *Black Diary* entries.

in the same house as him and he would tell him to come to the consulate when the *Liberal* arrived.

At lunch Mr Cazes reported that Lewis had come into the office and was to return. I requested that he should be sent to me at the Consulate on his return. As he had not come at 3 o'clock I sent Bishop down to the *Liberal* to ask him to visit me at the Consulate. Bishop returned at once, to say that "Lewis did not want to come, he did not know why." I said it did not matter that I should probably see him later on.

In the evening at dinner Mr Cazes said that Lewis had come into the store in the forenoon — and he had told him that there was a gentleman here from home who wished to speak to him. Lewis said he was in a hurry, pulled out a paper and said he had to go to the Prefectura and left at once. Mr Cazes told him to return and he said he should do so — but did not, and as is seen, when sent for directly by me he refused to appear. This man, a native of Barbados is referred to in two of the depositions made in Iquitos and published by Hardenburg.

... Sunday 11th ...

Bishop on coming this morning stated that neither Gibbs nor Lewis would come to see me. They "did not want to". I said that was foolish and he said he had told them so; that I had come here to help the Barbadians but they would not come.

It looked as if they had bad consciences and knew they had done wrong. I said that it certainly looked bad and that if they were frightened it was better to come and speak frankly to me, just as he, Bishop, had done — that that was the right thing to do and he had acted rightly ... Doubtless all the Barbadians have been talking together last night and the night before since the interview with the four men on Friday evening. I can later on compel Lewis and Gibbs to speak, but if I try to do so now I may do more harm that good. They are best employed on the *Liberal* at present, and I daresay when we are on board that vessel I shall find means to induce them to speak.

... September 12th ...

The launch I had chartered to go up to Copal Urco and bring the interpreter down has returned today without him.[112] The man

[112] The most blatant narrative inconsistency during the two weeks Casement spent in Iquitos regards the *Argentina*. The launch left late in the day of the 3 September and returned on the 12 without the interpreter, Santiago Vargas. Casement's

in question is said to be away at Aguarico — in Ecuador almost — and the long and expensive journey is fruitless. I must go up the Putumayo without an interpreter, trusting to the Barbadian F. Bishop, who says that he knows "a bit" of Huitoto, but no Bora to speak of. On the other hand I have succeeded in getting a Peruvian half caste as interpreter and guide for the Commission. This man was sent to me through Mons. Vatan as reliable and trustworthy. He was said to know Huitoto and Bora, having been for some two years in their service of the P.A.Co on the Putumayo. He is said to have left their service, voluntarily, (like Juan Garrido) because he refused to shoot two Indian chiefs he was ordered to kill by his chief of section. The last Chief of Section is now in Iquitos — retired and a highly respected member of the local aristocracy — seeing he is a Peruvian, a native of Iquitos and a former employee of Arana Bros. I did not interview this man but asked that he should be sent out to Mr Barnes the Chief of the Commission, who had asked me to try and get him an interpreter. Mr Barnes will now engage him and it will be on his interpretation we shall mainly rely I presume. His name is Viacara, and he stated yesterday to the members of the Commission that altho' he left the Putumayo some two years ago he believes things are just the same today. He accuses Miguel Flores of having hanged one man in his room. Flores was "degraded" — in the Company's service — but is still employed.

Viacara says he believes many of the Huitoto Indians if appealed to by anyone they could trust would come forward and state how they have been treated. The Commission will take down in writing Viacara's declaration and will give me a copy.

We now expect to leave for the Putumayo on Wednesday next, the 14th instant, and should arrive at La Chorrera about 23rd. That station will be our headquarters for some time and I propose making a journey on foot from it to various sections that supply it with rubber and where I learn that Barbadians are being still employed. Several of these men I am told are at Atenas and

---

straightforward reporting of the facts are confusingly serialized in the *Black Diary* as follows:

September 8th: ... *Hear that the Interpreter at Copal Urcu is not to be found. Nous verrons when* Argentina *comes* ... September 9th ... Argentina *returned 11 a.m. No Interpreter! Alack.* A few lines later this information is clearly contradicted with ... *It was not the* Argentina *after all so there may still be a chance.* Then on September 12th: ... Argentina *returned from Copal Urco without the Interpreter who was in the bush. A great pity in every way, but will get the Peruvian now.* A few lines later the information is repeated: ... Argentina *returned from Copal Urco. No interpreter!*

Savana — both of them sections with very evil names and "Chiefs" who are charged with horrible crimes. Every preparation will be made for our visits, so that we are not likely to surprise any flagrant wrong doing — but we may find the natives short of food, for instance, and learn its cause — also we shall see if they have been flogged, for as they wear no clothes it will not be hard to read the signs of the lash on their bare skins.

My chief hope is that some of the Barbadians will come forward and accuse themselves — in order to save themselves. Some of these men are accused of atrocious crimes — one, King, who is at present the baker of Sr. Loayza, the Manager of El Encanto, is said to have committed more than one murder.

I shall try to terrify this man into confessing — for, he knows, as a British subject, that murder is a serious crime, and altho' now buried in the wilds of a nameless forest in a debatable land claimed by two or three South American Republics I fancy he will not relish the visit of a British Officer specially sent out to investigate his relations with his actual employers and that he may prefer "to give these latter away" rather than incur the risk of being charged with murder by the Peruvian government, and made a scapegoat of — a possibility that I shall see is put before him (by his own countrymen who have told the truth) as by no means remote.

From La Chorrera I shall send word of my movements from time to time to Mr Cazes — but it is unlikely that any communication of interest can be received from me during the time I am actually in the Company's "territory" — as all means of exit and communication are in their hands and letters sent by their agency, as they must be, would not be very safe. It is therefore probable this will be my last advice until I get back to Manaos or Para in probably December next.

Bishop says this evening he had been telling Lewis and Gibbs that they were fools not to come and see me — that Gibbs had told him of the dreadful things he had seen (and done) with Normand. That he had seen people burnt alive and killed in all sorts of ways — and Bishop said Gibbs was afraid to come and tell me these things — he was afraid of the Company as he was still in their service and did not know what might become of him.

Bishop said the old Barbadian named Carlton Morris, who lives in Iquitos and is termed the Barbadian Consul wishes to come and speak to me alone — not before Mr Cazes. It is about young Barbadians being brought here as servants and ill-treated and not paid, and to know if I could get the Barbadian government to stop them coming. He does not wish to complain to Mr Cazes as he thinks there might be more result through talking to me. I said he might come tomorrow morning — at 9am and I would hear what he said. I shall tell Cazes of course.

Dr Jenaro Herrera, Editor of *El Loreto Comercial* — tried twice to interview me today but without success. First time I was lying down with bad headache and put him off — then he came at 8.15 and I fled straight to bed and refused to get up.

PRO FO371/1455 Consul-General Casement to Tyrrell

Iquitos, Sept. 12 1910

My dear Tyrrell,

Just a few lines more to tell you that I hope we (the Commission and myself) will leave for the Putumayo next 14th inst. Since my last letter I have got more statements of a highly detestable character from British subjects who have been in the Coys service and have secured Peruvian evidence of a similar kind which was sent to the Commission to take note of. I take up a Barbadian with me who is making a clean breast of it and declares he can prove all on the spot — and the Commission will I gather from them engage the Peruvian who assures them, they tell me, of his ability to also prove on the spot his charges.

Altogether what has been declared to us here in Iquitos is sickening and confirms the infamous character of the treatment of the Indians Hardenburg alleged. Incidentally I am convinced that whatever Whiffen may have been his statements to the Foreign Office were accurate. I believe I have got the Commission entirely with me and that we shall now enter the Putumayo region with a much clearer view of things and more instructed minds. Of course everything is prepared and ready for us — that we know. One of the witnesses said "if they could put up arches of roses for these gentlemen" (he was a Spaniard) "they would do it." So far as I can see the staff of the Coy on the Putumayo consists of "devilish criminals" — with a few exceptions and the attitude of the Peruvian government to it is — well hard to describe. The so-called "Comisario" on the Putumayo is a farce, and is undoubtedly an agent of the Company.

We are all of us acting with great caution, and secrecy even (as if we were the criminals) for it is clear the rascals are very suspicious — especially of me. I gave a dinner the other night to two of the principal criminals and drank their health in Iquitos champagne and said nice things! The dinner cost me £12 — but I fancy the toast will cost me dearer some day. They nearly choked me — but it was wise to do it, for I know they were awfully suspicious and their seeming show of being hoodwinked has helped a little. I am very sick of the whole thing — yet glad I came — and if my health holds out till December I hope to come out safe and sound. Putumayo is a "sealed book" even in Iquitos — it is amazing how everyone nearly is either afraid or "in the swim". No vessels of any kind come or go to that river save the launches of the Company — or those of the Government which are practically the same thing — and the distance is enormous — close on 1000 miles to the chief port — and it is not there the devilment goes on, but in the sections where the rubber comes from.

I am seedy — so is Barnes the chief of the Commission, both of us with fever and my eyes are bad — but I hear it is healthier and cooler on the Putumayo than here in Iquitos. It is over 90° every day (and night too nearly) and swarms of mosquitoes.

Adieu,

Yours sincerely,

Roger Casement

PRO FO371/968 Consul-General Casement to Spicer

Iquitos, 13 September 1910

Dear Spicer,

I send herewith copies of some of the declarations made before me since coming to Iquitos on the 31st August. Six of them are by Barbadians, one by a Spaniard, whom I referred to the Commission, and my note of his statements is my own, but Cazes, who did the translating, says it is entirely accurate.

No.1 The statement of Bishop was made partly before the whole Commission, partly before Barnes, Cazes and myself, and some of it to me alone. This man I have engaged as interpreter and guide at £12 per month and "all found".

We start tomorrow morning and I have no time to write properly, but think it well to send these statements and the map to you, as this will be my last chance of writing (except by a vessel of the Peruvian Amazon Company from the Putumayo) until I come out again. It is fully 1,000 miles from this to La Chorrera. As anything may happen to me up there, it is as well you should have these statements to know how things look to us before starting.

The Commission is entirely with me now; they are just as convinced as I am of the need for change, and we shall work together. We intend, at once, on reaching La Chorrera, the headquarters on the Putumayo, to make a rush for Atenas and Sabana [see map], and try to verify the starving of the Indians there by Martinengui.[113] Bishop tells me we shall have great difficulty in seeing active wrongdoing, such as flogging or anything of that kind, because they will be far too careful, but that the Indians will tell, if a good interpreter is found, and in any case we shall see their backs and buttocks cut and scarred.

I tried very hard to get an interpreter. I was told of one — an Indian — far up the Napo River at Copal Urco, and sent a special launch for him, costing £100.

We thought it over, and both Mr Barnes and Cazes thought there was nothing else for it. The launch returned yesterday without the man. He was even as far as Ecuador, in the forests. Meanwhile another interpreter had been brought to me — a young Peruvian half-caste, who had been two years in the Putumayo, and left, (he said) rather than shoot two chiefs he had been ordered to kill. I sent this man to Barnes, and as my Indian has not come, this man has been engaged by the Commission. He knows two languages — Huitoto and Boras.[114] My man, Bishop, knows Huitoto a little. The man I sent to Copal Urco for knew seven Indian languages, and it is a great pity we have not got him. I shall travel with Commission for first two or three months probably, and then I dare say I will have got all the Barbadian statements. Some of these men, I believe, have committed grave crimes, much worse than Bishop owns up to of flogging, and there may be difficulty in getting them to speak. A man came in to-day, Adolfus Gibbs, and told me his story. He was very frightened, and refused twice to come, but probably thinks it safer to keep in with me than with the company.

His statement is not included in those now sent, as I have only just taken it down, and it is incomplete. It refers to Abisinia and Morelia, and he was witness of the murder of an Indian chief (his head cut off by Jiménez, chief of Morelia), and of innumerable floggings for insufficient rubber, all last year. I shall see him again,

---

[113] The spelling of Elias Martenengui's name is consistently different in the Putumayo Journal to its spelling in the Blue Book where it is given as Martinengui.

[114] Huitoto and Boras were the main tribal groups of the Putumayo and together constituted around 90 per cent of the natives living between the Putumayo and Caquetá.

as he is a fireman on the Company's launch *Liberal*, in which we leave tomorrow for the Putumayo.
There is another Barbadian on board who is accused of misdeeds, and he has steadily refused to come, but I expect he will be frightened too, and will make a clean breast of it on board the launch.

We cannot get a cook — no one in Iquitos of the natives seems willing to go to the Putumayo. I am keeping a diary, and part of the statement of Bishop is really a leaf of my diary — the last part. It is only sent you in case I might get lost or disappear or something up there, or die of fever, and my papers might be overhauled long before they reached Iquitos, or they would be at the mercy of the people, who are in dread of our visit.[115] I am viewed with grave suspicion already, I think, but as I have got the Commission with me we are all right. The local prefect, Dr Paz Soldan, knows nothing about the Putumayo. He believes simply the stories told him by the interested people, and he has been in Iquitos, coming from Lima, only a year, and not on the Putumayo at all.

I hope to be out of the Putumayo and back in Iquitos, bound down-river by November or beginning of December, perhaps even earlier. The Commission will probably stay longer, as they have heaps to do of other things. My stay will depend on my health. Since coming to Iquitos I have been ill, and my eyes are very weak. The heat has been stifling up here, and mosquitoes day and night. I have been ill for three days and so have others. It is a ghastly hole this Iquitos and Colonel Bertie was right not to come on. He would have pegged out here, I think. God knows what it will be like on the Putumayo. The Spaniard Garrido says "if they could they would put up arches of roses" for us!

Apparently from the statements made there is not one decent man up there except Tizon.

The La Chorrera section embraces nearly all the stations on the Igara-paraná (the "very clear river"), with those over towards the Caquetá, while the El Encanto section embraces all the stations on

---

[115] It is clear from this statement and comments made in the previous letter, in which Casement stated that the Commission were "acting with great caution and secrecy even (as if we were the criminals) — for it is clear the rascals are very suspicious — especially of me", that there is a direct contrast with a far more easygoing mood that permeates the narrative of the *Black Diary*. The whole atmosphere of fear, suspicion and paranoia in which Casement and the Commissioners moved is almost completely missing in the *Black Diary*.

the Cara-parana (the "clear stream") and this section I shall visit last.

There are fewer Barbadians there, I am told. The worst stations are those towards the Caquetá, I am told, and the most dangerous to visit on account of the Indians, the Boras or Poras being stronger than the Huitotos, or more disposed to resist the gentle process of civilisation inculcated by the Peruvian Amazon Company. Altogether it is a charming place. Au revoir, and I shall be very glad to see your face again. This place is appallingly depressing.

Yours, etc.

Roger Casement

<u>N.L.I. MS. 13,087 (26/ii) Statements made at different times by David Cazes to me from 31 August to 14 September during my stay at Iquitos</u> [*This six-page note, written on single sheets of lined paper, looks as if it was drafted on the river trip up stream from Iquitos to La Chorrera.*]

Mr Cazes began our acquaintance by practically saying that he knew nothing or very little of the occurrences on the Putumayo. That river "was a sealed book" — no one came or went to it save agents of the Company and their steamers. Three Barbadians had once complained to him as Consul of the character of their employment on the Putumayo alleging they were illegally forced to hunt the Indians. Cazes seems to have taken no steps to verify or to elicit further information on this obviously important point — but he spoke to Julio C. Arana (this must have been 1908 or earlier) and said there must be no more complaints — Arana promised to do anything C[azes] wished as regards Barbadians and paid off and sent home some of them who complained. Beginning with knowing practically nothing, as the days have shown me more and more capable of eliciting the truth, Cazes has again and again admitted, incidentally, a pretty extensive knowledge of what was the state of things on the Putumayo. He also states that he had informed the FO "fully" — of "all he knew" — (that I knew was practically nothing and gave FO little or no help). When in London J.C. Arana met C[azes] more than once, I gathered, and appealed to him to stick up for the Company in the controversy then raging with *Truth*. This Cazes said he had told Arana he could not do — he had told Arana that what he knew would not be in the Coys favour — so he tried to steer a neutral course — and while not telling all he knew to the FO did not help them. This attitude he would have maintained had I not appeared on the scene at Iquitos — when he saw that as the truth was sure to come out, thro' me and the Commission between us, he might do best to stand in with H.M.Govt. and secure approbation for the undoubted help he has since given me. When I talked, quite early of the enslavement of the Indians as averred by Nordenskiöld,[116] he said that it was not true — "only on the Putumayo, where the whites did as they pleased."

He then, very soon after, told me the story of his buying an "estate" and the "cuentas" or debts of the Indians to the former owner. Several trading men then came to him and offered to buy their cuentas and so obtain the ownership of the Indian debtors. C[azes] refused, not because he objected to the system itself, but because in this case the would be buyers wanted to take the Indians right away to Brazil with them, and as the Indians had wives and families near Iquitos Cazes did not like to separate them and so refused these offers and unltimately lost £400 odd — and the Estate and its Indians did not turn out a success. Again and again I find slipping from his lips and those of others in Iquitos the unconscious admission of this system of wholesale slavery. Everyone nearly talks of "his Indians" just as if they were sheep or cattle — or rubber trees. For instance the trouble C. once had with Arana Hnos. [Brothers] over "an estate" both claimed and which Arana raided. Pensamiento was the place[117] — C[azes] said Arana wanted to get it in his hands chiefly because he could then check the Putumayo Indians fleeing to the Napo (where they would not be free men but would escape some of the sufferings and atrocities inflicted on them in the Putumayo). This "legal" contest over Pensamiento between D. Cazes of the Iquitos Trading Company and Arana Bros. offers a very interesting study of Peruvian legal administration. Cazes in his capacity as head of the Iquitos Trading

[116] Baron Erland von Nordenskiöld (1877–1932) was a Swedish ethnographer who travelled extensively in northern Bolivia and the Gran Chaco and wrote on the origins of the Indian civilizations of South America. At the start of 1910 he had contacted the Anti-Slavery Society in England regarding treatment of native populations in the montaña districts of Peru and Bolivia, where he had witnessed atrocities against the indigenous populations. In 1910 von Nordenskiöld published *Indianlif I el Gran Chaco*. Casement had been informed of von Nordenskiöld's correspondence with the A.S.A.P.S. by the Society's acting secretary the Rev. John Harris.

[117] Casement gave a clearer and more detailed analysis of the Pensamiento affair on 26 November after his return to Iquitos.

Company had claimed on Pensamiento for goods etc. advanced to its owner. Following the normal method of procedure in the montaña I presume in such cases Cazes went and took possession of Pensamiento to put in his "bailiff" and brought down whatever produce there was there (rubber) and shipped it to the value of something like £1,000 to Europe. Aranas also claimed Pensamiento on somewhat similar grounds, but were later in the field and found Cazes' man in possession and the goods flown. They turned his man out and put in as their "bailiff", Sr. Burga, actually Peruvian Commissary (or magistrate) on the Putumayo. (In this occupation of Pensamiento I find that Burga collected several "lots" of Indians and drove them back to Arana's fold on the Putumayo.) Ultimately Burga left Arana's service but is still Comisario on the Putumayo at the present moment! Arana went to law against Cazes in the Superior Court and got judgement in his favour, altho' Cazes declares all the evidence was overwhelmingly on his side. The court also ordered him to pay over, to a "trustee" they appointed, the full price of the rubber he had shipped home — say £1,000. Cazes at first refused positively to do this unless he got a "guarantee" of the court as to the safety of the money in deposit. The trustee they had appointed was a mere tool of Arana, a man of straw. During this strife over the guarantee between Cazes, as head of the Iquitos Trading Coy and the Iquitos court we get some eye openers. The court ordered Cazes' arrest! and put soldiers at the door of his private house which is the British consulate, with shield and arms and flag and half a mile from the store of the Iquitos Trading Coy. Where his trading is carried on. He was to be arrested if he came out of doors and finally the soldiers get orders to prevent anyone entering the Consulate or leaving it! Cazes at the early stage of this siege had gone out each day to his store but at length the Prefect begged him to stay in the Consulate — his private house as the court was writing imperative orders for him to be seized if he left the door. Finally, Cazes says he got a guarantee — the court gave it and so he paid the £1,000 over to Wesche and Cos agent, next door to the Consulate. Immediately after Wesche's man said he had received orders from the court to hand over the £1,000 at once — he had protested — but they said no guarantee was needed and the money was paid over immediately. He appealed to Cazes, for advice in his difficulty, who said he could not refuse and so the money was paid over without any guarantee to the Arana nominee. Cazes appealed from this "judgement" to the Supreme Court at Lima which gave judgement, he says, entirely in his favour, annulling the act of the Iquitos Court. On communication of this judgement to the latter potentates, they have annulled the order of the Supreme Court of their country, declaring that it was come to in ignorance of the facts and upholding their decision in favour of Arana and the disappearing £1,000 and that is the situation at the present moment, during my stay in Iquitos! Burga, the commissario of the Peruvian Govt. on the Putumayo told Cazes, he tells me, that he ceased to work for Aranas (altho' all the time nominal comisario or magistrate) because they put him to do "wrong things on the Indians" and he got disgusted. This is the "Peruvian authority" to whom I bear the order of the Prefect Dr Paz Soldan, to aid me in every way in my mission! What a tragicomic opera: a comedy indeed were it not for the gruesome tragedy of the enslaved and murdered Indians.

That every word of Nordenskiöld's letter to the Anti-Slavery Society is true I am quite convinced. The entire Indian population is enslaved in the montaña and whereon the devil plant, the rubber tree, grows and can be tapped. The wilder the Indian the wickeder the slavery.

Where he becomes "civilised" and can read and write and study "cuenta" [accounts] with his "patron" then he ceases to be an Indian and becomes a "Peruvian" and himself an enslaver. As to the laws — all these South American republics have excellent laws on paper — and no sense of equity in the man behind the paper. The laws are beautiful and simple books — a fool could turn the leaves and apply them — an honest fool would make an ideal judge.

But these people are not honest and are not fools, and to obtain justice in Peru or Brazil, or any other of these Latin States of the New World one must bribe and lie, cheat and corrupt, terrify and threaten so that your justice won leaves the soil rank with misdeeds.

On 14 September Casement and the Commission boarded the flagship of the Peruvian Amazon Company the Liberal *and cast off from Iquitos and headed back downstream towards Brazil. After crossing the Brazilian–Peruvian frontier they continued on to the mouth of the river Ica, the Brazilian name for the Putumayo, and started heading upstream recrossing the frontier into territory disputed by Peru and Colombia.*

Despite Casement's comment before he left Iquitos that he was "keeping a diary" there is only the Black Diary left as a record of the river trip. Just one fragmentary diary extract has survived in N.L.I. MS 13,087 (26/i) and refers to an incident at dinner with the Captain of the Liberal on 17th September 1910:

Up the Putumayo river on board the *Liberal*.

One of the Pilots (an Indian with a nice face) has parts of his left ear clipped away and a bare spot in the hair behind it. I remarked on this at dinner tonight and said to Captain Reigado "your Indian pilot has had part of his ear shot away" and he at once said "yes — by the Colombian up at La Union in January 1908". He, the Captain, was not on board then, but Zubiaur was in command. The chief engineer Colmenares said he was on board and the pilot was hiding in his cabin — "the only one hiding and got shot right through the woodwork as he lay down".

I asked if there was shooting on both sides and the engineer, Sr. Colmenares, said "Oh! Yes." I asked if Loayza was on board at the time and he said "Yes" and I asked if there were Peruvian soldiers and he said "They were coming after in the 'Iquitos'" — so that it was true the *Liberal* began firing and not the Peruvian soldiers.

This pilot's name is Samuel Pisgara.[118] He and Manuel the old pilot came from Punchama. Punchama, the Captain says, was founded by the Indians who fled from Borja when in 185? something, the Huambisas Indians wiped it out. They were the survivors. The Huambisas when they attacked Burga at Santiago had been armed by him against an old priest who had a settlement higher up. The old priest had also armed the Huambisas against Burga. The two "opposing" parties came down the same day and wiped out Burga and the old priest simultaneously and so "civilisation" was extinguished for ½ a century on the gorge of the Upper Marañon.

[118] The name Samuel Pisgara becomes Simon Pisango or Simon Pizarro in the corresponding *Black Diary* entry for 17 September although Casement was clearly confused by the pilot's name and corrected himself in an entry on 18 and 23 November, when returning down river to Iquitos from La Chorrera. Due to his poor working knowledge of Spanish, Casement had trouble writing the proper names of many individuals he met during his investigation resulting in frequent spelling inconsistencies in the text. While several of these incongruities are Casement's phonetic errors, other differences between the Putumayo Journal and *Black Diaries* are harder to explain and clearly suggest confusion on the part of the forger. The most detailed analysis of spelling inconsistencies between the Putumayo Journal and corresponding 1910 *Black Diary* entries was carried out by Maura Scanlon and the results were reproduced in E. Ó Máille, M. Uí Callanán and M. Payne, *The Vindication of Roger Casement* (1994).

The Liberal *made an unscheduled stop at a place called Indostan, a Company station below La Chorrera which they passed on the morning of 21 September. On going ashore Casement found a young Indian called Bolívar chained up in one of the outhouses and some feverish young Indian girls to whom he gave quinine and food. From subsequent references that Casement made to this incident it is clear that he made notes of what happened, but none have survived. The events at Indostan were subsequently corroborated by the Commissioners' report.*

PART THREE

THE PUTUMAYO JOURNAL

"I have come to give you some good news, a word of truth; at last, the land which is yours *is* yours."

President of Colombia, Virgilio Barco, following the return of 6,000,000 hectares of the Colombian Amazon to the Huitotos in April 1988. Quoted by Ghillean T. Prance F.L.S., Director of the Royal Botanic Garden, Kew, in his Foreword to *Vine of the Soul — Medicine Men, their Plants and Rituals in the Colombian Amazonia* by Richard Evans Schultes F.M.L.S.

DIAGRAMMATIC MAP OF THE ISSA-JAPURA CENTRAL WATERSHED
SHOWING LANGUAGE GROUPS
BY
CAPTAIN THOMAS W. WHIFFEN

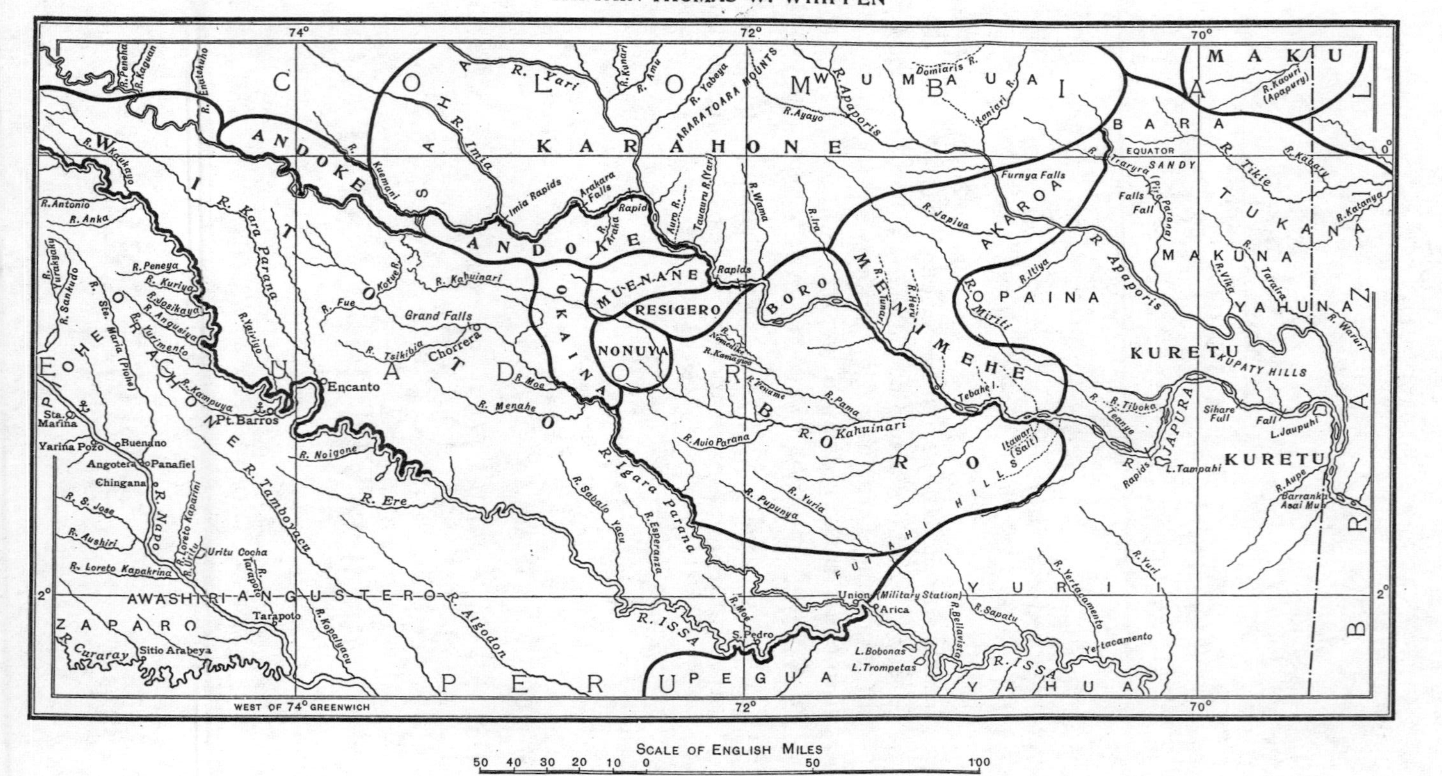

SCALE OF ENGLISH MILES

50 40 30 20 10 0 50 100

REFERENCE

Some language groups are enclosed by a thick line thus ▬▬
and the name of each is shown in this character — **BORO**

The region termed "the Putumayo" consisting principally of the area drained by two tributaries of the Iça or Putumayo River, the Igara-paraná and the Cara-paraná, lies far from the main stream of the Amazon, and is rarely visited by any vessels save those belonging to the Peruvian Amazon Company. The only other craft that penetrate that district are steamers of the Peruvian government sent occasionally from Iquitos. Brazilian vessels may ascend the Japura, known in Peru and Colombia as the Caquetá, until they draw near to the mouth of the Cahuinari, a river which flows into the Japura, flowing in a north-easterly direction largely parallel with the Igara-paraná, which empties into the Putumayo after a south-easterly course. The region drained by these three waterways, the Caraparaná, the Igara-paraná, and the Cahuinari, represents the area in part of which the operations of the Peruvian Amazon Company are carried on. It is impossible to say what the Indian population of the region may be. Generally speaking, the upper and middle courses of these rivers are, or were, the most populous regions. This is accounted for by the far greater absence of insect pests due to the higher nature of the ground which rises at La Chorrera to a level of about 600 feet above the sea, with neighbouring heights fully 1,000 feet above sea level. The lower course of the Igara-paraná, as well as of the Putumayo itself, below the junction of the Igara-paraná down to the Amazon, is through a thick forest region of lower elevation, subject largely to annual overflow from the flooded rivers. Mosquitoes and sand flies and the swampy soil doubtless account for the restriction of the Indians to those higher and drier levels which begin after the Igara-paraná has been ascended for about 100 miles of its course. In this more elevated region there are no mosquitoes, and far fewer insect plagues, while permanent habitations and the cultivation of the soil are more easily secured in the regions liable to annual inundation.[119]

---

[119] Blue Book p. 25. Casement's introduction to his report to Sir Edward Grey — 17 March 1911 — gives a good geographical overview of the Putumayo region.

I

LA CHORRERA

ARRIVAL AT LA CHORRERA

After a nine-day river journey, Casement and the Company's Commissioners arrived at La Chorrera, the headquarters of the Peruvian Amazon Company in the Putumayo, on Thursday 22 September. They were received by the Company's two main representatives — Juan Tizon and Victor Macedo. Tizon had been sent out to the district a few months previously in preparation for the Commissioners' visit and was a well-respected citizen of Iquitos. Macedo was one of Arana's longest serving Chiefs of Section and had an established history of brutality. The Putumayo Journal *proper begins at 2.15 on Friday 23 September in a rather abrupt way that suggests it was carrying on from a previous entry.*

AT LA CHORRERA, FRIDAY 23RD SEPTEMBER, 1910, 2.15

Assessing the situation with Bishop's advice

I asked Captain Camino Reigado to-day if he could spare the man Stanley S. Lewis[120] to accompany the Commission and myself as a servant. He at once demurred, (and I thought with alarm and suspicion) saying that he was bound by the port regulations of Iquitos to bring back every member of his crew, under a penalty. I asked what the fine might be, and he said he would look up his book of regulations. I said that, of course, my request depended solely on his ability to release the man, and also on his willingness to let him go — that if he needed his services on board very much there could be no question of my taking him — and, equally, that if

[120] Stanley S. Lewis {Blue Book Statement No. 8}. Casement conducted his first interview with Lewis on board the *Liberal* on 20 September, again on 22 September and subsequently at La Chorrera on 24 September in the presence of Tizon and the Commission. Lewis later testified before the Prefect of Iquitos in December.

the Port regulations of Iquitos were as he stated, then the matter ended.

On telling Bishop this (and Messrs. Barnes and Fox), Bishop said that already Sr Macedo was acting behind our backs. That this morning when I was speaking to a crowd of Indians through a Barbadian workman, who all were standing at the door of a store to get their rations, Sr Macedo had sent Lawrence, the Cook, to stand behind and hear what I said. My questions had been of the most innocent kind and made quite aloud and generally, such as any traveller would put as to the customs and habits of a strange people. The Barbadian to whom I was speaking pointed out one young Indian lad, a *muchacho de confianza*[121] presumably — who, he said, had "already killed plenty of men", but that he was "not yet civilised"! Mr Fox was standing by all the time we were talking and Sr Macedo himself came along too, and stood by grinning — but not following the remarks — hence the Cook!

Bishop says the men would all like to go away with me, that they don't think they will be safe after I leave. He says one of the Barbadians — the man I happened by chance to be talking to at the store door — Donal Francis — would like very much to get away, and come with us. That he has been employed on the usual dreadful tasks and is sick of them and also that he has an Indian "wife" about to give birth to a child and he is anxious to get her out too. (I said to Bishop that I might be able to take the man and the other Barbadian away when I went, but that I was not at all sure I could do anything about the Indian "wife" — that the agents here might keep her as she was a Peruvian and I could do nothing in the matter). I said that I intended asking for the loan of this young man, in any case, as I had already been asked by Mr Barnes and Fox to get a Barbadian for them, as the interpreter is sick and Garrido is also complaining and may not go on, and that I thought this young man would make a good servant. Bishop says all would like to go away now — they are frightened — and he adds that Sr Macedo is still more frightened! What a situation.

---

[121] *Muchacho de Confianza* — Confidence boy — these were specially trained groups of armed Indian quislings trained to act on the orders of the section chiefs and often used for murder and torture. Hierarchies imposed by colonizers often encouraged local tribal hostilities as a means of more effective control. *Muchachos* forcibly recruited from one tribe were often deployed in territories belonging to traditionally antagonistic clans. Such methods generally increased tribal tensions and manifested the state of fear. See Michael Taussig, *Shamanism, Colonialism and the Wild Man — A Study in Terror and Healing* (Harvard UP 1987) p.122.

I have told Srs. Tizon[122] and Macedo that I wished to speak to all the Barbadians on the Station to-day if convenient, and they have agreed and will send the men to me at 3 o'clock. Immediately after this I saw Macedo on board the *Liberal* talking in earnest with the Captain, who, of course, has told him of my interviewing Lewis and Clarke.

Casement's dilemma — request to interview the Barbadians

Here, at the very outset, we are face to face with grave difficulties, and there seems no way out. Any sincere interrogation of these five Barbadians here at La Chorrera must bring to light a state of things that cannot openly be tolerated, and both Tizon and Macedo will, at once, pretend that this is such serious evidence of wrongdoing, (of which they had no knowledge) that a Peruvian court must enquire into the charges. If, on the other hand, I intimate to the Barbadians that I am only going to make a perfunctory enquiry, as to whether they are happy, well treated, or in distress etc., they could truthfully reply, so that nothing real comes out, and that is an end of their evidence for any purposes of useful reform. If, however, I induce the men to speak out, under a promise of protection, it is clear their accusations would involve Macedo, and doubtless many others in the Sections at this moment, and I could not very well pretend that my enquiry has been an entirely pleasing one. Besides Tizon or Macedo may wish to be present, and I have thought from the first that one or other should be present, and then the fat would be in the fire at once and these Barbadians will practically be under arrest — or secret threats — or worse — unless I take all away with me, and even then there is the very real danger of Tizon or Macedo writing down to Iquitos to have "an enquiry" held there and take the depositions of all these men on their arrival.

Indeed, that is certain — and what sort of "Enquiry" would that be at all? Obviously one solely directed to screening Macedo and Co., and therefore inculpating the Barbadians. They would be made the scapegoats, both to justify Macedo and clear the Peruvian authorities too, and also to destroy any real evidence of the wholesale crimes that that have been allowed for years in this unhappy region.

---

[122] Although closely allied to the company Juan Tizon was despatched to the Putumayo to help improve its image before the arrival of the Commission. He had jumped to the Company's defence in a letter published in the Lima press at the start of 1910 and was a firm Peruvian patriot.

One is surrounded by criminals on all sides. The host at the head of the table a cowardly murderer, the boys who wait on you, and the whole bag of tricks. To go on through this District pretending one is hoodwinked and accepting at their face value all the things we see, will defeat the end in view — for we cannot, later on, bring forward as trustworthy evidence, tales and stories told to us in secret with men posted to see there are no eavesdroppers and acting as if we were the criminals afraid of being found out. And yet, if we don't act like this, I see that almost at once we shall be up against a dead wall, for it is obvious that these men, guilty and evil as they know themselves to be, are not going to sit down idly and see us steadily piling up a dreadful case against them. They will act to protect themselves, and that action will clearly only take one shape, namely, to "accuse" the Barbadians, or to say that, as such very grave charges are now being made to the Commission, and to me, it is the imperative duty of a Peruvian Court of Enquiry to investigate these charges, and all this comes back to the same thing.

The Barbadians will be nobbled and terrorised into denying everything — indeed, it would be only sufficient to lock them up in Iquitos, thus demonstrating my entire inability to protect them to get them to say anything the investigating court desired.

And so here I am with the clock on the verge of 3 p.m., waiting to interrogate the Barbadian hands of this Stronghold of wrongdoing. What shall it be? A real interrogating covering the ground of their relations to the Company and the duties they have been put to perform, or a merely sham one to allow me to "save my face" and assure Tizon that the men "seem happy, and all say they are well treated and properly paid" etc.

This last thing, or anything like it, once said, becomes irrevocable. On the other hand I cannot keep entire silence, neither will the men themselves, at least not all of them. One or other, perhaps the cook ("with £200 to his credit") will tell Macedo just what sort of questions the Consul put to them, and there is always, too, the question of whether it may not be the right thing, from the broad point of view, for me to invite either Macedo or Tizon to be present, just as I shall invite Barnes.

Interview with five Barbadians

7 p.m. I decided to invite Mr Tizon to be present when I interviewed the Barbadians — it was the lesser of two evils. I also asked Mr Barnes and, thus constituted, I had them brought in one by

one. The room with open door on the main verandah of the house, Sr Macedo came and planted himself at door for a time, but, as I made no sign to invite him inside he had to go away, and walked up and down the verandah during most of the time.

The Barbadians presented were the following:

No.1 — a liar — Donal Francis. Engaged 1905. He lied throughout.

" 2 — said nothing — Philip Bertie Lawrence — (Jamaican) Engaged by Juan B. Vega as servant-cook at Chorrera. In Chorrera all the time.

" 3 — saw little — Seaford Greenwich. Baker at Chorrera. Engaged in 1904. Well-treated and is a man of confidence. Has saved over £100. Was once only out of Chorrera, and that was end 1904, and beginning of 1905, when he was in Matanzas. Saw Cyril Atkins there shoot the Indian woman. Since then has been always in Chorrera.

" 4 — Saw much and said so — James Chase. Engaged 1904. In sections often on commissions. Witnessed floggings and killings — up to quite recently.

" 5 — Abisinia. Saw much and said so — Stanley Sealy (or Sily). Engaged in 1905. On commissions often and has flogged frequently himself for not bringing in rubber — but is ashamed to own up to it. That will come. It should be remembered that this man is in a very embarrassing position. He has no money — may soon owe money to the Company — he is sick now — his feet wrapped up in bandages and he has just come from a Section whose moral atmosphere is one of the worst in the whole of this land of crime.[123]

The fifth and last witness, Sealy,[124] spoke like a man throughout and my heart warmed to the ugly black face, shifting from side to side, his fingers clasping and unclasping but the grim truth coming

---

[123] These five statements appear consecutively in the Blue Book as {Nos. 10–14}. Francis, Chase and Sealey were all subsequently interviewed by Casement. Francis later went on to make a statement on 3 November which to a great extent contradicted this statement. It later emerged that Francis had been threatened with death by Macedo if he spoke out. Sealey was employed by Casement and Chase by the Commissioners as personal attendants during their journey on from La Chorrera.

[124] The name Sealy changes to Sealey in the Blue Book. Following this interview Sealey was employed by Casement as guide and escort, and remained with him until Casement's departure from the Putumayo, when he was taken over by the Commission.

out of his lips. Says he had flogged Indians himself — many times — very many times — at Abisinia; at Savana; always because he was ordered to by the Chief — who decided which Indian was to be flogged. It was always for not bringing in rubber — sometimes 25 lashes, some 12, some 6; and some only 2 even — according as the rubber was "short". The Indians would "lie down of themselves" and take the flogging — "like a dog, eh?" I threw in. Their backs — or buttocks rather — would be cut — often badly cut — and so the ghastly tale came out. The Indians were not happy and brought the rubber because they were afraid. They got food "in the Sections" — but not when collecting the rubber in the bush. He had seen women flogged just like men and a boy flogged in Savana.

I told Sr Tizon pretty well just what I thought of it when this last witness had gone — and he had to admit that it sounded rotten and infamous and must be swept away — but that all stations were not like Savana.

The two last witnesses, Chase and Sealy, both spoke out and the former asserted in the most painfully timid manner that was all the more convincing that he had seen Indians shot and flogged to death — not dying actually under the lash — but dying very soon after from the flogging and shot, both after flogging and shot also without having been flogged. Altho' Sr Tizon several times interrupted at this stage the man adhered quite firmly to his statements, and when asked if there was flogging now in Abisinia said yes — and then to please Sr Tizon who intervened said it was "not so bad" as formerly — but still he had seen Indians flogged up to quite recently — and always for the same crime — not bringing in Rubber, or not enough.

His evidence to my mind was very convincing. Barnes too felt as I did, altho' he thinks this man when he said that he himself had never flogged any one was not speaking the truth. I think so too — I think it highly probable he must have flogged Indians.

Had Sr Tizon not been present I am confident a great deal more would have been said — especially by Donal Francis, the first witness. This man, I am assured by Bishop, knows a lot and it is evident he could not have been at Matanzas, one of the very worst stations, for one year and nine months merely "planting yuca" and "guarding himself against the bad, wild Indians".

Bertie Lawrence, the Cook, seemed a decent lad — and as he has been here all the time in Chorrera it is possible he has seen very little altho' even here Indians have been flogged often enough it is clear, and the *cepo* [stocks] have been in evidence until not long ago. Is leaving in December.

The Baker, it was evident, did not speak all the truth. He tried to answer questions within the narrowest limit of reply. He is evidently well-treated, has made money over his job and wants to get away in December with all his earnings, and without being troubled or delayed by possible enquiries in Iquitos or elsewhere.

[*Some pages on in the manuscript Casement adds a further paragraph*:

Bishop told me that the Barbadians had all been tampered with — particularly Donald Francis — the first man who I thought at the interview had lied. There have been not only threats, but bribes — Francis told Bishop that Macedo had begged them and offered him £2 a month more.

The testimony of Chase and Sealy was direct and obviously given under great mental stress — these two men were afraid and yet did their duty. No one with any common sense could doubt the truth of their statements.

In evening Bishop told me that the Barbadian Dyall had come in and would he bring him to me? I said yes, in the morning early.]

AT LA CHORRERA — SATURDAY 24TH SEPTEMBER — 8 A.M.

Joshua Dyall

The man Dyall, referred to in John Brown's statement to Governor of Barbados, arrived down country last night Bishop tells me. I have asked Bishop to bring him to my room this morning — so that I may speak to him, if possible, before Macedo has been at him. I expect, however, that Macedo has long since seen him prepared by the Baker, so that it will be a well-worked up witness I shall see. One moves here in an atmosphere of crime, suspicion, lying and mistrust in the open, and in the background these revolting and dastardly murders of the helpless Indians. If ever there was a helpless people on the face of this earth it is these naked forest savages, mere grown up children. Their very arms show the bloodlessness of their timid minds and gentle characters.

Dyall came at 8 or 8.30 a.m. and I had Barnes in to hear his statement[125] — one of the most revolting character. The man is a brute but has been employed by greater brutes.

As his statements are so grave, he owning up to five murders of Indians by his own hands, two he shot, two he beat to death by "smashing their testicles" with a stick under Normand's orders and with Normand helping, and one he flogged to death, I thought it

[125] Joshua Dyall {Blue Book Statement No. 15.} Dyall's long statement gave a detailed account of widespread atrocities.

wise to have his evidence stated in full before the Commission and Sr Tizon. I therefore asked Tizon to meet them all in my room at noon where I had a very grave statement to read to him. Dyall came and I read his evidence, a statement rather, and he confirmed it, and then I had F. Bishop and Stanley Lewis up and all these testified as to the deeds they had witnessed, the illegal acts they had themselves performed under orders of their Chiefs of Section, and the character of the system of "trade" they were put to enforce over the Indians.

Their statements, particularly Bishop's, were convincing enough for any fair man I should think, that what he had been employed on could not rightly be called "commerce" or "trade" in any civilised or accepted sense of the term.

One of the punishments described by Dyall for Indians who failed to bring in the rubber required of them by Normand had been to haul them up by a chain round the neck high off the ground, and then let them drop suddenly, so that they were insensible and had to be brought to by pulling their arms about — in a way he demonstrated before us. (Bishop had previously told me exactly the same thing of Sections where he had been employed, and described one case of an Indian so hoisted, who when he fell, fell back insensible and bit his tongue through. He has volunteered to assert and "prove" this statement anywhere and before anyone.)

Sr Tizon in vain sought to weaken these three men's statements, but they did not vary them nor withdraw, and I asked both him and the Commission to put any questions they pleased to them. I said that, for my part, unless these statements were refused I was bound to accept them: not perhaps in every detail, but in the main as constituting a very grave indictment of the whole system and revealing a state of things that was wholly wrong and could not be allowed to continue. I refused to admit that flogging Indians for failure to bring in rubber required of them, even when they had "accepted advances" of goods, was to be tolerated for one moment, and that to my mind the state of dealing with the Indians that had been described was slavery.

It was immaterial who had originated it, Colombians or Peruvians — the company was a civilised institution, it had inherited the claims of the founders of this method and it must sweep away this system and establish a lawful and civilised and humane method of dealing.

With regard to the Barbadians they accused themselves, which, in great part, went to prove the truth of their statements. I could not see what motive should induce any man to charge himself with grave and dastardly crimes, as Dyall had done, unless it were that he was confessing.

If these men were guilty, as I believed they were, of criminal acts, it was not they so much as the men who had ordered them to do these things who were the real criminals, and if there was a question of punishing anyone, I should seek to defend these men and should ask for legal advice and help.

[*With reference to this episode Casement later adds*: "We arranged to take all the Barbados men up country and confront the accused, Tizon, Bell and I thinking it undesirable from various points of view, but Barnes, Gielgud and Fox desiring it, and as I stood aside and said I only wished to aid the Commission Tizon had to give in, and of course Bell accepted the majority view."]

Casement's private conversation with Tizon

Tizon was in great embarrassment and later on confessed that he was prepared to accept the men's charges "in the main" — and did not wish to confront them with the men they accused.

He said that no good could come of accusing Fonseca, Montt, etc. to their faces — that we were not a judicial body and that there is no one in the Putumayo empowered to investigate criminal acts and that there has been no effective administration in the past, owing to the boundary dispute with Colombia, by Peru — and thus lamentable deeds have been committed with impunity.

Later in the evening, in the course of a long conversation with me he practically threw up the sponge, said the system was slavery, that it would have to go and that these criminals who were dangerous men capable of anything, with their arms, their *muchachos* and their local power, might arm the wild Indians and do anything.

He confirms himself afraid of the consequences if we insist on charging these men face to face with the blackman as accuser that they will not accept such an accusation except from a Court — and that "anything would be possible". If the Commission will trust him, and the Company will support him, he will undertake to get rid of all these men, every one, as the Commission and he think it desirable and he will undertake to completely abolish flogging for "commercial" reasons — and to see that a far more humane and civilised method is adopted in the Sections where force has been or is still ruling, He appealed to me to use my influence with the

Commission to get them to agree to this course — I said it would lie with them and the view they obtained during our forthcoming journey of his ability and sincerity, of his ability to carry through the reforms he outlined, and of course of his sincerity which, for my part, I was prepared to believe in now. He thanked me warmly again and again — and said it was a fortunate and a happy thing that the British Government had sent a man of my experience, tact, etc., etc., (ad infinitum) out, that it was due to me that things would be set straight. (This at its face value!)

I think the man is sincere in his wish to perform things here — I only doubt his ability and strength. He says if the Company is swept away, as it will be if the Commission chooses — he quite recognises that — then a "far worse state of things will prevail" — and I am in full agreement with that.

If the Company can be kept going and he can have his hands strengthened, then he is prepared to make a sweep of all the criminals "prudently" but as quickly as possible. They would be called down to La Chorrera, one by one, and then got rid of — paid off and sent away, and not allowed to return. Better men would be obtained and put in their places.

Our conversation lasted till after midnight.

[*Casement repeats the above description some pages on.*]

At La Chorrera — Sunday 25th September

I told Barnes and Bell of what Tizon had said to me the previous night. They said that if he would repeat his statement to the Commission, then they would agree to the Barbadians not confronting the accused Chiefs of Sections. These Chiefs of Sections directly accused are Montt (Ultimo Retiro), Fonseca (Sabana), Normand (Matanzas); Aguero of Abisinia is also accused, but our proposed itinerary for the first journey is to go north to Ultimo Retiro, Atenas and Sabana, and back here — to cover the ground included in Dyall's and Lewis' statements.

I accordingly told Mr Tizon I wished him to meet the Commission and discuss certain matters at say, 4pm today, as it was very hot. We did not meet till nearly 4.45 in my room. I warned Chase I might want him beforehand.

p.m. meeting between Commission and Tizon

At the meeting I spoke at length. I explained that Mr Tizon thought it very undesirable to confront the Chiefs of Sections we were about to visit with the accusing blackmen who had been their servants. On the other hand, I pointed out that this confrontation was the only means in our power of establishing the truth or otherwise of the statements the Barbadians made against their employers. For my part I recognised the full force of Mr Tizon's objections, but, on the other hand, I could not allow it to be said that I had abstained from putting to the only test (in our power) the declarations of these British employees of the Company. Would the Commission, and would Mr Tizon, then accept at their value the declarations of the Barbadians? These men made them in good faith to me — an official of their Imperial Government sent specially to investigate their relations to this company — and, for my part, I was compelled to accept these statements unless the agents of the Company on the spot could disprove them. On the contrary, I was appealed to not to put them to the only test open to me, seeing there was no Peruvian authority of any kind, no Court, no magistrate, or any judicial body to which either the men or I could appeal on their behalf.

These men charged themselves with the gravest crimes — killing, and flogging Indians under the orders of men who were in the pay and employment of this British Company, some of them at spots only a few miles away. I could not allow it to be said later on that I had accepted testimony which had not been investigated, and was, therefore, one-sided or valueless. I was quite prepared to carry the matter to the fullest development, and, if necessary, to telegraph at once for legal assistance, and if these Barbadians were challenged and put on their trial — as they ought to be in any civilised country — to defend them, because, however guilty, they were not nearly so guilty as the men who had ordered them to commit these crimes. They said they acted under fear, under compulsion, and I believed it. I pointed out that the real criminals, in my opinion, were the supreme agents or heads who directed this system of wrong-doing, and enslavement of the Indians, and drew their profit from it, closing their eyes to the inevitable results of the application of such a system in such conditions of lawlessness — or absence of law — as prevailed on the Putumayo.

Therefore if the man's charges were not to be tested by confrontation with the accused agents of the company, I wanted to know would Mr Tizon affirm in the presence of the Commission what he had said to me the previous evening, namely that he would dismiss everyone of the arraigned men? That was the least that would satisfy me. I had now received the testimony of the majority of the Barbadians in the Company's service, and it revealed a disgraceful state of things. The few remaining men — eight in all, except one at El Encanto I should see very shortly, and then my work would be done, and I should be going home, leaving the Commission behind me. They would visit many places I should not; they would be engaged on other things, peculiarly economic and mercantile questions, and the memory of the Barbados men's statements would, to some extent, be effaced. Also there would be active influences at work to efface it. They had no interpreters, no proper interpreter to find out from the Indians how they were treated.

Any sincere enquiry must begin there with the Indians, the producers of the India rubber. It was obvious that unless they were questioned, the Commission would be quite in the dark, and might obtain very unreal impressions. I instanced Mr Gielgud's visit last year, and how at the station where Bishop was, the prisoners, Bishop stated, had all been removed. Mr Gielgud agreed. After a great deal of discussion — much of it irrelevant — with Barnes and Bell supporting my point of view, Mr Tizon agreed openly, in the presence of the Commission, that all the agents incriminated would be dismissed while the Commission was here. He would not question later on the statements of the Barbadians, he practically accepted them, and would act on them as if proved. He repeated this declaration emphatically. He pleaded for assistance and support, averred his sincerity and good faith, and appealed for our backing up of his authority in the very trying position in which he found himself. I said that I fully realised this, and I was satisfied. It was the best that could be obtained. There was no Law, no Authority on the Putumayo as the Company had assured the Foreign Office in their letters. We had been informed categorically in London that the charges against the Company were impossible, because the Peruvian Government maintained an efficient administration in the Putumayo, and here was Mr Tizon admitting that nothing could be done, even to investigate the terribly grave statements made by these British subjects against Peruvian citizens, because this was "a very peculiar region", and lay practically outside the jurisdiction of civilised authority.

Casement attacks the system

I abandoned, therefore, today, in deference to Mr Tizon's wishes, the strength of which I fully admitted, the only opportunity available of proving or disproving the charges made by the Barbados men, I must insist now that the Commission and Mr Tizon would agree that I had done so because to attempt to prove them would be in itself a waste of time, seeing there was no authority to appeal to, and highly dangerous into the bargain as Mr Tizon asserted, and likely to defeat all the good he hoped to effect by proceeding prudently and quietly to dismiss the incriminated men. But the dismissal of these men would not be enough. I must also insist that the system of obtaining rubber under terror by flogging and other illegal punishments must cease, and must cease at once. This Mr Tizon agreed to. He would at once issue a circular to all the agents warning them that anyone who was found to flog natives or ill-treat them would be dismissed and handed over to Peruvian justice for trial.

I said that the Company had assured the FO of this same line of conduct, and I read their paragraph from their letter, but the first statement made to me, on arriving at Iquitos (1st September) and one they had heard the previous day again repeated from the man Bishop, was that he himself had flogged Indians this year in the months of April and May at the Stations of Atenas and Cabana close to Chorrera, for not bringing in rubber.

Tizon promises to act

Something more than circular instructions was needed, it was pretty obvious. Mr Tizon gave the most emphatic assurances that he would act, and not merely circularise — that the guilty men would be dismissed, and flogging for rubber, wherever it still existed, entirely and promptly abolished. With this assurance I was forced to content myself, and I expressed myself as entirely satisfied — that is to say, within the obvious limitations imposed by the peculiar circumstance of the case. Mr Tizon is the only element of good I can see in the whole outlook. He has undertaken this task, and he promises to do his duty, and that is all one can ask of him. He will give proofs, so he says. He said, moreover, that if he failed he would resign; that if the company did not give him the power he needed he would not stay a day. He assured me later that he was very sorry he had ever come into the Company's service, that, had he known what he now knows, he would never have done so, but that, having given me this "compromise", this promise, he would not act on his personal desire and abandon so thankless, so well-nigh impossible, a task, but would try faithfully to reform and cleanse this evil region. He said he felt greatly tempted to go down on the *Liberal* on the morrow, to give the whole thing up, but that he could not, for the sake of his country, whose national honour was at stake to a great extent, and for the sake of the humanitarian reasons that were so apparent. If the company failed him, or if, by reason of these charges, the Company were to disappear, and he saw that the fate of the country lay with the Commission, then the last state of the Putumayo Indians would be far worse than the first. In the place of a powerful British Company, able to insist on change, there would be left these desperadoes up country, who would "form themselves into companies" — they would not go, they would unite, and make 20 companies of freebooters and robbers, where today one only existed. Let the Company be preserved; let the Company back him up and sustain his efforts, and he prayed for this support, and something much better could be brought out of this situation.

I told him that he, and his evident sincerity, were the only helpful elements in the situation; that were it not for him, I had really no hope, for I saw all that he said — that if the Company were to disappear the fate of these unhappy Indians would be far worse.

The man is a compound of weakness and sincere good intentions. The evil lies deeper than his weak effort at reform can reach. That I am sure of, but, still, his effort is the only one likely to be made; it is a beginning, a sincere personal effort of an honest Peruvian to right a state of things that no one, outside of Peru, can attempt to tackle. It is much to have succeeded in getting a Peruvian to attempt so much. One thing is clear — Tizon is not strong, but he is honest. He is not self-seeking or money-grubbing. He did not, I believe, enter the Company alone to make money. The task before him is a very hard one. I said I should do my utmost to help him, both in London and Iquitos. He said "Yes, please, but chiefly in Iquitos."

The Zumaetas, the Dublés — and, worst of all, the Aranas — should be eliminated, but, alas, they are the Company, the local company. The London shareholders and Board are merely the cloak of respectability, and the guarantee for cash. Arana and his gang in Iquitos are the real Peruvian-Amazon Company. When he finds no more money can be got from London then the Company will go, but Arana and his horde of infamous ruffians here will remain — the Mirandas, Macedos, Agueros, Fonsecas, Montts, Normands, Argaluses, Flores, Luiz Alcortas — and all the abominable rest. God help the Indians! Poor Tizon, too. He said to me at nightfall, "It needs prayer, it needs an angel to come to help me. Where are the better men to come from?"

I went to bed very sad and tired after this long talk with Tizon up to 12.30 a.m. I should think.

AT LA CHORRERA — MONDAY 26TH SEPTEMBER

The *Liberal* went away to Encanto, taking Dyall, also Lewis as steward again! and much of my evidence is thus disappearing. We are to go up country tomorrow, Tizon, the Commission and myself, in the 'Veloz', the small launch, above the falls to Ultimo Retiro, and then to work back to this via Entre Rios, Atenas, Sabana, etc. etc., probably.

A sick Bora Indian

The Boras Indians, who were here discharging cargo, etc., went away by *Liberal* under Miguel Flores, of all men! I did not know until he had left that this was Flores, — I believe Miguel Flores. One new Boras Indian appeared — sick, emaciated — walking slowly. I said to Gielgud "How like a woman he looks". That was while he was squatting on the bank. Then he rose and went to the "Botica" for medicine. I followed, and asked the attendant Whiteman if he was not sick? He said, "Yes, his belly". This was shrunken in like a starving dog's. The man patted it, and looked at me, as I bent over him, with the most pathetic eyes. He spoke in his native tongue, evidently asking for relief. He got no medicines! I saw that. The "Doctor" was at coffee all the time and never moved, and the assistant over at the Dispensary gave nothing, and at last the man had to go back to the steamer and sailed for Abisinia without even that small amount of medical help that we are assured this Chief Station supplies. All the other Boras were dressed in singlets and pants — for our eyes! This man had none. I gave the *muchacho de confianza* of Flores, the boy I photoed on Saturday, named Jay, a pyjama suit. I did not know then this miserable half caste was Flores — is it possible Miguel Flores? He was going back to Abisinia with these men, and a stack of Winchesters, and, as the steamer was near going away, a pretty half caste girl came down reluctantly, and was ordered on board — the last incident! Was this girl trying to avoid going? And were we actually looking on unconsciously at one of the "incidents" of this very incidental Putumayo? Was this, perhaps, the wife of one of the Colombians of the Caraparaná — of David Serrano? — or of another? Quite possibly, but we could not tell, and could not ask.

I showed Barnes the sick Indian at the door of the Botica, but he made no enquiry. I took him to the Baker to prove that the Doctor did not visit the sick. We saw John Brown's child, crying all the time, carried in the burning sun to the Doctor, and in a moment met it again coming back. The Baker had paid ten soles (£1) for a bottle of Scott's Emulsion from this store for his servant boy a few days ago. He admitted to getting drunk, and said he could buy liquor. He showed a bottle of whisky the Captain of *Liberal* had just given him. The men got drunk pretty often, in their own houses, Chiefs and all. He got drunk sometimes. Sealy had got drunk from liquor he gave. He bought it in the store on an order from the Chief, and he got it from the 'Cosmopolita' sometimes. I had seen him on Saturday morning, and this visit with Barnes was to confirm for Barnes the statements about the Doctor and the drink, and the cost of medicines.

Doubts about the Commission

Why have not the Commission themselves questioned anyone? They do nothing. They sit in their rooms and read, or they are occupied in the purely commercial and economic aspects of the Station and the Company's affairs. These points about sale of drink — denied by the Company in London — and the Doctor not visiting sick people in their houses could all be verified, and should be verified. They have not sought to find out why the Boras Indians were flogged. Of seven men here on the station, three bore obvious broad weals, deep-dyed across their buttocks and thighs. We pointed this out to Tizon on Sunday — they had done so they said on Friday, and I raised it yesterday — Sunday — as proof that they had no means of finding out anything without an interpreter. Here, I said, at the very first station we stop at, are Indians evidently flogged. No one says a word about it — it is quite natural — the accepted state of things — and you can't find out the reasons for it. It is proof of lawlessness, and of extreme lawlessness, for the marks are deep, and yet everyone takes it as a matter of course.

Then there was the case of Bolívar at Indostan[126] — in chains for 2 months there, and only released because I found him and

[126] This refers to the incident that occurred on 21 September, before the Commission reached La Chorrera where Casement found a young Indian called Bolívar in

drew attention. Bolívar, Tizon said, was a "bad man", but, if this lawless chaining up of "bad men" is to be indulged in, where is one to draw the line? One Chief will only chain up his "bad man"; another, a little further off, or more violent by temperament, will shoot him!

When is it to end? Witness Aguero at Abisinia. James Chase (and Bolívar) tell me that Aguero has shot 'Chico', an Indian. When Chase states this before Mr Tizon on Friday, Tizon excuses the act by saying "Chico was a bad man". He had revolted — he had stolen guns and tried to kill whiteman, etc., etc., and Aguero had to take action. Let us see how Aguero's action has worked out?

Casement redefines his mission — the search for proof

I am here on a Mission of Enquiry to find out how British subjects have been used and employed by this British Company. Here is a British subject, an employée of this company, who tells me, in the presence of the Chief Agent of the Company, that another British subject (Allan Davis) an employée of the Company had killed an Indian by shooting him, acting under the direct order of the Chief of Section. This within the last two months of this year, say in July last. Mr Tizon tells me incidentally that Mr Aguero is "a very nice man". I have nothing to do with that — with Mr Aguero's qualities — but I have something to do with the use he puts British employées of the Company to. If he ordered Allan Davis, as Chase states, to shoot 'Chico', or to bring him in "alive or dead", and Davis, acting on this order, has shot 'Chico', as Chase states Davis has admitted to him, then where are we? And where is the law and authority of Peru in this region that this British Company has asserted to be in supreme existence here?

It seems to me I need only prove this one case to convict the Company, the System, the Peruvian Authorities, and the whole thing of being a lie, and a very lawless lie indeed.

'Chico', I gather, was a *muchacho de confianza* of Abisinia. He got too much of the nice qualities of Sr Aguero and "revolted", and so a British subject is employed to shoot him. It is murder, but who is the murderer — Allan Davis or Aguero? The thing may be very grave for Davis. He might be arrested and sent to Iquitos, as Cyril Atkins was for shooting the woman long ago at Andokes "by mistake", as the baker stated to me, a man who was then at

---

chains and two native girls with high fevers. The rather fleeting reference implies Casement had made a more substantial note about the incident elsewhere.

Andokes. Cyril Atkins died in jail at Iquitos. This must be investigated — Cyril Atkins when I return to Iquitos — and the case of Allan Davis here at Abisinia. This I shall certainly do on my return from up country, and I think by proving this case before I leave, it will, perhaps, be the most convincing proof of existing lawlessness I can obtain. It is quite clear to me that the thing is entirely lawless and without defence.

Mr J.C. Arana has been astute enough to plant the Peruvian method of "handling" wild Indians on the British public and to float it as a company.

Out of the mass of difficulties that have surrounded my course, the great perplexities that have beset me since arriving in Iquitos, and that have accumulated within the last few days here at Chorrera as to how best to proceed this case seems to offer the most helpful way out. By proving it I may be able to convince and convict all round. No one suspects here that I am even thinking of Allan Davis. The matter was raised not by me. I knew absolutely nothing about it until Chase, in the course of his evidence before Messrs. Tizon and Barnes, said that Davis had confessed to him that he had fired the first shot and killed 'Chico' along with Juan Sellar. When this statement was made Mr Tizon said 'Chico' was a very bad man", etc. etc. It was only that point of view that struck him, and after I had dismissed Chase he said he thought Chase had lied, and "was accusing Davis because he was an enemy!"

I have left it exactly there — not mentioned the matter again — and I have even said I did not propose to visit Abisinia. Nor did I. It is only now, as I am writing, that the clear significance of this employment of Davis here within touch, only a couple of months ago, comes home to me. This is not "ancient history". It is yesterday. It involves not "cannibal" savages and Colombians, but a civilised British subject, engaged originally as an "agricultural labourer", and possibly later on a contract like Sealy's. In any case, a British subject has clearly been put to a grossly illegal task — ordered to commit a crime and to endanger his life. The facts are already known to Mr Tizon before my arrival, to some extent at any rate, for he knew 'Chico' had been killed certainly, and he had not only done nothing, he looked upon it as perfectly natural, but he defends it on the grounds that Aguero must defend himself and the Station, as there are no constituted authorities of any kind in the district to afford protection.

Incidentally, too, it illustrates the depravity entailed by the whole system. 'Chico' was one of the "civilised" Indians of Abisinia

— one of those armed and drilled to obey and execute the orders of the civilisers on the wild, or, in other words, defenceless Indians. With what result? He revolts. He becomes "a bandit", an armed terror "threatening the lives of white men even" (these were Tizon's own words to Barnes and myself), and so is shot out of hand by a labourer of British birth in the Company's service. The boy I photoed on Saturday was the *muchacho de confianza* of Flores, and he, I was told by Donal Francis on Friday, has "killed plenty of men", although only a lad, and was not yet "fully civilised!" When later on he "revolts", who will kill him?

This very afternoon at teatime, while Sr Macedo's little boy of 3 years old was at my bedroom door, playing with me, with his Indian nursegirl, and another little girl, not a nurse, but evidently the child of a Peruvian — a pretty child of 5 or 6 — Bishop seeing me pet the boy and glance at the girl whose hand he was holding, said to Barnes and myself, "That girl's father, Sir, was killed by his own *muchachos* a few months ago." I realised the significance at the time, but not so fully as now. Barnes was in a hurry and was pressing for something I had, and I asked no further question. But there you have it — the *muchachos* armed and exercised in murdering their own unfortunate countrymen, or, rather, Boras Indians murdering Huitotos and vice versa for the pleasure, or supposed profit, of their masters, who in the end turn on these (from a variety of motives) and kill them. And this is called "civilising" the wild savage Indians!

What a scandalous, infamous state of things to exist under the administration of a British Company, which indignantly denies that there is a word of truth in the charges brought against its past. Why, here at the present moment, I find at my very doors, playing with the children of the Chief Manager of the Company at the principal Station, living proof of the most extraordinary state of things — a white agent murdered, not by the cannibals and savages he is subduing to a beneficent civilisation, but by the very "boys" he has already "civilised" and used as agents for the betterment of their wild brethren.

Clearly the *muchachos* civilised and armed are more dangerous to civilisation than the poor, wild, unarmed Indians of the woods, who are the prey of the civilisers.

I must ask Bishop for details of this girl's father's killing — name, place, time, and facts.

Ask Chase if the Flores who left today is Miguel. If the *muchacho* who had killed many was known to him at Abisinia? The girl who did not want to go on board? The sick Boras Indian — the one without clothes or medicine? Why 'Chico' had revolted? and then prepare my case for a descent on Abisinia, on getting back next month, and proving this case.

God guide me aright. God help me for the help of these unhappy beings.

AT LA CHORRERA — TUESDAY 27TH SEPTEMBER — A.M.

It was Miguel Flores who went away yesterday in *Liberal* to Abisinia. The boy 'Jay' — Resigo in the Savana — is the *muchacho de confianza* of Abisinia. One of them.

'Rochipo' was the name of the man we have been calling 'Chico' — that Allan Davis shot by order of Aguero, and he was killed quite recently by Aguero's orders. Davis and Juan Sellar shot him. Juan Sellar is a Peruvian.

'Chico' was quite another man and was killed "long ago" — but this last man was 'Rochipo', and it occurred quite lately. I told Chase not to say anything about it until I told him to. That I would have it all brought to light later on. That there was no quarrel between him and Davis — as Mr Tizon said or thought — it was Davis told him quite voluntarily. He had confounded 'Chico' with Rochipo.

In conversation with Bishop

Bishop called by me to answer questions early morning.

Bouchel is father of the girl I saw on the verandah playing with Macedo's children. He was killed by his own "boys" — himself and three other "blancos" were killed by the banks of the Caquetá at the end of last year. It was their own "boys" who did it. It was one of the boys — Katofa — who went with Bishop and Robuchon[127]

[127] Eugenio Robuchon (d.1906) was a French explorer/anthropologist and member of the Geographical Society of Paris. Robuchon was commissioned by the Arana Hermanos in 1904 to make a survey on behalf of the Peruvian Government of their Putumayo rubber district lying between the Caquetá and Napo. Robuchon departed Iquitos on 18 September 1904 with his Great Dane 'Othello' and travelled to La Chorrera to begin his survey. After photographing and describing habits and customs of the Witoto and Nonuyas he travelled into the territories of the Caquetá where he mysteriously disappeared, although some of his photographic plates were later recovered. In 1907 the Peruvian Government published a book entitled *En el Putumayo y sus Afluentes*, with a text edited by Carlos Rey de Castro, the Peruvian Consul in Manaos, from Robuchon's diaries. The book claimed that Robuchon had been eaten by hostile cannibal tribes and dwelt at length upon the anthropophagous nature of the tribal people of the Putumayo. Other rumours

years ago. He had run away. He ran away at that time, and he and other *muchachos de confianza* attacked Bucelli and the *Empleados Racionales* referred to while sleeping on the banks of the Caquetá.

I also told Bishop to tell all the Barbadians left here that I might again require their testimony, and that, if so, they were to bear in mind their duty to God and to their Country's laws, to remember that I had been sent by the Imperial government to assist them, and they owed a duty to their country and citizenship to speak honourably and fearlessly, that it was only by the truth coming from their lips that these unhappy Indians could be helped and a change made. That there would be no other chance, that if now they were false to their manhood and did not enable me to convince these other gentlemen of what had been done, or was being done, then no other chance of doing right in this wrong state of things would offer.

Bishop said he had told Francis that he was as bad as any of the "murderers" here or elsewhere in the Putumayo for not telling me the truth the other day. Francis was a coward he had said, and he had told him so.

Later in the morning Casement and the Commission left La Chorrera on board the Veloz *and headed up the Igara-paraná. They stopped briefly at Victoria and Naimenes, slept on board overnight and arrived the following morning at the rubber station of Occidente.*

---

however suggested that Robuchon had been quietly murdered by Company assassins after he started to turn his camera on the atrocities committed by employees against the tribal people. Casement's copy of this book, containing his margin notes, is preserved in the N.L.I. Casement sent a translated précis of the book attached to his letter to Charles Roberts, chairman of the Parliamentary Select Committee Enquiry, on 16 November 1912 {R.H. Brit. Emp. Papers S.22}. He made further reference to the work in the Blue Book p.48.

II

OCCIDENTE

AT OCCIDENTE — WEDNESDAY 28TH SEPTEMBER

We arrived here at about 9 a.m., being greeted on landing by Fidel Velarde, the Chief of the Section, Manuel Torrico, his second, and Rodriguez and Acosta, whom we left at six last evening down at Naimenes. They had walked over this morning, and it is evidently not far by land, as Chorrera itself is only seven hours, or possibly eight hours by land.

Description of Velarde and Occidente's rubber production

Velarde looks a perfectly awful type — worse, if possible, than Miguel Flores, who left so evil an impression on me at Chorrera. I must look up Velarde's "criminal record". As I had been lying on a plank all night, and not a very level one, and it had rained too, I got very little sleep last night, so soon after landing I turned in the best guest room on a fine big iron bed, very kindly placed at my disposal by Tizon. I slept most of the day. The Commission decided on the route they propose taking from this, and also on what they shall do while staying here. I did not join these deliberations, as they were purely concerning the business of the Company, but I saw Velarde sitting there, and looking like a convicted criminal. I subsequently am told by members of the Commission that his examination by them had produced the worst impression. They believed he was lying, and had so told Tizon. He had been unable to give them any help in their "economic and mercantile" mission. He had told them that he had 530 rubber collectors or "labourers" on the list of his employés, this not including *muchachos* and "domestic servants". The former are the armed Indian boys kept at each stronghold, the latter are for sexual intercourse chiefly, and carrying water from the river. I expressed no opinion on the statement that this Station of Occidente has 530 "labourers", simply because I have "no opinion" of the statement. It is a lie. There are doubtless 530 Indians inscribed, whose duty is to bring in every three months some 30 kilogs of rubber against battle, murder and sudden death if they don't, but I must prove this for the satisfaction of the Commission before I openly question the "facts" they think they are eliciting. Velarde, I understand, told them, and Gielgud did, that this station produces 50 tons of rubber per annum. Let us see how that works. Say 30 kilogs per man per quarter gives 120 kilogs per annum plus 530 "labourers", gives 63,600 kilogs. The actual quantity collected per man must, therefore, be less than 30 kilogs per quarter. Yet in the Store today I weighed one of the one-man loads lying there, and it comes to 33½ kilogs, and I was told it did not represent the full amount for a *fabrico*, or rubber term. The *cepo*, or stocks, are also in this rubber store. There is nothing else. It is the whole ground floor of the big house, and is lined round the two long sides with shelves on which the rubber lies, according as each Indian "labourer" brings it in every ten days or fifteen days. To be accurate he does not bring it in, I am told. Although a collector, he is himself collected when the rubber is "due". The 530 labourers are scattered all over Sr Velarde's section, and they are collected fortnightly, we will say, by armed bands of *muchachos* under his, or Rodriguez' or Acosta's leadership. They are marched down to the Station here, each man (or family) with his or their load of rubber, which is here weighed. If correct, the man escapes back to his forest home to begin almost immediately collecting afresh. If not up to weight he gets flogged or put in *cepo*. Such is, mildly, the system. At the end of the fabrico, which is five of these collections, he receives not payment on the 30 kilogs, or whatever the exact amount may be he has gathered, but an "advance" against the next fabrico, that is to say, he is kept on "the books" of this commercial establishment as a debtor to the firm. He is not asked if he wants an advance, or what he would like, he is only too happy to escape with a whole skin, or with his wife and daughter.

The system

I did not gather any of this from the Commission. They merely told me they were convinced Velarde was lying. I am writing down what I believe to be the system, as I have both read it and had it described by the various Barbados men I have interrogated (see some of their statements). I hope to convince the Commission of the full working of the system before we part, but it will be very difficult, for I cannot question anyone save the Barbados men I have interrogated and they cannot question anyone save the

Agents of the Company, who have an obvious interest in lying. No one is to question Indians, the best witnesses of how the system works, because that would upset everything. Moreover, the Commission's only interpreter is the Barbados man, Chase, who joined them solely because I asked him to.

Velarde had issued invitations for a big Indian dance to greet us. Our coming had been known for long. The manguaré,[128] or Indian drum, in the *muchachos'* house was beating almost all the time — exactly like the native drums on the Upper Congo. The identical system I should say. These tappings and boomings were to say, "Come to the ball", "Come to the ball", and in the night the beating went on often for lengthy periods.

I sat up late at night hunting up the "record" of this man Velarde in my police news.[129] Did not get to sleep till after 3 a.m., as I had to go all through the 240 pages of typed document. I find he is one of the "principal criminals" of the Putumayo of that extraordinary record. There are not many incidents given against him, but several of the witnesses put his name down in their lists of the chief wrongdoers they had met in the region. (See Velarde's record attached.) I also am hunting up Rodriguez' record, but it must go for another day.

AT OCCIDENTE — THURSDAY 29TH SEPTEMBER

An Indian dance

From 11 a.m. the Indians began to arrive for the dance. Men, women, boys, girls and children "on back", not children in arms, the women mostly stark naked and generally painted, sometimes quite artistically in yellow and red, and feather fluff on their legs. The men are all under-sized, some half skeletons, at least very underfed, and with wretched arms and legs, some of them only in

---

[128] Manguaré — Pair of drums used by tribes of the Putumayo for forest communication. Hollowed out of tree trunks the small drum (male) is normally about four feet and the larger drum (female) about five and a half feet. By pounding these drums rhythmic messages can be sent for great distances through the forest calling tribal conferences and announcing dances. The heads of the drum sticks are made from congealed crude rubber. Casement bought a pair of manguarés during his Amazon journey that are held in the anthropological collection at the National Museum of Ireland in Dublin.

[129] "Police news" is Casement's secret name for the dossier of information compiled by Hardenburg and others containing the statements and press cuttings about the perpetrators of atrocities. Despite this private name for the dossier it does not cross-reference with the *Black Diary*.

fono,[130] their native work dress, but others came in "gala dress", that is to say, a soiled flannelette shirt and a pair of check pants, the two worth 3/6d.

The naked men in *fono* are better off, to my mind, than the poor specimens in shirt and trousers. The dance began irregularly in parties and processions, and gradually enlarged and developed. We photographed many — Gielgud and I. We visited the Indians' house (the *muchachos* house) where the Indians were dancing both in afternoon and evening. I saw many men, and boys too, covered with scars, and often drew the attention of the others to this, but they were looking for themselves. Some of the men were deeply graved with the trade marks of Arana Bros. across their bare buttocks, and the upper thighs, and one little boy of ten was marked. I called Bishop and we both verified it, and I tried to photo him. One boy had red weals across his backside quite recent. The Commission was more than ever convinced by Velarde's lying to them yesterday. He had declared that no one had been flogged at Occidente since he took charge in January last, and that only one "labourer" (that is to say only one forest Indian) had run away.

Tizon assured me he intended to close down Abisinia and Matanzas, the two worst stations, and open simply trading stores there, with rubber for the currency. I warmly approved. The stores would have to be guarded, of course. He said he had decided on this already before I came, but his decisions were being hastened, the need for change and immediate change was so apparent. I told him I thought his plan was excellent. At these two Sections, where possibly the worst crimes against the Indians have been committed in the long period of lawlessness and anarchy, he will abolish compulsion altogether, and leave the Indians perfectly free to come or not to the Stations. If, as he hopes, they now want things, they will try to procure them by bringing in rubber, and the deal will be a proper commercial transaction. The goods will have a fixed price and rubber a fixed local value. I said "good agents" would be needed, and he should see that more useful and civilizing articles were selected for this barter than any I had yet seen. The silly "caps" with a gilt anchor, worth 6d. I should think at outside, the worthless pants and shirts, no healthy covering at all in themselves, might be replaced by more useful and enduring articles. The present system is not merely slavery but extermination. A slave was

[130] The *fono* is a small bark strap adorning the penis and worn by Amazindian tribesmen.

well-cared for and well-fed, so as to be strong for his master's work. These poor Indian serfs had no master who fed them or cared for them, they were simply here to be driven by lash and gunfire to collect rubber.

The Indians danced all night till 5 a.m. One could hear their chants. No food was given to them, that is to say, presents of sardines and salmon occasionally. Many of the Indians brought in present, birds, game birds they had killed, fruit, and even a little *paca* alive. They presented these so courteously to Velarde or another of these gentlemen as they arrived. There were no fine feather head-dresses, these are all gone, if the Huitotos ever possessed them.

Our great height excited comment at the Dance. We were often surrounded by gazing and smiling bands of both boys and men. Barnes, who is 6'4" (almost) was actually measured by one elderly Indian man with a thin rod he had carried in (as a wand for the Dance) from the forest. He broke off the tip at Barnes' height, and carried off his measure of the tallest white man, or any other man, who has ever been in the Putumayo probably. He measured Gielgud and myself too — we who are both less than Barnes — and then returned to Barnes and took his stature definitely as I have described.

I think the Indians already perceive that something is up. This is a quite different *baile* to anything they have had before. Everyone is kind to them, even Velarde and "the others", surely an unusual experience. They came round us again and again and stared and smiled. Fox is highly popular, dancing with them, keeping step, and playing with the children. Hilarity increases. Bishop assures me this is not an ordinary dance. He says he has seen Indians at these dances, which are only permitted once at each fabrico — that is to say less than 4 times a year — who were cuffed and kicked, and at night he has known the *blancos* go out, excited with drink, and commit abominable orgies with the women and girls by force — even raping prisoners in the *cepo*. He blushed I think — he certainly cried the other day when telling me one of these filthy stories of crime. So, I must say, did I when listening to Dyall's relation of his own atrocious acts. He tells me that he has been roused from bed by the Chief of his Section more than once late at night and sent off to some Indian house near the station where a Dance was going on, to stop it. I thought this was because the Chief was disturbed and could not sleep. "No, sir," he said, "I was sent to stop the dance, because he said, they would not be able to work *caucho* tomorrow if they danced."

Poor Indians! Everything they like, everything that to them means life, and such joy as this dim forest at the end of the world can furnish to a lost people, is not theirs, but belongs to this gang of cut-throat half-castes. Their wives, their children are the sport and playthings of these ruffians. They, fathers of families, are marched in, guarded by armed ruffians, to be flogged on their naked bodies, before the terrified eyes of their wives and children. Here we see all before us, men and husbands and fathers, bearing the indelible marks of the lash over their buttocks and thighs, and administered for what and by whom? For not bringing in a wholly lawless and infamous toll of rubber, imposed upon them, not by a Government, as in the case of the Congo pillage, but by an association of vagabonds, the scum of Peru and Colombia, who have been assembled here by Arana Bros. and then formed into an English Company with a body of stultified English gentlemen — or fools — or worse — at their head.

" ... my celibacy makes me frugal of human life ..."

And the charming Lizardo Arana tells me in Iquitos I shall find "such splendid Indians" here, and he feels sure the result of my journey to the Putumayo will be more capital for the Company! Yes, more capital punishment if I had my way. I swear to God, I'd hang every one of the band of wretches with my own hands if I had the power, and do it with the greatest pleasure. I have never shot game with any pleasure, have indeed abandoned all shooting for that reason, that I dislike the thought of taking life. I have never given life to anyone myself, and my celibacy makes me frugal of human life, but I'd shoot or exterminate these infamous scoundrels more gladly than I should shoot a crocodile or kill a snake.[131]

[131] Casement's revealing comment about his "celibacy" appears to have slipped the analysis of Casement's biographers. Those who believe in the "authenticity" of both "black" and "white" diaries should ask themselves exactly what Casement means by this reference to his "celibacy" when, according to the *Black Diaries,* he was anything but a practising "celibate". It has been suggested that Casement might be using the word in the same sense as "bachelor" — but given the context of the word's usage this seems untenable.

At Occidente — Friday 30th September

Note about the Colombians

Remember to point out to Commission that if, as alleged by Mr Tizon, there are many "very good" stations on the Cara-paraná where the Indians are happy, etc., it must be remembered the Colombians were there first, and the Peruvian Amazon Company has only "taken over" their establishments, some quite recently. If, as is also alleged, the Colombians were so bad, such devils and even "tigers" (these were Tizon's own words to me) why did they leave such content and peace behind them, or are we to believe that these happy circumstances have only followed the murders of Serrano, Gonzalez etc., in 1908, the last of the Colombians who were brutally murdered by the agents of the P.A. Company in January 1908. Again, if the Colombians were so bad to the natives, why has the Company got so many of them in its service?

Here at Occidente we find one, Rodriguez, at Sabana another, Ocana, and a few miles further on Aquiléo Torres at Ultimo Retiro, although a few years ago the last was captured by Normand and kept a prisoner with a chain round his neck by our actual host Velarde. Was this to civilize him to the point of entering the Company's service? To tame him too, as the appalling Jimenez or Aguero tame their Boras and Caquetá Indians. There is far too much of this putting the Colombians forward as the "bad men of the place". Arana did it to the shareholders, by inference largely, the Prefect of Loreto did it to me openly at Iquitos, and Tizon has done it many times. For instance at Chorrera, deploring the evil system established by the Colombians, on which Arana had been obliged to more or less model his more "humane" methods, he said that the two first Conquistadores of the region, Crisóstomo Hernandez and Benjamin Larrañaga[132] (both Colombians whom

---

[132] Crisóstomo Hernandez and Benjamin Larrañaga are generally cited as the first two *caucheros* to enter the Putumayo regions and introduced the regime of exploitation of the Indian population. Both Colombian nationals, Larrañaga was a veteran of Rafael Reyes's campaign into the Putumayo in the 1870s to collect *chinchona* (quinine) and in about 1895 returned with his son Rafael and a group of rubber exploiters. They founded the first settlement at La Chorrera and through "co-operating" with the Aimenes Indians began to tap rubber. The business expanded quickly but problems began when Larrañaga, after personally delivering a consignment of rubber to Pará, was swindled of his earnings and subsequently forced into a financial partnership with the Morey family, rich Iquiteño merchants, and a Jewish moneylender called Jacobo Barchillón. In 1897 he began to trade with Arana Bros. and fell further into debt until his operation was Peruvian-

Arana subsequently enveloped) had committed atrocious "crimes" and that Hernandez was a "tiger". Also, when Dyall, the Barbadian, related his first journey to Matanzas in 1904 with Normand and Roman Sanchez, Tizon at once said, "But Sanchez was a Colombian". Nevertheless the Barbadians were all engaged by Arana as "agricultural labourers" or "labourers", and if Arana gave them to Colombian "criminals", whose "properties" he has since entirely acquired, and whose system he has maintained, if not indeed developed. I cannot see but that he is responsible quite as much as these Colombian "ruffians", and to the British Government he is solely responsible for the use to which he has put the labourers recruited in a British Colony.

And this brings us back to the Cara-paraná, where Tizon asserts are the happiest and best Stations of the Company, where he goes for days, he says, entirely unarmed. These were nearly all founded and worked by these Colombians for years, while the admittedly worst Stations — such as Abisinia, which he now proposes to abolish on the ground of its infamy — were created and worked by Arana, I believe from the first.

Indian Captains talk to Bishop

This morning Bishop came to me about 7.30 to say that during the night some of the Indian Captains had come to him and begged him to intercede, or to tell me, how badly they were treated. The chief of these was an elderly man, a captain whom the staff here call 'Francisco' but whose Indian name is Caimanabesa.

This man and another, whom Bishop pointed out to me, had declared to him, he averred, that flogging them for rubber had not stopped, but had been going on until not long ago, and that quite recently beating them with the flat of machetes across the shoulders and backs was taking its place. This latter form of torture, though very painful, left no marks. Also they were now being submitted to a new form of punishment. When they were

owned. Despite forging further business partnerships with Arana he was never able to escape from his Peruvian debtors. Crisóstomo Hernandez was compelled to abandon his rubber estates in the Caquetá in about 1897 for committing a series of unspecified crimes. He fled to the Putumayo and took refuge among the Huitoto, but before long had "conquered" many tribes and instigated a reign of terror. He was eventually shot by one of his own men whereupon his business fell under mainly Arana's control.

down at the riverside washing the rubber, one of the *Racionales*[133] (what a title) stood over them and latterly men would be held under water by him and his *muchachos* and half drowned by this process. They named Acosta particularly as the agent of this fresh "discipline" and Francisco said that within the last few months one of the Indians, whose name he gave as Feraze Pinaima of the Inonia "Nation" of Huitotos, whose Captain was Friapponaima, had been drowned by Acosta in this manner. I at once told Barnes and Bell begged them to interrogate this Indian. Bell was dressed, but Barnes not. He hurried to dress and I went to occupy "the others" and keep them from watching Barnes and Bell interviewing Francisco. Presently I saw Francisco going away — it must have been 9 a.m.— and the Indians were all breaking up and going back to their homes in the forest. I called Bishop and told him to go quietly off as if "to the bush", and to follow Francisco and stop him out of sight of the Station until Mr Barnes and Bell arrived.

I then begged them to hurry after, and as Bishop can speak Huitoto to use him as interpreter, while I stayed behind and kept "the others" occupied. I went to Tizon, Velarde, etc., and asked them to arrange groups of Indians for me to photograph. Barnes and Bell soon returned, having taken notes of Francisco's statement. After lunch Tizon spoke to me on the verandah, telling me of his hopes and fears, the former predominating, as is right if he is to succeed. I assured him of my very best personal support; that wherever I had any influence for good it should be exercized to the full for him, so that his fight against this evil system might be strengthened. I then told him of the Francisco incident, and asked him to interview Barnes and Bell. This he did, and decided to send for Francisco and examine him in private with a "faithful" interpreter he had (this is his Iquitos man).

He later on did this, for Francisco, I think returned to the Station voluntarily — and he told Barnes and Bell that the flogging with machetes and the putting of Francisco in guns was admitted, but that there was some doubt about the wilful drowning of the Indian by Acosta. An Indian had been drowned, it seems, by Acosta shoving him into the river — this was what his interrogation of Francisco led him to think. Of course it is not satisfactory. Tizon's interpreter may be better than Bishop, but in a case involving unquestionably the death of an Indian by an act of a

---

[133] *Racionales* were another rung in the hierarchy of the Putumayo, men of mixed race able to read and write. They received a small salary from the Company.

servant of the Company (who is often in charge of a sub-Station — that of Naimenes — with no one to oversee his acts) some fuller enquiry and the questioning of more witnesses than this one man Francisco is clearly desirable. Several Indians are said to have been at this rubber washing and to have witnessed the death. With much testimony available here the matter is left with two clandestine interrogatories, as if we were afraid of being found out! When Barnes and Bell told me this, my comment was that the probabilities lay with the first version being nearer the truth — as an Indian merely shoved into the river could easily escape by swimming. All can swim very well, whereas if he had been held underwater to frighten him, for any length of time and was struggling there and perhaps imbibing during this enforced immersion, it might very well be that when he escaped the hands holding him down, he could nevertheless drown, swimmer and all as he might be. He would drown from exhaustion caused by the struggle — exhaustion and fright together and want of breath. In any case, as Barnes remarked, there was no question of an Indian — one of the so-called "Labourers" and therefore a commercial asset — having been drowned here at this station, and quite recently, and by an act of Sr Velarde's inferior *racionales*, and yet no notice had been taken of it and no report of the death made to La Chorrera, and the information now only reaches Sr Tizon through my servant man Bishop being able to inspire the Indians with some confidence in our ability (or goodwill) to be their friends. Barnes and Bell told Bishop during their interview with Francisco to tell the *Capitan* to tell all his people that if any of them were flogged or maltreated they were to seek out the Commission, wherever it might be during the next month or two and lay the facts before them.

In the afternoon an Indian *capitan* came and embraced me, laying his head against my chest, and putting his arm round my waist. He did the same to Barnes who was standing by. Both of us were touched. I knew quite well what it meant. I bathed in the river, and 'Andokes'[134] and Barnes caught butterflies. I was not well today, and turned in without dinner.

---

[134] In this context the name 'Andokes' refers to one of the servants employed by the Company's Commission. It is also the name of the tribal group living along the Caquetá and is an alternative name for the station of Matanzas. While Casement is rather constant in the various uses of the word in this text and tries to avoid confusion, the *Black Diary* does the opposite and the name is used often and to muddle the sense.

At Occidente — Saturday, 1st October

Commission go for forest walk — Casement interviews Sealy

The Commission with Tizon went out towards the N.W. to see the Indian "labourers" of that section tapping the rubber trees on that part of the Estate. They were guided by Rodriguez (locally Juanito), Acosta and Torrico, who knew the labourers. I stayed at home, writing and sleeping — not well — and trying to avoid my host, Fidel Velarde, who came to enquire after me. I breakfasted alone with Bishop waiting. I got Stanley Sealy in to describe further, and at greater length, his experiences in the Company's service, the method of employing him, his duties, and then, as he desired to make it, I took down a statement as to what he had witnessed on a Commission headed by Jiménez from Morelia to the Caquetá, in very end of May, or beginning of June 1908. Chase was one of the Commission, he informed me, and could confirm or otherwise his statement; Chase being out attending the Commission in the forest, I took down in quiet and without eavesdroppers this statement of Stanley Sealy's. It reveals the most hideous crime I've almost ever heard of, absolutely hellish. I took down his statement almost word for word, and I shall never forget it. It was told with a simple truthfulness that would have convinced anyone in the English-speaking world, I think, of the man's absolute good faith and simplicity. I decided that I must have this statement confirmed in the presence of the Commission and Tizon, by calling Chase and Sealy again. Till that opportunity arises, I shall say nothing.

Casement debriefs Commissioners

The Commission returned about 1 o'clock. They had found two Indians, rubber tappers only, and had seen, Fox said, only three rubber trees. They seemed quite surprised. I said to Barnes I was surprised at his surprise. I wondered he had not already grasped that this story of Indian labourers was a lie. There were no labourers — there was no industry on the Putumayo. It was simply a wild forest inhabited by wild Indians, who were hunted like wild animals and made to bring in rubber by hook or by crook, and murdered and flogged if they didn't. That was the system. He was surprised that none of the accompanying white men of the station knew where the trees were — the so-called *estradas* — or where the Indians were working. I said I wasn't. The Indians knew by dire extremity where the trees were scattered, and they got the rubber by dint of journeying and misery and hunger — by a constant search, ever extending over a wider area, as they exhausted nearer sources of supply. The whites in the station did not care a damn where the trees were, all they troubled about was where the Indians were — that is to say, to see they did not "escape". It was evident, I pointed out, that the only system was one of sheer piracy and terrorization, and if you lifted the lash you stopped the supply of rubber.

That the forest was gradually giving out its stock of rubber seemed almost apparent to me, as we found these "sections" were continually changing their locality. For instance, this very one, Occidente, was higher up stream a few years ago. It has been transferred quite recently. Then look at Naimenes, only just opened. Look at the list of abandoned stations on the company's own map, abandoned or shifted. The stations were following the rubber trees. I understood that Fox was disappointed at the poor show of rubber trees he had encountered, and those, he said, exhausted and hacked to exhaustion. I am not. Gielgud admits that the supply has fallen off of late, at least he thinks so; but I can never find that he is quite precise or sure of anything I ask him. He is generally a little vague — not intentionally, but he has never grasped the significance of these things, has taken everything for granted, and did not test statements (save books and their keeping). Still, he puts the present output of the "estate" at about 400 tons. The prospectus of the Company gave 470 tons for 1905, 644 tons for 1906, nearly the same for 1907, and some 390 tons for 6 months to June 30th, 1908.

AT OCCIDENTE — SUNDAY, 2ND OCTOBER

An outing into the Forest

As the Commission are going out again today to another part of the forest to see some of the "labourers" working rubber, I accompanied them. We all went on foot, a big party. All Commission, Tizon, myself, Sealy and Chase, with Rodriguez as "guide" and Master of Ceremonies. Coming to a tree over a forest stream, a tributary of the Igara-paraná, Barnes had to turn back unwell. I enjoyed the walk. The forest extremely poor, small stunted trees, and I only saw one rubber tree in the whole 4 miles tramp, and it hacked to death. Fox, I believe, saw one other tree. We reached a small manioc clearing in the forest with a *manguaré* (drum) and then across a tiny stream to an Indian house. Here were two women with children (all stark naked) preparing cassava bread, and four Indian men (nude save for *fono*) appeared. Other Indians had come with us, including Francisco, the Captain, and one of his boys. We lunched there after seeing the four men work rubber. Only two did any actual working — one a lad of say 18 or 20, the other an elderly man. When I first saw this man he was coming up to the house with a baby boy clinging to his bare shoulders — a boy of about two years — just like a little monkey. The man's bare buttocks, thighs, and even lower back and loins were severely marked with lashes. All of us noticed it. I looked at the backsides of all four Indians, all bore marks of flogging, marks that will not disappear, although the older man's markings were far the worst.

Conversation about flogging

As the conversation before lunch turned on this flogging, and the traces of it that so frequently greet us, I said that I thought 90% of the Indians bore flogging marks, or, at any rate, had been flogged. Bell and Fox both thought this too high a figure. At the dance they said they had looked at many bottoms. I said I had done the same, and I really thought 90% not an exaggeration. We continued to differ on the percentage. Leaving them at the stream side watching the two Indians working the rubber, I returned to the house only a few yards away, as I was hungry, and during eating some biscuits I asked Sealy to ask the men present, who numbered nine Indians, if all had been flogged. They answered unanimously yes. They were boys and men. The only male in the house who had not been flogged was a boy of about 5 or 6 years. So here on this small haphazard enumeration, my estimate was less than the reality, for every one of the adult, or quasi adult males, had been flogged. I informed Bell of this on our gathering at breakfast. It stands for just what it is, no accurate test can be applied, unless we examine the posteriors of every Indian male we meet. Then there are the women who are flogged too, often, according to Bishop, Sealy and Chase, who are all prepared to swear to it. Bishop has flogged women himself. Sealy says only men, but "very many men". Chase says he only flogged once himself, but that he has seen hundreds flogged — very many.

Washing rubber

The two men washed the rubber well, to my thinking — no light task. It was soaked slightly, trodden out with the feet in curved plank receptacles stretched across the stream, pounded with wooden machetes while water was poured on it, and hot water more than once poured over it from a pot one of the men kept on a fire. As the older man washed the rubber the scars on his back were very prominent and conversation turned on it. Tizon was asked by Fox if no good could be done by asking this man here why, how and when he was flogged. Tizon said he thought no good could come. Rodriguez, of course, was standing by all the time. Finally, when the rubber was washed and done into two huge sausages nearly a yard long, we returned to the house, had breakfast, and then packed up to return. The others went back by the launch, which had come down stream to pick us up, but I decided to walk back and Gielgud accompanied me — Rodriguez and the Indians too. We wagered against the launch, and after a very stiff walk of 61 minutes we reached the Station some 8 or 9 minutes ahead of the launch. I won a sol (2/-) off Fox, who was prepared to beat us!

Rather hot and tired, I must say, and I was glad of a bath. I began the day at 6 by swimming nearly across the river. Bathed again in the forest in the stream before breakfast, and now a shower bath on return from this vigorous walk.

In the evening I turned in early, being tired, after a very brief rubber of Bridge. I had settled in bed to read, at 9 p.m., when Bishop came to my room with a pencilled note on a slip of paper. It was as follows:

Gusmán's note

Alfredo Montt — *Tiene Indios en cadena y les esta pegando por que elevan muy poco caucho, los indios estan con el culo roto todo rajados lo mismo las mujeres de los muchachos estan todas flageladas.*

Alfredo Montt: Has Indians in chains, and many of them flogged for being short of rubber, and others running away.[135]

I asked Mr Bell to come to my room and translate the note and decided to show it to Tizon in the morning, when the Commission

[135] Casement's rough translation of the Spanish note is indicative of his quite poor grasp of Spanish. It better translates: "Alfredo Montt: — Has Indians in chains who are being punished for collecting too little rubber, the Indians have lacerated bottoms and even the women of the *muchachos* have been flogged." Casement was not a gifted linguist and despite spending many years in Portuguese-speaking Africa it seems that he did not speak Portuguese well. His Castilian was worse and Peru was the first Spanish-speaking country he had actually worked in. The diplomatic language, French, appears to have been the tongue in which he was most conversant and he had limited comprehension of Gaelic and German.

are to meet at my request, to hear Sealy's statement about Jiménez. I have not told them yet, except that I have some matter to lay before them. It will be very hard to have a proper meeting, as we are overlooked and overheard on all sides. The statement of Sealy will be a dreadful one, and the name Jiménez will occur frequently, so that these men here can hear it and could warn Ultimo Retiro.

I am forgetting to say that the paper Bishop brought at 9 is from a man he calls Hermes [Jeremias] Gusmán, a fat *rapaz* here on the Station. I've never even said good day to this man, as he seems to be only a servant of sorts and does not live near us. Bishop says this man has an Indian wife from Atenas and her brother, an Indian, has come down tonight from there and says he has been quite recently flogged by Montt, who threatened to shoot him if he did not give him (Montt), his dog. Gusmán writes to me, begging me not to let his name out. Strange, he, a Peruvian, should appeal to a British Consul. I gave the paper to Bell to keep and will hand it to Tizon in the morning after the Jiménez raid is discussed.

AT OCCIDENTE — MONDAY 3RD OCTOBER 1910

Casement, Tizon and the Commission meet

Sent Bishop to Chorrera by launch, telling him to bring up stores and keep his mouth shut, and find out if any more Barbadians have been called in, and where Batson now is. Launch left at 8. Then I asked Tizon and the Commission if they could gather, as I wished to lay further facts before them. It was difficult to meet in the house. We were watched all round, and as every room is open, everything said can be overheard, besides the sight of the two Barbadians, Chase and Sealy, delivering themselves of the raid of the Caquetá, followed by Garrido, would have itself told its story to the eyes of the onlookers, and the name "Jiménez" bound to be repeated more than once would have been sufficient guide to subject of our investigation. So I proposed the Indian house at the back of the station, and we wandered off there pretending to look at the plants, sugar cane etc, with butterfly nets, camera, etc., as if just off for a stroll. And this is the way the Commission sent by the Company and the Company's chief agents, is forced to hold a meeting in one of the principal stations of the Company. I told Sealy and Chase to come as servants, and Garrido was asked by Bell, we thinking it perhaps desirable, after the Barbadians had told their story, to put him forward to convince Tizon of the recent enough state of things in El Encanto and La Chorrera itself.

I at once called Sealy and Chase, and told former to relate the doings of the "Commission" to the Caquetá in May or June of 1908 under Jiménez.[136] He told the story, simply enough, with less detail perhaps than when he gave it to me on 1st instant in my room (See his statement). Chase substantiated, and they were dismissed, after some objection raised by Gielgud had been disposed of.

Garrido's betrayal

Garrido, then put forward by Bell, went back practically on what he had related to the Commission, before Mr Cazes and myself at Iquitos in September. He gave practically nothing and presented a wretched figure — a contemptible cur. He has been "got at" clearly. We continued the discussion, dismissing Garrido who was hanging around, and after explaining my position very clearly, I obtained again from Mr Tizon and the Commission entirely with me, save Gielgud, who, at length joined the rest, that this charge against Jiménez must stand, and as no action could be taken to prove it, or even to confront the accused man, that the representative of the Company should consider it as actionable and dismiss Jiménez. Sr Tizon again asserted his intention to "dismiss all".

My position, I pointed out, was simply (as stated in the covering notes to Sealy's statement on 1st October) that, as the Company could not, and declined, to take any step to disprove these charges against their Agent, I must regard the testimony of the Barbados men as valid, and form the "independent and impartial" conclusion as to the relations existing between British subjects and the Company's agents, that I was required by my instructions to arrive at, on the only available testimony, namely, that of these British subjects themselves. I was debarred from asking questions of other employés of the Company, or making any attempt, on my part to verify the charges. It lay with the Company's responsible agents here to disprove them, if they wished to convince me that these British subjects were not speaking the truth to the Consular Officer sent to investigate the state of things as it affected these men, and their dealings with the Company.

---

[136] The word Commission was used by the Peruvian Amazon Company to describe the organized raiding parties sent across the frontier into Colombia in pursuit of runaway Indians.

I could come to no other conclusion than that the men were controlled by a lawless organization, lawless from top to bottom; that they had been put to wholly illegal work, and deliberately made into criminals. That my duty was quite apart from that of the Commission, that I was here to do one thing only, and I could do that only with the means at my disposal, viz.: to interrogate the British subjects I found in the Company's employ, as I was authorized to do, and to form my conclusions on this, the only testimony furnished me, and, I might add, the evidence of my sense and of my eyes.

Mr Barnes, as Chief of the Commission, fully agreed, and pointed out that the Commission itself had been indebted to me, and the testimony of my witnesses for most of the information it had so far gained, that the Company's agents (always, of course, excepting Sr Tizon) had withheld matter, and also had wilfully lied as Velarde had done to them at this very station, notably in the case of Captain Francisco, whose charge against Acosta of drowning an Indian quite recently, and of the flogging of Indians, and of the beating of himself with machetes across the back, and the putting of him "*in guns*" had been brought to their notice only through me and Bishop.

I handed Sr Tizon here the pencilled letter that Bishop had brought to me at 9 last night from Hermes Guzmán,[137] and explained how it came and the statement that accompanied it. I did not say to him that this circumstance, viz., that one of his Peruvian employés on this station, whom I had never even nodded to and did not know by sight save by the description given of him, had actually preferred to send his complaint to me, a foreign Consul, rather than to the head of the Company he was serving, was perhaps one of the most damaging facts that had come to my notice, but I did say so, subsequently, to Barnes and Bell when talking things over with them.

I merely remarked to Mr Tizon that he must, as a Peruvian (who had held high office in the service of his country), perceive the extreme danger of such a state of things, and this he instantly affirmed. "The man is a bandit," he remarked. Later on, when we had exhausted the immediate bearing of Jiménez' raid to the Caquetá, which, so far as the meeting was concerned, was to end in the general acceptance of the two Barbadian men's story and the dismissal of Jiménez by Tizon, the matter of Francisco, the local

[137] Referred to as Jeremias Gusmán elsewhere in the journal.

captain of one of the Indian tribes came up. I think it was Barnes brought it up as proof that, within the last few weeks, here at this very station an Indian had been drowned by Acosta, one of the *racionales*, and Velarde the Chief had not thought it worthwhile to report it. This, apart from the fact whether the man had been purposely drowned or not. Barnes put forward the very argument I had first raised. When there was doubt expressed by Tizon as to the deliberate drowning of this Indian by Acosta, the story, as told to him, being that Acosta had merely given the man a shove, while the Indians were washing rubber at the river bank, I had said that all these Indians, it was admitted (and obvious) could swim from childhood, and an Indian thrown into the river (here very narrow) if not previously greatly exhausted, would be very unlikely to drown. The story, as first related by Francisco, had been that the Indians were now being "held underwater", when washing rubber as a new punishment to take the place of flogging (prohibited by Tizon under apparently honest circulars), and that this particular Indian, struggling to escape from Acosta, who had him under, had got away and been drowned. My comment had been that inherent probability was with this argument, since, if the man had not been exhausted and dazed from immersion, I saw no reason why he should be drowned from being pushed into water he was accustomed to play in and swim in from early boyhood.

Barnes on bringing forward this story of Francisco, however, was at once greeted by Gielgud (and Fox) with the remark "Why were we not told of this? This is the first of this we have heard." The reasons for their not having been informed earlier were given by Barnes and Bell, and then on their understanding of these, Gielgud said "I regard this as much more important than anything brought forward by the Barbados men. Here we have first-hand information." I said quietly, "Pardon me, the other is first hand information too — the statements of eye witness. The only difference is one of date." He shut up like a trap.

They agree. The thing admits of only one explanation, the reign of terror that exists, and the absolute ignorance in which Tizon has been kept. I begged him to be very careful in his enquiry, as the man Gusmán had begged Bishop, when giving me the pencilled note, to explain that on no account was I to let "the others" here know that he had spoken. "The others" mean Fidel Velarde, Rodriguez, Acosta, and, possibly, the other *racionales* of the station. According to the *Planillas de Sueldos* [Pay Sheets] for September, I saw the other day the *racional* staff of Occidente consists of Velarde (paid by results — 2 soles (4/-) per *arroba* gross weight rubber and 7%), Miguel Torrico, Eugenie Acosta, Apolinar Atravea and Augustin Pena — the latter is the Cholo manservant from the Andes, who waits at table. He is almost a pure Indian, like the soldiers in Iquitos, and is a fine, sturdy, well-built young man of 27 or so, capable in the hands of a decent master and mentor of being a faithful and devoted servant, I should say. Here, in such an atmosphere as this, he has no doubt fallen with the rest. Acosta is now gone away again, I suppose back to Naimenes. Gusmán's name does not figure, but a Jeremias Gusmán appears on Atena's list.

The discussion in the Indian's house today after the evidence against Jiménez had been admitted more or less, took for a time a sharp enough aspect. Gielgud constitutes himself a sort of *advocatus diaboli*. First, too, in the story of the Barbados men he intervened in the same direction. When Sealy came to Jiménez crossing the Caquetá (into the Republic of Colombia) with armed men in quest of "Indians", Gielgud interrupted to ask him "whose" Indians these were? Whether they were men who dwelt across the river or fugitives who had run away from the "Section"? Sealy said: "He say they was Indians from dis side. I don't know. I think so." The habitat of the Indians was quite immaterial from any civilised point of view. The clear point established was that Jiménez, a servant of this English Company, was conducting an armed raid of the Company's servants in pursuit of human beings into the territory of a neighbouring South American state. Mr Gielgud's thought seemed to be, to more or less justify it, on the grounds that the Indians might be fugitives from the Company's territory, as if an English Company who indignantly deny the existence of forced labour, who speak to our Government of their purely "commercial" relations with these Peruvian Indians, "who are protected by an effective administration, etc." could claim to own Indians just like rubber trees. I let Gielgud's interruption pass in silence, but Barnes very justly struck in at once. "That's immaterial, the Company doesn't own the Indians, we are told they are free."

Not wanting to "rub it in", I did not add that "this much more convincing" statement originated, like every scrap of evidence so far submitted to the Commission in the same quarter, viz.: myself. Francisco's complaint had been made not to Sr Tizon on the Commission but to me through the Barbadian, Bishop. It was I who had told Mr Barnes and Bell, it was I who had sent Bishop to stop Francisco, and it was I who had the same day told Sr Tizon, and asked him to enquire from Barnes and Bell. Again, during our discussion, I said that, apart from all question of murder and ill-treatment of Indians, it was convincingly clear to me that, instead of the Putumayo being policed and administered by a civilised power, as the Company asserted to the FO, there was here a rule and reign of lawlessness, of an entire absence of law. The members of the Commission (save Gielgud) agreed, and so did Mr Tizon. Gielgud's interjection was that, in the absence of local authorities the local agents of the Company had to devise and apply law!

I again pointed out that this was the very objection raised from the first by H.M. Government in their correspondence with the Company which had been so indignantly met by the absolutely warrantless statement that the Peruvian Government maintained efficient and complete civil and military control. Gielgud shut up again, and poor Tizon said "The military were only for political purposes as connected with the disputed frontier with Colombia." I did not wish to further press this outrageously apparent point as against Tizon, but as against the Company and their mendacious assertions to the FO. I asked Gielgud where the Company had obtained their information from. I read the passage from their letter of 30th December last:

> Dealing with some of the minor points raised in your letter, I may point out that there is no ground for the imputation cast on the Government of Peru of leaving the district uncontrolled. In fact, they exercise complete control there, maintaining military ports, and appointing both civil and military officials.

This statement I observed was based either on knowledge or ignorance. If the latter, it was inexcusable; if on statements made to the Company which they relied on, where had those clearly untruthful statements originated? There was only one member of the Board who knew the Putumayo at first hand, and that member, moreover, was the man whose unsupported statements they had preferred to rely on to even discussing the condition of things raised by H.M. Government in their letter of November. This was Sr Arana, and I then informed them of his letter to Mr Cazes, as evidence to my mind of his bad faith, and of his effort to actually enlist a British Consul against his superior officer, sent officially by his Government, and to induce him to withhold his local knowledge and assistance, both from myself and from the Commission if they had sought it, as they were entitled to do. There was no reply possible to this. As to the equally mendacious assertion of the Company that their agents were in each case paid a salary, and not a commission on results, I said that here again they either wrote from knowledge, or categorically denied the FO complaint from no knowledge. As to the former, they knew so little of their business that here, I found, a monthly pay sheet offered for my inspection, whereon every single agent was paid by "results", one of them, Normand, even getting 20% of the gross output of his district, and that the furthest removed from any central influence or control. This was putting a premium on outrage, on that irresponsible tyranny which was bound to lead to the gravest abuses.

I carried the war into the enemy's camp today. I think it had to be, and I carried practically the whole of the Commission to my point of view, but that, unhappily, lands us in a hopeless position. Poor Tizon is the one solitary hope of the situation. Arana, it is clear to me, is a scoundrel, the most guilty scoundrel of the whole of this syndicate of crime. I used these very words — "syndicate of crime" — subsequently to Bell and Barnes, talking over the morning's events. Bell at once agreed, and Barnes has already come completely to my way of thinking. Bell still has a hankering after Arana, I can see, but it is rapidly being broken up by the dreadful logic of these days at Occidente — this, "the best station of the Company", the one that gives the biggest output, fifty tons a year, or even a seventh of the total rubber "crop" of the whole Putumayo, (according to Gielgud, the Company's expert).

Here we have, as our immediate host, the most guilty face, and criminal eye, I think, I have ever seen — it beats even that of Miguel Flores, which struck me as so repugnant at Chorrera. I told Tizon today, at the meeting, of Flores coming to bribe the wretched Dyall, by offering him £2 to exculpate him. Tizon said that Flores was a very bad man, and he had already intended to dismiss him. The wretched thing is that not one of these atrocious wretches has yet ever been dismissed. From the list of Chiefs of Section published officially in Robuchon's book in 1907, consisting of sixteen men, I find seven are still Chiefs of Section, one (Miguel Flores) is still employed, altho' no longer as a Chief of Section; another (Schulz) is still in the Company's employ in the Brazilian "properties", while seven have retired or died. Of the retired ones, I saw one — A. Rodriguez — flaunting it in Iquitos as one of the affluent members of its "upper class"; another, Elias Martinengui[138]

---

[138] The spelling of Elias Martenengui's name is consistently different in the Putumayo Journal to its spelling in the Blue Book where it is given as Martinengui. The incorrect spelling has been changed.

is the wretch charged by Bishop with the atrocious crime against the poor girl, Mercedes, now at Naimenes. This unspeakable brute left Atenas by the last *Liberal* before my arrival, and has retired on his "gains". Against every member of the Company's higher staff, so far as I can see, dreadful crimes are not merely alleged, but have been sworn to and published in Iquitos. I said nothing of this to Sr Tizon at our meeting today — at least I said, very quietly and sympathetically, — "Why, when these crimes were first publicly asserted in Iquitos nearly three years ago did your local authority not take action to investigate?" He replied that, first, the then Prefect had refused him power to proceed to the Putumayo, as he had himself desired, on the ground that Peru could not intervene since the district was in dispute with Colombia, and it remained to be seen whose territory it legitimately was(!) Second, he said that an 'Enquiry" had been opened in Iquitos. I remarked that Iquitos was 1,200 miles away, and that no enquiry could enquire into anything of moment except through the Indians here on the spot. These were the witnesses. It was they alone who could testify, it was they who "produced" the rubber, they who were flogged, they who were outraged and killed, who were robbed of everything from their manhood and their wives and children, to their poor despairing lives — these miserable "assets" of this powerful English Company. The thing was the most disgraceful I had knowledge of. I asked him and the members of the Commission how we were to go on to Ultimo Retiro and sit down at table and accept the hospitality of this man, Jiménez, accused here before us, by eye witnesses of the most atrocious crimes. For my part, I said I did not know how to proceed, it was the most repugnant task conceivable. He begged me to put aside this thought — that I was not Jiménez's guest, but his — I agreed, but I did so, I said, for his sake, not to increase the difficulties already in his path, but to aid him, if my presence could aid, to cleanse this "filthy stable".

I pointed out to Tizon, returning from the Indian house, that it seemed to me the "pay sheets" should include all the numerous lower class personnel of each station. He said they already knew at the Chief Stations all this local staff. I asked if they were sure of names and capacities, and he said yes. I then asked if they ever enquired what had become of, say, a *muchacho*, whose name might disappear from the list. He talked a little, but it had evidently never struck him, and it was clear that no enquiry is ever made, even if these lists exist in anything like correct form. The pay sheets of the higher staff are clearly inaccurate, as even I can see.

This man, Juan Rodriguez, for instance, the Colombian we find here at Occidente, appears on the Entre Rios list, and Chase, the Barbadian, appears on the Palmera list, whereas he states he was on the Abisinia strength when we left. Gusmán, now here, I find, on the Atena's list. As to the utility of the supposed lists now said to be kept, I need only Bishop's statement of the murder of the four *muchachos* of Ultimo Retiro by Montt, and this very man, Rodriguez, in January last to show how useless they are. I told Tizon of this crime, and asked him if these "disappearances" had been reported to La Chorrera. He saw the gravity at once, I presume. He was pale, silent and miserable. So am I.

I am sincerely sorry for the man. That I am, after all, the guest not of Tizon but of the local Chief of Station is apparent, despite Tizon's attempt to assure me otherwise. Here at Occidente I sleep in Velarde's bed , the sheets, pillow cases, etc. marked with his initials. An amusing demonstration occurred soon after our meeting.

Casement's washing

My washing came back, brought in by Sealy. I asked him how I could pay for it, which woman of the numerous domestic staff one sees here I could pay by giving a present to. He said simply "The Manager's wife, Sir, wash de clothes." I said, "Oh! Do you mean Mrs. Velarde. I can hardly give her a tin of meat. Did she wash them herself?" Then the grim Barbadian features expanded into a pleasant grin. "He got four or five wives, Sir", and we both laughed. I did so openly, and so did Sealy, who had been forced, blushingly, two days ago to inform me of his various marital establishments on the Putumayo. Sealy, however, had had only one wife at a time. It is reserved for Chiefs of Section and the higher agents of this commercial establishment to take their matrimony like their rubber, by a toll on the "gross product" of the district. Here is this Fidel Velarde who gets only "2 soles per arroba" with a mere bagatelle of "four or five wives", one of whom kindly does my washing, while Normand in far-off Matanzas, with his 20% on the *peso bruto* [gross weight] should have a harem of at least a hundred handy maids. I told Barnes and Bell — they roared with laughter — but their laundry, too, goes through just the same intermediary. We cannot escape from our surroundings, and I said that it was all very well for Tizon to say I was his guest, or the Company's guest, I was really the wretched Indians' guest. They paid for all. The food we eat, and the wine we drank, the houses we dwelt in, and the launch that conveys us up river — all came from their emaciated and half-starved, and well flagellated bodies. There is no getting away from it, we are simply the guests of a pirate stronghold, where Winchesters and stocks and whipping thongs, to say nothing of the appalling crimes in the background, take the place of trade goods, and a slavery without limit the place of commercial dealings.

Casement's nightmare

I am getting positively ill. My nightmare last night was a composite creature of all these criminals, a sort of Velarde-Jiménez-Aguero-Flores — indescribable and bleary-eyed, sitting at the door of my room waiting for me. That was all. Just waiting. No wonder I yelled in my horrid sleep, and roused the whole house!

In the afternoon, while the rest slept, all of us fatigued and worried and upset, I visited the "stocks" with Sealy, and took more measurements of them, while he explained their mechanism and method of work. Then Chase came, and said he wished to make a statement about what he had "seen" in Abisinia. I told him I should hear him later on sometime. I told Barnes and Bell of this further possible revelation, and said I might ask them to be present when I interrogated Chase, or when, rather, he unbosomed himself.

And now to bed. It is 3.40 a.m. I am tired, having wakened at 1 a.m. (or even earlier) and taken up my pencil to record the day's proceedings. It has been a very unhappy day. Garrido's treachery, for instance, shows how strong the influence of evil round us is. Fancy this man going right back on what he had volunteered to say to the Commission in Iquitos! Not that, as evidence it mattered very much, its only value now is that Garrido stands convicted of being either "bought" or intimidated — corrupted, at any rate, since coming to this district. The whole air of the place is atrocious. The one preoccupation now of even ourselves — this Commission and myself — is to see that nothing of the truth shall leak out. We, in search of the truth, proceed as if we were the liars and wrongdoers, and hold our meetings in secret, and constantly pledge ourselves to be "prudent" and "silent", and to show no one of our local hosts what we think of them or of the things we are hourly looking at. We play a part the whole day, and when investigating (as far as we can) a most appalling crime like that told this morning, pretend to be butterfly catching. And all this caution now is enjoined on us for the sake of ... the Indians!

In London the Company declined to investigate on the ground of the Peruvian Government; then, when I come out on the spot, with an order from the Peruvian Government, I find it worthless, as there are no Peruvian officials. And, finally, when I say all right, let us then proceed of ourselves, just as everyone round us has been doing for years, only they have been slave-raiding and murdering, let us, too, then proceed to act for ourselves, and find out the truth by merely investigating, and lo! the poor Indian appears in sight. If we were to inspect, even cursorily, any of these terrific charges of ill-treatment of the Indians we shall destroy the Indians! The only chance of saving them is to continue make-believe, to pretend we see nothing, and for Tizon to dismiss the local Chiefs one-by-one, to introduce "reforms", and sweep away the evil system, and this is only possible, provided the company is screened, and nothing of the truth leaks out! It is well-nigh impossible. I have said that, obviously, so far as I personally can do anything to help I shall, but many things may prevent the realization of this hope of reform. The principal is that I don't see how the Company can, or will, continue to exist. The English Board will resign, and what then? Arana returns to his vomit. The Zumaetas, the Dublés, and all the rest of the blackguards fasten their hold on the remaining Indians of the Putumayo firmer than ever. *Aprés moi le deluge* becomes indeed the motto of each separate Bandit. United they stand and divided they rob, each for himself, in his own patch of forest, and all together against the Indians and the outside world, Peruvian or Colombia — until the last drop of *Jebe debil*[139] has been hacked from the heart of this miserable forest, and the last Huitoto and Boras has been burned alive or civilised into a *muchacho de confianza* and has murdered his patron. This sounds incredible and unreal, and a gross exaggeration. It is nothing of the kind. It is no more incredible than what we hear daily, and, fact by fact, are beginning to accept as strictly true. At least I, for my part, see no reason to doubt the truth now of any of the crimes imputed to these men and the logic of the system, now

[139] *Jebe* was the most widely used name for rubber in Peru and derives from a native word used by tribes of eastern Ecuador. Its usage was reported by La Condamine. *Hevea* is the Linnaean classification for the tree and is the latinized form of the word *hevé* as given by F. Aublet, *Histoire des plantes de la Guiane Françoise* (1775). Nevertheless, it is intriguing that one apocryphal local etymological explanation is that *Jebe* derives from the Spanish pronunciation of GB (Great Britain) and that the latex was conveniently called after the country for which it was bound.

quite bare to our eyes (it always was to mine) admits of scarce any other conclusion.

AT OCCIDENTE — TUESDAY 4TH OCTOBER

Things seem to be getting worse. We are here nearly a week now — a week tomorrow morning, and the "Commission" (I begin again to use inverted commas) have seen about 8 rubber trees and four Indians — labourers actually at work — two, they told me, the first day they went out, and two washing rubber the day (Sunday) I was with them. Today they have been assembled at the dining room table all day discussing mercantile matters. I have been in my bedroom writing.

Indian girls

At 8 a.m. or so Sealy came to say that "Juanito" (Rodriguez, the Colombian) had accused Chase of trifling with the girls who carry water up, or, to be exact, with one of them. These are the only workpeople I have seen at work in nearly seven days of this, "the best station" of the District of Chorrera. They are a body of well-developed Indian girls, with busts and coloured chemises, and during the day they come and go from the river with kerosene tins of water for the various rooms — the bath, the pantry, the kitchen etc. Sealy says that one of them wished to take a tin in which Mr Gielgud had photo plates to wash, and Chase intervened, and then Rodriguez accused Chase of trying to "seduce" the girl, and further charged them both with "telling lies" to me, to the Consul. So he came at once to report. I told him not to pay any attention, and to tell Chase the same. I told Bell at once, who thought it serious — an attempt to tamper with or intimidate witnesses, and thought Tizon should be told. I said I saw no object in worrying Tizon on what was, after all, a squabble between servants. The Barbados men may quite likely be trying to get the girls to sleep with them, but in this place that is clearly the rule of life. They all have women, natives, and these water girls are clearly kept chiefly for immoral use. In any natural order of things native labourers would be paid for these duties, and men would be hired. Here the men are all at rubber, and the women play another part.

As regards the attempt of Rodriguez to intimidate the boys, that is futile. Garrido, doubtless has told the Staff here that these two men made statements yesterday to us all up in the Indian house. He was present during their tale of Jiménez and the Caquetá, as at that time the Commission believed him to be loyal to them. He understood much of the story anyhow — the names and gestures alone told much — and, as his subsequent attitude plainly showed, he has gone over to the scoundrels around. He has been bribed or terrified. I thought the Commission should get rid of Garrido; his usefulness was entirely at an end as his loyalty and sincerity were now in question, and Barnes and Bell both said they intended to dismiss him today.

Casement visits Barnes and Bell

I wrote nearly all day. In afternoon I visited Barnes and Bell in the next bedroom to myself, and we discussed various aspects of things which, to my mind and I think to theirs, are as unsatisfactory as they can well be. They again and again assert that Velarde lies to them, that he is wholly untrustworthy, and yet, when they want information, it is from him or his subordinates they must get it. They cannot question the Indians at all. I mentioned the method of collecting the Indians out in the forest houses and marching them in — that Sealy and others have stated to be the practice [see Sealy's statement of 1st Octobe] Barnes knows nothing, and confessed he has lost interest in the thing, as "it is rotten from top to bottom". Bell confines himself more or less strictly to his particular branch, the purely commercial, Fox to the rubber, and Gielgud — well, I cannot say that I have observed any particular branch save that of the Company's general interests, which is quite right. As Bell had been told a quite different story about the method of collecting Indians, in fact, according to him, there was no collection of Indians outside, they came in voluntarily with the rubber, and he points out quite truly that here there was not a sufficient staff to follow the method described by Sealy. I called Sealy to describe it, and he came to the bedroom and repeated the manner of tying up the Captain, etc. etc. He said he had done this at Sabana, Abisinia and Ultimo Retiro.

Interview with Sealy

He again stated he had repeatedly again and again flogged Indians for not bringing in the rubber. After this Bell asked Torrico to explain the method adopted here, and informed Barnes and myself at tea time of Torrico's explanation, which throws a wholly different light on this and other aspects of the relations of these Stations to the surrounding Indians. I append it later, and my comment on it. We are awaiting the return of the launch from Chorrera to leave this tomorrow morning for Ultimo Retiro.

I have been writing all day nearly. One has to, to keep sure of one's track.

After our talk (with Barnes and Bell) I again wrote. Bell went up to the Indian house, where Fox, Tizon, Gielgud, and the others had gone with a body of Capitanes, who had been called in to hear a lecture from Fox on the best method of collecting or tapping rubber. On their return tins, matches, etc. etc. were given to them, and Rodriguez talked to them glibly in Huitoto. Huitoto means "Mosquito" — a nickname given them by neighbouring tribes on account of their thin arms and legs. They are a wretched lot.

Conversation with Tizon and other commissioners

I talked to Tizon from 6.30 to 7 — again an interesting conversation. We discussed many things — the hope of the Company carrying on, the Iquitos house, etc. I told him that if the true state of things now came out the Company could not last a day, and also that I did not see how he was to reform things here with the Iquitos house dead against him, and in the hands of such men as Zumaeta, Dublé etc. I then told him frankly that I thought he was the "only honest man in the Company" — or that I had met — and that were it not for him I should pack up and go at once (and the Commission too I fancy!) I said Arana's action with the board and all I saw here convinced me of the fact that he had deceived the Board, and I could not trust him at all. In the end Tizon agreed to all, and said "If I followed my heart, I'd go at once. I'd like to see the Company swept away, and Arana, and all those men chased from public life", but he came back to the Indians. If Arana remained — as he would — and the Company went, the Indians would be far worse than today. He said "Here I have 150 pirates up here, and they would remain with all their knowledge of the Indians, who are children to be wheedled round their fingers." That man Rodriguez knows Huitoto like a book. He can talk to them like one of themselves, and do what he pleases with them. He could easily turn the Indians against us. We must be very prudent — very cautious.

Torrico, he said, was to stay here in charge. Velarde is to go. Bell says he has already over £1,000 to his credit in the books. Tizon says there is great waste, and that expenses can be cut down very much, so that with proper, or, at any rate, less improper methods, towards the Indians, the Company would carry on by paying expenses. I said I trusted his ability to reform things to any decent extent and pay expenses. Barnes and I are both of opinion that immediately anything resembling civilised dealings with the Indians is instituted, not 10% of the actual rubber produced will be brought in. That is to say, 90% of it "at least" in Barnes' view comes from vile oppression and slavery. I put it at 100% I think, and agree largely with the statement of Muriedas in the Hardenburg document — that, under the present system, the question is, which will be exhausted first, the Indians or the rubber trees.

The trees it is clear are very far apart, the labour of collection alone is very trying it is evident, and with the labour of carrying in and down to Chorrera, and the incessant and vexatious interference and robbery of food, women and anything these scoundrels need from the Indians, or fancy, I do not think the Indians will outlive the trees.

I suggested to Tizon and later to B(arnes) and B(ell) that they might telegraph for the Colonel, to try and return, or for a Director (one of the board other than Arana) to come out and join them before they finished. I go very soon, that is settled since our first field day at Chorrera, and they will then be alone and in a very trying position, trying to save what, morally speaking, should be destroyed, in the hope of "doing good", never seeing a step ahead, never sure that with the best intention they might not be doing the worst thing. I said this to both Tizon and the Srs. B. and B. Later alone, I told him to suggest it to them. Later to them, as my opinion for their guidance. They said it was useless now, too late. No one could get here before February probably, and they hoped then to be through. I told Tizon of the charge brought by Rodriguez against Chase, and, further, of Rodriguez accusing both men of "telling me lies". He said R. had been to him to say that the "water girls" complained that the Barbados men were touching them, and that he, R., had objected. I said there was more than the water girls in it, I thought — it was quite likely that the men and the girls were "carrying on", but I did not like the attempt to interfere between these men and their duty to tell me all they knew, and I thought there was a connection between this act of Rodriguez and Garrido's treachery and disloyalty to the men he had engaged in Iquitos to serve. It was he who had volunteered his statement to the Commission and had sought this engagement, and now, at the first test yesterday, he proved himself a liar and disloyal.

As we returned to dinner Bell told me that Garrido had "resigned"! This gives me furiously to think, also Barnes and Bell. I thought it out after dinner, while the others were playing bridge. I had cut out happily with the Queen, and went to my room, and there thought over all that has happened in this amazing tangle of lies, deceit and half-told stories, none of which we were even to be permitted to test by the only test open, viz.: to question employés of the Company openly. Neither the Commission in their purely commercial functions nor I in my investigation of the position of British subjects can hold any real examination at all. They have to rely on the statements made to them by these obviously interested agents. They say there are no books, no documentary proof practically of anything. When they ask for a certain account or paper required here to elucidate the matter under discussion, Sr Velarde says it's gone to Chorrera. One such document of commercial importance that they required today at their General Meeting, Barnes said he called for. Velarde said it was in his house and went over to get it. He stayed a long time, and then came to say he had sent it to Chorrera. And so, Barnes states, it is with everything they enquire into. They were to witness, for instance, the bringing in of the rubber from the different Indian houses in the forest during their stay here at Occidente. This was agreed on. This rubber delivery by the Indians was due they were told ?, it has not come; they were told it was "delayed", and would not be in till the 10th — several days after their departure. Hearing this, I said to Barnes and Bell,

"Why not one of you return by launch from Ultimo Retiro, or wherever we may be then, and see it and take notes."

Bell said "Yes, that would be a good idea."

Later he tells me that now they say the rubber won't be in "till 28th", by which date the *Liberal* is due to be back from Iquitos, and I am going away by her, and they are all to be back in Chorrera too! So it goes on, on every side. Wherever they turn for information they say — they who are sent out by the Company to aid and advise — are met by concealment or untruthful statements or an entire absence of any documentary evidence they may call for, and which should be forthcoming instantly. Here are no books at all, they say, nothing but *blancos* lolling in hammocks, idle (often absent) *muchachos*, who go and come into the forest armed, but never a stroke of work of any kind done on this so-called factory. No one works. Even the table boys go to their hammocks at 9 a.m.

and lie down three deep playing with each other.[140] All this is eminently unsatisfactory to them, and now comes the resignation of Garrido, following on Monday's exposure of his want of character. They say it is clear he has been "got at". I say so too, but as I think it over I see worse.

Later, after Bridge — conversation with Barnes and Bell

When Bridge was over and the party going to bed, I was walking up and down outside, and Barnes and Bell came and joined me. It was then 11.30 p.m., and we were quiet, and removed from eavesdropping, and I told them of the fear that these last incidents of today had wakened in my mind. My argument was this.

Here we are, all groping in the dark. So far the only "evidence" of any direct and open kind has come from Barbados men, made to me, their Consul, under belief in my power and ability to protect them. I was responsible for the safety of these men. They had relied on my obvious right to ask them to state the truth, as far as they know how. They had, more than once, shown and expressed great fear of the consequences to themselves, and it was their trust in and belief in me that led them first to speak, to offer to confront their Chiefs of Section, even face to face, and, finally, to accompany us up country. But I had no power to protect them, there was no law or authority of any kind in this country; the Prefect's letter to the "authorities" they saw themselves was a farce. Bell said its only value now was as a "curiosity". The men were now being assailed by Rodriguez, whose "record" was a very bad one, and whose influence Tizon had just declared to be very great for possible evil. Garrido's resignation was due either to fear, I said, or to bribery and the hope of making more out of resigning and telling lies against them in Iquitos that by remaining in their employ. The $20 a month he was resigning was far more than he had been earning in Iquitos, that we knew from Mr Cazes. Both agreed with all this. Why, then, did he resign? Fear or treachery? Fear, possibly of going on to Ultimo Retiro, where this murderer Jiménez was in power. Jiménez probably had already been warned

---

[140] The sense of this general, unspecific observation by Casement about the table boys lazing around in their hammocks has been twisted in the *Black Diary* into the following entry — 4 Oct.: "*Heavy rain last night and afternoon. River rising again. At 9 to bath and found 'Andokes', the light boy and a little boy in hammock outside bathroom, all doing what Condenhor once said of the boys of Rome, and Johnston of the Nyasaland Boys, without concealment! The other servants looking on practically while these three boys played with each other, with laughter and jokes! A fine beastly morality for a Christian Co.*"

of what took place on Monday, when Sealy and Chase had told us (in Garrido's presence and hearing) of the crimes of the Caquetá. Moreover, even if not, he would at once recognise both the Barbados men as having been with him on that journey. If he had really committed these atrocious crimes and in their sight, as they both stated, what would his frame of mind be seeing these two men our servants and in close touch with me? Obviously he would be alarmed, and more than alarmed. If the story was true (and there were many other witnesses against Jiménez, they must remember, to show his desperate character) such a man would stick at nothing. He would either get rid of the Barbados men, or try to convict them of some "crime" to assail their utility as witnesses against him. Both would be easy. At Ultimo Retiro he would be master of all, of everyone in the place. Nothing easier than to get these two young negroes mixed up with some of the women, either his own, or the "wives" of his staff or *muchachos* and have them shot in the act, and rush in to say that his Indian so and so finding this man with his wife had killed him in the struggle, and so forth. It was never necessary for these Chiefs of Section to do their own killing. I instanced Lewis' statement, made before us all, that Fonseca had threatened to make away with him, and had said he would not shoot himself, but would get it done by his Indians; also Macedo's threat to the Barbados men after Rutter had got the story of Dyall's ill-treatment by Montt. Macedo had said the same thing to them, so they had told Bishop on our arrival in Chorrera that he would easily "get them shot". Crimes about women were, we knew, amongst the most frequent up here. Considering all this, I went on, I was convinced these Barbados men were in danger when we reached Ultimo Retiro. I was, therefore, going to take precautions, and I should make the men sleep close to us, if necessary in our very rooms, and we should keep all our weapons loaded. Both Barnes and Bell fully agreed, and saw with me the extreme gravity of our position. Tizon, himself, has again and again warned us that these agents of his are "dangerous", are "pirates", that Jiménez is a "bandit", and that they have their cut-throat *muchachos* and the Indians entirely at their bidding and their mercy.

We have, therefore, agreed that the 3 Barbados men with us are to be warned to have nothing to do with any woman under any pretext, to be very Galahads of negro virtue (!), and to sleep close to us with Winchesters and revolvers loaded. This then led me to point out a further conclusion I had arrived at.

It was clear that, so long as I remained with them, the Commission would incur the suspicion and the fear of these men, which now, of course, was secretly directed against me. They were safe from any evidence against them, save through the Barbados men accusing them to me. No Indian would speak, that was obvious. The Indians were more completely at their mercy than any other people in the world could well be at the mercy of any men. My presence with them was not only a source of danger and discomfort all round, engendering this secrecy and midnight talking in the open, etc. etc., but it was hampering to their other duties and subjects of enquiry. It was, moreover, dangerous to Tizon's position, because, as they saw that he was one with me, they would all be banding secretly against him to dish him with the Iquitos office, where the head blackguards cogitated together. To all this they both agreed. Then, I said, I see no use my remaining longer with you and compromising your further work. My mind is made up as to the character of all we see around us — it is slavery, sheer, stark slavery. Do you agree? Yes — both — Barnes with sweeping emphasis — "absolute slavery from top to bottom". Do you require more evidence, such as it is, that it may be in my power to bring to your notice through the interrogation of the remaining Barbados men still out in the Sections? No. They both were fully convinced, absolutely. Can you carry the two members of your Commission with you in this? Yes, we fully believe so. Then you agree that it would be for your own good and for all the worthy and right objects of your coming here that I should detach myself from you as soon as convenient, and leave you now, fully convinced of the true state of things behind all we see to carry on your purely commercial and economic enquiry. Yes. They both agreed that it would be of service now that they should proceed without me. And there will be no going back on your present fixed declarations to me, no matter what happens after I have gone? None, absolutely none. Barnes emphatically declared that I could trust him up to the hilt, that his mind was irrevocably made up, and that no evidence now laid before him would change it. The thing was everything bad, rank slavery and crime from top to bottom.

We agreed to leave it at this, and I shall tell Tizon. My proposal is that he shall call in all the remaining Barbadians from Matanzas, Sabana, Abisinia, etc. to Chorrera, where I may see and speak with them, and if I deem it advisable take them all away with me. This can be done from Ultimo Retiro, say, by letters sent to Matanzas, etc., and to Chorrera, and I will stay on a reasonable time with the

Commission and then return to Chorrera in time to meet the men and return by *Liberal* at end of this month.

AT OCCIDENTE — WEDNESDAY, OCTOBER 5TH

In Casement's manuscript there is a roughly sketched ground-plan of the rubber station at Occidente.

A summing up of the situation at 5.30 a.m.

Having pledged them on their honour and good faith to adhere to their present attitude towards this execrable regime of man hunting, we went to bed after midnight. I did not sleep much. Here I am at 5.30 a.m. up again and writing out an "agreement".

The launch has not yet returned from Chorrera. This, too, gives me a little uneasiness. There may have been some devilment down there, and with Bishop alone, surrounded by those scoundrels, who knows what they might attempt? Make him drunk and pump him, and take down his "evidence" against us all, or me rather, and try to make trouble in Iquitos with it. It is obvious these ruffians will stick at nothing. If they are now assured, as is likely enough, that Tizon is an honest man and adopting our views and going hand in hand with us, they must all know their tenure of their lucrative posts depends on getting up a conspiracy, and a successful one, against him. To do that they must damage in some way the chief object of their fears — myself. It is solely through me and the loyalty and trust of these three or four ignorant blackmen to their Consul that the truth has come out. We three, late last night, agreed that the situation was really incredible — that no one could believe it. Bell (the sceptic at first) laughs and laughs at this aspect of it — that they, a Commission of Experts sent out by a powerful English Company to advance its interests, should be forced to act like guilty men, to hide their minds, to refrain from asking the most necessary questions, and to be forced to declare that of every agent of the Company they have met up to this, only one man, Tizon, seems an honest man. (Torrico doesn't count. We think him better than the others here, but we really know nothing about him.)

It is now 9 a.m. and no sign of the launch — over two days away, and she should have been back yesterday. Tizon says he gave positive orders for her immediate despatch. Either she has met with an accident (highly possible), or she is delayed at Chorrera through some devilment of Macedo.

Garrido, I am told, will be left here. His "resignation" relieves the Commission of the difficulty of discharging him, and giving their reasons. He will return to Iquitos by the *Liberal*, and Barnes is going to write to Cazes. Both Barnes and Bell say they need no further evidence as to the true state of things. I have entirely convinced them, and can leave them in the assurance that nothing will induce them to modify this view. As I am myself convinced, I see only possible grave trouble to everyone in continuing to take evidence under such conditions of peril as surrounds us here. To go to Matanzas would be madness — to the arch-murderer Normand. Torrico, Bell says, told him that the out Stations towards the Boras country, Sabana, Matanzas etc. were all really "forts". Nothing open below — all fenced in up to the ten or 12 foot verandah, and armed guard kept day and night! No one goes into the forest there save in numbers and well armed.

I should dearly love to see these things with my own eyes — to be able to record the methods used there in this "commercial" and "industrial reclamation" of the Indians, but how can I? The Commission will hardly go to Matanzas, they say, or to Abisinia, the roads are long and full of water. To me, personally, it would be a real pleasure, but I am gravely alarmed for the results — the possible results. It might mean the murder of the Barbados men, under our eyes almost. Of course, it would be the "cannibals" or the "savages" who had done it, or it would be the "injured husband" or something of that kind. No evidence possible of a crime. Besides, these men have never been punished for the most awful offences against humanity. Not one. They have been here for years committing the most hellish crimes, as we all now believe, and they were openly denounced in Iquitos three years ago, with many witnesses walking the streets of that capital city asking to be brought before a court. And what followed? Nothing, absolutely nothing. They have neither retired with a small fortune like Mr Rodriguez of Iquitos, or are still active agents of the Company, drawing very handsome incomes from their sections. Barnes says this man, Velarde, who is not worth £5 a year to any house of business, gets, he believes, fully £600 a year, and he has 4 or 5 "wives" free, a house built by the Indians, everything save European supplies, levied by crime from the surrounding defenceless population.

The others are out shooting at a target of an Austrian soldier as I write. It is well to keep up appearances, and this we do pretty well, although my constant writing in my bedroom is suspicious. I cannot help it. I try to do as much as I can at night, but one gets very tired in this climate, and often I give in and go to sleep. Poor Barnes is ill. He takes 40 grains of quinine daily, and is really looking painfully thin and haggard. Gielgud, who is still under 30, looks very well. For any serious purpose, however, I fear he is useless. The whole question doesn't strike him as serious, I fancy.

Charlie's Birthday.[141]

Observations about the captive women and washing

I was up at 5.15 a.m. Saw first a girl come out of Torrico's bedroom close to mine, on same verandah. Seeing me at my door she bolted. I stayed on verandah, and saw four girls or women come out of Velarde's house (where he and Rodriguez, and, I conclude, Aquiléo Torres, are sleeping), and, at same time, four of the water carriers appeared on our verandah to get empty tins and go down to the river. At same time I saw women at the doors of the Servants' rooms round the other side ... [text comes to abrupt halt and there is sketched plan of the station of Occidente]

Here we have a pretty big female entourage, all unaccounted for by any useful work, save these poor water girls who begin at 5.30 a.m. and are often carrying water up to 8 p.m. They, or some of these female slaves, wash our clothes. Last evening Sealy brought Gielgud's laundry and Tizon's, and I asked G. (on purpose) how he paid for washing here? "Oh!" he said, "I don't pay. I regard it as one of the things the Company provides." I nodded, and asked innocently, how were these women who did it paid by the Company. "Oh!" he said, "they get good food. They are not paid. They get presents and tins of sardines, and things." "I see," I said, "but if they are servants of the Company and engaged as such, surely there is some rule or scale of payment." He gave no answer. This was before Tizon, and all of them. Just before dinner, and this is what he finds "so good"!

10 a.m. Conversation with Sealy

Just now (10 a.m.) Sealy in my room cleaning up. I told him that when we left this for Ultimo Retiro I desired all three men to sleep near our rooms, and explained that there must be no tampering with the morals of the Indian girls, that it was dangerous and also wrong to me, that if charges were brought against them on this account, or even worse things, not only could I not protest, but

[141] Casement's eldest brother.

then all their testimony might be put aside, and it would be said indeed that they had "told me lies". So that everything required them to be chaste, their honour and loyalty to me, and their government. It is a pleasure in these abominable surroundings to feel that these simple, ignorant Africans have still enough manhood to understand when their honour and their hearts are appealed to. God bless their black faces!

Sealy swung his head from side to side as he does when moved, and said "All right, Sir. I know. I know." He then again assured me that Chase had not tried anything wrong with the girl yesterday, that he had only spoken to her about Gielgud's watercan, and Rodriguez had made that the pretext for the accusation. He said that Rodriguez, when recently in Chorrera had actually tried to steal his own "wife" from him, the one who is there now waiting his return — that "de woman" tell him so. Rodriguez had asked her to "run away". He then went on to say that "they were drowning Indians here." I said I had heard of one such case, but that it was denied. He said at once:

"Two, Sir — James Mapp was here then, and saw it, and told me when he came to Chorrera quite lately. He is in Santa Catalina now. You will hear when we gets there. These two Indians was tied. It's the way they punishes them now — they holds them under the water till they's half-drowned to frighten them, and these two men was dead."

I said again that I had heard of one, but it was stated that Acosta had only "shoved" him into the water.

Sealy said, "He lie, sir. They ties their hands and holds them under. Wait till we get to Santa Catalina." And there I left it.

And so the fearful tale goes on, quite unsought and unsuspected out comes this, when I was merely talking of the dangers of sleeping *en garçon* in these halls of Circe! Shall I tell Barnes and Bell? What use. They said last night they believed all, that they needed no more testimony as to the atrocious regime, and would not henceforth for their parts attempt to make any enquiries as they were convinced, that I had amply fulfilled my part, and there was no shadow of doubt in their minds.

'I am becoming the bête noire *of the Show'*

I am becoming the *bête noire* of the Show. Every time I approach these poor gentlemen it is with a new crime on my lips, or in my eyes. And I cannot help it. If I say nothing to anyone, and later on these matters have to be made public (who knows) the Commission might well say "But we were with Mr C. all that time, sleeping next door, meeting every hour, dining and lunching and playing Bridge together, and he never opened his lips, and yet he was receiving this dreadful evidence, and now states he believed it." However, this cannot arise now. They say they are convinced that I have done my duty by them in fully exposing and offering to any test they choose to apply the statements of these men.

Gielgud defends the system and accuses Casement of exaggeration

The most impossible person of the Commission is Gielgud. He is to a great extent committed to this evil state of things, and seeks many occasions to defend it. He would say, doubtless, to defend the Company, but his defence really is of a system that to any discerning eye is indefensible. Of course there are lots of people in this world who will defend anything that exists — merely because it exists, and they are so mentally constructed that they cannot imagine another state of things. Their thought is applicable to those circumstances, forgetting that circumstances are very largely of human contrivance. What is, and what has been going on for years may be, perhaps, not right, or the best, but the best under the circumstances, and, therefore, why not profit from it? This is very much the point of view of Gielgud, so far as I can gather, that he has any fixed point of view at all. His powers of observation are certainly not acute, and he cannot, so far as I can see, think very clearly. His heart may be all right, but his mental powers are distinctly deficient when it comes to a human problem of this kind, for his heart and head must balance each other. Thus today he and Fox, before luncheon, have been seeking to find good points in this system of slavery. They say in one breath it is slavery, and then that it is a "commercial transaction", that the Indian "owes" money to the Company. And this in face of all the lashes and scars, to say nothing of the murders, we have witnessed the last few days, or have been directly informed of. Gielgud passed through this district a year ago, slept in the very room I am now in, and found everything "all right" — rudimentary, perhaps, but quite suited to the surroundings. He will revert to this attitude of mind tomorrow, if the constant presence of well-nigh daily exposure that I have to make is relaxed, and who will keep it up when I am gone? That is why I told Barnes last night at midnight I should never forgive him if he went back on his promise to condemn the thing lock, stock and barrel on getting home. He had said that I could count on him, if no one else, that his mind was as fixed as mine. Fox is out of his depth completely in these surroundings, a man of most kindly heart and human sympathy, but of inadequate grasp of a complex situation like this. He can see a little way, but not far enough. Thus while he is horrified at the stories of Jiménez and the burning of the "old lady" of Sealy, or the beheading of the little boy, he thinks these are "individual outrages" — this is what I gather — and that because he can find Indians who dance, who sing, who smile like children, that this is evidence they are happy and not "all ill-treated".

It is the Congo question over again, with the same kind of careless-minded or not logical minded defenders. A thing cannot be slavery, and, at the same time, be a voluntary contract. When I contested to-day, for instance, in this talk with Gielgud and Fox, that the arrangement as to "paying" the Indians in advance after each *fabrico* was legitimate trading, or that it afforded any pretext in law or out of law for flogging an Indian subsequently who had taken these goods for not delivering the "price" put upon them, he demurred. He did not defend the flogging, but he did uphold the "contract". I said there was no contract, no proof that the Indians voluntarily accepted the goods or willingly contracted the obligation to pay for them with 30 kilogs of rubber or with anything else. Both he and Gielgud at once said "I was assuming" this, arguing on an assumption. I said my argument admitted of simple truth, but when even this or any other form of proof was called for we had been told that to question the Indians, to try to prove well nigh any statement affecting them would upset the whole show, and create "chaos". Thus flogging was not to be tested by direct questioning of the men whose scarified backs we could see, because that meant "accusing" the local whitemen and also exposing the Indian to his vengeance after we had left, and so wherever one turned the same difficulties to bring it to the only test available was apparent. One saw a thing that one's reason and one's principles, no less than one's common sense, question, and you were debarred from putting that question. Nothing would be easier than to test this matter of the "payment" of the Indians, for instance, were they prepared, was Mr Gielgud prepared, to put it to this test? At the next *fabrico*, for instance, would he let me ask, or would he ask, the Indians whether they wanted the "advance" or payment, or would rather not have it, and be released from the obligation to bring rubber. (This advance is indifferently called by both names, according to the line of argument advanced in its defence; sometimes it is a payment for rubber delivered, or even for rubber "sold". Then when the evidence of the lash or the *cepo*, or even the killing is pointed to it becomes an advance that has not been made good, and the whipping, a bit barbarous and so forth, is merely the rough and ready way of dealing with a defaulting creditor). These were not their words, but this is the theory of defence they distinctly put forward. In one breath they agree that the system is a bad one, that the people are slaves, and, in the next, that it is not all bad. And that to condemn it sweepingly, as I do, savours of exaggeration, because I do so without "proof", and on "assumption".[142]

I say "All right, then, I am prepared any time you like to prove my assumption, but you demur, on two grounds — one that this is "Peru", and the other that it is not Peru, and there are no authorities at all, it is impossible to investigate anything of this kind, because as your investigation will end in criminal charges — must, indeed, necessarily end in criminal charges — you must abstain from making it, since there is no one to arrest the criminal or punish the crime you may bring to light."

What delightful reasoning, if reasoning it can be called! It is really a waste of time and breath to try and convince this "Commission", apart from Barnes already convinced, and Bell. The latter still clings to some extent to some of the "commercial" side of the argument, and the duty to "make the Indian work" (for his own good, of course — it is always for his good a man is enslaved. This is not Bell, but me). But he is convinced, I think, that this system is "one of slavery" pure and simple, and I hope he will denounce it as such.

I don't object at all to Gielgud trying to defend his Company, that is loyal and right, but an Englishman educated at an English University should be able to smell right and wrong in a case of this kind. This thing we find here is carrion — a pestilence — a crime against humanity, and the man who defends it, is consciously or unconsciously, putting himself on the side of the lowest scale of humanity, and propagating a moral disease that religion and

---

[142] Accusations of exaggeration, made mainly by Peruvians, were levelled against Casement throughout his Putumayo investigation and arose partly because people simply could not swallow the scale of horror which Casement described. In 1913 when the Foreign Office tried to extract themselves from the embarrassing predicament resulting from Casement's investigation they too began to insist that many of the stories were exaggerated. The *Black Diaries* were clearly tailored to try and emphasise Casement's desire and ability to exaggerate and is most clearly seen in the apparent fascination for idle phalloplethysmography (penis-measuring).

conscience and all that is upright in us should uncompromisingly denounce. I find Tizon, the Peruvian ex-official, who was ignorant of much until we arrived at Chorrera far more sympathetic, far more humane, far more lofty-minded than this product of an English University.

First principles of right and wrong

Every day the battle has to be renewed, and when I think I have won and established once for all the principle that should guide their investigation, I find one or other of the Commission (not Barnes, he is now, and since Iquitos, with me) breaking away and harking back to the Leopoldian arguments — expediency "the only way, "the beginning of things", etc. Yesterday it was Bell with Torrico's explanation of how the rubber is brought in, and the rubber conveyed to Chorrera (and the houses built) another *chacara* or so-called plantation here made by the Indian women, a description that is the very definition of slavery (see it), and which he yet found "all right". This was how he described it to Barnes and myself, as he came fresh from Torrico's version, and I give Torrico's version in Bell's words. Then I get today Fox and Gielgud assuming that my condemnation is based on "assumption", is even "exaggerated", and that, putting aside individual outrages, the thing is not "so very bad". It has its bad features (these to be suppressed), but also its good ones. To say, as Fox does, that it is not altogether bad, that there are some good features about it, is about the same as to say that human nature is not altogether bad. Of course not. But one does not spare a criminal, or seek to maintain a crime, or any part of a crime, because the criminal was a human being and had a human heart. This thing that we see here is either good or bad; either decent or indecent, either defensible or indefensible. We are dealing here with first principles of right and wrong, and all the argument in favour of this damnable thing is, originally, inspired by greed, and only maintained by concealment of fact.

Here we are confronted on every hand with concealment. When I said that the Indians were slaves, then Gielgud (as I shall call him now) and Fox demurred and wanted my "proofs". I said to Gielgud "I'll prove it very soon if you, that is to say the Company, permit the test." He said the demand should be addressed to the Government of Peru! Harking back at once to the old yarn, the lying yarn told to the FO I said, but you admit there is no government here — of Peru or any other State — that has been put forward more than once as reason for *not* taking any action, or submitting any of these charges of the Barbados men to investigation. Therefore, they don't appear on the scene. Our proof lies with the Indians, your Company's "creditors", as you assert. Let me, at the next *fabrico*, ask (I'll find the interpreters) whether they wish, man by man, to take the cap and pants, or whatever the things are you give them, for a further supply of rubber, or whether they would prefer to be free of this obligation? It's a very simple test. If they are "free" they have an absolute right to refuse your 3/- or 4/- worth of stuff, or whatever the goods may be. But do you ask them? You know you don't. You compel them without question asked or put, to take these things. It is immaterial whether they *select* them or you bestow them. And then, when they have gone off to their houses, — poor sacrificed devils — you follow them up and intrude upon all their home life, and force them to bring you in rubber at a rate of exchange *you* prescribe mind, and if they don't satisfy you, you flog them, as well nigh every male stern in the district can testify, and you challenge my condemnation of this thing, and say I argue from assumption. Why, the test is the simplest in the world, and you won't apply it! Line the Indians up here before me, or before any of us, and let them be told that they need not bring in any more rubber unless they like, that you won't "ask" them to kindly take a pair of cheap pantaloons, a 6d. cap, and a flannelette shirt for the ensuing term, and let us see who then is reasoning from assumption?

Condemnation of the System

There is an even simpler test. I may wish to *walk* back to Iquitos. This is a free country, so we are told. The natives are citizens of Peru, so we are told. Well and good. There is nothing to prevent me sending out to engage as many Indian carriers as I wish to carry my things to Iquitos. May I do it? You know perfectly well I cannot, and may not. It would not be allowed by your Company. These Indians then become their "labourers" on the list of your local agency, and they have received "advances of goods" from your Company, and so are not able to go away, and so forth. All right. I'll admit even this. Produce your account with your contract with these labourers. I'll pay their debt, I'll even pay it with 100% added. Will you consent? No you won't, and you know it. You want not your "debt", not your trumpery trash of a few shillings' worth of cheap and useless goods, but the 30 kilograms of Indian Rubber, that at 5/- per lb., or maybe 4/- per lb. is worth £15 or so to you, and your contract is null and void in all equity, since it is made, not between man and man, for value preferred and accepted, but is violated every day of its existence by the application of force, on one side, of punishment with law (where there are no magistrates), of stripes by the lash, of invasions of domicile, and forcible capture, and detention in stocks and cells, and all the damnable expedients we have been hearing of since the beginning of last month. It is the system that is the crime, not the criminals who administer it, and you, when it becomes demonstrably indefensible, adopt the argument that this English Company is not responsible, because the Government of Peru is callous, indifferent, absent, or non-existent. I did not say all this to Fox and Gielgud, but a good deal of it, and a good deal more that it is impossible to recall or write down, for man's speech is sometimes fluent, and I said a good deal, and they too. To write all would mean a shorthand writer every time and all the time, and even then much irrelevance from both sides slides in. I put this forward only as a part of my argument that they say rests on "assumption" — the main and unchallengeable argument being that they dare not allow me to put any assertions at all to the test, and that they — I mean the Company — while denying much, demonstrate nothing. So far as my eyes can convict them, all that any man of sanity and decent thinking sees here must convict this system they have sought to defend.

I don't wish to be unjust to Gielgud in thought even, and so I sometimes try to provoke argument in order to allow him to recover lost ground, but it is hard work and dispiriting. Perhaps I am too belligerent. I try to be cautious and even enquiring.

Goods advanced to the Indians

As regards the "goods" they advance or pay to the Indians at each *fabrico*, there should be the very simplest proof here on the spot of their actual value, of their worth to the Indians and of their relative value to the goods the Indian is forced to supply in so-called exchange for them. This station gets 50 tons of rubber per annum (more or less) worth, say, £10,000. Where is the Goods Store, and let me see the goods you have in depot to meet the forthcoming *fabrico*, of, say 1/4th of this total, or delivery of £2,500 worth of rubber? (As a matter of fact there is no Goods Store. There is a small room where Gurusi the Steward, and Garrido sleep in hammocks, with the smallest assortment of trash I've ever seen anywhere. It knocks any Congo Store, of Bula Matadi or

Domaine de la Couronne[143] into a cocked hat. There is not at the present moment in this Store anything that a Congo native would give a for.)

Failings of the Commission

I asked yesterday Barnes and Bell, as Chiefs of the Commission, to take an inventory of the store. They refused, from laziness I think. Bell said they could always find out what goods came to Occidente by consulting "the books" at Chorrera. The task of taking this inventory would not be half an hour's. I've looked in the store more than once, but I cannot go and do this. It would give great offence, and would at once provoke the question "What are you doing here?" The Commission can, if they will, and ought, to do this. One inspection of this kind, along with one visible "payment" of these "530 Labourers" for a seventy five days supply of rubber would remove many doubts, and prove who was exaggerating, or reasoning from "assumption". But here, again, all demonstration is denied or withheld. I cannot wrangle with the Commission. My wish, and earnest and constant wish, is to convince them, but it is very hard to be alone, to be the only one with a constant and absorbing wish to get to the bottom of the whole thing. To find Englishmen of the type of Gielgud, more keen, I fear, to defend than to reform, more swift to find the good than the evil, in a thing that is evil, is a very great disappointment. Here a man who defends becomes, to my mind to some extent *particeps criminis*. I want more than ever the Colonel. Oh! how I wish he had come on with us. How I wish I had begged him to come, implored him to come. When I said to him at Manaos "Do, please, impress this point of view on the others" and he answered "But it is fact, not opinion we want", I had said "Yes, but much, very much depends on what point of view a man holds of this sort of thing. Facts fit in

[143] Domaine de la Couronne was a concessionary area in the Belgian Congo under the direct control of Leopold II — revenues from that area were due directly to the king and were not accounted for in any way whatsoever. During Casement's investigation into the Congo in 1903 he learnt from witnesses at Impoko that many of the worst atrocities had been carried out in this area. Bula Matadi (deriving from the name of the prophet Francisco Bullamatare) was a settlement within the Domaine and means — "Breaker of Stones" — this was the nickname originally given to Henry Morton Stanley, the man who first explored and eventually claimed the interior of central Africa for Leopold II. Stanley was proud of this African tribal naming. Twenty years later, however, the phrase had come to signify "abusive white administration" and instead of "breaker of stones" its meaning was "breaker of men."

with it, or can be made to. There are fixed principles to be held fast to, and once you let go your grip of them, acceptance of anything becomes possible in the end, and there are your facts."

I suggested twice last night telegraphing for him still to come. If they do I'd wait for him even, although my work is done. Barnes is the only one whose instinct is right in this matter, and his knowledge and ability to direct others are inadequate. There is no Chief to the Commission as it is, each one goes his own road, no collective enquiry beyond a certain point, and up to this that has been very much due to my dinning and insistence on one line of investigation.

Putumayo worse than Congo

This Putumayo Slavery is, indeed, as Hardenburg said, and as I laughed at when I read it a year ago in *Truth,* a bigger crime than that of the Congo, although committed on a far smaller stage and affecting only a few thousands of human beings, whereas the other affected millions.[144]

The other was Slavery under Law, with judges, Army, Police and Officers, often men of birth and breeding even, carrying out an iniquitous system invested with monarchical authority, and in some sense directed to public, or so-called public ends. It was bad, exceedingly bad, and, with all its so-called safeguards, it has been condemned and is in process, thank God, of passing or being swept away.

But this thing I find here is slavery without law, where the slavers are personally cowardly ruffians, jail birds, and there is not authority within 1200 miles, and no means of punishing any offence, however vile. Sometimes Congolese "justice intervened, and an extra red-handed ruffian was sentenced, but here there is no jail, no judge, no Law. Every Chief of Section is judge and law in one, and every Section itself is only a big jail with the Indians on the treadmill, and the criminals as the jailers. As Barnes and Bell said last night, it is "incredible". And yet, here are two kindly

[144] As with any genocide, exact figures are hard to pin down but recent estimates suggest that around three million Africans died under Leopold II's regime in the Congo Free State. Figures regarding extermination of Amazon tribal people during the rubber boom are even harder to calculate. In the Putumayo around 40,000 Indians were exterminated from the time of first contact with *caucheros* to the end of the boom. It seems likely that death figures rise well into the hundreds of thousands, possibly millions when all the vast rubber districts of Amazonia are considered. But the details of the Indian slave hunts and killings went largely unrecorded.

Englishmen not defending it — that I will not say — but seeking to excuse to some extent, and actually unable to see its full enormity or to understand its atrocious meaning. No wonder there were French Sheldons and Montmorres on the Congo, and Colonel Harrisons and even Boyd Alexanders.[145] The world, I am beginning to think — that is the white man's world — is made up of two categories of men — compromisers and Irishmen. I might add and Blackmen. Thank God that I am an Irishman, that I am not afraid to "assume", that I won't shirk the charge of "exaggeration". Let that be. I shall drive home this nail, and if these unhappy, these enormously outraged Indians of the Putumayo, find relief at last from their cruel burden, it shall be through the Irishmen of the earth — the Edward Greys, the Harris', the Tyrrells, and even the Hardenburgs and the Whiffens.[146] The "Blackmailers" are far better men than the Company promoters. Tizon spoke from his heart last night, when he said "I, too, if I acted from my heart, would sweep the Company away and chase the Aranas and those men from the public and social life of my country."

Poverty of the store and Torrico's statement

The explanation of the poverty of the store here in anything resembling trade goods is now given me by Bell. I returned to the charge today with Barnes, Bell present, as to taking an inventory of the "trade goods" in this trading agency. Bell said nothing at the time and Barnes did not move. I had just told them, privately of the unsought confirmation of Francisco's statement of the drowning here that had come from Sealy, reporting James Mapp's statement to him as to the two Indians drowned here. I had told them this assertion, but said I did not propose doing more, that they had told me the previous night that they needed no more of this evidence of crime, and that they were convinced. Moreover, we had now ample demonstration of the futility of discussing further these aspects of the situation — since nothing could follow. No action could be taken by anyone to verify the statement; there could be no "accused" and no prosecution, any more than defence.

---

[145] There is scope here for further research by specialists in the field.

[146] Despite the fact that none of the names mentioned was an Irishman, Casement seems to be using the term "Irish" to mean those who are not prepared to compromise and wish to expose the truth. The five names listed here were the five individuals most involved with Casement's investigation into the Putumayo atrocities.

All was swallowed up in Tizon's reiterated assurances that he accepted all, without going into details, and would act as if the charge were proven.

With that they were content, and I was not a prosecuting counsel. As they were satisfied, no more need be said. Barnes remarked that when they got back to Santa Catalina they could interrogate James Mapp. I said no more, because it is obvious that interrogation would end when it began. In the extraordinary state of things around us it is quite farcical to call this a Commission of Anything, just as it is equally farcical to call this Company a trading Company. Here at one of its chief trading stations it has not in store sufficient trade goods to meet the demand of a tenth-rate Banyan Store outside, say Delagoa Bay. Its rubber store, on the other hand, is vast. It occupies the entire basement of the larger section of the house — of the very much larger section of the house — while the room in which the goods are (and the two stewards) is about 12 feet square, and all it contains of trade goods could be easily put in one trunk.

The explanation, as furnished through Bell, is this. (It comes I am told from Torrico). When the *fabrico* is completed, that is to say, the last yield of rubber is delivered up by the Indians for the term, (75 days) for which they have been paid, they all come into the Section House with it. It is sent down to Chorrera by the launch, and the Indians, who have supplied it, are asked here at Occidente to state what they want "as advance" for the next term, or *fabrico*. They go back to their *chacaras* and work (under supervision and direction of this Staff who visit their various settlements in the woods to compel them to acts of tillage) on their *yuca* or cassava patches, and so forth, so as to have their food supplies assured, while their women are retained at the Station to clear up its "plantations", such as the draggled and disordered sugar cane we see around us here. The goods the Indians have asked for come up in the launch on her return from Chorrera, and are ultimately delivered to the Indians as an "advance" (not a payment — mark the difference), for which they are held bound to bring in an assigned quantity of rubber.

This is, in brief, Torrico's statement — not all of it — which Bell relates. In addition to the foregoing, Torrico asserted that the Indians here at Occidente, and at all of the Sections, came in of themselves with the rubber, and were not collected as described by Sealy. They gathered voluntarily under the direction of their own captains on each occasion, and brought the rubber into the

Station. Torrico has been in the Company's service for over a year certainly, as Mr Gielgud states he was already here at the date of his visit last year. I had been told, incidentally on arrival at Occidente, that Torrico had been only two months here, having come from Pará, and this statement seemed to be accepted by Barnes, as well as by myself to cover his service with the Company. We now find we are wrong.

The rest of Torrico's statement dealt with the transport down to Chorrera of the rubber, and the work of the women here, and of the men out at their own *chacaras*. To my mind it reveals as extraordinary a way of conducting an English Company's business as can well be imagined, not to speak of the total invasion of the natural rights of the Indian. To take 20 men down to Chorrera to transport the rubber there from Victoria to the Station, keeping them away from this without pay or any surety of it all for this extra weeks detention, and absence from their homes, is to me a new feature in this industrial enterprise. The retention during this period of the women of the "530 labourers" to clean up the Station grounds and plantations (also for no pay) is equally remarkable. Torrico says they are "paid", but when I ask for definite particulars they are not forthcoming. The pay then resolves itself, like Gielgud's laundrymaid's salary, into "things". They get "presents" — of meat, sardines, etc. But presents are not payment, any more than "advance" is. Here, in a matter easy of control, susceptible of disciplined treatment, the vicious disorder and irregularity that runs through the business side of this unbusiness concern again appears. Besides, if they are paid where does the money come from? There is nothing in this store.

And then, again, what is one to think of the statement that it is necessary for these (so-called) white men to go out to the Indian houses to compel the men to work up their own food supplies, otherwise they would not do this essential work (and so starve!). Just think of it. The women here, as in all tropical states of savagery, do the actual cultivation, the men only the hard work of felling the forest. The crop is almost invariably sown, or planted and harvested, just as the food from it is prepared by the women — and these forest Indians are no exception to the ordinary rule of primitive agriculturalists.

Were the condition of things here not so extraordinary no extraordinary compulsion of this arbitrary kind would be called for. The "justification" of this interference with the Indians' home life that is put forward is indeed the condemnation of the Company system, and yet Fox, Bell and Gielgud are prepared to swallow it. Not Barnes, I fancy, but he pays so little attention to anything — is obviously so ill and unsuited to the task — that he counts the least of all in local decision, altho' I count more on him at home, when all is closed, and the summing up has to be delivered.

EN ROUTE TO PUERTO PERUANO — THURSDAY 6TH OCTOBER, 1910

Left Occidente at 9.20, and got to Puerto Peruano at 7 p.m., where we slept. For today's notes see pages 13–19 green notebook.[147] As I was on the launch all day cooped up, I could not write much, except on my knees at odd moments.

From Puerto Peruano in 'Veloz' to Ultimo Retiro. Butterfly day. For notes on journey up to Ultimo Retiro see my green notebook, page 20–27, which carried me up to the beach at Ultimo Retiro.

---

[147] The "green notebook" is referred to on a number of occasions in the course of the journal at points when the text becomes sparse and was apparently used when Casement was travelling in uncomfortable situations where it was difficult for him to write on loose leaves of foolscap. Such a notebook, however, is not to be found either in London or Ireland, although we know that it survived the voyage and remained in Casement's possession because of Casement's reference to it in his letter to Charles Roberts of 27 and 28 January 1913 {R.H. Brit Emp S22 Casement to Roberts}.

III

ULTIMO RETIRO

ARRIVAL AT ULTIMO RETIRO, FRIDAY 7TH OCTOBER

Arrival at Ultimo Retiro — catching butterflies

From Puerto Peruano in 'Veloz' to Ultimo Retiro — butterfly day — (for notes on journey up to Ultimo Retiro see my green notebook page 20 to 27) which carried me up the beach at Ultimo Retiro. It was not Jiménez but the head *muchacho*, I presume — a nice looking Indian youth, with red painted face, black shirt, blacker hair, and white duck knickers — but down came the redoubtable hero of the headless boy and burnt woman and burnt man of the Caquetá raid of June 1908. A burly young ruffian — looks 26 or so, sturdy, with that far-off touch of the nigger you see in some of these Peruvian lower-grade men — not so much as Dublé has, but still just the touch of it. Rodriguez, with his cruel mouth and glinting eye, had it too.

We were all presented by Tizon, and to relieve our feelings we began an elaborate butterfly chase there and then on the sandy bank of the river. They were certainly magnificent specimens, and the soil was aflame with glowing wings, black and yellow of extraordinary size, the glorious blue and white, and swarms of reddish orange, yellow ochre, gamboge and sulphur. Fox got one of the splendid big black and green and yellow.

The river here is narrow, some 30 yards, between cleared banks, and the Station house stands like a fortress stoutly stockaded on the apex of the rising ground some 50 feet or 60 feet above the water. The house is built like a ship, with its bows facing the river — a high stockaded peak bow, in which is the dining room, open all round, the tops of the stockade forming a bulwark some 2 feet above the verandah. The rooms being about 13' x 13' at the outside — I'll measure to make sure. One of these with a wicket gate open to the air, is the store with a still smaller assortment of goods in it than even the miserable thing at Occidente. I counted 13 "jerrys" and lids in Fauver emailler [sic]. (John Bull would call it tin-pot) — these for the higher civilisation of the upper Igaraparaná! A few flasks of powder, four or five hammocks, and a few odds and ends. I'll try and get an inventory of it by looking through the bow. It is a tiny room, smaller than any of the others. The "Staff" was grouped on the verandah amidships, by the *cepo*, which is where the principal object in view, and bowed to us with "Buenos Dias, Señores" as we came up the rough ladder. They all looked unmitigated blackguards. Among them one Barbadian, named Crickley,[148] Bishop says. The worst looking blackguard is a big hulking young Peruvian with the eyes of a wild beast, who is named Zancorra, Bishop tells me. I'll get the whole list later on. The Indians here are finer specimens than those at Occidente — bigger, stouter limbed altogether and more cheerful faced. Lots of them about. The Indian house quite a small structure, an open floor some 9 feet off the ground with women, &c. there, and on the ground underneath a lot more indians, chiefly women and children. Women greatly predominate. They are everywhere. I counted 7 concubines at once outside, three down by the verandah where the "staff" resides. Here is the plan of the house, or ship, — the pirate ship.

[*Despite Casement's reference the plan appears to have disappeared.*]

ULTIMO RETIRO — SATURDAY, OCTOBER 8TH

Commission interrogate Jiménez

While I write on morning of 8th the Commission are interrogating Jiménez as to the "trading" methods employed here. Fox is the only man asking questions. He is asking sensible questions, Tizon putting them and translating Jiménez's replies; but these are contestable. If Fox goes further, and asks others (the Indians here and there), he will get the truth. Not from this man. He asks questions as to "payment" of Indians — God save us — and the treatment of sick Indians, smallpox cases and so forth. They segregate them, and the Indians themselves do this — so Tizon translates. (We saw something of this yesterday on the river bank in the measles cases from Atenas.)

---

148 Although Casement clearly, but incorrectly, writes the name Crickley in his journal and goes on to call the Barbadian Crichley on several occasions in the following days, the *Black Diary* does not contain the same inconsistency. October 8th: "... Examined Edward Crichlow ..." and on blotter "... Edward Crichlow very damaging statement."

I don't know what view the Commission take of their questioning of Jiménez. It endured about ½ an hour, and in my hearing, although I lost words occasionally, and was not listening, and from what I heard it was far from illuminating. Fox did almost all the questioning, Tizon and sometimes Bell translating to him Jiménez' replies. I heard Fox ask how the rubber was collected, and Jiménez' answer was that the *blancos* did go out to the house of the capitanes and "advise" them of when the rubber was due, and bring them in — this twice in the *fabrico* — except Parvenir, whose rubber went direct to Occidente.

The "payment" was an "advance". The Indians named their goods, and these came up from Chorrera subsequently. Fox asked how "prices" were fixed? What quantity of rubber was demanded for a gun, say. Jiménez said the Indians did not understand prices or quantities; they brought what he told them. He fixes the quantity and prices and decides quantity required accordingly to the "advance". No question of any kind was asked as to payment for other services, such as the buildings we see — the clearing, the various services these people are constantly performing.

Crichley

Bishop has come to say that Crichley, the Barbadian, told him last night that A. Montt had sent to move the bones of the four *muchachos* killed in January last when he heard we were coming. He also says that a few days ago a man called Solar, came from Chorrera with a letter to Jiménez from Macedo, and that he, Crichley, was then called aside by Jiménez and told that he was not to say anything to the Consul, that his pay would be increased. This man they sent on to Atenas to warn Montt. This was last night in quiet with Bishop. I asked Bishop if Crichley would speak the truth when interrogated by me, or would he do as Francisco did and lie for the sake of this bribe. Bishop said that Crichley did not want to speak out, that he was anxious to make some money now; that he had been promised a good "gratification" for his silence, and he was anxious to go home to Barbados with some money. I said I would see about that. That, in any case, his duty was to tell me the truth at all costs.

I have determined to tell Crichley that unless he speaks the truth to me in answering my questions, he shall not be permitted to remain in the Company's service, that he is bound to answer with truth questions put to him by a British Consul, and that if I find him lying I shall request Señor Tizon to dismiss him. Tizon has already volunteered in Chorrera to send away all the Barbados men if I desire it. I consider that this is perfectly fair and just. The man is being bribed by the Company's Chief Agent to lie to the Consular Officer sent to assist these men, and I am fully justified in meeting such disgraceful action by depriving this man of the bribe and continued service at higher wages he counts on as the price of his falsehood. It is his duty to answer truthfully, and if he fails to do this for the sake of the money inducement, then I shall deprive him of this price of corruption, and have him dismissed and sent to Iquitos by next steamer. If he speaks the truth I may ask that he be retained on, with a clear warning that any flogging or ill-treatment of Indians by him, no matter who orders it, is illegal; that he must not obey, but at once inform Sr. Tizon.

I told Bishop to tell Crichley of my determination that if he answers me untruthfully — and I shall find out — that I shall request his immediate dismissal. His duty is to speak the truth to the Officer sent to this country, and if, for the sake of a bribe, he does not do so, then this bribe shall be a very poor reward for his dishonesty. Bishop understands the position, and has just returned to say that he has warned Crichley as I directed him; that latter said he did not at first intend to tell me the truth, and that now he will do so, that whenever I send for him he will reply truthfully to my questions. So far so good.

Indian women at the river bank

I took a moment's change, and sent 'Andokes' with the butterfly net to catch the lovely beings that infest this foetid beach. We went down towards the "lavatory", newly constructed for our coming, Gielgud says. One of the *racionales* was directing the putting in of logs to make steps down the slope to this house, which squats astride a small brook. Here is the picture.

I found eighteen women with machetes squatting and cleaning the ground, two of them fully grown, stark naked; a third, a girl also naked as when born, and the fifteen remainder (wives of *muchachos*, or from the bush) dressed in the cushuca skirt, with strings of beads or coins. How are these beings paid? Not out of this store, surely. Nine of the male Indians have a straw or stick through the nose tendon. All wear *fonos*, although some of the small boys are naked. Last night at dinner eleven captains and *muchachos* sat round the bulwarks looking at us feeding. They were cheery, and seemed in no fear of Jiménez and Bishop says he has done more with the Indians since Montt left. I heard Tizon say the place had been "in disorder" when Montt was here, yet Montt is in Atenas.

Inventory of the Store

I have taken the Store inventory as well as possible. The "Commission" went there after questioning Jiménez, and I stood at the door and looked in. They merely glanced at the guns, handled one or two, and came away, but my searching eye and Sherlock Holmes soul[149] did the rest. It would not take 5 minutes to take down every single article, and appraise it too. There is not $5 worth of stuff all told, or anything like it, apart from the guns.

Here is the inventory :

27 "guns" and Winchester rifles.
13 old Sniders and Muzzle loaders (6 with Bayonets)
c. 140 Winchester cartridges
15 enamel iron "chambers", 13 with lids, 2 in use.
3 glass candle lamp globes.
c. 10 enamel iron plates
1 " " jug
1 " " cooking pot
c. 50 x ¼lb. flasks of powder
75 Packets of matches
12 Cotton Hammocks

Some drugs of different kinds, one or two tins and paper packets.
3 small rolls of cotton lampwick.

The above to meet the daily and weekly needs of a Station, founded for many years now, "employing" some fifty or sixty people in one way and another, with cleared ground round it of over a 100 acres, three houses, and, the Devil knows how many concubines. There are surely more concubines than saleable articles in this store, but I suppose these ladies are not saleable. They give their all — like virtue, above price.

---

[149] The Sherlock Holmes stories were serialized in the *Strand* magazine between 1891 and 1927. Coincidentally, the Doctor on board the SS *Hilary*, who treated Casement's eyes on the voyage to Iquitos, was called Dr Watson. Conan Doyle first became associated with Casement when he lent his name to the Congo Reform movement. In 1916 he was the leading public figure to try to save Casement from the scaffold.

The Commission are now "inspecting" outside, and Gielgud taking happy snapshots of interesting natives with painted faces and sticks in their noses. What I should like would be a photograph of all the female staff of the establishment, and then their names, capacities, salaries, and cost to the Company or surrounding Indian population given below each place. Not a difficult thing to do. The place is like a rabbit warren with them, but it will not be done.

Visiting the stocks

As soon as convenient I want to have the stocks or *cepo*, tested publicly. These are the same stocks in which Dyall was confined all night by Montt. They have nineteen holes, very small, and I can well believe that to put a big man's leg in here, sit on the heavy beam, and then lock it down on him was veritable torture, as Dyall said, and as his deeply scarred legs showed. I will go in them myself and try and put Bishop and Sealy in! I certainly think the brute beast Montt ought to be made to pay dearly for having put the unhappy Dyall in this torture-box for a night with his legs lacerated, and then to hang him up to the beam above, by a chain.

I went to the stocks at about 10.30, and tried them on Sealy — there was quite a gathering. They would not nearly close on his legs, the internal measurement being, I think, less than 3", nearer 2½" . We put in a sturdy Indian, and they fitted him just. He could move his foot a little up and down, but his leg was thin round ankle. Here are its measurements ... His name was ... ? ...[150] As we did this Barnes, Bell, Fox, Gielgud and I, he began to talk in Huitoto and poured out a lot. It was translated for us partly by Sealy and Chase. He turned his thighs and buttocks, and showed us the broad weals on both, right down the back of the thighs, and he said he got this for not bringing *caucho*, and that they were put in this *cepo* here and starved to death — that they died in it; that many, that all of them there had been flogged. Many had died in this *cepo* — his injured countenance protesting as much as his words.

A boy Huitoto chimed in too, and pulled up his shirt. He had only a small mark or marks, but said he, too, had been flogged

---

[150] The name of the Indian, according to an entry on the blotter of the *Black Diary*, was Waiteka, and the statistical information left blank in the journal is as follows: *age about 35–40, weight say 120lbs Height 5'6" Chest 35" Thigh 17" Calf 1¼ (his ankle in cepo just fitted) Biceps 9½ Forearm 8" Stomach 32"*. Casement probably wrote the information in one of his notebooks — a source available to the forger but now lost.

once. Lots of people were gathering round. I said to Bruce, who was grinning and saying, "He has been flogged for not bringing *caucho*," as if that justified all.

"Yes, and I'd sooner beg my bread than live from that," pointing to the scarified limbs of this poor old Capitane.

Then I said so that all should hear, "This was not intended for a place of detention, but for an instrument of torture."

The holes would hold only the emaciated legs of these poor Huitotos, whom even the neighbouring tribes call "mosquito legs".

The Barbadians enjoyed it, it was first-hand evidence at last — an Indian actually daring to speak out. The man had grasped the situation, and it poured out. All were laughing, but in different ways. I was smiling with pleasure that this fearless skeleton had found tongue and the innocent-faced lad beside him, and that these two incontrovertible bottoms with the sign manual of "Casa Arana" were being flaunted in the faces of the Commission. I said (to Chase) aloud, and with my finger measuring the required depth, "Tell him the next time he doesn't bring in enough *caucho*, and they are going to flog him, to spread the Indian rubber an inch deep all over his back side and legs, and let them fire away!"

All roared but the thrust went home. The "staff", with their Idol thus opprobriously made game of and before the Indians too, who had trembled so long in the grip of this monster, did not know whether to smile or protest at this slighting of the Stocks. The latter they dared not do, so they laughed too.

I then said, "As we are discussing this instrument of torture — I would suggest that the Commission should signalise their visit to Ultimo Retiro by having it publicly burned. That's what I would do if I were in charge here."

All looked grave, only old Fox approved, and he actually brought it forward later on to the members, as an official suggestion, but they thought it "wiser not" to do anything quite so glaring as to burn the *cepo*. That would make a flare.

Lots of people were gathering round, and I thought it as well to stop. The matter was getting embarrassing. Sr Tizon, poor man, came along and I walked away.

Luncheon

At luncheon we saw a party of women ferried across, and start under one of these scoundrels to prepare the path for the "Commission" tomorrow, who intend to visit some locality near at hand. Nearly all were women — the man with a gun — the male animal to direct and the women to work, and these swine of the underworld actually reprove the Indians for that the men don't work their plantations! These pigs who loll in hammocks and wait for the rubber to come in, who never do a hand's turn of work, and could not earn 6d. a day in any decent community, are the lords and masters of these unhappy people — body and soul — and exercise more than feudal tyranny in the name of a great English Company, over a large tract of country inhabited by these gentle, timid beings we see around us, starved and flogged, and humble as dogs that lick the hand that beats them.

Another complaint from the Barbadians about their food. Bishop begged me to allow him to give a tin of my meat to a very thin little girl he saw outside working. I said, yes, of course, but he lost sight of her, poor wee soul.

Crichlow's interrogation

After lunch I called Edward Crichlow and asked Barnes and Fox to be present while I put questions to him. He spoke out — my injunction of the morning had done its work.[151] His details of some of the bestiality of Fidel Velarde and Aurelio Rodriguez flogging Indians, men, women and children, the latter extending them in a double *cepo*, one for the legs, the other for the head and arms, a *cepo* that moved up and down, so that it could fit the stature of children — was revolting. I was glad Fox was present. He did not hear the last part of Crichlow's statement, when later I recalled him and interrogated him as to the Expedition to the Caquetá in March–May of this year when Jiménez invaded Colombia, and brought back 21 Indian prisoners and 3 Colombian white men

Jaguars

Just before dinner, two *muchachos* with guns, came in to the dining room to see Jiménez. They looked such weird little things (one pale and thin, with his long black hair draped round his thin mummyish face), and their high staccato, Chinese-like speech, every word cut from its fellow. They were like ghosts in an opera. They began excitedly telling Jiménez of their doings, and he laughed, and told us that it was another "tiger" scare. The head boy had just been stalking a *pavon* (peacock), and was aiming at it up in a tree when a jaguar aimed at him behind. He rose with a

[151] Edward Crichlow's {B.B. Statement No 16 p.87–92}. To avoid further confusion the name Crichley has been changed to Crichlow.

yell, fired in the air and leaped after. The jaguar went in one direction and the Indian in the other, and here he happily was, to tell the tale.

Two fine Puma skins were drying outside the house, just newly shot, Jiménez said. The Capitanes at dinner time told us that an Indian with a gun and machete had just recently been killed by a jaguar, and the man at the *chacara* (the clearing across the river) lately saw a woman killed by the jaguar, probably the same, but could not get in time to save her. This man is Montozo.

We are all going out to the forest tomorrow — 2½ hours out — and will take arms, and try for one of these numerous panthers or jaguars — here, of course, called "tigers".

Poor 'Andokes' (the Camereiro mayor, as I call him) fell off the launch today while it was going up river with the Commission to visit the *chacara*, and was nearly lost. He came to the top, however, and was picked up, but is ill tonight. Angry with himself, they say.

The Commission have decided to leave on Tuesday, back to Puerto Peruano by the Launch, and then on foot (7 hours), then on to Entre Rios to "O'Donnell's country". To think that a name so great should be dragged so low! That an Irish name of valour, truth, courage and high-mindedness should be borne by a Peruvian bandit, whose aim is to persecute these wretched Indians, his "fellow citizens", to rob them of all they possess, in order to make money from their blood. The only cheering thing is that this Andrés O'Donnell has the best name of the lot — the least scoundrelly record. It is not much, but still in the kingdom of the blind the one-eyed man is king, and it is something here to have it said of you that "O'Donnell did not kill Indians with his own hands, all the others did."

Zumaran

Sealy came to say that I had asked him before at Occidente to point out when we reached Ultimo Retiro the other man who used to flog at Sabana when he was there. "Here he is," he said, "the cook there, Zumaran." I looked to the kitchen, and saw this undersized underling, in blue pajamas, one of the gang Bell said yesterday looked "all cut-throats". This was poor Sealy's co-executioner before — now our cook. When I looked at Sealy's decent, good natured black face — a really good darkie's countenance, and see him grinning from ear to ear with delight when I sometime rub it in to these cowards, in public, as at the Stocks today, I wonder how it was he was saved from sinking altogether to the animal state of his surroundings.

After telling me of Zumaran being the other flogger at Sabana, when he was there as executioner, he said Jiménez had called Crichlow aside this afternoon, after being interrogated by me, and had talked to him apart, and that Crichlow would not tell them what Jiménez had said. I asked Bishop if this was so, and he said that Crichlow had said that Jiménez asked him to say nothing against him — that he had always treated him well — which was true — and had then gone on to talk about the women of the Station, and had told Crichlow to keep a good guard — "a good eye on them to see that no one interfered with them". This is exactly what I had been expecting. I told Bishop that he and the other two men were on no account to sleep apart, but all in the room where they are together. The remainder of what Jiménez had said to Crichlow, the latter had refused to tell, even to him, Bishop said. He admitted that Jiménez had said more, but refused to say what it was.

The end of a long day

I am tired now after a very long day of hard work, uninterrupted almost, in much heat, and with a good deal of disgust at the presence of this beast Jiménez at table, and the necessity I am under of being even civil to him, or to any of this gang of dirty cowards. Bruce's laugh at the stocks today that "he got flogged for not bringing *caucho*, that's why" was as selfish an exhibition of the inner cur as I have yet seen. He is a sickly, pale, lame youth, flushing easily, with a washed out skin and a profile and nose like Lefroy,[152] the murderer of my boyhood — just like him. I've been wondering where the resemblance lay — now I have it.

I turned in early and tried to sleep to the tread of the sentry pacing the verandah all through the night. The sentry, I believe, is Zumaran, the special looking cut-throat, quite the worst cast of face I think we've struck yet in this Chamber of Horrors' collection of criminals.

---

152 Casement shows a penchant, characteristic of the period, for phrenology and the work of Cesare Lombroso on criminal archetypes.

ULTIMO RETIRO — SUNDAY, OCTOBER 9TH

The Commission visit an Indian village

We left for the "Nation", as they call it, of the Meretas Indians, to see *Hevea* trees. The whole Commission, Tizon, Jiménez, Bruce, and a train of servants, the cook and empleados, and a lot of press-ganged Indians had gone before. We were to walk 2½ hours through the forest, and the ordinary forest track had been prepared yesterday by the force of women and a few men we had seen going off at lunch.

As we embarked in the *batalon* to cross the river, two elderly Indian men came down with more camp equipment for us, nude save for their slender *fono* of white bark cloth. Their sterns were both terribly scarred, indeed the two broad patches on one man's buttocks looked like burns. They were the scars of an extra deep cutting of the lash. All of us saw them, but I broke silence, and said, at large,

"Two very incontrovertible burns, I must say."

These instructive backsides climbed in and squatted beside us, their elderly owners asking me for a cigarette. "Chigarro, Chigarro" has become the greeting we get wherever we go, but especially myself, for I give cigarettes with a lavish hand. The poor souls, young and old, love them and, God knows, they have little pleasure. Whenever they get a present they stroke one's hand or shoulder affectionately, and say, "Bigara, bigara" (Good, good). They apply it now universally, and we are constantly hailed with cries of "Bigara", so I christened them this morning "the Begorrahs". It sounds exactly like an Irish begorrah. The name has stuck, and Barnes and all of them speak of our poor Indian hosts as the Begorrahs, and we made much play with the word during the day.

As we went along the path we found constant evidence of yesterday's work for our benefit, the rough places made smooth, and, I added, when we noticed this — "At the expenses, I fear, of their smooth places made rough," — patting my haunches. I am certainly becoming the enfant terrible of the Commission, but I mean to rub these highly instructive backsides well in their faces until they admit that it is the lash behind and not the "advance" in front that collects each *fabrico* of rubber.

The path had indeed been smoothed for us — trees felled, saplings and trunks laid over wet spots, and bridges made over many streams with a liana rope banister to hold by. Over three traversings of a large deep river, a tributary of the Igaraparaná, we found very large trees felled, and a strong bridge thus made at great labour by these poor people. The road was fully six miles long I should say, all through rich forest with many *Hevea* trees, mostly young saplings, some fine palms, with the cries of birds, toucans and parrots, and the most variegated display of butterfly wings we have yet encountered.

I pointed out more than once, in remarks to those near me, that I could not see how any of this heavy labour of preparing this path was to be paid for. It was clear that there was no intention paying these people, for there was nothing in the Store to do it, and even the pretence of "feeding" them could scarcely be sustained, seeing the want of food everywhere visible. Perhaps they would assume that these lady workers were to be remunerated with the enamelled iron "chambers" with lids we had observed in the Store, but even then it was clear you'd have to divide one pot between a dozen ladies. I have certainly been nasty today, and have handled my weapons truculently, the enamel iron utensil being so prominent in the tiny Store that it pays the price of obviousness.

Crichlow, Sealy and Chase came also with us — all armed with Winchesters — as were the "staff", the cook and general parade of scoundrels who precede us everywhere. Crichlow said once "This section used to have plenty of Indians — they've been killed mostly." This was said quite aloud — for general use — but I fancy only Barnes and I, who were leading, heard it.

On the way we met a small party coming in under a Captain with a dead monkey, just shot and trussed. This they at once handed to Jiménez, who told them to take it to the Station, and some cassava bread a woman was carrying. These "gifts" of these poor fugitives, shot by themselves in their own wild forest, or made by their patient wives from their tiny patches of cassava, are another part of the unlimited tribute laid upon them by each of these strongholds of robbery.

Arrival at the Meretas village

We met several of the women of yesterday's smoothing process, returning to their "homes", I presume, after having been out in the forest, or at the Meretas Indians house all night. On arrival there we did nothing but eat a luncheon prepared for us by the cook and those who had gone ahead. I photographed the whole of the Meretas tribe or nation, which Jiménez said reckoned seven head, all told. There were two gentle-eyed men with tin and bead ear-rings, and their small families all living in this one house — surrounded by a small patch of cassava. We did not go on to see any more rubber trees — as Fox had seen enough on the path out — so soon after twelve we started back in hot sun, and, arrived at the river in a thunder shower. I swam across, and the rest got into the batalon and followed. It was very hot and Bell was rendered ill by it.

Crichlow asks to leave Ultimo Retiro to seek indemnity

Crichlow came to see me to say that he wished to leave Ultimo Retiro with me, and not to stay on any longer. I asked "Why?" and he said "To give my evidence, Sir", with a cunning look. He evidently hopes now to get back at the Company for his ill-treatment, and, no doubt, to recover damages. He certainly is entitled to indemnity for the gross ill-treatment and abuse that he received from Aurelio Rodriguez and Velarde at a time when this company had been formed, and for which it must legally accept responsibility. But he could never get a ghost of a chance in Iquitos by any civil action — that is clear, and I imagine his hope is that if I take him away he will get me, or rather the government behind me, to champion his claim against the Company. As a matter of fact, there is no doubt all the Barbadians have a very legitimate claim against the Company — for illegal employment forced upon them, for illegal punishment inflicted on them, and also for breach of contract as regards food. All this is clear to me, but to prove it is another thing, and even then to establish the claim successfully by law would be out of the question.

The Iquitos headquarters would win in any law proceedings started there — witness, if witness is at all needed, the fact of this very man's detention for fifteen months without trial on a mere letter from Loayza and Juan Vega on the Putumayo, and his expenditure of £29 (earned while in jail!) on a local lawyer to defend him.

I said to Crichlow that if he really wished to go, and asked me to assist him to leave, I should do so, but that I should talk the matter over with Sr. Tizon, and advise him later on.

Conversation with Gielgud

I asked Gielgud to discuss the matter with me. I pointed out to him the perilous position in which the English Company stood with regard to all these men still in its service. There was no question, as he now knew as well as I did, that they had been illegally employed, illegally treated (witness Dyall's disgraceful torture here at Ultimo Retiro) and put often in grave peril; witness this recent raid into Colombia or the shooting of Rochipo by Allan Davis at Aguero's orders. This man, Crichlow, was astute enough to understand this — he hoped that in Barbados, or wherever it was possible for him to state his case, that he would get a ready hearing, that he could appeal to his statement made to me in my official capacity, and thus the whole question of the conduct of affairs in this region would be raised publicly, and in the most damaging way to the Company. My own view was that these men were entitled to compensation, and that possibly when my report was handed in the FO would also take this view, and might possibly so inform the Company. As to that, I knew nothing obviously, but I should personally support the men's claim if it were ever referred to me for support. In all this he fully agreed, entirely from start to finish, and frankly admitted that the Company's position vis à vis its British employees, these Barbadians, was not sustainable, and that by far the best course would be for some indemnity, or the principle of it to be admitted here and now. This was my object in raising the question. Would he and Mr Tizon, as representing the company, listen to the statement of Crichlow, also to that of Bishop here on the spot where evidence is obtainable, either to sustain or refute their case, and if they made it good, would these two as representing the Company assure the men in my presence that the matter would be referred to the London Board with their favourable opinion on the men's claims so that a suitable sum might be paid to them as compensation for indemnity later on? The sum could not now be fixed. I had no authority to claim compensation for these men, or to do anything, but to find out the exact nature of their relation to the Company, and whether they were in distress, and, if so, from what cause. But it was clear that many of these men were, or had been recently, in distress. They were often put to the most singularly illegal duties under threats and compulsion — they were even made to imperil their lives illegally and on illegal tasks that would entail capital punishment by our laws, and all this done by authority of a British Company!

Mr Gielgud admitted the full force of all that I put forward, he would not contest it all or attempt to defend the actual or recent situation — and thanked me for stating my views so clearly. I said I could not muzzle Crichlow if he went away, and chose to create a horrible scandal against the Company, as it was clear he could do, for he could always say he had stated these things to the British Consul General specially sent to investigate, and that it was this officer who had "taken him" out of the country. After a long talk on these lines, Gielgud said he would discuss the situation with Tizon, and he believed they could both come to an agreement that might be, he hoped, honourable and straightforward all round.

There was no wish or intention to "buy" the silence of the Barbadians. What they said was admitted, what they had suffered or endured would be equally admitted — the only question would be to endeavour to do what was now right and called for in their cases with the ultimate approval of the FO and the Board. It was clear that to discuss the matter in any way in London this preliminary investigation and admission of right must be made here.

The need to save the Company

So I left it for today, and Gielgud parted from me in a happier frame of mind, I think, than has been his for days. What we are all doing is clear. To try and save the hideous scandal of a public exposure of what has occurred here, not even in the remote part of, say, 1907, but right up to today, to this very month, in order to save the Company. That the Company as such should be saved neither Tizon nor I think nor care, but the Company is the surest guarantee we can lay hold of for more humane treatment of the Indians, all that are left of them. The destruction during the last few years has been abnormal. This region, bordering on the Japura, has always been, or for a very long time has been, the happy hunting ground of the Portuguese and of other enslavers of the Indians. See Lt Maw's account[153] of what he heard in 1827 when passing down the Amazon from Peru. Then even Portuguese raiding parties went up the "Japura river" to catch slaves, and the methods he described nearly a century ago are exactly those of Jiménez and this English Company today in 1910. But if you can keep it going, as really an English Company, and not merely as

[153] Henry Lister Maw was a British naval lieutenant who made a journey across northern Peru in 1828 and entered Brazil via Tabatinga, continuing down the river to Belém do Pará. He was shocked by the lot of the "civilized" Indians he encountered in their state of slavery and degradation. The following year John Murray published *Journal of a Passage from the Pacific to the Atlantic crossing the Andes in the northern provinces of Peru, and descending the river Marañon or Amazon*. Casement was clearly impressed by Maw's journey and referred to it frequently in his work. In a number of respects Casement was Maw's successor.

Arana Bros., registered in London, then radical changes can be effected and this disgraceful state of things brought to a more or less speedy ending. The difficulty will be to keep the gang — to prevent the board from resigning at once. Every pressure that can be brought to bare upon them should be brought by the FO and other influences to induce them to hold on even at a loss, so as to repair to some extent the wrong they have innocently helped to inflict on these unhappy, these mercilessly persecuted people. They who have made money from the slavery of the Indians must now be begged, compelled, if it can be, to even lose money to redeem the remnant of the Indians. This is what we are all trying for, Tizon, I think, perhaps more than anyone, save myself, while Gielgud, admitting to the full the moral claim and the dire need, fears that the body of shareholders will kick. So do I.

And then there is always Julio Arana himself! He is the danger spot. If he finds he cannot hoodwink any longer the English Company, then he will destroy it and restart the past and actual piracy on even worse lines with the Peruvian Government behind him to wring out the last pound of rubber while one Indian is left alive to procure it in all this stifling wilderness. God help the poor beings — only He can help them.

I intend taking a boy home to try and interest the Anti-Slavery people,[154] etc. etc. and the Missions,[155] so that possibly some of the wealthy people, who are also good people, may, possibly, — who knows? — it is a wild thought — take shares in the Company not to get rubber but to save Indians. If the Company goes, as I fear must be the case, then all is lost. The last hope of these poor beings disappears for ever, on their green trees, their blue skies, their rushing rivers, their innumerable woodland signs, and then deliberately and lovingly slay each other. Better far! Die once and

[154] The Anti-Slavery Society had amalgamated with the Aborigines Protection Society on 1 July 1909 and the Putumayo atrocities became their first main cause. Following Hardenburg's disclosures in *Truth*, the A.S.A.P.S. took up the case and lobbied hard to force the FO and P.A. Co to take action. They continued the pressure until 1914 and were the most effective humanitarian group involved in the affair. Most of the Society's papers relating to the investigation are held at Rhodes House, Oxford University. {Brit Emp. S22.}

[155] This refers to the large number of British missionary groups which Casement felt might be interested in trying to relieve the situation. Once the Congo reform movement began, Catholic and Protestant missionaries had played an important part in bringing about change. Here Casement expresses his first interest in taking back an Indian boy to try and stir up wider public interest in the plight of the Amerindians. Taking Indians back to Europe was a tradition maintained by many New World explorers and travellers since the moment of first contact.

be done with it. Not only do you end it, but you also pay back in the only way left you these scavengers of crime, their atrocious treatment of yourselves. With you all dead and gone these forests are worthless, these thousands of miles of Upper Amazon tributaries go back to the wild beasts and the human beasts, who have infested them these twenty years past, go back to their sordid and mean lives in the streets of Peruvian and Colombian towns without rubber and without *pele*,[156] and might soon be forced to work for their living.

Proposed itinerary

Our proposed itinerary I find from the Commission now is as follows:

October 11th — Leave Ultimo Retiro by the launch to Puerto Peruano, where disembark and march for Entre Rios.
October 12th — Arrive at Entre Rios, where stay some days and go on to Matanzas and Andokes.
October 20th — Arrive Matanzas.
October 24th — Leave Matanzas
October 27th — Arrive Entre Rios
October 28th — Arrive Atenas
October 31st — Leave Atenas for Chorrera, where we should arrive about 2nd November or earlier.

The *Liberal* will be there then with our mails from home, and to take me back to Iquitos. Our mails will be of 26th July, and that on, up to perhaps 15th August. We have had no letters since the mail the 'Hilary' herself brought out with ourselves on board dating from 25th July as the last date, we ourselves having sailed on 23rd July.

Starving Indian carriers

On ending the talk with Gielgud we saw a lot of Indians on the opposite bank of the river, men with boxes ("Chop boxes") on their backs, carried in the usual fibre slings from the forehead. Poor beings they were, limping along, and sat down to wait for the canoes. We were told they had come from Occidente with more of our food loads we had left behind there — too much for the Launch to bring on. There were about three canoe loads of them,

[156] Animal skins — before the advent of rubber, fur-trapping had been an important means of livelihood for Amazon frontiersmen.

and there were coming in until 6 to 7 p.m. When about a dozen or more had arrived I called Bishop, and we found out that they had been 2 days on the road, and as they looked starved I asked him to enquire what rations they had received at Occidente for this journey.

Bishop said, "They've had nothing, Sir, can't you see those Indians are starving. They never get any food given for any journey at all — rubber or expeditions — or anything — they've got to find it as best they can, or get it from their friends. That's why they chew the coca.[157] They say they can go two days without food on the coca."

I said "Never mind, ask them all the same". So he did, in Huitoto. There was a perfect howl. A "hugh", and two men turned their scarified bottoms, a boy also, and we saw the most enormous weals and scars I've seen yet.

I called Fox and Gielgud, and one of the men, a captain, who was sitting on the bulwark, told us, or rather Bishop, with gestures suiting the words, "We asked Velarde for a tin of sardines for the road, and he told us to eat our private parts," and he put both hands down there and made pretence of doing what Velarde had done. I was glad I had got Fox and Gielgud and Barnes to be witness of this recital.

Casement feeds the starving Indians

I gave these poor starving wretches a tin of meat or fish between every two men. There were over 20 of them, and it made a hole in my supplies, but I never gave food with greater pleasure in my life. They literally wolfed it with the loudest "begorrahs" I've got yet, and such smiles of delight. All squatted down there and then, all over the verandah, in the door of my room, anywhere two by two, and tore the tins open and swallowed in a brace of shakes, sheeps' tongues, herrings, salmon and other preserved meats. We all enjoyed the spectacle, almost as much as they did. One boy swallowed the greasy paper round a sheep's tongue, inside the tin, and another opened a tin with his teeth. The "Begorrahs" were

---

[157] The leaf of the *Erythroxylon Coca* is still widely used throughout the Andes and Amazon to assuage feelings of hunger and fatigue. The leaves are generally mixed with small quantities of lime and chewed slowly. From the leaf is distilled the alkaloid cocaine which has been harnessed to the needs of modern medicine as a good anaesthetic for eye, ear and throat surgery. But it is best known as the raw material for the multi-billion dollar international illicit drugs trade.

one genial flow of eructation. It was only a snack, but was a welcome one and unexpected.

The spokesman, a young capitan, gave forth the rest of their charge, against Velarde — that he had "been frightened" (their very words) when we were there, but now he said he should flog them again, and do so as he pleased with them, and hold them under water and drown them. Here again was the same charge uttered by these men, and Tizon only a pace or two away. I was delighted, and Bishop translated for us all with equal pleasure. Fox said it almost made him cry to see them — these poor lacerated, emaciated beings, like children in so many ways, biddable and gentle, and the absolute, entire slaves of these damnable scoundrels. Gielgud too was moved to hearty indignation, the first time I have had the pleasure of hearing him out with real, unmitigated reproof. He said Velarde ought to be hanged, or handed to these very men and flogged by them till he died. I said I'd like to flog the brute myself, but he was only one of many and the System that had been planted on these poor serfs by Arana & Co. had introduced these ruffians and employed them and their methods for years at highly remunerative terms. It was no use denouncing Velarde as an individual blackguard, it was the entire system of slavery had to go and its substitution by some rational and faintly legal treatment for the Indians.

Jiménez

Jiménez and the "staff" stood afar off regarding us, and the extraordinary sight of white men interested in and caring for Indians. Crichlow, quite innocently, I find, speaks always of the staff as "ordinary men", in contradistinction to the Manager. The gang here would be hanged on their photographs in any country that has police — all, perhaps, except Jiménez. Bad, atrocious as we know him to be, his face rather wins upon you. He is brown and sturdy and strong; never flinches, is intelligent, and answers clearly and well. He has courage, and has made up his mind to play his part, and it looks like a winning one. While his deeds at Abisinia and Morelia, and on the way to the Caquetá are undoubtedly true of this awful ruffian, he is actually a winning ruffian, and the Commission are favourably impressed. But if he is kept on because he has turned over a new leaf, how discharge the others? They would complain that they had done nothing worse than Jiménez.

Jiménez draws a fine percentage of profits here on his 25 tons (mas ou menos) of rubber supplied by the "260 workmen" of his district. I wonder if the 21 Indians brought from far beyond the Japura in Colombia, figure among these.

Death of an Indian

Bishop in the evening brought in a paper on which he had written what an Indian had told him last night. It said that an Indian had been here in chains and in the stocks in January last had been shot by order of Montt, the executioner being one Velasquez. I find Velasquez figures on the list of Station hands, but, of course, he is not here now, any more than Aquiléo Torres, who is "on the move". None of these *racionales* have a stroke of useful or natural work to do, for all their human use the whole lot could go. They are merely the instruments of torture, to bully and oppress and dragoon the peaceful, timid children of the forest.

Ultimo Retiro — Monday 10th October

A sore eye at dawn

Up at 5. Eye (left eye) very sore and swelling again, so that I have to bandage it.[158] Out at 5.30 and saw the poor Indians of last night sweeping the Station! They got rice last night by Gielgud's order. I doubt if anyone would have given them a thought, only my tins and the demonstration they evoked caused so much scandal. If I, a stranger, gave them all this food, valued up here at perhaps 2 pounds (for I gave some fifteen tins), then the people who had press-ganged them and used them like beasts of burden with no thought of paying them, had to give them at least a meal.

First thoughts

They all returned across the river to return to their homes at 7. I gave the Captain and others some cigarettes, and gave him a couple of flasks of powder, and a bag of shot.[159] His joy was boyish,

[158] Despite the references to Casement's eye problem made from the outset of the voyage, the *Black Diary* remained completely silent on the matter until this day (10 October), when the corresponding entry reads: " .... My eye is very bad indeed — left eye, and I have it bandaged with Boracic lotion and the Dr of *Hilary*'s stuff. Turned in early with wet bandage over eyes."

[159] Casement here is admitting to supplying ammunition to an Indian Captain. His efforts to mount effective resistance to Arana continued throughout his subsequent voyage to Iquitos in 1911, when he tried to spur a local anti-Aranista group to ac-

he fairly hugged it. One boy I saw, and really thought of trying to get home with me to interest the Missions and Anti-Slavery people in the fate of these poor people. If a Mission were started it might help a lot, but it can only come on two conditions — that the Company (I mean the English part of it) is strong enough to crush Arana and dismiss his gang of murderers, and put in decent men, and then that the Company itself will consent to carry on — even at a loss, as it must be for some years. Then a Mission here would be first rate, but a Mission with the present system would mean only more victims.[160]

Casement describes some methods of treating the native people

The others all went away (except Bell) to visit rubber trees in the forest, the Indians going home to Occidente were pressed in to carry part of the grub, tables etc. Tizon had treated them all well, and given each of them two tins of sardines, and 10 kilogs of rice among the nearly 30 men, so he told me. This is, of course, very exceptional treatment, due to the strange circumstances we are here, and Tizon is here, and sees our point of view. But of course no one dreams of pay. To pay them has not entered any head but mine, and yet even on the Congo there would have been payment (of a sort) as well as food. This Company has not got the means of paying for anything in its *Provedura* or Store, and yet it daily imposes onerous tasks (apart altogether from rubber collection) on the surrounding people. And they perform these tasks, patient, humble beings, with smiles and compliments and gentle speech to their oppressors. From building these huge houses (this one is fully 45 yards long and as strong as an old three-decker) clearing great tracts of forest, making plantations of yucca, mealy, sugar cane, &c., constructing roads and bridges at great labour, for these men to more easily get at them — to supplying them with "wives", with food, with game from the chase, often with their own food just made for their own pressing wants, with labour to meet every conceivable form of demand. All this the Indians supply for absolutely no remuneration of any kind, this entirely in addition to

---

tion. Casement was eventually arrested in 1916 off the west coast of Ireland after disembarking from a German vessel carrying 20,000 rifles for the Easter Rising.

[160] Casement's first mention of a mission, which he clearly felt was the only genuine way of protecting the Indians. At the beginning of 1912, Casement set about raising funds to establish a Mission on the Putumayo through the Putumayo Mission Fund. Four Franciscan missionaries were eventually sent out at the end of 1912 and remained in the area for three years.

the India rubber which is the keystone of the arch. At Occidente it yields £10,000 a year, here, possibly, £5,000, and the expense of running these Stations after the Chief's percentage is subtracted is scarcely anything, for even the *racionales* are robbed. Getting nominally, say £5 to £7 or £8 per month and food — they get so little food that much, if not most of the £7, say, goes back to the Company at fully 100% profit, for such things even as rice and sugar beans and candles and matches and tinned meats. I am dealing fully with this in Crichlow's case, his accounts are in my hands. I sent for him again today, and got fuller account of the expedition to Caquetá (see in his statement). It is incredible — ordered, too, by Macedo the General manager.

Claims of the Barbadians

Then I got Tizon and Gielgud to hear Crichlow and Bishop, and former admitted the principle of their claim (under pressure), and it was left at that. The men's claims were to be presented in London, and urged to the favourable attention of the Company, and meantime Crichlow would stay here and work on. I told him before Tizon and G. that he was to be put to no illegal tasks — that flogging the Indians was an unlawful and punishable offence, no matter who ordered to do it, and that if he were ordered to do this, or any other unlawful task, he was to refuse obedience and to at once inform Sr. Tizon. Tizon agreed to this, with Gielgud nodding approval, and said "You are to write to me at once." Bishop's case is a claim for compensation for lost and stolen property, and for his services at the time when Robuchon was lost in 1904, I think — a long time back, and before the Company arose on the scene.

Casement debriefs the Commission

The party out on the forest got some harrowing scenes of flogging, they told us on return — "the worst yet", Barnes said. One, a boy of about 10 or 11, "cut to ribbons" by Montt, the other, the nice-faced gentle old man that Fox liked so much who brought the shot monkey yesterday on the road. They made him take down his cotton check pants — part payment for 30 kilogs of rubber — and he was terribly marked, Fox and Barnes say. Fox is furious and disgusted — told me he was glad I had not come, it would have made me ill. I said I was glad they had seen it, and to Barnes that perhaps now they would begin to accept my 90% of floggings. He said "100% more like it."

Fox told me later he was getting sick of it all, it filled him with nausea, and he wanted to get away. He had called Tizon in the forest, to see the little boy, whom he had sent up a tree for some specimens, and then it was he had noticed the terrible markings on the poor little chap's back and legs. He told Tizon, when the little boy was explaining "Montt, Montt" as the cause of his injuries, that if he saw the brute now he would shoot him. This will be our next host in a few days at Atenas. Bell, who talked things over at lunch with me, is also much more convinced than before, "Sheer slavery from top to bottom", he now admits.

Gusmán's river bath

The man Gusmán came in from Occidente with three more loads of ours on the backs of Indians, as Bell and I lunched. He had not been able to keep up with the poor wretches who arrived last night, and had slept in the forest. His "wife" of course accompanied him. These creatures never go anywhere without their "wives". The Cook who goes out ahead each morning to prepare the lunch of the Commission struts off with a herd of male and female Indians carrying the utensils, always carrying his Winchester and followed by his "wife". The rifle and the rifled wife go together with these civilisers. Gusmán, soon after arrival, went down to wash in the river — the only bath the *racionales* have. The water is beautiful, deep and clear, and the Indian boys and girls too are often in it swimming like ducks. Gusmán washed on the bank and I happened to catch sight of his naked body. His "wife", clothed in her long cushma, was in attendance, holding one of his hands to steady him as he soaped himself, washing his feet and performing all the services of a bath attendant. This on the broad open beach 40 yards from the house front. There was nothing wrong in it, but it shows clearly how these Indian women are regarded. I called Bell to see it and we both stood and watched — the stark naked white man attended by his clothed girl "wife".

Bell said, "Of course, she's a slave, and there's an end of it."

When she had finished serving her lord and master, she herself, cushma and all, jumped into the river and swam about! The Indian women I find do this generally — jump in clothed and divest themselves of their garment when in the water. The men and boys are extraordinarily modest — clothed and unclothed all alike. When they go to bathe they carefully conceal with their hand that part of them exposed when they strip off their narrow *fono* or bark cloth.[161] Certainly these Indians are in every sense but one (that of brute and brutal force) incomparably higher in the human scale than any of the agents of the Peruvian Amazon Company I have met, save Tizon and Gielgud.

Casement's left eye

My eye is getting very bad, and I have to do all my writing now with one eye — the right — the left is carefully bandaged up.

Conversation with Tizon

When I explained to Tizon today that, in addition to the gross ill-treatment inflicted upon him by Aurelio Rodriguez and Velarde, Crichlow had also been quite illegally employed this year, from March to May, on a lawless raid into Colombia, rendering him liable to be shot possibly if any Colombian troops had been there, he said

"That expedition was a very stupid thing of Macedo's. He wanted to send another, but I stopped it."

I said that if the Colombian Government made representations on the matter, as this was an English Company and certainly responsible for the acts of its chief representative out here, I thought the Company would cut a very extraordinary figure before His Majesty's Government.

As to the claim of Crichlow, he was at first disposed to assert a *nonpossumus* on triple grounds.

1st. That by Peruvian law the Company is not responsible for criminal acts of its employés. I disposed of this by saying Crichlow's claim was a civil one, for compensation for injury sustained.

2nd. That if he admitted, or the Company admitted, claims of the Barbadians injured, it would have to admit all other similar claims, and these would be legion. Innumerable people had been injured, and how could all these claims be met? I said that that did not concern me, that I was here to look after the interests of the British employées alone, and I could not stand aside from supporting them when I thought they had right on their sides, because the Company's agents had also injured many other people.

[161] Casement's very direct statement about the bathing manners of the Indians is written in an innocent and asexual way — what Taussig describes as Casement's "ethnographic realism".

3rd. That some of the offences and injuries occurred "a long time ago", and it was scarcely fair now to put them forward against the Company. I met this by saying that the men had had no means of obtaining redress, or a hearing even, until now; that their complaints to the Chief Agents at Chorrera had been treated as offences and only met further illegal punishment, and, finally that (as with Velarde) the agents accused by these men were still in the Company's service and drawing large incomes as a part of its highest personnel.

He admitted this, and gave in, and agreed to put the matter before the London Board on the lines of my statement, that they were to investigate the charges and honourably and justly deal with them now that these statements were first brought to their notice.

With regard to Dyall, I said it would be a matter for a higher amount of compensation. The offence was committed, it is true, before the Company took over from Arana Bros., but Alfredo Montt, who so brutally injured Dyall, was still in the Company's service, and one of its principal agents. Here again, Tizon agreed.

No sums have been mentioned, nothing specifically at all. Gielgud hazarded a guess — a tentative proposal — "say from £20 to £50", according to circumstances, in each case of an aggrieved Barbadian who has a trustworthy account to give of the facts.

I said that, with regard to Dyall, I thought much more would be needed — in other cases I could not say. I named no sum, I merely brought the cases to their attention here, as it was clear the question of indemnity would be, and must be, raised at home, and I should support it. It was, therefore, only fair to let them know that the men were bringing their claims to my notice, so that here on the spot they, the representatives of the Company, might investigate the evidence laid before me. Crichlow was a servant of the Company, and they could question him and take his evidence. For my part, I would give them a copy of his statement to myself, of that part of it dealing with his proposed claim based on the specific acts of ill-treatment alleged against higher agents of the Company.

Both Gielgud and Tizon thanked me for thus bringing the matter to their notice, and so, for the present, we leave it. I told Crichlow, when I called him in the evening, that if he left the Company's service he must tell the British Consul in Iquitos where he was going to, and leave an address, and report himself to the authorities in Barbados when he arrived there.

Heavy rain in night. We are to start for Puerto Peruano, sleep at an Indian house in the forest, and arrive at Entre Rios on morning of 12th, where we spend some days.

IV

THE ROAD TO ENTRE RIOS

DEPART ULTIMO RETIRO — TUESDAY, OCTOBER 11TH

Rain delays departure

Heavy rain, so heavy that it was decided to lunch here and start afterwards and sleep at Puerto Peruano, and do the whole march to Entre Rios tomorrow. The weak brethren are Fox and Bell, who shrink from a 7 hours' march. Rain stopped at 10 a.m. Crichlow brought for my inspection the remains of the bottle of lotion for his knees for which he is charged S/3.84 = 7/8, as for *remedios extraordinarios* in the Chorrera accounts. Fox was in my room reading Whiffen's letter to F.O when he came with the bottle, and I called Gielgud to hear Crichlow's statement. The stuff was some soap or turpentine liniment in a very small bottle, worth 6d. at outside, but this man was entitled to medical help and medicines free. I told Gielgud plainly I thought it was robbery, not an "extraordinary remedy", but an "extraordinary robbery".

How the evil system evolved

Fox is pretty well convinced now. I have been seeking to disabuse his mind this morning on another point. He has been told that the evil system he sees in full swing was a sort of natural and inevitable growth based on the fact that the first "settlers" had to hold their own against the Indians by terror.

These latter would have murdered them and so forth, and so, step by step, this armed abomination grew up as "a cruel necessity for self defence". I bore him to my room, read over Arana's statement to the shareholders, in which this lying plea is put out, and asked him if he believed it, and he said "No, it is untrue". So I said with the rest of that tale. These men came here not as settlers "to trade" with the Indians, but to appropriate the Indians. It is not the rubber trees so much as the Indians they wanted and want. The trees are valueless without the Indians, who, besides getting rubber for them, do everything else these creatures need — feed them, build for them, run for them and carry for them and supply them with wives and concubines.

They couldn't get this done by persuasion, so they slew and massacred and enslaved by terror, and that is the whole foundation. What we see today is merely the logical sequence of events — the cowed and entirely subdued Indians, reduced in numbers, hopelessly obedient, with no refuge and no retreat, and no redress. Here, this very year, is this very man, Jiménez, heading a large armed band of the "Company's servants" far into the Republic of Colombia, many days beyond the Caquetá, the indisputed frontier of that State, and putting three Colombians in Stocks for 21 days on their own soil, and bringing them and 21 Indians down here as prisoners. These 21 Indians had fled many days' journey to escape from this regime, and they are not saved by flight, even into another so-called civilised country. The whole thing from top to bottom is slavery without law — the most lawless state of things imaginable in this stage of human progress, for these Agents are not savages, but are the highly paid servants of a great English Company — citizens of a civilised state and amenable, so we are told, to an "efficient administration of justice."

I intend taking home, if I can, some of the flogged Indians to convince humane men and women of the dire need for helping these poor people, which incidentally must mean helping the Company. A strange outcome of this raid of Jiménez into Colombia is that one of the three Colombians taken prisoner, Bishop says, is now working at Atenas. This is the man Crichlow, termed Ramón, and Bishop says his name is Ramón Vargas, whom I find on the September pay-sheets as at Atenas for $50 per month. What has become of the other two it is hard to say. They may have refused to "enter the Company's service", and may be, for all we know, kept prisoners somewhere until sufficiently reduced, like Aquiléo Torres, to become agents.

The story of Aquiléo Torres

The story of Torres is really like a story from medieval fiction. Captured in 1906 by Normand, along with many other Colombians, as related so circumstantially by Roso España to the Manaos *Jornal do Commercio*,[162] he was kept for a very long time as a pris-

[162] *Jornal do Commercio* was the main daily newspaper published in Manaos during the rubber boom. Roso España's story is partially reproduced in *Hardenburg*'s *The Putumayo, The Devil's Paradise* pp.220–225 giving the facts of this cruel raid by Peruvians on an Andokes village

oner with a chain round his neck and feet, and passed on from Section to Section in this State. He was beaten, reviled, and spat upon, and several of the men who wrote to Hardenburg or *La Sanción*[163] at Iquitos related how and where they had thus seen him up to May 1908, when he disappears from that recital of the crimes of the Putumayo, in the letter of Celestino López of 15th May, 1909, as having been at Abisinia in May 1908, when López left that Section. He had already, in those Documents been converted into an agent of the Company, for López, in his letter, says that Velarde at Oriente who had kept Torres at Port Tarma "about a year and a half" had "compelled him to the ignoble task of flagellation".

On my coming to La Chorrera, I began to hear the name; it was mentioned in passing, by James Chase in his first statement dealing with flogging, &c. at Abisinia quite recently. This the day of the first interrogatory of the first five Barbadians (23rd Sept.) when Tizon was present, and only Chase and Sealy were brave enough to speak out. When the name occurred, Tizon said "Torres is a Colombian", and, later on, Sealy told me that Torres was actually one of the existing staff at Ultimo Retiro, and then on the *Planilla de Sueldos*, or pay sheet for September, 1910, I find him as one of the superior Staff of that Section, drawing $100 (or £10) per month. He had already sunk to the level of his employers, for Chase said he flogged the Indians like anyone else, and brutally.

Then one evening, the 3rd October, while we were leaning over the verandah at Occidente, a dirty "blanco" appeared with a puppy dog and three or four Indians carrying his gear, coming from the north. Sealy said, "That is Aquiléo Torres," and he passed on under the house to Velarde's house where he slept the night. Next morning early he was gone, and I was told, when I asked, that he had gone to Chorrera "on business".

He now reappears in Sealy's and Chase's narratives, and finally, in that of Bishop. The former had him as a colleague or *racionale*[164]

[163] *La Sanción* was a small Iquitos-based newspaper and the first effective voice of the local anti-Aranista party. Set up by a Peruvian Jew and active socialist, Benjamin Saldaña Rocca, the paper was instrumental in alerting local attention to the horror. Evidence of atrocities described in the articles helped Hardenburg's efforts to expose the situation. Saldaña Rocca was evicted from Iquitos at the start of 1908 as a result of local pressure from Arana and died four years later destitute in Lima. Casement had respect for and sympathized with Saldaña Rocca. A story appeared in the paper on 22 August 1907 describing Normand's cruel treatment of Torres, see Hardenburg, *op. cit.*, p.225

[164] Casement's mistaken singular form of *racionales*, which should be *racional*.

in Abisinia and Morelia, and Chase says he was as bad as any of the other murderers and ruffians there. Chase says he flogged the Indians brutally and killed them too when he, Chase, was with him at Morelia.

Finally, Bishop, in one of his reminiscences told me that once he was on a *correría*[165] from Matanzas hunting Indians for Normand, and on the track between Atenas and Entre Rios he met Fonseca at the head of a "Commission" going towards Ultimo Retiro. Bishop accompanied them a bit of the way as their paths lay together until he reached the point where he branched off into the forest after his prey — the fugitives from Matanzas section. Bishop had previously seen Torres kept, heavily chained and guarded, at Atenas whither he had been brought by Fonseca chained up like an animal. On this road Torres was still chained, and Bishop says the chain was heavy and about 10 feet long. He heard Torres beg Fonseca to stop, as he was tired from dragging and carrying this heavy chain. Fonseca replied that "it was better for him to walk as fast as possible, for if night took him on the road he would have to carry his (Fonseca's) *tula* — or Indian-rubber road bag.

The tula

The tula is often 25 kilogs or more in weight, depending on the contents. I have seen a tula well packed weigh some 34 kilogs, quite as much as a good African carrier's load. These wretched under-sized Indian boys and men look like shivering ghosts going along under a huge tula, or carrying a big box of provisions strapped behind their puny backs from the forehead by a fibre thong.

The raid on the Caquetá — May 1908

The killing of Indians by Aquiléo Torres — that Chase says he was often an eye-witness of — took place in latter part of 1908, and in 1909, as it was only in May 1908 that Chase went to Abisinia. Torres was one of the party, I believe, and went with Jiménez on the awful march to the Caquetá in June 1908. That may have been his first "service" in the Company, for it was in May 1908 that López states that he left him still a prisoner in Abisinia. I will again

[165] *Correría* (meaning "slave raid") was a widely used term in Peru during the rubber boom. These are Indian hunts organized by the *caucheros* who sought through these lightning attacks on Indian settlements to force more Indians into slavery and terrify them into submission and subjugation to the white man's authority.

question Sealy and Chase as to how they found Torres, whether free or still controlled, on their arrival at Abisinia in May 1908.

I have sent for Sealy, and he says that when he came to la Chorrera on 12th May, 1908, Aquiléo Torres was there not a prisoner, and that he accompanied him and Chase to Abisinia then, and took part in the "Commission" of Jiménez across the Caquetá when the Indians were burnt alive. Torres, Alberto, Urdinitra and Forman Vasquez were among those who crossed the Caquetá with Jiménez, and Torres returned in a short time from the other side of the river to remain with Sealy and Chase until Jiménez came back.

When they returned to Morelia Torres stayed there, and Chase stayed there while Sealy returned to Abisinia early in August 1908. Sealy did not up to this see Torres kill any Indians, although he saw him, on this very journey from the Caquetá strike an Indian boy over the head with a stick and cut it badly. It was on the march back from the Caquetá. He saw Torres again, in August, at Abisinia, when he came for a day or two from Morelia, and Sealy was sent to Ultimo Retiro in January 1910, but Bishop had already left then, and Torres arrived there a few days after Sealy — about 6 days after. Torres was in Ultimo Retiro all the time — say four or five months — January to May 1910, that Sealy stayed there. Torres was one of the expedition to the Caquetá in March–May this year as described by Crichlow, but Sealy was left at Ultimo Retiro, as he was sick. The three Colombian prisoners, Sealy says, were sent down to Chorrera after himself had gone there — that would be about the end of May. They came down about ten days afterwards to Chorrera in the *Veloz*, and Sr. Macedo sent two of them (these would be Mosqueiro and Tejó, according to Crichlow's statement of last night) down river in the 'Liberal', and one named Ramón he sent to Atenas. (This man is the Ramón Vargas on the lists of that Station for September.) This Ramón, Sealy says, came down to Chorrera with Alfredo Montt, the Chief of Atenas, the other day. Sealy says he is a young man, about 28 or 29. We will verify this at Atenas.

Corroboration of Hardenburg statements

As regards some of the other statements in the Hardenburg letters, Sealy corroborates here and there, and again both he and Chase deny the truth of certain statements.

As regards the statement, for instance, of João Baptisto Braga[166] (pp. 135–136) that he escaped from Morelia on 28th July 1908 along with the Colombian prisoner Felipe Cabrera and a Peruvian named Melchor Sajamín, Sealy says this is absolutely true, as related by Braga. Braga took advantage of Jiménez being away and got three canoes together with food and Indians and said he was "going on a Commission". He tried to "borrow" Sealy's panama hat, but Sealy, knowing the Commission story was a blind and that they were escaping, refused the loan. On the other hand, he stopped Chase from preventing the flight. Chase said they should stop these men escaping, but Sealy said it was not their business, and they ought to let them go. When Jiménez returned he was furious at the escape, and pitched into them all. Sealy says Braga was a kind man and very good to him.

On the other hand, both he and Chase deny the truth of Braga's accusation against Jiménez of setting fire to the Chief Tiracahuaca and his wife with kerosene, as described on p.135. Braga states that this crime took place "recently in the month of July" at Morelia — this means July 1908.[167] Sealy says he never heard of it, and does not believe it, because he was there at Morelia that very month up to Braga's escape, and Chase, who had remained long after Sealy left the Section, says that Tiracahuaca is still alive, that he escaped from the *cepo* and is at large, but that his wife was murdered by Armando Blondel, who "beat her to death". This Blondel was in charge of Morelia two months ago, when Chase left for Chorrera, where I found him on 22nd September. His name appeared on the Abisinia list of employés for September, 1910 at $100 (£10) per month. Morelia and Palmera are both under Abisinia, and have now only a *racionale* in charge, since Jiménez has been transferred from that Section to take charge himself of a District.

---

[166] See Hardenburg *op. cit.*, pp.237–40. Casement's page reference refers to his own document containing Hardenburg's evidence.

[167] Hardenburg *op. cit.*, p.239: "Here, recently, in the month of July, the tuchana known as Tiracahuaca and his wife were held prisoners in chains. When Jiménez — who had been temporarily absent — arrived, he had them brought into his presence and told them that if their tribe did not appear within the space of eight days, he would show them what he would do with them.

The eight days passed, and as the tribe did not come, he ordered a can of kerosene to be poured over them, and then, striking a match, he set fire to these unfortunates, who fled to the forest uttering the most desperate cries."

The man, Celestino López, in his letter to Hardenburg of 15th May, 1909,[168] at Iquitos, speaking of the bad time he had in Abisinia and Morelia, with Aguero and Jiménez, says (p.148), "I also saw the two unfortunates Paz Gutierrez and Felipe Cabrera (the leading Colombians along with Aquiléo Torres captured by Normand in 1906) "who were prisoners, shut up in a small dirty room under sentinels: to these unhappy wretches they gave almost no food at all, and abused and insulted them vilely and cowardly. One of them," (this was Cabrera, who got off with Braga on 28th July 1908) "at last succeeded in escaping, but the other still remained in the hands of his jailers at my departure from Abisinia." This latter with Paz Gutierrez, and I now learn from Sealy that he too escaped, and got to Chorrera when he (Sealy) was there. This was during the five to six months he (Sealy) spent at Chorrera after leaving Abisinia, and before going to Cabana. Gutierrez arrived in a canoe one day, he thinks it would be about March 1909, along with a Peruvian named Molino. Macedo was angry with Molino, who had helped Gutierrez to escape, and put him in *cepo*. He said if he wanted to run away from Abisinia he should have done it alone — without Gutierrez. The latter he put into a room and fed. Sealy heard that both men were sent down river in a canoe by Macedo, but does not know if that was true. He did not see them again, and was told in Chorrera that they had gone down in a canoe. (This may or may not be so. Macedo may have had them murdered, although that is unlikely. They might be traced through the Colombian Consul at Manaos, whom I shall see on my return to that city.)

Departure from Ultimo Retiro

We left Ultimo Retiro at about 1.15 p.m. the rain having cleared up. Before leaving I called Crichlow again. It was to ask him if the double *cepo* that Aurelio Rodriguez had used at Santa Catalina for flogging victims raised off the ground, with the more able "leg stocks ... so as to fit children" was still in existence, as, if so, we might photograph it. Gielgud and I had been regretting that we had not photoed the *cepo* here, which is such a big one. Crichlow said that Rodriguez had had those stocks destroyed when "Capt. Whiffen was coming, and then added that it was he (Crichlow) had made it "to the plan of Rodriguez". I said — "You must be quite a good carpenter then", and he grinned, and said "I make all the

[168] Hardenburg *op. cit.*, pp.243–50.

furniture here, sir," pointing to the strong wooden benches with moveable backs, on which we had been sitting at meals every day. It is for this extra work that Jiménez is giving him 20 soles (£2) per month over his ordinary pay of 50 soles per month. Then, as we were leaving, I said to Crichlow in a loud voice, so that all could hear "Remember, any illegal work, such as flogging Indians or beating them or maltreating them, you are not to perform. It is illegal to ask you and illegal for you to do it, and is a punishable offence, and if you are ordered to do it you must refuse, and at once inform me if I am still here, or if not Sr. Tizon, and write to the Consul in Iquitos." Everyone heard this, I think, certainly the *empleados* and Jiménez did, for they were standing close at hand.

Jiménez accompanied us to the beach to wave affectionate farewells with his white military cap. I raised mine to this thrice, triple murderer! And shook hands, too! His face is not so bad — that of a sturdy, rather good-tempered ruffian, strong, healthy, brown and courageous with a thick-set, very strong and sturdy body. He looks well under 30.

I don't know what the Barbadians must think of me — of us all — shaking hands affably with this man whom they saw commit the most appalling crimes, but it will be made clear to these simple dependants later on that we are not so black as this would paint us.

Arrive Puerto Peruano — more starving Indians

We steamed well down stream to Puerto Peruano, arriving there at 4.34, when we find about 40 Indians — boys and men — sent by O'Donnell from Entre Rios for our baggage. We have some 60 loads I believe, so Bruce tells me, so part of the goods must be left behind. These poor beings were starving — literally starving, as we dined about 7 they sat around on their bare haunches with gleaming eyes and shining, smiling teeth, giving the most hungry looks imaginable at every mouthful. I could not stand it, and by stealth I slipped all the food of my plate as each course was handed me, and collected it up beside me and gave it to two small boys of the group, who divided every morsel with their friends. Tizon ordered them rice and beans, which were boiled subsequently for them.

To bed with bandaged eye

I turned in very early in the house where I slept before — the two-roomed palm house, and it poured with rain. The 40 Indians and the others merely slept under these rooms on the ground or on the billets of firewood stored there for the launch. This firewood constantly stored here is another of the tasks laid on these wretched people, without the shadow of any payment.

My eye continues very bad and is bandaged tight over, so that I have only the right eye to see by.[169] Slept fairly well in spite of some very long-legged mosquitoes, just like gnats or daddy long-legs. They did not bite but buzzed.

ON FROM PUERTO PERUANO — WEDNESDAY 12TH OCTOBER 1910

Caravan through the forest to Entre Rios

We left Puerto Peruano before 7 — the Indians taking the loads given them without the slightest discussion or refusal or disorder. The most obedient, docile carriers I've ever seen, and God knows I saw enough giving out of loads and starting of caravans in Africa. Here never a murmur — and they are half-starved too. The others started quickly, but I came more slowly with Tizon, as my eye is under a heavy bandage and the road very bad. Up hill and down hill and across streams innumerable flowing from right to left into the Igaraparaná or Coddicé as the Huitotos call it. The land rises often 100 feet or more and then sinks again to another stream — often with steps and big trees and stakes laid — all the work of the Indians. Every stream is well bridged. Some have five big trees laid parallel and notched so the feet won't slip — and often a liana rope banister. This road alone is a big work — seeing too that the wretched workers on it are drawn from far-off homes, many hours away, and get no scrap of pay and only just the food to sustain a starved existence — even when they get food at all, and are not forced to look for leaves and "seeds" in the forest. I saw many of our carriers plucking seeds to-day.

We arrived after 4 hours of this at a deserted Indian house — called a *maloca* in Brazil. This was of the Monones Indians, but they abandoned it (we learned subsequently from O'Donnell) on

[169] The handwriting in Casement's genuine journal is quite clearly affected by his increasing eye problem and his pages of pencilled script become unusually untidy and scrappy during this journey through the forest when his vision was clearly impaired by his ocular infection. The corresponding entries in the *Black Diary* for 12–13 October are neatly written in black ink — the tightly-packed script shows no signs whatsoever of the shakiness evident in Casement's own hand. Future handwriting experts seeking to make a judgment about the *Black Diaries* should begin with a comparison of these days. On the strength of handwriting analysis alone of these parallel entries, it becomes extremely difficult to believe that the same man wrote both journals.

account of the robbery of their food committed by *blancos*, *empleados* and Indian rubber carriers going and coming from Matanzas, Atenas and Entre Rios to Puerto Peruano.

The house is not so big as the Indian house at Occidente, but is clean and nice. No *chacara* round it — the undergrowth is growing up fast. We met three Indian women on the path, one with a little boy of 6 or so clinging round her neck and asleep. She, the gentle-faced mother (an elderly woman, and, of course, stark naked) carrying her tired boy. They all look semi-starved.

Lunch at Monones

At Monones we found a horse and mule sent from Entre Rios under one of the empleados named Barbolini. After lunching here and a siesta we went on at 1.15 for Entre Rios — Fox and Bell riding — I came last on purpose, as I can walk quicker, and on the way Bishop told me that last night when I was in bed down at "the port" some Indians had told him, in secret that they had been flogged quite lately, and that this man Barbolini was the executioner.[170] One boy had shown his buttocks with raw marks, and Bishop had shown him to Mr Fox. I was glad of this, and told him always when he got a chance to convince any member of the Commission — and Mr Tizon too — of the recent character of these "punishments". We got to Entre Rios soon after 3, about 2 hours from Monones. The whole road from Puerto Peruano is styled a 7 hours march, but could be done by any good walker in 4 or 4 ½ hours. I reckon it from 12 to 14 miles. The first part, say 8–9 miles, is in the watershed of the Igaraparaná, all the streams flowing into it — and then after Monones a flatter stretch occurs and the streams flow from left to right clearly into the Cahuinari — a big tributary of the Caquetá which rises, we are told, just here at Entre Rios.

---

[170] Casement is clearly told this story by Bishop on his march on Wednesday 12 October, but the brief reference to the story appears in the *Black Diary* in the previous day's entry: "... An Indian recently flogged within 30 days by Barbolini — the white executioner at O'Donnell's. Showed himself to Bishop who showed him to Fox."

V

ENTRE RIOS

Description of Entre Rios and ingenuity of Indian buildings

Entre Rios Station is in the centre of a great clearing of fully 200 or more acres — probably 300 acres. The forest walls it round — a silent arch of dark trees, and in their midst this 1 mile or 1½ mile in diameter circle of clearing. Some of it is planted, but most of the cleared ground is neglected — the felled trees lying where they fell, or were burnt — in other places the undergrowth springing up again. There are a good many acres, however, under *cassava* (here called *yuca*), sugar cane and maize. The station house is a fine building — not so big as Ultimo Retiro — in the middle of this great clearing. Like the rest, it is entirely the work of the Indians. Not a nail used in construction. The big beams and trees of the uprights and rafters are peeled of their bark and lashed always with a tough liana called "Spanish soga", but by the Huitotos. The thatch is splendid — cool and dry and of immense extent. This is the leaf of a swamp palm.

The walls and floors are made of the bark of the *frona* palm, so called in Quichua[171] — which is, I believe, the *Ariartea Orbigniana.*[172] We saw immense quantities of it on the banks of the Putumayo, but have not seen it so much here. It is always cool.

---

[171] Quichua (or Quechua) is the name for the family of languages spoken by the Andean tribes of South America, including the Incas. Quichua is still spoken in increasingly isolated pockets in the Peruvian Amazon

[172] Named after the nineteenth century French explorer Alcides D'Orbigny. Casement's botanical knowledge was quite considerable given that he had no formal training and was self-taught and certainly botany remained one of his side-line interests throughout his Putumayo voyage. See M.J.P. Scannell and O. Snoddy, *Roger Case-ment's Contribution to the Ethnographical and Economic Botany Collections in the National Museum of Ireland* in *A Journal of Irish Studies*, Vol III No.4 (Winter 1968). Although this deals mainly with his time in the Congo, it establishes him as an important amateur botanist. Casement was also a good friend of Augustine Henry (1857–1930) who spent many years plant collecting in China and from his frequent references he was clearly familiar with the English naturalists who travelled in South America during the nineteenth century.

The floors of this open-work bark are light and airy, and give to the tread. The houses are splendidly built, and are only another tribute to the skill and knowledge of these poor Indians. This house at Entre Rios must have fully a dozen rooms in it — a wide verandah all round — and, like that at Ultimo Retiro, it is built something like a ship, though of less solid structure. In Ultimo Retiro the "bows" pointed due West over the river, 50 feet below, while here the "Bows" front due north across the great wall of forest that bounds the clearing towards the Japura.

O'Donnell

O'Donnell[173] came down the steps to greet us as we arrived, and Tizon presented us one by one. He is far and away the best looking agent of the Company we have yet seen, quite healthy-looking and clear-eyed. His reputation in my "Police News" is also much better. He appears here and there by name among "the chief criminals of the Putumayo" but never with any single specific act of crime alleged against him.

He is merely lumped up with the others, by two or three of Hardenburg's correspondents, as those who have committed atrocities. One of these writers, the M.G. of page 109, whom I find from S. Lewis is Marcial Gorries, says in his letter of 16th July 1907 to Dr Saldana Rocca, which letter appeared in *La Felpa* of Jan 5th & 12th 1908, as follows:

"The principal criminals are the Chiefs of Sections:

Armando or Felipe Norman
José Inocente Fonseca

[173] Some have tried to suggest that O'Donnell became one of Casement's sexual conquests see Robin Furneaux, *The Amazon; The Story of a Great River* (Hamish Hamilton 1968) p.193: "In his journey up the Amazon he left a long trail of male conquests behind him, white, black and brown from Pará to Andokes. His own account shows him having affairs with Sealey and Leavine among the Barbadians and, more discreditably, with O'Donnell, the rubber collector." Although Casement certainly found O'Donnell the least offensive of the Section Chiefs he had encountered on his journey thus far, it is wholly untenable that his feelings towards the man went beyond this. O'Donnell had at least three wives and as many children by different women. On his return to the Amazon in 1911, Casement found O'Donnell living in Barbados and about to marry the daughter of a local British dignitary. Despite O'Donnell's reformed ways Casement tried to have him arrested and put on trial for his part in the Putumayo atrocities. O'Donnell eventually escaped to New York and was never heard of again. The only thing Casement seems to have liked about O'Donnell was his Irish name, and that he hadn't turned quite as brutal as his Putumayo colleagues.

Abelardo Aguero
Augusto Jiménez
Aristides Rodriguez (he is dead — died on way from Europe, I learn)
Aurelio Rodriguez (now in Iquitos in deep mourning)
Alfredo Montt
Fidel Velarde
Carlos Miranda
Andres O'Donnell

With the exception of O'Donnell who has not killed Indians with his own hands, but who has ordered over 500 Indians to be killed, all the rest — every one of them — have killed with their own hands, the least criminal like Jiménez ten in two months; others like Fonseca more than 100 in one year."

Bishop's view of O'Donnell;

I mentioned O'Donnell's better character to Bishop who spent over a year here with him. He came at end of 1908 or beginning of 1909 he says, and left this section for Ultimo Retiro early in January 1910. He did not see O'Donnell kill anyone during this year, nor did he know of his own sight any Indian killed by his order in the Section during that time — but floggings! These, he states, went on just the same as elsewhere, and he himself flogged here lots of Indians. He has heard O'Donnell send *muchachos* to kill Indians in the forest if the rubber was not forthcoming, but does not know if anyone was killed. He says O'Donnell may be better than the others, but that he is just the same — that he does anything to get rubber — and I have known him get 2000 sols (£200) in a quarter from the rubber these poor Indians bring in.

In the room I am given — the best in the house — Bishop points out that the door and washstand and all the pieces of rough furniture there, and says he made them all — every one of them — and never got a cent for it, but had to go on "commissions"[174] too to hunt the Indians. He produced a pair of trousers, things that in Whitechapel would not be bought for more than 3/- by any sane work-lad, and states these cost him 25/- (£2/10/-) at Chorrera! I intend taking them home with his accounts. So here we have the only evidences of civilization, the fine big house and the cleared

[174] Although Casement himself was on a Commission, the title was already used in the Putumayo to describe the parties of company employees who set out to conquer and enslave Amazindian communities.

ground, due to the unpaid, beflogged Indians, and the "furniture" of this dwelling due to the Barbados employé, who is robbed out of his salary of a few pounds a month and is not paid for the extra work at all, while the Chief he serves makes hundreds of pounds per annum out of the illegal uses he puts these people to, to coerce and maltreat the surrounding Indians.

I insisted on paying the eight Indians who had carried my things up from Puerto Peruano, and got 8 tins of Salmon and Beef out of the store from O'Donnell to pay for it in Chorrera when I settled my account with the Company — the poor beings were delighted!

Casement's eye

As I was ill, and my eye very bad, I did not go to dinner, but lay down right away in this guest room.

Bishop reports

Bishop came in the evening and said this brute Barbolini, who has been the chief flogger of the Indians, had got drunk after dinner and was kicking up a row with him. Barbolini accused him of "telling on them" to me, and that now we wanted to turn the Peruvians out for the things they had done to the Indians, while he, Bishop, had been as bad as any of them, and had done just as bad things. Bishop said he came to tell me, but that he had told Barbolini he would not talk with him in his actual state.

He added that all he had done he had done under compulsion as already confessed — but he had hidden nothing from me of his own misdeeds, but that he had not even deliberately killed an Indian. Barbolini, he said, had — he had seen him at Urania long ago (this station is now abandoned) cut off an Indian's head. He had wanted Bishop to do it, and he refused, and then he called a *muchacho*, and the boy's heart failed him when he had begun to hack the neck, so Barbolini took the machete from him and finished the job. This was long ago, soon after he, Bishop, had joined the Arana gang, probably in 1906.

Martin Arana and the Section staff

There is a man named Martin Arana[175] here among the staff who is, so Bishop says, "a brother of Julio Arana" — I think it means a

[175] During a journey across northern Peru in 1994 the editor met and interviewed a man called Martin Arana in Rioja, the birthplace of Julio Cesar Arana. In physical appearance he looked strikingly like Julio Cesar Arana. This Martin Arana claimed

half-brother (by an unwedded woman); possibly only a cousin. He is a sort of servant — looks after the store, gives out food and cleans lamps etc., also makes cocktails. He has a look, certainly of Lizardo Arana, but is much younger.

The staff of this section I find is the following :

Chief — Andrés A. O'Donnell. 3 Soles per arroba & 7%

Sub-Chief — Juan B. Rodriguez 50 cts per arroba & S/80 — (Now at Occidente)

Florentino Santillon 125 S/ (£12.10/-) per month — (Actually at Atenas)

Martin Arana	80 S/ (£8) per month here
Abel Ortiz	70 S/ (£7) "
Basilio Cama	60 S/ (£6) "
Pedro Garcia	50 S/ (£5) "
Abel Valle	50 S/ (£5) "
Maximo Barbolino	70 S/ (£7) "
Eusebio Pinedo	60 S/ (£6) "
Miguel Castillo	50 S/ (£5) "

Not one of these scoundrels does a hand's time of useful work, be it remembered — and here we get a wages bill of over £60 a month without the huge commission the Chief gets of 4 Soles or 8/- per arroba (say 33lbs) of rubber and the 7% whatever that means; or Rodriguez 1/- per arroba and 80 soles. It is clear there is very great waste here of the Company's money — or rather of the poor Indians money — for they supply all. The rubber pays for it all — and they house and feed this gang of idle ruffians into the bargain. This is merely a centre of terrorization — that is all. The rubber is collected from a certain area of the forest here, and then goes down to Chorrera, say every 4 months (at end of each *fabrico*) and the "payment" is made from Chorrera. This "store" has merely the few things the station needs, or O'Donnell orders for his own wants. I've not seen it yet — as the door is a closed one, and Arana keeps the key. It is really outrageous to see this handful of lazy cut-throats armed to the teeth and living in absolute idleness on the whole of the surrounding population. All these men, except O'Donnell and Arana, go barefooted, and are dressed

that he was directly descended from Julio Cesar Arana through his brother Martin Arana. He said that he had other relations living in the U.S. and Switzerland. Even today the Arana family remains a powerful force in Rioja where they own the main hotel and an ice-cream parlour.

like "beachcombers". All have "wives" and several of them children by these poor women. O'Donnell has a "Harem" apart — a house like Velarde's in the compound.

There is a circle of fine popuna palms round the house and some very fine bananas.

O'Donnell's map

O'Donnell has been here at Entre Rios seven years. He is now 27 he says, and left Lucia in 1901, when he could have been only 17. He speaks Huitoto fluently — better than anyone else in the Company's service, so Gielgud and Tizon say. He produced a sketch map[176] of his section this afternoon which is interesting, and which I should much like to copy. It was drawn by himself in 1908 and shows the "houses" of each Indian sub-tribe (or "nation") in his section, with the paths and principal streams. The Cahuinari rises quite close to the north of this, and flows some 250 yards below the house on the East, down through the cleared ground. The bathing place of the *blancos* is down there — a dressing house by the stream which is 4 feet deep. Even to go down to this stream everyone carries his rifle! It is "a custom" O'Donnell says — and dates from the days when the Indians used to attack them. "Before they learned to work — now they are quiet, and very content — muy contentos!" I did not express any doubt. On the map he has places marked four crosses showing where "los Indios" had burned "houses of the Colombians" — and then a red patch showing where the "last rising" took place against him — and another patch quite close to the house — only a few miles away to the north where he had "fallen into an ambuscade." I only said "more power to the Indians", but as he is not an Irishman, in spite of his name, he did not follow.[177]

He has been shot at here while bathing down at the bath house — but that was in the bad days before the Indians took to *trabajar*. Since they adopted working rubber for him they are very happy and content and don't shoot any more at their patriarchal imported High Chief.

There are a great number of women here. Indian "wives" and water girls like those at Occidente — the place is more

[176] This sketch map is still to be found amongst the Casement Papers in {N.L.I. MS13,087}.

[177] Casement here makes his first proper connection between the plight of the Indians and the plight of the Irish, whom he clearly considered to be an oppressed tribal people.

"respectable" than Ultimo Retiro — that was the absolute pirate ship without pretence. Here the plantations, the bananas and palm trees close up to the houses — the evidences of cultivation and the superior appearances and address of O'Donnell certainly create a favourable impression after the recent horrors we have been living with — the snake-like Velarde and the burn-'em-alive Jiménez.

It was at this Station last year that Bishop was when Gielgud came round inspecting the books. He used to clean Gielgud's gun — O'Donnell had the prisoners cleared away when Gielgud came — some of them — four or five were actually locked up in a room near the kitchen, Bishop says. The kitchen is always detached out here and communicates with the dwelling house by a raised bridge level with the verandah.

We intend staying here several days I believe. I heard the others at Bridge as I gradually fell asleep. Eyes both bandaged all night.[178]

ENTRE RIOS, THURSDAY 13TH OCTOBER

Early morning

Up early and a very heavy day. Eye better and took bandage off and started writing hard right away. Visited the rubber store and some enormous sausages of rubber and bigger loads than any I have seen yet either at Naimenes, Occidente or Ultimo Retiro. I must get some weighed. The *cepo* here is a fine one — 24 foot holes — or leg holes — larger than either Occidente or Ultimo Retiro, with a central head hole. Bishop says he once saw a woman put in the head hole. She was one of the "girls" of the house, and she "stole" some food from the plantation around, so O'Donnell had her necked in.

As to the going down to the stream with rifles, there is an interesting notice on the Store Room door on the verandah here close to my bedroom.

It is an *Aviso*:

Advertencia

Es prohibido que los empleados vayan a banares e a lavar ropa sin avisa antes el jefe.[179]

---

[178] Casement here realises the fear of having "a complete breakdown of eyes in the wilds of the Amazon forest." {see Letter to Tyrrell 14 August 1910}

[179] It is prohibited for employés to bathe or to wash clothes without notifying the Chief of Section.

Entre Rios — en 25 de Avril de 1905
(Sg) Andrés A. O'Donnell

This was during the "state of siege" when these surrounding placid rubber workers were taking pot shots at their benefactors who were teaching them the beauties of labour.

Statement of James Chase — Commission examine O'Donnell

I got James Chase into my room to make his statement while the Commission out on the verandah were examining O'Donnell. Chase had said to me in Occidente that he had something he wished to lay before me, and I told him I would hear it later on. This rest here is a good occasion, so it happened that I was hearing from Chase of his experience at this very station of Entre Rios while O'Donnell was lyingly telling the Commission that no Indian had been "flogged for four years"; that they were "muy contento" etc.

Chases's statement is dreadful. I think in some way the worst yet, and his record of the awful crimes he witnessed only four months ago on the "*Commission*" after Katenere,[180] the brave Boras chief who killed Bartolomé Zumaeta in May last year, would sweep the Company to perdition. While O'Donnell was lying on the verandah, Chase was telling me, almost within their hearing, quite so if they had not been talking, of how he had seen O'Donnell have an Indian murdered from this very verandah by one of his "boys" right under the eyes of the whole station. Chase cannot recall dates, but this occurrence was before 1907, as he came here

[180] Of all the Indians, Casement came to sympathize and identify most with Katenere {B.B. p.45–46} "Perhaps the bravest and most resolute opponent the murderers had encountered had met his death only a few months, or even weeks, before my arrival in the district. This was a Boras cacique or *capitán* named Katenere...This man...but young and strong, lived on the upper waters of the Pamá...He had, from necessity no doubt, consented to bring in rubber, and for some time had worked voluntarily for Normand, until, through bad treatment, he, like so many others, had fled. He had been captured later on, along with his wife and some of his people, and confined in the stocks of the Abisinia district, to undergo the taming process. While thus himself a prisoner, his wife, so I was informed by a Peruvian white man holding a well–paid post in the Company's service, had been publicly violated before his eyes by one of the highest agents of the Syndicate ... Katenere escaped, aided, I was told, by an Indian girl, who lifted the top beam of the *cepo* when no one was looking. He not only got off, but succeeded then or later in capturing some Winchester rifles from *muchachos* of the Abisinia district. With these he armed others of his clan, and thenceforward waged an open war against the whites and all the Indians who helped them or worked rubber for them ..." See entry for 31 October

on foot from Chorrera before the launch *Veloz* was put on the river, and that I find took place on the 7th May 1907. I was interrogating Chase all fore-noon — long after the Commission had ended.[181]

Conversations in the afternoon

I told Barnes and Fox, in afternoon, of what Chase had related. Both said they knew O'Donnell was lying about the flogging, because they knew of the men recently flogged by Barbolini, and we have decided to get one of these with the freshest marks on him and bring him before Tizon and O'Donnell and ask when these marks were given. All the Indians are coming in for a dance tomorrow, and I am telling Bishop to look out for these men and bring them to me. Fox seems deeply moved at last, and said it was a sense of duty alone kept him going at all — to end this happy state of things. He will speak out to the world, he says, if Tizon fails to reform or Arana goes back on Tizon. Arana is clearly the danger. He knows and knows all and when he knows we have captured Tizon and that he is determined to end the atrocious slavery of the Indians, Arana may kick and kick Tizon out. In that event the English Company smashes at once, the FO will be at complete liberty to publish my report, and Fox says he will let himself loose on the world too — nothing will keep him back. He will only keep silent to give Tizon and the Company a chance. If they fail, and the thing goes back into the hands of Arana and the Iquitos clique and of these bandits here, then the whole world must be moved and Lima compelled to intervene.

Such is poor old Fox's plan now. I got more statements from Bishop in the afternoon, down by the Cahuinari. I went there for quiet and took him and the camera, pretending to photo but really to question him further. He told me more to-day of Francisco, Bartolomé Zumaeta and many more, which I noted down as he spoke and will use from time to time to make things clear.

In the evening we had a lot of details about the Indians from O'Donnell, who knows them well. Very interesting indeed, and I wish I could have taken them down verbatim. I will try and recall them and put them down in a special note I am preparing about the Indians and their customs.

---

[181] Chase first gave evidence at La Chorrera on 23 September.

I played a rubber of Bridge tonight, the first for a week nearly, but turned in early. Tomorrow we should have lots of Indians at the Dance.

ENTRE RIOS — FRIDAY 14TH OCTOBER

Thinking ahead

We are a month to-day away from Iquitos, and my work is nearly done. I gave Tizon a list of the remaining Barbados men who are to be called in to Chorrera by end of this month so that I may see them there. We go to Matanzas from here, where are two Barbados men one of whom, Levine, has been there with Normand from the very first. Bishop says this man could tell very much if he liked, but he thinks he may be as bad as the men over him, by this time, and that like King,[182] the murderer at Encanto, in Loayza's confidence, he may be bribed to confidential secrecy. I can make him speak if I like, but it does not matter much now, as we practically know all. Fox confirmed yesterday that he was quite "full up" and accepted all, he saw through the whole thing and needed no more proof. He said I had done my work here — as on the Congo — and I might rest assured that I had convinced him. Thank God! it is indeed, providence that has moved some power to send us all here, in time maybe to save the remnant of these persecuted people.

Number of dead Indians

Gielgud admitted last night, at dinner, to me, that he knew "the Indians were very much reduced in numbers" in the Company's "property". The first time he has said anything so damaging. I had said it was clear to me that Mr Tizon's estimate of 14,000 was excessive — at least I thought so — and I put them only at 10,000. He said there were more than that because he had data of the "workers" in each section. That of course, I did not posses, but there was not doubt they had decreased considerably. Arana, the scoundrel, put them at 40,000 in his lying prospectus.

I have been busy writing all day to day from early morning, taking further statements from Sealy and trying to test Whiffen's and other statements when these referred to Abisinia and Morelia.

The remaining Barbados men, after the two in Matanzas whom I shall see in a few days, are four at Sabana (under Fonseca) two at Santa Catalina (under Serninano) and at Abisinia. These eight men

[182] See above, Section I p.33.

are to be awaiting my return to Chorrera by the end of this month, and I expect another royal tussle there, as I am determined to get the truth out of them. Macedo will have been bribing or threatening, or trying all he can to get them either to lie or deceive me .

Peruvian types

The Peruvians I find, hate confrontations of accusers and accused. We Northerners like it. It is the only way of thrashing a matter out and getting to the truth. They prefer letters and secret intrigue behind one's back. The lower class Peruvian half-caste is a cur; the higher class are good like Tizon or the Prefect; while the lowest class, the Indians and Cholos, are fine fellows. They are really Peru, the backbone of the country. It is that "blanco" type that pulls down the nation, the people with the skins of whiteness only, and certainly not the hearts of Indians. The Zulus were proud of their colour, they honoured black, their Chiefs were "the great, great black one" — a man had a black heart — and we speak of a "white man" meaning an honourable man by it. Here a "blanco" can mean only a scoundrel, and to the Indian a murderer. These three Barbados men with me have proved themselves far straighter, honester and straighter than any Peruvian we have met. They have told the truth, under great stress of fear, (and shame too, I hope) have accused themselves and have manfully stuck to their guns — while the one "whiteman" the Commission were to rely on (Garrido), and whom they paid £20 a month to, turned tail at the first confrontation and revealed himself a coward and a liar.

Sealy came just now to say that the man Pinedo, here on the staff, was with him at Ultimo Retiro, and was a member of the recent Commission to the Caquetá when Crichlow went with Jiménez. Crichlow had declared to me that no one was killed in this raid, and Sealy says that Pinedo has twice, last night and this morning, told him of how Aquiléo Torres killed an Indian boy on the road back, and that Jiménez, Crichlow, Reuben Phillips (the other Barbadian on the expedition) and the rest of them saw it done. The boy was tired and Torres called him, and putting the muzzle of his Winchester out to him, told him to blow down the barrel as if for a joke, and when the muzzle was in the boy's mouth he pulled the trigger and killed him. I said I should see to it later on.[183]

[183] {B.B. p.92. Pinedo's statement to Casement and Commission}

Indians arrive for a dance

The Indians were coming in to the dance, but later than anticipated. O'Donnell said to get a good dance needed 10 to 15 days notice, as many of the men were out at rubber-getting and their wives would not come without them, and also it took time to paint themselves nicely. Parties came in from 3 o'clock on to 5.30, just as at Occidente, save that there were more here to-day I think, and many more necklaces of teeth — some of these of "tigers", jaguars and pumas, were splendid, and I saw Indian men in two cases hide them as they passed us. One of them, the Captain, an elderly keen faced Indian, explained to O'Donnell that he had hidden his necklace because it might be taken from him. Bishop said this was constantly done, everything the Indians had was taken, their spears, all their bows and arrows, their "gods", and these splendid collars of teeth. I bought several for tins of powder and tins of meat, the recipients of the powder being so delighted that they gave me their feather arm rings "on top", and said they would bring more teeth when I returned from Matanzas, as this was good business. A flask of powder is worth about 6d it is sold even at Chorrera at 2/-, and here its value to these poor beings is enormous. I am confident many a man has supplied a whole fabrico of rubber — the collection of 75 days, varying from 30 to 40 kilogs — for this, or less. The rubber in the Store here is often of enormous size, the lump brought in for each *puesta* of 15 days being here the biggest I have seen yet. I intend weighing them on first chance. The purchase of collars of teeth went on all evening, by Bishop and Chase and Sealy acting for me — and sometimes for the "commission" — Barnes and Bell &c.

A lot of the ladies were stark naked and beautifully painted, even better than at Occidente, the young girls too, and down even to children. About half the men and lads (or less) were nude, that is to say in their *fonos* only, and they too, were stained black in various patterns, or painted pale green or red. Many of the men, I fear most, had the trashy and dirty raiment that is paid to them by the Company, a vile flannelette shirt (worth 1/-) and a pair of soiled pantaloons, worth certainly less than 2/6d, being a garment fit for a *Capitan* here, and the payment fully for 50 kilogs of rubber. The naked and painted men with their *fonos* (called "agafe" in Huitoto) of white bark tightly clothing their loins, their pale bronze figures elaborately and artistically designed in violet-black stains, with bars of red and yellow, where they had kept their long black hair were almost handsome and certainly imposing figures, beside their diminutive wives, whose tiny but shapely bodies were beautifully painted, and their calves covered with rubber of some kind, and then a yellow ochre paint like cork thrown on it, just as in ships one finds the iron ceilings often painted with broken chips of cork. The different "tribes" or families of Indians came from their houses in the forest, and wait a few hundred yards away until the whole party is united, when each family makes its entry to the house giving the dance. The manguaré has been distributing its invitations for long before, "come, come" one single resonant bass note, followed no doubt by specific directions. No tribe wishes to arrive first, the object is to make your entry when the House has already got some arrivals to witness your coming. This is very much like our smart set at home, coming late to the ball or theatre. When the family or tribe has united all its members, and the women see that their painted limbs are renovated after the march through the forest and the last touches given to feathers and other decorations, the party comes forward at a run towards the house giving the dance.

The women and children tip lightly in, the men, with bunches of trees and ferns, palm fronds, or anything "pretty" they may have plucked on the way, then assault the house with loud cries (firing off their guns as well) and as they pour in at the door they flog the low eaves and thatch and make a tumultuous eruption upon their hosts and the assembled guests. This sham fight is, I take it, to show their independence. They come to dance to-day in friendly gathering, but they could come if they liked as attacking warriors. The survival of an old past no doubt. The new-comers join the dance, and so it grows with each new party or "nation" that comes on the scene.

Today O'Donnell said at 6 o'clock there were over 500 people present, and fully 200 men he thought with their wives and children. These latter were few for so many parents, and in one case a tiny baby only 8 days old was carried on its slender mother's back in a fibre thong, and slept and cuddled throughout her prolonged movements. This dance was in full-swing by 6 or 7, and after dinner we went out again and visited it. The songs and chants varied constantly and the step with them, and often the manguaré broke in with a sudden call or beating time movement.

No food is given to these guests of the Company, invited many miles to this worthless entertainment, yet to them it is clearly a great pleasure. Since the coming of the Arana marauders all their social customs and home life have been destroyed, and no dances are permitted now save when the Chief of Section allows. These are usually now held at each fabrico, when the five puestas or deliverings of rubber are completed. Then all the Indians of the Section have to come in to make up their quarter's delivery of rubber and carry it to the nearest river port, or La Chorrera, as the case may be. On these occasions, which vary at each Section, and may number from three to even four in the year (the fixed period is 75 days per fabrico generally speaking) the assembled Indians are "permitted" to have a dance in the Section Indian house. To-day's dance, like that at Occidente, was purely an honorary one, got up in our regard. The Indians apologised to O'Donnell on arrival, that, owing to the short notice, they had not been able to paint themselves as nicely as they would otherwise have done. Many of the men brought in gifts of game, birds they had shot on the way, and smoked monkeys, a dreadful sight. The poor things, shrivelled and dried, with grinning teeth and smoke blackened hands are trussed and carried in along with *pavons* (peacocks) and other wood birds. One crested bird they offered O'Donnell was a very handsome woodpecker.

Treatment of women

Their gifts of food are generally annexed by the "ladies of the household" I find. They certainly were to-day. I counted eighteen of these ladies in the first "cotillion" of the early arrivals at the dance. This party was made up of seventeen men and seven boys, nine women, from the forests, and then these eighteen ladies of the household, including the actual three Mrs. O'Donnell's Mères, and I hesitate to say how many Mrs. O'Donnell's who have not yet given this proof of devotion. There are three young O'Donnell children by separate mothers, and Bishop says he knows of five other ladies of the Establishment who reside in the harem across the compound. My laundry, as usual, is in their hands. Blondini, the executioner, has two "wives" here in the house, and each of the other men has his. Young Rodriguez (who belongs to this Section, but is temporarily lent to Occidente) has three wives. All these are taken, by force, or death, or simple appropriation from the surrounding Indian "nations". As a rule, an Indian wife is not taken thus, although many cases have been related to me, of Jiménez or Fonseca, or Montt, taking wives by force and killing the husbands who resisted, but as a rule I gather the actual wife of a full grown Indian man is — well, not respected, but left to him.

The reason is not solely benevolent respect for the Indian's conjugal rights. Sealy put it quite tersely this afternoon, when telling me of Aguero of Abisinia having nine "wives" when he was stationed there, and taking as many women as he pleased, just as Whiffen described in his letter to FO.

"Did he take wives of Indians?" I asked.

"No sir, not their wives."

"Why not?" I asked.

"Well," he said, "If you takes an Indian's wife he won't work *caucho*."

"But you flog him, you can make him work *caucho* by flogging."

"No, not if you takes his wife, he won't work *caucho* then, you may flog and flog, he will die, some of de Indians loves their wives very much."

What a pitiable people to think of it! The one provision that saves even their wives from the lust of these Satraps is the greed of their men, they cannot get the rubber, or as much rubber, if they don't leave the poor hunted Indian his one wife, the sharer of all his miseries, but the mother of his child.

Indian Chiefs at dinner

At dinner we had the Chief of the Mimanes Indians and the Captain of the Inonokomas, who came on the verandah. The latter a very intelligent looking man, with bright piercing eyes. They sat beside O'Donnell before dinner, and he made the Captain take off his soiled and hideous pantaloons and shirt because he said these smelt after the dance.[184] This gave the Inonikoma Captain his chance. He knew, in a dim way who we all were, and that we were here to "change things". That word has gone round. So he stripped at once and stood in his *fono* and painted bronze limbs, a

---

[184] Casement here includes his own ethnographic footnote: "As a matter of fact there is no offensive odour from these Indians' skins. They have the most wonderfully clean bodies considering their conditions, and when nude one can stand in the midst of a crowd of them in the hottest hour of the day without perceiving the slightest smell. Their skins are extraordinarily dry, I have not yet seen one perspire, although carrying a heavy load through the forest on an atrocious road. They are weak and frail to the eye and to the leg under the heavy loads, but get along cheerfully and quietly without a word of complaint. As they get scarcely any food and are sent on their marches for days with literally nothing but what they can pick up, it is perhaps no wonder they do not perspire, but it is a marvel they can live and move and carry such weights. They have nothing to exude at the pores, they are chips of this old forest, dried vegetable products rather than flesh and blood."

much finer object, but he turned upon O'Donnell, who was sitting on the bench and delivered his soul. I said to Tizon:

"That seems a very intelligent Indian, he can talk quickly and is evidently saying a lot."

None of us knew a word of his rapid speech, save O'Donnell. He tried to stop him, and waved his hand, but the Captain went on with flashing eyes, and after pointing to his buttocks, now bare, but painted, and extending his hand. It was clear he was saying more than O'Donnell liked, who remarked he was a great talker, and we laughed agreement, for the Huitoto words, sharp and hard, were pouring out in a continuous stream. I felt certain this was an Indian "witness" at last, one who has got the whole Commission before him, we were all at dinner by this time — and was determined to get a pronouncement from us in the face of O'Donnell. The latter, it was clear, was ill at ease, he said the Indian was saying he was glad to see us (he didn't look it a bit!) and that once he had been O'Donnell's great enemy and had tried to kill him, but that now they were friends and he worked *caucho* for him and we were to see he got nice things for it. In fact, he was another voluble example of the "muy contentos" Indians. As soon as possible I slipped from the table under pretext of getting a cigarette and told Bishop to come and have a look at the man, and afterwards to find out from him what it really was he had been saying for our benefit. Bishop came to show me a collar of leopard teeth, as a pretext for looking at the man, and I agreed to buy it, another pretext, and when our dinner ended, I waited to hear the result of my stratagem.

What the Indian said

It was as I suspected; he was the spokesman for all. He had said that O'Donnell was working his people to death, that many had died, and now they were all being flogged for not bringing in the rubber put upon them, and they could not work harder than they did, and he wanted the flogging stopped to save his people. This was the gist of his long speech and the Muinanes chief had said the same, and further that O'Donnell had given him a "carabine" (a Winchester) but what was the use of it without cartridges, and we were to tell O'Donnell to give him cartridges, too, and to pay them better things for all the rubber they brought in. I told the others, Tizon and Gielgud had left for the dance, while we played Bridge, of what I had done in setting Bishop on the track and of what he had reported. Bishop further tells me that Blondini was sent up the road to stop any badly flogged specimens from coming into the dance. I have noticed O'Donnell eyeing the bare backs and nether parts of the unclothed Indians rather closely. He made a bad break, however, when he suggested that old Inonikomas should undress, the old chap took the bull by the horns.

Bishop's opinion of O'Donnell

Bishop, I can see, has no feeling of respect or regard for O'Donnell, he says he is not the worst, perhaps the best of this infernal crew, but that he has flogged and terrorised and caused Indians to be killed for the same pure greed of rubber. I said that I thought Julio Arana was the most guilty of all. I was amazed to see how, at once, the coarse, black face flushed, and he said with vehemence,

"Indeed he is, Sir, that's my opinion, and I've thought that always. He knew perfectly what was done here and how the rubber was got, and these men are not so bad as he is."

Fonseca he says is a maniac, a murderous maniac. He relates how, he saw him have 2 Indians taken out of *cepo* at Ultimo Retiro, two mornings running at 6 a.m. and shot for mere sport by a man called Luiz Silva at Fonseca's order. Fonseca, he said, shouted for this to be done, just like ordering morning coffee, there was no earthly reason for it. The poor wretched Indians were starving in the *cepo* and for sheer diversion, or as Bishop put it, "just for pride", he had them killed. This Luiz Silva is now dead, or rather very righteously slain by the Andokes, alongside with Bucelli, in the Caquetá country. He had murdered many Indians, Bishop states, to his knowledge.

The shooting of the two unfortunates at Ultimo Retiro by Fonseca's order was in 1906 and soon after, he, Bishop, had come there. Bishop came from Urania (now abandoned) where he had been under Martenengui. This Silva was one of the "executioners" at Ultimo Retiro, and again, later on, at Occidente, under Fonseca; and at both places Bishop states he saw him flog Indians most brutally, cutting them to pieces. The marvel to me is that so much that is good can have survived in Bishop, himself, after five years of this hellish work. He came to me today to ask who was the Consul in Manaos in 1905. I explained that there was no regular Consul there at all, but an unpaid Vice-Consul who had been for many years an agent, or the acting Agent, of Booth's S.S. Co.. He said that when he had first come there in 1905, many people had told him and the other Barbados men, that they were not going to be used as "agricultural labourers" but to go out and "fight the Indians" and that they would be killed by them. He had gone to "the Consul" in Manaos, he and others, and had complained and asked for advice and help. The Vice-Consul had said he could not help them, that they must abide by their contracts and go on. Later on, he said, he had complained to Sr. Loayza at Chorrera of the work he had to do, as he had more than once done to Macedo, and when some Barbados men were being paid off sick and sent away, he, too, had been asked to be paid off and sent back. Loayza had refused. He was not ill and was serviceable as a flogger, so he had to stay on and "do this filthy work." He had resigned himself more and more to this; had got into debt in the books of the firm, and latterly had tried to save money, to make the best of the bad job and get away with something in hand.

At Iquitos, when Pablo Zumaeta had asked him if he would not return to the Putumayo — he had brought down a good character from Macedo — he had told him that no sum would tempt him to return to the Company's service. This, he admits, was after he had spoken to me and knew that the old state of things must change. He says that one of the witnesses to the letter of Reynaldo Torres in the Hardenburg Document page who signed as "Arthur" was a young American who had been at Matanzas with Normand. He resigned and came down to Chorrera, and when Macedo pressed him to stay on and offered him better pay, this young man replied that he would have "None of your blood-stained money." So two Americans have libelled this Civilizing Company. Well done, Uncle Sam!

End of the dance and the enslaving of the Indians

Although dancing gaily and making these simulated attacks as they arrive, there is a pervading gloom about this festivity that never leaves human things on the Putumayo. Whatever it be, one sees and feels it. These rejoicing Indians are sad savages indeed. There is an absence of gaiety, of reality even, in their rejoicings, and one cannot help feeling that their dance even is "got up". Such indeed is the case; they come because they are summoned, just as they would have to do if the order had been to go down to Puerto Peruano and carry loads.

All native joy died in these woods when these half-castes imposed themselves upon this primitive people, and, in place of occasional raid and inter-tribal fight, gave them the bullet, the lash, the *cepo*, the chain gang, and death by hunger, death by blows, death by twenty forms of organised murder. One sees it in their eyes. You have only to speak suddenly to any man around, and an instant silence falls on him, and those near him who may perceive to whom you are speaking. I sent Bishop today to get two of the biggest men among the guests, to photograph, with a typical negro, Sealy, standing between.[185] I wanted to show how much bigger the stature of the negro is and illustrate the different build. Two members of the Guamaraes "family" were brought by him, with painted and designed bodies, and guns — trade shotguns — in their hands. Both looked more than disconcerted. It was not that they could not understand it, but they were afraid; there was the whole thing. To be called out from their fellows by a man they had often been flogged by and brought before the *Viracucha* (the white man) meant trouble. I told Bishop several times to reassure them, and when I had taken two photos of Sealy standing in between them they were told they might go. They went as they had come, without a word or a glance. Had I ordered them to be shot, to be cut up with machetes the thing would have been quite the same, I believe, and among the *muchachos* around, accustomed to these tasks, one could have found instant executioners. Before the white man came, if these people can be called white men, the Indians between the Putumayo and Japura must have been among the most numerous and most desirable of the Indians of the whole Amazon valley. The reasons for this one can only guess at, so little is still known of the region. I have a theory which will be developed later on when I come to deal more closely with the Indians and their customs. Of the fact of their recent numbers there is no question. It was up the Japura the Portuguese slave raiding gangs chiefly came. Lt Maw, in 1827, noted this when at Egga. This raiding for men, or rather boys and girls of the Indians, has been going on for over 100 years, and up to recent years by the Brazilians or Portuguese. Until the rise of rubber in the early nineties, and the rapid development of the trade, there was little or no attempt at organised settlement by white men in these forests. Iquitos was still a village, and the early trade in sarsaparilla,[186] "Peruvian bark",[187] &c. had scarcely disappeared

---

[185] This photograph can be found amongst the N.L.I. collection of Casement photographs and shows Sealey, wearing a hat standing between the two Amazindians.

[186] Sarsaparilla — a prickly climbing plant found in tropical America from Mexico to Peru of the genus *Smilax*. Its large aromatic roots and heart-shaped leaves were

along the main course of the Amazon. The Putumayo was known only to Brazilians, as the names of these two tributaries, Igaraparaná and Caraparaná denote. Both are Guarany[188] names. This river, the Igaraparaná, is known by the Huitotos as the Cottué, which may mean merely "the River", like Njali and Nzadi on the Congo — "the water way". The Cahuinari, too, is a Guarany name, I fancy, it is called locally. It was up this stream which enters the Japura, a long way east from this that the Portuguese and Brazilian slaving bands chiefly came, Tizon says.

The search was never for rubber, or trees, or commodities, but for men — men and women, boys and girls. They surrounded a house, set fire to it, shot down the old, and captured the young. When not strong enough to do this, they might "trade" in people, but I think it very unlikely the Indians were ever disposed to deal largely in their kith and kin, nor even to sell their enemies. They preferred killing them and possibly eating them. O'Donnell says the father of my Muinanes Chief was a "noted slave dealer with the Brazilians," but I doubt this. It sounds suspiciously like the indictment formulated against the Boras and other strong tribes who "won't work", that they are cannibals. It is like Mark Twain's grandfathers[189] — "Grandfathers are always in the wrong". The Indian, who is stout enough to resist enslavement, is always in the wrong, and therefore a "cannibal".

I have assured Gielgud that some of the nicest people I know on the Congo were cannibals.[190]

---

dried and distilled into a herbal tonic used in the treatment of psoriasis. The tropical forests of South America were widely plundered for this plant in the two hundred years before the advent of rubber.

[187] Peruvian bark was the common English term used for the bark of the Cinchona tree from which was ground a powder used as a febrifuge and in the distillation of quinine used widely in the treatment of malaria and yellow fever. In 1894 3,000,000 lbs. were shipped to England from Peru alone. While in Colombia Cinchona was the most valuable foreign export during the nineteenth century. Both Sarsaparilla and Peruvian bark were the most important commodities in the extractive economy of South America's tropical forests until the advent of the rubber boom.

[188] The Guarany language was widely used during the seventeenth and eighteenth centuries as a result of the Jesuit and Franciscan missions in southern Brazil and Paraguay. The language was given a written form and a grammar and was widely used in the proselytising of the Indians to Christianity as far north as the Amazon.

[189] Mark Twain wrote *King Leopold's Soliloquy* (1907) — a biting satirical indictment against Leopold II's Congo Free State which became a useful work of propaganda for the Congo Reform Association.

[190] Casement considered cannibalism to be in the most part a myth used to justify the process of civilization and the subjugation of the Putumayo Indians and ex-

Sealy reports

Sealy came again to say that Pinedo, the white employé here, was telling him of the misdeeds of Aquiléo Torres on the recent Commission to the Caquetá, and that he wished to tell me directly, but not to let the other white men know. It is Gusmán at Entre Rios over again. These men see that the end of the outrageous system is near and want to make terms with the incoming reform. They look on me, I presume, as the chief cause of the change portending, or rather my official enquiry is on foot. Otherwise they would be as they were with Gielgud last year, who passed through with the pleasing impression that this was a garden of Eden. He represented to them merely the existing order of things; the interests of the Company, the method of account keeping, and, although an Englishman, even Bishop never opened his lips to him. It is true Gielgud was singularly obtuse, for the naked limbs of the Indians told a tale that is obvious to any thinking, much less humane man of civilised upbringing. I told Sealy I would hear Pinedo's story some time tomorrow.

O'Donnell's Irish roots

O'Donnell is full of Indian lore, and has told us much of the habits of the Indians and their thoughts. I wish I could take it down, but I miss a good deal of his Spanish. He says his grandfather went to Spain from Ireland, and father came from Spain to Peru.[191] I

---

pressed these thoughts in his article for *The Contemporary Review*. Certainly the debate on the anthropophagous nature of the South American Indians is one that remains controversial. Casement was one of the first to try and demythify the question. For an interesting recent argument, see W. Arens, *The Man-Eating Myth — Anthropology and Anthropophagy* (O.U.P. 1979). Taussig also deals with the subject specific to the Putumayo in *Shamanism, Colonialism and the Wild Man*.

[191] The most interesting Irish–Peruvian connection regarding rubber was the figure of Carlos Fermín Fitzcarraldo (Fitzgerald), the legendary rubber baron and son of an Irish-American sea captain. Fitzcarraldo entered the lands of the Upper Ucayali river in 1879 and ten years later emerged as the overlord of the territory. In 1894, using hundreds of enslaved Asháninkas and Piros, he hauled a motor launch the *Contamna*, across the isthmus separating the headwaters of the Ucayali from those of the Madre de Dios, giving *caucheros* working the rubber rich territories of the Madre de Dios, Beni and Madeira rivers access to the cheaper markets of Iquitos. In 1897 Fitzcarraldo's empire fell following his premature death on the river and his business concerns were taken over by his partner Nicolás Suárez. His house still stands in the Plaza de Armas in Iquitos and he is buried in the town cemetery. The only known chronicle of his life is Zacarías Valdez Lozano, *El verdadero Fitzcarraldo ante la historia* (Iquitos 1944). His death is described by Tony

doubt the grandfather. It is probably further back. Still the man is certainly the best by a long way of any agent of the Company we have met, and with seven years of this cruel savagery behind him it is remarkable he has remained so outwardly untouched and with so clear and straightforward an eye. His manner, too, with the Indians is far better, and they seem to have almost an affection for him. Strange that such gentle hearts should be so abused, or rather it is not strange, but, I suppose, human nature. Were these poor savage beings like the Africans, this paltry handful of filibusterers and pirates — for the whole gang numbers only about 150 — would have been swept away, after the first few murders. But the simplicity of the Indians and their fatal obedience have been their undoing, and their childish weapons, blow pipes and toy spears, thrown three at a time in their fingers, are a poor substitute for the African battle spear and axe. The African never feared blood; he liked its flow. These child-like beings, even in their wars, took life secretly and silently with as little flow of blood as is possible. The Winchester rifle in the hands of one desperado can overawe and subdue a whole tribe here, although they are not cowards. Their humble simplicity and humility are more dangerous to them than the weapons of their enslavers.

ENTRE RIOS — SATURDAY, OCTOBER 15TH 1910

Indian building methods

Down to the Cahuinari to bathe — a nice little dressing house built by O'Donnell with steps into water — I should say built by the Indians, as is every house we have passed through. They are excellent builders and put up these huge Station houses to harbour a dozen "whites", and perhaps twice as many "wives", without a single nail used in the construction, or a single penny expended. Nails are used only when, as here at Entre Rios, rough European doors have been added to some of the rooms by the Barbadians or other civilised employées. The river has dropped a great deal since my earlier bath. Then you could dive into five feet of water — now there is but three. It is a small stream — a forest ditch or drain.

Weighing the rubber

On return I had some of the rubber *puestas* in the Store weighed, just as they have been brought in by the different individuals, and

---

Morrison in *Lizzie: A Victorian Lady's Amazon Adventure* (BBC 1985). His myth is best served however by the epic Werner Herzog films *Fitzcarraldo* and *Burden of Dreams*.

which in each case they await one more *puesta* to complete the *fabrico*. O'Donnell assisted. There is a much greater diversity in the size of the *puestas* in his Store here than I have noted anywhere else. This would seem to imply a more impartial mind on his part than with the Occidente or Ultimo Retiro managers. It looks as if he permitted to weaker members of the community a smaller contribution; that his assessment was made more in proportion to the strength and capacity of his individual "workers" and their families to bear it. All the *puestas* as they come in are placed by the man bringing them with his lot and tied up by him, like immense sausages, together in one place. Each Indian knows his load, and in addition O'Donnell knows them, and can tell at once the name of the "owner". Some are marked with the name of the Indian, or an indication to show whose they are. One large "load" was pointed out to me as being that contributed by my friend of overnight, the Chief of the Muinanes Indians. It weighed 63 ½ kilogrammes = (140)lbs, and still needs one *puesta*, to be delivered by the end of this month, to complete the *fabrico*. O'Donnell stated that he required now only two *fabricos* in the year, and that each *fabrico* at present yielded about 16,000 kilos or, say, 33,000 kilos per annum. Bishop, who was weighing the loads for me along with Sealy, said this was scarcely the truth. When he was here last year — the whole of last year he found a *fabrico* came to 24,000 kilos., and that there were nearer three than two *fabricos* in the year. O'Donnell gets now 4 soles or 8/- per arroba (Portuguese) of 15 kilos with 7% in addition. The "payment" made to an Indian, he himself told me, varied. For a very good load like this of the Muinanes Chief he might give a gun, a hammock and a pair of pantaloons. The European value of these things would be under £1, I should say, judging from the samples of each I have met with here in the hands of the Indians. The "guns" are the worst trash of the kind I have yet seen anywhere, and could not have found purchasers, at any price, in Africa. As for the hammock and pantaloons, well, I shall buy specimens at Chorrera and leave them to tell their own tale. When the final *chorizo* or sausage is brought in, the load of this Muinanes Chief will be fully 75 kilos, which, at present prices, would give fully £40 on the London market.

Transporting the rubber

All the labour of transporting this down to Chorrera falls on the unfortunate vendor, or did fall on him. To-day this burden is partly lightened by the *Veloz* being now stationed on the river. He, and his family — wife, daughter, son &c., — however, have to carry it down by the dreadful road, some 14 miles, to Puerto Peruano on such food as they can bring with them, or that O'Donnell can or will supply. What he gives comes from the plantations round the house that they themselves have been forced to make without getting one cent of payment. Thus, the handful of cassava — dried, granulated starch — and a lump of sugar-cane, which is all I have seen given here to a carrier up from the port with a very heavy load, is equally the product of their own unrewarded labour — unrewarded save by stripes.

When the *fabrico* is transported down to Puerto Peruano, on these terms, it is shipped by the bringers and their families on the *Veloz* and the big canoe or *batalon*. She tows, and some 50 or 60 of them have to go down with it to tranship the rubber again from above the rapids into the Store at Chorrera. This is even a bigger task than the carrying down to the port — although the latter is no light one and must, under all the distressing conditions that prevail of want of food, exposure, fatigue, compulsion on young and old, infirm and sick, entail many deaths in each year. Bishop says he has known men often carry 40 or even 45 kilos down to Puerto Peruano, although that is above the average, and for these frail Indians, always in a half-starved condition, could not be performed by all. Let us put the average "load" at say 30 kilos. the *fabrico* is, say, 16,000 kilogs, so that 5,333 persons or valid men must be needed for this. These have to travel, most of them, many miles before reaching Entre Rios to take up their loads. Some of the Indian families live 8 hours march away, or fully 25–30 miles of these awful forest tracks.

The fifty men who go down to Chorrera have to carry the whole of this mass of rubber from Victoria, about 1½ miles above the rapid down to Chorrera — a distance of probably 3 miles. At 30 kilos again per load the 16,000 kilos gives each man 10½ to 11 loads to carry, involving 11 journeys of 6 miles. When the rubber is unloaded and stored he will be kept at Chorrera doing any dirty or heavy work at the Station, just as the Boras Indians we found on arrival had to discharge the cargo from the 'Liberal'. He will also be compelled to load the rubber on the down-going steamer and his detention at Chorrera, including the journeys up and down the river in the launch will be not less than 7–9 days. For this he gets no pay, possibly a shirt, or a cap, or a pair of the things called "pantaloons" may be given him, in sheer benevolence before he re-embarks at Victoria to return upstream. He has not yet been "paid" for the rubber either. This function takes place on his return to Entre Rios, the fifty men who had gone down with the *fabrico* bringing back on their shoulders the goods that the Agent has ordered for this purpose. The distribution of these goods is made by the Agent on the reassembly of all his "workers" summoned for the purpose. These have by no means been having it all their own way in the interval. The women have been retained at the Station to clear up the plantation, or extend its cultivated area of maize, sugar cane, &c. &c., while the men who returned to their own homes are forced under supervision of the "rational staff" (the barefooted, rifle on shoulder, revolver on hip half-castes who draw a salary) to cultivate their patches of cassava. This the Indian man of himself does not do. It is his woman's task, while he would be hunting or fishing or doing the heavier work.

The process of civilization

But the Company objects to the habits and customs of the Indians. They are not civilised — moreover, they would not produce rubber. So the woman of the Indian household is kept at Entre Rios, or Occidente, or Atenas as the case may be, for a space of from a week to ten days to cultivate the fields of the Company, so that its staff may have cheap food, while her husband, under the "directions" of a half breed much more ignorant of agriculture than the wildest Indian in the world, is forced to plant and hoe yucca in order that his body may be fortified against the next *fabrico*, which begins right away. If this uncongenial task is not performed to the satisfaction of the *Empleado Racionale* sent to his village to chase and hunt him to it, he will not receive his "payment" (or "advance" — the terms are synonymous and transposable) for the last *fabrico* of 40 or 50 or 60 or 70 kilogrammes of rubber he has delivered to the Company — not until he has satisfied this agricultural expert. This seems to me almost the chief refinement of cruelty of this truly devilish system of cruelty. The whole thing is hard to beat, and it has been going on for years — longer than I like to think of, and will go on, I fear, until the last Indian had delivered up his last *puesta*, and, with it, his poor, starved, beflagellated ghost to the God that sent the *veracucha* to be his moral guide and friend. Alas! poor Peruvian, poor South American Indian! The world thinks the slave trade was killed a century ago! The worst form of slave trade and of slavery — worse in many of its aspects, as I shall show — than anything African savagery gave birth to, has been in full swing here for 300 years until the dwindling remnant of a population once numbering millions, is now perishing at the doors of an English Company, under the lash, the chains, the bullet, the machete to give its shareholders a dividend.[192]

Methods of transporting rubber

Later on photoed many of the men carrying sample loads as they would go on the road. These are done up in palm-stem baskets very much as on the Congo, but the load is borne on the shoulders and backs, stooping suspended by a strip of bark fibre from the forehead.[193]

I weighed another haphazard medium size load in Store still awaiting its first *puesta* and it gave 53½ kilos.. One large *chorizo* or sausage was then weighed — it came to 18½ kilos. This was the product of twenty days collecting of one Guamaraes Indian, O'Donnell said. Bishop discounted some of his statements as to payment. He had seen a man bring in two *fabricos* of each 50 or more kilogs before he got one of these cap "guns". They are the frailest things of the kind I have seen get given as trade goods. Another quite among the smallest size in the Store gave 35 kilogs. This belonged to a Mintofigis Indian and, like the others, still needed its final puesta of from 7–8 kilogs.

Physical descriptions of the Indians

Later on I measured an ordinary sized carrier — a young Indian of the Guamaraes who carried my bed the other day, and is going up with us to Andokes on Sunday. I have photoed him more than once. His measurements, I should say, are those of an average young married man.

The Indian "ladies of the Household" and those "boys" who get food from the table soon swell out and shew fine development, especially of chest and shoulders, but also their legs and arms become bigger and stronger. The poor Indian rubber collector is just like a starving native dog one finds nosing for bones round a

---

[192] Here Casement unequivocally lays the blame for this long process of genocide at the feet of the white man and latterly targets British trading interests involved with the exploitation of wild rubber resources. Casement's resentment and anger regarding British involvement in financing the slave-kingdoms of the Amazon went deeper as his investigation continued. It was a matter, however, that he could only express in private.

[193] Casement's photograph of Indians carrying rubber loads can be found in Carlos Valcárcel, *El proceso del Putumayo* p.224.

camp fire on the march. I have seen these poor beings after we had finished a meal on the road eagerly collect the very crumbs of biscuit that have dropped from the table. Before the "white man" came they were stronger and handsomer too, and perhaps the healthiest people in the world. Venereal diseases, smallpox and other ills we have bestowed, along with the weals and welts of this outrageous fortune we drag from them were formerly unknown. They grew old. There are no old people now, I have not seen one old or even elderly man or woman since we reached Chorrera, and I have seen over a thousand Huitotos by now, possibly a tenth or fifteenth of the whole people. The oldest face I have seen is that of a man of the Muinanes tribe who goes with us as a carrier on Sunday, and he is not more than 54. The reason for this is to be found in the story Labadie told me in Iquitos, of Carlos Miranda (now at Sur, only two hours from Chorrera) cutting off "the old woman's" head and holding it up by the hair as "an example" to the rest. This was because she was a "bad woman", i.e. gave the younger people bad advice. Bad advice means not to work rubber. Thus the old folk are always the first singled out. Bishop says in the Andokes country, where we go next, the old men and women were killed long ago — all Normand could get hold of. The same thing with the Boras, but these are the boldest and the strongest of the Indians the Peruvians have yet to handle in this part of the Montaña. The Boras hit back. "They don't want to work" is the cry I constantly hear going up like an accusing incense before the *maloca* of these forests. The Boras are "bad people"; they have killed white men; they kill other Boras who do want to work; they produced a Katenere who shot Bartolomé Zumaeta at the sacred task of rubber washing. Gielgud threw a fresh handful on the flame yesterday at dinner, and in comment on some remark of mine about the Boras, said "that's why they won't work." Old Fox smiled grimly and said — "No, not on the terms". The Indians who actually prefer their forest freedom to the whip, the *cepo*, the bullet and the raping of their children are spoken of in terms of reprobation as lazy, idle and worthless — and this by men who never leave their hammocks all day, and whose only "work" is to work crime. They have not cultivated a square yard of ground or done one useful thing with their hands since they came here. Their only use — their sole purpose — is to terrorise and rob. And this is the function of the paid employees; the higher staff of a great English Company! Truly Mr Arana has planted a strange rubber tree on English soil!

Interview with Pinedo

I interviewed Pinedo later on; saw him hanging around and looking at me, so I went out, and as I was not sure of his identity I asked "Are you Pinedo?" in Spanish and he at once nodded, so I told him to follow me. I had told Bell to come after, and together we took his story. It was all against Aquiléo Torres, whom he evidently hated. There were a few moral maxims about treating the Indians kindly thrown in for our benefit. I presume to give us the impression that he disapproved the lash and the cutlass of the ordinary *racionale*. Anyhow, Torres, according to him, had not only killed the Indian "boy" by inviting him to blow down the muzzle of his Winchester and then blowing his head off, but had also killed two women, for sheer brutality of sport — all this quite recently. Jiménez had kicked him out from Ultimo Retiro as impossible (the word he used, *botar*, means about that), hence his passage through Occidente on 3rd instant. He has evidently a spite against Torres, and is trying to kill two birds with one stone. I told him through Bell I should tell Mr Tizon, and that he must tell him what he has told us, to which he agreed. We left it there and returned by separate paths as I did not wish, for Pinedo's sake, that his companions should suspect he had been giving anything away to us — the intruders who are so manifestly here to upset time-honoured customs.

Lunch with the Muinanes chief

Bell told Tizon who said he would speak with Pinedo. At lunch we had the Muinanes Chief again. He had a lot of his men and other Indians have been kept back, after the Dance, from returning to their homes to carry our loads to-morrow up to Matanzas. The Muinanes Chief whose name is Hatima, looked through Fox's field-glasses, especially liking the small end which diminishes the object viewed. This, he said, is just what things look like when "we have taken Una[194] — very clear and distinct and very far off!" This was translated for us by O'Donnell. It shows perception and a

[194] *Una* refers to *ayahuasca* — the Vine of the Soul — the sacred vine that allowed the payé or shaman to enter cosmic communication. Putumayo Indians had one of the most advanced medicinal cultures of any South American Indian people and the sacred hallucinogenic *Banisteriopsis Caapi* was one of several plants used for entering different psychic regions. When mixed with *Psychotria viridis*, known as *Chacruna*, the effects of the *ayahuasca* were enhanced. [See Richard Schultes, *Vine of the Soul — Medicine men, their plants and rituals in the Colombian Amazonia* (1992).]

comparative mind. A minute later he came out with a much apter remark that caused an appalling silence.

Handling the glasses affectionately, he said, "I suppose you buy these with the rubber we produce" — O'Donnell translated it too — and I nearly laughed aloud. It was on the tip of my tongue to add, "Yes, indeed, and this lunch too that we are eating and you get none of — " but I couldn't do it for the sake of Tizon who looked really distressed. He is very unhappy, I think, at all that is being so clearly revealed to him, and I am sincerely sorry for him, altho' glad to think there is a Peruvian gentleman trying hard to set right all this great wrong, built up by his own countrymen.

Indians watch Casement writing

I had lots of Indians in the afternoon watching me writing. They came into my room just like Congo men of old and talked to me and smiled. They even bring their biscuits in, or something given them, to eat in peace. I give them lots of cigarettes which they like very much, and everything I can spare from my own tins. Poor starved, flogged and murdered people, how I pity them.

The very idea of keeping back these 40 or 50 men for our long march to Matanzas shows how absolutely enslaved they are. They came to 'a Dance' by special invitation and now they are to wait here — on very short commons — and carry our heavy loads for 10 hours thro' this awful swamp and tree-littered forest, and mighty little food for the road and not a penny of pay or reward at the end of it.

We hope to start early tomorrow. It is the first time (except from Puerto Peruano to this) I have travelled with a caravan of unpaid men; all the years in Africa, bad as I have seen them, I never knew this.

VI

MATANZAS

Before leaving Iquitos, Casement had been warned that the stations nearest the Colombian frontier were the most dangerous and of those Matanzas — the Slaughters or massacres — had the worst reputation. In a number of respects it might be compared to the "inner station" of Conrad's "Heart of Darkness" and if there is a single figure that resembles Kurtz in this journal it is Armando Normand.

THROUGH THE FOREST FROM ENTRE RIOS TO MATANZAS — SUNDAY 16TH OCTOBER

8 a.m. departure

Fox stays behind; he cannot stand these dreadful forest tracks and his leg is bad.

Our start was delayed till 8 a.m. A lovely morning — very bright sunshine and delicious blue sky — but not like Pará with its wonderful glancing light on green leaves and its radiant skies. Our 40 odd men and boys under the leadership of the Muinanes Capitan were squatting all along the verandah, each to get a handful of dried *cassava* meal — a large coarse *farinha* that the Indians make here — and a chop of sugar cane, about a foot or a foot and a half to each man. Not a very sustaining preparatory meal for a march of five hours, or say eight hours with stoppages, as we shall go. I gave the Muinanes captain a white serge suit, with large mother of pearl buttons on the jacket, that has shrunk for me. He donned it at once in great delight — "muy contento" as O'Donnell says. We were soon across the Cahuinari and slushing through the forest over many streams and some biggish rivers flowing into Cahuinari, I was told, but these are bigger than it, and it seems clear to me that the true Cahuinari cannot be the stream at Entre Rios, but rather one of those larger rivers of the forest, into one of which it flows.

(For my diary of the road, see pp.41–44 of Green Book.)

ON ROAD FROM ENTRE RIOS TO MATANZAS — MONDAY OCTOBER 17TH

(See pp. 45–50 of my green pocket book for the road diary up to near Matanzas.)

Arrival at Matanzas

After lunch at the big stream I pushed on with Bishop and Sealy and a few of the quicker Indians. A very heavy thunder-storm broke over us — a rain-storm rather — and we got soused. A perfect deluge, but it was cool and delicious, and the road improved too. The Indians plucked instantly palm fronds and big leaves and made themselves quite smart umbrellas — as much to shelter their loads as themselves — although I can well think they do not like the cold sluice on their bare and singularly dry, soft skins. But neither leaves nor true umbrellas availed anything, and I go wet with a Dublin "brolley" — the first, I'll wager, ever seen in these forests. I was a long way ahead of the rest, and after a clamber over a fallen tree across a dry stream-course — flowing, I am sure, to Caquetá at last — which was filling with the storm, I found myself at the verge of a clearing, and saw the roof of Matanzas or Andokes Station, and the Peruvian flag flying. I decided to wait for the others, rather than to go on to meet alone and be civil to this evil-reputationed man, Armando Normand, with whom I wish to have as little and as brief intercourse as possible. The Commission and Tizon arrived about 3.30., perfectly soaked, and we all went on over a knoll into the Station in the midst of the tail of the storm. Found Mr Normand away at the other Station, where he lives, La China, named capriciously like Indostan, or Abisinia — which is 10 hours away, or, say, close on thirty miles.

Casement sizes up the situation

He is said to be on a *correria* after Indians. The staff here are upset at our coming — only heard yesterday we were coming — and they sent off for Normand at once. We are received by a Señor Bustamante, the second in command, a pale-eyed man who gives a nasty impression. But he is clean in garb, and that is something after the specimens seen in Ultimo Retiro. The usual gang of scoundrels peer round corners, and I catch sight of a black Barbados face, one of the two, Levine or Lane, up here. Levine, I am told, has been here right from the first, with Normand, nearly if not quite six years. What things he must have seen, and what evil things done too during that spell! This place, along with Abisinia, are those which occur most often in the dreadful record of crime and horror compiled by Hardenburg and Normand's name probably more often than that of any other. The Commission and myself have for some time now come to the conclusion that the Hardenburg document is true. The part written by Hardenburg certainly is, and I think many of the declarations too. There are obvious exaggerations and misstatements, and often no doubt actual falsehoods, but on the whole we believe it gives a faithful enough rendering of the class of crime and the evil of the system these men were mixed up in. Nothing in the Hardenburg book exceeds in horror the account given by the two Barbados men of Jiménez burning alive the old Boras woman and the young Boras man in June 1908 — or again, the dreadful series of murders perpetrated by Vasquez only five months ago by the Pama river. Bishop tells me that he firmly believes the stories related of Normand dashing children's brains out against tree stumps and burning them alive. He declares that Donal Francis who was here for nearly two years with Normand at the beginning, has told him more than once of these things, and of the dogs tearing the bodies of the dead to pieces and bringing up an arm or leg to the house to gnaw. Donal Francis, when questioned by me before Tizon and Barnes, had only "planted yucca and sugar cane" during his year and eight months.

Bishop says he reproached him after that interview as being a coward and as bad as these murderers to lie to me for a bribe — for a "dirty bribe". Now, at last here I am in Matanzas, the centre of such dreadful things with one of the very Barbados men who has been through them all to stand the fire. I expect he will lie too, like Donal Francis.

Description of Normand's sitting room

I got Normand's sitting room given to me; it is pasted round with pictures from the *Graphic*,[195] largely dealing with the Russo–Japanese War of 1904. There are also a lot of cocottes taken from some low-class Paris paper, and several photos of brutal faced South American people — one in particular I should imagine to be Normand himself "when a boy" — it looks like a low typed East End Jew, with fat greasy lips and circular eyes.[196] There are also

[195] Popular illustrated Edwardian magazine dealing with current affairs.
[196] Despite this derogatory remark about East End Jews Casement did not generally hold the same anti-Semitic views as many of his contemporaries.

certificates from The London School of Book-keepers of 1904, giving him a certificate as "book-keeper" and a certificate from some senior school of earlier date.

Normand arrives

About 5.30 we heard a rifle shot in the woods to the South and a murmur of "Normand" was heard from the boys and servants. It was like the advent of a great warrior! He is quite a remarkable walker, Gielgud says, the best "commander" out here.

He arrived a few minutes after, but I did not meet him until dinner. I heard him talking English to Gielgud in the next room and complaining of Chase as having been "impudent" to him. I had heard the conversation between himself and Chase a few minutes earlier, just across the partition. He had called Chase to bring a candle, and Chase evidently had given it to one of the Indian carriers or boys to take to him, and Normand's voice said, "Bring it yourself; bring it yourself; aren't you a servant?" Chase had come with heavy foot and in slow voice I heard, "I am a servant — but" — he was going to add "not yours" it was clear, but stopped there. I waited until sent for by Tizon's servant to go to dinner, and then was duly presented to the man. He came up, I must say, to all one had read or thought of him, a little being, slim, thin and quite short, say, 5'7" and with a face truly the most repulsive I have ever seen, I think. It was perfectly devilish in its cruelty and evil. I felt as if I were being introduced to a serpent. All through dinner he spoke Spanish only, but whenever by chance a word came to me, I answered in English. As soon as dinner was over, he bowed and left us. Barnes and Bell are in his bedroom, next to mine, so he has moved down to another room towards the staff's quarters.

Description of Matanzas

The house is the usual big ship-shaped building, but in very bad repair, the very house, I believe that Dyall in his statement declared they had built on arrival here, with Ramón Sanchez and Normand in 1904. The underneath space is quite open, no wall or trees or stockade, simply this one storey raised some ten or twelve feet from the ground, with one ladder to get up and down. The house is on a hill-top with slightly higher hills around it, partly, but badly cleared. The area under any kind of cultivation is very small, a little Cassava down in the valley, and round the house splendid plantains, quite African in their height and thickness of stem, two

Casement seated on board Amazon riverboat in 1910.
(courtesy National Library of Ireland)

Walter Ernest Hardenburg (1886-1942), the "tropical tramp" who brought the case to the attention of the A.S.A.P.
(The Anti-Slavery Reporter)

Sir Edward Grey (1862-1933), British Foreign Secretary 1905-16, who sent Casement to investigate the Putumayo atrocities.

Casement and the Commissioners: *(from left to right)* Juan Tizon, Seymour Bell, H.L. Gielgud, Walter Fox, Louis Barnes and Roger Casement; while Casement went to investigate the truth behind the atrocity reports, the other Commissioners were acting on behalf of the Peruvian Amazon Company and reporting on ways of improving the Company's commercial prospects. (from Brian Inglis, *Roger Casement*, 1973)

Starved Amazindian woman in hammock.
(PRO FO 371/1452)

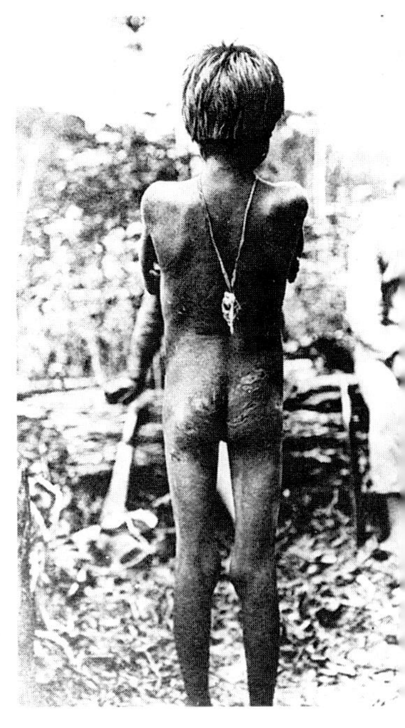

The "photo of the poor scarred child".
(PRO FO 371/1455)

Chained Indian rubber-gatherers in the stocks on the Putumayo river.
(from W.E. Hardenburg, *The Putumayo: The Devil's Paradise,* 1912)

Julio Cesar Arana (1864-1952), rubber baron and managing director of the Peruvian Amazon Company.
(from Richard Collier, *The River that God Forgot,* 1968)

Pablo Zumaeta, Arana's brother-in-law. He ran the Company's operations in and from Iquitos.
(from Eugenio Rubuchon, *En el Putumayo y sus afluentes,* 1907)

Eleven chiefs of section of the Peruvian Amazon Company.
Standing left to right: José I. Fonseca, M.F. Torrico, Paroles, Aristides Rodríguez, Escurra, Alfredo Montt
seated: Miranda, Dr José Rodríguez, Macedo, Matas, Andrés O'Donnell.
(from Sydney Paternoster, *Lords of the Devil's Paradise,* 1913)

Victor Macedo, one of the most evil chiefs of section, who accompanied Casement during large parts of his Putumayo investigations.
(from Carlos A. Valcárcel, *El proceso del Putumayo,* 1913)

Andrés O'Donnell – chief of section at Entre Rios, Casement found him the most tolerable of the "vegetable filibusterers", sympathizing with his Irish name and knowledge of the Amazindian dialects.

The *Liberal* – the principal steam-launch of the Peruvian Amazon Company that conveyed Casement and the Commission to and from the Putumayo.
(from Eugenio Robuchon, *En el Putumayo y sus afluentes,* 1913)

...ly – slept fairly well – in spite of some very long legged mosquitoes, just like gnats or daddy long legs. They did not bite – but buzzed.

already typed from here
number on

Wednesday 12 Oct.

We left Puerto Peruano before 7 – the Indians taking the loads from them without the slightest discussion or refusal, or disorder. The most obedient, docile carriers I've ever seen, & God knows I saw enough giving out of loads & starting of caravans in Africa. Here never a murmur – & they are half starved too. The others started quickly, but I came more slowly with Bishop – as my eye is under a heavy bandage – & the road very bad. Up hill and down hill & across streams innumerable flowing from right to left into the Igaraparaná or Cododié as the Huitotos call it. The land rises often 100 feet or more and then dives again to another stream – often with steps & big trees & sticks laid – all the works of the Indians. Every stream is well bridged. Some have five big trees laid parallel and notched so that the

Handwriting comparisons: a page from the Putumayo Journal shows Casement's handwriting was affected by his worsening eye infection.
(courtesy National Library of Ireland: MS 13,087 (26))

82 October, 1910.

10, MONDAY

11, TUESDAY

12, WEDNESDAY

His pencilled scrawl of 12 October was not mirrored in the corresponding *Black Diary* entry where the hand is deliberate and in pen.
The whole problem of Casement's eyes was neatly edited out of the sexual narrative and not mentioned until 10 October, two months after Casement had first mentioned the ailment and two days before he had a complete visual breakdown. The handwriting experts who have examined the documents have clearly overlooked this.
(courtesy Public Record Office: Folio 32, PRO HO 161/3)

Putumayo Indians *(top)* dressed in bark costumes and headmasks, and *(below)* a group of girls in ceremonial body paint preparing for a dance. These photographs by Casement are among the few to have survived from the seventeen rolls of film he shot during the course of his 1910 journey. (courtesy National Museum of Ireland and National Library of Ireland).

avocado pear trees, young and in fruit. The stream lies close to the house, down a very steep hill. It flows to the Caquetá which is some six hours away. The forest here is far bigger and stronger than any we have yet seen since leaving Chorrera. Large trees, like those on the middle Amazon, began to re-appear in to-day's march. We are clearly in the watershed of the Japura, and in what is a less populous country, I should say. The big, original vegetation shows this. Where the Huitotos have been, I think the poor forest we have noticed is due to a lengthy native occupation. They have practically cleared it all at one time or another, and moved up from spot to spot. Here we are getting back to the primaeval forest.

I turned in early, being tired and not anxious to see more of Normand than I could help. I have already made up my mind that as soon as Levine, the other Barbados man arrives from "La China" I shall return to Entre Rios.

Casement awakened by the harem

At 2.30 a.m. was wakened by feet pattering round the verandah, and low voices saying at the door of the next room, "Normand, Normand". I jumped from bed and went out. A man with a lantern and rifle was guarding a huddle of female figures, five or six of them with bags and road equipment. Some voices shouted down the passage and they all bolted to the room Normand is sleeping in. It was the arrival of the Harem, making for the room where they presumed their sleeping lord was lying. Barnes had been wakened too, and we both turned out and viewed them, and laughed heartily. They looked tiny little things from the glimpse I got. Poor little creatures pattering all day and night through the forest after this beast. I suppose he set out at once as soon as the messenger reached La China with news of our hourly expected arrival at Matanzas, leaving the household to follow under care of some of the *muchachos* of his guard.

MATANZAS — TUESDAY, OCTOBER 18TH

Casement decides to leave

I told Tizon I should leave Matanzas tomorrow and go back straight to Entre Rios, after I had interviewed the two Barbados men. Lane is here now and I shall call him at once, and if Levine does not come in from "La China" in time, he can follow me down to Entre Rios. Tizon at once assented and I told Bishop to get everything ready for a long tramp tomorrow, as I intended starting early with Sealy and himself and seven Indians for all our loads, and making the thirty miles to Entre Rios before nightfall. I told Barnes and Bell that I could not stand another hour of Normand; it made me sick to look at him. They fully agreed and Bell called him an "absolute monster" capable, from his face, of any crime. They are interviewing Normand officially at 9 a.m. to give the usual account of the administration of his district, which is a foregone lie, and I am calling James Lane at same time to be interrogated. The double inquiry going on within earshot with only these thin palm-bark screens between, will be interesting.

Interview with Lane

Lane's interview has been fruitful.[197] I did not prolong it, as the man very soon said he wished to leave the place, and would be grateful if I could get permission for him to go; Normand had twice refused to allow him. He was slow and halting in speech and rather unwilling, I thought, to speak out and I once taxed him with untruthfulness and called Bishop to warn him. He said he was only trying truthfully to answer my questions. On the whole, I think he did this, but it is obvious my questions can only cover a small area, and the thing will be later on to get a fuller statement from him of what he has done and seen since his arrival here. He came from Iquitos with Sealy and Chase, it appears, arriving at Chorrera on 12th May 1908 and coming straight up at once to Matanzas, where he has been ever since. According to him, he has not witnessed many gross crimes, nor has he taken part in killing or flogging. He states he has never flogged; that he has been exempted from that as he has no "arm" for it. He has very fine muscular negro arms as big as two of mine, and is a healthy, strapping youth of some 22 or 23 years of age. So that this "no arm" for flogging may mean that, despite his strength, he was so poor a hand at laying on the lash on a bare body that he got let off this degrading task. Chase's account of his own exemption at Abisinia is practically the same. He too is a typical big strong negro and yet he says he only flogged once. Swears it again and again, and say this was because "he don't know how to flog".

Stanley Lewis after flogging Simona never, he swore, flogged again. In his case he suffered for this refusal. Fonseca beat him and put him in *cepo*, and had it not been for Juan Castanos he might

[197] {B.B. Statement No 17 pp.92–96}

have starved. And here is this big, strong boy stating pretty much the same thing; Levine, he says, does much of the flogging. He has only hit Indians with sticks. He has seen three Indians, however, die from flogging, two here at Matanzas and one at La China, and his account of the death of this last one, a man named Kodihinka, is one of the most atrocious things I have heard yet. It makes me sick to think of it, and it occurred only last month! while we were at Iquitos or Chorrera. This unfortunate man, captured with five others (his wife and child among them) far across the Caquetá in Colombia, was brought down tied up at wrist and elbows for several days' journey to La China. Here they were all flogged, three males and three females. This man was the elder male — the head man of these poor fugitives, who had fled many days to escape the "advances" of this captivating English Company. They preferred freedom and flight to the gifts lavished upon them for the rubber that we are told they so gladly work in order to obtain nice things. So they are pursued. The Commission going after them, headed by this assassin Normand, is actually 21 days engaged on this exploit, six of the days spent in open violation of international law in the territory of another nation state.

The flogging administered to these "workers" of the Company on arrival at Normand's house, kills this man. He is put into the *cepo* alongside the five others, all with bleeding backs and limbs, and there he dies within three days of receiving these lashes. His flesh, according to Lane, stinking and rotten — his wife and child alongside him, pinned like wicked animals with their feet in iron-wood holds. God! what a state of things! And the human beast that did this is telling the Commission across the partition that he has not flogged for three years; that all he does now is to give some of the most recalcitrant "strokes on the hand with a round piece of wood with holes in it." My old friend, the Congo "palmatory"[198] emerged at last! As Normand was actually stating this in my hearing, Lane was declaring — unwillingly declaring — that within a month he had seen a man beaten to death, beside five others, three of them women, by the very orders of this man, and giving me the name of the employée, José Cordoba, who had laid on the lash.

I told the Commission immediately after Normand had been dismissed what Lane had declared to me. In the midst of my in-

[198] Casement here shows how the instruments of torture used in both the Congo and Amazon were similar. The wooden *Palmatoria* is still used in Brazil to discipline miscreants at school.

terrogation of him I heard that Levine had arrived from La China. At lunch I told Tizon that my mind was fully fixed on leaving at day-light for Entre Rios, that I did not wish to stay an hour longer than I could help in this company.

Interviews with Westerman Levine and Normand

In the afternoon I summoned Westerman Levine; Levine is his full Barbadian appellation.[199] He is a small-sized, mean-faced negro with a smirk, a face that at once awakens distrust and dislike; a lurking grin always in the eyes, and a weak sloppy mouth. I did not take to him, and it very soon became clear that he was not merely concealing things, but answering direct questions untruthfully. He left Chorrera with Normand on 17th November, 1904, so has been here almost six years. I made no attempt to get a general statement from him concerning this period, but confined myself to putting questions and requiring categoric replies. He confirmed in very much the account given by Roso España, of Aquiléo Torres and the other Colombians in the beginning of 1907. The "two Barbados negroes" referred to in that declaration were himself and Donal Francis (the man who at Chorrera had only "planted yucca and sugar cane" all his 20 months at Matanzas!).

After admitting modified flogging, and even a case of shooting an Indian by himself, "done with orders of the Manager", I asked for particulars of the flogging and death of Kodihinka last month at La China. Here his replies very soon brought him into direct conflict with the statement of Lane. When he committed himself definitely to the statement that Kodihinka had not died in the *cepo*, and had died, not from flogging administered in La China, but from the beatings he had received on the road back when in the custody of James Lane and two *muchachos*, I called Lane, and confronted the two. I said one or other was lying and I must find out which. I read Lane's replies to my questions about Kodihinka and then Levine's, and the two men faced each other, but only for a moment. Lane adhered to every word of his and openly accused Levine of being a liar. I taxed the other with it, and asked if he would now speak the truth. He couldn't face more of it, and gave in — with another lie — that he had forgotten.

"What!" I said, "Forgotten and only a month ago!"

---

[199] Westerman Levine's name changes to Leavine in the Blue Book. {B.B. Statement No.18 pp.96–99.}

He admitted that Kodihinka had received 30 lashes from José Cordoba. He himself had given "3 cuts"; that he had died in the *cepo* alongside the other Indians as described by Lane. I asked Mr Tizon to come in and be present at this confrontation and hear the charge, admitted by both men, and he did this in great distress. Levine, then, in answer to my further questions, admitted he had been employed for six years only at this work, going out with a rifle to hunt Indians, to flog them and maltreat them to bring in rubber, or to flog them for having "run away", and had done nothing else all this time, except keep guard at night. And all this explicitly by the manager's orders.

Tizon said it was no use asking Normand — I said apparently not. The matter was clear enough already; no fuller evidence seemed possible to obtain. Here we were on the spot, with Normand a room off (and he could hear what I said), and both these employées of the Company directly charging him before its Chief with ordering these crimes to be committed. I dismissed both Barbados men, on the distinct understanding that they were at once to leave Matanzas. Lane is to accompany me in the morning — Levine to follow with the Commission next day. I refused to allow him to come with me, as I told him I looked upon him as not only a liar, but a cowardly scoundrel. He had said that he gave the "3 cuts" to Kodihinka when the prisoners arrived at La China tied up. Kodihinka, according to him, when he admitted these "three cuts" was then half moribund. He was tied up and his back cut and bleeding and bruised from the blows he had got on the road from the *muchachos* under Lane. It was when in this state that he had given this wretched man three lashes with the twisted tapir hide.

"I give him the cuts, Sir, because he no pay me for a box of matches I gave him on de road."

"I see", I said "You gave three lashes with his hands tied, his back and limbs bruised and bleeding and himself, as you say, in a dying condition?"

"Yes , Sir, but it wasn't from these three cuts he died; he died from the beating on the road."

I told him he was a coward and a scoundrel and that if he were in Barbados he would be hanged for such an act, or for any of the murderous crimes I was now sure he had committed; that to plead Normand's order was no excuse; and that I had a good mind to hand him over to the Prefect at Iquitos for trial there. I said all this before Tizon, Lane and Bishop — this and much more — for I added

"Guilty and contemptible as you are, you are far less guilty than the brute who employed you to do these things for his profit."

Casement's view of Tizon's duty

When they had gone, Tizon seemed dazed, and said he could not stay in the Company, he could not go on with it,

"To think I am mixed up with this", was his cry.

I said that he was honourably mixed up with it, he must stay and do his duty. He had a duty to his country and to these Indians to perform — higher than to the Company, and that he must keep a brave heart and get through with it, and all the moral aid I could give him was his. Wherever I could strengthen his hands he might count on me. He then told me he had always told Normand he was to go, that he had hoped soon to get him away by the very steamer I was going in, but certainly by the next, at end of November. He added that Matanzas Station should be closed right away, and that in time he hoped the Indians there might be induced to come into Entre Rios voluntarily and sell rubber at a fixed price.

I said this was the only thing to do. The road down to Puerto Peruano was impossible for human transport with such loads as these unfortunates were now compelled to carry, and all this hideous state of crime and outrage on them as well, before they start. He promised me again that the whole staff at Matanzas and La China should go, and go at the very quickest date possible, and the same should be done with Abisinia and Morelia, and also he trusted with Sabana and Santa Catalina. He would confine the sections (save Entre Rios) to the waterway of the Igaraparaná and abolish these dreadful inland posts that could not be inspected or controlled, and would get mules for the transport from Entre Rios down to Puerto Peruano.

I warmly commended all this and pointed out that in the end it might even mean a financial gain, for the Indians, relieved of this dire pressure of the long marches with enormous burdens, without food, would have more time and greater strength and contentment to collect rubber, and Entre Rios might be made, by wise management, a collecting centre for all the Andokes, and much of the northern Boras country. The task before him, I said, was a very hard one, for I feared he would find opposition all round among the "staffs" and Chiefs of Section, when they realized that the change involved the doing away of their lucrative posts. This man Normand gets 20% of the gross yields of his district!

What an incentive to crime, this alone! He has the biggest staff of any section, all well-paid, armed ruffians, simply here to terrorise and enslave. Tizon said that Matanzas was not merely wrong, but a "financial folly". It had not yielded any profit but was run at a loss! The commission to Normand and the heavy salaries and expenses of keeping it up (as well as the other administrative expenses, for Macedo, too, comes into the Commission account), eat up all the "profits", and it had been run at a dead loss for some time.

I gather Normand gets only about 8 tons of rubber a year — so he said, I am told — but I have not yet got the figures from any member of the Commission. They are convinced that he did nothing except lie to them. While Levine's statement was being taken, in the afternoon, a lot of Boras and Andokes Indians were coming in with very heavy loads of rubber. This was Normand's *fabrico*, this first part of it. He is getting it in now to take down to Puerto Peruano to ship to Chorrera by the *Veloz* in a few days.

Watching rubber arrive

When I had finished with Levine I went out to see the rubber arriving. They came up the hill, men, women and children, largely the two last, staggering under perfectly phenomenal loads. I have never seen such weights carried on roads — and such roads! — in Africa or anywhere else. Lots of the men were Boras, big, fine-looking fellows, with broad faces, very pale skins, almost whitemen indeed, simply bronzed by the sun, and frank open air and manner. Their bodies were slim and graceful, and their bodily strength very remarkable. I tried to carry one load of rubber, made Chase lift it and put it on my shoulder, Normand standing on. I could not walk three paces with it — literally and truly. My knees gave way and to save my life, I don't think I could have gone 50 yards. Yet here they were, coming in from 8 to 10 hours away, 25 to 30 miles, and with 45 miles of that atrocious path through the forest before them to get to Puerto Peruano, and their only food such as they could bring with them, made by their poor wives who were tottering along under loads of 50, 60, 70 and 80 lbs. The little boys, some of them 5 or 6, without even a *fono*, stark naked, dear little things with soft gentle eyes and long eyelashes were coming along too, often with 30 lbs or more on their tiny backs. I saw one lad, looked about 15, with a boy's frank voice, with a load of fully 75 to 80 lbs.

Conversation with Normand

I asked N. for his balance to weigh some of them. He said he had none there, that the rubber was weighed either at La China or at a house in the forest where the Indians had to collect it. Several loads he admitted had not come in because the bearers were sick. Six were sick and he sent back some of the stronger Boras who had already come in, to bring in these other loads. Not one scrap of food, he admitted, was given to anyone. He had the audacity to tell us that the natives "preferred their own food"! — that it was so nutritious, and much more "alimentary" than rice or beans. It consists of rolls of *cassava* bread, half cooked and rolled in with the rubber, in leaves, and carried with it in the palm basket, that holds their enormous *chorizos*. Some of the loads I could not lift at all. I could raise them just off the ground and no more.

Description of Boras carriers — the "noble savage"

The Boras men were the finest Indians I've seen yet. Not tall or big really, yet wonderfully graceful and clean limbed. They walked as steadily as machines. Short, quick steps, but the leg never moved or the knee-joint relaxed. With a big sigh, each man slipped down and slid the load from his back to the ground, releasing the fibre band from his forehead; he sprang up, straight as an arrow, and walked firmly and strongly away. Many of them had fine limbs, strong arms and beautiful thighs and legs, although nowhere any remarkable development of muscle. It was simply that they were all over well and perfectly made children of the forest, inheriting ages of its wild free life, until their bodies had grown like the very trees, to be a part and parcel of the soil. They sleep on it naked, walk or run upon it all the day, and never perspire with a load of 100 or 150 lbs on them. Many of these loads must weigh fully 150–170 lbs, of that I am sure. I hope to weigh some at Entre Rios, and I shall be going down the road with these first fruits of Normand's last *fabrico* to-morrow.

They are to dance tonight, so he tells us, but it will be entirely off their own bats — for they'll not get a scrap of food or drink from him. There is not even food for us, so Tizon says. He has had to send messages down to Entre Rios for further supplies, some of which arrived this evening by special runner, one of O'Donnell's *muchachos*, who got in at 4.30 with a load of something to eat and drink. A great many of the men were flogged and showed bad traces of it. One tiny boy child of not more than eight, so small he had no *fono*, but was quite naked had his little backside and thighs covered with scars — broad weals and lashes. An abominable sight. He had a biggish load of rubber too. There must have been fully 30 boys and children carrying, some of them mites of five or six. These latter had only food baskets, the youngest with a load of rubber was seven I should say, and they ranged on from this up to ten or twelve. One of the big Boras men with raw red scars of a recent flogging, Bustamante hid from us, or tried to. He was taken upstairs with a handkerchief on his bare buttocks. I spoke to several of the men and boys, but all seemed half dazed and wholly frightened, and when I got some to stand for their photos they looked as if under sentence of death. It was impossible to reassure them, as neither Sealy nor Bishop could speak Boras or Andokes

A visit to the cepo

Normand spent the whole afternoon under the house, arranging the rubber loads for the morrow, and calling over the lists of names. Lane had told me that the *cepo* had been hidden away on the morning of our arrival, and was lying behind the native house and kitchen covered with leaves. We visited it and found it covered with thatch, in two big pieces, it looked like a double *cepo* as both parts were quite separate. Lane had also said that the previous evening when word had come that we were on the road, Bustamante himself had hurried the two prisoners away that were in it. He had taken them out to some house in the first and sent them on, guarded by two *muchachos*, presumably to "La China".

I told the Commission of the bare facts of Lane's and Levine's evidence, and took them to see the hidden *cepo* along with Sr. Tizon.

At dinner

In the evening at dinner we had quite a farce. Tizon said that neither 'Andokes' nor 'Lincoln', the two local boys he had brought with him, were anxious to stay now in their own country. He had asked both whether they would not like to stay at Matanzas and be near their own people, and both had protested. Normand rose to the occasion.

"That's what I like to hear," he said, "It shows that civilization is at work."

I said to Barnes out loud "This nearly chokes me", and put a piece of bread in my mouth. The whole of us were speechless for a minute, and I was afraid I'd laugh out loud.

Two rebellious muchachos

Sealy came late to tell me that two of the *muchachos* who had shot Bucelli, Luiz de Silva etc. last year, had been kept here with long chains round their necks, and had recently escaped. He was in great excitement,

"They had them down there", pointing to the native house, "and they got off with the chains, and Levine did not tell you, Sir. They sent after them everywhere, and haven't got them."

I said, I hoped they would not. I asked if the Indians had any means of getting chains smashed, seeing they had no hammers and chisels, and Bishop, who was standing by, said "there was never an Indian yet who was long troubled with a chain once he got away. If they have a hatchet or an axe they'll soon get rid of the chain".

This seemingly is the end of the great Caquetá Rebellion. I've heard several times of the "four whites murdered by the cannibals". The two survivors of the killing party I hope are in security and safety somewhere, poor beings. When they killed that party of rascals, they only did what should be done to every single agent and empleado of this damnable Syndicate of murderers, with the single exception of Tizon, who is clearly out of his element here. However he will have to stay to try and end the lot of them. I hope these two *muchachos* will keep clear. They are not Andokes or Boras, however, I gather, but Huitotos.

VII

ENTRE RIOS REVISITED

FRIDAY, 21ST OCTOBER 1910

I got back here yesterday, after quite an adventure on the 19th on leaving Matanzas.[200] I had got the Muinanes chief and six men to carry my things back to Entre Rios and with Bishop, Sealy and Lane, I left Matanzas at 7 a.m. Many of the Andokes or Boras rubber carriers had already started on the road, and I wished to photograph some of them, particularly the small boys and girls, with their heavy loads on the way. I set out before Bishop and Sealy and soon overtook the rubber carriers. Poor chaps, they shook hands with me as I passed, and one wretched woman was crying and groaning and spoke to me in Andokes, pointing to her trembling legs and the big load of rubber she had. Some of the boys were awfully nice little chaps, and now that we were alone together, away from the shadow of Matanzas and the eyes of Normand, they were quite cheery and laughed when I patted them and held my hand again and again. A lot of them called me "Capitan, capitan", and pointed to the stripes and scars over their hips and thighs.

Groans in the pathway — Casement helps a feverish muchacho

Bishop and Sealy overtook me about one hour out and we passed on rapidly, leaving all the rubber carriers behind and passing my own carriers who had started before me. When about 7 miles out

[200] Although the date preceding this entry is Friday 21 October 1910 at Entre Rios, it refers to Casement's return journey from Matanzas on Wednesday 19 October. This entry was clearly written up two days after the events described. Despite the clear and logical order of the narrative as reported by Casement, the whole sense of what happens has been hopelessly confused in the corresponding *Black Diary* entries and shows a misunderstanding of events. Most revealing is the entry for 21 October "*I am writing up my diary since Monday* ... ", a clear error, as Casement states in two genuine contexts that he was writing up his diary since Wednesday, the day of his departure from Matanzas. A comparison of the narrative describing these days shows two conflicting accounts — one fact, the other fiction.

from Matanzas, I heard groans in the pathway ahead and saw a pale smoke stack. I hurried forward and found a boy, a *muchacho* evidently from his Winchester lying alongside him, stretched on the ground. He had a raging fever and was groaning, and trembling all over. When Bishop came up we questioned him. He said that he was one of the *muchachos* of Matanzas. He had been sent out 12 days previously without any food to look for the "wife" of one of the empleados named Negretti, who had run away. He had not found her, had been starving for days, and was now absolutely played out and unable to walk. I stopped then, got some brandy and gave it him, and then when my carriers arrived, I stopped the "chop box" and got a tin of soup and some biscuits out and heated the soup over the fire and made him drink some. He did not want to, but we made him little by little. He drank a great deal of the tea to quench his raging fever. I rarely have seen a more pitiable sight. At length, after an hour or more, I asked him if he could walk a bit, and if so, I'd try and help him along to the Muinanes house, where I now decided to sleep and give him plenty to eat in the night and morning, so that then he might either return to Matanzas, or if he preferred it, to come on to Entre Rios where I intended to hand him over to Tizon. He said he would try to walk, and so we started. Unfortunately I had let all my carriers go on, they were in a hurry to be off. The boy stumbled a few steps and fell with a groan. This was repeated again and again, and I saw it was useless to attempt to go far with him.

So I sent Bishop on to overtake my carriers at the first river he could, and get them to stop and light a fire and wait. Then with Lane and Sealy we tried helping this starved being along. He said again and again it was hunger had him, that when he tried to walk the road went away from under his feet and down he fell. At last I got a big Boras man who overtook us with an enormous load of rubber, to lay it down and shoulder the boy. This he did, and carried him up a steep hill and laid him on a bed he made of big leaves he cut. Then, poor chap, he had to trudge back for his huge load of rubber. At last, about 12 noon, I got the boy down to a stream where I found Bishop halted with the two lost men, who fortunately were there with my food supplies. So we had our breakfast. I tried to make the sick boy drink more soup, but I had to force it down his lips. He could do nothing but groan. Soon after he started by himself to try and walk on, and when we broke camp I found him fallen in the track just up the hill at the burnt Muinanes' house which 'Andokes' had told us on the day of our coming had been burnt by Normand. There I was forced, very unwillingly to leave him, as my carriers were far ahead. A rain storm was coming on, so we rigged up a shelter over him of palm fronds and wild banana leaves and I then put my umbrella over him inside this. We promised to send back three of my Indians from the Muinanes' house to help him on there. Bishop and Lane said that the *empleado* coming behind us at the tail of the rubber caravan who was the very Negretti who had sent the boy out to look for his "wife" would certainly drive him back to Matanzas. I was afraid of this before they spoke. So I wrote my name on a piece of paper addressing it to Entre Rios — and then, on second thoughts, wrote inside a slip in bad Portuguese to say that the bearer, by name Ramón, was to follow me to Entre Rios. I was in hope this might serve as a protection if the oncoming man interrogated the poor creature. With this paper and some biscuits and meat I left him, and his last words were to send the Indians quickly, as there would be moonlight, and he would try to get into the Muinanes house to-night. I then hurried on — hours had been lost, and all hope of reaching Entre Rios was over.

A sick Andokes woman

We had not gone far, however, when a second case occurred — even worse. The woman who had appealed to me in the morning was unable to go further. She was crying bitterly and trembling all over, and as I came up the most pitiable sounds arose to the poor creature's lips. I knelt beside her and took the load of rubber off her shoulders and the band from her head, and told Bishop to lay it beside the path and cut a cross in the tree it was leaning against. The woman cried still more, and kept saying Normand would kill her, Normand would kill her. She was an Andokes and Bishop had to do, or try to do the translating. I told him to tell her not to be afraid — that Normand would do nothing with her — that I would be responsible for taking her load away, and that she was to come on with me to the Muinanes' house where I would give her food and medicine and clothes. She was, like most of them, stark naked, and her poor straight back had been battered and beaten. She pointed to her thighs and legs showing the bruises and marks. She seemed to have a severe attack of rheumatism too, and had not a scrap of food. When finally she really understood she was to go on in safety with me she wept still more bitterly and held my hand, pressing it to her forehead again and again. I gave her tea to drink from my bottle, and by this time a lot of the other carriers had arrived and squatted all around us — looking on with a sort of hopeless resignation on their faces. Only the small boys — boys all the world over — grinned and laughed.

The woman could hardly walk, and the task of getting her on was a very slow one. She fell several times, and I gave her my walking stick to help her trembling legs. She gave way constantly at the knees and fell. I cried a good deal, I must confess. I was thinking of Mrs. Green and Mrs. Morel[201] if they had been here and could have seen this piteous being — this gentle-voiced woman — a wife and mother — in such a state. Her load had been one of between 50 and 60 lbs, I should think — three fairish *Chorizos*. Her "food" for this journey of some 70 miles (she came from 25 miles beyond Matanzas) down to Puerto Peruano, consisted of a small bundle of palm frond wrapping less than 2 lbs. weight of farinha, with a tiny bottle of 'aji' — or notin pepper. This we took from the load and carried on for her. On getting near the Muinanes' house I heard the *manguaré* beating — a welcome sound — and soon after a shot. A minute or two later we met four of the genial *muchachos* from Entre Rios going up to Matanzas with provisions for Tizon and two letters for him, one from Chorrera and one sent off by O'Donnell that morning at 6 a.m. with the boys. I stopped them and abstracted two bottles of ginger ale, two tins of sausages and a tin of prawns, and wrote a chit to Tizon telling him why, and explaining that I was delayed by these sick people on the road.

Arrival at Muinanes maloca

We were very glad to reach the Muinanes house at 4 p.m. and the woman fell, a groaning heap, by the fire. I got her, rigged up in pajamas, on my bed sack, and put a warm coat over her — and several times Sealy fed "de ole lady," as he persisted in calling her, with oxtail soup and sausage and biscuits. She ate protestingly, but all the same it went down and would help the poor battered body to revive. She was a woman of some 40 or 45 — and her husband was one of the men who had sat watching me giving her the tea on the road. The Boras and Andokes men and boys and many women

---

[201] The wife of E.D. Morel, whom Casement admired as a public-spirited woman. She did all she could to support her husband's long campaign to bring about the cessation of atrocities committed against the central African people under Leopold II. Casement's efforts to promote the Morel Testimonial were as much to do with creating some financial security for his wife and family as with bringing to the public's attention Morel's humanitarian work.

— some of them sick too — kept on coming in by twos and threes up to about seven. Then my three Indians, who had been sent back by Sealy to get the sick boy and the three loads of rubber left by "de ole lady", came in empty handed to say that before they reached the boy they had met Negretti, who turned them back. He said he had already turned the boy back to Andokes. Poor lad — I lay awake thinking of him out in the forest all night. The brute Negretti had told them, they said, the boy belonged to Matanzas, and was not to go down to Entre Rios, so my stratagem with the note addressed to myself was in vain. I was grieved and wretched. For all I knew he could not reach Andokes alive — certainly not, unless the food I gave him should later on work some restoration.

Casement attends to the wounds of the Boras carriers

The sick woman groaned all night, and some of the other women came for medicine and help. I gave them what I had in the shape of relief, and then the big men, seeing this, came round me with their bruised buttocks and scarified limbs. One big splendid-looking Boras young man — with a broad good-humoured face like an Irishman — had a fearful cut on his left buttock. It was the last scab of what had been a very bad flogging. The flesh for the size of a saucer was black and scarred, and this crown of sore flesh was the size of a florin. I put lanoline and a pad of cotton wool over it. Many more came for the same treatment. One youth I had already noticed on the road with a bad cut on his back — he said José Cordoba had given it. On the road I gave him my handkerchief to try and keep the strong wood of the palm basket in which his rubber lay from pressing too hard on it. He was grateful, poor soul, a very thin Andokes boy, I think. In the evening he came and showed me many more cuts all over him, fresh ones and raw; one over the shoulder blade. I lanolined all, and with tufts of cotton wool all over him, he and the others roared with laughter. Some had cuts on the feet and shins, these from sticks and trunks. I put plaster on these as well as I could.

Casement sleeps among the Indians

The man Negretti did not arrive. I lay awake a long time with my revolver loaded, for I thought he might come in and begin abusing the poor woman whose load I had left in the wood, and, if so, I was determined to prevent it at all costs. His hammock came on and some of his *muchachos* with rifles, but he did not turn up. I was relieved but could not sleep. I heard the wretched woman groaning and crying all night. At 2 the moon broke through the broken side roof of the house, and I looked round on all the weary forms of these poor men and women. Several of the latter were awake and crying softly; occasionally a man would give a sort of groan of weariness as he moved in his sleep. Some of them awakened and rose from time to time to stir the fires aflame, and then lay down with their backs or feet to the warmth. I was glad of a blanket, and I had put two of my jackets over the sick woman to keep her warm, but these sturdy forms lay naked and almost white in the moonlight and firelight.

Chieftaincy

The Boras are the fairest skinned Indians I have seen yet — some of them are almost white in colour, a very handsome set, and with the children particularly winning, and their forms are graceful in the extreme. One lad of about fifteen hung to my heels often during the day — whenever I came up he ran over and took my hand and held it. This indeed all did wherever I passed them, in the most winning way, men and boys. This boy's name was Doi, he told me. I wrote it in my notebook, and he repeated it slowly twice over, laughing all the time. I then tried to find out his tribe, but am not sure if I understood his reply. It was "Otaniko", and then he said "Capitan" striking his chest. I gathered that he was one of the people of a Boras Capitan or *cacique* named Otaniko, although he may have meant that his tribe was the "Otaniko" one, and he its captain. Several of the Capitanes are boys, I am told. The office is hereditary, like the chieftainship of a clan, although some system of election may enter into it too. O'Donnell and others have told me of several cases of boys being Capitanes, and Bishop, when on the march yesterday from the Muinanes' house into Entre Rios told me of an old woman Capitan he and Robuchon met on the Caquetá in 1906 who was very good to them and gave them food. I am recording Bishop's account of his journey down the Caquetá elsewhere; it is most interesting, and I shall try to give it just in his own words.[202]

I was glad the night passed without trouble from the man Negretti. Bishop and Lane told me that when the Commission were questioning Normand at Matanzas this man had been vapouring before them, and saying that he wished "the Englishmen" would send for him to question him and he would enjoy insulting them.

---

[202] This statement does not appear in the Blue Book.

I spent thus the night of 19th–20th in some anxiety, for I did not want a row with a low-class brute such as this empleado was sure to be, and at the same time I was determined to protect the woman.

Departure early on 20 October

At 5 a.m. of the morning of the 20th the Boras men and boys and the women with them got up; and, after a warming over the big blaze of the fire, and a handful of Cassava bread, without a word they passed away out of the house, each of them getting their enormous loads up and off. They were gone at 5.15 a.m. I stayed on and got coffee and gave some to the two sick women, on top of some of Bishop's Eno's fruit salt, a bottle of which he had bought at Iquitos. I had not made up my mind what to do. At one time I thought of sending back to look for the famished boy, but finally decided to go on to Entre Rios and to leave Lane with a note for Barnes and Tizon explaining about the boy and sick women here — for there were two of them now. I wrote a note to Barnes telling him what I wished done, and then Negretti arrived with the tail of the rubber carriers. There were over 40 of them — mostly women and children. Out of 47 of the rubber people and *muchachos* then in the house, I counted only twelve men and lads — the rest were women and children. Negretti brought the three pieces of rubber the sick woman had left and threw them down with a vicious snarl, and then came truculently towards me and asked for the rifle of the *muchacho* I had taken from the starved boy on the road. I gave him this and then asked where the boy was, and he answered at once, a deliberate lie, "Oh, he's in Matanzas now", and added, to my further enquiry, he had sent a boy to help him. (I found out later that this was absolutely untrue). I then asked if he had seen my umbrella, and he said he had sent it back to Matanzas. (This too I find out is a deliberate lie; Gielgud found the umbrella where I had left it). I then asked if he had not seen the letter I left with the boy, and he said he had not seen it. "Never saw it."

The sick woman was lying by the fire, and the other sick woman by another fire, and two more, mere girls, fell beside her groaning. He called out to Lane, whom he gathered that I was leaving behind, to tell Sr. Normand, who was coming with the rest of the rubber, of these four women and the pieces of rubber he was leaving behind. He then hurried on with his rifle on his shoulder after the rest of the unfortunates who were being hunted down this awful road to Puerto Peruano. What is wanted here is a

Hanging Commission with a gallows — not a Commission of botanists and commercial experts. Leaving Lane with the note for Barnes, and with a verbal message to give to Normand if he should attempt to ill-treat the woman or scold her for leaving her load, I left at about 7.45 or 8 a.m. I told Lane to say to Normand that the woman was not responsible for leaving her load — that I had taken it from her on finding her sick and unable to proceed, and that if he desired an explanation it was to come from me. Lane promised faithfully to guard the women and feed them throughout the day and to stay there by them till Tizon and the Commission should arrive from Matanzas, which I hoped would be about 4 p.m. I then hurried on, and soon passed the "human animal" Negretti, as I call him. He is a vicious-looking, thin half-caste from Moyobamba,[203] I should say. A mean ferret face and teeth like a wild animal, and a fierce hungry glare in his eyes. Almost as evil a face as Normand's. and his sole duty is to slave-drive, flog and threaten with death, when he does not kill these thrice unhappy beings.

On the road

The whole road along I passed the Boras and Andokes carriers — going slowly and steadily on, often resting against trees or squatting for a moment's pause in this awful track of slush, fallen trees, roots, deep streams to cross by a single log or fallen tree, and all the obstacles a bewildering forest can throw in a track such as this. For me, a famous walker once, and still pretty good on my legs, the route was excessively wearisome. I was bathed in perspiration half an hour after starting, and the constant ducking one's head, or balancing on a slippery pole, or falling over the ankles into the mud, wearied the mind and the attention more even than the body. Here were these men, many of them with loads far over a cwt. on the lightest diet man ever lived on, to get over this path, with no hope of relief before or behind them, and with this human devil and his armed *muchachos* behind to flog up the stragglers. Every time he appeared in sight it was "Hiti, Hiti." — "Get on, get on" and a volley of Boras and Andokes I could not understand. I was so sick of the sight that I hurried past at full speed and did not slacken until I had left the rubber carriers well behind.

---

[203] Town in northern Peru about 50 kilometres east of Rioja.

Bishop and Sealy tell atrocity stories

I was furious at the whole thing — the most disgraceful form of slavery left among mankind — of that I am certain. Slavery in the interests too, of this miserable gang of cut-throats. Bishop and Sealy told me, as we walked more quietly when we got well ahead, of many things they had seen or knew of. Of Normand, Bishop said that nothing related by Hardenburg was untrue. He believed it all. He had not seen Normand kill people during the six weeks he had been with him at Matanzas, but Donal Francis had told him of the dreadful things he had seen at that section — of the burning alive and the dogs eating the dead.[204] Young Rodriguez, Bishop says, is to succeed Normand. The boy Lincoln had told him this. Lincoln (who speaks Spanish, and is confidential boy to Torrico at Occidente) said that Normand was to have two more *fabricos* and then "Juanito" (Rodriguez' name with everyone) was to be appointed to Matanzas to succeed Normand.

Bishop added that these men were so false even to each other that Normand, believing Juanito was to come after him, had been telling the Indians that Rodriguez would ill-treat them dreadfully, so that one "nation" had already taken to flight. This to ruin Rodriguez' chances from the start of getting a good haul of rubber. There is evidently no honour among these thieves. I said from what I had seen of Rodriguez at Occidente I thought him quite as big a scoundrel as Normand, if that were possible. Bishop laughed, and then told me the following of Rodriguez' conduct once at Sabana. Bishop was there at the time.

It was this year in April, Rodriguez had come over for a "visit" to Fonseca, and every morning when he got up he visited the prisoners in the *cepo*. To these poor Indians he administered sundry cuts with a whip, laughing all the time. This he did for morning sport. As he flogged them he called out "Here's your tea and coffee — you like tea and coffee — here they are" — and as he lashed them, Bishop said, a big black dog that was there jumped on the man or woman flogged and worried them. Bishop's statement was that the dog "took bits out of them." It is too atrocious, and yet one has only to look at these men and the dumb, terrified faces of the Indians when they speak to them to read it all. Sealy then chimed in with another illustration of Rodriguez "humour".

The day we had spent out in the forest at Occidente, at the rubber washing, when we breakfasted in the Indian's house, we

[204] This story was corroborated in Dyall's statement (see above).

had had two pineapples. Sealy recalled this, and I said "Yes, I remember the pines well — they were very good ones". Rodriguez, I remember, too, had brought them along near the end of lunch, and we had had them, there and then, cut up and eaten them, not thinking anything about where they had come from.

"Well, Sir," said Sealy, "them two pines Juanito took from an Indian girl behind the house. She wanted a tin of salmon for them. He gives her two bats over the head — I see him do it," and Bishop threw in grimly,

"That was her tin of salmon!"

So they regaled my march. Sealy then told me another story of our friend Velarde when Chief of Sabana where Sealy spent some months.

One morning he sent two small boys out to fish in the Cahuinari. They caught nothing, and came back at nightfall empty-handed. "So next morning he gives the two boys six cuts each, good hard cuts, and sends them out to fish again. That was to make them catch fish. They don't catch no fish, and they was so frightened they stayed away for three days. Then they had to come back because they gets nothing to eat — but he didn't flog them when they came back".

The worst story of all, perhaps, Bishop told me of Elias Martenengui, the man who has recently gone to Lima with his "fortune". He saw an Indian woman he liked, the wife of one of the local Indians. He took the woman, and told the Indian he would keep her until the man brought in a certain quantity of rubber. The poor husband had to go and get the rubber. He brought it in after fifteen days, and Martenengui said it was not enough. He sent the man back for more and still kept the woman in his harem. Again the man returned and again the same answer, and the woman was still kept. Finally on the third or fourth return of this unhappy husband, Martenengui refused to give up the wife at all, but gave the man a girl instead, who had been nursing one of his children by one or other of his "wives". The man protested in vain, he was driven off with blows by the *muchachos*. Bishop said he could do nothing — he had to look on — passive at this. By and by, the man was killed, because on account of this robbery of his wife, he refused to work rubber at all, so some of the *muchachos* were sent to chastise him and he was not seen again. Bishop believed he was killed, he did not know it for sure, but the girl Martenengui had given the man in place of his own wife was brought back to Atenas and again added to Martenengui's "Harem".

On one occasion when Bishop was in Chorrera, Martenengui came in from Sur (the nearest station to Chorrera only two hours away) with his harem. Two of his wives had recently borne children — "twins"! They were born almost the same day and where they were openly carried in by their respective mothers along with this highly civilised gentleman to the Chief Station of the Company. An American named Arthur was there at the time, and he said to Bishop,

"There's something you won't see with any civilised people in the world, a whiteman like that."

I got on at last to within sight almost of Entre Rios. A shower came and wet me without cooling the air. The road was indescribably bad and I was getting tired. When near the Indian house, *Huascar*[205] (O'Donnell's favourite boy) and two others, hove in view with tea, coffee and food sent out by O'Donnell on hearing of my coming. It was very welcome and I was glad of it. We hurried on after this and I plunged into the Cahuinari and sent Sealy up for dry clothes, and while in the river Fox and O'Donnell came down to see me. Sealy had arrived at 12.50, and I got up to the house about 1.20 I should think. I would have been in by 12.30 had I not stayed for the tea and the bathe in the river.

Conversation with Fox

I told Fox of all that had occurred at Matanza and on the road, and at my deep disgust at the slave gang I had seen driven along by the brute Negretti, and the lamentable condition in which many of these wretched people, especially the women, were. I lay down to rest.

Boras and Andokes carriers arrive

At 5.15 the long line of Boras and Andokes carriers — men, women and children, appeared on the path coming up from the Cahuinari, with Negretti the footpad, rifle on shoulder, bringing

[205] *Huascar* is inexplicably changed to Inca in the *Black Diary* see 20 October: "Inca sent out by O'Donnell just past Indian house." The original Huáscar (1495–1533) was the son of the eleventh Inca ruler, Huayna Capac (*c.*1450–1525). After Huayna Capac's death his great Andean Empire was divided between Huáscar and his brother Atahualpa. But the brothers quarrelled and Huáscar was defeated in battle in 1532 and duly executed. It was this civil war that allowed Pizarro and his few hundred conquistadors to overpower the Inca empire with surprising ease.

up the rear. I begged Fox to observe them closely and to take some photos of the children with my camera. This he tried to do, as they arrived, but Negretti appeared and called "Hi-ti, hi-ti", go on and the poor beings had to stagger and shamble off through the plantation and on along the road towards Puerto Peruano. It was just twelve hours since I had seen them leave the Muinanes' house in the morning, and a 12 hours march under such loads, upon such roads, with scarcely any food, God alone knows how they do it and live! I was furious with anger, and disgust, and told O'Donnell I thought it brutal and wanton brutality. Here was a big empty Indian house with room for several hundreds of people where they could have passed the night in comfort, and yet they were driven on relentlessly into the forest after such a march. In some ways I think it was the most disgusting exhibition of brutality I have seen yet. The man Negretti was raging, I could see, at Fox taking photographs of them, he only got two poor ones in the fading light. I have failed to get any photo that will show, I fear, of the lithe, tiny little boys, staggering under 30 or 40 lbs. of rubber. I have seen nothing like this on the Congo, and it is indescribable, and makes me positively ill.

Evening chat with O'Donnell

In the evening O'Donnell was very civil, and both Fox and I agreed he is the only man of the Chiefs we have met, with whom we can shake hands, and yet he has done dreadful things too, or more often allowed or directed to be done. He came here a boy of 20 and had to fall in with the accepted method of driving the Indians, and he has probably sunk far less than anyone else. Besides, he is certainly ashamed of much of it, one can see that, and would wish to minimise as far as he can the evil of the beastly system he administers. The true criminal is the government of Peru, far off, uncaring. Arana has been free to erect the individual acts of lawless squatters, Colombians and Peruvians, into a system of robbery under arms. The Government of Peru has stood by passive, and when called on for help (as with David Serrano and Gonzalez) ready to kill too, and so extend the frontiers of Peru and get more revenue-bearing territory. The two have gone hand-in-hand, Arana, the arch criminal and the administration of the Department of Loreto. Both Fox and I were sick with disgust all night.

I turned in very early, very angry and very sad and now I am trying in the quiet of a day off to write up the happenings of the last three days.[206] What with taking down the depositions of the Barbadians, no light task in point of time, questioning them and trying to check their answers, then looking around me for confirmation or otherwise each day, leaves little time or energy, always with only the night for writing. At night I am very tired, and on the road it is almost impossible to write; the sandflies at Muinanes were a dreadful pest up to about 6 p.m. and then I had the sick Indians, and all my anxiety about the poor famished boy in the forest and the sick woman beside me. If only I could write shorthand, never felt the need as now. So much depends on noting at the time and writing down at the time, leaving as little as possible to memory and the vague chances of recalling correctly, or not recalling at all. Much is lost in any case, and all I can do is try and record as promptly and as clearly as may be my thoughts, my perception of things and such facts as arise.[207]

Interruption of writing

I am now quite tired out. I've been writing all day nearly, except when occupied with Fox and O'Donnell, and now by the carriers of rubber, who turned up belated and footsore from 11 to 1 o'clock and then with Normand's coming. He arrived at about 1 o'clock, we saw him trying to slip past the station over the plantation, ¼ of a mile away, but seeing that we had seen him, he left the carriers to go on through the forest and came to us by the Atenas road, which he was cutting across, so as to strike the Puerto road beyond this.

I'll record this day's events later on. I must go out to talk to Tizon, Barnes and the rest who arrived very wet from a strong rainfall at 3 p.m. to 3.30. Normand, too, is waiting to try and talk to me. He has already begun with a string of lies, perfectly infantile in one way, but astounding illustrations of impudence and assurance.

---

[206] Contrast this to *Black Diary*: October 21: "... I am writing up my diary since Monday ..."

[207] This categorical statement about Casement's writing methods seems directly to contradict everything that the *Black Diaries* stand for. The latter portray Casement's state of mind as muddled, inaccurate and exaggerated. It should be remembered that as well as writing thousands of words of his journal each day, Casement also copied out in longhand the statements made by the Barbadians. In the seventy-five days covered by his Putumayo Journal, Casement wrote a total of around 250,000 words averaging well over three thousand words each day.

It recalls Leopold in the Palace at Brussels in November 1900 — before I had written "How I found Leopold".[208] But this hyaena is a poor Leopold. This wretch is only fit for the flogging triangle and then the gallows, and yet he dares to seek me to-day with assurances of his regard for and care for the Indians. I'll record it later on.

ENTRE RIOS — SATURDAY 22ND OCTOBER

The interview with Normand yesterday afternoon was really amusing, but it shows the man in a new light and a dangerous one. Most of these criminals I have met here are fools. This man is not. He has courage, courage of a dreadful kind, and cunning. He realises to the full, I can see, the position he is in. He was partly brought up in England and, no doubt, wishes again to go there. He knows perfectly well how such crimes as he has committed during these six years at Andokes are regarded, and how punished in England. He also knows perfectly well that the Barbadians have been illegally employed, and that a share of the responsibility for

---

[208] Casement had an interview with Leopold II on 18 October 1900, before he had made his investigation leading to his official report, *Administration of the Independent State of the Congo* {Cd.1933 Africa No.1 1904}. Casement is referring to this meeting, but he is also hinting at the effect that his discovery of the horror at the heart of the Congo Free State had on his psychological state. The changes in belief derived from his Congo investigation were conveyed in a letter to Alice Stopford Green shortly after arriving in Santos as Consul in 1907. It is the earliest occasion when he laid bare his reasons for turning against British imperialism. N.L.I. MS 10,464 [3], Casement to Green: "At the Boer war time I had been away from Ireland for years — out of touch with everything native to my heart and mind — trying hard to do my duty and every fresh act of duty made me appreciably nearer the ideal of the Englishman. I had accepted Imperialism — British rule was to be extended at all costs, because it was the best for everyone under the sun, and those who opposed that extension ought right to be "smashed". I was on the high road to being a regular Imperialist jingo — altho' at heart, underneath all and unsuspected almost by myself I had remained an Irishman. Well, the war gave me qualms at the end — the concentration camps bigger ones — and finally when up in those lonely Congo forests where I found Leopold — I found also myself — the incorrigible Irishman. I was remonstrated there by British highly respectable and religious missionaries. 'Why make such a bother', they said — 'the state represents law and order — and after all these people are savages and must be repressed with a firm hand.' Every fresh discovery I made of the hellishness of the Leopold system threw me back on myself alone for guidance. I knew that the FO wouldn't understand the thing — or that if they did they would take no action, for, I realised then that I was looking at this tragedy with the eyes of another race — of a people once hunted themselves, whose hearts were based on affection as the root principle of contact with their fellow men and whose estimate of life was not of something eternally to be appraised at its 'market' price.."

engaging them as "labourers" and turning them into criminals might be attributed to him. Not legally of course, but then none of these men are quite sure of law, one way or another. All he knows is that I am out here on an official journey, with an unknown purpose, and that I am obtaining very damaging evidence, both of the system of enslaving the Indians and of the individual crimes of the enslavers, of whom he is one of the worst. He knows perfectly that Lane gave him away first, and then that I compelled Levine to confess all and to accuse him in the presence of Tizon. He is, doubtless, seriously alarmed for his personal safety. Even with such a conscience as he must have, such crimes committed and now, as he fears, going to be exposed by the British government, possibly himself denounced (for so he fears it must be) he is trying to guard against consequences. The bribing of Levine is one way, the other, the course he adopted yesterday of approaching me to "disabuse" my mind, as he put it, and not allow me to be deceived, so that I might alter my "assertions". However, I will relate the happenings of yesterday, to tell their own story.

I got up late and tired still. The last 4 or 5 miles of the road from the cross roads of Jiménez to Entre Rios is so bad that my feet were swollen. Also they were cut with the roots and spikes of the numberless trees and stumps and a good deal scratched. This, in spite of thick socks and good shoes. The sandfly bites too, had been particularly bad, and both ankles and calves were itching a good deal, as well as my wrists and finger joints. The irritation from these sandflies is worse than from mosquitoes. I had found a huge chigger in a toe of my right foot at Muinanes on the way back on night of 19th, and it too, was sore and raw when I had cut out the bug. This is the first chigger I have had since leaving the Congo. Strange that, in all my time in Brazil, whence this pest came to Africa in 1868, I have not seen or felt one. Here this insect came, I am sure, when we stopped at the Muinanes house on the way up to Matanzas. The house is now really a sort of caravan or rest house. The Muinanes family of Hatima, the Chief with me, whose home it was, has moved away from the road on account of Normand's people going and coming from Puerto Peruano. The *cassava* and plantains are still around it, but to all intents it is an empty (and partly unroofed) house. As caravans of Andokes and Boras sleep here, they no doubt leave a certain amount of chiggers (and other vermin).

I spent the morning of yesterday bathing in the Cahuinari and talking to Fox. I told him of all that we had noticed of things at

Matanzas and my experiences on the road. He saw for himself the type of man employed there in the person of the blackguard Negretti. This brute, after having hunted on these weary beings the evening before, had stayed here all night and got good food and rest. He left about 6 a.m. to follow after the rubber men, who must have continued their weary march towards Puerto Peruano very early. Fox and I got talking of many things and suddenly he himself broached a subject that has often been in my mind. The way the Commission are carrying out their investigation.

He said that they were not proceeding properly at all and he bitterly regretted the absence of Col. Bertie. They needed a President and someone of greater experience to keep them together and collect their work. Barnes had no capacity for it and did nothing. Since he had himself raised the question, I told him I had long since noted this and regretted Col. Bertie's absence fully as much as he. I had suggested, I told him, at Occidente, to both Tizon, and Barnes and Bell that they should telegraph for him or someone else to come out. As things were, they were not a Commission at all, and on the few occasions when they met once for an hour, perhaps at each station house to interrogate the Chief alone, I had noticed that practically all the questions, and certainly answers to the point had come from him, Fox. There was no collective action it seemed to me, and no Secretary to take minutes of their proceedings, and no method in their enquiry. All this he said he felt so strongly, and had already made up his mind that he might have to write a separate report. We discussed this quite privately and confidentially and were in full agreement. I advised meeting the Col. as soon as they arrived in England and getting his advice and help in compiling their report. This, too, had been his idea he said. Barnes had told him he was no good at writing, and moreover Barnes has told me that he is so disgusted that he takes no interest in his part at all. That may be, but then he should not stay on. The whole thing is far too haphazard, each one goes his own easy gait, and were it not for Fox, the collective notes of the party (Barnes, Bell and Gielgud) would not be of the least value.

Gielgud, I said to Fox, I frankly could not look upon as a member of the Commission, he stood simply for the Company. Fox agreed, and added "Didn't the Colonel let him know that in Manaos too!" The only cheering thing is, that, as Fox admits, no shadow of doubt exists now in any of their minds as to the reality of the system of slavery we find here. Here they are at one. I said I hoped so, that I could not think any of them, even Gielgud now, would for an instant defend it in any aspect. He said not for an instant, and that if the Company proved powerless to reform, then he should denounce the state of things out here by every means in his power.

Indian carriers arrive exhausted

We were still discussing these things when some stragglers from the rubber carriers came along up the path from the Cahuinari. I hurried down to try and snapshot them as they passed, but the poor things were so frightened they almost ran, and I lost a fine chance to get one of the tiny boys with a rubber load. The little chap was not more than six I should say, a mite, and he fairly bolted with short steps before I could focus on him. I got, however, one or two bigger boys, three in a group, but they were quite big lads, and two of them fat boys as well. Then a lad of perhaps sixteen, I had seen at Matanzas, the whole afternoon nearly, sitting wearily on the ground, over his load, came along by himself and we called to him and stopped him. Bishop assisting, I got a better one of him and then I decided to weigh his load. He looked terrified when we laid hands on him and it, and as we could not speak Boras there was no chance of reassuring him. We took him into O'Donnell's store, and he and Fox came down to join me. This boy's load was 37½ kilogs. He had no food in the basket, not a scrap. Bishop said all my tins were gone, our last feed with my own carriers on the road and the sick people had finished all. There was only a tin of Libby's Asparagus, the last of those I had got from Cazes in Iquitos.[209] This, I said, was food anyhow and told Bishop to fetch it, and gave it to the boy. O'Donnell said sardines might suit him better. I said yes, and if he liked to give the boy two tins of sardines, I'd give him the asparagus. The poor boy looked on with big sad eyes all the time and gave up the asparagus when Martin Arana brought the sardines. I gave him a packet of cigarettes too. He hurried off at a trot almost, when we let him go.

[209] Casement not only brought a large amount of supplies with him from London, he also stocked up while in Iquitos. Before leaving England, Casement went to W.J. Allison and Co., who fitted him out for the trip with basic travelling necessities as well as a large stock of food — mainly cans, bottles of fruit and biscuits. Before setting out for the Putumayo from Iquitos, Casement bought further supplies from the Iquitos Trading Company, the list included: cans of mushrooms, Irish stew, Dutch cheese, pressed beef, salmon, asparagus, herrings, tinned milk, mutton, sheep's tongue, Rioja wine and sugar.

The others, who had passed, said Normand and more were behind.

Then just as we were going to breakfast, a weary being with body bent double nearly came up the incline from the road. I watched the slow approach and called Fox. The man came on step by step, and when he reached the shade of the house he fell like dead, he and his load of rubber, and lay groaning. I sent Bishop down, who came saying "He says he's dying". I hurried down, he lay inert and almost senseless, only groans coming from his white lips. I took some Irish whiskey and poured it down his throat and thus got him up, with Bishop, and got him into the store and down on one of O'Donnell's mule rugs hanging there. Fox came down, and we both eyed the piteous spectacle. O'Donnell too. The man was an Andokes too, and O'Donnell said he could not understand. The load was meanwhile brought in by Bishop and Sealy and we weighed it. It was just 50 kilogs, say 111 lbs. and not a scrap of food with it. He had eaten all on the road to this, and was now half dead with hunger, as well as the crushing weight. What infamous cruelty! Both Fox and I were furious and there were tears in our eyes too. At breakfast I felt I could not eat, and at last I apologised to O'Donnell and sent my soup down by Huascar, his boy, to the tired man. He said he would give him food himself, that he never ill-treated "his Indians" like that, and when he sent them down to P. P., it was only with loads of 30 kilogs at outside, and the whole of the people of the district helped to carry it. I quite believe that the whole of the population of the section is compelled to carry it, but I don't believe that he limits his loads either to 30 kilogs. Bishop told me he had seen just as big loads sent by O'Donnell, and the Indians staggering along just the same, O'Donnell having a better cultivated *chacara* (all done by the Indians remember) has more food to give away. With regard to this carriage of rubber, it should be borne in mind that it is wholly unremunerated. Neither food nor pay of any description is given for this extra burden, involving these terrible hardships, and exposure and long absence from their own homes and work. No wonder the Indians have no food and no time to cultivate. How one finds such sleek bodies among the Boras I cannot say, except there may be more rubber, there probably is, and so the time spent collecting is less than in this more peopled and less-forested Huitoto country.

While we were at breakfast after seeing this poor beggar provided for in some way, another straggler appeared coming up the hill with a huge load. He was not so bad as the last man and managed to get past at a snail's pace. I was moved to go out and call him in too, but did not wish to be too officious, and I feared for the man himself later on when Normand got at him. That beauty was still behind.

We had finished breakfast and about 12.30 I noticed a white hat and some Indians over on the other side of the *chacara*, making past by a circuit so as to avoid the house. I called Bishop and he said it was Normand. O'Donnell came and Fox and the whole station, and looked to try and make out. O'Donnell got his glasses. The figures appeared and disappeared in the burnt margin of the forest and thus would have to cross our field of vision over a strip of cassava planting, and O'Donnell said it was Normand passing round to intersect the P.P. road lower down through the forest.

He and N. he said were not good friends and had not held any intercourse for six months. Still this was the first time that N. had ever passed Entre Rios like that, actually leaving the road and going round over the stumps and through the forest. We could see *muchachos* of course, and finally, bringing up the rear, the blue and red costumes of the harem, also of course. The Mrs. Normands appeared to be travelling fast, all were scurrying. The white hat bobbed and bobbed and finally all disappeared into the deep forest beyond the Atenas road. The thing was a mystery, and it was only when in bed pondering on it all I hit upon this reason for this evasion of us. Just as we thought we had seen the last of Normand and that he would flounder through the forest until he struck the P.P. road with the rearguard, we saw the white hat out again, alone, on the Atenas road, and then the figure hurrying down towards us. Soon a couple of rifle shots announced the Paladine's approach. O'Donnell replied with a revolver volley. These knights of the road all salute each other. Hoping the man would only stay a few minutes I did not remain on the verandah — Lane had turned up shortly after (1.45) — come in from keeping guard at Muinanes. He said that Normand had arrived first, before the Commission, and had pulled the two coats off the "old lady" and had ordered her to go on to the neighbouring Indian house. He had given her rubber load in pieces to some of the stragglers to bring on. Normand had gone on and slept in the forest. Then the Commission and Tizon had arrived and he had given Barnes my note. They had looked for the boy and had given the old woman, who was still there, unable to walk, medicine and food, also the other sick woman.

Normand I found was staying on here, so there was no chance of not seeing him again. The Commission arrived in sections from 3.30 to 4, first Gielgud and then the others. All were soaked, a rain storm in the forest had broken over them, but we had got only the tail of it.

Normand came out dressed and cleaned to tea and made up to me at once with a sweeping bow. He began by thanking me elaborately for being so kind to his people on the road and said he wished to explain how it was I came to encounter these cases, as he thought I might have a mistaken impression of his way of dealing with his Indians. Then followed a very contradictory statement, from the famished *muchacho* and the "old lady" to his recent transit across the *chacara*. Bishop had said he only returned to face us because he saw we had all seen him from the verandah. But as the man spoke to me I saw another intention revealed. His insistence that he wished to "disabuse" my mind, that I should alter my "assertions" ("I make no 'assertions'," I replied quietly), and his frequent references to the old woman and his regret that I should have thought him capable of ill-treating her. Lane had told him, he stated, that I left a message he was not "to flog her", showed me clearly that he was playing a game. He invited me repeatedly to put any questions to him I wished and he should answer and explain anything he could.

He said "many people don't like us (who the 'us' was never transpired), and I do not wish a gentleman in your position to go away with untruthful statements uncorrected. There are bad people, I know, who tell lies about us, and from your message to me by Lane, I am afraid you believe them".

I said that Lane had no message of that kind from me, but only that I was responsible for removing the woman's load, not she, and that as for the beating of her, it was really she herself, poor soul, who, in my hearing, had repeatedly expressed fear of him, Mr Normand. I said the woman was clearly terrified as well as very ill.

"Oh, no, no I assure," he replied, "she was not at all frightened, not at all. She knew perfectly I would not, I could not touch her. I never ill-treat my people. My system is a quite different one you see. When they are sick I go to visit them and take them medicine, and when they go like this, carrying rubber, of course, some must fall out because they hurt their feet or get ill (the old woman had "knocked her leg", that was all) and that is why I came last, as you see, so that I may attend to the sick ones. I carry medicines and spare food with me. I always bring several women carrying food (the Harem! Oh! heavens). And when I find people like this man here who fell down to-day, you see, I give him this food and make them rest like this and help to divide their loads among the stronger ones. I have left several loads of rubber behind on the road, and by and by the strongest of those who have already gone to Puerto Peruano will be sent to their homes, and after they have had a good time there (he actually used those very words — "a good time there") they will be sent out, with presents, of course, you see, to take down those other loads, later on, later on".

This and much more. As regards the starved boy in the forest he had begun with him. This had been without his knowledge. The boy had been sent out to look for the wife of one of the men without his knowledge, (I said Yes, I knew that, as the boy had told me) and the boy had not found the woman and had lost his way coming back from Occidente. Lost his way, and "got hungry". I said he was "starving", absolutely and literally, and quite unable to move. "Yes, yes," he said, "I heard of that — I knew he was coming, and that he was sick, and I was sending out for him when you so kindly found him and cared for him". The boy is now "quite well" and gone to his "home" at Andokes.

His last touch was perhaps the funniest of all — it was a volunteered explanation of why he had not come directly up to the house here at Entre Rios, but had tried to slip past through the *chacara*. His rubber people, it seems, always robbed Mr O'Donnell's fields, so he had given orders that none of his people were ever to pass through this station, but to go round it without spoiling anything. I remarked that fully 150 had passed through the evening before without robbing anything — clearly in defiance of his order that none were to come this way — "Yes, yes," he went on, looking two ways at once — "I never allow them to come this way, that is why, you see, I took all my people round over there, because then they could do no harm, until I saw them past Mr O'Donnell's fields, and then I came here."[210]

---

[210] The *Black Diary* makes a complete nonsense of the chronology and facts of this most important conversation between Casement and Normand. On 21 October, the day of this conversation, the relevant parallel entry reads: "Then Normand himself. Wonderful fright across Chacara and then he came — two shots and then the Commission with news of the boy and the 'old lady'. Both better. Thank God. Normand tried to talk to me. I left him to Fox." A further entry clearly trying to

Arrival of Normand's harem

The Harem had arrived, and now five strong, one of them a child, positively a child, they floated over to Mrs. O'Donnell's quarters, where they were multitudinously received by that household of similar beauties. I nearly said "But I don't see them carrying the food you speak of, Mr Normand" — but it really was not worthwhile. I had listened almost in silence to this tissue of lies and absurdities. The only thing clear was that he was seeking to pose me in a difficulty. If I asked for explanations I'd get them galore, and if I did not, and then persisted in my "assertions", he could always say he had voluntarily offered to correct the "misstatements" I was relying on.

Fox traps Normand

Fox came in and listened to the end of our talk, or rather of his talk, and I went away. Fox's description of it is quite amusing. When, after a long rigmarole of silly lies, he had got to his good, kind treatment of the Indians, the medicines and "spare food" etc. and how they worked so gladly for him, Fox had asked

"How then do you account for the scars all over them?"

This had brought him up with a round turn, Fox said. He had stopped dead with his "yes, yes" and "you see", and had not found a word until Fox, deliberately laying a trap, as he told me, had said,

"But perhaps the Indians fight among each other."

"Yes, yes, that's it," he said, "they fight, you know, tribe against tribe."

"I see," said Fox, "and that's how they get these blows and scars, they flog each other?"

"Yes, yes, that's it. I've often seen them fight — sometimes 30 or so. They are savages, you see," and so the stream of idle lying went on. He had actually told the Commission, Barnes tells me, that he had no *cepo* at Matanzas. This in the morning, and I took them out and showed it to them at 4 p.m. — under the banana leaves and palm thatch.

---

correct this error has been squeezed above the entry for 20 October: "Normand came to Entre Rios (without Levine) who passed on road to Puerto and stayed the night. Tried to talk to me to convince me of his gentle treatment of the Indians and to make me change my 'assertions'. I said 'I make no assertions'."

Normand stays the night

Normand stayed all night, and his grievous face upset all our equanimity. It is a perfectly atrocious face — but there is no doubt the brute has courage — a horrid, fearful courage, and endurance, and a cunning mind too. He is the ablest of these scoundrels we have met yet, and I should say far the most dangerous. The others were murderous maniacs mostly, or rough, cruel ignorant men like Jiménez — half a Cholo servant man badly brought up. This is an educated man of a sort, who has lived long in London, knows the meanings of his crimes and their true aspect in all civilised eyes. Hence it is, I am sure, he is more alarmed at my coming than any of the others. He probably too wishes to return to England some time, and he fears, perhaps, that things might go badly with him there — or he may even fear that I am going to inform the Prefect at Iquitos.

This Levine may have put in his head — because I told that young ruffian that if I handed him over to the Prefect it might go hard with him. It was only later on I fully realised this. I asked Bishop where Levine was — if he had not come with Tizon and the Commission — and he said no, he thought Levine had passed through the *chacara* with Normand and gone on to Puerto Peruano. I called Lane, and he said yes, that Levine had gone on with Normand from the Muinanes' house. Later I asked Tizon why he had not brought Levine with him to Entre Rios, as I had understood he would do — that had been the arrangement. He said Normand had asked for him to help with the rubber people on the road, as he was short-handed, and so he had allowed Levine to go with him to Chorrera. I said it was a pity, as I feared Normand's real reason was to bribe the man, or boy, to unsay what he had stated at Matanzas — Tizon said nothing, but looked a bit sick. I let it rest there, but in the night, when alone, I thought things over and I think see the game of this crafty gentleman. He will get Levine down to Chorrera with him and he and Macedo can very easily bribe or frighten him. Levine is already terrified, and thinks I may hand him over at Iquitos. Of course he and Normand have exchanged confidences fully. Normand has asked and been told all that passed when I got Levine to admit his guilt before Tizon, and that he had done it "by the Manager's orders".

This clearly is why he wants Levine — and then another danger came before me. The eight other Barbados men will soon be at Chorrera — some of them certainly — to await my return at end of this month. These men will all be tampered with by Normand, Macedo and Levine as go-betweens. Levine with a good bribe, and with his tale of terror of a furious Consul going to "hand over any man who has flogged Indians" or some such story, might upset the whole applecart, and these men could be got at before my arrival. With Levine then to deliberately retract what he had said at Matanzas, and these men all waiting to depict an idyllic existence of "planting yucca and sugar cane" like Donal Francis, I should be left with only the unshaken testimony of Bishop, Sealy, Chase — and possibly Lewis and Dyall. Crichlow's they can discount by saying he has been sent to jail in Iquitos as a thief! Lane's is not very much to go upon — save for Kodihinka and the raid into Colombia — and this Levine would deny and say it was all a lie, and he had only agreed to admit it because he was terrified by me. As I am playing with the Devil I won't take any risks. I'll not go spades and let him double when I have such a good hand of Barbados Clubs.

Casement despatches Bishop

So very early this morning (the 22nd) I jumped up with my mind made up, and before I got hold of Gielgud and asked him to request Tizon to tell Normand that Levine must be sent back from Puerto Peruano. No reasons to be given — merely that I wished it. I then called Bishop, and as we were surrounded by ears, and all can be heard in these houses, I told him to stroll out to the Indian's house, where I followed him. I then told him plainly what I feared was up, and that I wished him to go first to Puerto Peruano and see that Levine came back, and then on to Chorrera and to see that the eight Barbados men were not tampered with. He grasped the situation instantly, and said

"I see, Sir, I see very well what you want."

I said I had to trust him, and did so — that he was to be very wise and discreet and let the Barbados men know exactly the truth, and that they must not be deceived or bribed or misled. I said, too, that I thought it very likely that Levine would not be sent back from Puerto Peruano. Tizon, Gielgud said later on, had given Normand positive injunctions to this effect. We will see how Normand carried them out. Perhaps with Bishop there he may — otherwise I do not think he would have obeyed. He would have explained this at Chorrera after the mischief had been done. Bishop fully saw how easily Levine could be bribed and moulded by Normand. The boy has been six years with him and is now his black counterpart. Lane has been saved by a sturdy denseness of body and pate — the other has become Normand's best flogger and whipper in.

So, after breakfast, when Normand got up and again bowed elaborately and shook hands all round — I sent Bishop marching off with him and an Indian boy from O'Donnell to carry his *tula* or Indian-rubber bag. Normand will be cheerfully surprised! I think I have spiked his gun. I wrote to Macedo (Bell did it for me in good Spanish) to say I was sending my man down to despatch something to me I needed, and I begged him to look after the man until I arrived. A nice touch. Bishop is to look after him and his charming Lieutenant, and I think the faithful black man will beat the two treacherous white men. So now for a week I shall be more or less anxious until we get back to Chorrera. I expect a pretty big row there as a finale. I have nothing but tension all the time, but I hope it is a winning game I play — anyhow it is for the right — for these helpless people against their abominable oppressors. If Levine returns tomorrow, Sunday, it will be a little relief. In some ways, now that I have forestalled their game, it might be even better if Normand disregarded Tizon's order and took Levine on to Chorrera. It would help to prove so much of his game. I told Gielgud and Fox what I had done. Former says that he is confident Normand only stopped here yesterday in order to try and "convince" me of how wrong I was in believing anything against him. Gielgud agrees that he is "seriously alarmed and that he is a cunning rascal, capable of anything." I shall be heartily glad — oh! so glad — when I see the last of Iquitos, and my nose is sniffing down the broad Solimões for the far-off breakers of Bragança and the sea breezes of Pará.

Pará seems a delicious dream up here in these awful crime-stained forests, with this hopeless race of human beings hunted and slain and tortured worse far than the wild beasts. It is now 5.15 p.m. on this Saturday afternoon, and we have had a tremendous storm of rain, badly needed. It has been dry for over ten days, O'Donnell says, and the river he calls the Cahuinari has shrunk to an 18" trickle of muddy water. Today's shower should fill it up, and I am just off now to look at it and get a breath of fresh air. Counted forty-five ripe or ripening bunches of bananas and plantains around the house. Some of the red variety like those at Andokes are very fine plants. There are four different kinds here, and some of them delicious. With any care at all enough of this fruit alone might be grown to feed the carriers passing with rubber. But nobody cares a rap about them. The rain comes on again — two of the Pupunha palms shedding the pollen from their buds with a noise like hail on the fresh banana leaves. Some of the girls of the harem are lying below.

AT ENTRE RIOS, SUNDAY 23RD OCTOBER 1910

Questioning James Lane

Up again at 5.15. It had rained nearly all night and has done it practically all day. Didn't go down to Cahuinari to bathe this morning. The others did and said it was full. My right eye now is swelling up and I do not intend going to Atenas to-morrow with Tizon and the Commission. Called James Lane at 8 a.m. and put him to further questions dealing with Normand's effort to bribe him and silence him before me. In the course of this he blurted out how Solar had reached Andokes also with letters from Macedo about my visit and how Normand had actually declared before all the employés that he would reward Donal Francis for not having told me anything at Chorrera. This was "in the letters", so Lane said, and Normand had spoken openly of it only a few days before our arrival in praise of Francis. I called Barnes and Gielgud in to hear the further confirmation of the shameless bribery going on and attempt to tamper with these Barbados men.

I forsee plenty of trouble

No sign of Levine yet — at 2 p.m. — it is still raining and he may be sheltering in the Muinanes house, but I think it more likely Normand has, on getting away from this, decided to take him on to Chorrera, in spite of Tizon's order to send him back. I expected this at the time, and told Bishop I was pretty sure Levine would not come back — that he and Normand were now one. It is well I sent Bishop especially with this further proof of Normand's intention at bribing Donal Francis, or rewarding him. I could have got Francis to tell all in Chorrera had I then cared to recall him and ask him to confess that he was bribed. Bishop said he would very likely tell me everything if I recalled him, but I did not care to do it or to raise the question of Macedo's criminality to further embarrass Tizon. I am half sorry now. I forsee plenty of trouble still before me. Normand is evidently seriously alarmed and will stick at nothing to disarm the witness against him or even attack me. I fully think he will go round to Iquitos with me on *Liberal* whether Tizon likes it or not. He will be afraid to let me go away with what he knows to be so much incriminating testimony, fearing the use I may put it to. A man like that, with such a guilty conscience, will naturally suppose I am after him, instead of being after the miserable and criminal system he has been administering. The fate of the system is of no concern to him, he has made his pile from it; it is his own safety and future he is now thinking of and, like all criminals, he is thinking only of how he personally may come out.

How the system is financed

Tizon says Normand had 18,000 soles to his credit before this *fabrico* came down. That means £1,800 — and this *fabrico* will bring in possibly another 3,000 soles — or say £300 more. The "20% on the gross product of his district" is calculated on the value put down upon the rubber at Chorrera. This, Tizon says, is calculated at 20 soles (40/-) per arroba of 15 kilos. This, I am told, does not pay the cost of the upkeep of Matanzas. There are eleven employés, or *racionales* there — and their salaries come to £77 per month, according to him, or £924 a year.

Let us work it out. Normand admitted to the Commission that he got two *fabricos* in the year, of say each 8,500 kilos. — or 17 metric tons of rubber. He has 120 men "working", so he says, and each man brings in 140 kilos (or 16,800 kilos) per annum. In his talk with me on Friday afternoon, he said that "to my surprise, I find 15 more men have brought in rubber than I knew of"! How delightful! He had thought these men had "gone away", but they suddenly turned up of their own accord, coming from nowhere, each man with 40 or 50 kilos of rubber. It was very nice of them, I said. If we put the yield of his district then at 17,000 kilos and its Chorrera value at 40/- per 15 kilos, we find it yields say 1,134 arrobas at 20 soles, or £2,268. 20 % of this would give Normand about £450. He probably makes more.

Then we get the salaries of the Staff and Normand's commission, giving £1,374 which leaves only £894, calculated on the Chorrera value of the rubber to meet all the other expenses of the Stations of Matanzas and La China, not to speak of the payment of the Indians for bringing in these 17 tons! Their share must be very small. I am convinced that the value of the goods paid to the "125 workers" (plus even the 15 who came from nowhere) for a whole year's supply of rubber does not amount to anything like £100 in the year. I mean even the Chorrera value. An *escopeta,* or trade gun, is charged 15 soles there or 30/-. This James Lane states he has never known one to be given for a whole year's rubber to any single man, and Normand told the Commission each man brought 140 kilos per annum. The Iquitos value of this would be, at 9[1]/[3] arrobas at 40/- £18.13.0; its European value (say 360 lbs. at 4/6d. per lb.) £67.10.0 or £68. For this amount probably a hammock costing 5/- and a pair of check cotton pants worth 4/- and a shirt worth 2/- will be given — and not in every case by any means. The recalcitrant, the "rebellious", those who have failed in some other way to comply with the ceaseless demands upon them; the dead and those in *cepo* or who have "escaped", must all be deducted. The cost of carriage of the rubber from Normand's section to Chorrera is nil — Tizon admitted that to-day. The rubber gatherers carry it down at their own charge — neither pay nor food being supplied.

The £894 over after salaries and commissions at Andokes are paid is left them to meet the following further charges:

* Payment to rubber gatherers — termed "advances", say £100
* Commission drawn by Sr. Macedo at Chorrera.
* Food to Sr. Normand and 11 *racionales*.
* Material needed for 2 stations such as rifles, cartridges etc.
* Sundry charges and wastage of one kind or another.

These probably eat up all the £894, leaving nothing to good on the rubber as it leaves Chorrera. Of course 4% of the arroba at Chorrera is a wholly arbitrary calculation and does not really represent anything like the actual value of the rubber there. Then again the salaries of the staff are to a great extent not paid in sterling, so that a profit is made out of them. The Stations are so ill-supplied with food, etc. that many of the employés have to buy it out of their salaries, and it is charged to their accounts at an exorbitant, quite extortionate value. (See for this Crichlow's and Bishop's accounts). So with the £100 of goods "paid" to the rubber gatherers.

Treatment of the tribal people

These are not only murdered, flogged, chained up like wild beasts, hunted far and wide and their dwellings burnt, their wives raped, their children dragged away to slavery and outrage, but are shamelessly swindled into the bargain. These are strong words, but not adequately strong. The condition of things is the most disgraceful, the most lawless, the most inhuman, I believe that exists in the world to-day. It far exceeds in depravity and demoralisation the Congo regime at its worst. The only redeeming feature I can see in this system as compared to the Leopoldian is that whereas Leopold's legalised tyranny affected many millions of people and played havoc with the heart of a Continent, this lawless tyranny affects only a few thousands. It is true that a very evil condition prevails, I believe, all through the Peruvian montaña and the Bolivian rubber districts as well, as described by Baron von Nordenskiöld (and other writers) — but the sum total of the poor outraged humanity suffering under it is less than two or three decent-sized African native tribes. The whole Indian population of the Peruvian and Bolivian rubber forests probably amounts to no more (at the outside) than 250,000 people.

Population of Indians

This Putumayo region, which is doubtless suffering the worst tyranny, has, according to Arana, 40,000 Indians, but Tizon claims only 14,000 all told, and I should think there are less than that. Still these quarter of a million Indians and these 14,000 Putumayo slaves have a great claim on the conscience of civilised mankind. The slavery under which they suffer is an abominable, an atrocious one. Although few to-day, they are the survivors of a far greater people once. It is appalling to think of all the suffering so-called Spanish and Portuguese civilisation has wantonly inflicted on these people. I say wantonly because there was no plea of necessity, as, say, in the case of the North American Indians, to put forward here by their enslavers and exterminators. The conditions are or were rather totally different.

The inevitable disappearance of the North American Indian before an advancing stream of colonists who came to possess the soil and till it and found families, great cities and a mighty people, differed from the mere enslaving invasion of Latin Exploiters who came not to till the soil, or possess it or found a great civilised people — but merely to grow individually rich on the forced labour of the Indians whom they captured and have held for centuries, in rapidly diminishing numbers, as perpetual and hereditary serfs. As Tizon said to me: "Peru has many inhabitants, but very few citizens".[211]

[211] Casement believed firmly that the methods of colonization between North and South America were essentially different. While the settlement of North America and the wars of extermination carried on against the North American Indian in the nineteenth century had given way to ordered settlement, the land and people of South America had been brutally exploited. The argument is laid out more fully

Una

Several plants brought in to-day. Among them the 'una' — a creeper, O'Donnell says. This is the plant that provides the Indians with the strange narcotic that sends them off into a trance when they want to discover who it is has bewitched them. O'Donnell described it to us one of the first evenings of our arrival at Entre Rios — and I am going to take notes from him to-morrow on some of the Indian customs. Robuchon does not mention this. Hardenburg's narrative of the customs, etc. of the Huitotos is very largely a translation of Robuchon's, I find — often word for word.

2.30 p.m.

The first of the returning Andokes and Boras rubber carriers have just appeared, coming back from Puerto Peruano, but no sign of Levine. I hurried out to try and see them, but they had already passed the house and were well down the road to the Cahuinari. Poor souls! — in this rain — although it is now stopping. I see Lane on the watch for the men. I told them this morning to look out for them and bring up certain individuals, and I am now in hopes I may get these two fresh witnesses up this afternoon — although Normand may take the men down to Chorrera. We'll see. I find Bishop cannot send me any goods up, as the *Veloz* is kept at Occidente to await our arrival at P.P., so Tizon tells me.

Letter from Bishop

Here is Bishop's letter — just brought to me at 2.35 p.m.. It tells how he overheard Normand and Levine plotting together and how Normand told him (Bishop) that Levine was "too ill" to return to Entre Rios and that "the Consul" must do without him. Bishop added that both were going down to Chorrera by land, and he was going to stalk them and stay here till I arrived and warn the remaining Barbados men who were being called in to be questioned by me that their best game was to tell me the truth and the whole truth. It also says Levine refuses to return — as I expected.

I have read it to Tizon, Gielgud and Fox — and former (who is angry) is at once sending a *muchacho* to P. Peruano to bring in Levine with a letter to Normand. I said I did not require this to be

in Casement's essay, "The Putumayo Horrors", which Casement wrote at the end of his journey.

done. I do not need Levine. I was merely desirous of proving to him the utter dishonesty of these men, and I told him then of Solar's coming to Matanzas with letters from Macedo first as to Ultimo Retiro and Normand's pleasure at Donal Francis refusing to speak out. Also of the attempt to bribe Lane himself the night we arrived at Matanzas. I told him I had been sure from the first when I heard Levine had gone past this without showing that Normand was taking him on to bribe him and that this had been the explanation of his going round this station through the plantation instead of coming by the road past the House. It was to get Lane away without my stopping him here. It was quite clear that he was bribing Lane to retract all he had stated to me in his, Tizon's presence. Then at Chorrera he and Macedo would further bribe Donal Francis, and bribe or intimidate the Barbados men who might already have arrived there to await my return. I told him I had sent Bishop down to counteract, by his presence, as far as possible, this attempt to suborn these British Subjects. I added that it was, of course very reprehensible action of the part of these high agents of this Company to attempt anything of this kind.

"Yes" he said, "but it is human nature."

"Low human nature", I replied

"That is little", he replied, "men who are murderers will not think much of being merely dishonest and liars."

I said it was, in one way, a matter of indifference to me as I felt sure he was already as convinced as I of the terrible evils that existed here. He replied, "Yes, I was convinced before you — not by you — but by my own sources of information."

The messenger was despatched with a written order from Tizon to Normand to send Levine back. I sent also a note for Bishop, acknowledging his letters and saying that he was to carry on to Chorrera and follow my instructions and I added that he should tell Donal Francis to be a <u>man</u> and speak the truth when I came down. I asked Tizon if Normand would not open this letter. He said "No, that was not possible, I might send it all in safety." I have my doubts, very strong ones. I sealed it with three seals, wrapped it in oiled paper and asked O'Donnell to give it to the *muchacho* who was to give it <u>only</u> to Bishop himself. We shall see if it reaches him. I am now fully convinced that Normand means danger. I can quite guess what the "other things" were he said to Bishop, especially after something Lane stated this morning at the end of his replies to my questions. He said that when Normand had spoken to him on the morning of my leaving Matanzas after I had left the station one of the things he said to him was — translating Lane's imperfect English.

Normand's words to Lane

"Do you trust these Englishmen? Remember the one who came before and how he failed you. You complained through him and what came of it." This was the gist of it. I asked Lane — "What did he mean?" He said "I don't know, Sir — that's what he say." This, I fancy refers to Whiffen. Normand wanted the boy to realise that just as Whiffen had failed in his encounter with Arana, and things had gone on just as these people chose after Whiffen's exposure — so it would be with me. The Barbados men who trusted me would find me powerless, a broken reed to lean on — that was the intention I imagine.

Assessing the situation — the worst scenario

I have thought it over since writing the above and feel sure that Macedo and Normand will now stick at nothing to save themselves. They are afraid that I am going to inform the Prefect at Iquitos of the things I have seen, etc. and that I am relying on the Barbados men as my evidence. They will, therefore, try to forestall me either by complaining of me even — or else by getting the Arana house in Iquitos to charge the Barbados men (any pretexts would be sufficient for their purpose) and getting them in jail. Once in jail they would rely on being able to force every man of them to retract anything they had stated — and even to say a good deal else that suited the needs of the scoundrels, or they could charge them, the Barbados men, with committing crimes on the Indians. Nothing would be easier, and the witnesses might be the very Chiefs of Sections who had compelled these men to those very acts.

The thing is perfectly possible. Gibbs and Cresset (the latter has not yet been spoken to by me) could be arrested as deserters from the *Liberal* the day we left — even as 'thieves' because they had advances of money from the Captain. Poor Stanley Lewis, the boy of that rascal Reigado,[212] the Skipper, could also be locked up on any trumped-up charge. This could be done with Dyall too, now at Encanto with Loayza who is evidently one of the cleverest rascals of the crowd. Possibly Dyall has already been bribed, or terrorised

[212] The name Reigado has been clearly changed in the manuscript version to Reigada on the three occasions it appears on this page.

into recanting — a possibility I foresaw when I allowed him to go to Encanto to await my return.

I told the Commission then that I was parting with much of my evidence. There would then only remain to me Bishop, Sealy, Chase and this thick-headed boy, Lane, who does not count for much in the way of sense or reliability. These men they could not bribe or terrorise. They will be true to me as Blackmen can be to their "Massa". Bishop, moreover, has plenty of intelligence and will be more than true. He knows quite well what it is I am striving for. But true as steel, would not perhaps prevent them suffering too. All might be arrested — charged possibly with 'libelling' Macedo and Normand. They might even go to the length of imputing this to me — anything to discredit me. They have already as I told Barnes long ago in Iquitos would be the case, accused us all of being drunkards. This by Captain Reigado on the *Liberal*. Lewis told Bishop he had more than once heard Reigada and the Engineer saying this up in the bows together and again at Chorrera. This Bishop told me coming in from the Muinanes' house on the road together on Wednesday last. He was speaking of the duplicity of the these men, even to each other, and then told me this of Reigada whom he said, — "You gentlemen thought so pleasant and straightforward on board ship".

Fears for the Barbadians

I told Bell and Barnes of my fears as to the plot that is being hatched at Chorrera, and that I had, as a matter of fact, expected that something of this kind would arise sooner or later. Indeed I am surprised it has not come before. Already in Iquitos I told them, I had discussed the possibility of this with Cazes and had told him that I thought it highly probable I should not return to Iquitos, but would get off somewhere in Brazilian territory with all the Barbados men, I might have with me, and wait on the bank of the Solimões for a downgoing steamer to Manaos. I had said then that if I suspected any attempt might be made on the liberty of the Barbados men who had testified truly before me I should not risk their safety by returning to Iquitos with them, but should go straight down to Manaos, by a passing steamer. I now told Bell and Barnes that if, on getting to Chorrera, I saw the likelihood of this game being played I should not return to Iquitos.

At all costs of inconvenience and exposure I would go down the Putumayo on a raft, if necessary. I would not expose those men who had been true to their sense of duty to all the evident risks that might await them in Iquitos. It is I who have put them in peril. Bishop at the outset asked me in Iquitos if there was any "political" trouble, because he was "a poor man". I said that he was to trust in me, that no trouble should come to him and that if it did it would have to fall on my head first.

Both Bell and Barnes agreed with me. I asked them not to say anything about this, it was, perhaps, too soon to anticipate evil, but they knew as well as I did that these scoundrels, now thoroughly alarmed, would stick at nothing. Had I gone to Matanzas alone, I am pretty sure they would have made away with me. I might have "died of fever" and who would have known? Even Gielgud admitted that this was highly probable. Normand clearly would shrink from no crime to save himself or conceal his infamies. But it is not myself that is in question. It is the whole case against this wrongful system and the hope of reform that we have been planning together.

If the Barbados men should be arrested in Iquitos, I should have to defend them. My first step would be to telegraph home and to ask for legal advice and help. In any case, a "trial" or imprisonment of the Barbados men would upset the whole apple-cart we have been toilfully dragging through these miry forest tracks. All question of the British Company surviving such a trial and the attendant expenses would be at an end. Our work here would be swept away and the Company with it, and all would again fall into the hands of the Arana gang, and their hired murderers on the Putumayo. More too, the British government would be involved in nasty questions with the government of Peru on the imprisoning and trial of the Barbados men. The Peruvian government, if it found itself committed, by intrigue at Iquitos, to these arrests and prosecutions, would then, right or wrong, to save its face, ensure the conviction of the men as having been guilty of grave crimes on the Indians. The real criminals would all escape, the guilty would survive and, the company swept away, they would revive their worst forms of pillage and murder to get the last ounce of rubber out of these forests.

That was the position I foresaw as likely to arise on my return to Chorrera, and I wanted them to understand the dangers, and accord me their full support if, as might become necessary, I should decide not to return to Iquitos but go down the Putumayo with the Barbados men and seek "reform by flight." Like Sir Peter Teazle[213] I

[213] Sir Peter Teazle is a character in Sheridan's comedy *The School for Scandal* (1777) — an old man who has married a young wife. The reference is to the moment when Sir Peter, on leaving the company of the scandal-mongers, Sir Benjamin

would leave my character behind me, and I should count on them, the members of the Commission, making quite clear later on why I had taken this course and that they had better come too with their full approval and support as being the best thing to do under the circumstances.

Plenty of law and little justice

All this is not fantastic conjuring up of dangers. Take only three cases within my knowledge — that of Cyril Atkins, sent down by this very man, Normand, to Iquitos, and who died in jail there, without a trial — of E. Crichlow, confined for 15 months in Iquitos jail on mere letters from Loayza, without one single witness or scrap of personal evidence against him — and finally the case of Braithwaite, that was on while I was in Iquitos, where all the influence of Cazes was powerless to obtain a trial, although the charge against the man was flimsy in the extreme — merely one of disorderly conduct on board one of the river launches, and at the worst of threatening the Captain, while the man alleged the Captain had done more than threaten him. Tizon himself admitted to me only a few days ago (when on the march from Puerto Peruano here) that in Peru "they had plenty of law and little justice".

The Prefect would be probably powerless to intervene. The Casa Arana would get the warrants for arrest from the Court on any sort of pretext sufficiently backed up by a bribe, and then the Prefect would be powerless in the face of the law. Why, even in civil matters the Iquitos court does as it pleases. Cazes' case is one in point, his house surrounded by troops, the British Consulate guarded so that the Consul dare not leave his doors to transact business. The Prefect confessing himself powerless and that, too, in a case where the Aranas were the other parties in the suit, and the matter was purely a civil one, a case of mere commercial dispute. Finally, as Cazes asserted, the Supreme Court at Lima gave a decision in his favour and the Iquitos court has quashed it! The Iquitos Court, one of quite inferior jurisdiction, sets aside the order of the highest Court in the republic and persists in maintaining a judgement already annulled by law. It is clear that no trial of accused Barbados men in such an environment could be a just one. The witness against them would be the very criminals who had compelled them to perform the very acts they would be charged with. I must at all costs, prevent this — even

Backbite, Lady Sneerswell and Mrs. Candour, makes the classic remark, "Your ladyship must excuse me ... But I leave my character behind me."

by flight down the Putumayo and the Amazon until I can put these men in safety in Brazilian territory and telegraph home for advice.

Casement's counterplan

My plan then would be, if FO sanctioned, to return alone to Iquitos and with Tizon and the Commission behind me convince the Prefect of the true state of things here and of the imperative need for the government of Peru to intervene promptly and decisively to sweep out all this den of murderers. The Commission would I am sure, back me, and Tizon I hope, too. I shall wait till we reach Chorrera and then tell him all my fears, if I see that Normand and Macedo etc. are intending to carry out the plan I attribute to them, and also my counterplan and claim his full support.

Muchachos return from hunting

In the evening one of the *muchachos* brought in a fine puma he had shot some two hours away. He had cut off the snout or jaws for the teeth, and the paws, too, for the claws. This was a fine specimen. The "boys" took it to their house and ate it — a good dish for them, poor beggars. There is plenty of game in these forests round here. So much so that O'Donnell says he cannot plant beans as the deer come out of the forest and eat the young shoots. The beans eaten at all the sections come from the Ucayali.

AT ENTRE RIOS — 24TH OCTOBER

The Commission were to leave for Atenas to-day. I had decided not to go there, but to stay here with O'Donnell until the time comes for our going down to Puerto Peruano to catch the *Veloz* for Chorrera. This is timed for 27th or 28th. The *Liberal* is due to leave Iquitos any day now, and should be at Chorrera before 5th November. Velarde I find is already dismissed by Tizon, or by Macedo acting on Tizon's instructions. He will go back to Iquitos on *Liberal* with me. Nice company. If Normand goes too, with his wretched tool Levine, I shall be in charming society for the ten days back to that centre of intrigue — supposing I were to go to Iquitos by the *Liberal*. That had been my intention up to yesterday — now all may be altered. We shall see at Chorrera.

A wood ibis at lunch

A great wood ibis at lunch suddenly sailed down from the North — coming from the Caquetá, O'Donnell says, and alighted quite near the house. There was a hubbub and a rush for the guns by Whites and Indians. Fox and I intervened to save its life to the disgust of all. I tried to photo it, but could not get within sufficient distance. It stayed some twenty minutes, preening itself — quite close, not more than twenty yards away from O'Donnell's harem — and Fox and I guarded it until at length, rested and refreshed, it sailed away on great white and black wings and soared high into the air. It looked like a stork and was almost as big. I will try to verify it in the Pará Zoo on my return.[214]

Later the same *muchacho* who shot the puma brought in three fine forest birds — one a big partridge, as big as a pheasant and like it but with only a fine soft tuft of speckled feathers in place of a tail; and a glorious speckled pigeon — and quite different in plumage — more like a hawk's — except for the amethyst and opal shading on the breast feathers.

An early afternoon swim

I went down to the river to bathe at 2–3. It was full and delightfully cool. A decent Indian lad about seventeen went with me, and I gave him soap to wash and to six little boys — dear wee chaps of seven or eight who swam like fish. All revelled in the soap and laughed and lathered. The big boy was terribly scarred with the lash right down his thighs, all across the buttocks and round on the hips on both sides. Poor lad! I pointed to them and asked how they came and he bent low and said "Huh" — yes — with the look of grave reminiscence that comes across all their faces when you touch these scars.

Many of the Boras and Andokes men and women passed back up country again to-day from carrying down Normand's rubber to Puerto Peruano. None had a scrap of food. Two were quite old men and very sick, they could hardly walk although empty handed, because empty bellied. I never witnessed anything of its kind worse than this forced march of these poor beings and this

[214] The Pará zoo that Casement refers to is the Museo Emilio Goeldi in Belém do Pará, set up at the end of the nineteenth century along the lines of a European zoo. In the large gardens a number of birds and animals of the Amazon were held including tapirs, capybara, snakes, crocodiles, monkeys, araras, toucans and turtles. The museum also held a fine collection of minerals and items of local anthropological interest such as Amazindian tools, weapons, weaving and pottery. Casement seems to have had close contact with the Institute and was responsible for introducing a number of Amazon animals to Dublin Zoo. Casement also told this story about the Wood Ibis in the piece he wrote for *The Contemporary Review* in September 1912.

return to their homes, 40, 50 or 60 miles away, without an ounce of food to carry them home. It is revolting. Several of them had been further pressed in to carry up to us some boxes of provisions etc. left at Puerto Peruano. That is fifteen miles away. They brought these and only asked to "escape", fear was in their eyes all the time. O'Donnell gave each a lump of *cassava* bread and a tiny tin of sardines, and, taking this they pointed up the path and asked if they might go, and with a "Huh" were off with their short quick steps.

He has little in his store. On getting back from Matanzas, I wanted to pay my seven Indian carriers. I had promised them a shirt apiece. He had only three shirts and one pair of pantaloons in all his store! It speaks for itself. So I gave each man a "good for" and am sending the things up to O'Donnell when I get to Chorrera, and leaving a bit of all these men and their sub-tribes with him for identification, so that he can pay them for me when the things come. I got some tins of meat up from Chorrera on return from Andokes and have been able to give some of it away to the poor starving Boras going home. How I pity these people — God help them!

O'Donnell told me about four that my letter to Bishop had been delivered, and that they had all gone down in the *batalon* to Chorrera. The *muchacho* messenger had returned and reported this. No sign of Levine or word from Bishop. It is exactly as I foresaw. Normand is keeping the boy in defiance of Tizon's positive order to send him back. Each rogue is now the support of the other — united they stand to make as much trouble as they can, so as to prevent me denouncing them — as they fear I am intent on doing.

Tizon's letter from Normand

About 5 p.m. Tizon came with a letter he had received from Normand, sent back by O'Donnell's "boy" who had taken down his order for Levine's return. He was pale and angry.

"Here is the beginning of the trouble", he said, handing me the letter. "I sent him only four or five words, to send back the man and he disobeys."

The letter said Levine was ill, this time a "sore leg," (it had been fever before) and that he could not oblige a sick man to take the road. It is a palpable lie, and Tizon now admits it to the full. We talked the matter over fully, and I told him all my fears as to the line Normand would now probably pursue. I pointed out how the man was thoroughly alarmed, and that a criminal afraid was a desperate man. It was his neck, his skin, he was scheming for, and he would have the support of everyone in the Company, even Tizon himself, in concocting a story for consumption at Iquitos that, by implicating the Barbados men, should shield himself. I said there was no doubt that Zumaeta and Dublé, not to speak of Macedo, Velarde etc. would be behind him. He saw it clearly and the danger too, just as I have put it down earlier. He promised to stand by me and the Barbados men to the end, and when I suggested his possibly coming to Iquitos, either with me, or surely in time to forestall Arana in December and get his ear, (and the Prefect's) before Dublé and Co., he admitted the strength of my argument.

"If Normand goes to Iquitos" he said "then I go with you. I'll hear the Commission here and accompany you straight to the Prefect and make everything clear and plain to him. You can count on me to the end."

Casement fears the worst

I pointed out the lamentable consequences that would ensue if the Barbados men were arrested, and if Normand provoked a scandal in Iquitos in hope of getting off under the smoke. Any such course I said would inevitably end the Company, Tizon's projected reforms and all the good we had been planning together for the Indians. It would also bring about the hideous scandal we wished to avoid, and call down upon Peru the universal reprobation that such deeds as these merited. He saw it all, agreed with every word, and said it must be stopped at all costs and that I could rely upon him, and he felt sure on the Prefect (his old school chum) doing all that was possible to checkmate the game of Normand and the Iquitos house. He confessed frankly that they were the danger, that he had no one to rely on in the Company at all. Until we came he had been alone. Now he felt isolated among the employés of the Company — he saw in the manner of all toward him that he was no longer "persona grata" with any of them — he had joined us, "the enemy", and stood for entire reform and change and they knew it. All would be against him. None would fight in the open — but in intrigue and lying — behind his back. Dublé he admitted was the leader of the gang — kept for his skill, chicanery and ability as a schemer. When they saw their occupation going they would stick at nothing to get rid of him. (I said every word of this to the Commission yesterday and here is Tizon saying it himself.)

"But", he said, "we are fighting in the good cause, they in the bad, we can and shall fight in the open — we will have the whole world behind us if it comes to that — my country too, and we shall win."

I said I had never doubted that. I had been convinced from the first of that, and as he was so entirely with me in all I felt and thought we should never doubt for an instant that we should prevail and sweep this place clean of these ruffians and found a wholly changed method of dealing with the Indians. It would be impossible to record all we said — for our talk was a very long one. We have at any rate established a plan of campaign against the rascals for the immediate future. For the later danger — the attitude of Julio Arana himself to any sincere reform and the possibility of the London shareholders kicking and the Board resigning when they know the truth — we can do nothing. Tizon said he had read the correspondence between the Coy. and the FO (I presume he had asked for it from Barnes or Gielgud) and was annoyed at the folly of the Coy. in adopting such an attitude. It annoyed him — both their truculence and their stupidity — for both to some extent he blames Gielgud, as is obviously right. Everybody knew, he said, that the agents were paid a commission on results and Gielgud knew it well, and if he did not he was more than stupid. The childish attempt to play off his Government and to pretend that a British Consul could not accompany the Commission without possibly giving offence to the Peruvian Government he deprecated.

He said "You see, my government welcomed you as was perfectly right. But in Lima they knew nothing of the truth, now I know it all and they shall know it too."

Tizon's statement has greatly cleared the air. I always trusted him — as I told him — from the first day we had our big tussle at Chorrera when I won, and he gave in. Since that we have not often had any long talks, because I did not wish to worry him — knowing he was doing his part and that he was alive to the need for action. However, we are more clearly of one mind than ever before and I told him he could count on me to the end. He went so far as to say, that if Arana would not give in and whole-heartedly join the reform scheme he would devote his life to ending this state of things. That he would go to Lima, and ask me to send him some of the evidence I had collected from the Barbados men, go to his government, publish it and move every good man and woman in Peru to join him in saving these Indians. He said again and again, "I mean to fight, and to win."

He realised as I pointed out to him the danger of Arana joining the Iquitos lot and kicking over the Coy. How can Arana make his explanation to the London board? He has grossly deceived them Tizon admits, for he said "Arana knew, he must have known". I said the only thing will be for him to eat humble pie, to say he had been deceived and bitterly regretted his attitude and to make amends would do his utmost to help the English Board to reform things here. For this I urged him strongly to go to Iquitos in time to meet Arana before Dublé and Zumaeta have "got him".

Also to get the Prefect completely informed. He said he had written to the Prefect (after our big field day at Chorrera) and had told him frankly things were "very grave" and would need all his strength to deal with. He had also written Arana in the same sense — and more hurriedly.

Casement's revolutionary blood starts to rise

Another danger we discussed was that these pirates on the spot will not accept dismissal when it comes, but will go off on their own to *conquistar* more Indians and upset the reforming agents. To conduct, in fact, private wars against the Coy. as they have done between themselves and Colombia for years. He said this was a real danger and he would require troops. I have seen this since Occidente when I took the measure of "Juanito" and the d****d young scamp Rodriguez. Tizon over-rates these men's influence with the Indians I think. He fears that they could "turn the Indians against us," because they know them so well and the Indians are "such children", and they alone speak the language. I said that was true, but that any decent Peruvian officer with, say, 150 good soldiers, would clear the lot out very soon.

Once, I said, the Indians saw one of their murderers hanged and were told it was done for their sakes to save them, they would be with the soldiers as guides, as allies and trackers down. A few good Boras armed with rifles, with the military force of Peru and a military magistrate behind them, would end the *correrias* and *commissions* of the Juanitos, Velardes, Montts and co. in a very short time. Something of the kind will have to be done — that I told him — and he sees it well, in his heart. I said, three weeks ago, at Occidente, when we had our last straight talk, that I should strongly urge him to write them for troops and a military magistrate — what in West Africa would have been a District

Commissioner. Hanging, I fear, would not be possible — as Peruvian courts come in and the lawyers — but shooting a few of the scoundrels would be easy enough. Tizon said he would like to do some of it himself.

We kept the Commission waiting for dinner with our very protracted yarn, but I am much happier in my mind. My position is a very difficult one. Here I am quite alone officially, and a heavy official responsibility on me too, to steer clear of all trouble or friction with the Peruvian government. That I can accomplish, but the situation is an extraordinarily difficult one, for at any moment I may be landed in a row, the end of which no one can see, by any of these guilty men who are now all awake. I am "the enemy" because it is only through me and the Barbados men that they fear the truth coming to light. Tizon said they had "built a wall round him, so that he should not see the truth" — but he had seen it all the same — "And now", I added, "we've pulled down the wall altogether and you see clearly, and everyone of them will be against you." We shall win — not merely against the Normands and Macedos — they are contemptible beings — but against all the bigger intrigues in Iquitos, or wherever they may be.

The Bridge Game

Played bridge — 33 hands in two rubbers.[215]I should think a record. First rubber was 17 hands and second 16. I kept the score of the first to send to John Gordon. Turned in at 11.30 only and read an amazing melodrama by P. Oppenheim called *The Yellow Crayon*.[216] It is too funny, and yet extraordinarily interesting and

---

[215] This is another revealing slip of the forger's pen. In the parallel entry in the *Black Diary* it states: "Played 33 hands and 2 Rubbers Bridge." The importance of the rubbers for Casement is that they played 33 hands "in" two rubbers, which was clearly a freak, given that the average rubber has from between 6 to 12 deals. The bridge that Casement played with the other Commissioners and Tizon during their Putumayo investigation was 'Auction' Bridge which developed from 'Whist' and 'Bridge Whist' and was first played in 1903–04, and gradually died out after the development of 'Contract' Bridge in about 1926. Although Casement certainly played bridge quite often on his journey there are more references in the *Black Diary* to the game. Bridge has long appealed to tacticians and plotters, because of its partly revealed/partly hidden nature. Among twentieth-century enthusiasts can be counted Ian Fleming, Chairman Mao, Eisenhower and Somerset Maugham. The figure of John Gordon, to whom Casement wished to write about the two exceptional rubbers, has not been identified. It is probable that the high number of games was due to incompetent bidding.

[216] *The Yellow Crayon* by E. Phillips Oppenheim (1903) was a popular Edwardian drawing-room novel filled with soft sunlight, magnums of champagne, oysters and

just the thing I wanted to make me laugh and forget these surroundings. I read it nearly all night.

Entre Rios — Tuesday 25th October[217]

Apology for O'Donnell

The Commission and Tizon left for Atenas at 8.30 or 9. I staying with O'Donnell. How strange, with this man of Irish name, whose record in any civilised land would consign him a hundred times to the gallows, and yet here I like him actually. We all agree he is the best, and are prepared to forgive his crimes as being part of "the System" he was engaged to administer. It is the lowest system of slavery in the world, and this man who came here a boy of 20, 7 years ago, has probably sunk less than the others and got his rubber with cleaner hands than any of his neighbours. He is not so low as the system he has worked — that is my apology for him and for my mental attitude towards him. I heard Tizon ask Gielgud how to spell 'gaol-bird', last night. We all smiled and mentally applied it to the agents of this great English Company. I have gone one better, because I called them to-day "the excrement of the jails of Peru".

I am sorry for O'Donnell, as we all are, and really feel that he has not fallen nearly so low as the others; yet if the crimes committed here in Entre Rios, in this far and away best of the stations, could come to light, what a ghastly record there would be. The lashes on the limbs of the Indians are far too conspicuous, they tell their horrid tale. Still here I am staying with O'Donnell rather than stay with Montt and I feel a sort of kindly feeling for the man, and a belief that under other direction he would have done well even. As it is he has done well compared to all the men around him, and his Station is a model one among these detestable penitentiaries. Fancy having a gaol where the gaolers were all the criminals and the prisoners the innocent and the wronged!

---

good old-fashioned love and indiscretions — a comedy of manners. The frontispiece of the book shows a man and woman elegantly attired and seated in a plant-filled conservatory and staring into one another's eyes. She says to him in the caption below: "You are not like these fools of Englishmen, who go to sleep when they are married, and wake in the divorce court." The drawing-room drama builds to a climax in which a British Cabinet Minister is assassinated.

[217] Up to this every entry in the journal is in pencil. Entries from 25 October to 2 November are written in pen and black ink. These entries would make interesting candidates for further handwriting analysis.

At luncheon to-day, which included Martin Arana, the reputed brother of Julio Arana, O'Donnell told me something of the Indians killing the Colombians in this neighbourhood. I said I had "great sympathy for the Indians" — and he could only smile.

Casement desires to arm and train the Indians

I have more than sympathy — I would dearly love to arm them, to train them, and drill them to defend themselves against these ruffians. I said to Tizon last night that I only wished this were British territory for a year and with 100 men what pleasure I should take in scouring it clean. Poor chap! he agreed saying "Alas! but your government is a powerful one, and mine is not". We both agreed that we should have great pleasure in hanging, if needed with our own hands, many of the Company's staff. Tizon said, too, what I have several times averred to Fox and other members of the Commission privately, viz. — that if, by chance, he surprised any of them in the act of flogging an Indian, as this horrid act has been so revoltingly described to us, he would shoot the man without a moment's hesitation. I told him such had been my intention for sometime back. I did not add that I had loaded my revolver and had it ready on Wednesday last in the Muinanes house, on the road down from Andokes, in case Negretti had arrived in the night and begun to maltreat the sick woman. It is a strange thing perhaps, the only time I have thought even of using a revolver has been against a *racional* employee of the Company. I have never otherwise had it near me, it has been carried by one of the servants or locked up. I never carried a revolver against African natives, and I certainly shall not begin to do so against these very human South American Indians who are so much gentler and less able to defend themselves. The innate gentleness of their dispositions is revealed in a score of ways. But it is strikingly visible in their countenances. I take exception to Whiffen's phrase in his letter to FO, wherein he attributes much of the criminality to the *muchachos* or to the innate cruelty of the Indians.[218]

---

[218] Casement here leaves a blank for Whiffen's quote. He is referring to Whiffen's report to the Foreign Office sent on 21 October 1909 {FO 371/722}. Casement's copy of this letter is held in N.L.I. MS 13,087 (9) and contains margin notes made during his voyage. From this version it is clear that the comment made by Whiffen to which Casement took exception was the claim that many atrocities were committed by Indians on other Indians. "This is partly due to the policy of the company taking as 'boys' Indians of tribes hostile to tribes being dealt with, thus putting them at the mercy of their hereditary enemies, partly from the fear of death on the part of 'boys' if instructions are not carried out, and partly on account of the sav-

Cannibalism

There is not, so far as I am aware, any specific act of cruelty or torture attributed to these people even by the very men who have so cruelly wronged them for years, and who so richly deserve torture. When the Indians have killed these so-called white men, they have simply slain them outright, and think what this killing has meant to them — the rescue of wife and child, of all that was dear to them. The *muchachos* have been brutalised, and made to behead and shoot, to flog and outrage. They are only another instance of the hopeless obedience of these people. What the white man orders they are only too prone to execute. Their very weapons attest the bloodlessness of their minds and customs. These childish spurs and deadly blowpipe — noiseless, stupefying and not blood-letting. Contrast such a weapon with the battle-axe, the six-foot spear with its 18" blade, or the beheading knives of the African inland tribes. Those robust savages rejoiced in blood-letting, just as the heroic Zulu saw red and well-nigh bathed in it. These soft-voiced, soft-eyed, gentle-mouthed people have never slaughtered, they have killed. Even their cannibal feasts, as recounted by Robuchon in 1906, or by Lt Maw in 1827, have never been orgies of blood-letting and seem to have been attended by as little cruelty to the victim as is possible to attach to such a ceremony. Moreover, these feasts do not, in truth, appear to have been banquets at all, and I doubt much if the killing and mastication of an enemy, as described by Robuchon had anything to do with feeding the body upon him. It is more like the feeding of the spirit with his spirit; of the heart with his heart; of the soul with his soul.

The subsequent vomit, deliberately provoked, would seem to strongly support my theory that they killed not to eat, so much as to survive. So it has been in all their attacks upon Colombians, Peruvians, Brazilians. Grievously wronged beyond all human endurance, they have sought to free themselves and their hunted

---

agery and innate cruelty of the Indian character." Casement's margin note states: "I should be disposed to say not 'innate cruelty' so much as innate thoughtlessness. These Indians are extraordinarily obedient — 'dangerously so' — as Tizon put it. They do what they are told without question. A good man could direct them to good object — a bad man to evil, as has been done so very often by the very evil men in many of these sections. The Indian leaves his thinking to be done by those over him — he naturally has never seen human life venerated as with us, save in his own narrow family circle. To abuse his child-like ignorance of the meaning of life and convert him into a murderer, from boyhood up, is not the least of the crimes of these scoundrels."

wives and children from the most atrocious bondage and fiendish outrage.

The tragedy of the South American Indian

The tragedy of the South American Indian is, I verily believe, the greatest in the world to-day, and certainly it has been the greatest human wrong for well-nigh the last 400 years that history records. There has been no intermission from the day Pizarro[219] landed at Tumbes, no ray of a dawn to come. All has been steady, persistent oppression, accompanied by the most bloody crimes. A race once numbering millions, practising many of the arts, adapting itself to a wholly gentle civilisation imposed rather by precept and advice than by force of arms and conquest has been reduced to the wretched Andean serfs — the Cholos of Peru, a race "without rights". Truly Tizon could say "Peru has many people but few citizens". Here in these primitive forests we are back with Pizarro, without the saving influence of the priests. All restraint, even that of a mediaeval and inquisitorial church, is here removed.

Submerged types

Only the blood-letting, blood-thirsty conquistador seeking not gold but rubber, not rubber so much as Indians — these are the real prey — without a soul, without a God, without one single ideal of decency or self-respect, this alone remains, not even a white man as Cortes[220] and Pizarro were, but in 8 cases out of ten a *mestizo*, a

[219] Pizarro, Francisco (*c.*1470–1541), conqueror of Peru, was born in Trujillo in Extremadura. He first arrived in America in 1509 and settled in Panama in 1519, and joined Almagro in his voyage to explore the west coast of South America in 1522. In 1526 he explored the Gulf of Guayaquil and subsequently returned to Spain to seek permission from Charles V to conquer new territories for the Spanish crown. In 1530 he returned to Panama and the following year the expedition got underway. In 1532 he overcame the Inca chief Atahualpa and subsequently executed him. In 1535 he founded Lima but soon the Conquistadors were involved in their own feuding and Pizarro and Almagro fought each other (1537–8), Pizarro eventually being killed by Almagro's followers. See John Hemming, *The Conquest of the Incas* (Macmillan 1970).

[220] Cortés, Hernán (1485–1547), conqueror of Mexico, was born in Medellín, also in Extremadura. He arrived in Hispaniola in 1504 and was elected officer on an expedition to Cuba led by Diego Velásquez in 1511 and in subsequent years explored the coast of Mexico and Yucatán, guided by Jerónimo de Aguilar who had knowledge of the Mayan language. He led a massacre of the Indians at Tabasco and took an Indian mistress, Marina, who became his interpreter. He founded Veracruz and destroyed his fleet so that there would be no turning back. Entered the Aztec capital Tenochtitlán (Mexico City) on 8 November 1519 and took Montezuma hostage. In 1520 he was forced to retreat to Tlazcala following an Aztec

mulatto, a half-caste of some submerged type or other. I have seen nothing of so low a type, even on the Congo as most of the men met here are. The lowest Belgian is a gentleman compared to them. They are people of another world. And the Indian, the more they outrage and flagellate and degrade, when they do not destroy him, is of our world. He is a far better man. These lords and masters, the undisputed givers of life (they all have harems of ravished girls and women) and death, they all murder — they are infinitely inferior to the man they hunt with whips and firebrands through his primeval forests. The caged and chained Indian gives his soul to God, let us indeed hope that the conquistadors go down to the bottomless pit. They are, I verily believe, the worst people in the world, this is certainly the greatest crime. It is so hopeless, so devilish — so wholly damnable.

Failure of the Monroe Doctrine

If the United States cannot let light into the dark places of South America then she must stand aside or be swept aside. The Monroe Doctrine[221] is a stumbling block in the path of humanity. Instead of being the cornerstone of American Independence, it is the block on which these criminals behead their victims. If the only great power in America cannot do her duty, in a matter so vitally concerning America's honour, then the Greater Powers of the

---

revolt; prepared new attack on Tenochtitlán and captured it August 1521. In 1523–4 sent expeditions into Central America whereby Pedro de Alvarado overcame the Mayan tribes of Guatemala. Stripped of the governorship in 1526, he returned to Spain in 1528. He returned to Mexico in 1530 and in 1536 discovered Baja California, returning to Spain in 1540 to die. See Hugh Thomas, *Conquest: Montezuma, Cortés, and the Fall of Old Mexico* (Simon and Schuster 1995).

[221] The Monroe Doctrine refers to President James Monroe's message to the U.S. Congress on 2 December 1823 whereby he established a principle of U.S. Foreign Policy that opposed the influence or interference of non-American powers in the Americas. The most important element of the Doctrine stated, "With the Governments who have declared their independence and maintained it ... we could not view any interposition for the purpose of oppressing them, or controlling in any other manner their destiny, by any European power in any other light than as the manifestation of an unfriendly disposition towards the United States." In 1904 President Theodore Roosevelt added the Roosevelt Corollary to the Monroe Doctine, declaring that if a Latin American republic failed to respect its obligations to the Doctrine, the U.S could intervene in order to prevent European intervention. The Corollary was denounced by several Latin American governments as an expression of Yankee Imperialism. Casement reflected this view. America became heavily involved in the Putumayo atrocities in 1911 after Casement's reports had been circulated at a "diplomatic level". It led to their own official interpretation of events: *Slavery in Peru* — House of Representatives Document, Washington 1913.

World must step in. The Monroe Doctrine has more than served its purpose. It is to-day but the selfish instrument of a grasping diplomacy that, while refusing to act itself, would prevent others capable of action from doing their work. To-day the Monroe Doctrine is challenged and Europe protests with shot and shell against this greedy assertion of Yankee ambitions the better for mankind. This blight in the forests of Peru and Bolivia would end to-morrow were it not for the Monroe Doctrine.

Casement rides around Entre Rios

Four Boras Indians came down to-day guarded, as usual, by one of the footpads of Andokes section. This man, a stout *mestizo* named Villota. The Boras were very light-skinned, a handsome young man and a boy of 12 or 13, each with a load of rubber, and two women — one doubtless the "wife" of Villota. Both women looked despairing. I gave them a tin of meat. The boy bore brands of flogging all over his nether parts, poor little chap. I photo'd both of them. The young man smiled and shook hands. Bathed in Cahuinari, and then rode all round O'Donnell's *chacara* with him. I should say the area cleared of forest is some 300 acres, of which probably 50 or 60 are under crops — chiefly *cassava* and *yucca*.[222] The young maize is coming along splendidly in parts. All of this is the work of the Indian men and women, and they have received never one cent of remuneration for it. Found ruins of the old house of the Muitidifos Indians in the midst of it, with a long dancing pole across. O'Donnell says only the pretty girls stood on it, and swayed it up and down, while the painted men danced around it.

In the new Muitidifos House — half a mile away — there is no dancing board — it went by the board with the gaiety of all these once happy "nations". Poor souls! As Macedo is alleged to have said:

"The Indians are not here to plant *chacaras*. They are here to get rubber."

O'Donnell's standing crops are *cassava*, maize and sugar-cane. Near the house bananas of nine varieties (so he says, although I have noticed only five kinds) and popunha palms.

Muchachos return from hunting

One of the *muchachos* brought in a beautiful little brown-red squirrel he had shot in the forest. I got the tail mounted, but he

---

[222] Casement's clearly written Yucca is spelt with only one 'c' — Yuca — in the corresponding *Black Diary* entry.

spoiled it by cutting off some inches of the tip. He reports a fine buck deer as shot by himself also out in the forest some 2½ hours away. It was too heavy to carry, so he came in to get help. The deer was brought in by one of the big *muchachos*, a fine young man with skin like copper. Very handsome figure he presented, standing 5ft 9in. or 5ft 10in with beautiful limbs, only in his white *fono* with the brown deer slung by its legs from his coal black hair. The deer had been cut open to lighten it, and even then weighed 36½ kilogrammes. The Cook said he had seen one bigger once, carried by two men on a pole. The horn is a stag's horn — without tines — only about 7in. long. Round the root there seems to be a socket with tiny little tines on it.

Heavy rain both in afternoon and night. The 40 or 50 Indians pressed in to carry the Commission to Atenas began arriving back from 6.30 onwards up to nearly 9 o'clock. The late-comers came with blazing torches of palm fronds, and it was fine to see them emerging from the distant forest and coming gradually across the *chacara* waving these flaming fronds. Poor chaps! they were foot-sore and hungry, and yet nothing for them that I could see given. Their homes too, are far off in many cases, they will sleep tonight here in the Indian house and then go home on empty bellies and empty handed. It is truly an expensive system of transport.

I have decided to go to Atenas tomorrow, to go and come, arriving for lunch and returning before sunset. It is put at 3 hours' march — but of quick marching — so should be about 11 or 12 miles.

I have put down in my Indian notes[223] what O'Donnell told me to-day of the Indians in his district. I wrote a note to John Gordon with the Bridge record of last night.

Casement's Indian Notes

I — Chingamuni

"Today O'Donnell at lunch tells me more about the Indians here. When he came in 1903 there was a great *Cacique* of the local Indians — a Captain of energy and character, who was highly respected and liked by all the Huitotos of this part named

[223] Casement's "Indian notes" recording these conversations with O'Donnell are to be found in MS 13,087 (26/iii) and the page is titled "Fragments of conversations with O'Donnell at Entre Rios on 25 Oct 1910 — Various Notes on the Indians from O'Donnell and other quarters". Significantly, there is no reference to this long and important conversation in the corresponding *Black Diary* entry.

Chingamuni. This man had influence through force of character. The chief before O'Donnell — was Elias Martinengui — who had only one *fabrico* here before O'Donnell took charge.

O'Donnell was once coming back from Chorrera with Chingamuni and latter's wife got ill on the road so Chingamuni stayed with her. The Colombian Rafael Calderon who lived at Atenas was going down to Chorrera and met Chingamuni on the road. They were enemies and fought. Calderon killed Chingamuni — shot him twice — and himself was shot in the wrist (Chingamuni's death was to be regretted. He was another powerful Indian removed from the path of these people.)

II — The Colombians and the Indians.

O'Donnell says that the Colombians were here at Entre Rios and all over the country before he came. They had "treated" the Indians "very badly" — much worse than he and the Peruvians have done. So he says. They had no goods to trade with them — it was simply "conquering" Indians and holding them as slaves — killing them and their women and living entirely on them (This is exactly what he and all the agents of the P.A. Co. do today — only with less killing). He says there were far more Indians when he came here 7 years ago. Many have died from smallpox and "other causes". The Indians got back on the Colombians sometimes. One notable "massacre" occurred before he came here. It was carried out by Gutierrez and sixty men, Colombians and Brazilians he brought with him up the Caquetá. They came in a launch. Gutierrez landed with all his men and goods and was well received apparently. The Indians brought food and presents and gathered around in friendly guise. He was deceived. He had no lamp and he even did not put guard that night. He said "these Indians are good and will be our friends" — So all slept and some of the Indians slept beside them. At night many more Indians came and surrounded the house — and crept in upon them. They were all surprised in their sleep and seized and cut to pieces with machetes. First the Indians took their guns while they slept and then fell upon them. All the heads were cut off and the arms and legs. The teeth were drawn from the head as trophies — the bodies tied with a rope were put in the river and kept as "souvenirs" — to be hauled out and exhibited until decomposition set in. The skulls were suspended in rows on the *manguarés* in the Indian homes. He himself found twelve of the bodies on stakes and buried them — those of this killing and a later one.

Then Rafael Calderón and many others were killed, he says, on the Purus by the Brazilian Indians there. The shooting of Chingamuni took place "five or six years ago".

III — Another killing of Indians took place in the Andokes country after O'Donnell came here at about this time. Four Colombians, very hungry and quite without food got to an Indian house and were received well. The Indians brought food but gave it to each separately and gradually got them sitting apart. A "friendly" Indian sat beside each man, and little by little edged him away from his companion in the act of eating. Then when they were quite separated in the house the Captain and his other Indians appeared with more food and presents and eggs etc. As he drew near with these he gave a loud "Heu" — and each Indian sitting by a Colombian threw his arms around him and held him fast. The Captains and the others ran in and cut them to pieces with their machetes. These were not eaten. He says the Indians had a repugnance to eating white men — they hated them and did not eat them. I said I sympathised very much with the Indians — and that I found these killings of such men "very natural".

He and Martin Arana laughed. How sincerely I cannot say.

IV — More Colombians were killed here than these — all over the country the Indians did it until the house of Arana brought "peace, order and content." The Indians were never safe with the Colombians (Are they with the Peruvians?).

The Andokes Indians tried to kill him. So he says. Four Capitanes came here to see him soon after he arrived and invited him to visit their country. They promised him rubber if he would come. He said he laughed and declined their invitation. Later on the Guimaraes Indians, incited by the Andokes "rebelled" and attacked him. They and the Andokes took *chupe del tobaco* together. The Andokes had said they would kill them if the Guimaraes did not join them against the *blancos*. He does not tell how this rebellion was suppressed. However he was often fired at even here in the station. I can imagine that the suppression of the Guimaraes rebellion was something to be remembered. Those I saw at the dance looked distinctly cowed. Besides all — the native arms of the Indians have disappeared — their spears and arrows etc. These have been seized and confiscated and others sold or kept as curios. I have not seen, since leaving Chorrera, a single Indian with a bow, arrow, spear or blowpipe — or any form of native arm. The spears I have actually seen are a few O'D[onnell] has as curios — of the throwing spears with light shafts of wood and very poor iron tips. Three are thrown at a time in one hand, gripped between the fingers. Bishop says he saw women armed thus, on an island in the Caquetá who came to oppose Robuchon landing, thinking he had come to catch them to work rubber.

The chief of the Muinanes, Hatima, O'D[onnell]'s "best friend" has a Winchester and I gave him 12 cartridges (secretly) for this. I find the back sight was removed from it before giving it to him — and, as a weapon of precision it is useless. He bought it out yesterday to shoot the wood Ibis and was greatly disappointed at my refusal. He wanted the plumes. Also he said the Ibis was a bad omen — it had been sent by another tribe to bring disaster.

Tizon, in the course of our lengthy talk yesterday evening, after Normand's letter had come, spoke much of the Indians and of all his hopes. His views are practically my own. He says they are starved — starved to death — it has killed "hundreds and hundreds". That they have no time to attend to their own wants, or to make plantations and prepare food. They are literally done to death. The thing must be stopped and at once. If not he will join me and go to Lima and denounce it openly and ask me to give him some copies of the depositions of the Barbados men. He will write to me and I to him.

As to the Boras he says they are worthy of a far better fate. They are braver, stronger and more intelligent than the Huitoto and have been treated "shamefully-awfully". Jiménez, he says, has told him of the things done to them by himself too. Jiménez said they were good people and if properly dealt with would be far more useful — but they had been outraged beyond words. Jiménez he says is a humble man. He did what he was got to do — because he is (a *cholo*) obedient and will obey good orders when they are given him.

VIII

ATENAS AND THE RETURN TO LA CHORRERA

A Walk to Atenas and Back — Wednesday 26th October

The walk to Atenas

I went to Atenas with O'Donnell today. The times were as follows and we walked very fast. I made O'Donnell often hop, skip and jump to keep up with me, and wherever the path was flat we went five miles an hour:

Going:	Left Entre Rios	8.05 a.m.	Time Walking	2.45
	Arrived Atenas	10.50 a.m.		
Return:	Left Atenas	3.00 p.m.	Time Walking	2.54
	Arrived Entre Rios	5.54 p.m.	Total	5.39

We did not stop at all going and returning were delayed by tremendous rain storms stopping for water at streams. The rain comes in cataracts and began as soon as we left Atenas and lasted nearly into Entre Rios and made our walking harder. I am sure the distance is 12 miles, so we did 24 miles today — not so bad for me in my 47th year — and in these awful, humid sloughs of despond. Sealy had to stretch out to keep up with us. He carried my revolver by special request. I asked him if he wanted it to shoot Mr Montt, and he said "No, Sir, but he ought to be shot."

Arrival at Atenas

Found Commission enjoying the pleasure of Mr Montt's society in a horrid, abandoned pirate stronghold. All looked pulled down and ruinous and utterly neglected. Saw only one Indian outside the staff and *muchachos*, he was terribly thin, a skeleton, and scarified all over nether limbs. Sealy and Chase brought him up to the veranda to show me and I called Barnes and we inspected the poor being. He was one of those sent to carry the Commission's baggage down to Puerto Peruano tomorrow. He looked more fit for a hearse himself. Barnes said he would photo him.

Barnes tells me that Atenas is "played out", so Montt had said in reply to the Commission's "inquiry". All the rubber trees for miles around had been killed by Martenengui's driving of the Indians. This also accounts for the famine stricken district. The *cepo* or stocks the Commission found dismantled.

Montt's system

Of course "no flogging for years"! The Indians were "very bad" according to Mr Montt, and he has only 3 *empleados* — he can do nothing! He cannot send any of his *blancos* out to the forest as they are not enough — so the *Muchachos* have to go. Nevertheless he gets 24 tons of rubber a year out of them — so he says. The Commission were informed at Chorrera that there were 790 rubber "workers" in Atenas Section. Montt tells them he has only "about 250". Where are the rest? The Barbados men who have been stationed here all say that the women here have to work rubber, not merely to carry it — that they have to do in all the sections, poor souls, with their tiny children and all — but here women are on the "lists of the workers" and have to bring in rubber just like the men — hence the starvation that the Barbados men say prevails in this district.

Description of Atenas

The clearing round Atenas a very large one — as big as O'Donnell's in area of felled trees and burnt and decayed stumps, but little or no planting of foodstuffs. Only a very little *cassava* recently put in. The Cahuinari here a fine stream, fully 8 feet deep or more. (I tried it) and liable to sudden rises of 10 feet or over even, O'Donnell says. The frame of an old bridge, high above the water shows, where the track goes down to Chorrera. Some of the rubber from the forest goes direct to Chorrera — so Montt said — the rest nearer at hand goes down to Puerto Peruano. The Colombian Ramón Vargas who was captured by Jiménez in April across the Caquetá is here at Atenas. He was not in the station — out getting the road ready for the Commission tomorrow to Puerto Peruano.

The rubber at Atenas is done up in quite thin *chorizos* like the long sausages of a butcher's shop. It is the "true Putumayo sausage" I am told. As a matter of fact it is. It is the entrails of a people.

Return to Entre Rios

Got back to Entre Rios gladly enough despite the terrible downpour — and turned in very early indeed. Our dinner consisted of deer steaks and *cassava* — very good indeed, but I lay down too soon after it and wakened at 12 midnight and lay awake most of the night — a prey to the most venomous sandflies. My legs, wrists and hands are now a mass of sores from the scratching.

Leave Entre Rios — Thursday 27th October

Depart Entre Rios

O'Donnell says he will come with me to Puerto Peruano. I on horseback, he on the mule. My baggage — 6 loads in all, including two *tulas* of Lane and Sealy — will be carried by some of O'Donnell's *muchachos*.

Staff list at Entre Rios

I find the following to be O'Donnell's list of his station hands; it is taken from a list hung up in his office. (Names &c. in Notebook) These do not constitute all — but they are the rubber executive. All the armed men — 23 in all — are the local force for controlling the life and limb of every Indian in the district.

In addition to these there are many more small boys and innumerable girls and women. O'Donnell's harem have a three-roomed house of their own — in which the four Mrs O'Donnells, their three children, and a bevy of handmaids dwell. Then every empleado has a "wife". Borborini has two, and many have children and these require Indian nursemaids. Little girls coming on to make into spare wives. Then there are a train of girls carrying water all day long — as at Occidente, up from the Cahuinari. Those often counted 8 together at one filling. Then the *muchachos* I should say all have their wives — some of the *muchachos* are really only boys or lads — but others are men of 25 to 30. Altogether O'Donnell's station numbers fully 65 to 70 persons, and they are all fed at the expense of the surrounding population. They do not cultivate a yard of ground themselves. All they do is to hunt, bully, terrorise, flog and otherwise compel the local Indians to bring in rubber, or to come when called on for any task that may be put on them. All the women do is to wait upon the men, breed for them and be their docile servants.

The road to Puerto Peruano

The road down to Puerto Peruano with O'Donnell was quite agreeable. My horse went well and with a very little work the path could be made quite serviceable for mules, to carry the rubber and relieve these poor human beasts of burden of that part of their burden. We lunched in the abandoned Muinanes house, Borborini coming bare-legged along and cooking the lunch. O'Donnell caught several splendid Blue Emperor butterflies for me with his hands and Sealy two also. Caught Commission up at their lunch at a stream and then all on together to Puerto Peruano.

Heavy rain at 2.30 just as we reached the Nimué — the river that flows into the Igara-paraná and makes "the port". From that on some 25 minutes in heavy rain. We passed for fully 2 hours through the once enormous clearings of the Iguarase Indians. Tizon said they had once been very numerous. There must have been hundreds of them — now none at all. All is desolation. The ruin of a Colombian house in the midst. All this destruction of the Indians has been since the last 15 to 18 years at outside. When the rubber boom began about 1893 the Colombians came, later to be followed by Peruvians, like a crawling pestilence and fastened on these wild people and "tamed" them — as we see.[224] The population has undoubtedly decreased by far more than half in the last few years. If there were 40,000 Indians, as alleged, a few years ago, there are certainly no more than 10,000 I believe all told, in the whole Putumayo district administered by Arana Bros. They put it at 12,000 sq. miles in their fraudulent prospectus when launching the Peruvian Amazon Company.

[224] The dates of the Amazon Rubber Boom have been defined by Barbara Weinstein in *The Amazon Rubber Boom (1850–1920)* (Stanford 1983). Rubber prices began to soar following the production of the bicycle in the 1890s and most steeply with the setting up of the motor-car industry at the dawn of the twentieth century. The mass production of the Model T Ford in 1906 turned rubber into a raw material more valuable than gold and the Putumayo atrocities were a direct consequence of the spiralling market demand. Plantation rubber began to make a significant influence on the international rubber market from about 1907 and by 1912 had captured about 18.51 per cent of the market and almost 40% by 1914 when it had surpassed Brazilian production levels. See P.W. Barker, *Rubber Statistics 1900–1937* (U.S. Department of Commerce 1938).

Condition of carriers

The Commission's carriers are over 40 Atenas Indians, many of them boys, several are literally skeletons. I never saw anything much thinner than four boys of from 15–20. We photographed them — one had dreadful sores as well, and the back of one had been flogged raw. It was heartrending. God help them! I gave orders to Sealy to give all the tins of meat I had left to them, poor creatures. Tizon had a good meal of rice and beans and sardines cooked for them too, and he says they shall have another in the morning, before they return to Atenas.

We found lots of the forest trees with berries pulled down and lying across the track. O'Donnell says this was done by Normand's starving carriers. Here is the literal illustration of what the Barbadians have said to me that when on the march with rubber the Indians "live on seed, Sir." Here were the very seeds. I found two varieties of trees had been dragged down, often the path blocked by the fallen trunks and the branches torn away. Tizon was saying just what I did all the way, that it was time this Commission of ours has come if indeed, it is not far too late. I feel quite hopeless in my heart, as I do not think any effective and humane control can be set up. Effort to establish it will, no doubt, be made, and Tizon will do all one man can do; but he is the only honest Peruvian I have met, except the Prefect. One man cannot cleanse this place, and the English Company is only English in name.

A night at Puerto Peruano

Played a rubber of Bridge and lay down in the front hut, with all the Indians sleeping below, and O'Donnell there too, along with Garece, Borborini and Arévalo, the Iquitos Captain of the *Veloz*. Bruce is down the river, and Normand, Bishop and Levine I find all had to walk from Chorrera. The launch did not come up for them and Normand's rubber (most of it) is lying in a *batalon* at Puerto Peruano, waiting the next up-trip of the *Veloz*. I don't know where the army of carriers have disappeared to. Only (as far as I could see) some 70 or 80 returned through Entre Rios — and all the rest can hardly have gone back via Chorrera or Occidente perhaps?

I am on the look out for one lad, named Doi. If I can see him I will try and take him home. I have half a mind to take some of these poor starved Atenas beings to Chorrera. If I were in any authority here I should certainly do so — take the whole lot down and feed them.

Journey from Puerto Peruano to Chorrera — Friday 28th October

Left Puerto Peruano	7.18 a.m.		h. m.	miles
Passed Occidente	11.10 a.m.		3.52	say 25
" Naimenes	3.11 p.m.	slow current	4.1	say 20
" Victoria	5.28 p.m.	" "	2.17	" 18
Arr. Chorrera . (above rapid)	5.37 p.m	swift stream	0.9	" 1
				say 57

(For incidents of to-day's journey in launch, see pages of my green notebook.)

A document held in the N.L.I. {MS 13,087 (29/i)} gives a detailed explanation of the expenses Casement incurred during his weeks away from La Chorrera as he went on his tour of investigation of the Company's rubber stations. What is interesting is that he insisted on paying each of his Indian carriers with food and money — despite, and probably because of, the fact that the Company paid them nothing.

IX

THE EXODUS FROM LA CHORRERA

Arrival at La Chorrera

On leaving launch at the beginning of the rapid above Chorrera we walked to the house, arriving at 6.10 or so. Carriers sent for our baggage — mostly Normand's Andokes and Boras — some of whom I met on the way hurrying up the hill to get our things. They recognised me and grasped my hand and shoulder as they passed with broad smiles — poor naked souls.

Bishop's diary

Welcomed by Macedo and at dinner found the usual staff — including Normand — who looked as beastly as ever and bowed very low. The man Solar who has been all over the sections before us to warn the Chiefs and the Barbados men, is back again. This is the gentleman who went to Ultimo Retiro to bribe Crichlow — and to Andokes with the news of Francis' hoodwinking of me — as they thought. After dinner Bishop came with a sort of written diary of his doings since he left Puerto Peruano.[225] It is entirely off his own bat. I read it to Tizon after dinner. Here it is. He says he will settle Normand's little game very soon — that if Normand wants a row he shall have it — and it may be a hanging game for him!

Casement and Tizon make plans

We talked till nearly 11.30 (after a game of bridge) and fixed up our line of action both as regards Normand and Macedo. Also I told Tizon that I was determined to try and get Colonel Bertie to come out and meet the Commission before they leave the Amazon and take command of things, and that their report shall be one worthy of the needs of the case. He fully agreed and was delighted at the thought of the Commission being so strengthened, and said,

---

[225] The reference to "Bishop's diary" is recorded as follows in the corresponding *Black Diary* entry: "Bishop brought a written statement of all that has transpired since he left me. Amusing in its way."

if I could impress this need on Colonel Bertie it would be indeed a good thing for the Company, and the best interests of those we are all trying to serve.

I said I should be home (D.V.) some months before the Commission and I could see the Colonel privately, urge on him the course I suggested, and he could join them at Pará or Manaos, and en route home put things into shape in this report.

I had told Fox of this idea of mine before dinner, to his great content too, for he says he will not be satisfied with any report drawn up by Barnes (who admits he cannot do it) or by Gielgud. I said I thought a report by Gielgud — who has already committed himself to such inaccurate statements — and who is a paid servant of the Company — could scarcely be that of an impartial man, and Fox fully agreed. There remains only Bell — and I greatly doubt his capacity for such a task. Fox says, if the Colonel does not come, he will write a separate report — his own — and let the other three men go as they please. It is certainly not a Commission. There are four decent men walking about together, but there is no point of common union and action — and all headship and direction are wanting. Moreover, there cannot be said to be any real collective enquiry. Fox alone, to my mind, fully realises his responsibility.

At Chorrera — Saturday 29th October

General observations

Back again at this more open station — out of the forest with the broad part of the river before us. The river has dropped here, below the fall, some 16 feet — with only some 6 or 7 above it. That is strange. The great pool here ¼ of a mile — or nearly half a mile across on the diagonal — is shrunk enormously and two sandbanks shine white across it. Above, the river is pouring through the rocks into the pool in a greatly diminished volume and is almost hidden by the rocks, that when we left a month ago were covered by a raging flood of water. The little boys are having a fine swim over to the sandbanks, and kicking about on logs, they swim like fish. So do the girls. They swim as easily as they walk.

Decision to dismiss the Barbadians

I have not spoken to Bishop to-day, altho' he tells me that Francis is behaving very badly. This man now has quite joined Levine, and is clearly acting under the bribes of Macedo and Normand. Last night at midnight he quarrelled with the young cook — the

Jamaica negro boy, Philip Lawrence. Philip, it appears, has told Bishop some of the things Francis had confessed to him — of the bribes etc. etc. and killings in Andokes — and Francis drew a revolver on the cook at midnight and threatened to shoot him for telling these things to Bishop. Macedo had to be sent for to try and keep the peace and of course they are afraid I may hear of it and press for Francis' dismissal. This I shall do in any case and Tizon agreed last night that all the Barbados men ought to go. I think so too. They have all committed criminal acts — under compulsion in most cases I believe, but they cannot very well be now retained. If they tell me the truth they are in danger afterwards from their local chiefs — and if they lie like Francis and Levine, they are no fit employees for a British Company. They are being bribed (with that Company's money!) to lie to a British Consul sent out specially in their interest — and by so lying they are injuring that Company — for they are helping to maintain an evil state of things that the Company must be the first to wish swept away.

Therefore from no point of view can I see any justification for the Barbados men remaining on and this is Tizon's view too. I have called no one to-day, only thought over things and what is the best line of action to follow. First I have asked to be supplied with a statement showing the actual state of the Barbados men's accounts with this, the Chorrera Agency. Here it is as now brought to me by Gielgud, drawn up by Parr the accountant.

Accounts of the Barbadians

It shows, incidentally, that the bribe offered by Macedo to Crichlow to lie to me was even larger than I had reason to believe when at Ultimo Retiro. The accounts are compiled to date, as near as possible, and Crichlow instead of having a debt against him of 120 soles, is actually owing S/P 247.69 or £24 14/-. This was a considerable sum of the Company's money to offer this man to be untruthful and fail in his duty. But as Tizon said "What can you expect from such men? Murderers will not stick at bribes and dishonesty." Last night he confessed that Macedo could not stay on, and his departure, too, I gather has been decided on as soon as the more general clearance is effected.

This is a precious document! Most of the men, it will be seen, are deeply in the Company's debt; one of them, Joseph Minggs (who is, I find, down here from S. Catalina) to the extent of some £46 (S/P 463.47). Most of this "debt", it is true, is for things that are grossly, nay extortionately over priced, and many of them, things that, by the men's contracts (such as medicine, food etc.,) they are entitled to free. Thus Bishop brings me to-day all his accounts with the Company and with Arana Bros. before them. He has kept all. From 10th April 1906 to 15th Feb., 1910 he has paid for medicines alone (the full list is attached) S/P 104.90 or £10, and most of it since the Company was formed in July 1907, or exactly S/P 70 say (£7) from 8th July 1907 to February 1910. He asks me if I will aid him to try and get some of it back, as well as S/P 66.40, or over £6 for the clothes that he left at Ultimo Retiro in January last which Plaza stole and gave to the Indians. The price list of this clothing he gives me too — all of it goods he had bought from the Company and which the Company's representative (at the time) robs him of and while the Chief Agent of all illegally confines him here at Chorrera and puts him "in guns". If ever a man had grounds for compensation he has.

Sealy and Chase came to say they had been cheated, that their pay is reckoned at S/P 10 per pound sterling whereas their contracts in Iquitos are at £5 per month, a £1 sterling was reckoned in all transactions out here at S/P 10.50. They claim the refund of this 50 centavos for each £1 of their salary carried to account at S/P 10 only. I called Gielgud and he agreed instantly, as he obviously has to. What book-keeping! He (and everyone else) knew it was a swindle and yet they carried it on for years. A shilling in every pound is not bad to rob a poor workman of, on the top of all the other robberies and extortions practised on them. But what can one expect from a business founded on robbery and a system maintained by murder and outrage and lying and bribing.

Enough. I'll write no more to-day. I am sick of the whole thing, and thank God I am back so far on my way out of this den of thieves. God! if I could only take all the Indians with me! Where to? Poor souls. No hope for them, I fear.

Casement buys some goods at the store

I got some things in the store to-day, the greatest trash imaginable. I am sending them up to O'Donnell to pay my Indian carriers. The trousers, I find, are made here in Chorrera! The slave women cut them out and sew them! Talk of sweating! This bangs Banagher.[226] Young Parr in the store told me this when buying them. He said he could not tell me the price of anything! (I smiled

[226] A phrase derived from a proverbially corrupt pocket borough in Ireland and meaning "that surpasses everything".

to myself grimly). He has been instructed. I am no doubt to be charged a special price much lower than to the Barbados men. We'll see. It is so foolish of them to do this, as if I can't see the Barbados men's accounts and compare the prices of the same articles. I bought a hat, a hammock, shirt, singlets and pantaloons. I'll append prices to each and take a sample home for valuing in London. I know, too, the quantity of rubber the Indians have to bring against each article. A hammock is anything from 40 to 60 kilos or even more at some stations — although, doubtless, they have otherwise informed the Commission. But as there are no proper books kept, it is hard to check any statement made. One must proceed by deduction or inference.

While in the store, I saw the goods prepared and done up ready for the Oriente fabrico which is due to come in to-morrow. It was Mr Parr pointed them out to me. There were two small bundles, in sacking, each about 30 lbs. weight of shirts and pants, the whole easily carried by one man. And this is the whole payment for an entire fabrico![227]

Parr said some "ammunition" would be added, caps, shot and powder, but there it is, two tiny parcels of this utter trash for goodness knows how many kilos of rubber. I'll find out what quantity Oriente sends to-morrow.

I mentioned the circumstances to Barnes in the evening, urging him, or the Commission rather, to have clear, precise details furnished of the exact payment made in each case. A section yields a given quantity of rubber each fabrico, the exact amount is known and the names of the Indians who have supplied it, and the quantity each man (and his family) brought in. There must be a definite record of what is given each man in return. So far the Commission, I learn from Barnes, have not been supplied with these particulars. I asked Gielgud if this were so and he declared that the "books" at each section did show in effect the actual advances made to each Indian and he had seen them. I asked how it was that Barnes, the Chief of the Commission, had no knowledge of this, and his answer was, that Barnes "would not understand the books if he saw them!" This I can well believe, not that Barnes is a fool, but that the books "are intended for fools". As I am on the subject to-day I will try and thrash it out. So far as I can gather

[227] See R.H. Brit. Emp. S22 [G355] containing Casement's "diary extract" copied from these passages referring to Parr, the English store-keeper at La Chorrera. It clearly was attached to Casement's letter to Roberts dated December 1912 (no day) when he made his earliest reference to his Putumayo diary.

from the members of the Commission the answers given to their questions varied at each section, but it is amply clear that the value assigned to rubber and to the articles given in so-called exchange for it are left entirely to the discretion of the Chief of each Section. Not only that, but he may withhold an advance whenever he pleases and substitute for it a good hiding with a tapir-hide thong. This is not a joke, but entirely true, and Gielgud admitted it to me to-day when I thus put the statement that "It might be so — there was nothing to prevent it". And yet this is the gentleman who last year found everything ideal and the Indians so happy!

AT CHORRERA — SUNDAY, 30TH OCTOBER

Remaining Barbadians to be interviewed

I am now awaiting the arrival of the remaining eight Barbados men. There were ten instead of eight, as I believed, at the out stations that I had not already seen, and these have been ordered by Sr. Tizon to be here by to-day. Two are already here, Batson from Abisinia originally, and J. Minggs from Santa Catalina. Both came here some weeks ago and have been kept working here until my return. Batson, Bishop states (in his paper handed to me Friday night) although Bruce tried to get at him, will tell me the truth. Of Minggs, I know nothing, except that I see him often with Levine and Francis, and I know that they are already brought by Normand and Macedo.

Contracts of employment

I think the wise and right course will be to insist on the dismissal of all the Barbados men in the Company's service. Those of them who owe money to the Company will have to go away penniless, and the Government may even have to pay the balances due by them. If necessary I shall do this by a bill upon FO, and then leave the matter to be thrashed out at home. There is little doubt the men have been robbed. I have just sent for the contract of Greenidge, the Baker here. It is the original made in Barbados, and I am taking copy of it. It is made between Sr. Abel Alarco[228] of Putumayo (Igara-paraná) Peru, South America as Employer.

[228] Abel Alarco was a brother-in-law of Arana and part of the immediate "family" who had done a lot of the company's dirty work over the years. In 1904 he went on behalf of the company to Barbados to recruit a labour force although his mission effectively amounted to slave trafficking. After the flotation of the Peruvian Amazon Company, Alarco was sent to London and lived in style in a large Ed-

This is the only one of the original made in Barbados I can now find here on the spot. Bishop's was lost when all his things were lost with Robuchon long ago, and none of the other men have their original contracts. Both Bishop and Greenidge and others of the men who have been here from the first have been working on since this contract expired, and since the foundation of the English Company, that is to say since 1st July, 1907, without any form of contract. It is merely a verbal promise, but it is unquestionably binding, I should think. A more slipshod way of doing things, it is hard to conceive.

Fraudulent contracts

This contract of Greenidge's has been violated again and again. The medicines, for instance, the not being left destitute, and many others of the clauses. Also that referring to work to begin "the day after arrival at the above-mentioned place." Here a double fraud was committed. There is no such place as Putumayo, nor as Igara-paraná. The former is a huge river, fully 100 miles long, the latter a tributary river about 400 miles long. Bishop declares that he had to begin working at Colonia Rio Jano, cutting firewood and no pay was given for this. He states Chase came with him and he, Chase, and several others protested at Manaos and went to the British Vice-Consul to claim protection. They had learned of the duties they were likely to be put to and the character of their employment, and did not wish to proceed.

Consul Fletcher

The Vice Consul (I wonder who was Vice Consul then — probably Mr Fletcher) refused to help them, saying they must fulfil their contract, and as several of them still protested and actually declined to go on board the vessel waiting to take them up the Amazon, police were sent for and they were conveyed on board in custody. As I am now so fully convinced of the lawlessness of the whole proceedings of this Arana concern, I shall, before leaving Chorrera, get depositions on this point from Chase and from Bishop.

---

wardian mansion house. After a botched attempt to bribe a newspaper reporter, George Thorogood, in September 1909, just after the Putumayo story broke in *Truth*, Alarco was sent back to manage business operations in Manaos.

Solar

Solar, who went up country as our avant courier is, of course, back at Chorrera and thick as thieves with Normand who returns to his section to-day but without Levine. He had wished to go to Iquitos but Tizon stopped it, so he tells me. He goes, for good, however, next steamer, and Tizon I fancy will go too, both to ensure his quietude there and to see that Julio Arana (and the Prefect) are fully advised of the gravity of things here and of the absolute need for their support of the reforms the Commission are going to urge.

Solar, I find, was formerly a police officer in Iquitos, whom Tizon, when acting-Prefect of Loreto, dismissed for misconduct. Tizon was surprised to find him here, in the Company's service, on his coming in March last! It is only another proof that all the scoundrels in Peru are at home here — poor Tizon, to be in such Company.

Some more Barbados men arrived to-day from Sabana I believe — but I have asked no questions. Tomorrow, Monday, I shall begin with Batson and go on through them as they arrive.

Normand's effusive goodbye and offer of Indian boy as present

Normand left at 2.30 for his Andokes by *Veloz*, and gave me an effusive good-bye — coming to my room to shake hands. He is also to send down a boy — the boy Doi, I saw carrying a heavy load on the road whom I wish to take home if the lad is willing to come. I did not ask him for this. I spoke to Tizon about the boy, who told Macedo and Macedo gave orders to Normand to find the boy and send him to Chorrera as he "wished to make him a present to someone"! These are Normand's own words. They reveal, innocently — if that word can be applied to such a man — the attitude towards the Indians of these ruffians. "A present of a man" — fancy it!

Casement's answer

I said to Normand that there was no question of this kind, only that if this lad wished to accompany me I should take him. But the position is disgraceful. Here is an entire population, titular freemen in Peruvian law and in the eyes of civilisation, who, without question can be sent for, a hundred miles away, and sent down country to be "given as presents". If they only knew that I hope to do the Indians a service by choosing two or three good types and getting them introduced to the right circles in Europe whereby to elicit sympathy and help for these people, then they might be far less willing to "make presents" of these human beings.

Indian children swimming

The river has dropped fully one foot to-day, and the sandbanks now fill almost half the expanse of the pool of the Chorrera. The Indian boys and girls revel in it. The little house boys and the slave girls who wait upon these animals and serve their every want are down in the river now — swimming like water rats — out to the islands and back. Some paddle logs across and kick their heels like paddle steamers. Little things of five and six swim as well as the big ones. Perhaps nothing illustrates their love for the water more than the following.

The house girls this morning took large tins of cooking pots, plates, etc. down to the waterside to wash and scour with sand. But they did not stop at the waterside. They actually embarked, pots and pans, plates and all and swam across to the island, 50 or 60 yards of deep water — to begin their cleaning operations. Others — the lads — go there and play in all sorts of jolly ways and I have been admiring their graceful figures on the clean sand. The women are extraordinarily modest, as are also men and boys. Although the latter take off their *fonos* their hands are always available and the women keep their *cushmas* or long shirts on.

Thoughts of Herbert Ward

One lad to-day had a splendid figure — a young Boras boy on one of the launches. I would like to take him, or one like, home for Herbert Ward[229] in Paris. It is a good thought, why not do it? Herbert Ward might help materially in the cause. This Indian world of South America is unknown to Europe. H.W. might help

[229] Herbert Ward (d.1919) was a civil missionary turned sculptor who became a close friend of Casement while in Africa, a friendship recorded in *Five Years with the Congo Cannibals* (London 1890). In 1910 he published a volume of memoirs entitled *A Voice From the Congo* (London 1910) — telling his story after his return from Africa, when he became an artist and built his reputation through his sculptures of life-size bronzes of primitive African warriors and tribesmen. On reaching Europe from the Amazon on 1 January 1911, Casement went straight to Paris to visit Ward, who had a beautiful studio lavishly decorated with thousands of African weapons, spears and axes. Casement hoped that Ward would try to turn his attention to sculpting the Amazon Indian and help Casement's new crusade to stop the widespread destruction of the Amazindian tribal world. Ward's admiration for Casement extended to the naming of a son Roger Casement Ward, but in July 1916 he refused to sign Conan Doyle's petition to save Casement from the gallows and could never come to terms with Casement's conviction. Gertrude Bannister claimed that despite knowing that the *Black Diaries* were forged he refused to take the issue up or help her in her efforts to vindicate Casement.

materially with a bronze figure in the nude of a "Putumayo Indian".

Casement reiterates his wish to take an Indian back to England

I will see if I can get hold of any lad or young man willing to go. Bishop said the whole of Entre Rios would have gone with me if I had been able to take them. Several of the carriers of my baggage told him that. There is no question of the Indians gladly going, the question is that the Company's agents will not let them go. Each lad represents some 120–140 kilos of rubber per annum, at the cost of a hammock, a shirt and a pantaloon, or put thus — 300 lbs. of Rubber @ 4/- per lb. = £60 sterling — versus cottons costing 7/6d. The profits are high! It is true much is swallowed on the spot by the "Peruvian" Section of the Company.[230]

How civilisation tames the Indian

I got copies to-day of some of the statements made to the Commission by Chiefs of Section showing the prices they set upon the various articles they exchange or advance against rubber. I will append them later on. They speak for themselves, although they are quite untrustworthy as business statements. Of course, there is no business about the whole concern, it is simply slaving on a big scale and the worst in the world.

The Commission had no means of testing any of these statements. I have some slight means, through the Barbados men's actual knowledge of the "payments" they have for years seen made to the Indians. From these it is clear that all the Chiefs of Section have, as the Commission state openly, lied to them and the values they state against the goods are far less than those they actually compel the Indians to take the goods at. Moreover it must always be borne in mind that the Indian is no party to the contract. He is compelled by brutal and wholly uncontrolled force — by being hunted and caught — by floggings, by chaining up, by long periods of imprisonment and starvation, to agree to "work" for the Company and then when released from this taming process and this 5/- worth of absolute trash given to him he is hunted and hounded and guarded and flogged and his food robbed and his womenfolk ravished until he brings in from 200 to perhaps 300 times the value of the goods he has been forced to accept.

[230] The MS. ends rather abruptly here, indicating that Casement was either interrupted mid-sentence or that there is a missing page.

If he attempts to escape from this commercial obligation, he and his family as defaulting debtors are hunted for days and weeks, the frontier of a neighbouring state being no protection and when found are lucky if they escape with life. The least he can expect is to be flogged until raw, to be again chained up and starved, to be confined in the stocks, in a position of torture for days, weeks and even months. Many Indians have been so kept for months.

When he has acquitted himself of the commercial obligation and has carried in at great fatigue and physical deprivation of many kinds the quantity of rubber assessed upon his unhappy shoulders there is no escape. An enormous load of this, often, as I have seen, in excess of 50 kilos. has to be carried for distances of 40 to 70 miles to the nearest "port" on the Igara-paraná, over roads that even a mule cannot traverse — more fit for monkeys to scramble over than for men — and this without food save such as his wife and children can bring along with the heavy loads of rubber laid upon them also. Death on their road often attends them — death from hunger, from exposure, from fever and from sheer physical and mental break up.

All that was once his has been taken away from him — his forest home, his domestic affections even — nothing that God and Nature gave him is indeed left to him, save his fine, healthy body capable of supporting terrible fatigue, his shapely limbs and fair, clean skin — marred by the lash and scarred by execrable blows.

His manhood has been lashed and branded out of him. I look at the big, soft-eyed faces, averted and downcast and I wonder where that Heavenly Power can be that for so long allowed these beautiful images of Himself to be thus defaced and shamed. One looks then at the oppressors — vile cut-throat faces; grim, cruel lips and sensual mouths, bulging eyes and lustful — men incapable of good, more useless than the sloth for all the work they do — and it is this handful of murderers who, in the name of civilisation and of a great association of English gentlemen, are the possessors of so much gentler and better flesh and blood.

The Commission have not asked yet for a Statement of the exact quantity of goods he took back with him for the next *fabrico*, that is to say to purchase some eight or nine tons of rubber. It is here on "the books" somewhere and could easily be verified, and I have twice suggested that this should be done, but I have doubt of any united attempt being made to trace it. Fox is the only man who persistently enquires. Barnes, Bell and Gielgud are practically quite useless for any serious purpose of investigation, much less serious reform.

Barnes admits this — he simply says reform is impossible — the whole thing is impossible from top to bottom and the outlook so hopeless that there is really no use enquiring further or suggesting any remedy, because he can see none. The Indians are doomed to extinction and the Peruvian Amazon Company to liquidation and prompt disappearance.

Such I am afraid will be the case — and what then. Can any international outcry, and intervention be effective to compel Peru, Bolivia (and Brazil too) to protect their Indian peoples? I fear not. Still the attempt can be made and with God's help I'll make it.[231]

[MS 13,087 (10) — At La Chorrera

30 October 1910 — Handed to Sr. Tizon — 10.30 a.m.

Sir,

From the statement furnished to me showing the state of the accounts of the Barbados labourers actually in the service of this agency of the Peruvian Amazon Company Ltd., I observe that a sum of S/P 301.85 stands to the credit of one John Brown, no longer in the employ of the Company. This man, who is a native of Montserrat, I learn from the Government of Barbados is seriously ill and will in no circumstances be able to return to claim this money. I would, therefore, suggest that a draft for the amount due to him, calculated at its equivalent in sterling, should be remitted to the Governor of barbados, or as I understand that the Company has no direct means of remitting money to that island the payment might ne effected through me or through His Majesty's Government in London as may be convenient.

I am Sir,

Your most obedient, humble, servant

Roger Casement,

Consul General]

---

[231] This statement is an extraordinary confession on Casement's part for a number of reasons. His brief from Sir Edward Grey had stated that he should investigate the state of British subjects employed by the Company, but after weeks of travelling in the Putumayo and his exposure to the entrenched atrocities, Casement's own attitude towards his investigation quite clearly began to change. After returning from the Putumayo, Casement campaigned solidly for another two years to raise public awareness of the plight of the Amazon Indian.

AT CHORRERA — MONDAY, 31ST OCTOBER

Evelyn Batson's statement

Up early 5.30. Lovely sunrise flowing over the great pool in a flood of salmon-tinted light. Told Bishop to bring Evelyn Batson to see me at 7.30. He came before 8. He is a fireman now on the launch 'Huitota' which is going down to-day to St Julia to bring up the Abisinia *fabrico*. I presume Aguero will come. Batson's statement is a dreadful one. The man answered every question put to him simply and quietly and with every sign of speaking the truth. It is a horrid record and incidentally throws light on the truth of Crichlow's and Chase's statements, the former's as to his treatment by Aurelio Rodriguez at Santa Catalina in 1898, and the latter's as to the capture of Katenere's[232] wife and the other people on the Pamá a few months ago this year. The state of things at Abisinia must be as bad as ever, the crimes committed by Aguero and his subordinate, Juan Sellar (N.B. A misspelling. I found later on the man's name was Juan Zellada but the blackmen always pronounced it to me as if it were "Sellar".) that Batson knew, are as dreadful as anything ever recorded I think. They include a shocking case of cannibalism, a man cut up and carried past the house by the *muchachos* under Aguero's directions and the limbs taken away to be eaten, and a group of the Pamá prisoners cruelly murdered — three by deliberate starvation and the fourth man shot by Sellar.

Also a woman killed by Armando Blondel at Morelia, by blows of his fist and further the actual shooting of Katenere himself at Abisinia by the *muchachos*. This latter incident is like a page of romance.

Katenere's guerrilla war

Katenere was the hero of the Boras — the brave Captain who resisted and tried to give back blow for blow. Bishop who saw him once, a year ago when he was under Normand at Andokes, says Katenere was a fine, tall, strong young Boras *cacique*,[233] who worked rubber at first but fled from Normand's ill-treatment of

---

[232] Although Casement spelt the name of the rebel *cacique* Katenere in his reference of 13 October, the name seems to have changed here to Katendere. For the sake of consistency, the name has been changed here to its previous spelling. Casement makes an interesting margin note about spelling a few lines later.

[233] *Cacique* is the term used in Brazil and throughout Latin America to describe a tribal chief.

him. He it was who shot the scoundrel Bartolomé Zumaeta in May 1908 at a stream in the Boras country while that villain was directing the washing of rubber. Since that Katenere has been "on his keeping" to the hills — as we said once in Ireland — and every effort to kill or capture him failed until this last actual attack of his own on the station of Abisinia itself. What a pity he did not succeed.

Batson's long interrogatory took me until 10.30 a.m. It fills eight pages of foolscap.[234] I told him I should require him later on to return and sign it. He has to leave at once almost in the 'Huitota' so it cannot be done to-day. J. Minggs, I hear, has to go down in her too. On the other hand every Barbados man has arrived, Bishop tells me, except Allan Davis from Abisinia. I presume he will come up with the 'Huitota' in a day or two with the *fabrico* from that Section, and possibly bring Aguero too. They know already, I can see, that Batson has told me everything. I can see it in Macedo's face. The lurking dread and shifting eye — willing to wound but yet afraid to strike.

He is reduced to impotence in his own headquarters, the wretch who bullied and terrorised for years obliged to smirk and grimace before a man he must detest. He sees the Barbados men he sought to terrify or bribe fall from him one by one and where, two months ago, he would have put them in the stocks, he is now forced to ask them to come to my room knowing that all the atrocious crimes they have seen committed or have themselves committed will be categorically laid bare before me. His face when we meet at dinner or lunch is a picture. A mixture of servility and dread. He even waits on me himself — taking the dish from the hands of the servant and handing it to me.

Francis repents

Bishop has just come in to say that Donal Francis sent him to me with his humble apologies for having lied and been bribed! He says he repents and is ashamed! That he sees his countrymen who have stated the truth walking about "with their heads up" — and he is ashamed to face them or me. He begs I will send for him and he will confess everything — that he was bribed and lied to me and that now he wishes to put himself right by confessing and so recovering his self-respect!

---

[234] Evelyn Batson {Blue Book — Statement No.19 pp.99–106}. Batson provided the longest single statement yet given to Casement.

A black man's heart is very like a white man's too. I told Bishop to say that I would consider it — that as he has lied to me before, deliberately and in a cowardly way, and had preferred to take his stand with the cowards and murderers, it was a matter I should have to think over. That it was not for my purposes or in any way to serve me that he had been called on in the first instance to speak truthfully, but for his own sake too — for his manhood and honour. Strange words these.

So called "Whitemen" here wouldn't think to apply (them) to a negro — and yet the negro has a better heart and a better conscience than they have — and is a far better "whiteman" at bottom. I told Tizon this, to his secret amazement I think.

Arrival of the Sur fabrico and Carlos Miranda

The Sur *fabrico* under Carlos Miranda began to arrive just before lunch. He first with a huge dog. He was formally presented to us all by Macedo. He is a fat, gross-looking whiteman, with a fair complexion. I thought, as he shook hands with me, of the "old woman" in Labadie's statement at Iquitos. That seems a trivial incident now after the more recent first-hand horrors I have had — but it was an atrocious act. The "old woman" had given "bad advice" to the Indians. She was a "wise woman" that counselled them not to work rubber — not to be slaves. So her old head was cut off with a machete and this whiteman who has just shaken hands with us and sits down beside us to lunch, had held it up by the hair to the assembled Indians and told them that that would be their fate if they did not obey him and work *caucho*. What a curse there is in those words — *to work caucho*.

Weighing rubber

Fox and I went out to the store and watched the rubber coming in. Huge loads of it, men, women and children. Dear little bright-eyed boys — tiny girls — mothers with infants — two quite old women and two old men even — almost the very first old people I have seen. Three of the Indian men, too, had beards — stray hairs, it is true, but still beards — one 2" long. These are the first men with hair on the face I have seen.[235] We weighed several loads — one

[235] Lack of facial and bodily hair was a characteristic of the Amazon Indians and most tribes practised depilation and extracted the hair from all over their bodies and face except their heads. See Capt. Thomas Whiffen, *North West Amazons* (Constable 1915) Appendices I and III, also Rafael Karsten, *The Civilization of the South American Indians* (London 1926) — Chap. II.

was just 50 kilos — on a thin spare enough man too. Then I went one better and collared two small boys with their loads and got these weighed first and then the boys themselves.

One mite had a load of 22 kilos. of rubber on his tiny back and then when put on the balance himself he came to just 25 kilos. The next, a little boy whose name he gave as Kaimeni, weighed 29½ himself and was actually carrying 30½ kilos of rubber! One kilo more than his own weight. This had been for many miles. The Station of Sur itself is only 2 hours away, but this rubber we are told came from Kaimenes on the way to Encanto — a much greater distance. Fully 100 people came in — more than that I should say — and even as they deposited these enormous loads of rubber in the big Rubber Store they were collared and made to carry off boxes of things and bags for the 'Huitota'. Two birds killed with one stone! They had not time to sit down or get a drink before this further task was put upon them — to load the departing steamer with goods for Abisinia. Fox and I watched this confirmation of so much — it told its own tale — with a sort of grim joy I think.

Casement buys an Indian boy — Omarino

I sent to the store for a case of salmon and distributed tins galore to men, women, boys and mites — also some of my own tins still left from Iquitos. They clicked their tongues and lips with joy poor souls and I photo'd a good many of them. They are nice bright-looking people — and I picked one dear little chap out and asked if he would come with me. He clasped both my hands, backed up to me and cuddled between my legs and said "yes". After much conversation and crowding round of Indians it is fully agreed on, he will go home with me. His father and mother are both dead, both killed by this rubber curse — and his big brother — a young man — was shot by Montt. Out pat came the story — the boy's Captain standing by and explaining. The Captain asked for a present on the agreement — virtually the sale of this child — of a shirt and a pair of trousers which I gave him, and Macedo with great unction made me "a present" of the boy. The child's name is Omarino and he comes from the Naimenes village, towards El Encanto. He had carried a huge load of rubber down too. I will get him and it weighed to-morrow. The wee chap clung to me often, both hands, and I gave him several tins of salmon to give to his friends as "parting gifts". He so asked for the Salmon — to give away — and I watched him running round and giving those joyous tins — for such they are to these starving folk. Several tins of it went to an elderly woman, who had a mite of a boy nude entirely without *fono* at all.

Parr confesses

After lunch I went with Parr to the Rubber Store and got a load of 63½ kilos weighed — and not by any means the biggest load I have seen. Some of Normand's Boras' loads were a good bit bigger, but this is a pretty fair one. The rubber is coming in wearily — plodding along. Macedo said at lunch it is a fine *fabrico* for Sur "from 9 to 10 tons". Parr, in the Store, got confidential, and let himself go. He said the whole thing was disgraceful — robbery and slavery — and that the people to-day were being well-treated because we were here! Parr is only a young, decent-looking English boy of about 24 I should say — or less.

Rubber at sunset

More rubber from Sur itself came in at sunset. Enormous loads — men and women staggering under them — it went on all evening nearly and late at night I saw road lights on the surrounding hills. Plaza, who stole Bishop's clothing at Ultimo Retiro, and second in command of Sur, arrived with these last loads. I find he is in debt to the Company S/P 436.27 or say £43, so it will be hard to make him stump up Bishop's 61 soles claimed.

Casement approached by Indian during afternoon swim

I bathed in afternoon and a boy or young man came and sat on the bank — 'Andokes' and other boys were swimming like fish. This young man is a *muchacho* of Sur and I had photo'd him along with others as they brought the rubber in. I had noticed him looking at me with a sort of steadfast shyness and as I gave him and others salmon his face flushed. He now came and eyed me in the same way and when I came out from my swim he followed me up to the house and begged me to take him away with me. Again and again, I called Bishop and he said he would go above all things — to get away! Bishop says the whole country would go if they could get out. This youth is married too! He says, however, his wife has gone to her "family" and that he will gladly forsake all to get away. He is a fine youth, quite strong and shapely with a true Indian face. I'd gladly take him, but I already have Omarino and Doi is on order from Matanzas, and Tizon says will come. This youth is a bigger boy than either — a married man of 19, probably or 20 and would make a fine type for Herbert Ward in the group I have in my mind for South America. This has been for some time in my thoughts, to enlist Ward (and France) on the side of these poor Indians and to do it through their artistic sense. I'll gladly take the boy if Macedo and Coy. don't kick up too much fuss. Of course they could not lawfully refuse and I could put it that way If I chose, but that would indeed be a challenge!

Physical description of Arédomi

To actually declare that a Putumayo Indian was free to go and come as he or a civilised man thought right. Ruat coelum rather than that. This youth's name is Arédomi, but he has been called 'Pedro' by these civilising gentlemen! He has the fine, long strong hair of the Indians, the cartilage of the nose and the nostrils bored for twigs and a handsome face and shapely body. I gave him a pair of pantaloons, and he stripped the old ones off, and stood in his *fono* — a splendid shape of bronze and I thought of Herbert all the time and how he would rejoice to have the moulding of those shapely limbs in real bronze. I told Arédomi to wait till the morning and I would see if I could take him — Bishop seemed delighted. He has already got the tiny Omarino in harness, getting clothes made for him to carry him as far as Iquitos and he is to sleep in Bishop's hammock to-night, Bishop taking to his cot.

Playing cards for an Indian

I played four rubbers of Bridge — won two and lost two. Like Dean Swift[236] I was playing for Arédomi, had I got clear conqueror I was to take him — I had to fight terribly to get this mere tie and so the Bridge did not decide Arédomi's fate. It is really buying the freedom of a slave. I shall not pay in goods or coin for him here — although in some ways even that may be called for, but the expense of conveyance etc. is heavy. My hope is that by getting some of these unknown Indians to Europe I may get powerful people interested in them and so in the fate of the whole race out here in the toils. Harley House and the A.P.S.[237] will help and

---

[236] A reference to Jonathan Swift (1667–1745), the political satirist, pamphleteer and poet who became Dean of St Patrick's Dublin in 1713 but is best known as the author of *Gulliver's Travels* (1726).

[237] The A.P.S. refers to the Aborigines Protection Society. Despite the fact that the drive to abolish slavery had been well-established before the passing of the Emancipation Act in 1833, aborigines and their status and protection had been completely neglected. In 1835 Thomas Fowell Buxton obtained the appointment

exploit the boys for all they are worth if it ever comes to raising the question in public campaign against this hellish slavery and extermination.

Lots of the Indians — men, women and children, lay all night under the House — on the cement platform — cold and hard. One trod on them almost at the foot of the stairs and I heard the faint murmur "chegarro" (cigarette) from two or three non-sleepers and gave them this dearly prized gift. I've given away a "quare load" of cigarettes since I came to the Putumayo. They like tobacco of course, but they drink it only[238] — and these things to smoke are a new pleasure to them — poor souls — of the few things pleasant that get into their awful lives.

The river is falling so fast that it is said the *Liberal* won't be able to come up to Chorrera. She will only get some eight hours below it — so Tizon and Macedo says. In that case I may charter the

---

of a Select Committee of the House of Commons to look into the matter and in 1837 a Blue Book drafted by William Gladstone, was published and Dr Thomas Hodgkin established the Aborigines Protection Society "to assist in protecting the defenceless, and promoting the advancement of civilized tribes ... the Collection of authentic information concerning the character, habits and wants of uncivilized tribes ... to communicate in cheap publications those details which may excite the interest of all classes, and thus ensure the extension of correct opinions." Among the Society's honorary members were Baron Alexander von Humboldt and Charles de Tocqueville. Despite the efforts of the Society to protect aborigines, the mounting level of atrocities committed behind the curtain of empire at the end of the nineteenth century fell outside its sphere of influence, most obviously in the case of the South American Indian. A new phase in the Society's history began in 1889 with the appointment of H.R. Fox-Bourne (1837–1909) as Secretary. Fox-Bourne continued crusading hard for aborigines' protection, especially in Africa. He became one of the most virulent spokesmen against the "scramble for Africa" and denounced Euroimperialism as a military crime — targeting Belgium, Britain, France and Germany as the main offenders. On his death in 1909 the A.P.S. was amalgamated with the Anti-Slavery Society.

[238] Casement's reference here to the Indians drinking tobacco is to the ceremony known as *Chupe del Tabaco* — literally the sucking of tobacco, another magico-religious ritual when the leaves of *Nicotiana tabacum* were imbibed, after being boiled down to a concentrated liquid with the consistency of molasses. Hardenburg described the ritual as follows, "Upon the occasion of a fiesta or to solemnise any agreement or contract, they have recourse to the celebrated chupé del tobaco ... A numerous group of Indians congregate about a pot ... which contains a strong extract of tobacco. The *capitán* first introduces his forefinger into the liquid and commences a long discourse ... Then they became more excited, until finally the pot is gravely passed around, and each ... dips his finger into the liquid and then applies it to the tongue. This is the Witoto's most solemn oath." The ceremony was normally associated with story-telling or with swearing of oaths against the white man. See Eugenio Robuchon, *En el Putumayo y sus Afluentes* (Lima 1907). Taussig also has much to say on the ritual.

'Huitota' altogether and take the Barbados men and all down to the Solimões in her — some 650–700 miles and wait at the mouth of the Putumayo for a passing river steamer. Macedo says if it does not rain on 2nd November it will not rain for six weeks. A local St Swithin evidently.[239]

Hallow eve this and I walked about till near midnight with the sleeping Indians all around — one or two of them getting up and talking to me.

AT LA CHORRERA — TUESDAY, 1ST NOVEMBER

Interview of Augustus Walcott

Up early — and saw Arédomi waiting — poor boy.. Sent for Augustus Walcott, a Barbados man from Sabana and his statements took me up to breakfast at 11.30 and again in afternoon too. He spoke so slowly and was prolix — but truthful.

When finished with him called Preston Johnson and Sidney Morris,[240] two other Barbados men from Sabana, and their statements took me to 5.30 — even hurrying up the latter's. All wish to go away with me and as they have left most of their things in Sabana they have to return there. So I was obliged to hurry to get things explained to Tizon so that they might leave early in the morning with an order to Fonseca. This took till 6 p.m. and meanwhile the 'Huitota' came up with Aguero and Alcosta from Oriente and a lot of Ocainas Indians and the rubber of Abisinia and Oriente. I missed all this. At dinner met Aguero and Alcosta — former a rapacious-faced individual — bold and hawk-like — the latter taller and thinner. Very heavy rain at 1 o'clock till 4. Poured and river began rising almost at once. By sunset it was visibly on the move up and the cataract roaring and leaping. No time for

---

[239] The legend is that St Swithin, Bishop of Winchester and adviser of Egbert of Wessex, who died in 862, desired to be buried in the churchyard of the minster, that the "sweet rain of heaven might fall upon his grave". At canonization, the monks thought to honour the Saint by removing his body into the cathedral choir and fixed 15 July for the ceremony, but it rained day after day for 40 days, thereby, according to some, delaying the proceedings. The legend gave rise to the popular saying that if it rains on St Swithin's day, there will be rain for forty days. The *Black Diary* entry entry for 2 November says: "*Very little rain today, but still it passed St Swithin's with rain.*" The forger seems to be purposefully cryptic here or has just been confused by Casement's reference to a local St Swithin. Whatever the reason, the sense in the *Black Diary* is both misleading and wrong.

[240] Sidney Morris {Blue Book — Statement No.20 p.106–109}.
Preston Johnson {Blue Book — Statement No.21 p.109–111}.

diary today. I swam over to the island in the early morning at 7 a.m. and then began the Barbados statements right away.

Allan Davis has come up too from Abisinia — so I have all men here now. Six more to interview and then I am through.

Told Tizon of Batson's and Morris' statements and read part of Batson's to him about Aguero. Also of Katenere's death. Told him of Normand's setting people on fire and burning them alive as Sidney Morris witnessed it. Perfectly atrocious. Tizon told me all were going. Velarde is down from Occidente to go with me — Normand by next steamer. Aguero and Fonseca are to go very soon.

The Commission went to inspect the payment for the 9–10 tons of Sur rubber. It consisted, they said, principally of a tin jug for each load. One of those I saw was 63½ kilos and others I will swear were 70 kilos. I wish the Commission would be more systematic, they could easily have seen exactly what was given in each case. No time for doing anything myself now till I settle up the Barbados men.

Heavy rain today — began soon after lunch and poured steadily. The river at night could be even heard rising on the banks.

The Ocainas Indians who have come up with Alcosta from Oriente are fine men — tall and well-built — like the Boras. Some of the latter have also come with Aguero — but not many. His rubber has not come. The Abisinia *fabrico* is not till December I hear.

One of the Barbados men who spoke today, Augustus Walcott, was shamefully ill-used by Normand at Matanzas at end of 1904 or beginning of 1905 — just after they arrived. He was hung up by his arms tied behind his back for a very long time, and beaten with swords or machetes. He became unconscious and when let down was ill. Remained ill for a long time and had to be carried down in a hammock to Chorrera. Could not use his arms for two months.[241]

It is shameful that this infamous scoundrel Normand should get off scot free. He will leave it in a month with a fortune —

---

[241] Augustus Walcott {Blue Book Statement No.22 — p.111–118}. It is interesting to note that the *Black Diary* says, "Took statements of Sidney Morris, Preston Johnson & Augustus Walcott." — The names appear in the chronological order of the statements that were subsequently published in the Blue Book. But this is different to the order in which they were taken down on the day. Walcott's long statement was taken before those of Morris and Johnson but was not signed until 6 November and for this reason the chronology was changed in the Blue Book.

£2,000 in hand here at once — and whatever else he has saved in the past and invested and here is this poor blackman, outraged and criminally treated with a debt against him of £38 after six years of service. I spoke strongly to Tizon on this aspect of the case — but not so strongly as I intend doing.

La Chorrera — Wednesday, 2nd November

Interview with James Mapp

The river has risen steadily. It is now fully 5 feet up and the sandbanks are rapidly covering. Did not bath. Saw Arédomi who is cutting firewood and fully decided to take the poor boy with me. Told Bishop I had decided. Carlos Miranda came to bid me good-bye, going back to Sur. Then called James Mapp and got a long statement from him lasting up to 11 a.m. He is one of the first to come here. He saw Velarde have the Indian drowned at Occidente this year — as described by Francisco the Captain. Saw it with his own eyes — four poor beings were taken down to the river with their hands tied behind their backs and held under water by an Indian acting under Acosta's personal direction until they were filled with water and nearly drowned. One of them struggling to escape got loose from the hold of the Indian and was never seen. With his arms tied, and his "bowels full of water", as Mapp described it, the poor soul had not much chance. His body was recovered on 24th June at the mouth of the river just below the Station.[242]

I brought Tizon in to hear James Mapp repeat the statement and when he learned that this had actually happened the very day he left Occidente, to go on to Entre Rios he was pale with anger. I was glad of this striking confirmation of the truth of what I have been driving into his soul the last four weeks — that he has been dealing with murderers and liars and cowards. Mapp's straight-forward testimony was good all round. It took me all the morning to record it.

Afternoon interviews — Hoyte, Phillips, Quintin and Davis

After luncheon I had four men in — Alfred Hoyte, Reuben Phillips, Clifford Quintin and Allan Davis[243] — the three first from S.

---

[242] James Mapp {Blue Book — Statement No.23 — p.118–124}.

[243] Alfred Hoyte {Blue Book — Statement No. 24 — p.124–125}.
Reuben Phillips {Statement No. 25 — p.125–127}.

Catalina — the last from Abisinia. The same stories — the same stories all through — are confirming one another. Quintin had been tied up by Normand and flogged — got 50 lashes and is very ill too — was again beaten by Normand and Bucelli. The marks of the first lashes — 6 years old! — are on him, one dreadful scar across the ribs. His foot is poisoned by a spike the Indians put in the ground at Santa Catalina to protect themselves from visits of these civilising gentry. Poor man — he is a wreck — completely broken in body and spirit.

Three of them return by my direction, at once to Santa Catalina to get their things back here in time to go with me by the *Liberal* — Mapp, Hoyte and Phillips.

Poor Quintin, in addition to all the gross ill-treatment done to him by Normand was forced at Santa Catalina to cut off an Indian's head by Rodolfo Rodriguez now second in charge of that station. The list of horrors has grown every hour to-day and yesterday and Monday. So completely are the Barbados men now vindicated that Tizon actually to-day asked me "as a favour" — his own words — to let him have a list of the names of all the Agents of the Company incriminated by the men. High and low, — he asks now they shall be judged by the blackmen! What a change from the first days of my coming to La Chorrera. Through the faithfulness to me of these despised men, and their dependence on my power to protect them they have placed the truth full in the light. So that there is now no attempt to dispute it. These statements to-day practically complete my work. There remain only two Barbados men in the Company's service I have not yet interrogated. One of these, Joseph Minggs, is here now, but there is no time to-day to have his statement, and he goes down to Providencia this evening on the 'Huitota' with Alcosta and Aguero who are returning to their sections after dinner. She will be absent three days. Batson is on her, as assistant, or fireman, and Levine is going down too — all with rifles just to guard these poor nude Ocainas that brought Alcosta's rubber.

Arrival of rubber from various stations

We have seen a great deal of a general *fabrico* from all the sections arriving under our eyes — from up river and down at the same time. The Occidente rubber is coming in on the backs of the poor

---

Clifford Quintin {Statement No.26 — p.127–130} Quintin made a further statement on 5 November.
Allan Davis {Statement No.27 p.130–133}.

meagre men and women of that district, across from Port Victoria; some 50 or 60 have been brought down to transport it this 2 miles or so. Velarde is here, dismissed on his way to Iquitos, owing the Company £160 odd, but this *fabrico* will square it. Rodriguez and Acosta are also here.

Vasquez Torres is down from Atenas with some of its rubber, the rest to come by Montt himself in a day or two. Normand's rubber has also begun to arrive and then we have had Sur giving a clear 8 tons of the best of rubber seen yet, and Oriente. There remain still several sections to deliver before the *Liberal* goes. Entre Rios, whence O'Donnell comes in person at the head of his contingent, Ultimo Retiro, and Santa Catalina will send its rubber back by the 'Huitota' on 5th or 6th.

I am trying to find out what are the actual payments made in each case. The euphemism that the goods now given are an advance for the next *fabrico* and not a payment for this meets one instantly, but it is of no account. The real point is that an "advance" is already a payment — and as we know the quantity of a *fabrico* for each station it follows that the "advance" of to-day is the payment for the next *fabrico* for 3 months hence. That *fabrico* will have to be the same as this — so that whatever Sur took to-day is payment for 8 tons of the best rubber the Ozu produces, I shall try and get young Parr, in the store, to give me lists of all the goods he has issued against these recent fabricos.

Casement measures a Boras Indian

I measured a fine young Boras Indian to-day come with Aguero 37½ inches round bare chest — not inflated — 12½ inches round biceps — not distended — 23" round head at forehead. His skin was exceeding fair and he was tall and very well built. I am told some of the Boras are white almost. Some I have seen are as white as a Spaniard or Portuguese.

My little boy Omarino was weighed to-day too; he weighs 25 kilos, and the load of rubber he brought in weighed 29½ kilos!

Arédomi is hanging round, Bishop says. They want to take him back to-morrow to carry the *tula* of one of the Sur empleados who returns. We shall see. I will ask Macedo in the morning. The poor lad has tasted the hope of liberty. I shall see that he gets away.

Aguero and Alcosta leave

Aguero and Alcosta happily left before dinner. They did not go in fact, but dined with some of the other ruffians here sending their boys to the table for food. They prefer not meeting our somewhat cold and rigid faces. The 'Huitota' did not leave until 8 p.m. and I heard crying on the beach.

The river still rising — although only very slight rainfall to-day.

La Chorrera, Thursday, 3rd November 1910

Arédomi and Sealy

Arranged early this morning to take Arédomi with me. Sent Bishop with the lad to Macedo who at once consented, so that is happily settled.[244] Arranged also that Stanley Sealy, my tall, faithful Barbados man, shall enter the service of the Commission, like Chase on my leaving. He wanted to come with me but I pointed out the advantage to him of going with Barnes and the others. Barnes promises to continue his pay of £7 per month and when the Commission leaves — probably not before March or April next — to have Sealy's passage to Barbados paid. So he will be able to go back home with a good bit of money in hand.

Aguero's new concubine

Bishop tells me that another dastardly outrage took place last night under our very eyes. The *Huitota* with Aguero and Alcosta did not leave till 8 or later. Aguero took one of the poor work-women here. Macedo gave her to him to swell his harem. He always has eleven at Abisinia, Chase tells me. This poor woman is a Huitota, one of the local slave staff. She used to sweep the verandah every morning and Fox and I had both noticed her gentle patient face. Bishop says she wept bitterly and begged to stay. She has been working here for years, since her poor Indian husband "disappeared".

She had been given, of course, as a wife to some of the *empleados*, but these had gone too, or died, and she was for some time working here, sewing, making "pantaloons", etc. under Mrs. Macedo's direction and performing house tasks and now she is handed over to that degraded infamous wretch to swell his pen of unfortunates. She begged, Bishop says, to stay and even asked why

[244] The word "Arranged" shows an interesting discrepancy with Casement's usual capital "A". A comparison with the same word that begins the entry for 3 November in the *Black Diary* shows a completely different formation of the letter. The most revealing inconsistencies in the script of the *Black Diaries* concern the fabrication of uppercase letters that generally lack Casement's fluency and often look as if they have been touched up.

Aguero, who had so many wives already, should want her. I told Fox, Bell and the others of this fresh outrage and when I am quite certain of all the facts I shall speak to Tizon.

Garece and the Rodriguez brothers

Gave Garece, the Steward who accompanied our march, tip of £5 to his amazement. He is an Argentine, married to a Peruvian with two children here. A decent man, one of the few, the very few, I should trust. Tizon says he is honest and told him of the absolutely disgraceful things done to the Boras Indians at Santa Catalina and Sabana by the two Rodriguez brothers — Aurelio and Aristides, the latter happily dead. They were a "Company" of themselves in the old days. Arana got hold of them and they made a combine. He left the two in charge of the two Sections, each to have 50% of the product of the district! Arana made nothing out of it, even lost. Aurelio has retired on what Tizon admits is quite a big fortune and is one of the leading lights of Iquitos Society. The crimes he and his brother committed would appal mankind.

The testimony of the Barbados men, especially Quintin, the last few days is perfectly awful. He and Batson were at Santa Catalina during the latter years of Aurelio Rodriguez — Quintin up to the very end. Wholesale massacres of the Boras — men, women and children — endured up to June last year.

Quintin, I find, concealed some of his own crimes, as Batson says that in addition to cutting off the man's head he has killed other Indians at Santa Catalina. When I bring him up to sign his Statement I shall get the whole confession. The man is in a miserable state mentally as well as bodily. He has been converted into a criminal, a murderer of the worst kind.

Sent for Donald Francis at last and he came to make his full confession. He begged again and again I would hear him and let him confess his lying to me on 23 September and tell me all. I read him a homily, he apologised humbly, and I told him I did not now want his story of wrong-doing, that I knew all and had already received all the information necessary for my mission. He is really sorry and anxious to stand well with me and with his own conscience.

The "public opinion" of all the other Barbados men has been too much for him. He wants to "hold up his head" with them. Now he can do it. I don't want criminal evidence against Macedo, it would only add to Tizon's enormous difficulties to add Macedo at once to the black list. He is perhaps the worst of the lot, as he has been in control and has allowed and stimulated all this dreadful crime, besides the things I know and suspect he has done himself, including the burning alive of the 45 Ocainas Indians here at Chorrera.[245] But Tizon assures me that Macedo too is going, so let him go in peace, for the sake of Tizon's work of cleansing and reform.

Swindling of the Barbadians

I went through a lot of the accounts of the Barbados men to-day and find the grossest overcharges. They have been robbed incredibly. 10/- for a tin of butter, 10/- for a pair of thin wretched carpet slippers (about 9d a pair at home) and food that should be supplied them charged for at outrageous prices.

I analysed one account of Allan Davis — from January to March 1909 coming to S/P 120 and S/P 80 of this were for foodstuffs alone. I took it to Tizon and pointed out how excessively unjust these charges were. His whole manner has changed with regard to the Barbados men. He admitted much of what I said, but sought to plead the excessive prices charged by the Iquitos house for the goods it sends here. That is no argument as the men are concerned. Because this Company allows the gang of swindlers in Iquitos to rob it right and left by false prices, and by buying in the dearest market for personal gain and for bribing all the "commerce" of Iquitos is no reason why the employés should be swindled.

The whole of the goods required for the needs of the Putumayo are bought in Iquitos — some £30,000 a year, I am told, — instead of getting them direct from Europe. Close on £20,000 a year by abolishing the house altogether. The whole thing is an inconceivable swindle — founded on incredible crime as the bedrock of all its income.

Macedo offers 25 per cent reduction on Barbadian accounts

Macedo came into Tizon's room while I was discussing this account of Allan Davis and, learning that I thought the prices charged the men "rather high", he at once and quite spontaneously offered to

[245] This refers to the burning alive of twenty-four Ocaina *caciques* on 2 November 1903, an event which had effectively instigated the P.A. Co.'s rule of terror on the Putumayo. Under Macedo's instructions *caciques* were called together by the Chiefs of Section and after some preliminary talks were set upon and tied to individual stakes in the ground and then burnt. See Neftalí Benavides Rivera "Los crimenes de la Casa Arana" in *Cultura Nariñense* No. 84, (June 1975).

strike off 25% on all their back accounts since the Company's formation. Tizon asked if I would agree to this. I said I should find out the men's opinion. As far as they are concerned it is an amazing boon. It is really a bribe to me! Macedo wishes to pose as the just, kind man and to have my good word to the end.

It is, incidentally, again robbing the Company, however. What a way of doing business. Here are nearly 3½ years' sales, amounting to possibly £1,500 — to the few remaining Barbados men, — to be now tampered with like this and one fourth of these "sales" profits of the Company to be calmly wiped off its books! And this by a minor agent without any consultation or permission of those who employ him!

I spoke to Bishop and others. They are delighted and thank me warmly. It means much to them, but I am in doubt about the justice of it.

Here is the full list of men it will affect.

List of Barbados men who came with Stanley Sealy on Contracts made in Iquitos on 25th April 1908 — arriving at La Chorrera on 12th May 1908. These contracts were for Five Pounds per month — "cinco libras" — and the men have been credited with only 50 soles per month — whereas a pound is 10s 50. I claim, on their behalf, that they should receive credit for this 50 cents on each £1 since 13th May, 1908. It means S/P 2.50 per month, equal to S/P 30 per annum. On 12th November it will be two years and a half since their pay began — a difference in their favour of 70 Soles. I have put the matter before Mr Tizon who agrees to this. The men affected are:

Stanley Sealy	S. Greenidge
James Chase	P. Lawrence
Reuben Phillips	Jasper Dyall
Alfred Hoyte	E. Crichlow
James Mapp	E. Batson
Preston Johnson	A. Walcott
Sidney Morris	Clifford Quintin
James Lane	(?) James Layne
Allan Davis	W. Levine
Donal Francis	F. Bishop

and I have given him a list and he promises to have this difference carried to their credit.

Compensation for ill-treatment

Apart from this petty robbery I find the men have all been robbed in a variety of ways — the exorbitant prices charged for the things they need, for food, shoes and petty necessaries of existence and for medicines. Food and medicines are free in their contracts, and yet far the greater part of their indebtedness to the Company is for food and is charged at the most outrageous prices.

I have just handed to Mr Tizon an analysis of one factura of Allan Davis taken at random that I made out this morning. It covers the period January to March, 1909, the sum total being S/P$120.60. Of this amount, S/P$80.20 is for foodstuffs including rice at 60 cts the kilo = 6.60. 2 tins butter at 5/- each or almost £1 for 2 tins of butter! Tizon agrees with me it is excessive. Moreover, I am told by the men that the Chiefs of Section and other Employés, such as Bruce and Burke, the engineers of the two launches — get their goods at Iquitos prices, whereas these poor Barbados men, at £5 and £6 a month, are charged these very high prices. Bruce gets £25 a month salary — and the Chiefs of Section anything up to £1000 a year. The rich men who rob the country and the Indians get their goods cheap — the poor man, who is beaten and starved and put in cepo, gets all his pay, and more than his pay, taken back for the necessaries of life. Macedo came into Tizon's room while we were discussing the matter — and Tizon showed him the analysis I had made and opened the subject. Macedo promptly fell into line and, off his own bat, without any suggestion from me, offered to wipe out 25% on all the back accounts — and Tizon suggested my concurrence rather than carrying the question home. I said I thought I would counsel the men to accept this — that it seemed a reasonable offer under the circumstances — the best that could be looked for.[246]

I have told Bishop and he is delighted and says the men will be very glad and very grateful to me. Some of them will now have a good sum in hand. Allan Davis, for instance, I find will get about S/P 400 back — £40 — under this arrangement. The men never dreamed of such a thing I can see and I fancy I am doing well in counselling them to accept it.

Sealy and the seven others will also get their S/P 2.50 per month for the last 30 months — and I gather that Tizon will strike out the medicine charges altogether, so that the actual gain to many men will be more. Bishop, for instance, will get 50 or 60

[246] This paragraph repeats information that has been noted a few pages earlier.

soles, at least, back for medicines he bought since 1st July, 1907, and thus 25% on all his other purchases.

There then remain the four grave cases of ill-treatment of J. Dyall by Alfredo Montt; E. Crichlow by Aurelio Rodriguez and F. Velarde; A. Walcott by A. Normand and (the worst of all) Clifford Quintin by Normand. I mentioned these cases to Tizon and pointed out how shameful it was that the men who so criminally maltreated these men should get off scot free with large sums of money to their credit, while these poor beggars who had been so injured were without redress. He begged me to try and let him arrange these cases here in a friendly way. That is I would find out from the men what they would take as compensation he would try and get it from these Peruvian Agents named.

Any prosecution of these men is hopeless — that we know — and the actual ill-treatment occurred in three cases long before the Company was formed. It is clear the men injured can recover nothing by law, and not I think by any pressure in London, as the Company is not responsible for these acts committed long before its inception — or even, in any case, I should think, for crimes committed by its agents.

There is only the moral responsibility of having had these Agents for 3 years its powerful representatives in many districts and never having attempted to find out what was being done out here. I asked Clifford Quintin what sum he would take. He said "£50 or £60" — poor soul — with a grin. If I could get him £50 it will be well.

The sound of crying

Normand, they all say, loves money. He robs even these Barbados men. Levine told Bishop that Normand got 110 soles out of him last month gambling. They gamble for anything — tins of food, old clothes etc., etc. and here is a Chief of Section who gambles with a black boy — his servant — and takes nearly two months of his wages in one note of hand! Truly a civilising Company.

Bishops says the crying last night was that of one of these poor Station women, the one who swept the verandah each morning. She was taken to Abisinia by Aguero — to add to his concubines — a gift from Macedo at his request. How revolting! Bishop says she wept bitterly. Perhaps, who knows, she had a husband here — at any rate, here is a case, infamous in all its aspects, and occurring right under our eyes — while we sat at the dinner table. We heard the voices and heard the whistle of the launch 30 yards away, and never knew that this poor woman was being handed over to gratify the lusts of this rapacious monster. I told the Commission of this.

Busy all rest of day with Barbados men's accounts and with Tizon over getting him a Black List of all the actual employés in the Company's service actually seen committing gross crimes. The list includes one of the most revolting crimes yet mentioned by Fonseca — witnessed by Chase at Ultimo Retiro in 1906 or 1907. Also another by the brute down at the Pescaria — in the Putumayo — similar to the atrocious crime on the poor girl at Naimenes — and other revolting acts by others — cutting off ears, and throwing babies away or into the river at Santa Catalina. What a miserable herd of cut-throats and assassins![247]

Donald Francis came at 2 p.m. sent for by me. He came to apologise, and recant — to ask me to forgive him for lying and to wipe out his statement as untrue and let him now tell me all.

I forgave him for the matter and said I should add to his statement his retraction of it — but that I did not want him to make any fresh one. It was useless now — I knew all — and needed no further evidence. He begged, but I declined — and read him a little homily on the virtues of manliness and truthfulness. He is physically the typical blackman — with a good face, too — and very strong body. A young Hercules — he went off very grateful and glad — entirely "rehabilitated" he thinks and able to hold up his head again with the rest — because I have listened to him.

Bishop told me of the prices of goods here — some queer things and then of the payments he had seen for a whole *fabrico* of rubber — from 30 to 40 kilos at different places — with the climax in a storyette related by Chase that really for comicality relieves the baseness of the motive.

The Pup Story

First O'Donnell and the Pup, also the 4 tins of meat for a whole fabrico; then Aguero's pup going round for many *fabricos*.

[247] The *Black List* compiled by Casement had the names of the worst criminals, against whom Casement felt the Iquitos courts should bring criminal proceedings. The *Black List* was given by Casement to Tizon at the end of the voyage and all the names on the list were duly dismissed from the company. Macedo's inclusion on the list was a delicate matter since he stood so close to the Commission and knew pretty much their every move.

I learn that the Atenas Indians who came down with the rubber from that Section were not allowed to cross the river. They feared we should notice the starvation! The poor beings were turned back after 13 hours' march with no food, too. We saw the lights on the opposite hills and wondered last night the cause. This is the explanation.

DAY TRIP TO SUR — FRIDAY, NOVEMBER 4TH

The road to Sur — a visit to the cemetery

Commission started to Sur at 7.30. I followed alone with Sealy and Arédomi at 8 and caught them up just entering Sur — an easy 1½ hours walk, — about 4½ miles, I fancy. Much of the road saplings, fully 30,000 young trees and saplings, felled and laid across for well two miles of the way. Saw a strange orchid — lovely bamboo palm — exquisite thing.

On the way to Sur I visited the so-called cemetery on the top of the hill above Chorrera. It is merely the bare hillside used as a burying-place and very largely for the unfortunate Andean soldiers — the Cholos — who were round here recently owing to the alleged, but wholly fictitious, Colombian invasion. Macedo says that 80 died out of some 120 all told — but most in the Encanto district. Here most of these poor chaps were buried with no cross or mark at all. A few have just a rough stick with the name, or date, rudely painted by some other soldier — but even these are broken or lying on the ground.

There are three masonry graves of whitewashed stone.

The first to Benjamin Larrañaga,[248] the founder of La Chorrera — a Colombian born in Pasto in 1851 who died here on 21st December 1903 (?). J.C. Arana had already entered into partnership with him and has ousted his son, Rafael who erected this monument.

The next tomb is a Peruvian Officer — a Lieutenant Serapie Valenzuela of the 'G.M. de La Chorrera' (I presume the

[248] Benjamin Larrañaga was the founder of a colony at La Chorrera and the leader of the first wave of Colombian *caucheros* to enter the Putumayo district. He had formed part of Rafael Reyes's original troop who entered the territory in the 1870s to collect cinchona. He returned at the end of the 1890s, leading a party of *caucheros* to start exploiting rubber. After initial success he was forced into debt and made a series of trading alliances with moneylenders and Iquitos-based *aviadores*, including Arana. As Larrañaga's debt to Arana increased, the two formed a partnership but the alliance was short-lived as Arana's aims for territorial expansion on behalf of Peru demanded the expulsion of Colombians from the region.

'Guarnicion Militar de La Chorrera') a native of Cuzco who died on 29th December 1904.

The third and last is the most interesting. It is that of the Mr Richards James Mapp served under years ago at Gondan and Abisinia — the co-partner with Aguero in the founding of that appalling section. His name is Enoch Richards on the tomb and it curtly says "fallecio el 3 de Septem. de 1905". This "places" Mapp's separation from the man and his going on to Puerto Carlos with Miranda. Sealy says only the bones of Richards lie here — they were dug up in Captain Whiffen's time and brought here. The Boras Indians, in defence of their homes, killed him — and from 1905 to 1908 the body lay buried somewhere in the country. It is to be hoped the spirit rests somewhere else.

Description of Sur

Sur a wretched place — no plantation or food visible, but Miranda says soil is bad and he is removing the Station 40 minutes off to a new *chacara* he — or rather his Indians — are making. The house a poor place, although better furnished than most and the man himself a more civilised man. James Mapp gives him a good character — better far than most of the others — and the only grave thing I know against him is what Labadie asserts of his cutting the "old woman's" head off. I fear there is no doubt it is true.

Return to Chorrera

I bathed in the stream and after lunch returned with Sealy and Arédomi, starting at 4 p.m. getting an enormous shower on the way and arriving drenched at Chorrera at 5.30 or so. The river rising steadily and every hour now makes the approach of the *Liberal* surer.

I turned in very early — not wishing to stay longer than necessary with Macedo and this lazy brute of a so-called Doctor Rodriguez, who is too lazy to walk even round this tiny Station to see his patients. They have to be carried to him! — unless they are racionals in which case he may go to see them. He gets £50 a month for this — and his board and lodging and that of his wife, too, and has a paid assistant.

Bishop tells me that Juanito Rodriguez threatened a poor Captain in Occidente with a good flogging after we left because I gave him some food and a knife. The Captain was a friend or Bishop's from old time and has come down here with the Occidente Rubber. Juanito said "the Englishmen" were not his father and brothers and he was not to speak to them and after we left he would be given a good hiding for having spoken to me.

I have put Juanito on the Black List for Tizon. It is now about ten names — it should be all the actual employés of the Company — but I restricted the Barbados men to things they actually saw with their own eyes.

La Chorrera — Saturday, 5th November

Comparing prices at the store

Long talk to-day with young Parr, the store-keeper as to accounts and charges. He gives me much information and is quite *au courant* with the infamous system of working the Indians and the wholesale robberies, too. It is not only the wretched Indians who are robbed — but the London Board and shareholders. The system of buying in Iquitos is bare-faced robbery. An account for goods bought there, or rather invoiced from there, is shown to me and I have copied it out entirely.

The Invoice is No.7291 made out to the Casa de la Chorrera due to the Peruvian Amazon Company, Ltd., and it happens to be the very cargo we bought round here from Iquitos on 14th September last — consisting of 402 packages of an invoice price of S/P 13,766.63 (say £1,376) to which are added S/P 3314.57 (or say £331) for freight 20%, Porterage, Wharfage, Customs, Despatching, Mojonazgo and 1% Insurance, bringing the invoice total up to S/P17,081.20 or roughly £1,700.

Most of the goods are provisions — and are invoiced at ridiculous prices — fully 100% over European prices or more. I will have them compared with even Cazes' Iquitos prices. I find, on doing this that the prices charged to this Agency by the Iquitos Agency are practically the same as the Iquitos Trading Company charged to me retail for the £40 or £50 worth of goods I bought from them. My butter I see I paid 1.05 for, and that is a little less than Chorrera pays Iquitos for theirs — a fraction less. Then the Barbados man taking a ton of butter pays 5.00 soles for it! I bought a Winchester carbine from Iquitos Trading Company for S/P 39, and this is exactly what the Peruvian Amazon Company at Chorrera pay for it to their Iquitos house!

I paid S/P 5.50 a 100 for Winchester cartridges in Iquitos and I see the poor Barbados devils have had to pay S/P 18.00 per 100 — or say £1.16.6 per 100 as against my 10/-6d.

Rice which is invoiced to Chorrera at S/P 12.00 the sack of 60 kilos. is sold here to the Barbados men at 60 cts the kilo or S/P 38.00 the sack — an increase of just 200% to them. So with every item I find — some more than this — some less — but very few less, I fancy. The Winchester cartridges are sold to them at nearer 400% on the Iquitos price — at really far more. For it is clear this invoice of the Company's to the Company here in Chorrera is a fraud. Not any original invoice from the Iquitos firms the goods were brought from is sent. The house there, or rather Pablo Zumaeta, Dublé &c. but wholesale from their friends there — it is a syndicate of robbery. They certainly do not pay what I paid to Cazes' house — that is clear. They then invoice to the House here at a figure which is obviously much higher than the one they actually paid in Iquitos, and they pocket the difference. The London Company pays the piper. Before the rubber that these wretched enslaved Indians have to bring in gratis — for puppy dogs, tins of meat, 9d. shirts and 6d. belts plus, battle murder and sudden death — finds its outlet on the English market, it has enriched the O'Donnells, Normands, Montts, Macedos and other murderers here — the Zumaetas, Dublés and all their accomplices in Iquitos — and the Arana–Alarco syndicate in Iquitos and Manaos. What remains for the English shareholders is a mighty small portion — it is like the Barbados men's share at this end! The thing begins in robbery and ends in robbery. I have kept a copy of this last invoice — and with the samples I take home of the actual goods I hope to be able to convict these atrocious swindlers of the wholesale robbery of everyone they come in contact with.

The position of the English Company seems hopeless. To carry out any reform they must smash up the Den of Thieves in Iquitos — that is clear — and yet it is these men who own the Putumayo and the Putumayo Indians and when they see their reign of wholesale plunder threatened, they'll smash the Company and let the English Shareholders whistle for their money.

Then it will be that the exposure of the whole thing must be made to the world — to the whole world — and yet it might be better to do it earlier.

Anyhow I see clearly Tizon will have to go to Iquitos, as I told him, before Julio Arana arrives, and tell the Prefect of the situation and of the grave peril to Peru and her claims to be a civilised State if he allows Arana, Zumaeta, Dublé and Co. to carry the day and defeat and drive out Tizon.

What Gielgud could have been doing in passing such books and such accounts for a firm of London auditors bangs me. It bangs Banagher.

Commission return

The Commission minus Tizon and Gielgud, returned this morning before lunch — the two latter are staying on in Sur to see an Indian dance arranged for this evening by Miranda. The river is rising by jumps — positively leaping up — and with a very heavy downpour that came to-day it ought to go up still more. The fall is a foaming mass of white and by tomorrow the pool will be again a swirling mass of water. Signatures of several Barbados men taken to their statements which I read over to them.

La Chorrera — Sunday, 6th November

Morris, Walcott and Johnson return with Fonseca

The three Barbados men, Sidney Morris, Augustus Walcott and Preston Johnson who had gone up to Sabana to get their things have returned — along with Fonseca. They came down by the Atenas road last evening and I saw them and sent a canoe to bring them over. Fonseca arrived just after Chase had made his final declaration before me about this awful wretch killing a man in the *cepo* at Ultimo Retiro by smashing his testicles and private parts with a thick stick, — a poor young Indian who had simply run away from working rubber.

He is a stout, rather gentlemanly-looking man and to some extent realises Tizon's definition of him as "a very nice man" when, in the first days at Chorrera, Stanley Lewis brought the first charges against him of shooting the girls at Ultimo Retiro. I shuddered, positively, when I had to shake hands with this monster. He came in while we were at dinner and was formally presented by Macedo to Barnes, the rest and myself.

Rising river

This morning the river has risen fully 4 to 5 feet from last night and the cataract is now a roaring mass of snowy water. Beautiful in the extreme. The water is lapping the banks and one can hear it rising, like the incoming tide on the shore. Throughout to-day it has risen enormously and the rise now as I write at 5.30 p.m. is fully 8 feet from last evening at this time.

Reading over the Barbadians statements

I have been busy getting the statements of the Barbados men read over to them and signed before me both yesterday and to-day. Yesterday I went carefully through Sealy's, Chase's, Quintin's and James Layne's statements, reading them out slowly and then getting the men to sign them. This took a good long time.

To-day I have repeated the operation with the three men from Santa Catalina, Preston Johnson, Sidney Morris and Augustus Walcott. I then got them to bring their accounts and have gone into them more thoroughly than has yet been possible. I have compared the prices charged them with those figuring on the Iquitos invoices of the Company's which I copied yesterday as well as with my own invoices from Cazes' house in Iquitos — and the more I look into the figures, the less I like Macedo's proposal to wipe out the 25%.

Suspicions and doubts about Macedo's offer

It is not good enough. Moreover, the very readiness of the proposal coming from him so instantaneously without the slightest suggestion on my part that anything of the kind should be done makes me suspicious. If he is so ready to give away this money, it is because he fears the question being raised at home. Am I at liberty to compromise? My instructions are to arrive at an "independent and impartial" conclusion on the relations of the men to the Company and then to report on to the Government.

If I sanction this deal between Macedo and the men I practically close the question of their treatment by the Company — and my report to the government is robbed of much of its value. Any representations they might feel disposed to make in London to the Peruvian Amazon Company would be shorn of their weight as the Company can reply — and will, of course, reply — Your representative on the spot was satisfied with the settlement come to there, and the matter is settled to the satisfaction of the aggrieved men and with the full approval of the Officer you sent out in their interests. This would not, perhaps, be the worst of it however. Might not the much larger question of the case of these poor Indians be also compromised? To some extent yes. The more I think the matter over, the less disposed I am to sanction this deal on the spot. The men will be bitterly disappointed, it is true. To them the offer comes as such an immense surprise that they are all rejoicing at it. Bishop, for instance, tells me that on going through his accounts he finds it will mean some 500 soles coming back to him — at least that. That is a big sum to a blackman — some £50 to £60 — and if I counsel him and the others to reject it, they may ultimately get nothing and will not thank me — yet my duty seems to grow clearer in that direction the more I ponder the matter.

Casement asks for a sign to relieve his doubts

I asked for a sign — and lo! it has come — the most extraordinary utterance — I have been in grave doubts all the afternoon — feeling that by purchasing the present ease of the blackman I might be selling the Indians — giving up the game that is, to some extent in my hands. And I rose from dinner with this thought heavy on my mind — I left Fonseca and the murderers and the Commission — and walked to the end of the Verandah — far from them, by myself, revolving the whole question and what I should say to Tizon and Macedo to-morrow when they bring me the accounts of the Barbados men with the reductions all round. I said, as I walked the Verandah, to myself, how shall I put it? Shall I accept or say no — and if the latter how say it? The answer of my mind was "Say No — say it thus — Say, I am grateful for your offer and thank you for it very sincerely. I appreciate it much and on the men's behalf would gladly accept it, but on full consideration I feel that I am not empowered by my Commission from H.M. Government to accept such a proposal without reference to them. I shall therefore refer your proposal to them in the spirit of goodwill that prompts it — and meantime leave the matter in this state — namely, that you freely offer on behalf of the British Subjects to whom it is made, I will beg to be allowed to refer the offer to His Majesty's Government."

A sign from the heavens — a lunar rainbow

Just as this thought raised itself, I looked up from the verandah to the eastern sky — and saw, to my amazement, an arc of light across the dark, starless heaven. For a moment I did not realise what it was — then I saw it — a lunar rainbow — a perfect arch of light in the night. The moon was in the West — with stars and a clear sky round her in the East, obscure sky and coming rain — and this wondrous, white, perfect bow spanning the dark. I called Fox, Bell, all of them — everyone came — none had ever before seen such a sight. It was about 7.30 — as near as could be — and as we looked at the perfect arch, curving from forested hill to forested hill right across the Eastern heavens, the rain began to gather over it. It was slowly dissipated — broadening and fading away. We watched it for nearly ten minutes — I take it to be a good omen — an omen of peace and augury of good, — that God is still there — looking down on the sins and crimes of the children of men — hating the sin and loving the sinner. He will come yet to these poor beings — and out of the night a voice speaks. I shall not sell the great question of the Indians and their hopes of freedom for this mess of pottage for the handful of blackmen. These shall get their rights, too — but they shall come as rights — freely granted — and I shall not be the agent of silence, but I hope of the voice of freedom.

I have decided — or rather I do feel that this extraordinary sight, coming as it did, when my whole soul is seeking the right path, points the way. It was a direct answer to my question. I think it can only be read one way. Superstition, I suppose — yet are we not all children of a very ancient human mind that has sought in the heavens for its god and read His will in the clouds.[249]

And so to Bridge with my mind made up — and to-morrow alack! instead of peace and smiling Macedo and Tizon — the old uncertainty and suspicion and possibility of trouble at Iquitos. I sacrifice my own ease and the present good of the Barbados men — but so be it. It is in the right cause!

La Chorrera — Monday, 7th November

The river is stationary — not risen an inch since last night at 11.30 when I went to look at it. They have put the barge *Putumayo* in to the water this morning — it was just touching her keel.

---

[249] It was perhaps another sign from above that here the forger makes his most blatant chronological mistake so far. The sighting of the lunar rainbow happened on the night of Sunday 6 November and yet in the *Black Diary* it is written clearly in ink under Monday 7 November, "At night a lunar Rainbow 7.30 to 7.50 in due East & then rain." An effort to rectify the mistake has been made by scrawling "This is on Sunday Night" in blue crayon across the entry and then writing a corrected entry on the blotting paper opposite Sunday 6 November, "Lunar Rainbow at Chorrera. 7.30–7.45 p.m. seen first by me who called Fox, Bell, Barnes, 8, Tizon, Macedo & F. Velarde all saw." The notes scribbled on the pink interleaves of blotting paper in the *Black Diaries* are often of greater significance than they might appear and become a method by which mistakes or omissions are rectified by the forger. The mess continues with the following entry written under Tuesday 8 November, "Lovely morning at 8a.m. Reading Lt Maw again about the Indians & Putumayo in 1827. Hope *Liberal* comes today. They are trying to put the "alvarenga" or barge *Putumayo* into the river today — the high waves are awash of her." This whole entry has then been lightly crossed out and a new entry for Tuesday 8 included, "Made a mistake of a day since Saturday!"

The *Huitota* not back yet from taking Aguero and Alcosta away. They left on 3rd. and Macedo said would be back at latest on 6th. There is also no sign of *Liberal* which Macedo said was due to leave Iquitos on 25th to be here by 5th. Normand may be back any day from Andokes now. He and O'Donnell will probably come in together. Several of O'Donnell's men — Indians — are down here. The poor beings are sent all that way just to carry the rubber over from P. Victoria — some 2 miles away — above the cataract. They get wretched food while here — half cooked rice or beans twice a day — and are kept away from their homes all this useless time — and of course no cent of pay for this. What a system! It is insane as well as criminal.

Davis called away

Take this instance. Allan Davis, the Carpenter, Barbados man, who has returned from Abisinia and who, at his earnest request, is to be allowed to stay on in Coy.'s service until he earns more money — enough to take him, his Indian wife and two children home to Barbados — was to be put to "useful work" here in Chorrera. Any of the men who may remain after I go are to be kept here at useful (and highly necessary) tasks round this station — repairing the houses — making roads, etc. Such was Tizon's assurances. On Sunday morning I sent for this man, Davis, to read over to him his statement to me of 2nd. instant, and get him to sign it. He has been sent to Encanto — such is the answer. Went there on Friday, while I was at Sur, to guard some Indians sent there to fetch soap. There is no soap here; the *Liberal* is expected daily; yet they send off Indians, under a guard at 70 Soles per month, to do this simple thing. Encanto is a good two days walk away. The Indians sent, I find too, are Occidente men kept here permanently, across the river on the other *chacara*, on the hillside. They are not allowed to go home to their own place, but are retained here at what, I presume, is termed agricultural service. If they were paid and properly engaged men there would be no necessity to send an armed guard with them to Encanto. They would go and come gladly as free men — as slaves, they must be winchestered along the path; and the man chosen for the task is the man whom I was told would be kept in Chorrera at "useful tasks".

Summing up the surroundings

The whole method of handling their human surroundings is so greatly stupid as well as wicked that one stands in amazement at it.

The waste and extravagance on one hand, accompanied by gross speculation — and the absolute starvation and penury on the other. No food for the Indians — no peace for the Indians — but highly paid servants of the Company do never a hands-turn of work except swing their hammocks. There is a square mile of clearing round Chorrera — and not a yard planted on it. The only man who is "athrive" is Greenidge, the Barbados baker — with his two little houses, his servants, his *maracujas*[250] and poultry yard. The Doctor and his assistant eat up fully £1,000 a year and they hardly give even a dose of Epsom salts out. Macedo makes from £2,000 — £3,000 a year. His salary is £30 per month with 6% on the profits of the whole of his Agency. I judge his annual income from the fact that — in the paper I have seen — he raised his balance from S/P 1852 on 31st December '09, say £185, to S/P 13,786 on 30th June '10, say £1,378, or say £1,193 increase in the six months. During this period he has done absolutely nothing. He has ordered raids into Colombia — I know positively of two, one by Jiménez, the other by Normand, both accompanied by grossly criminal acts and the murders of several Indians, as well as the illegal imprisonment of three Colombian citizens on their own soil. He has, in a score of ways, injured and imperilled the interests of this British Company. He has threatened the Barbados men here with being shot — with "having them shot" if they told anything on him — and he has been the principal directing Agent in a series of appalling crimes committed on the native population whereby the Company's "workers" have been reduced in numbers and in physical capacity for work. Of trade, of commerce, of anything to be called traffic or human dealing between man and man there is no trace. And yet he gets probably £2,500 a year for being the leading spirit in this policy of destruction — of all round destruction. The Zumaetas in Iquitos draw £5,000 all told for the "upkeep" of that wholly useless office — and probably rob some thousands more of the Coy.'s money from the Commission they obtain on the local purchases from their friends there. The £30,000 a year expended in Iquitos on goods for the Putumayo is one of the keys to the situation.

---

[250] *Maracuja* (*Passiflora incarnata*), sometimes called "purple granadilla", is a member of the passionflower family (*Passifloraceae*) which is widely cultivated in the Amazon basin. It has a berry type fruit made of a hard yellow rind and acidic tasting seedy pulp that is mixed with water and sugar to make a soothing and nutritious drink.

Velarde and Bishop

Bishop tells me Velarde came to his room the other evening to try and pump him. He began by offering to buy my shot gun for £5! This is a useless weapon I got in Iquitos for 42 soles — say £4, and have not used as we could not fill the cartridges. He then said that he knew he was going to be sent away by this *Liberal* because he had been drunk at Occidente while we were there. He wanted to know if Bishop knew anything. A fine enquiry for a Chief of Section to make of a Black Man — a despised Negro!

Gambling debts

This is nothing, however; I now learn that a lot of the Barbados men's indebtedness is for gambling debts — and that they sometimes gamble with their Masters! Thus Normand quite lately "won" 110 soles from his tool Levine — the Barbados boy of 20 or 21 he has been bribing. He holds Levine's note of hand for the sum to be debited here to his account. The men's accounts are full of these debit and credit notes between themselves and the Peruvian employees of the Sections. Thus Preston Johnson began last half year, 1st Jan. 1910, with a balance to his credit of S/P 582.48, or say £58. He ends it on June 30 with a debit of S/P 42.52 — £4 — to the bad despite the fact that he is credited with S/P 300 for his wages, S/P 50 per month — so that he has spent £92 during the six months while earning only 30. The late Chief of Section, Elias Martinengui, figures for the following bills drawn by Johnson in his favour — S/P 34.30, S/P 242.90 and S/P 10.50, or a total of S/P 287.70, or about £28, paid by this negro at £5 per month to one of the principal servants of the Company, for "value received". I am told it is not gambling in Martinengui's case, but for the sale of things and "raffles". The Chiefs of Sections often raffle their clothes, and the employees take tickets for them. This, on top of the gambling, leaves them in constant debt. Of the S/P 980.75 of indebtedness Preston Johnson incurred from Jan–June of this year, only S/P 68.56 are for things he bought from the Company, while S/P 912.19 is for notes of hand he has given in favour of a long string of employers to whom he has incurred indebtedness one way or another. No doubt much of it is gambling — but no respectable company has any right to allow such a condition of things to prevail among its staff — and to actually debit and credit these shameless transactions in the books of its Chief Agency with a Manager drawing £2,500 a year to superintend the book-keeping!

Concerns about Arédomi

Owing to my long spell of work with the Barbados men to-day is the first day I've had much leisure to write up my diary — and I have missed some incidents of the last few days. For instance Arédomi's wife — a young girl — has come in and begs to be allowed to go away with him. Arédomi is quite willing to give her up in order to get away. I don't know what to do. I don't want the woman — it is an awful handful to add to the menagerie I am taking down stream — yet I am sorry for her. If I leave her she will be "all right" Arédomi says with her mother. I daresay she will — but it seems inhuman. If I leave the boy with her he goes back to slavery. Bishop says he would swim away to get off with me — the door of freedom has opened and given him a glance of a life beyond and I have not the heart to shut it. I daresay it will end by the girl going too — in which case I shall leave both at Pará to get work there and become free Brazilian citizens. It will be a step up for them indeed. They will soon learn Portuguese and Arédomi can work and earn his living — without fear of the lash, the bullet, the machete and the *cepo*.

"Mare Capitan" — the Good Chief

The Sur Indians of the Naimene and other tribes are fine-looking people — the best Huitotos I've seen. They all smile at me — Arédomi and Omarino have given me a great character — the "Mare Capitan" — the good chief. Yashios, a young Capitan, came down from Sur and visited me — a fine young fellow of 25 or 30 — handsome and quite rakish . He spoke a few words of broken Spanish and shook my hand warmly.

Further discrepancies over the Barbados men's accounts

Another feature of the Barbados men's accounts is that some of them declare they have not received all the goods charged against them at these outrageous prices. Crichlow complained of this at Ultimo Retiro but said he had kept a careful list of the missing things and would reclaim them. Now P. Johnson brings me all his back invoices and accounts for the last 2 ½ years. In May, 1908, in one invoice of S/P 65.30, goods to the cost of S/P 21.40, were not given to him and have never been given to him. The things are:

3 small tins biscuits	2.40
2 pounds bread	2.00
2 tins chocolate	2.00

2 pairs of Slippers	5.00
	21.40

In Jan. 1909, 50 Winchester cartridges charged to him at 9 soles = 18/- were not delivered and in May 1909 he was short 12 tins of Sardines, S/P 3.60, and 2 combs (for his "wife") S/P 1.20, while in May 1910 he is short 2 tins of Biscuits (quite small), S/P 1.60, and 6 tins of beef, S/P 6.00 — a total of S/P 42.80 short in four invoices only. Getting on for a month's pay. He says he spoke of it more than once — and to Mr Macedo and has got no satisfaction. Of course, now, I have only to mention it and he will get the money and some lying excuse will be made to me. I am keeping all these invoices and will take them home with me. They speak for themselves. Fancy charging these poor blackmen S/P 7.50 or almost 15/- a pair for these corded slippers that don't cost a shilling in Europe and are invoiced from Iquitos, even, at 25 soles the dozen, or S/P 2.08, say 4/- a pair. They cannot cost anything like 4/- a pair — I am certain not a shilling a pair wholesale in Europe. I take a pair with me also to London and will have them priced.

Wild ducks on the river

The river is stationary or even falling. It has fallen since last night an inch or two. Yesterday a flock of small wild duck, beautiful birds, came on the tiny patch of sand left where the big island had been. The Barbados men and a lot more went to shoot at them with Winchesters and winged one poor bird which fell in the river and was swept away.

Casement photographs Arédomi

To-day an afternoon of fearful heat. I took Arédomi up to the hill to the cataract — and photo'd him in necklace of "tiger" teeth, armlets of feather plumes and a *fono*.[251] I also photo'd the falls from the steep cliff above through the dense bushes. We went on to the upper river, to the landing place and sat there and talked, or tried to talk, I asking him names of things in Huitoto, and he telling me as well as he could. He actually clings to me I can see — poor boy. We saw 14 splendid Araras or Macaws fly slowly by — one alit on a tree quite close with a flash of crimson under-wing.

[251] This photograph was subsequently published opposite p.152 in Hardenburg, *The Putumayo; The Devil's Paradise* (Fisher Unwin 1912) with the caption "A Huitoto Indian Rubber Gatherer".

Omarino says he wants to learn to write and came to my room and got a blue lead pencil and covered a sheet of paper with weird signs. In the evening a shower or two of rain — but the river still falling.

La Chorrera — Tuesday, 8th November

O'Donnell arrives with letter from Crichlow

River fallen a foot I should think since yesterday. No sign of *Liberal* or 'Huitota' either. O'Donnell arrived about 10 from Entre Rios by *Veloz* bringing down his rubber and the Atenas rubber. He brought me a letter from Crichlow at Ultimo Retiro dated 29th October asking to be recalled as he is not safe there, since he spoke to me. Things have changed and he begs to be sent for at once, and if I don't take him away with me at least to ask that he should be kept in La Chorrera where he will be safer.

I have done very little to-day — the heat is great — but rain came at 2.30. Fonseca returned to Sabana, going away at 1 a.m. in blazing heat, with three poor Indians carrying his 'tulas', a fine head *muchacho*, a fair-skinned Boras and a fine little boy. I saw no Harem come with him. He left without attempting to bid any of us good-bye — a sign of grace! He hardly came to meals, even at the big table, sending his *muchacho* for food. Barnes says he saw Velarde also in walking kit this morning. Surely they are not sending him back to Occidente. That would be almost a breach of faith.

I wrote out a black list of the Employés charged with recent crimes by the Barbados men for the Commission's private use and help, at their repeated request. It is by no means a complete document and is merely an outline of some of the cases involving men still in the Company's service.

The mules are being kept busy, ridden by the Barbados men mostly, going over to Port Victoria to return with Entre Rios and Atenas rubber landed from the *Veloz* there.

Igara-paraná

The rain has lasted only a few minutes and will do nothing to swell the river. It has risen some 16 feet in the week and now is dropping again. This river is fully 450 miles long or 500 and both Macedo and Tizon say it is the chief tributary of the Putumayo. From its mouth they reckon 250 miles up to Chorrera and Macedo says 120 miles on to Ultimo Retiro where it is still a fine deep stream. I put Ultimo Retiro at only 80 miles above Chorrera and reckon that there the river has already come 100 miles at least. The quantity of water now flowing over the fall is far greater than any river in Great Britain or in Ireland brings to the sea and yet there is only about one map of S. America even records its name as a tiny dot on the expanse of water that marks the Amazon.

Casement feels out of touch

I need a barber badly. My hair has not been cut since the very beginning of September at Iquitos. My beard I cut myself at Entre Rios — very badly. No news from Europe since 25th July save official telegrams from FO and the one or two telegrams I saw in Pará papers up to 8th August, since when everything is a blank. My last three months have been Amazon and Putumayo only.

Barbadian accounts

I am expecting the rectified accounts of the Barbados men to be presented to me daily for approval, with the 25% reductions made in them and when I say I am not going to counsel the men to accept there will be a strained feeling again. I shall not ask to see them and shall wait until they are completed before making my refusal. I'll simply ask that they be referred to the Board in London who ought to be consulted, while I feel I must lay the matter before the FO to decide. It will be best. The Barbados men have high hopes, poor souls. Three of them have been in this morning to make further claims of promises of special "gratifications" of S/P 100 and S/P 50 that have not been kept to them. I made a note of their claims that are of interest in two cases as illustrating the lawless character of the work they were put to. Both claims refer to raids into Colombia directed by the Company — one by Jiménez this year and the other by Jiménez in 1908 when he killed the three Indians on the way, two by burning alive and the poor wee boy by beheading.

O'Donnell's rubber is weighed

I did nothing all day — or very, very little. In afternoon I went out to see O'Donnell's rubber from Entre Rios being weighed. He came down to-day with a lot more men, by *Veloz*, bringing 14,000 kilos of rubber — his *fabrico*.

About 20 or more of O'Donnell's Indians are down — poor hungry beings — and several of his *Empleados* (Ortiz and others) who here do no work either. They are dressed up and squatting with their friends — the poor nude Indians are going and coming all day — with mules too under Barbados men — to the port for rubber. I went and had several of the loads weighed that have come in. Here is the list :

1@ 80 kgs
1@ 77
1@ 67 ½
1@ 52 ½
1@ 50
1@ 63
1@ 77
7@ 467 kgs = 66 ¾ per man

Arebalo, in charge of *Veloz*, was at the Store during the weighing, and said that they were one man loads but it seemed incredible. Later the Barbados man, Sydney Morris, who was with the mules said they were not necessarily carried by one man, but represented his share of rubber brought in by him, with the help of his family. The *chorizos* might be carried separately, but had been all tied together at Puerto Peruano in these loads to show exactly what each man was responsible for.

I walked up to the stream, by the hill, but did not bathe. Arédomi brought me a feather head-dress from his house, poor boy it is a gift of gratitude and he went away home to-day to get it. River dropping fast, it has gone down a good deal, but is still very high. Very weary of this long delay at Chorrera doing nothing.

Not very well.

La Chorrera — Wednesday, 9th November

Child slavery

River still dropping. The sandbank showing out of water a couple of feet at least. Rain yesterday afternoon and a threatening of it to-day and some fell but not enough, I think, to influence the rise or fall of the river. I did nothing all day — am not very well indeed — and I am sick of this horrid atmosphere of crime. Fonseca returned to his Sabana to-day, without attempting to bid any of us good-bye. He went off in the glare of the sun by the Atenas road — across the river. I saw the ruffian going and watched him up the hill, three poor Indian slaves bending under his baggage loads &c., then he, and then his favourite *muchacho* (a handsome young Boras Indian who, no doubt, has committed many crimes at his orders) and a little Boras boy. He is the first, he did not bring a "wife" — at least I saw none. All the others, whenever they appear, as sure as the rifle on shoulder is the little Indian girl at heel. Normand brought five actually to Chorrera! O'Donnell's *empleados* each has brought down his poor slave — crouching and running patiently to heel. God help them.

Casement helps injured mule

Went out at 4 and watched the mules bringing in the loads of rubber. Every beast is maltreated, and one poor thing with its lips and mouth cut to pieces by the hide thongs passed under the jaw on a slip knot, that has cut near to the bone. Called Barnes and Tizon and made a row. Got out the mule man (Pelayo's his name) and told Tizon to see a change made.

Arrival of Liberal

Just as we had finished this, heard the people say the *Liberal* was coming and then at 5.45 she appeared, steaming up — her white mast and funnel showing over the point of land and bushes. We nearly cheered — some of the people did. She, of course, fired off a great rocket into the sky followed by a sound signal that was like the outbreak of a volcano. Saw several passengers on her. She anchored just at 6 p.m. and Bishop came to tell me John Brown of Montserrat[252] — Whiffen's old "boy", was on board and then brought him up to me with a letter from Barbados government explaining how it is they came to send him. It is a nuisance — a waste of money — but I suppose cannot be helped. The man is worse than useless now — merely an incumbrance. Told him he had come too late and would have to return at once by the *Liberal*. A Captain Delgado with a file of Peruvian soldiers on board — going to Encanto I believe — and two fresh "agents" (God save the mark)[253] for the Company. Have not yet made the acquaintance of

[252] John Brown of Montserrat was the interpreter Casement had tried to get hold of from Barbados before he arrived in the Amazon. Brown had served as Whiffen's interpreter during his journey through the district two years earlier, spoke the local Indian languages well and knew the terrain. He arrived too late to be of any help.

[253] This phrase is defined in the *Oxford English Dictionary* as "an exclamatory phrase. ... used by way of apology when something horrible, disgusting, indecent or profane has been mentioned. In modern literary use (after some of the examples in Shakespeare), an expression of impatient scorn appended to a quoted expression or to a statement of fact." Casement's usage might be considered to incorporate both these interpretations.

any of these folk. The soldiers, poor youths, the Andean hill folk of Peru, the Cholos of the Cordillera — far too good and fine a race to have such disgraceful masters. If only the Monroe Doctrine could be challenged by Germany, and successfully challenged, there would come hope for the hunted Indians and gentle beings of this Continent who have had 400 years of "Latin Civilisation" to brood on.

Dr Crippen and news from home

Got lots of letters from home — but none of great interest to me here in these surroundings. Crippen[254] is caught too! but what a farce it seems — a whole world shaken by the pursuit of a man who killed his wife — and here are lots and lots of gentlemen I meet daily at dinner who not only kill their wives, but burn other people's wives alive — or cut their arms and legs off and pull the babies from their breasts to throw in the river or leave to starve in the forest — or dash their brains out against trees. Why should civilisation stand aghast at the crime of a Crippen and turn wearily away when the poor Indians of the Putumayo, or the Bantu of the Congo, turn bloodstained, appalling hands and terrified eyes to those who alone can aid?

I wish I could see some ray of hope. I read letters a bit — wearily and with no interest in anything of home news — except Mrs. Green, Morel[255] and a fine little bit of Irish news.

[254] The dismembered body of Dr Hawley Harvey Crippen's wife had been found buried in the cellar in their house in Camden Town in early July 1910 and a warrant had been issued by Scotland Yard for the arrest of Dr Crippen and his mistress Ethel le Neve. Travelling under the names of Mr Robinson and son, the two fugitives were finally apprehended by Chief Inspector Walter Dew in the North Atlantic on board the SS *Montrose* on their way to Canada. The Captain of the Montrose said his suspicions were alerted when he saw two "men" holding hands. On 23 November Crippen was hanged and buried at Pentonville prison. Following Casement's execution on 3 August 1916 his body was thrown (coffinless) into the same limepit as Crippen's body, and in 1965 when Casement's "remains" were returned to Ireland and buried in Glasnevin following a full state funeral "on a beastly day in Dublin" rumours circulated that Casement's and Crippen's remains had been confused. (See *The Daily Telegraph*, Thursday 19 October 1995 — "Coffin Secret that went to the Grave".) More recent research shows that the position of Casement's body was carefully marked and exhumed under the strictest vigilance of Irish officials. See Deirdre McMahon, *Roger Casement: an account from the archives of his reinterment in Ireland* (Irish Archives Spring 1996).

[255] From further references to this letter over the following days it is clear that sent to Casement via the FO on 13 October. LSE Morel F8/24:

"My dear old Tiger,

LA CHORRERA — THURSDAY, 10TH NOVEMBER 1910

Up at 4.30

Liberal alongside the steps. Busy writing early morning. This will be a very long day. Allan Davis, A. King (the murderers of Justino Hernandez at Encanto) and J. Dyall all came from Encanto yesterday afternoon. I must interview all as soon as possible.

Huitota *arrives — plot to ambush Barbadians*

Found *Huitota* there too, on going out. She came up in the night from Providencia bringing back the three Barbados men, Mapp, R. Phillips and A. Hoyte, but without their things or wives. They had not been to S. Catalina. They were frightened to go! On sending for them and interrogating Mapp I find the following the reason. They declare that a plot was hatched by Aguero, Armando

---

I wonder where you are and what you are doing! beware of Bell: he is a snake in the grass. Curiously enough, he knows a lady friend of my wife's, and he is writing home to her blackguarding you, so keep a weather eye on the scallywag.

I do hope that you are keeping your health and not having too bad a time.

My sailing time is now definitely fixed for the 22nd, Saturday week, from Liverpool. I hope to be back about the middle of March, and shall look forward with avidity to shaking your hand here, as I hope you may be back by then.

I cannot tell you much about the testimonial. I enclose you an extract which I see in to-day's papers. I was told privately by Brabner that they were going to cut a dash in Liverpool next month or this month, and that dear old Holt, Guthrie and others were coming forward handsomely; but I really know nothing more and I don't want to.

On the 20th October there is to be a demonstration at the City Temple at which Conan Doyle, Israel Zangwell, Archdeacon Beresford Potter, a Dr Orchard and Campbell are speaking. It is called "E.D. Morel and the Congo". You will be glad to hear that.

My wife and I went to say goodbye to poor old Holt the other day in Lincolnshire. He was much affected. It was most pathetic. He is paralysed all down one side, wears his left arm in a sling, and can only get about supported by two people or wheeled about in a bath chair; but his brain keeps wonderfully clear and he is showing extraordinary courage and pluck. He spoke most feelingly of you.

We follow you so much in our thoughts, and trust you may be preserved from all the dangers of men and climate which beset you. Herbert Ward's book is out and there is a fine tribute to you in it, I am glad to say — the best description of you I have read anywhere, I think.

My wife and two of the kiddies, Stella & Roger, will attend the meeting at the City Temple, but I shan't.

I have got my credentials from *The Times* (special correspondent to Nigeria), and all my things are pretty well packed up now ready. It has been a big job tucked on to the usual palavers.

Goodbye, old chap. May we meet again in the Spring, Bulldog."

Blondel (Bruce in it too) and the others who went down, to return to Abisinia to have them ambushed on the way by some of the Boras Indians, or *muchachos*. Aguero would not allow them to go to Santa Catalina by daylight! Ordered them to wait at the port until Rodolfo Rodriguez and the rubber from Santa Catalina had come down there and then to go by nightfall. Bruce to give them a lantern! They were to return by same road too — this an injunction on them by Aguero who they say made very disparaging remarks about the "English Commission" not omitting myself.

A Brazilian negro at Providencia named Pinheiro came and told them of what he had heard Aguero, Blondel, Bruce, etc. saying up at the house and warned them against going on the road. Armando Blondel tried to throw them off the launch by force and make them go but they refused to budge and have come back in her. Solar, they state (the ex-police officer from Iquitos dismissed by Tizon there and now Macedo's lieutenant here) also made disparaging remarks of the Commission (and myself) and said that if any Barbados man stayed on after I left it would be a bad thing for him. He would pay for the rest! Burke, the engineer, even said lately — Greenidge and Bishop heard him — that if he were a Chief of Section he would have these f*** Englishmen shot and he knew one Chief who could do it, Aguero.

I have warned the Commission — particularly as regards Chase and Sealy who will be with them when they go to Abisinia and Morelia. These poor lads might very easily be made away with by a stray Boras or two and then it would be put down to the "Cannibals".

Mingg's and King's Statements

Very busy all day getting the remaining Statements of the Barbados men read over and signed by them. Also took J. Minggs' and Armand King's fresh statements.[256] Latter is a mulatto with a wholly evil face. A murderous looking ruffian. He admitted to shooting Justino Hernandez but pretended it was in self-defence. I put no questions to him of his services beyond the bare record — as the man is so clearly a villain and in Loayza's pay as a "confidential agent".

[256] Joseph Minggs {Blue Book Statement No.28 p.133–135}.
Armando King {Blue Book Statement No.29 p.136–137}.

Dyall's charges against Normand

Dyall reaffirmed categorically his charges against Normand of smashing the two unfortunate men's testicles. He also, incidentally, admitted to Tizon and myself that he had nine different Indian women given to him by Macedo and other Chiefs during his stay here.

He has one child, a boy of three but the woman now with him is not its mother. Poor Huitota women — what a fate — passed from one to another by these horrid wretches without any voice or question in the matter — as in the case of that unfortunate woman from this that Macedo gave to Aguero a week ago. The whole thing is a pig-sty.

Colombia's plans to invade the Putumayo

Tizon told me that the Prefect had written to him to say that he had definite news, the Colombian Government was going to invade the Putumayo! They were making a road from Porto to the upper river and would soon be invading this region. He appeared pleased I thought. I think he sees political kudos in it. He added that he didn't think the Company would have a long lease of life! I told him I had doubt as to my ability to interfere in the proposed settlement of the accounts of the Barbados men, that I did not think I was authorised to make a settlement here, that was for the Government and the P. A. Coy to arrange. He said that if the men did not take this offer they might certainly get nothing as the Coy. "might smash" long before then! This is quite conceivable.

Tizon's Power of Attorney

He later shewed me a Power of Attorney he had received from Iquitos giving him full power over the whole business here, to dismiss any employé of "whatsoever rank and to appoint others and to liquidate and wind up" and take any steps he pleases.

His position is strengthened greatly. On the other hand I don't like his way of viewing the future. He is (I think) already losing sight of the Indians and their future and that of the Coy. in the larger view of a possible conflict with Colombia in which he could play a big part for Peru. There could be a "victory", an "extension of the national territory" and things of that kind to fight for, and the poor Indians would be between the Devil and the Deep Sea.

Lima press reports of judicial enquiry

He also showed me a copy of the *El Comercio* of Lima of 10th October containing an article on the "Indians of the Putumayo" and a forthcoming judicial enquiry to be held by the Iquitos Courts (!) by order of the Peruvian Attorney-General.

The article states that the Lima authorities are acting on the evidence raised by M. Deschamps[257] in his letter to the Barcelona press and on the facts alleged by the London Anti-Slavery Society and quote from Carlos Soplin. If there were any hope of this being a real enquiry with a desire to find out the truth and to punish the guilty then it would be for good. I have no such hope. Tizon believes, or affects to believe, that it is meant for an honest effort to protect the Indians. I certainly don't. If any such desire really existed in Peru among the governing class of the country, they would long since have given expression to it much nearer home than on the Putumayo. Are there no oppressed Indians in the montaña save on this tragic river? When the charges were first made in Iquitos now three years ago, why did they not enquire into the matter then? Had they no national honour to safeguard, until it is assailed in the press of the World, and when a very powerful Government has begun to actually take steps on the spot to find out the truth? It is not the truth they seek now — but to suppress the truth being established, to their shame, by others.

I got lots of letters from home, from Morel and many others. The National Testimonial to him, Conan Doyle writes to me,[258]

---

[257] Despite the sensational press coverage of the Putumayo atrocities in British newspapers, the Peruvian government did not act until this letter from M. Deschamps, first published in the Barcelona press, was reprinted in Peru's national paper *El Comercio* on 7 August 1910. Deschamps talked about the Anti-Slavery & Aborigines Protection Society's efforts to try and motivate the British government to action. The letter was answered in *El Comercio* on 9 August by the Attorney-General of the Supreme Court, Dr José Salvador Cavero. He stated that the Peruvians would mount their own investigation. {see FO 371/968}. The Peruvian government remained suspicious of British government intentions behind their interference in the Putumayo atrocities from the very outset, believing that the British were using a humanitarian issue to screen their commercial interests. Certainly the timing of the investigation coincided neatly with British intentions to switch investment away from wild Amazon rubber towards Southeast Asian plantation rubber.

[258] This refers to Conan Doyle's letter to Casement dated 5 August 1910 [N.L.I. MS. 13,073 (28ii)] written from The Beach Hotel, Littlehampton, which goes into some detail about his efforts to stir up support for the Morel Testimonial amongst MPs. The end of the letter reads as follows:

amounted to £1,300 early in October and he see his way to making it far more before the end of the year. Morel has now sailed for the Niger in John Holt's ship. God bless him and old Holt too.[259]

On board the Liberal

I went on board the *Liberal* and saw Captain Reigada and two "agricultural experts" the P. A. Coy. had sent out. The Captain Delgado and a file of Cholo soldiers who came round by the *Liberal* left for Encanto to-day, to march overland. It is a good two days' march and is said to be very unhealthy with plenty of fever there — in strong contrast to this very healthy river.

LA CHORRERA — FRIDAY, 11TH NOVEMBER

The accounts of the Barbados men, handed me by Mr Tizon this morning are as follows:

Date 1910 Former State of a/c 29 Oct

"I envy you your journey up the Amazon. What an experience. I have a sort of wild boy's book in my head. The idea roughly is that news reaches a group in England of a peculiar place up in the unexplored parts at the head of one of the tributaries of the Amazon. At this spot a considerable plateau has been elevated long years ago, and left with cliffs all round which forbid access. On the 40 square miles of the top the extinct flora & fauna still live, dinosaurs, maslodaurs (?) & a weird prehistoric race up the trees. My group go there, take photos & have wondrous adventures. It is a fine idea, I think. Now if you hear of anything weird & strange out there let me know, and I'll sew it into my patchwork quilt."

The book, published in 1912, was *The Lost World*, one of the most popular adventure stories of the century and later made into a Hollywood epic. The character of Lord John Roxton is based loosely upon Casement and there are a number of references to Roxton hunting Peruvian slavers in the Putumayo. See *The Lost World* chapter VI:

"I was the flail of the Lord up in those parts, I may tell you, though you won't find it in any Blue-Book. There are times, young fellah, when every one of us must make a stand for human right and justice, or you never feel clean again. That's why I made a little war on my own. Declared it myself, waged it myself, ended it myself. Each of those nicks is for a slave murderer — a good row of them — what? That big one is for Pedro Lopez, the king of them all, that I killed in a backwater of the Putumayo River ..."

Conan Doyle had become acquainted with Casement as a result of his interest in the Congo Reform movement and in 1909 he had published his own attack on Leopold II's regime in *The Crime of the Congo*. The following year he teamed up with Casement to raise public attention and funds for the Morel Testimonial. Casement and Conan Doyle remained friends to the end. Doyle spearheaded the most public of the petitions demanding Casement's reprieve in the weeks before his execution. Signatories of this petition included Arnold Bennett, G.K. Chesterton, Sir Francis Darwin, Sir James G. Frazer, John Galsworthy, Jerome K. Jerome, John Masefield and Beatrice and Sidney Webb.

[259] This refers to Morel's trip to Africa in 1910. Despite Morel's long campaign against Leopold II's Congo regime, he had only brief knowledge of Africa gained during his time working for the Elder Dempster Company before he turned his attentions to humanitarian journalism.

No.1166		81.04		383.66
S.Sealy				
No.1167	171.77			200.00
J.Mapp				
No.1168	463.47		92.96	
J.Minggs				
No.1169		641.36		766.34
J.Layne				
No.1170		55.83		306.54
A.Hoyte				
No.1171	113.96			139.04
S.Morris				
No.1172	102.47			183.42
P.Johnson				
No.1173	113.42			162.95
R.Phillips				
No.1174	189.87			97.43
J.Chase				
No.1175	385.57			80.70
A.Walcott				
No.1176	72.92			210.71
C.Quintin				
No.1177	59.58			258.18
W.Leavine				
Deduct	1,673.03	778.23	92.96	2,788.97
credit:	778.23		Deduct Debit:	92.96
Debit			Cred. Balance	2,696.01
Balance on 29th Oct:	894.80			
			Add debit:	894.80
			Amount gained to the men:	
				3,590.81

The concession of 25% off the back accounts by these 12 men (nos.1166 to 1177) converts a total debit balance of S/P 894 into a credit balance of S/P 2698, or a gain of 3590 soles to these 12 men. F. Bishop, my actual servant, who left the Coy's service in August last, obtains a sum, additional to the above, of S/P 535.39

Bishop's a/c shows the following:

Chorrera, 31de octubre de 1910

Snr FEDERICO BISHOP

en cuenta corriente con The Peruvian Amazon Company Ltd

Bonificacion que se le concede de 25% sobre S/P 2141.56 de todas nuestras facturas a S/Cgo desde el 1 Julio 1907 fecha de la fundacion de esta compania.

Haber S/P 535.39

Nuestro giro S/P 594 sobre Iquitos, Deb. de su cta. y orden cancelación

Deber S/P 535.39

Deber	Haber
535.39	535.39

The accounts of five of the men still in the employ of this agency are not handed to me. These are :

E.Batson — actually fireman on 'Huitota'
E.Crichlow " at Ultimo Retiro, but asking to be recalled
A.Davis " at Chorrera — to stay on as carpenter

also

S.Greenidge and Donald Francis — remaining on at La Chorrera, one as Baker, the other as headman.

There are also: J. Dyall, heavily in debt to the Coy. by last A/C, who is staying on at El Encanto as baker at his own request, and A. King, with a credit balance also at Encanto as cook.

I call up Sealy first on the list and show him the a/c as it stands, explaining the situation to him. That it is a free gift made by Mr Tizon and Macedo in order to effect a friendly settlement with the men and one pleasing to me. That there is no question of legal rights or claim — the goods bought by the men having been bought by them with their eyes open knowing the prices and paid for cannot now be the subject of any legal claim. The Coy. in London will resist and rightly any legal claim — but none could ever be urged. The only thing that remains is a friendly settlement by a conciliatory offer by this kind and this is the offer made here, to me, for the men — and is he willing to accept it. He looks at the account and says yes, provided I agree. He will leave the decision to me as I know best. Personally he would accept without question were I not here, as this is a gift he had no reason ever to anticipate.

He will forego his claim for the gratification of S/P 100 for his stay in Abisinia and go only to Caquetá in 1908, altho' that was clearly promised in writing, but thinks he should have it. But he leaves the whole question to my judgement.

1. S. Sealy (1166) a/c correct, will leave decision to Consul.

2. Called James Mapp (1167) and showed him his account. He protests it on three grounds. First the promise of S/P 100 gratification for his stay in Abisinia promised in writing to all employés in that section who stayed over one year. 2nd., that he holds debit notes against other employés of the Coy. amounting to S/P 125 which he produces; and 3rd that Sr. Macedo promised him his pay to rise to S/P 60 per month from July last, 1910.

3. Called J. Minggs (1168) whose a/c shows him still in debt to the Coy. S/P 92.96 say £9. He admits that the account is correct as it stands, has no claim, but prefers a request for the gratification of S/P 100 for his stay in Abisinia.

4. Called J. Lane (1169). Show him his account, he is quite content and thanks me.

5. Alfred Hoyte (1170). Showed him his account, which gives him a credit of S/P 306.54. He admits it is correct as it stands and thanks the Coy. saying he is absolutely content. Claims gratification for services in Abisinia S/P 100.

6. Called Sidney Morris (1171). His account which showed a debit of S/P 87.82 now gives him a credit of S/P 139.04. He states the account is correct as it stands, but he brings *giros* of J. Dyall and Reuben Phillips to his credit.

7. Preston Johnson (1172). His account now stands at a credit of S/P 183.42, from a debit of S/P 102.47 on 30th June. The a/c is not correct.

He claims refund of S/P 42.80 on goods not received according to invoices produced, also S/P 1.20 for medicines. Also claims S/P 151 against James Mapp on *giros* given to Sr. Macedo a few days ago.

Also claims £18 for a Mauser rifle bought by Sr. Macedo a few days ago. (This is privately allowed I am told. They did not wish to enter such a transaction in the books.)

8. Reuben Phillips (1173). a/c presented. He disputes a debit of S/P 89.25 in favour of E. Crichlow and A. Antas. States he owed Antas S/P 33 and nothing to Crichlow.

He also claims S/P 50 as gratification for a Commission to the Caquetá as by *Aviso* of Sr. Macedo of 25th February 1910 at Ultimo Retiro.

9. James Chase (1174). His a/c on 30 June showed debit of S/P 41.82 and with the changes made in it, as now presented to 31st October it stands at S/P 97.43 credit.

This is presented to him and he admits it is correct as it stands. He accepts it. He claims a gratification of S/P 100 for his stay in Abisinia over 1 year according to the Aviso in this Section.

He states that the following employés got it:

A. Blondel
Juan Zellada
A. Jiménez
Renes
A. Lopez

and a man named Galon, a *cholo*, who went to Iquitos in August last — that all these got this special remuneration.

10. Augustus Walcott (misspelled Walker in all accounts). He cannot read so Consul explains the account to him).

It shows a debit against him on July of S/P 254.42 and a final balance on 31st October of S/P 80.70 in his favour.

He disputes one item — Factura 2668 — goods debited to him on 30th September as supplied by Chorrera for S/P 97.60. He states he sent a *pedido* [order] for these things but never received them. He claims refund of this amount. He produces roll of tobacco which cost him S/P 8 = (16f) which is half rotten — and asks if he can recover that. I keep the roll of tobacco and say I will see into it. (His claim of S/P 97.60 for goods not received is allowed I am told. It is admitted the goods were despatched too late to reach him.)

11. Clifford Quintyne. His account stands thus:

	Deber	Haber
July 1st — Saldo de cuenta entregado	260.92	
Sept 30 — n/factura 2349	12	
Oct 31 — Sus sueldos desde Julio 1		200
Bonifacion 25% en S/1202.52 valor		
de todos n/factura a s/cgo desde Julio 1907		300.63
s/giro orden Santillon	17	
u/giro H596 de su cuenta y en cancelacion	210.17	

Total	S/P 500.63	500.63

He cannot read well and asks it be read for him.

13. W. Leavine (1177) His account showed a debit on 1st July of S/P 152.08 — and now gives him a credit of S/P 258.18.

A forgery

Later. Took Leavine to Sr. Tizon to whom he repeated his statement that he did not sign a *giro* for S/P 120 in favour of Borbor. I ask both to go to Macedo and repeat to him. The actual *giro* is produced with "Westerman Leavine" written on it. He denies it is his signature and says it is a forgery. He says Borbor did it and Bustamante (2nd at Andokes) has done the same. I compare his signature with another of his admitted and I think he is right. He adheres to his denial. Mr Tizon says as he admits owing Borbor S/P 120 the matter will be dealt with as if the *giro* were signed by Leavine. I make no comment beyond pointing out that the man protests against it as a forgery — and otherwise it is a gambling debt between himself and Borbor.

He disputes the *giro* in favour of F. Borbor for S/P 120. Never gave Borbor any *giro*. He admits that he owes Borbor S/P 120 but never gave him any *giro* or signed any paper for it. The debt he states is a gambling one — and he gave no *giro* for it — and he protests against it being charged to his debit. He is otherwise content with the account and is grateful for the *Bonificación* of 25% off his purchases.

The accounts of the other men will be ready by this evening — so I am told. Going through these accounts and finding out from the men if they admitted the debit amounts, etc. has taken me the whole morning. The view I take of the transaction is that it is one that solely concerns the men. If they choose to accept this *Bonificacion* of 25% off their bank accounts, offered as a gift to them by the local representative of the Company, I shall not stand in the way of their doing so. My attitude shall be a purely negative one — and I shall make that quite plain. The transaction is between the Company and its employees — and just as I could not prevent them robbing the men by extortionate charges, I cannot legally stand between them making any allowance they like to the men.

I have asked for nothing on the men's behalf — neither as a favour nor anything else. I have pointed out to the Representative of the company that I consider the men have been grossly overcharged for the necessaries they had to buy — and further that I think they have often been gravely maltreated, and illegally employed — that is all.

I presume the idea of Macedo (and to some extent of Tizon also) in making this proposal was to shut my mouth — or to secure a more favourable report from me to the FO of the condition of British Subjects in the Company's employ. I cannot prevent them indulging that presumption, but if they should seek to obtain any statement from me to that effect I shall undeceive them.

This being so, I think I may safely stand aside and let the Barbados men accept, as they feel disposed to do, this purely voluntary offer of partial restitution. It in no way realises my conception of what, under any sense of impartial dealing, these employés of the Company are entitled to. I think at least 50%. In strict justice 70% should come off.

The actual charges from Iquitos to Chorrera by the company's own showing are 25% — rather less than 25% — as by their Invoices of 14th September, 1910.

However, as the men are many of them destitute and might never get a penny if I induce them to refuse this offer, I think my best course is to say:

"Accept if you choose — I leave you perfectly free to do as you please without any interference. I have no right to hinder you and I have no power or authority to decide for you, or to accept in your name — you can do as you think best in your interests."

A lot of Indians from Sur, the nearest Section, have been brought down to unload and load the *Liberal*. Another instance of the complete servitude of these poor people. These men all have to get a large quantity of rubber for Carlos Miranda by next *fabrico*. They are called here, miles from their homes, to this extra work — without a penny of remuneration — merely the wretched tin of boiled rice or beans twice a day ladled out to them.

The Indians having completely discharged the *Liberal* are now loading her with the rubber already in Store.

This rubber is as follows:

Sur Section	: 8 tons
Occidente	:
Atenas	
Entre Rios	: 14 tons
Andokes	: say 8 tons
Oriente	: -

To this will have to be added that from Ultimo Retiro expected down by the *Veloz* in a few days and the Santa Catalina rubber, partly here already by 'Huitota', with more to follow, I am told.

The two sections of Sabana and Abisinia will only have their *fabricos* by December, so I am told.

Boat times

The *Liberal* I am told will be free to leave for Iquitos in about four days — probably it will be nearer a week. 'The Manco' which arrived at Iquitos on 1st November will sail on 15th, so I shall miss her. The next is the *Athualpa* due to leave Iquitos on 27th, which vessel I hope to catch and go down to Manaos in her with such of the Barbados men as choose to go — some say they wish to stay in Iquitos to try and find work there — in spite of my warning that I strongly urge them against staying in Iquitos. I will be able to judge better when we get there — but I am very much opposed to their remaining near the Peruvian "Courts of Justice" — and prisons!

Peruvian enquiry

With this forthcoming sham Enquiry, ordered by the Peruvian Attorney-General at Lima, to be conducted by the wholly corrupt Judges, &c. of Iquitos, it is clear the object will be to whitewash Peruvian administration in the Putumayo — and as it will be known that the Barbados men's evidence is very hostile to existing and past state of affairs, they may quite conceivably interrogate the men in a very arbitrary and unfair way and then quote their evidence against their own statements to me.

Remaining Barbadian accounts

The remaining accounts of the Barbados men have now been handed to me. The claims made by all the others have been admitted — the "gratification" of S/P 100 each for services in Abisinia and other sections. The one that comes worst off is Clifford Quintyne, whose foot is so bad from the poisoned spike. He is to get a "gratification" of S/P 100 — nearly £10 — for that — or for services in Santa Catalina. It is put both ways — either one or the other! Reuben Phillips gets his S/P 50 for the raid across the Caquetá this year! I didn't claim it. He asked for services at Ultimo Retiro according to an order of 25th February 1910 (Macedo's own order!) which I copied.

The remaining accounts are as follows:

	Former a/c Debit	29th Oct. Credit	Debit	Credit
No.1178 S. Greenidge		1057.85		1,888.15
No.1179 D.Francis	47.62			433.72
No.1180 E.Batson		200.97		583.64
No.1181 E.Crichlow	247.69			290.56
No.1182 Allan Davis		570.30		896.41
No.1183 J.Dyall	441.48		7.55	
	736.79	1829.12	7.55	4092.48
	Deduct Debit:	736.79	Deduct Debit:	7.55
	Cr:	1092.33		4084.93
		Deduct	previous credit:	1092.33
		Increase to men:		2992.60

The gain to the men by first a/c was: 3590.81
The fresh gain on these other a/cs is: 2992.60
Total 6583.41

Brought forward: 6583.41

To this must be added the following additional gratifications —

James Mapp	S/P 100
J. Minggs	S/P 100
A. Hoyte	S/P 100
R. Phillips	S/P 50
J. Chase	S/P 100
Clifford Quintyne	S/P 100
S. Sealy	S/P 100
A. Walcott	S/P 100
J. Dyall	S/P 100

Further claims for gratification.

E.Batson	S/P 100
Allan Davis	S/P 100

The gain to Bishop, so far, is = 535.39

He also claims for medicines he bought and for clothes that Plaza confiscated some S/P 139 — which may be allowed or in part allowed. Then there is E. Crichlow whose a/c is in my hands, pro tem, to look at and see if it is correct. It must await his arrival from Ultimo Retiro — which will take place in a few days now.

The total gain to the men, through this spontaneous offer of Macedo and Tizon will be well over £800, divided among nineteen men — or an average of perhaps £42 to £43 per head. No small gain to them, poor chaps, and they will obviously be grateful for it. They have all told me so — and thank me. I tell them it is not me — but a "free gift" from the Company in order to content them.

The trouble will now arise when Tizon finally brings all the rectified accounts to me — as will be done. He will expect me to distribute them to the men — and to "accept" the settlement on behalf of H.M. Government — that is his hope. I shall, of course, refuse to do anything of the kind. I shall say that he has been pleased to offer the men, voluntarily and in a friendly spirit, certain sums and that, so far as I am concerned as a Consular Officer, I have no advice one way or the other to offer to the men. They are quite free to follow their own wishes in the matter. I neither agree nor disagree — I am not authorised or sent here as a judge between the Company and the men; but merely to report on their relations to the Company. That is all. There will be further unpleasantness — it cannot be helped. I have little else but that since I set foot in this unhappy wretched district.

Forging of Levine's name

The forging of Leavine's name by Borbor is but a fresh instance of the disgraceful state of things prevailing and the determination to allow a forged note against a man who protests it is a forgery is a very singular one for a man like Tizon to arrive at. It throws further light on the wholly demoralising influence this accursed atmosphere of crime and of holding daily relation with criminals exercises upon even high minded men. In Iquitos an accusation of forgery would be met at once by legal action — here it is treated with a shrug of the shoulders and the forged bill dealt with as if authentic! And this by the Representative of the Company in dealing with two of its employés.

Water level

The river still rapidly falling to-day. Rain for a few minutes only — and great heat after. The *Liberal* is to leave on Tuesday for Iquitos. The *Veloz* expected down to-night from Ultimo Retiro with Crichlow — and perhaps Normand! I hope not — but I fear it.

Some men arrived from Atenas Road at 1 o'clock, — a young Peruvian — with rather a decent face. Don't know his name yet. Lots of O'Donnell's Indians and other from Sur carrying the rubber on board the *Liberal*.

Casement gives away gunpowder

Several of O'Donnell's men came and spoke to me. I gave two of them two tins of gunpowder to their huge delight.

LA CHORRERA — SATURDAY, NOVEMBER 12TH

Completed statement of the Accounts of the Barbados men at La Chorrera Agency, handed to me to-day by Sr. Tizon — after all corrections and additions in their favour are made.

No.

1165 F. Bishop ....nett gain....................... 676.29
1166 S. Sealy.....(claimed on 14th back-pay).............. 483.66
1167 J .Mapp... 365.00
1168 J. Miggs.. 72 .04
1169 James Lane.. 766.34
1170 Alfred Hoyte.. 406.53
1171 Sidney Morris.. 182.64
1172 Preston Johnson. 227.42
1173 Reuben Phillips..212.95
1174 James Chase +(claimed back pay) ....+197.43
1175 A. Walcott (Walker).. 178.30
1176 Clifford Quintin... 310.71
1177 W. Leavine... 258.18
1178 S. Greenidge (at Chorrera).............................. 1,888.15
* 1179 Donald Francis (at Chorrera).........................433.72
1180 E. Batson... 683.64
1181 E. Crichlow+(see corrected a/c., 14 Nov 1910) 531.26
1182 Allan Davis.. 996.41
1183 J. Dyall.. 7.55

* Also claimed S/P 30 extra for cutting boards at Occidente — as Crichlow did. Claim allowed by Tizon in my presence on 14 Nov. and promise that it would be credited to him in his final a/c on leaving. R.C.

Comparing these totals with those, as handed to me on 29 Oct the men have a very great gain.

I analyse this actual gain now.
The clear gains that have accrued to the men are as follows:

1165 F.Bishop	25% off his purchase:	535.39	
	Refunds for:		
	Clothes & Medicines:	140.90	
			676.29
1166 Stanley Sealy	2.50 per month:	72.50	
	25% off goods:	230.12	
	Gratification Abisinia	100.00	
			402.62
1167. J. Mapp	2.50 per month	72.50	
	25% off goods	299.27	
	Gratification Abisinia	100.00	
			471.77
1168 J. Minggs	2.50 per month	72.50	
	25% off goods	292.51	
	Gratification	100.00	
			465.01
1169. James Layne	per month	72.50	
	25% off goods	87.48	
			159.98
1170. A.Hoyte	per month	72.50	
	25% off goods	126.08	
	Gratification	100.00	
			298.58
1171. S.Morris	per month	72.50	
	25% off goods	314.90	
	Medicines bought	67.10	
			454.50
1172.Preston Johnson	2.50 per month	72.50	
	25% off goods	91.89	
	Goods not received	44.00	
			208.49
1173. R Phillips	2.50 per month	72.50	
	25% off goods	293.12	
	Gratification	50.00	
			415.62
1174. J.Chase	per month	72.50	
	25% off goods	214.80	
	Gratification	100.00	
			387.30

1175. A.Walcott	25% off goods	547.52	
			547.52
1176. C.Quintyne	25% off goods	300.63	
	Gratification	100.00	
			400.63
1177. W Leavine	25% off goods	297.26	
			297.26
1178. S.Greenidge	25% off goods		712.30
1179. Donald Francis	25% off goods		481.34
1180.E.Batson	25% off goods	418.77	
	Gratification	100.00	
			518.77
E.Crichlow	25% off goods	546.65	
+ also 75.00			546.65
1182. Allan Davis	25% off goods	396.91	
	Gratification Abisinia	100.00	
			496.91
1183. Joshua Dyall	25% off goods	399.03	
			399.03
1184.Philip Lawrence	25% off 905.15	226.28	
		75.00	
			301.28
			7965.56
	Add		676.29
	Bishop:		
			8641.85

Crichlow will probably have a further claim — certainly S/P 60 gratification like R. Phillips and I fancy he claims the 72.50 on Exchange.

No, I see Crichlow did not return on that contract — so his claim may be limited to the S/P 50 for the Caqueta expedition. That brings it to S/P 8,390 gained to the men through my representations to Tizon — or say £830 — not a bad concession. It represents a good deal to them — and for 19 men it gives over £43 per head.

Reports in El Comercio

Read the article in Lima *El Comercio* of 9 August on the Putumayo Indians. The Fiscal of the Supreme Court of Peru, Dr José Salvador Cavero, corresponding to our Attorney-General, has ordered the Iquitos Court to open an urgent enquiry into the charges brought against the Peruvian Amazon Company by the Anti-Slavery Society. He requires a judge to be sent to the spot too. It is based, he states, on the letter from Emil Deschamps, written from Barcelona to *El Comercio* which that paper published on 7th August. Tizon has shown this to me as well. It is a good letter — an excellent letter.

Tizon writes to press

Tizon tells me privately he has written to the Editor or proprietor of the Lima *El Comercio*, who is his cousin, saying the Government must take action. He is also writing to the Prefect at Iquitos, begging him to come round here as soon as he can. He tells me the Prefect has written to him too — and he begs me to go and see him and speak frankly to him. This I have said I shall do privately. He says it will be a friendly act — an act of goodwill and kindness. Our conversation was long and very friendly , as indeed my conversations with Tizon always are. He has repeated all his former assurances and with emphasis — that the gang at Iquitos must be broken up and Arana eclipsed, and the London Board take complete control. He says the criminals here will fly to Brazil as soon as the Judge appears — and that that will be the best settlement. There they will drift into the Purus[260] and other rivers — to repeat their crimes!

Compensation

Meantime there are Crichlow, Walcott, Dyall and Quintin gravely injured by Velarde, Montt, Normand and Rodolfo Rodriguez. Tizon said last week, that if they would tell him how much they wanted as compensation he would try and get it out of the accounts of these men. I sent Dyall to him last night and Dyall tells Bishop that he told him that he would talk to me on the subject.

So far this is all. I asked Quintin and he said "£50 or £60". I fear nothing will come of it out here, and I don't see what can come of it at home, as the Company is not responsible for the acts complained of.

Talk with Sur Indians

A very hot day and the afternoon blazing. I walked out to the stream and bathed in the soft brown water of the hillside brook. It is delightful. Talked to some of the Sur Indians down here. They

[260] Another rubber-rich river valley in Brazil.

are nice chaps, and several speak Spanish — broken Spanish. The others played bridge after dinner. I walked up and down in the moonlight till near 9.30 and then turned in, reading the latest *Daily Mails* with their shocking screams against Germany. It is a dreadful little cur of a paper — a regular yapper. The *Liberal* is repairing her screw shaft. There are over 40 — nearer 50, I should think — Sur Indians down here helping to load her as well as O'Donnell's men — many of whom came to talk to me, saying they were on our caravan to Matanzas.

Planning ahead

The *Liberal* is to leave on Tuesday I am told. That is 15th and she should be in Iquitos on 24th. The *Athualpa* is due to leave Iquitos on 27th, but it will be 30th before she does so I am sure, so that I may be in Manaos on 4th or 5th and Pará perhaps on 9th December. After that it is hard to say, as I'm thinking of going to Barbados, for many reasons and trying to fix up some things there. I see no likelihood of getting home before end of January.

La Chorrera — Sunday, 13th November

Borborini attacks an Indian

Sealy came early to tell me that Borborini, O'Donnell's principal footpad, who is down here with the Entre Rios Indians, had hit one of the Sur Indians over the head last night with a billet of firewood. These billets of firewood are thick, nearly a yard long, and with very sharp edges, and as hard as metal. He said the Indian's head was badly cut; Phillips and another Barbadian had seen it done. I asked him to find out who the Indian was and let me know. He said "the Manager" had sent the boy up to Sur, to get him out of the way. A few minutes afterwards he returned with the lad — a fine young Indian I had noticed yesterday. He had a nasty cut — the skull laid open and the long black hair clotting in the blood — some of this on his neck and cheek. It must have been a beastly blow. I sent for Gielgud at once and asked him to take the Indian straight to Tizon and tell him. Tizon was at breakfast and he at once acted. He sent for Borborini and dismissed him on the spot — ordering him to leave by this steamer. This is the first action that has been taken of this kind — and for a mere cut on the head! All the *blancos* will be thunderstruck.

A panic has fallen on the gang of *empleados* from the sections who are down here. They looked pale and askance at lunch. Borborini will be a nice fellow-passenger for me on the *Liberal* — knowing that he is dismissed through me and the Barbados men. There will be 16 of them on board — happily — enough to look after themselves. Tizon and I were photographed later on, each to have a picture of the other — by Gielgud.[261]

Borborini, Bishop has already told me, killed two people at Urania long ago when he was there — an Indian he shot and another he cut the head off. How many more he has killed since goodness only knows. He was the principal flogger at Entre Rios up to the date of our arrival there in October — so the Indians told us at Puerto Peruano.

Colombians building road from Pasto to the Putumayo

Tizon told me to-day, in our conversation, he has decided to visit Abisinia and stay there a long time when he starts the real "trading" venture with the Boras. He says the Colombians are again in the Cahuinari — at the mouth of it — and that the road being made from Pasto to the head of the Putumayo is a serious thing, and the threatened invasion may come off.

Indian wives

Several of the Barbados men have Indian "wives" and children and want to take them away with them. I say it can be done if they marry the women — not otherwise. John Brown is one. Explained situation to him. Again a very hot day, and the river falling steadily. It is now down 7–8 feet from the highest water on Sunday last, I think. That was also the day (or night) of the Lunar Rainbow.

Barbadian accounts

I have told Tizon I shall ask him to distribute the a/cs to the Barbados men to-morrow — and will ask Gielgud to be present. I told him (Tizon) I should be there, but would not counsel the men one way or the other that I was not here to arbitrate between them and the Co., and that this offer of the Co's was a free one to them which I should leave them quite free to decide on as seemed best to themselves. Miranda came down yesterday and is here to-day.

---

[261] This is probably the well-known photograph of Casement and Tizon together published in *The Sketch* (London 2 December 1914).

Arédomi's wife

I told Arédomi I could not take his wife, the poor little Indian girl, away with me. I spoke to Miranda about her. Arédomi is quite willing she should stay behind, indeed I think anxious for it. They are only boy and girl — and he does not really care. She is afraid of being taken by one of the *empleados* of Sur, a man named Zarate, I think, who has already told her Capitan he would take her. Arédomi explained this to me through Bishop. I asked Miranda to promise (through Bell) that the girl should be safe — and he promised on his honour that he would see no one took her against her will. Arédomi is to "send for her" — if he elects to become a European — or to return if he wishes it.

Bishop had translated to the girl and he says she is very unhappy. It is not Arédomi she cares about, but simply to get away from the Putumayo too! He says her brother has been in talking to him and saying how much he too would like to fly.

Indians take flight

I wonder if the 6 Occidente men and the tall Boras Indian, who are believed to have been the men who broke into the Store ten days ago and "stole" 2 bags of rice and other things and levanted in the night in Greenidge the Baker's boat, have fled for good and all. They might have got right over into the Putumayo and may get to Brazil. Heaven grant they do — poor souls. Fox and I are praying for them!

Casement's fears

It is exceedingly hot. I am rather dreading my last day to-morrow and this final settlement by the Barbados men's accounts. I may be wrong in allowing the thing to go through! but I cannot quite see where. If I stand aside and leave Co. and men to deal together it can in no wise tie the hands of the FO in any subsequent representations they may wish to make on the grounds of the general ill-treatment of the men.

Then there will remain my few days at Iquitos, when I must be hourly on my guard. I shall not feel safe or happy until I see Tabatinga and the Brazilian flag waving over its mulatto-troop of soldiers. Brazil and freedom are synonymous up here in this benighted region.

Revolutions in Manaos and Portugal

The Iquitos letters told me there had been a "revolution" at Manaos between the Neris and the Bittencourts and that the Federal gunboats had bombarded the town.[262] This on top of the Revolution in Portugal and flight of King Manoel and his mother to Gibraltar means great news of sorts.[263] Poor Portuguese — they will be out of the frying pan into the fire. A handful of educated rogues will rob 6,000,000 peasants more cleverly and to a bigger tune than any one-man show on earth. The Portuguese monarchy was not sufficiently a one-man show — that was its weakness. Had Dom Carlos' effort at absolutism but carried through and João Franco not failed to guard his King then Portugal to-day might have been on the high-road to financial integrity.[264] She will now lose not only her revenues — "gone astray" into strange channels — but her African colonies. These have only been saved to her by the friendship of England. Had England and Germany ever laid their heads together, indifferent to Portuguese feeling, they would have divided the spoils. The influence of the Portuguese crown secured European friendship — everyone "liked" the Braganza monarchy. It was old, it was illustrious — the monarchy was coeval with the people, and as long as Portugal kept her king she stood the best chance of keeping her overseas territories. All this friendly feeling will be dissipated to-day. No one will feel the slightest reverence or kindliness for a Portuguese republic run by a gang of half assassins, half card-sharpers. The first serious squabble over natives or any other cause in East or West Africa will bring about the beginning of the end.[265]

---

[262] The Néri family dominated the Brazilian state of Amazonas during the rubber boom just as the Arana family did in Iquitos and Loreto. At the elections for Governor in 1910 they had chosen Antônio Clemente Ribeiro Bittencourt (1853–1926), a veteran of the Paraguay War and a figure of immense local influence. Following his election the Néris grew anxious when Bittencourt started to act independently and against their wishes and to collude with the Lemos family who governed the neighbouring State of Pará and were the Néri's arch rivals. In 1910 the Neri's sought federal support to oust Bittencourt from office and an army officer and naval gunboat were duly despatched to deal with the situation. On 8 October Federal forces began to shell Manaos, and Bittencourt was forced to flee. He subsequently returned to Manaos to take up his post. Casement had a meeting with him on 30 September 1911 when he returned to the Amazon.

[263] A more important revolution had happened while Casement had been out of touch with current affairs. The Lisbon revolution of 4 October overthrew King Manoel II (1908–10) and saw the flight of the Portuguese royal family to Gibraltar.

[264] Dom Carlos I (1889–1908) of Portugal had tried to force monarchical dictatorship upon the Portuguese people and inaugurate a plan of "Regeneration", inspired by his chief minister João Franco, for Portugal and its global empire. Dom Carlos I was assassinated in Lisbon in February 1908.

[265] The Braganza family had ruled the Portuguese empire since 1640 with a short interlude between 1808–22 when the Court was forced to flee to Rio de Janeiro,

A swim with Arédomi

I went up the hill with Arédomi and bathed in the river above the rapid. There was a *batalon* and a *balsa* or raft there. Many of these Amazon trees will float and when nearly green, for the raft seemed of very fresh timber, all the sappy bark still on the logs. Arédomi and I swam out to it and towed it to the bank where we used it as a sort of wash-board for lathering ourselves. We came back by the swamp and hills behind the house and found an extraordinary caterpillar of pale yellow hairs, with a tufted crown like a cock-a-too. Arédomi said it was poisonous — presumably their irritating spines of yellow downy hair.

Borborini, the coward who struck the Indian boy from Sur will not go away by my *Liberal* on Tuesday. He returns to pick up his "wives" (he has two of them, the beast!) and things and will go over to Encanto to catch her next trip when she will go there for the Caraparaná rubber. This will save me the unpleasantness of having him on board.

A lovely day, but very hot and poor Fox suffering from asthma. The Commission will come down with me as far as Port Tarma whence they go up to Oriente to Alcorta's land. They will then continue to Sabana, I believe, Santa Catalina and Abisinia Sections. The latter is being run at a dead loss, so Barnes tells me, of S/P 36,000 soles per annum + £3,600! And this money is wasted on a District that is kept going on Murder, Massacre and Cannibalism and every human crime that depraved men can conceive.

Played Bridge (Tizon and I partners) and won 2 rubbers out of three — easily — against Barnes and Gielgud.

LA CHORRERA — MONDAY, 14TH NOVEMBER

Dogs

Up very early at 5.20 and out on Verandah. Found a glorious morning looming, so out with all the dogs — the dear old Scots deerhound 'Duchess', 'Boff' the mediator of new smells, 'Blackie'

---

while Napoleon's forces occupied Lisbon. At the declaration of Brazilian Independence in 1822, Pedro I became the first Emperor of Brazil while his father Dom João VI reluctantly returned to Portugal to rule. Pedro I and his son Pedro II ruled in Brazil until the declaration of the Republic in 1889. Though the Braganza's dynastic rule did not end until 1910, Portugal's empire, the oldest in Europe, persisted. The Portuguese continued to fight a protracted and gruesome campaign in their African colonies of Angola and Mozambique up until 1974.

of the Dugs, and the all-round 'Ladybird', the dog who attached herself to us up country at Entre Rios and now tries to attach herself to every male dog she sees. Had a delightful scamper in my pyjamas and French felt bath slippers — soaked — through the dewy grass and up the Sur hill, where the Hound and the dogs gave chase to the Company's with 'Lady' leading, of course. And now here I am back to my last "field day" in La Chorrera. I have to get Tizon and Gielgud to give out the a/cs of the men to them. I will have all up on the verandah and will be there and explain to Tizon and Gielgud exactly my position as a highly interested onlooker — no more.[266]

The field day

The field day lasted from 8.20 to breakfast time — 11.15 a.m. All the morning of it. The men were twenty all told, as Philip Lawrence, the Jamaica cook, a lad of 19, came this morning to me and said he was going too! He had intended staying on, I understood, along with Donald Francis and S. Greenidge for some months — but, I fancy, he and Macedo have fallen out. By the copy of his a/c which he brought to me yesterday, no allowance of 25% had been made to him. All his purchases are at the same rate as the rest of the men, viz., from 200% to 400% over Iquitos prices! — and yet he was not to enjoy the reduction of grace that was being made to the other men. I suppose the damned swine Macedo thought I should omit to ask this boy about his a/c and so, after I had gone away, he would have whistled for his redress. However, I had told Philip Lawrence on Saturday to ask for a copy of this a/c as it stood on 31st October, and when he brought it to me I saw at once he

---

[266] Casement's love of dogs was well-known and they accompanied him wherever he went. A vivid image of Casement and his dogs can be found in a letter of 26 December 1903 from Joseph Conrad to the Scottish socialist, South American writer and horseman-adventurer, Robert Cunninghame Graham: "I send two letters I had from a man called Casement, premising that I knew him first in the Congo just twelve years ago. Perhaps you've heard or seen in print his name. He's a Protestant Irishman, pious too. But so was Pizarro. For the rest I can assure you that he is a limpid personality. There is a touch of the conquistador in him too; for I've seen him start off into an unspeakable wilderness swinging a crookhandled stick for all weapons, with two bulldogs, Paddy (white) and Biddy (brindle), at his heels and a Loanda boy carrying a bundle for all company. A few months afterwards it so happened that I saw him come out again, a little leaner, a little browner, with his stick, dogs and Loanda boy, and quietly serene as though he had been for a stroll in a park." In Frederick R. Karl & Laurence Davies (eds.), *Joseph Conrad. The Collected Letters* vol. III, 1903–07 (Cambridge 1988). Casement picked up five stray dogs during his travels in the Putumayo.

was being "done". I did not tell him so, but merely suggested that he should see me again on Monday, as I had intended asking Tizon and Gielgud why he was being omitted from the general *bonificación*. He evidently made up his mind in the interval to go altogether and I think rightly. Out of the 20 men only 2 remain, Donald Francis and S. Greenidge — all the rest, 18 in number, will go away with me on *Liberal*. Crichlow arrived early from Ultimo Retiro, in the train of Jiménez who with some of his footpads and several Indians came down at 7 a.m. from Ultimo Retiro by the *Veloz*, bringing the rubber from that Section.

Barbadians accept bonificación

The men all accepted the *bonificación* and I suggested they should thank Tizon and Macedo. There was a fair amount of chicanery all round, from which (I am sorry to say) not even Tizon was exempted. For instance the a/cs of the men are closed on 31st October, whereas most of them have been working up to-day. E. Batson, J. Minggs and Crichlow have all been at work on the launches and at Ultimo Retiro and most of the others have been bringing the rubber over from Victoria. They are all done out of half a month's pay — right off the reel. Then again Crichlow was not told by Jiménez, at all, that he was sent for by me, merely told that Jiménez had need of him to look after the rubber coming down, so he left all his clothes behind, and his "wife" too. He put this forward at once — along with several other objections he made to his a/c as it stood. My attitude was one of strict aloofness. I explained to the men that (with Bishop first) they had no "legal" claim, as they had bought these things at the outrageous prices charged, with their eyes open, that is to say they knew they were being swindled. The local representative of the company made them a free offer of ¼ of these prices, and it lay with them to accept or not as they pleased. The men knew that their chances of obtaining more was remote and they accepted — and so, as far as they are concerned, the matter ends. But it certainly does not end, so far as the prices charged them is concerned.

Sydney Morris already had his cheque in his hand for the balance before he appeared in the room. What a method! Before this examination of the men to see if they wanted this settlement, they had actually tampered with the weaklings by giving them the cheque of an a/c that was already *sub judice*. Tizon has sunk to-day in my estimation — pretty low.

They have been systematically swindled for years, grossly maltreated and converted into criminals in order that this criminal association of footpads and vagabonds might grow rich by murdering and robbing the Indians and swindling their less guilty employés.

Casement disgusted

I was disgusted with the whole performance — Gielgud and Tizon pretending that this was a "remarkable concession" made on my account &c., that prices in Iquitos were very high and if they bought things, say, up the Purus, or "on the Amazon" they would pay quite as much. I merely pointed out that these men were employés of the Co. and there was no question of their buying things in a Store, but purchasing necessaries from their Employers and that the ordinary retail prices of an Amazon store to the general public could not be brought into the question at all. Moreover, my own a/c for the things I have bought since coming to Chorrera is made out, in the most barefaced way, at "Iquitos prices, plus 25% for freight". My bill for a whole lot of things, since 23rd Sept. to 12th November., is only S/P 261.52 plus 25% = S/P 65.38 = S/P 326.90. The same things to the Barbados men would come to fully S/P 1000.00 or £36 to me and £100 to them! I shall go through the a/cs of the men and compare in parallel columns the prices they have paid against the prices charged to me.

Talk with Gielgud

After the settling up of the B. men's a/cs I had a long talk with Gielgud, just before lunch. His mental attitude (or moral?) is a strange one. Frankly at heart I think he is as bad as any of these Peruvian scoundrels. He is a cold-blooded, selfish guzzler, who thinks of himself first and always. He clearly thinks that by the acceptance by the men of this *Bonificación* their mouths are stopped, or the FO's mouth is stopped as against the Co. I told him after breakfast that nothing was altered, so far as I was concerned, or the representations I should make to the FO as to the treatment of the men. I am glad I am leaving this ghastly hole.

Interview with Jiménez

After breakfast an extraordinary thing occurred. Jiménez came with Bruce to translate for him, to ask for an interview. I was sitting by Barnes on the verandah and I said certainly, here now, and sat on, so he began, through Bruce, to say that he learned he was charged in *Truth* with atrocities &c. and he wanted to disabuse my mind, so that I should stand well with him.

I said that I had nothing to do with what appeared in newspapers and that if an English newspaper had libelled him he had his remedy at law. He said he would take this but that he wanted to stand well with me. I was a *Caballero distinguido*[267] &c. and he did not want me to believe ill of him. Barnes, O'Donnell, Adolfo Castro Pol and a young Peruvian boy (about 6' tall or more) from Sabana came and sat listening.

Jiménez spoke again and again, there was a clear intention to get me to say that I did not believe Braga's[268] or *Truth*'s charges against him and accepted his denial. This I refrained entirely from saying. I pointed out I had nothing to do with these matters which concerned him and *Truth* and the Government of Peru and that while, personally I might even have a good impression of him it was not my business to deal with *Truth* charges one way or the other. As he persisted to seek an expression of opinion I said "Very well, as you ask me, I will say quite frankly I cannot carry away a good impression of you. It is not *Truth* alone, but I have heard from many quarters of things you did and while there may be some exaggeration I don't believe all is and I leave you to your conscience. You know what you have done, and if you have done wrong before you may try now to do good."

I suggested he should bring a libel action against *Truth* if he thought himself aggrieved, and this he said he should do!

Bruce confesses

He looked flabbergasted and so did the rest and after some more of the same kind of remarks he shook hands and went. Bruce stayed on to talk to me and he gave the whole show away. He admitted that the whole system of dealing with the Indians was an infamous one, and that if the Indians shot a whiteman they did quite right. All the chiefs he said had flogged and if any told me they did not they lied. I said I knew that — that the system had been a bad one from the start, and some men were better than others. It was an extraordinary attempt to draw me. Jiménez knows a Peruvian Judge is coming here and he wanted to get a statement made by me in the presence of witnesses, that would have whitewashed him. There is fear all round. I wish I could

---

[267] Distinguished gentleman.

[268] João Baptista Braga ,who had made a declaration referring to Jiménez's brutality, see Hardenburg *op. cit.*, p. 238.

think that any sincere and honest enquiry by Peru was likely — but I believe the whole thing is simply to whitewash. Tizon is delighted, because he says that it will prove that Peru has acted herself before any foreign pressure was brought to bear upon her! A fine idea — after waiting 3 years and when the fat is in the fire and all is known, — she begins tardily to move.

Casement in a fix

The truth is all these people are liars — I would not trust one of them — and as I write this late at night this Monday evening, I feel that all the trouble I have dreaded may rise again at Iquitos. Tizon is profoundly afraid of me and of the testimony of the Barbados men. He knows quite well that their evidence, which I hold in written form, seals not only the fate of the Co. for which he does not care very much, but the honour and credit of Peru for which he cares a good deal. It is quite on the cards that he is writing round to the Prefect urging that, on my arrival at Iquitos with these eighteen very black witnesses against Peru, they should be questioned, i.e. interrogated by this examining Judge. The method of interrogating would be their own — their very own. The object would also be their very own. To damage these the only witnesses — to obtain discrepancies, denials, recantations, &c., so that the only evidence Peru has to dread should be in her possession before it reaches England, that she might play havoc with. I am seriously perturbed. This rushing of a settlement on the Barbados men out here has so clearly been inspired by unworthy motives. I told Tizon I did not wish it. His leg began to jerk — the South American sign of agitation and I told Gielgud — that incomprehensible ass — the same thing, and he said he thought it should be decided on by the Company. They have practically forced a settlement on the men here — involving me as far as they possibly can as an assenting party. The object is clear, that as the men's claims are settled — and in my presence, there remains no ground for representation on their behalf to the Company — or to Peru. Step No. 1 accomplished (as they think) at Chorrera. Step No. 2, the complete robbery of all the evidence of the Barbados men at Iquitos and then Mr Casement and his 18 very black witnesses to be bowed out of the country. I am in a regular fix.[269]

[269] Casement here is accurately predicts the Peruvian reaction. Sure enough, once Casement had helped the Barbadians escape from the Putumayo and Peru, the Peruvian authorities claimed that he had robbed them of the criminals involved in the atrocities and valuable witnesses in the trial of other perpetrators.

Conversation with Barnes — Casement's crisis

I spoke to Barnes very late at night and told him of my fears or of my renewed fears. He quite sees their force. He says I cannot break the journey at Javari, or anywhere else, unless the "passenger" is booked there. That Reigada, the Captain of the *Liberal*, told him that last voyage. So if I leave Chorrera with all my Barbados men bound to Iquitos they must go. I want to leave them at some place in Brazil and pick them up on the way down river. This I cannot do unless I give notice here and say the men are landing at say the Javari mouth. Then I shall know how I stand or how the intention in regard to the Barbados men stands. I shall say this and test them — and if I see there is a deliberate intention to compel me to take the men to Iquitos then I shall have at least unmasked the enemy and I can fight openly. I shall then refuse to go by *Liberal* at all! The raft may again appear floating on the waters of the Igara-paraná! I cannot get down to the Amazon if these people will not assist me. It is 650 miles away and I could not get food even. They would not let me have the 'Huitota' or any means of transport down to the Amazon. Even the Barbados men (some of them) might join the enemy. The crisis of my journey to this accursed river has come, with its gang of villainous ruffians. The *Liberal* is delayed now until Wednesday 16th, so I shall have to-morrow to prepare for the fight.

LA CHORRERA — TUESDAY, 15TH NOVEMBER

The anxiety grows

I am up at 4.50 thinking over the problem. I feel pretty sure that Tizon is determining this. The very settlement with the Barbados men takes a new light. It incidentally compelled their return to Iquitos, whereas I had already once suggested that I might not go there.

I shall ask Bell to find out from the Brazilian Customs Officer if and how landing of passengers at Javari[270] is effected and then

[270] The Javari is a southern tributary of the Amazon rising in the Acré and meeting the Marañón–Solimões divide just above Benjamin Constant. For much of its course it defines the frontier between Peru and Brazil. It, too, was an important wild rubber river and the fact that each bank belonged to a different nation meant that it became the refuge for a dispossessed criminal element wanted by authorities either in Peru or Brazil. Casement made two voyages up the Javari in 1911 in pursuit of Putumayo criminals.

request Tizon and Gielgud to make out my passage and that of all the men to the Javari. If they refuse, or demur or raise difficulties I shall know what is in the wind and shall act accordingly, taking Barnes and Commission into my full confidence and if necessary even appealing to them to come away with me.

Bishop's advice

I told Bishop of my fears about taking the men to Iquitos, that with the forthcoming enquiry by the Peruvian judge they might take advantage of the men being in Iquitos to question them as the first witnesses — and possibly to go further. Some of the men stand confessed of dreadful crimes — Quintin for instance (three murders) and well nigh all of them of flogging and shooting Indians in one way or another. Bishop saw the danger at once and I said that as I could not trust any of the Peruvians I had decided to ask for passage tickets for the men optional to land on the way to Iquitos if desired. If this were refused I should know where I was and might not then go at all in *Liberal*. I should try to charter the *Huitota* to go down the 650 miles to the Amazon — or walk! Bell did not go to find out from the Brazilian Customs Officer about the formalities needed for landing at the Javari, where the Brazilian customs place is — so lunch came and I was no wiser. This is typical of "the Commission". I had not cared to raise the question of the tickets and destination until first aware as to the Brazilian Customs law. After lunch I told Gielgud I wished the passage orders for the men to be made out as for Iquitos but with liberty to break the journey at intermediate ports and he went to see Macedo. He returned to say that this would be done but that Macedo was not sure if the men would be allowed by the Brazilian authorities to land, that there was some treaty between Peru and Brazil regulating the river traffic. I saw Macedo instantly go on board *Liberal*, to talk to Reigada and then go up, I think, indeed, I am sure, to talk to the Brazilian Customs officer. He stayed nearly half an hour on board.

I pointed out to Barnes what I had said to Gielgud and Macedo's immediate visit to the *Liberal*. I waited a reasonable time and then myself went on board the *Liberal* and asked Senhor Mathias, the Brazilian Customs Officer, if there was any objection to passengers being booked from this to the mouth of the Javari or other Brazilian place — and he said none at all. He promised every facility and pledged himself to all sorts of personal services on my behalf including the loan of a steam launch up the Javari, if

I wished to visit Nazareth. I told Gielgud of this and asked him to make sure that the tickets or passenger lists rather, for no tickets are issued, were made out with entire liberty reserved. This he said he saw actually done. I rested most of the afternoon after this — for I have really been very anxious since last night when the fear of the collaring of the men at Iquitos became, if I may, so acute.

It is not by any means allayed, but I have at least now secured an alternative and I no longer feel a cooped-up prisoner hundreds of miles from anywhere and with no means of getting out save on the terms of the enemy. I should have got a launch round from Iquitos to meet me here, that would have been the wiser thing to have done. I should then have been free, not in this imprisoned position with my hands tied. I have revolved the pros and cons of the men's going to Iquitos until I am tired. They know nothing of what is in my mind — any more, poor souls, than they know what is intended about this Peruvian Court of Enquiry, only Bishop knows what I think and partly fear and he is not to say a word to the men until I wish it spoken. We shall go on board in the morning and anyhow get as far as the Javari — and if by that time I am still of the same way of thinking I shall counsel all the Barbados men to disembark there. I shall make some arrangements for their keep until I can return on the *Athualpa*, either with the Brazilian Customs Officer, at so much a head, or else at one of the trading factories along the bank of the river.

I could take up all their orders for the balance of wages due them, amounting to a good big sum, to Iquitos, and collect the money there through Cazes. The P.A.Company owes several of them return passages to Barbados and that, too, I presume could be got also. I could arrange with Booth & Co to issue tickets for all the rest, either to Manaos, Pará, or Barbados, as the men will tell me before I dump them down at the mouth of the Javari.

My mind is much easier since I have settled that I have freedom of choice as to taking the men or not to Iquitos.

Crichlow's accordion

Crichlow came to complain that, among the things he had left at Ultimo Retiro, of which he had handed a list to Gielgud and Macedo, was an accordion he had bought on 17th October here at Chorrera, after we had left U.R. He had sent down for some reason, and had run up a bill of S/P 240, although already in debt S/P 193, as far as I can see, to this Company. If he is a fool they are rogues. Here is a man at £70 a month, already in debt £19, and they allow him — nay tempt him — to go £24 further into debt. This accordion, it appears, Macedo had dangled before his eyes in the Store here, and he had bought it for S/P 105 or £10 !!! The instrument was even damaged too, and Macedo had promised to take off 35%, so Crichlow avers, and adds that Mr Parr was a witness to the promise. Well now, a few days later, he is forced to leave this instrument and all he possesses behind him, and he comes to know if I can do anything to help him. The question had been raised by him quite frankly yesterday at the settling up. It was partly the Company's fault too that the things were left behind, because Jiménez did not tell him he was sent for by me, but merely that he was to come down to "help with the *caucho*", i.e. to "shepherd" the poor Indians down on the way.

Therefore he had left all his belongings, including his "wife" in Ultimo Retiro, as he had had no reply from me to the two letters he wrote me. I explained to him, Gielgud and Tizon hearing, that I had got his two letters together almost, and had on receipt of the first asked Mr Tizon to write up at once an order for his recall to La Chorrera, and that this had been done. It was this order to Jiménez that had not been communicated to Crichlow.

I said then it was most unfair he should lose his things, and as the fault might be held to be partly mine, I would pay half the cost of the things if the Company would pay the other half. Even to this offer — surely a generous one — both Gielgud and Tizon demurred. First, they proposed that the man could wait here a month, get his things down in the interval, and go by next *Liberal*. I asked, would he be paid during this month, and they said no, that they would feed him here at La Chorrera! I did not say all I thought of this offer, but pointed out merely to Crichlow that his time was his money, and that I thought he would be foolish to stay on idly at La Chorrera for a month just to get these things, but, of course, it was his affair. He said that he had no intention of staying under any circumstances, that he was here to go home to Barbados, and go he would with me. He said he would let the Company have a present of most of the things, if he could get back say a hammock, a blanket and the value of the accordion. Tizon said he would see, and that he would certainly give him a hammock and a blanket, and see if the Company could buy back any of the other things.

This was yesterday. Tonight Crichlow comes to say that neither hammock nor blanket has been given to him, and that he is to lose his accordion too. Such is Macedo's decision. I took the man to Gielgud and he shrugged his shoulders, and said as the man was going at his own wish, and had been "very generously" dealt with in getting back 25% off his purchase, he thought the matter should end at that. I said that Tizon had certainly promised in my hearing that a hammock and blanket should be given to Crichlow, and that others of the things would be bought back from him, such things as were useful to the Company, so that his loss might be reduced as much as possible, and this was the way the promise was being fulfilled. I left Gielgud there, and went into the matter of the account with Crichlow, and showed it to Fox and Bell, who both agreed with me it was an abominable swindle.

I told Crichlow that I should pay him for the things myself, and do what I could to help him. This, I fancy, stirred Gielgud, because he went off, and finally came back to say that the value of the accordion would be returned to Crichlow and a hammock (S/P 15, I find), and a blanket (S/P 30) would be given to him. So much for Crichlow.

Walcott's tobacco

Then poor, simple-faced Augustus Walcott appeared, and said that his pathetic 6 inches of tobacco twist, for which he had paid S/P 8 (almost 16/-) was still there! I had produced it yesterday at the settling of the accounts when Walcott's came along, and had "playfully" suggested that possibly the Company might see its way to give him a whole roll in place of this half one. They had not acted on this inspiration, neither Gielgud nor Tizon! So Walcott came to tell me now. I sent Bishop round to the Store, and bought a roll, a miserable lump of Peruvian tobacco worth about 1/-, and sold to these poor beggars at 16/-. Bishop says it used to be S/P 9 = 18/-. The thing is such a curio I could not part with it, so I sent for another, and gave one to Walcott, and kept one to go in my Museum of "Curios" from the Putumayo.[271] The hearts of the Peruvian army

[271] Casement is referring to the exhibits and artefacts he had collected during his Putumayo investigation. Part of this museum of curios would later serve as evidence in the Parliamentary Select Committee enquiry — a gun, a pair of trousers and this roll of tobacco, but he had also collected a large number of ethnic artefacts. The centre of this collection was a pair of Manguaré drums and beaters that are still kept in the anthropological archive at the National Museum of Ireland in Dublin along with another fifteen or so objects he had acquired through trade or purchase. These include a bark dancing costume, *fonos*, and two stone axe-heads. They are recorded in the N.M.I. Loan Book (1881–1956) Item 756. The N.M.I. also contains some forty-six objects that Casement collected in Africa, mainly during his 1903 investigation. They include a small fetiche identified as a Nkisi figure. See U.C.L.A. *African Arts* Vol. XXVIII No.2 — Spring 1995.

or Directors will be stirred when these "goods" are exhibited at the Board of Trade say, or in the Under Secretary's rooms at the FO! By heaven I'll do it.

Quintyne's foot

Poor Quintyne came for a pair of slippers, and showed his wounded foot. I got a pair for him, too, of these S/P 5 (10/-) carpet slippers, and paid for them. My own account was then furnished me completed up to date. I had told Gielgud that I must pay my own hospitality bill, and he bought me a beauty. I pay S/P 10 a day for myself for 54 days — £54, and S/P 5 a day each for Bishop and Sealy, or another £1 a day. I fed these two men almost solely out of my own pocket. I bought £44 worth of foodstuffs with me from Iquitos, and bought a lot more here for them out of these Stores — fully another £15 worth. It is really amusing. Gielgud's ideas of value received are quite on a par with some of his ideas of equity.

Burke, the engineer

Burke, the Engineer of the 'Huitota' spoke to me after dinner. An amazing story, worthy of the "goodness" of Alcosta of Oriente. He spoke of Normand "dashing children's brains out" as a thing Alcosta had never done. Also he had not allowed his *muchachos* to eat a man! Also, when one of his "wives" went wrong with an Indian, he did not shoot her, as Aguero would do, but actually made the man take her. Zumaran at Indostan flogged pieces out of a woman up there. Burke saw her — lumps an inch deep out of her. Also Velarde, the same with 2 men. Alcosta is keeping them "to show the Consul". Burke admitted, like Benn, everything: A volunteered statement to put himself right with me. He knew that Jiménez had spoken and said "Of course, everyone knows about Jiménez having killed Indians." Bruce yesterday actually said that, under the present system, the Indians would not last more than six years. I had said 10 years, and he said, "No, indeed not 6. When I came here the Company had 10,000 Indians, and it has nothing like that now."

Two strange avowals to come at this end of my stay. Rats leaving the sinking ship. Seeing that I have won, and know all, they wish to stand well with me. Bruce also said Bartolomé Zumaeta had outraged the wife of Katenere before his eyes while Katenere was in *cepo*, so he shot him.

X

THE *LIBERAL* RETURNS TO IQUITOS

DEPARTURE FOR IQUITOS — WEDNESDAY, NOVEMBER 16TH

Casement and the Barbadians board the Liberal

Thank God! I left Chorrera and the Peruvian Amazon Company's "Estate" to-day. I am still their involuntary guest on their steamer *Liberal*, with the eighteen Barbados men, four Indian wives of these, and the children of John Brown, Allan Davis, James Mapp and J. Dyall.

Dyall's "tenth" wife

Dyall made a hard fight to carry off an Indian woman — his "tenth" wife. He came at 8 a.m. to say the woman Loayza had given him in Encanto refused to be left behind, and insisted on going with him. I went to Tizon who, for reasons I think justifiable, refused to allow her to go. Of course Tizon's refusal is illegal. The Company does not own the people, and only a government authority could refuse to allow this Indian, or any Indian, to leave. Tizon says that Dyall has no means to support her, which is true; that he refuses to marry her; which is true; and that she is not the mother of his child, which is true. Dyall admits all this, but says the mother of his child was taken from him by Velarde at Occidente, that he has no woman to look after his child, and that, final and best reason, the woman herself wishes to accompany him. The woman came weeping, and protested against staying, and made a regular scene. Tizon was obdurate, and I told Dyall I should not intervene, that I thought Tizon's reasons were good. The woman even tried to get on board the boat, but was turned off on the plank, and made to go ashore.

Donald Francis breaks down

Poor Donald Francis came to my room, and broke down, and cried like a boy. He did not want to stay when it came to the last. He said he would be "done bad by", and it was only his wish to get more money to go home which had led him to wish to stay on, and now even that he regretted. He spoke of his "old mother" at Barbados, how he had promised to help her, and had not done it, and sobbed, with his head on his arm like a boy. I comforted him, and said I'd go to see his mother in Barbados, and that he could stay on until December next and go then, or, if he really wished it, he could go now, and I would stop the *Liberal* until he was ready. I called Barnes in, and begged him to look after Francis, and see that he got off when he wanted to, and I later spoke to Tizon also. Everyone came down to see me off. Burke, the Australian, brought me a letter to post addressed to :

Mrs. P. Hefferman
2 Gladstone Grove
South Melbourne
Victoria
Australia

with the request that I would see it went safe. He said there was something "queer" with his letters, as he got no replies. Young Parr, too, brought me a batch of home letters to post, and I took them —

Mrs Parr
47 Savernake Road
Hampstead
London N.

Goodbyes

Also Barnes and some of Gielgud's. Everything was finished. I bade Miranda and O'Donnell special goodbyes, and after a last shake-hands with Tizon, Gielgud, Barnes, Bell, Fox, we cleared off the ropes and moved into the stream. Two fearful explosions of sound signals, and we were off. Sealy and Chase had come to bid me a special goodbye, and I saw them last — they, and Francis and Greenidge on the top of the steps waving farewells. We quickly slipped down the still water between the sandbank and the shore and with our nose in the downward current were in a moment swept out of sight. The last thing I saw was by an upward glimpse, the great white cataract pouring into the upper end of the pool. My last view of the scene of such grim tragedy as I believe exists no where else on earth today. It was just 9.45 as we left Chorrera.

Other passengers and seating arrangements

Two employes of the Company are on board, one of these Jeremias Gusmán, who wrote to me at Occidente to complain of Montt having Indians in chains, and the other our old friend Garrido. This miserable coward has been at Chorrera waiting to return to Iquitos, since he was dismissed, or "sent in his resignation" at Occidente the day when he turned tail and refused to answer Bell's question as to his statements made to the Commission in Iquitos. There is another employé, whose name I don't know (I hear it is Pineira), and these, with the skipper, engineer, and the Brazilian Customs Officer, Mathias, constitute my society. I find Garrido, Gusmán and the other employé are at table too with us! In the Sections these 'Perus' are obliged to eat by themselves, and when we came up river Garrido took his meals with Bishop. Bishop and John Brown are at a sidetable on the upper deck, where the servants got their meals before, on the upward voyage; finally Arédomi and Omarino are on the upper deck too, and a dear little *chiviclis*[272] that Macedo got for me.

Arrive Port Tarma — the Commission's itinerary

We found Port Tarma at 10.30, and some Indians ran down to greet us — two nude women and a man — from a wretched little hut. This is the "port" for Oriente — Alcosta's station, of which I have been getting such glowing accounts from Burke. The Commission go down to it tomorrow, and on to Oriente. From Oriente to Sabana, and back to Port Tarma, whence they go down to Providencia for Santa Catalina, and then to Abisinia &c., and back to Guarunes (Gwarunes) port and up to Chorrera again. This will take them the best part of a month. From Chorrera they go overland to El Encanto, and visit the stations on the Caraparaná. The *Liberal* is to return at once, on reaching Iquitos, and go straight to El Encanto for the rubber of that river. This, Reigada says, will be about 4th December, and nine days to Encanto at quickest will bring her there on 13th December. The Commission do not expect to see her again before the end of January, when

[272] This is a small rodent-like animal with a reddish-brown fur that looks a little like a cross between a guinea pig and squirrel.

they finish with the Caraparaná. I expect they will get to Iquitos some date in mid–February probably. They then go down the Amazon and ascend the Purus to visit some so-called "Estate" of the Company's in the Acre territory — the only property left there. They do not expect to finish that until end of April, and get home in May.

Thoughts on the Commission

I am going to try and get Colonel Bertie to come out and join them. Fox has begged me again and again to do this, and I see clearly that with all the goodwill in the world they cannot compile a report. They are all united as to the facts — at complete harmony with me. Gielgud, of course, I omit. He has practically long since disappeared as any serious factor from the Commission. He simply stands for a nonentity, a paid servant of the Company with really no mind of his own — an absent-minded beggar.[273] However, my preoccupation is in no wise about the Commission. I have them entirely with me, as convinced and overwhelmingly convinced as men can be, and pledged up to the hilt to damn the whole system, lock, stock and barrel.[274]

Port Tarma to Providencia

From Port Tarma (sic) we slipped down river, to Providencia — the port for Santa Catalina. A little hut on a clear hillside stands for the port. It was here the Aguero gang tried to make James Mapp and the other Barbados men go by force and by night up the road to Santa Catalina to ambush them on the way. We passed Providencia at about 5 p.m. Before noon we had passed through the high ranges — 600 feet fully — of hills that come to the right bank in great forested slopes. These are the boundary of inhabited land, I fancy, on that shore, the Southern limit of the Sur Section and of the Huitoto country. Thence on to the mouth of the Igara-paraná; I fancy there are no Indians, but heaps of rubber trees. But the

[273] A reference to Rudyard Kipling, "The Absent-Minded Beggar" (1899):
He's an absent-minded beggar, and his weaknesses are great–/But we and Paul must take him as we find him–/He's out on active service, wiping something off a slate–/
And he's left a lot of little things behind him!"

[274] The other Commissioners returned to England in April 1911 and together wrote a detailed report on the affairs of the Company — although Gielgud refused to sign it. The content of the report concentrated mainly on aspects of improving rubber production and had a comprehensive analysis of the Company's estates and assets. The report also confirmed the disgraceful treatment of the local Indians and confirmed the Barbadian statements detailing the long history of horror.

trees without an Indian population to enslave are worthless to these hammock warriors. Tizon confessed to me three days ago that he was sure there was much more rubber in the land down towards the Putumayo, and on along its banks, but "no Indians". On the left bank the inhabited tract stretches further down, to a point below Guarunes, which we passed at 6 p.m. This is the "port" for Abisinia, like all these "ports" a mere untidy, open shed on the bank, at the mouth of a small *quebrada* or tributary. We saw several cases lying there in the shed, left, no doubt, by Aguero to be fetched later on. A great number of rivers emptying in during the last few miles, in the last 20 minutes we have passed three fair sized openings on the left bank, showing where the Boras country rivers are draining that swampy region.

Glorious sunset and total eclipse of the full moon

The moon rose bright after a glorious sunset, one of the loveliest I have ever seen. We noticed the brilliant gleam over the tree-top as she rose — a full moon, too. As soon as she was clear of the trees we saw an eclipse was in progress, and as she rose we got a magnificent view of it. A total eclipse by Reigada's almanac. The whole visage of the moon was obscured by 8, and then clouds came and covered the subsequent stages.

I turned in early, but wakened at 2.30 with a glorious moonlight, and the lovely palm-crested forest slipping past silently and softly against a pale blue night sky. I looked long at it, and thought of the fate of the poor Indian tribes, who have been so shamefully captured and enslaved, and murdered here in these lovely regions, by this gang of infernal ruffians. I thought of Katenere, the brave Boras chief — of all the murdered Indians of these forests; of the incredible and bestial crimes of these infamous men, and wondered at the peace God sheds upon the trees. The forest, with its wild creatures, is happier far than the "centres of civilization" these Peruvian and Colombian miscreants have created and floated into a great London Company.[275]

---

[275] The corresponding *Black Diary* entry for 16 November contains a series of discrepancies over time. There are in fact numerous statistical differences between times and weights stated in the Putumayo Journal and those given in the *Black Diary*, but they are often too insignificant to bother about. In this entry, however, the concentration of mistakes makes it worthwhile.

16 November: "The skipper C. Reigado gave me assurances in front of Tizon, Gielgud, Barnes, that the men could land where they pleased. So off on my last fight! Passed Port Tarma at 11.30, naked Indian women, the last I shall ever see probably. Came to the great highland forested ridge at 12.15 — it is over 500 feet

ON BOARD THE *LIBERAL* — THURSDAY, 17TH NOVEMBER

The chiviclis

I took the chiviclis into my cabin last night, and it played long with me, and nestled up and chirruped, and then I put it in the nasty cage, and covered it up warm. This morning I made Arédomi take it out to play with and feed. He and Omarino and Bishop all slept on the upper deck. A lovely morning. The river now is broad and deep, and the banks lower and lower. All suspicion of high land has passed away, and we are in the swampy region near the low, flat shores of the Putumayo. The Captain tells me that he has 66 tons of rubber aboard, and 35 tons of firewood.

Cost of Liberal *and Captain's intentions*

The *Liberal* cost £7,000 in Iquitos, including costs of her passage out from England. The Company has just lost two launches in the Amazon, by accident, he tells me, and are getting a new steamer at home. He also says that he is going into the Yaguas river on his way down. This is a big tributary of the Putumayo, which comes in on the right bank above the Cotuhé. Its headwaters are somewhere behind Loreto or Pebas, I fancy. He says he entered the Yaguas last voyage, too, on returning from Encanto in October. He then had Captain Delgado and 14 Peruvian soldiers on board returning to Iquitos. An Indian "prisoner" was handed over to him at Yaguas, a man who had shot a Sr. Fonseca, — another Fonseca! — on the Yaguas. This Fonseca, I presume, is the Company's agent there. They claim to exploit the Yaguas too! This man had brought the Indian up from boyhood, so it seems, and yet he shot him! Reigada says the Indian gave "no reason" for shooting Fonseca, merely that "someone had told him to kill him" and so he did it. He blew his brains out. I shall carefully note things in the Yaguas River, doubtless it is exactly the same state of affairs. The Captain

---

high — fully 600–700 I think — a curving sweep — three or four parallel ranges, of forested upland."

In addition to the different spelling of Reigada to that adopted in the genuine manuscript (a name the forger seems constantly to confuse) there is an error concerning the arrival of the *Liberal* at Port Tarma. This is given as 11.30 here and as 10.30 in the Putumayo Journal. The relevant entry in the Putumayo Journal continues: "Before noon we had passed thro' the high ranges — 600 feet fully — of hills that come to the right bank in great forested slopes". In the *Black Diary* they reach the same place at 12.15 and the height suddenly takes on a definite but incorrect 500 feet qualified by the comment "fully 600–700 I think".

tells me later that the place is 4 hours up the Yaguas there, and is called Recreio. It does not belong to the Company. They merely bought rubber to supply this "trader" with goods. I presume it is one of Arana's "other" houses to drain the Company surreptitiously.

Casement's plans to disembark the Barbadians in Brazil

I have not said a word to any of the Barbados men (except Bishop) as to my possible, nay probable intention, of disembarking them all at some point in Brazilian territory, most likely Esperanza at the mouth of the Javari. I shall wait until we are out in the Amazon itself before I broach the subject. If only I could meet a vessel of the Amazon S.S. Company,[276] with the green flag of Brazil flying, I'd transfer all of us, bag and baggage, to her. There may be a chance at São Paulo de Olivença. If I saw a downgoing Brazilian steamer there — what luck — I'd ship all hands for Manaos with a letter to the Vice-Consul to pay their passages on ship's arrival, and to provide for the men until I got down there. That would ease my mind. I could then go up to Iquitos in this boat alone, or with Bishop, say, and give the Prefect all the information he wants, and perhaps a good deal more; collect the balance due to the men, and come down with my mission accomplished by the *Athualpa* early in December. Failing this I think the safe thing will be to leave all hands at the Javari, and perhaps stay there myself a day or two to see them safely booked for Manaos. The men may not like it, and may even refuse. They have a perfect right to, but if I point out that I have good reason for not wishing them to go to Iquitos they will obey me.

Possible Peruvian intentions — the control and perversion of evidence

I may be quite wrong in fearing anything of the kind, but, on the other hand, it is such an obvious thing for these dishonest people to do. The only evidence that they do not entirely control is here with me on this boat. For all the rest they can answer. Tizon and

[276] In 1910 there were four main transatlantic shipping companies running regular services between Europe or the U.S. and the Amazon. The Booth Line, established in 1866, was the oldest and largest and had five transatlantic steamships and over forty smaller vessels working the river itself. The Brazilian–Lloyd company mainly dealt with north American traffic as did the Hamburg America line. Germany was served by the Sudamerikanische Dampfschiffahrts Gesellschaft. The bulk of Amazon traffic was served by the Amazon Steamship Navigation Company, a London registered Company.

the Prefect would give anything to avoid a scandal, and if they think this can best be effected by getting hold of the Barbados men in Iquitos it can quite legitimately be done. The court here has a perfect right to summon them, fresh from long service on the Putumayo, to give evidence, and can compel them to speak. The object, I fear, is not the men's evidence — that is all for good, but the perversion of their evidence. If this Court of Enquiry is not sincere, and I cannot see how it can be, composed of Peruvians who have known for years of these abominable crimes (and all of them probably even bribed men) the investigation of the Barbados men would be carried out to establish just the opposite of the truth. A town that can tolerate a man like Aurelio Rodriguez as one of its leading citizens will have no qualms about protecting its well-to-do murderers against exposure. The Lima government will have a similar wish to prevent a hideous international scandal. The Prefect will say "I am going to do what is right in the Putumayo, cleanse the place of its ruffians, but I cannot allow the evidence in the hands of the Consul to go away thus, it will be held over our heads, and, instead of our action being spontaneous, it will be due to the fear of British representations."

Something of that kind. Besides these arguments there is a stronger. If I can get off with all my evidence intact then, knowing that this array of witnesses is held in reserve, the action of the Peruvian government on the Putumayo will be all the more vigorous and sincere. They will try to convince us that, of themselves, they have done right, so that we may never be forced into shaming them by publishing the Barbados men's evidence, or even communicating it to them.

Despite, therefore, every objection, and all the trouble, expense and anxiety I shall be put to by leaving the men camped at the Javari for a week or so, I think it is far the safer plan, and if my mission is to be assured of being successful and not a failure that this course is my duty. It is very distasteful to me, and will cause me a lot of trouble, but I think it must be done. I should never forgive myself if, trusting to luck, I took all on to Iquitos and found I had landed them just where the Peruvians wanted, and I don't think the FO would forgive me either. I must succeed — not fail, and to do the former I must take no risks.

4.30 p.m. — Arrive at Pescaria — beautiful sunset

Arrived at Pescaria. Here is the blackguard Cerron Quintyne told me about. The river is lower than when we came up in September last, I think. It is a noble stream and Arédomi and Omarino are looking on a new world. Arédomi says they call it Cottué — the Igara-paraná, and Harmia, the Putumayo. Whence the name Putumayo comes from it is hard to say. Lt Maw, in 1827, knew nothing of it as applied to the river, but heard of it as a place and as a tribe of Indians. It is probably Quichua, and was doubtless first applied to the Indians of the upper waters, as *mayo* is the word for water or river in Quichua, I believe.

Depart Pescaria — swarms of sandflies

We stayed at Pescaria one hour, till 5.30, and then off again. Got some firewood there; very poor stuff, and a lot of plantains and bananas, also myriads of sand flies. An incredible swarm of these pests attacked the men, carrying the firewood on board. The sunset was again magnificent, and the night came gloriously. After a fierce sun the cool of the evening was delicious, and the moon rose with a veritable column of gold, clean cut, in the river below, shining half across the stream in angular reflection. The palms stood out above the forest. We are back in the land of the myriad palm trees again. I stood in the bows till 9, talking to the Captain, and by the wheel, where a young *practicante* of the Punchana Indian pilots is learning his trade. He fell asleep at the wheel! Tomorrow I mean to try and go through the Barbados men's accounts again, and get a clear statement of the final amounts. I know all except Sealy and Chase. I don't know what was done in the final settlement with them, but it was only very small change, if any, which was made in their case. I think I have gained about £900 for the men — 20 of them all told, including Bishop and Philip, the cook.

ON BOARD THE *LIBERAL* — FRIDAY 18TH NOVEMBER

Steaming beautifully down the Putumayo. Got the Barbados men up, one by one, and verified their final accounts. All save Walcott are satisfied. He was swindled out of his gratification of S/P 100 for his services in Abisinia — poor soul! — after Tizon and Gielgud promising me it should be given! All but two are anxious to avoid Iquitos, most of them are anxious to clear out. Eight go, in any case, straight to Barbados, and I hope the 'Javari' (of Booth line) can arrive in time at Iquitos to allow of their going in her. Arrived at mouth of Yaguas river (on right bank) at 10.07 a.m. A fine, broad entrance, but no current; turned up it, and steamed in practically dead water for nearly 4 hours up to Recreio, a tiny house on a high bank with a little clearing of yucca round it. The river some 110 yards broad and deep, and only ½ a mile or less current. Took in firewood there. A canoe came down from Triunfo with a man and woman and four Indian boys paddling. All dressed and civilised. The Captain says the boys are Huitotos he "brought" from Chorrera. A gift from Sr. Macedo! There are no Indians — Yaguas — near this. This man gets his *caucho*, or *sernamby*, five days or more up the river by canoe, and then up a *quebrada* where he has "people working". For what, I wonder? We took about 5 balls of *sernamby*, each apparently a man's load. We also took a lot of firewood, which the *Liberal* will pay for, either in cash or by bill. This man, Reigada says, does well. He lives on the forest, the cleared space, the river (with plenty of fish) and — the Indians. He owes nothing to the Company, and gets cash for his rubber.

Triunfo

We stayed here about ¾ of an hour, and then steamed on up to Triunfo, about a mile further up the river. It has also on right bank, on a high cleared space, a kitchen, and actually an ox, the remains of a former sugar cane mill for making *cachaça*, and several lime trees, and a full citron with ripening fruit. Also a lot of pupunha palms, with ripe fruit.[277] Here were several people — three men (so-called Peruvian *blancos*) and a lot of similar skinned women — the sisters, cousins and aunts, and several Huitoto and other Indian *muchachos*. The house a veritable pigsty. The Barbados men landed and bought biscuits and cigarettes with spare cash — I presume the extra amount some of them got for working on after 31st October, the date when their accounts were closed.

I landed with Bishop and Arédomi, and took a photo of the place, and of the sisters, cousins and aunts, promising them copies to their great delight. We bought firewood here, too, and stayed a

[277] *Bactris gasipaes* — A palm tree reaching twenty metres in height, initially isolated, over time it forms a clump of trees. The trunk is covered in rings of black thorns which may also occur on the spathes and veins of the leaves and the axis of the infloresecence. It has long fronds, up to three meters, and flowers of separate sexes of a similar colour and size, appearing on the same cluster. The small conical fruit, red or yellow when ripe, has a thin skin and a yellow or orange edible pulp that is very acidic and is always cooked before it is eaten. Each cluster may produce over two hundred fruit and it is widely seen in market places throughout the Amazon. It was the only palm to be successfully domesticated by the Amazindian who used the root as a vermicide, the trunk for making walls, fences, bows, arrows, clubs and fishing rods while the leaves served for thatching roofs and for weaving baskets.

long time getting it on board. The Captain says there is little or none to be had in Brazil, and he is glad to come up the Yaguas to get it.

The man Fonseca, lately shot in this neighbourhood, was a relation of "our" Fonseca at Sabana. Bishop had heard of him. One of the boys here told Bishop that Fonseca was shot three or four days off "watching the Indians getting rubber", so I presume it is the same thing on a smaller scale. The prisoner is now in Iquitos — the "boy" of this man Fonseca — I expect one of the captive Huitotos that were brought here. The Captain says there are no Yaguas Indians, or any Indians nearer than three days from this up stream. The proprietor of Recreio told me there is a *veradero* across country to Caballa Cocha of ten days, and that a canoe will go up river for seven days, and then there is a *veradero* to Pebas of 2–3 days. Bishop says that when he came down in the *Liberal* in August last, on finishing his time, they brought seven Huitoto slaves and left them at Pebas.

He says, too, that the Pachiko[278] killed only a few weeks ago in Abisinia by Simon Angúlo and Zellada was a Ricagaros indian, whose wife had been outraged by one of the Peruvians, so he went on the warpath, like Katenere and for 2 years had shot at all rubber workers and others. He then gave himself up at Abisinia, being tired of the hunted life, and his end was to be brutally murdered by those two scoundrels a month ago.

Passed Recreio, going down, 4.27 p.m. it is a good mile below Triunfo. The water of the Yaguas is like that of the Igara-paraná, clear enough, although it looks muddy yellow from the deck. Several streams enter near Recreio and Triunfo of darker water. There are no tributary streams from Recreio to the mouth, the Captain says. I reckon Triunfo is about 28 miles up the Yaguas, and seven days in canoe would be about 160 miles above this, where they get the *veradero* to Pebas. The river is probably 250 miles long in extreme length, of which probably 60 miles (even at low water as at present) would be navigable for the *Liberal*, and fully 120 for smaller launches. There is an apparent rise from actual water of 8 to 12 feet. 8 feet more would be normal high water — 12 probably the utmost of flood height.

[278] This seems to be the same figure elsewhere referred to as 'Chico' and 'Rochipo'.

Gusmán's fury

Gusmán, who is on board going away for good, is furious, Bishop says, at them not allowing him to bring his Indian "wife". He vows vengeance, and says he will go and tell the judge everything in Iquitos about the treatment of the Indians. He wants to know if I won't help him about his wife, Bishop says — also to help him to relate everything. Bishop told him I would not do anything in a matter of that kind. I told Bishop to tell him he should go to the Prefect, and tell him all about the way the Indians are treated. I could easily get a dreadful statement from Gusmán, if I liked, but it is not my place to question a Peruvian, and I should not be justified in doing it. Still, it is strange that at the very first this very man should have volunteered to tell me rather than Tizon what Montt was doing at Atenas.

Bishop says Gusmán wants me very much to advise him, and, he adds, that he is sure he will make a row in Iquitos. He is so angry at Macedo refusing to allow him to take his "girl" away with him. Poor little Indian girl, she has returned to her "family" at Ultimo Retiro, Bishop says. Some other ruffian will get her. The man chiefly responsible for driving Pachiko out on the warpath was one Saldana now in Iquitos. He used to abuse the women of the *muchachos* — Pichako was a Sabana *muchacho* — and when his wife was outraged he and others went off on the war path against "the House." They got cartridges from the wives of the employés, so Bishop says. These steal from their husbands, and send out to the rebellious Indians by friendly *muchachos*, who are in with them. Then they lie in wait for *muchachos* and kill them, and get their guns and cartridges, and so it goes on. Pichako had carried this on for 2 years, until he got tired of the flights and shifts of such warfare, and walked into Abisinia and gave himself up. Then came his rumoured league with Diké, another rebellious Indian out on his keeping, and so Juan Zellada and Simon Angúlo first flog him cruelly and then shoot him.

It is a pity I am not going on to Abisinia and Morelia, with the Commission. Bishop says Pichako's brother is still there in chains, and was sent to Morelia the other day to be kept there when the Commission comes to Abisinia. It is a hundred pities I am not going there. I'd make those scoundrels sit up.

There was a considerable look of scare on the faces of the three Peruvian *blancos* up at Triunfo this afternoon when I came into the house. They all knew who I was, because the Recreio man had already addressed me as "Sr. Consul", and I can't help thinking there is no more in the shooting of Fonseca than the simple narrative of Reigada that the boy shot him, because "someone told him to". There has been some of the usual devilment here, too, and these rascals thought, in their ignorant way, (they are all half-castes) that I had come in some way about it. All these people nearly look upon me now as a sort of Enquirer Extraordinary, who has got to the bottom of things.

Slave trade

The Captain tells me that this Fonseca killed here was uncle of the villain now in Sabana. His widow in Iquitos has sold "the business" here on the Yaguas to the man I saw in the house, Azambriga by name — a Portuguese name.

The skipper tells me queer things. He has now a Huitoto sailor, a strong-limbed, very sturdy chap, about 22 or 23 years of age. This youth "belongs" to a man named Grosso in Iquitos, but won't stay with him. He came on board the ship as a sailor last time, and Grosso came and wanted the Captain to give him a promissory note for £50 for the boy! Reigada refused, and told him he could take the man to the Police if he liked. He said Grosso dared not, because they could not have kept him. He then told Grosso he was going to pay the boy himself, too, not give the wages to him, the master and Grosso could only grin.

Reigada admits that there are plenty of Huitoto women and boys who have been sold in Iquitos, that there is always a market for them. I asked how it could be, since they could always claim their freedom, and he only laughed. Men were known to give £40 for a boy or girl, so he says. He then wanted to tell me of the two Huitoto sailors he had last voyage, when I came up. Neither is with him now. One is staying with the elder pilot, Manuel Lomas, at Punchana. When Reigada paid him off with £6 last trip he asked this boy what he would do with the money, and the boy said he was going to buy "a cap and a pair of pantaloons." The skipper then told him the money was sufficient to buy 20 caps and pantaloons, and he only laughed and said he would give it for one of each. So Reigada handed the money to Manuel, and asked him to look after the boy, 'Julio' is his name, and see he was not robbed. He said "the Jews" in Iquitos would not rob him, as they did all the Indians. The other boy "belonged" to the present Portmaster of Iquitos, who had got him from the Putumayo somehow or other, but he would not stay with him, and "came to sea". He has now gone back to the Portmaster, because he was ill. Bolívar I asked after. He was taken to Iquitos, and ran away there on arrival. Reigada says he wants to be free, and will not return to Putumayo. Pablo Zumaeta tried to get him, but failed, as he cleared out promptly. Well done, Bolívar.

The younger pilot, Simon Pisango, has changed his name to Perez — not Pizarro.

Arédomi bitten by sandflies

Poor Arédomi is bitten badly by sandflies, and has just been to see me for the Colonel's lotion I got in Manaos from the old man before leaving. I rubbed it all over his chest and arms. He is washing up plates on board, and making himself useful, and smiles constantly — very happy. We have brought a young girl from Triunfo, a sister of Mrs. Azambuja, I think.

I intend asking Reigada why Zubiarr left the services of the Company. Whiffen stated to FO it was for dealing in stores from the Chorrera, poaching on Pablo Zumaeta's and Macedo's special private preserve. I have no doubt it was so, and I think in his actual mood of confidences Reigada will let it out to me. The whole game is pretty nearly up, and they all know it, and will, if I press, tell me pretty nearly all — one against the other. They are a fine pack of rascals.

Re-enter the Putumayo

Re-entered the Putumayo at 7.35 p.m. We have lost 9½ hours up and down the Yaguas, but I am glad I got a glimpse of it. There seems to be more palm trees on the banks of the tributaries than of the main river. The evening was close and the moon obscured. My little *chiviclis* is quite jolly. I let him run about all day, and at night only is he put into his wretched little tin cage. Saw some splendid butterflies today — different from any we got up the Igara-paraná — one small variety of orange and black round spots was exceedingly fine, and a great big yellow ochre and burnt Sienna winged chap made quite a flutter along the deck as we lay at Recreio and Triunfo.[279]

[279] The collection of butterflies that Casement made during his journey in the Igara-paraná was eventually presented to the Zoological Museum of Dublin and remains part of the collection.

ON BOARD THE *LIBERAL* — SATURDAY, 19TH NOVEMBER

Arrival at Brazilian frontier

We got to the Brazilian frontier post at 2 a.m. and stayed there some time, and then on to the next Brazilian so-called military post — where another delay occurred. I got up and noticed that the river seemed considerably lower than when we passed up in September. The Captain says the Amazon is much higher. He reckons it 15 hours downward steaming to the Amazon from the Brazilian frontier, or from 120–130 miles. By this down-stream reckoning of Reigada's the distance from Chorrera to the Amazon is only about 570 miles. He reckons 8 knots only down stream, but I think the vessel does more, especially in the Putumayo itself, where the current is stronger than in the Igara-paraná. The Captain says he lost 3 hours altogether at these two places, as he bought firewood at the military post.

Passed several Brazilian *seringueiros*' places — huts among the trees on shore, on right bank nearly all. A fine big river at 11 a.m. called 'Uruté', and then a long side reach of the river, into which we steamed looking for firewood at a place of a Colombian — a hut in a clearing. This is the Ticuna Indian[280] country, but the Captain says these people mostly do their own rubber getting. One place we passed at the mouth of the river — their private property — the usual "estate" nonsense. Everyone we pass is a lawless squatter. This place is served by two steamers from Manaos. The Captain says up the river they have Ticuna Indians who form the "labour" of this place. We stopped again at 1 p.m. on right bank for firewood. The skipper pays £3 per 1000 billets = 1½ tons, he says. This last place is a tiny open hut in a patch of maize taller than its roof, in a clearing of about 30 yards square. The men got fruit and sugar cane — the old man with a half Indian wife, and two grown up sons, the Captain says was once a Peruvian from Tarapoto,[281] but now talks Portuguese — as most of these Peruvian or Colombian squatters here do. They have lost their Spanish, so

[280] Ticuna or (Tucuna) Indians occupied the forest on the northern side of the Solimões. First mentioned by Cristobal d'Acuña, and frequently referred to by Bates *op. cit.*, the most important study of these people was carried out by Curt Nimuendajú (1883–1945), who eventually died while living among them in 1945. See C. Nimuendajú, *The Tukuna* (University of California Publications in American Archaeology and Ethnology 1952), also H.S.I Vol III *The Tucuna*.

[281] About one hundred and twenty miles south-east of Rioja in the Peruvian *montaña*, Tarapoto is nowadays a centre of northern Peru's cocaine industry.

he says. There is no life on the Peruvian Putumayo, but here, on the Brazilian Putumayo, we pass huts and clearings every few miles. Also we have met several canoes, one quite a big one going up stream under sail, another, going down, had a middle-aged negro, his wife, and a boy. He waved many salutations to us. The forest is much loftier than up the Igara-paraná, and there must be a good deal of rubber here, but "no Indians".

At 3 p.m. we are approaching a very fine line of trees.

Leavine tells atrocity stories

Leavine today, called up by me, simply confirms the very worst stories against Normand — of burning and dashing brains out, and all the rest of it. The man is an absolute fiend. I find our friend, Vasquez Torres, as we thought him — the brute from Atenas that Gielgud, Barnes and we all disliked so much, — is really Alejandro Vasquez, one of the most infamous of the ruffians referred to in the Hardenburg document. He is charged by Collantes[282] with revolting murders.

Bishop says Velarde gave Aristides Rodriguez S/P 7,000 to get Sabana when he went away! Aristides had got 30,000 kilos in one *fabrico* out of Sabana, and Velarde thought he would do the same, and so he tipped him £700 for this Section. Truly an interesting method for an English Company! The high forest land proves, on rounding a bend, to be quite a high sloping hill, cleared from the waterside up to near the top with houses showing — the first real Brazilian settlement I have seen. There is smoke at several of the huts we pass, showing where the rubber is being smoked.

3.40. Passed the high ground. It is quite a civilised little place, with steps, and a paling up to a neat little house, with the verandah painted blue and white, and the figure of a man and woman inside. The hill is cleared up to the summit, about 100 feet above the river, and is planted with bananas. Lower down, 50 yards, is a second clearing of cassava, and an open hut, of the workman or men.

We are steaming well, I should think doing close on 10 knots with a fair current with us. Tonight, about 9 or 10, we ought to be in the Amazon, and turn our noses up stream for that dreary stretch of close on 600 miles to Iquitos, where I have no wish at all to go. I questioned Leavine, P. Lawrence, Batson and Crichlow

[282] See Hardenburg *op. cit.*, pp.262–63. The description of Vasquez's murder of three Indian women with sticks of wood was so disgusting that it was edited out of Collantes's statement.

again today upon some points I was reading in the Hardenburg document. Incidentally, Lawrence, who has been at Chorrera since 1904, confirms the beatings and floggings of Indians there when loading and unloading the steamers.

Murder of the Ocainas

The murder of the Ocainas Indians and the burning of them, some not quite dead, took place there in 1903. Bishop says he often heard it spoken of. Rafael Larrañaga[283] took a leading part in it. The Ocainas were charged with killing Colombians.

Casement's verdict on the Putumayo criminals

There is no doubt the Hardenburg papers are in the main true. Here and there details are wrongly given. There are lies and exaggerations, but the main facts and charges are substantially correct. Moreover, hundreds of crimes not recorded there have taken place. Normand, Aguero, Fonseca, Montt, Jiménez, the two Rodriguez brothers and Martinengui, have between them, murdered several thousand of these unhappy beings. There is no doubt of it. Tizon admitted to me in Chorrera last week that the two Rodriguez "had killed hundreds of Indians", and that Arana gave them 50% of the produce of these two sections, S. Catalina and Sabana. Normand is again and again charged by the Barbados men with killing many hundreds. Leavine today said "over 500", that he had seen 20 Indians killed in five days in Matanzas alone, and the dead bodies eaten by the dogs and stinking round the house, so that he could not eat his food. These seven monsters have probably killed by shooting, flogging, beheading, burning, and got rid of by starvation some 5,000 Indians in the last seven years. Barnes said the Indians of the Company numbered 10,000 when he came, and there were "nothing like it now", and he has been here only two or three years at outside. Fonseca had killed hundreds, too, — and Martinengui.

The least criminal are probably O'Donnell, Miranda and Alcosta — of the rest it were hard to choose, save that Montt lacked probably the courage of the other monsters. And this is done in the name of civilization and industrial development!

[283] Rafael Larrañaga was the son of Benjamin Larrañaga and was part of the initial party of Colombian *caucheros* which entered the Putumayo forests.

Decision to leave Barbadians in Brazil

I have decided to leave the men at the Javari — conte qui conte. There are probably two of the Booth steamers now at Iquitos — the *Athualpa* and *Javary*, and I hope one or other will be downward bound, perhaps within a day of my arrival there. I will hear something of them at the places we stay at tomorrow on the bank of the Amazon.

RIVER AMAZON — SUNDAY — NOVEMBER 20TH

Maturas

We entered the Amazon about 2 a.m. and soon after got to Colonia Rio Jano, in the dark. We whistled there from mid-stream, but I think no one came off, and so we went on. At 6.15 we got to Maturas, where we stayed for firewood. I went on shore, and visited the church. No priest for three years, and the two men who came to show me round said there were many children to be baptised. Also their dead were buried without rites. I said I should see if anything could be done in Manaos. The church built by themselves — they apologised for its poverty — poor souls. All are half-castes — chiefly mixed Indian and white blood. Saw no negroes, but some pure whites. The place is one street of about 20 huts, well built of boards and palm thatch. The church has a big Cross in front — "*nossa cruz*", as one said, and two bells on a piece of wood outside. 17 children lately died from measles — otherwise healthy. A fine stream of black water — 80 yards broad, — comes in there. They work *caucho* and *borracha* up this river; about half-a-dozen pure Indian families — *mansos*[284] — I was told, lived there, but no "Indios bravos". They have long since gone — gentle, kind-hearted, timid Indios bravos! Many children. I got coffee from one of my guides, and his children looked happy. The house clean and well-kept; a sewing machine in every house, a child's coffin being made in one. One of my guides — a man of 50 — had never been in Manaos; was born here at Amatura. The other was a Clarence, and had visited Manaos more than once and lived there.

A heavy drizzle all the time — like a Scotch mist — very wetting rain. The river has risen since September, but I cannot yet see how much until we get to some point where I stayed before. Matural, these people say, is Amáturá. There is a fine church up at Belem —

[284] *Manso* means tame, timid or harmless as opposed to Indians *bravos* — untamed, aggressive and dangerous.

a little higher, as the Captain says. It cost S/P 30,000 = £3,000, built by one man. A priest, he says, has gone up the Javari quite lately, and will stop at every place and baptise, &c.

We heard that two English steamers had gone up, to Iquitos, the last week. They passed Amáturá. One of them on 14th, so my guide said. This may be the *Javary*, due there on 15th, and to leave 21st.

I spoke to Mathias, the Brazilian Customs Officer, about leaving the men at Javari, and he says all right, he will do his best, but there is no house and little or no food! A fine outlook for them.

Steamed on all day. Close to right bank most of the time. Saw a troop of *ronsocos*, really capivari,[285] just below São Paulo de Olivença at 5 near the mouth of the Jundiatuba River, which enters in a fine stream close on 200 yards broad. Many houses along the banks, of half-caste Indians and often pure Indians of the Ticuna tribe, but all clothes just like ordinary Brazilian squatters. From Jundiatuba up to São Paulo is near an hour's steaming, and a lot of palm-thatched houses along the bluff for a couple of miles below S. Paulo. We passed closely into that dirty little township of evil memories (See Bates' description of it in 1856.)[286] It is a shocking thought that this wretched agglomeration of mean huts — they can be called nothing else — and dirty neglected foreshore, represents 100 years of Brazilian citizenship. In 1827 Lt Maw found a *delegado* here. It is now the second town on the Brazilian Amazon after Manaos, but the headquarters of the district have been moved, the Captain tells me, up to Benjamin Constant on the

---

[285] Capivara are the largest of the Amazon mammals and the world's largest rodent — the name means "master of the grasses". Average weight around 50 kilos with front legs shorter than the hind limbs, no tail and the eyes, ears and nostrils set high on the head so that they are out of the water when the animal swims. Partially webbed feet help the rather clumsy animal move easily through the water. They are still intensively hunted throughout the Amazon. Casement possibly introduced the first pair to Dublin zoo.

[286] São Paulo de Olivença is the town where Bates was forced to turn back towards England as a result of an attack of ague. His impressions of the place were not good, "The inhabitants were utterly debased, the few Portuguese and other immigrants having, instead of promoting industry, adopted the lazy mode of life of the Indians, spiced with the practice of a few strong vices of their own introduction ... The principal residents ... were the priest, a white from Pará, who spent his days and most of his nights in gambling and rum-drinking, corrupting the young fellows and setting the vilest example to the Indian ... I remained at St Paulo five months; five years would not have been sufficient to exhaust the treasures of its neighbourhood in Zoology and Botany. Although now a forest-rambler of ten years experience, the beautiful forest which surrounds this settlement gave me as much enjoyment as if I had only just landed in a tropical country."

Javarí, to the great disgust of the São Paulo folk. These, the skipper says, have preserved their habits and customs as described by Bates. When a launch puts into their beach they crowd on board to drink and gamble, and try to get the money of the crew.

Brazilian inflation

The Captain told me at dinner that the Brazilian Customs Officer on board makes him pay £1 sterling now at S/12.50. This is a further drop of 2 milreis in the pound, since I left Manaos on 17th August last. When will it end? The customs man says the latest payers report the milreis at 1/6d. now. I shall be ruined if I have to live in Brazil now. Twelve milreis to the pound is a drop of 25% in my income since I left Rio in March, when the exchange was 16 to the pound.[287] How can trade of any commercial dealing flourish in a country where the value of the medium of exchange jumps in such a way? The variation from day to day and week to week can easily upset the best commercial venture in the world.[288]

Peruvian man-of-war, America

At 9 p.m. a big steamer passed down river close to us. She had green and red light, which the Captain says none of the river craft carry — only sea-going vessels. He thinks it is the 'Javari' outward bound again — for Barbados and New York. A great pity if this is so. I hardly think it can be, although the masts were high and the funnel black. I think it was the Peruvian man-of-war *America*[289]

---

[287] Casement left the Brazilian capital Rio de Janeiro and his position as the British consul-general in March 1910 and after travelling by train south to São Paulo and then into Argentina to Buenos Aires and Mar del Plata for a holiday he returned to Europe, stopping briefly in San Salvador de Bahia. Despite the fact that Casement remained consul-general of Brazil until his resignation from the Foreign Office in June 1913 he would never see Rio de Janeiro again. A situation that suited him since he detested the place.

[288] Despite frequent stabilization programmes, most recently the Plano Real, chronic inflation has remained the curse of the Brazilian economy throughout the twentiethth century and, indeed, throughout most of Latin America.

[289] The Peruvian gunboat *America*, constructed by the Camel Laird Company based in Birkenhead, Liverpool, arrived in Peru in 1905 and was immediately deployed in patrolling the waterways of the Peruvian Amazon. Equipped with two large cannons, it was capable of carrying up to 50 soldiers and was one of a number of British-built gunboats sold to the Peruvians at the start of the century. See Jorge Ortiz Sotelo, *La Cañonera America* (Lima 1989); also Fernando Romero, *Iquitos y la Fuerza Naval de la Amazonia* (1830–1933). Britain was almost single-handedly responsible for arming both the Peruvian army and navy in the sixty-five years before the outbreak of the First World War and the *America* played a dominant role in 1911 in the war against Colombia and the battle of La Pedrera.

bound, perhaps, from Iquitos to the Putumayo. It has rained most of the day — a dreary drizzle like a Scotch mist, fine and wetting.

ON SOLIMÕES — MONDAY, 21ST NOVEMBER

Firewood

We stopped a long time in the night getting firewood at Boa Vista, and did not leave it until 6 a.m. in a drizzle of rain like yesterday morning. The Captain complains of the increase in price of things here in Brazil. Not content with the milreis rising in value, these people now ask the most absurd prices for everything they possess. Here with the biggest world of firewood in existence, a forest literally without bounds, and dry wood for the mere felling of it at their doors, they asked us yesterday MR$ 72 per 1,000 faggots, roughly 1½ tons of firing. This represents at 12,500 almost exactly £6, or £4 a ton, rather more than coal is at Iquitos! The skipper refused to pay this, and got the wood for less, by pressing gold on the man.

The landing list

I asked this morning what men wished to stay at Javari, and who would go on to Iquitos? I find that all but Philip Lawrence now wish to stay at the Javari, and go down to Manaos by first boat. Only Bishop and John Brown, with his wife and child, will go on with me, and Philip Lawrence the ex-cook of Chorrera. No danger from these if interrogated, and little or no danger of their being interrogated under any circumstances.

Here is the list now, as I have given it to the skipper for his landing lists at Javari and Iquitos.

LIST OF PASSENGERS DISEMBARKING AT
ESPERANZA — 21st November, 1910.

James Mapp — wife and child
Allan Davis — wife and child
Alfred Hoyte — wife and child
Reuben Phillips and wife
James Lane
Clifford Quintin
Joshua Dyall and child
Sydney Morris
Evelyn Batson
Augustus Walcott

Preston Johnson
Edward Crichlow
Westerman Leavine
Joseph Minggs

14 men — 4 women — 4 children

The following go on to Iquitos:

F. Bishop
John Brown, wife and child
P. Lawrence, also two indian boys
Arédomi and Omarino

The chief difficulty is the food question, as I gather there is no food at Esperanza. I mention it to the Captain and find he has plenty of spare grub he can sell. He brought an extra stock, he says, and did not leave it at Chorrera. I calculate quantities with Bishop and Allan Davis and James Mapp, and decide on buying the following approximately:

140 lbs rice
80 lbs beans
70 tins of meat
100 tins of sardines
1 Barrel biscuits

Salt, sugar, tea and 10 tins milk for the infants.

I will leave Davis and Mapp in charge of the party. I have written letters for the Captains of downgoing steamers to convey the men to Manaos and recover the passage money from the British Vice-Consul at Manaos, and I wrote to latter asking him to look after the men until I arrive. So everything is ready, except to get the men's cheques (or *giros*) on the Company's branch in Iquitos, and then I am ready for everything.

Palmares

4 p.m. — We have had quite an interesting day. At 10 a.m. we stopped at a lofty bank on left shore of the river, steep and fully 35 feet above present level, with steps at top. This is Palmares, a line of huts below Belem. Here we got firewood and I went on shore. The two houses at this point were very cosy and well fitted, the most comfortable one could imagine for this locality, and such people — the soil amazingly rich, everything planted looked gi-

gantic. Sugar cane as thick as one's arm almost, and a great variety of fruits, and hibiscus flowers too. A turtle pond, with plenty of turtles, 25 bought this morning, one of the men said. Fine pawpaws, and delicious pink cherry peppers and pineapples as fine as Pernambuco[290] ones. The yucca or cassava very fine too and plenty of hens and chickens, some of which we bought. I saw a couple of lovely green parrots with blue heads, and, of course, their wings quite uncut.[291] They were perched on one of the houses, and very tame. The owner asked £4 each! Then a very fine *mutum*[292] — a beauty — and he was offered for £2, but I declined. Finally, the *dono da casa* came down to £1, but I further declined. It was not the price so much as the distance to carry him, and I believe I can get one in Pará cheaper.[293]

Everyone nearly on shore enjoying this beautiful natural history store. The forest round was lovely, only a tiny clearing, but each yard of it fruitful. Near the edge of the cliff the grass grew luxuriantly, and there was a patch big enough to feed a cow and sheep or goats. These people might live in absolute clover, if they would only work. They do nothing but rubber. "The rubber pays for all", just as in the South it is "coffee pays for all". There everything needed is bought with money from coffee — here it is pretty much the same, except that even the things needed cannot be bought, so that the money goes in absurd tomfoolery and waste. Then just up above us we can see Belem with its far famed church costing £3,000. This corresponds to a nobleman's private chapel at home — without the chaplain. No priest within a 1,000 miles, and Belem itself is only a one man's place — what in West Africa we should call a "factory". I don't object to the Church, however, it shows some mind and soul above the ordinary along this melancholy river, but most of these people, when they have money,

[290] Pernambuco is a province of north-east Brazil still famous for its succulent, sweet-tasting pineapples.

[291] From Casement's brief description this would appear to be the Blue-fronted Amazon (*Amazona aestiva aestiva*) — one of the more common species of Amazon parrot. Once captured, most birds have their wings cut so they are easier to domesticate.

[292] A type of Amazon chicken.

[293] Casement brought a number of birds and animals on his Amazon trips, many of which he later gave to Dublin Zoo. Pará remained, however, the main marketplace for captured wild animals. Today, the largest black market economy in the Amazon after illegal wood sales is in the sale of endangered birds and animals. On his 1911 trip to the Amazon Casement brought a hyacinthine macaw, which spent a lot of time perched on his shoulder and which he eventually gave to William Cadbury.

waste it on jaunts to Manaos, or on silly things quite unneeded. Houses with no beds, never a book within a week's journey or a schoolmaster, but accordions that cost £10, and a diamond ring, or gold watch chain for flashing down the pretentious sidewalks of Manaos, and often much more paid for much worse there — ladies from Poland.[294] Food at this place is lavished on these people by Nature. I never saw such vegetable profusion, right up to their doors, otherwise they would be starving, for it is not the labour of their hands gives them this.

Ucayali beans

At Iquitos, the skipper says, you often pay S/10 (£1) for 25 lbs. weight of Ucayali beans. These beans are very similar to the brown bean of Portugal, and constitute one of the chief articles of diet along the river. They are often imported, he tells me, from Portugal, more and more, in fact. In front of us here at Palmares stretch one of the great island sandbanks of the Solimões. This one is over ten miles long I should think. It goes far out of sight, and we have been steaming between it and this northern or left shore of the river for a long time. It is still exposed to a great height above water, and is now covered with arrow grass and shorter, softer grass. There must be some thousands of acres of this splendid soil on this one island, and for six to seven months each year it lies there fallow. Beans could grow like wild fire in it, and a score of other things. It is the silt of all the banks and lands right up to the Andes washed down each flood, and is rich as the Nile lands. All that is wanting is human labour to sow it. With beans at £1 for 25 lbs. in Iquitos, here alone is a field of profitable labour, far better than spending dreary and miserable days (at the best) in the depths of the forest gathering rubber milk, or (at the most) murdering and torturing the poor forest Indians to make them do this gathering.

Mafra, the rubber magnate

We left Palmares at 11, and steamed on past Belem at noon. It is a fine clearing, belongs to a man named Mafra of Italian descent, but a Peruvian, like many of these Solimões magnates. A fine tiled house, and some big iron-roofed stores, and a line of palm-thatched huts for the workpeople — just beyond it a river mouth.

[294] This reference is to the large number of Polish prostitutes in Manaos during the rubber boom. In March 1997 Manaos was once again denounced in the Brazilian press as a centre for child prostitution and child sex tourism.

Every proprietor has his own river, with a steam launch snugly stowed away. The clearing round the houses a big one, and the famous church has two towers. The skipper says the priest when he comes here makes a good thing out of it, as Mafra is devout, and has a regular flare-up on these bi-annual occasions. He works rubber on this river and another beyond it, which we come to at 12.30. This river is broader, fully 160 yards broad at mouth, and has an *alvarenga* or lighter anchored in the middle of the mouth. This to receive cargo — goods or rubber — for or from the passing steamers, also to guard the mouth of Mafra's main *quebrada*. Every "estate" its own river, and woe betide the stranger or rubber pirate who intrudes. This one our chief pilot, Manoel Lomas, says he has ascended for 6 hours in a big steam launch, or say 50 miles, at high river. He says Mafra owns Ticuna Indians up it, and they work the rubber. No Brazilian Government launch, I presume, has ever, since the world began, been up this river, and, God knows, what may go on there, in spite of the Church and its towers out here on the high banks of the Solimões. Mafra himself may be a godly man, but when it comes to owning Indians in these Amazon forests I fear for the body of the Indians, more even than for the soul of his owner.

A sandbank

The great sandbank continues far beyond Belem, bounding our left view up stream for miles. One such bank of soil — for it is not sand but a rich blackish soil — with a thousand chinamen upon it, would feed a kingdom. There is no felling of timber or clearing required. The great river does that. It just piles up millions of tons of gleaming drift, washed clean and harrowed and shining as the water subsides from the crest, and leaves them stretched out for miles to sun and rain for enough time annually to raise two crops each year. Before the water covers them again they are covered with rich grain, and as each rising river will gradually deposit more silt, the central parts rise annually, and then first the embauba or sloth tree comes, to be gradually followed by all the forest growths until one sandbank turns into an island forest. This island will some day again disappear, mile by mile, tumbling and swirling away with topping trees and ripping leagues of forest into some new opened chasm of the mighty waterway; channels that this year have 60 feet of water, and are the main route for the Liverpool steamers will close up, and become island the year after.

Casement's millennial dream for the Amazon: Teutonic civilization

Now, as I write, a stretch of fully 4 miles broad of river opens to left and right between the islands. I am sure of this, that in a reorganised South America, when the Monroe Doctrine has been challenged by Germany and happily dispatched under her shot and shell, the valley of the Amazon will become one of the greatest granaries of the world. Also, too, I believe it will be peopled with a happy race of men. It supplies practically for the asking all the essentials of human existence, and this in a climate that for an equatorial latitude is superior to anything else in the world. All it needs is the touch of a vanished hand.[295] The Portuguese (and Peruvians and others) have killed off in a shameful and cowardly fashion the aboriginal Indians, who, had the Jesuits[296] gained the day over Pombal[297] and the Colonists, would have today numbered millions. The murderers have put nothing in the place of those whom they destroyed, neither civilization to replace savagery, nor white humanity to replace the copper — all they could do and have done was to pull down, not to build up or create. This mighty river, and far beyond its shores of this great continent, awaits the

---

[295] A passing allusion to Tennyson, "Break, Break, Break" (*c.* 1834):
And the stately ships go on/To their haven under the hill;/But O for the touch of a vanish'd hand,/And the sound of a voice that is still!

[296] In 1608 the Jesuits were authorized by Philip III to christianize the Guaraní and a network of missions or *reducciones* was established throughout the territories of southern Brazil and present-day Paraguay. Each mission was set up as a self-sufficient theocracy governed by two Jesuit missionaries, one charged with domestic affairs, the other directing spiritual matters. Though the Indians were under the constant supervision of the Jesuits they were at least offered protection from the white settlers and *bandeirantes* (Brazilian slaver hunters). In 1759–60 the Portuguese crown, feeling threatened by the power of the Jesuits, ordered their expulsion from Portugal and Brazil and seven years later they were expelled from their missions in Spanish territories. The most effective missionary on the Upper Amazon was Father Samuel Fritz (1654–1724). Born in Bohemia, he was the first man to preach among the Amazindians living between the rivers Napo and Negro and set up the first mission on the Putumayo. See *Journal of the Travels and Labours of Father Samuel Fritz in the River Amazons between 1686 & 1723* (Hakluyt 1922). Casement sympathized greatly with the Jesuit cause and considered their missions as the only example of successful colonization in the Americas. He expressed this view in an unpublished book review for the *Manchester Guardian* written as he sailed from England for the Canary Islands at the end of 1912 — a draft of the review is still preserved in the National Library of Ireland {MS 13,073 [10/ii]}.

[297] Marquis of Pombal — Sebastião José de Carvalho e Mello (1699–1782) — was a Portuguese statesman and Prime Minister from 1756 to 1777. Regarded as Portugal's first enlightened despot, he tried to implement liberal and anticlerical legislation and ordered the expulsion of the Jesuits from Portuguese colonies.

hand of civilization. Four hundred years of the Spaniard at its sources, and 300 years of the Portuguese at its mouth have turned it first into a hell, and then into a desert. No sight could be pleasanter than the flag of Teutonic civilization advancing into this wilderness. The Americans have got their part of America, and it will take them all their time to civilize themselves. Germany, with her 70,000,000 of virile men has much to do for mankind besides giving us music and military shows. Let loose her pent up energies in this Continent, and God help the rats who have gnawed at it so long. Law and order would have meaning then, and justice and labour advancing up this mighty river would subdue the forest and found cities, and realise here in these glorious wastes the glowing words with which Bates closes his book — "for I hold to the opinion that, although humanity can reach an advanced state of culture only by battling with the inclemencies of nature in high latitudes, it is under the Equator alone that the perfect race of the future attain to complete fruition of man's beautiful heritage — the earth."

I share Bates' belief, and I believe that the people for the task are "neither Saxon nor Italian", but our friends the Germans. Not the Americans or Canadians, or anything Latin or Latinised. The curse of this Continent has been its Latinization. With everything in its favour — incomparably ahead of the desolate prairies of the northern America, already peopled by millions of gentle, docile and industrious beings — what have 400 years of "Latin civilization" done for it? Reduced the many millions of the Andean plateaux to a tenth of their number and to a condition of slavery that is unique among white governing races of the East, and murdered the wilder dwellers of the wilderness in every conceivable barbarous manner — not in order to replace them with white settlers and agriculturists, but solely in order to enslave their survivors in the interest of a handful of sordid, mean-souled and ignorant squatters. And to this has succeeded the pillage of the forests — vegetable filibustering replacing human filibustering, in order that the ignorant mob of Pará, Manaos and Iquitos may visit Paris or Lima, and indulge the sensual appetite with the vices of both.[298]

---

[298] Casement's support for Teutonic civilization as opposed to Latin or British colonization was a preference born of his increasing disillusionment with the British empire and his closer association with the movement for Irish independence. But in the times he lived he was not alone in holding such an opinion. In 1911 Casement began to argue that Britain's increasingly anti-German stance would

On Solimões — Tuesday, November 22nd

Disembarkation of the Barbadians

We did not arrive at Esperanza until 1 a.m. this morning. I had long since turned in, and had hoped we should lie there until daylight, so as to arrange for the landing of the men. However, the Captain called me to say the young Customs Officer in charge had very willingly allowed the men to land, and to sling their hammocks under the house. This young man came on board, and in true Luso–Brazilian amity embraced me, and I cordially responded, each patting the other's back. It was a pleasure to see the frank brown face of a decent-looking warm-hearted Brazilian, after the unmitigated murder type I've been accustomed to in the Peruvian Putumayo. He begged me to give directions to the men not to get drunk. We landed plenty of food for them, and I wrote orders on any down going steamer and to Mr Dening, the Vice-Consul in Manaos, to look after the men on arrival and pay the conveying vessel.

The S.S. *Javary*, I learned to my regret, had gone down river four days ago, and the *Athualpa* had passed up to Iquitos on 13th — eight days ago! It will take us all our time to catch her even now.

Bishop's puppy

Bishop reports two occurrences typical of these people. In the night one of the crew threw overboard his pup — the fat dog Greenidge gave him at Chorrera. Such a cowardly act! He thinks it is the 2nd cook — a tall, lanky, pock-marked Peruvian of pure white blood, looks like a weedy Spaniard. It appears this coward had threatened to throw the dog over if it came near the galley. At 9.30 p.m. it was playing with Bishop, when he went below, but at 1 a.m. when the men were roused for shore it was gone. Poor, podgy baby! It has met a horrid death, either by his young struggle in the great river or else eaten by an alligator.

---

bring the world to war, a prediction that proved correct. Nevertheless, Casement's view of German civilization was overly romantic. German methods of imperialism, mainly in the Cameroons, and in south-west and east Africa, led to disgraceful crimes against ethnic minorities and tribal people. The German suppression of the Hereros uprising in Namibia between 1904–07 is now held to be the first genocide committed by Germans this century. Casement's views on Germany were most concisely argued in an essay "Why I went to Germany", written just before he left Germany for Ireland in April 1916 and published a week after his execution in the *Evening Mail* (New York) on 10 August 1916.

Dyall's son

Second circumstance — the attempt of the Chief Engineer of this vessel to get hold of Dyall's baby son. Dyall is a blackguard, it is true. Bishop says Dyall was going to "give" his son to the Chief Engineer, as the Indian woman on board tells him he is not its father, that it is the son of an Indian man, as well as of an Indian woman. For this reason Dyall does not treat it well, and the Chief Engineer tried to get it from Dyall. I gave orders at 1 a.m. that, as Dyall had brought the child from Chorrera as his, he should certainly look after it, and refused to allow this deal in humanity. So the little Dyall disembarked too along with the rest. We got off at 3 a.m. in a clear enough night, and soon reached the second or main mouth of the Javari, where a great conflict of rivers occurs. There is often an overfall here, but tonight none — only a terribly strong current. Although the distance from Esperanza to Tabatinga is only 6 miles we took 3 hours doing it!

Tabatinga — The Brazilian/Peruvian frontier

At Tabatinga at 6 a.m. with the Brazilian green flag flying, and the Khaki-clad artillerymen of "the great Republic". The Sergeant, a handsome young *caboclo*, with five red stripes on his arm, came quickly on board, and we got our papers on the instant, and off again. He was very spick and span, with starched collar and cuffs showing, and well polished boots, picking his steps through the mud and sedge of the bank to the gangway. A true type of Brazilian — clean, nice-looking, and conceited, but with amiability stamped on his features.

Delays at Leticia

On to Leticia, the Peruvian frontier post, 1 mile up stream, and here we were delayed over three hours. We got there at 7 a.m. and did not get away until near 11. I could not understand the reason for delay as the skipper had told me he intended pressing on at all costs to catch the *Athualpa* in Iquitos. He told me after we had got under way, saying he was ashamed to have to confess to me what kind of authorities his country possessed.

Peruvian deserters

It appears that last night four of the *cholo* soldiers of his garrison had deserted — escaped down to Brazil in a canoe. They had been on the opposite bank of the river in a hut to arrest contraband at night that was alleged to be slipping by there in canoes, and they took the opportunity themselves to slip off in a canoe, and had gained the sacred soil of Brazil. Well, the Commissario and the Peruvian Lieutenant in charge of the force at Leticia had actually insisted on trying to compel the *Liberal* to go back down river, into Brazilian waters, to catch the 4 deserters. The Captain had refused, pointing out the illegality and the pains and penalties attaching — how it was quite impossible for a Peruvian vessel to arrest men on Brazilian soil, and that the *Liberal* would herself be arrested. They had declared they would take soldiers and manage it themselves! All they wanted was the vessel to return so that they might chase the deserters! His refusal had so preoccupied them that it was near 11 before he got away.

I hope these four deserters will be happy in Brazil. They have escaped from the vile slavery of Peru to a better life. Perhaps they are the very same young Cholos I saw first at Leticia in August, to whom I gave cigarettes. Anyhow, I am very glad that these young men have got away to a country where they will be free, and may earn good wages too.

It was very hot at Leticia indeed, and a cooling rain storm gathered and fell soon after we left. The river there has risen some 8 feet I should think since I passed up in August and found the *Esperanza* high and dry. The sticks, &c. of the framework she erected show their noses out of water, but the bank itself is completely out of sight.

Ancient Loreto — Pinheiro confesses

Many beautiful butterflies on board; some I have not yet seen, quite different from our lovely Igara-paraná varieties, notably today a green and black swallow-tail of vivid colouring, and a white and black, beautifully ringed. The Captain says the river has fallen an inch or two last day, but otherwise is rising. The big rise of the Upper Ucayali is due now and should shortly begin to appear down here. Anyhow there is now plenty of water for the *Athualpa* to steam by night as well as by day, so if I can catch her at Iquitos we should be in Iquitos in 3½ days, not bad going for 1200 miles. We stopped at a wooding place on north bank, in the midst of the ancient Loreto, and bought 1500 billets of wood from a Spaniard at S/P 25 per 1000. This is £2.10.0 as against £3 (cheapest) in Brazil, but the Captain says the Brazilian wood is better value. The clearing we stopped at is clearly old, the grass short and clipped by 4 head of cattle. No plantation at all, but many popunha palms and with ripe fruit too.[299] We got a lot of these — my little boy Omarino climbed one clean stemmed palm, from which the spikes had been removed. He tied my handkerchief round his ankle, and went up in a jiffy. The Brazilian negro, who was at Providencia when Mapp and the other Barbados men were to be ambushed by Aguero's cannibal *muchachos* is on board, going away after five years' service in the Company. He was very busy getting the fruit off the nearest palm with a long stick I passed up to him. I wandered further into the cleared space to gather some flowers, and saw two lovely black and yellow birds up a tree, by several hanging nests. They did not fly away but looked at us. Pinheiro came after me and told me the name of the bird — Jaura, I think he called it, and then he hurriedly said he wished to make a "declaration" to me of what he had seen in the Putumayo during his five years. He spoke with bitterness, and I gathered at once that here was another, like Gusmán, who desired to give the show away. I said nothing to Pinheiro, but later on told Bishop that if the man came to see me in Iquitos I should find out from him the facts as to the attempt to ambush the Barbados men, but that, of course, any declaration he had to make must be before his own Consul. It is another witness, however, ready to speak out, and that is all for good. I have broken into the Den of Thieves, and there will be many now will turn King's Evidence if the Prefect wants the truth.

A splendid race

I gave the Cholo sailors some cigarettes while they were getting the firewood on board — or rather I gave a packet to one sailor, and he at once distributed all round, keeping only one for himself. They are fine lads, always smiling and willing, and if properly handled by decent white men, would make a splendid race. The owner of the house was away when we arrived, but he returned in time to get payment for his firewood — a Spaniard, the Captain says. I presume he squatted here, as all have done along the river banks. The ancient town of Loreto has quite gone, only two or three scattered huts like this in the forest with here and there the remains of a fruit palm or other planted tree. This Spaniard had two small canoes, the ordinary dug-outs of this river, and one rather larger dugout — boat-shaped — with gunwale and a palm-

[299] The *Black Diary* records this incident as follows: "Got wood & popunha peaches at a clearing at ancient Loreto." Peaches is completely the wrong words to describe these small, acid-tasting bunches of fruits.

thatched *pamalcari* over the stern. I asked out of curiosity the price of this. He said he had made it himself, and it was not for sale. When asked, however, what its current value was he said £30, and added he had refused £25 for it, offered him in gold. The thing would have been dear in Europe at £4. Here its intrinsic value was much less — for all needed for its making was an axe, saw and adze. The forest gave the timber free for the cutting and the palm for the thatch, the whole of the materials were entirely free, and there was only needed the human labour with the few needed tools. I saw to-day one of the bits of sandbank planted with Yucca or cassava. The plant had shot up splendidly, and all this quite recently grown — only a tiny patch of it. It shows what might be done with this fruitful soil, for this cassava was not two months old I am convinced.

The Engineer is driving the engines all he can, and they still hope to get into Iquitos on Thursday, although I see no hope of it. Loreto is 248 miles from Iquitos, and we have not done more than 100 miles per full day yet, since we got into the Solimões from the Putumayo.

Just above Loreto saw the mouth of a *quebrada*, this is the Amaka-yaco, a small river that goes up to a veradero with the Yaguas, the Captain says, but on my map its *veradero* is shown as connecting with the Cotuhé. The Pebas river goes to the Yaguas.

At Pebas, the skipper, says we should have stopped to take cattle up to Iquitos, but now, as he is afraid of missing the *Athualpa*, there is no time for this visit. I am sorry for this, as he says the Yaguas Indians there still wear their forest garb of fibre, something like the Bangola women's dresses on the Upper Congo. I have one of these dresses given me by Tizon in Chorrera, but I've not seen them worn by any Indian yet.[300]

Tizon's cousin

As a strange enough illustration of things out there, the Captain tells me the little *mestizo* table boy, Victor, is a cousin — a first cousin — of Tizon! It appears an uncle of Tizon's, in some government position, passed this way once, and this little boy of 12 or so (as under pantry boy) is one of the souvenirs of the journey. An Indian mother, of course. The boy is a very nice looking, polite little chap. It is a pity his father did not do his duty by the little fellow. Tizon does not

[300] These bark costumes are still preserved in the anthropological department of the National Museum of Ireland.

know of the relationship, Reigada tells me. He has refrained from telling him, and possibly the little boy does not know anything of his parentage. He is a charming little chap, clean, bright and very good-looking. The steward boy is almost pure Indian, and a fine young chap, slim and graceful with good limbs.

Today has been trying from its heat, but the increase of pace we are now trying at nightfall gives more breeze. The Captain says (to his disgust) that neither the Comisario nor the Lieutenant had the slightest conception that there was anything wrong in their going down into Brazil and recapturing the four runaway soldiers by force. It is easy to see how raids across the Caquetá into Colombia, and wholesale catching of Colombians and Indian tribes en masse can be conducted by the Normands, Jimenezes, and other agents of the Peruvian Amazon Company in those wild, unknown regions, where here, at this century guarded frontier of Brazil and Peru, where each country has maintained troops and officials for almost quite a hundred years, a Peruvian magistrate and Military Officer were anxious to do the same thing and to requisition a steamer belonging to an English Company for the adventure. Fortunately, Reigada's better sense, and, to some extent, I fear, my presence on board, prevented this escapade. It gives a pretty good measure of the lawless minds that reign up here, when two of the high officials of Peruvian authority were actually furious at not being able to carry out what would really have been an act of war against Brazil. I must get the names of these two heroes — I shall report them to the Prefect; in the interest of Peru herself it is only fair he should know what dangerous guardians he has on the Eastern frontier.

Every hour now draws me nearer to my interview with him, which will, I think (and hope), be of much interest. I shall speak very plainly, very civilly and kindly, too, but I'll call a spade a spade, and a slave shall not be termed a "labourer", or this atrocious slavery of the Putumayo referred to as an industry.

If necessary, I'll call in Bishop and Stanley Lewis, whom I hope to find in Iquitos, and will give the Prefect Gusmán and the Brazilian negro Pinheiro as further references. If I can get three days in Iquitos it may be the best part of my journey.

STEAMING ON MARAÑON TOWARDS IQUITOS — WEDNESDAY, 23RD NOVEMBER

We made a fairly good night's run. A glorious sunset last evening across the wide reaches of the river. The river seems to me today to be surely rising. Quantities of the little floating weed, like miniature water lilies in bunches, are being borne past, and quite a tide of sticks and half submerged trees, all showing the rise of tributaries higher up. We are now well in the Peruvian Marañon, and in the more thickly inhabited reaches of the river. Many little huts and embryo clearings, and sometimes quite an estate. One of these we passed about noon called San Tomás was quite an edifice — a two-storied house with a sawmill behind it, and several other signs of industry. The first — indeed the only indication of industry in the proper meaning of the word — that is seen, I fancy for a good thousand miles of this great highway. Elsewhere the evidence of industry lies only in a house or store "waiting for the rubber to come in."

The rubber industry

The rubber industry so-called, even when unattended by crime and oppression of the Indians, is on the Amazon — throughout Brazil or here in Peru — one of the most harmful pursuits a people could have given themselves up to. Every man has long since abandoned himself to this wretched rush for "black gold",[301] as some one has called it. All else is neglected, not even thought of. Agriculture and the uses of the soil; the comforts of life; the joys of society, and the welfare of the community have been sacrificed in the rush to get rich. The demoralization of the Spanish methods of dealing with a subordinate people has here reached a climax. Regular work, the great need of the region, the one thing that would have reclaimed the wild Indian tribes from their irregular and fitful life has been entirely lost sight of.

Every man flies to get rubber — by hook or by crook; and all who can try to get it through the labour of someone else. The petty trader is the next step in the commercial ladder. He gets the rubber from the vicarious collectors by comprehensive swindling it would be hard to match anywhere else in the world. Iquitos, which has no church, has a large colony of Jews. It also has a big colony of Chinese, half-castes — that is to say a Chinese cross with the Cholo Indian, and quite a good physical type it is. The Jews are the predominant business factor in Iquitos, and since I have struck this Peruvian Amazon I have solved a riddle that has often puzzled me. In Johannesburg, before the war and probably since it, a Jew

[301] "Black Gold" was the vivid term used to describe rubber during the boom period.

was habitually written of in the press and spoken of colloquially as a "a Peruvian". I never heard an explanation or reason given — now I see its force.[302]

Catching butterflies

We have stopped once looking for wood, without success. We stayed at quite a pretty beach with a nice little house embowered in a beautiful garden with a high fence round it. The men all landed to get oranges, which, the skipper said, were plentiful. Omarino and I stalked some glorious butterflies — green and black spotted, and a magnificent crimson or scarlet and black barred. We went about it in a half-hearted way — with our fingers. Omarino caught one thus — a white and red, but I let him go at once, and he flew away uninjured. I could not bring myself to crush the little palpitating body between my fingers.

A heavy storm in afternoon — not much wind — but a sultry rainfall. We are due to reach Pebas sometime this evening, so I am told, where we shall stop for firewood. Here, the Captain says, the Yaguas Indians come quite in their original native garb — a dress of Chambira fibre plaited into a voluminous garment covering the whole body. Tizon gave me one, but I have not seen it worn yet. We shall not reach Pebas by daylight, however, and I fear there will be little or no chance of seeing these Indians. The strange thing is how have they survived and preserved their native customs, and dress, when all elsewhere along these 2,000 miles of river every Indian has merged in garb and external show into the ranks of his so-called civilizers. Generally this garb is a shirt and dungaree or cotton pants, with a wide, coarse straw hat. It is singularly unbecoming, and the bronzed, beautiful limbs of these men are so picturesque it is a crime to replace the *fono* or bleached bark loin cloth with this miserable gear.

After dinner a conversation with the Chief Engineer. This man looks a thorough ruffian. He took part in the attack on Serrano and the subsequent murder of the Colombians on 12th January, 1908.[303] This subject was raised on our way to the Putumayo in

---

[302] This South African usage as a term of contempt for Central and Eastern European Jews probably derives from the setting up in Kimberley of the Polish and Russian Union (P.R.U.).

[303] This is the battle between Colombians and Peruvians that Hardenburg and Perkins had witnessed and led to their capture, imprisonment and loss of their property. As a result Hardenburg stayed on in Iquitos to build a case against the Peruvian Amazon Company.

September, over the piece out of the young pilot, Pisango's ear,[304] and I noticed the Engineer's face during the talk at dinner. It was hard and nasty. He said never a word, but I thought he realised that Reigada was being "pumped". I mistrust him thoroughly, and don't wonder at Hardenburg's reception on this boat, as described by himself, with this man as one of his hosts.

Expenses of the Liberal

Our talk tonight was on the expense of running the *Liberal.* He says she cost £6,000 to £7,000, and has been at Iquitos since December 1904. Her running expenses are £3,000 p.a. at least. The following are some of the items, according to the Engineer:

The Captain — salary	£30 per month
1st Engineer — salary	£25 per month
2nd Engineer — salary	£20 per month
1st Pilot (Manoel Lomas)	£18 per month
2nd Pilot(Simon Pisango)	£15 per month
1st Cook	£12 per month
2nd Cook	£9 per month
1st steward (Colmenares)	£12 per month
3 table boys (each £3 per month)	£9 per month
5 or 6 Quartermasters – young Cholo sailors who can steer, each £9 per month	£45–£54 per month
	Total: £195–204

The rest I don't know, but the crew, all told, comes to 30 hands.

The food is very dear, too, and firewood also, so I should put the running expense at well over £300 per month.

Corrupt company methods

How, on earth, anything is left over for the English shareholders after all these Peruvian parasites have had their thwack at the rubber, beats me. Put the total output from the Putumayo now at 450 tons per annum — much of it very inferior rubber — average price now when things are good cannot be above 3/- a lb. or, say, about £390 a ton. I doubt if it fetches so much. Put the European gross return at £80,000 per annum, and I believe it represents the maximum received. The initial expenses out here under the

[304] The only fragment referring to Casement's upriver journey includes this incident {MS.13087 (26/I)}17 September 1910: "Up the Putumayo river on board the *Liberal.*"

scheme of elaborate swindling of everyone — Indians and shareholders — these people have carried through, must walk off with pretty nearly the whole of this sum. It must be borne in mind that nothing is paid for the rubber. I don't for a moment believe that the goods paid to the Indians come to £1,000 per annum prime cost. Young Parr, the storekeeper at Chorrera, thinks that 1/- to 1/6d. represents the true value of what is given to each Indian for a whole *fabrico* in many sections, and I am inclined to agree with him.

The *fabrico* at Occidente yielded about 12 tons brought in by about 400 "workers". They would get, perhaps, £30 to £25 worth of pots and pans, powder, fish hooks, a hammock or two, and other trash — if so much — for some £3,000 worth of rubber. Velarde would get probably £250 commission on it, and Macedo, perhaps, the half of that, and then the Iquitos house eats up £5,000 a year in salaries and £30,000 a year in "goods" bought.

I reckon that if the total income be, say, £80,000 from rubber sold in London, at least £65,000 of that sum stops here to enrich this handful of thieves and murderers. Pablo Zumaeta with his £2,000 a year, Macedo with his £3,500 to possibly more per annum, Loayza probably £2,500 per annum, each Chief of Section £1,000 per annum, and then the Dublés, Rey de Castros,[305] and other official and non-official hangers on must eat up a pretty big sum, too. The people who are robbed are — at this end, first and foremost the Indians, and then the lower employés, like the poor peons and Barbadians. These with nominal salaries of S/P 50 to S/P 80 per month really get at the end of a long spell of work perhaps £10 to £20. Some of the Barbados men, after five years or six years almost of work, have not a single penny. Their salary, say at S/P 50 per month came to £60 per annum. But instead of this being paid to them they were compelled to buy all sorts of things at from 400% to 600% profit, so that I doubt if the actual cash expenditure to the Iquitos house for a S/P 50 empleado ever came to or comes to more than S/P 20 per month.

---

[305] Carlos Rey de Castro was Peru's Consul in Manaos but was also receiving significant funding from the Peruvian Amazon Company for looking after the Company's interests in Brazil. The Commission discovered, when inspecting the Company's books at Manaos, that Rey de Castro had been "loaned" £4,600. Rey de Castro was also the figure responsible for "editing" Robuchon's book *En El Putumayo y sus afluentes* (Lima 1907), the Company manifesto which justified its work as "civilizers".

At the other end, of course, the English Shareholders are being magnificently robbed. They have put up some £130,000 in cash, and Arana himself has 700,000 shares to exploit. In return they are the accomplices of a gang of thieves, who don't own a yard of land and exist on piracy and murder. Enough — I am sick of the whole thing, but Please God, I'll make some of these ruffians sit up yet, as well as save the Indians.

The Negro in the New World

Reading Harry Johnston's *Negro in the New World*, which I like. He sent me the "first copy" (so he says) and I find it interesting in the extreme, and well done. I wrote him a long letter today on the modern slave trade here in S. America, which the great world does not respect.

Pebas — Yaguas Indians in the electric light

Did not turn in, sat up waiting for Pebas which we reached about 11 p.m. just up the mouth of its own river. Men on shore for timber and big logs. An old Peruvian named Julian Ruiz owns this place, so Reigada says. He came on board, and then I saw two Yaguas Indians[306] in their fanciful costume by the dim lantern light on the beach. They were helping our crew with the scantlings, and carrying enormous beams on board with the utmost ease. I got them brought up on deck in the electric light, and was truly amazed. The costume beats anything I have ever seen. They are bound round the bows with immense streamers behind, and the whole body clothed in this soft rustling fibre. It is all dyed a rich soft terra-cotta red, and the pale, handsome features of these two men looking out from these filaments were a revelation. One was tall, the other shorter, both young and handsome. The faces were exceedingly agreeable and shy and modest. Both looked down on the deck as we examined them. Their skins were coloured too, pink with annatto,[307] I fancy. It looked like African cam wood powder. The taller young man might have stood for an Inca prince. regular features, soft gentle eyes, a beautiful mouth and downcast, pensive glance. I lifted his face twice to try and meet the eyes, but he smiled gently, and looked down again. He had two

[306] The Yagua are one of the Peban tribes, occupying the region of the lower Putumayo and Napo rivers. See H.S.I ,Vol.III, pp.727–36,

[307] Anatto, *Bixa orellana*, was the standard body stain and dye used by the Amazon Indians, known as achiote in Peru and Urucú in Brazil. Made from the crushed skins of the pod-like fruit.

bunches of red parrot feathers over the ears. Their two wives were on the beach, and I went to visit them, but they both held down their heads and put up their arms to cover their faces, so I could not do more than glance at them by the lantern — the old man, Ruiz, introducing me in Yaguas. The Captain says these Yaguas are "free", but the word needs definition here. I presume they are all in debt to this old man Ruiz. He looks 68 or 70 at least and the Captain says was born here at Pebas, and is "the boss of all the Yaguas". He is also the "Governor" of Pebas. When I asked how it was these Indians had not disappeared or merged like the Ticunas and others along the river into the "civilised" squatter type, Reigada said he did not know, but a minute later the explanation came. There are priests here — a mission of Augustinians, and paid and maintained to some extent by the Peruvian Government, keeps two priests in the Yaguas country, and this has been going on apparently for a very long time. This is, I think, the explanation of the salvation of this noble, graceful tribe. Lt Maw's description of them, as he saw the canoe arrive here at Pebas in 1827, would apply today. They have been saved by the missionaries — that seems clear. Reigada says that few Yaguas go to Iquitos, and when they do it is in ordinary garb. Some three young men came on board after midnight, as we left, sent up with bundles by old Ruiz. He and the others went off up the hill by lantern light to the house, which lay hidden away in the darkness. I much regretted we had not come here by daylight so that I might have photoed these four Indians. I gave the men cigarettes, and they smoked them with pleasure. Both were seemingly very strong, for I saw the tall young man lift tremendous big logs and carry them easily on board at a half trot, and the other man once lifted four of the scantlings together and brought them along on his shoulder. The crew carried only one scantling each at a time. I suppose these poles are for building in Iquitos.

Pebas is said to be 20 hours' steaming from Iquitos up stream. The *Huayna* reckoned it 120 miles, so I think it is more than 20 hours against stream to the *Liberal*. She has taken a good 24 hours from Leticia, which is only 120 miles from Pebas. However, the Chief Engineer says we shall arrive in Iquitos at 6 p.m. tomorrow, Thursday. I hope so sincerely.

I stayed up till after 1 a.m. looking at the banks, and thinking of this Yaguas tribe. It is a pity I have no time to visit their country. According to Reigada, they work rubber for Ruiz, and also for some other man lower down the river, but they appear to be quite untouched by the proximity of mail steamers, Prefects, &c. &c.

The older man, Ruiz, however, is the "Governor" of Pebas. See Lt Maw, Herndon and others for the definition of this term of governing in the Peruvian Montaña. Reigada says that Ruiz is the governor, and the "Indians work rubber for him". It is like the old sarsaparilla business in Maw's and Herndon's time. If the tribe is untouched, the Peruvian method of "administration" is equally so. A century has brought no betterment of method, while on the Putumayo we have Pizarro and the crimes of the sixteenth century in full swing. What a country!

Casement's health

I fear I am going to have an attack of gastritis as in Pará in July, 1908.[308] That awful memory is with me still, and the symptoms that have developed today recall the beginnings of that attack. A nasty bitter taste in my mouth after everything I eat or drink. It doesn't matter what it may be — food or drink, meat, bread, tea or wine — as soon as it is swallowed this acrid, unpleasant taste, as if my mouth were filled with quinine follows. And this, accompanied as it is by the extraordinary irritation of the skin that has arisen since we left the Putumayo, makes me fear very much I am in for another bout of that dreadful infirmity of stomach that laid me low for 3 months in 1908. I shall go to the Doctor of the *Athualpa* as soon as we arrive, and knock off all meat &c. from tomorrow.

NEARING IQUITOS — THURSDAY, NOVEMBER 24TH

Heavy rain and thunder clouds all along the sky. Great quantities of weed, &c. drifting down, and the river is surely risen much the

---

[308] After spending the best part of 1907 as Consul in the Brazilian coffee port, Santos, Casement was posted at the start of 1908 to Belém, capital of the Amazon state of Pará. He arrived there on 21 February 1908 on board the S.S. *Clement* and, coincidentally, travelled from Madeira with Julio C. Arana, another first-class passenger. Casement appears to have enjoyed his first few months in Pará. He set about reorganizing the Consulate with his usual zeal, which he found was totally disorganized and improperly situated given the level of British investment in the city. In late April he made a journey to report on the progress of construction of the Madeira–Mamoré railway. In July he was struck down with an attack of acute gastritis and on doctor's orders was forced to leave the fever-ridden climes of the Amazon and travel to Barbados to convalesce. He left Belém on 26 July aboard the S.S. *Cearense* and spent several weeks in Barbados before returning to Belém. He finally left his post on 17 November 1908 and sailed for England aboard the S.S. *Lanfranc*, spending Christmas in Ireland before taking up his new position as Consul-General in Rio de Janeiro.

last few days. I shall be very glad to reach Iquitos now, especially as I feel worse today, and fear much that it is a gastric attack. My Pará attack was acute gastritis, and I don't want another up here, too, with this long journey before me to get to anything like comfort or care, and to be sick on the *Athualpa* with a landing in Manaos and worry there over the Barbados men would be the last straw. If we get to Iquitos in time I shall go straight to the Doctor of the *Athualpa*.

Today is cool. The *cholo* sailors are clearing everything up and getting the ship smart for her arrival at the local capital. I looked through Congo letters and others I got on 9th November, and have arranged them for answering when I turn my face downstream, I hope on Sunday next the 27th in *Athualpa*.

Spent a lazy day, not writing much or doing anything. I played with my little chiviclis in the morning, it is a dear little thing, and will soon be as great a pet as the one we had up the Madeira river in May 1908,[309] which got blown overboard in the tremendous tornado that swept our decks coming down river one afternoon. I keep it warm and cosy in my cabin every night, and early morning Arédomi or Omarino come and take it out, and much of the day I leave it free to play run and chirrup — and eat.

Anchor opposite Napo

We are passing many more houses — *chacra* as they are called here — mostly of Indians, in tiny clearings. At about 2, we sighted the mouth of the Napo on our right, and anchored alongside the main bank on the opposite side — the south bank of the Marañon — at a line of houses embowered in trees that is called Muruku.[310] Here we got plenty of firewood, and fowls, ducks, eggs, &c. The

[309] Within a few weeks of arriving as Consul in Pará in 1908 Casement went on a long mission to make a report on the progress of the Madeira–Mamoré railway — possibly the most ambitious railway construction folly ever undertaken. Efforts to build a railway around the 225 miles of unnavigable rapids of the Madeira river and so improve access between rubber-rich lands of northern Bolivia and the main rubber markets at Manaos and Belém had been undertaken as far back as 1872 but each time met with disaster. Following the signing of the Treaty of Petropolis in 1903 and the ceding of the Acré territories by Bolivia to Brazil, Brazil in return was bound to build the railway for Bolivia and in 1908 Percival Farquhar, the American entrepreneur, began work. Casement arrived a few weeks later and sent an encouraging report {Casement — Cheetham FO 128/324} about the work in progress. Despite the loss of thousands of lives in the construction the railway it was finished in 1912 at the moment when the bottom fell out of the Amazon rubber market.

[310] In *Black Diary* the name of the village is given as "Murupa".

settlement is one of Indians and half-castes, gentle-faced beings, and all clad like the ordinary dwellers of Peru or Brazil. I went on shore with Omarino and the young pilot Pisango, who is a fine young chap with a handsome pure Indian face. He bought ducks for his home in Iquitos. I merely looked at the houses, three or four scattered along the bank about 100 yards from each other, with agreeable garden and grounds between and around them. I saw bread, fruit, guavas, cocoa, cassava, plantains in great quantity, peppers, maize, sugar-cane and other fruit trees I did not know, all scattered in great confusion mixed up together "through other", as we say in Ireland. Also, of course, the beautiful Popuña palm, called here Pifwa, and chontadura in Colombia.

We left this Muruku village at 3 p.m. and the skipper now confesses that we cannot possibly arrive tonight, as I knew all along. It is 8 hours' steaming, he says, from the Napo up to Iquitos, and so we shall slow down presently, so as to arrive at daylight. This is better than going alongside at midnight, and getting noise and mosquitoes.

As regards the Yaguas Indians and the Pebas river, I passed last might, I have got further particulars from the Captain. He says old Ruiz works the Indians for rubber — that his son has "charge of them" 6 days' journey inland or up stream, and lives at the headwaters of the Yaguas river. The man Azambuja we saw at Triunfo on the Yaguas river has others of the Yaguas "to work for him".

Also "traders and others" go up the Yaguas to "trade with the Indians". I wonder what are the exact conditions of such trade. The Indians are clearly the Sons of Obedience today, as they were in Maw's time. The two young men last night were both from far away, and had obviously only reached Pebas last night, as their wives were sitting by their bundles on the bank, while they helped so vigorously to load the *Liberal* with the old "Governor's" logs and saplings. We did not take nearly all he had there piled up waiting shipment, as we were pushed for time, and he has made some arrangement for a down-going Brazilian steamer to call for them for Manaos. One of the young Indians, old Ruiz said, came from 6 days away — the other, the taller and better looking youth, from only 4 hours away. I never saw gentler faces, or more agreeable expressions on any faces than on those of the two young men in their truly extraordinary garb. I shall get Arédomi painted and clothed in it at home, and have him photographed and presented to Dilke[311] and the Anti-Slavery people at a great meeting! That will be an idea to enlist sympathy.

The Pongo de Manseriche

The Captain tells me the Pongo de Manseriche,[312] which was successfully passed in May or June of this year by the P.A. Company's '*Cosmopolita*' under Captain Lores is not even a rapid — merely a compression of the Marañon between the two last buttresses of the foothills of the Andes. After passing the Pongo de Manseriche, however, rapids soon occur, and the river is not navigable for steamers. A boat with 10 knot speed, according to Lores, could always pass the Pongo. A Peruvian Company called the Cia. Gomera del Marañon, is working the rubber (*Jebe Debil*) and Indians above the Pongo de Manseriche. Reigada describes it "as a poor thing": it sends its produce down to Iquitos on balsas — i.e. rafts. The P.A. Company doubtless have some interest in helping the U.S.A. Syndicate to try and open up the Santiago. This river comes in just above Manseriche, and it was to begin the survey of the river and "conquest" of its "warlike" Indian tribes that the *Cosmopolita* went up this year.

As to the future of all these concerns, they can have only one — failure and rank failure. The reasons I'll not put here, but they may be summed up generally speaking, in the faults of the Peruvian character, which will quite eat up the overseas energy and vicarious control of European or U.S.A. Boards of Directors.

The Ucayali

Take, for instance, the Ucayali river. This, the true Mother of waters of the Amazon system, is still the principal feeder of the Iquitos export market. It used to send *caucho* — the rubber of the Castilloa tree — now none — and it is taking up "rubber", i.e. the milk of the *Hevea brasiliensis*, or 'fine Pará', as they call it. The

---

[311] Sir Charles Wentworth Dilke (1843–1911) published *Greater Britain: a record of travel in English-speaking countries during 1866 & 67* (1868) about his travels in America and the Pacific. He became a Republican and Radical MP in the same year. Nevertheless, he held office as under-secretary for foreign affairs under Gladstone, and was regarded as a potential successor to the leadership of the Liberal Party until he was defeated at election of 1886 after a marital scandal involving accusations of adultery. Dilke rendered important services to the A.S.A.P.S. during his time in the Commons, to which he returned in 1892.

[312] A famous stretch of the Marañon above Borja where treacherous currents and eddies render the river impassable. It is here that the Amazon ceases to be navigable.

caucho was a great source of wealth, but the *caucheros* have destroyed in ten years, the Captain says, every milk-bearing *Castilloa*, within reach of the banks of the Ucayali. How many Indians of the riverine tribes have also been destroyed, God alone knows. An entire industry ruthlessly killed in a decade. The exactly similar characteristics of the Spaniard of Pizarro's time holding the field today. The Putumayo bears full testimony to that. There is an English Company, and see the fruit of the alliance! The rubber and the Indians — the Company's property is fine — hopelessly ruined in less than ten years, and this by a syndicate enjoying the full support of the highest authorities in Peru. Arana Hermanos, as the Prefect assured me, had "performed distinguished services" to the Government, &c. and were an eminently civilizing agency. If this be so, what of the lonely *cauchero*, himself by no means milk-fed, who goes after the milk of the *Hevea* or the *Castilloa* — machete in hand, and murder in his heart? God help the tree and the Indian it shelters who stand in his path. We have, too, the added element of swindling — witness Israel's magnificent success with the Pacaya Company — his "Estate", if you please, just up the Ucayali. I see no hope for the Amazon under Peru at all, and very little for the Amazon under Brazil. Peru has, far and away the better and finer people — I mean her rank and file — her Indians who constitute the population of Peru, but her governing classes are too few, too weak, too corrupt to raise or enlighten the Indian mass. While pretending to the name of a Republic, she is not even an oligarchy.

The day has passed wearily. Lots of houses all the afternoon. After passing the mouth of the Napo at 3.30 we went by a side or north channel between islands, leaving the main channel to our left. We got to a place called Santa Thereza at 9 p.m. where the *Eliza*, a launch of P. P. Morey & Co.,[313] was lying at anchor, and we sent a letter to her. The Stewards and all were there, and 'Lincoln' told me her name and gave me further information. He is almost a pure Indian, a lad of 18 or 19, with a queer broad face, gentle and loving, and grey-black eyes with a wild look. Fine limbs, like all these Indians, and a very gentle, kindly manner.

Turned in at 10, after talk with 'Lincoln' in broken Spanish.

---

[313] The Morey family was another established Iquitos commercial dynasty with a fortune made from rubber, whose local power matched that of the Aranas. In 1911 Casement also started to attack the Morey family as he tried to undermine the commercial control of the Aranistas.

XI

IQUITOS

Arrival at Iquitos — Friday, 25th November

In sight of Iquitos

Arriving at Iquitos on getting up. Passed Nanai, and at 7 a.m. are abreast of Punchana, the Indian village below Iquitos, where Simon Pisango lives. Its church, too, in ruins! The *Athualpa* clearly in sight, made fast at the mole of Booth & Co . Hurrah! I'll welcome the sight of the English flag. I! Ever so, since there is no Irish flag — yet. I am glad to think there is a flag — red and all — that stands today for fair dealing and some chivalry of mind and deed to weaker men.

I have packed up, and all is ready for landing, and today will see my last fight on the Putumayo question. I shall call on the Prefect at 2.30, and then there will be a frank, if confidential, exposing of the situation to him, and I'll make it clear that Peru has got to deal with this hideous evil, or stand the consequences of loss of prestige and reputation, to say nothing of the shutting off of all financial supplies.

I must now put my diary away, and go and stand on the fo'c'sle to talk to the skipper.[314]

Saturday, 26th November

Catching up on the day before

Landed yesterday at Iquitos, and got all things up to Cazes. Mr and Mrs Cazes very well, and took up my quarters in the very hot bedroom of before: Bishop, Arédomi and Omarino to quarters in town I am renting for them. Mrs C. sniffs at their being here, and suggests a bath. I said the Indians are, generally speaking, much cleaner than whites as regards their

[314] Casement's very short entry for 25 November then comes to an abrupt end. He catches up on the day's proceedings in the next day's entry.

bodies. Took both boys to a barber — a Spaniard — to have their hair cut, and my own mop shortened. He was enchanted with their Indian hair — beautiful, long and strong. Received a visit very soon from the Prefect's A.D.C., a young *mestizo*, who couldn't look me in the eyes, but rapped his knees with his riding whip. Prefect sent complimentary message after my health, &c., and my stay in the Putumayo, &c. I said I should call on him in person tomorrow, or next day. Pablo Zumaeta also called, but I was fortunately out then. Visited Booth & Co and down to *Athualpa*, to find to my disgust she does not sail until Friday (2nd December) at earliest, and probably not till Sunday, 4th. The S.S. *Clement* is due to leave Manaos for New York via Barbados on 9th, and I hope to catch her with Bishop, Brown and all the men, to get rid of those who are not staying on in Brazil.

Punishment for drunk cholos

Visited Reigada on the mole, he was superintending the discharge of the Putumayo *chorizos* or sausages of vile rubber. All his poor *cholo* boys of crew today, he says, got drunk, and he cured them by putting them down the hold and covering them with the hatches battened down — "to sweat it out", he said. It is a barbarous and infamous method of dealing with men, and I find a favourite one with these Peruvian river skippers. Bishop tells me, Zubiaur, the brute so often mentioned in the Hardenburg depositions, and who is now Captain of David Cazes' launch, the 'Beatriz', put a Peruvian "down the hold" of the *Liberal* once, and the man died from suffocation, Nothing was done to Zubiaur. I can well believe anyone would die from even ½ an hour down the hold of a tiny launch like this — the depth is not more than 4 feet, and there is absolutely no air or breathing hole of any kind once the hatch is on, and iron walls all round, in this climate! The poor *Cholo* boys were working the rubber when I saw them, having "sweated it out", and some of them looked pretty pale.

Casement's homily on the virtues of drink

I told Reigada that the people who were not afraid to get drunk had conquered the world! — the English, Irish, Scotch, Teutons and Northerners generally, while the sober races had failed! The man who was not afraid "to give himself away" had probably a temperament that made for greatness lacking in the more discreet man who feared in vino veritas. When English gentlemen went to bed on their servants' backs, a drunken English cabinet had smashed France and conquered the world! My homily on the virtues of drink v. sobriety ended. (I said it on purpose, as Reigada had accused "these Englishmen" — the Commission and myself — of being "whisky drinkers" and thinking only of that.)

I returned to Booth's and had a cocktail.

Talk with Cazes

Long talk with Cazes about Putumayo — his mental attitude is not a desirable one. Every time he opens his mouth on the subject he shows how very much more he knew about it all than he admitted to the FO when asked for information. He was cheek by jowl with Arana in London at that time. He knew of heaps and heaps of things, and yet in his letter to FO he pretended that he knew practically nothing — even that Huitoto slaves were brought and sold here in Iquitos. Why, I already know of several. There is the sailor boy Julio on the *Liberal* this voyage, the property of the present Portmaster of the town, who tried to make Reigada sign a bill for £50 when the boy engaged on the *Liberal* on 1st October.

Bishop told me yesterday that the woman in the house where he has got a room for himself and John Brown has a Huitoto servant girl, and yesterday morning he heard her tell John Brown that the girl had cost her S/P 500. Brown had known the girl somewhere in the Igara-paraná and was asking her about the girl, and she said, "Yes, I paid £50 for her."

In the evening another long talk with Cazes. I must say he does not inspire much confidence. For instance, he had the effrontery to try and cram down my throat that he often sold goods at Iquitos at below their cost price. This apropos the reform the Commission will suggest that in future all goods shall be bought in England and not in Iquitos. He thinks that "a possible saving of 10%, at most 15% might be effected thereby — not more! He adds that the House here in Iquitos (Zumaeta and Co.) do not buy here, even at the cheapest local rates. They make no effort to obtain the best prices locally obtainable. That I had long since guessed. They buy from their friends. He admits that there is an enormous amount of inside swindling in this and other respects, and that the London shareholders don't get a penny out of the rubber.

Every cent goes out here; or to those who have advanced the money in one way or another.

As regards the Yaguas Indians, Cazes knows them. He says they are "nice looking but stupid".

The old Governor, Ruiz, is a trading client of his, he is godfather to two of Ruiz's children. Cazes does not think the Yaguas are enslaved, but he evidently knows very little about it, and cares less. He did not know that Ruiz's son was established, for instance, up at the head waters of the Yaguas river 6 days from Pebas, although he has such close dealings with the father. He says the present service of rubber is very good for him — plenty of it.

The Pensamiento affair

As to Zapata, the former Prefect, he says he knows, from personal knowledge, that he was bribed by Arana in the Pensamiento affair. That affair, of course, hit Cazes very hard, so he took trouble. He said he has proof that the Aranas bribed Zapata — private proof.

Pensamiento was an Estate that he and Arana claimed. The owner of it died, leaving, as trustee of his property, a man called Plinio Torres. The defunct owed Cazes, or the Iquitos Trading Company rather, a sum of money, one of these customary trade debts up here that everyone incurs so readily, and every merchant is so pleased to venture. On the man's death Cazes put in an embargo on the Estate, and got all the rubber, &c. there was on it (and sold it too) as part settlement of his claim. Arana sent Burga, the then Commissario on the Putumayo, and again now the actual Commissario there, to seize Pensamiento for them, as they also alleged claims on the house of Pensamiento. Cazes says they had bribed Plinio Torres, and that their real reason was to seize Pensamiento because it was the best loophole of escape to the Napo by the Huitoto Indians fleeing from their oppressors. Shutting this door (and then the murder of Serrano &c. later on) closed the only routes of exit from the Cara-paraná to these wretched people. There is an account of this seizure of Pensamiento by Burga acting for Arana in the Hardenburg Deposition made by Fermin Torres, the brother of Plinio Torres (see page

137).[315] It is dated Iquitos 22nd May 1908. Cazes does not know I have this statement to go on, too, and I shall seek to check his account of this Pensamiento transaction with it. In any case, here is proof from two questions that Burga, who was at the time "the Peruvian authority" on the Putumayo, was paid and employed by Arana and despatched about the country with soldiers, in the private interest of that firm, and, further, Cazes' positive statement that "he knows absolutely" that Zapata was in the pay of Arana in the same transaction.

Cazes' further statement as to the action of the Superior Court here in Iquitos in supporting Arana in this Pensamiento affair, and ousting him (Cazes) and making him pay up to £800, is a perfect romance. It is too long to put in here, but I will try and write it out for future reference. It incidentally shows how very undesirable it is to have a merchant also a Consul, for the Consulate here was guarded by soldiers with orders to arrest Cazes if he went outside, and finally Zapata (the Prefect) told him in a friendly way to give in and pay the money to the Court, or the soldiers would invade the house and arrest him in the Consulate, which is quite distinct and far away from Cazes' business quarters.

Cazes could have given the FO invaluable information had he chosen. Jensen[316] and Vatan are far better guides, to my mind, to the true state of things as regards the Indians and what is called "trading" up here. They are better educated and far more thoughtful men, and have a very much clearer and more enlightened intelligence.

Cazes now, for instance, admits that when this Pensamiento business was on, the man in charge there, who did not want to hand the place over to Burga and Arana, actually came to Iquitos with a lot of Huitotos who had fled Pensamiento who were dreadfully scarred from flogging. Cazes saw them and tried to have them put forward as evidence, but he says the whole thing was hushed up. Zapata and the Court had these Indians sent away. Cazes forgets the name of this man, so he says, but says he tried to assist him in that matter, as it

---

[315] Casement here is referring to the page number in his large Hardenburg dossier of statements. The account was not reproduced in Hardenburg's book.

[316] Jensen was another local trader, who gave much worthwhile information to Casement. They would become much better friends on Casement's return to Iquitos in 1911.

incidentally assisted his own claim to Pensamiento. This man must have been either Fermín Torres (the brother of Plinio) or else the man Perez Torres refers to in his letter to Hardenburg. I'll find out later on. This man, Cazes said, had refused to deliver up these Indians when Burga came and demanded them, and got them down to Iquitos to prove the iniquity that went on in the Putumayo. And yet Cazes in London this year assured the FO he knew nothing about the Putumayo tragedies, and told me more than once when I came here that "it was a sealed book", and repeatedly averred that until he heard Bishop's and Labadie's statements he had known nothing definite. Every fresh conversation I have with the man convinces me that to be a trader in Iquitos is a very perilous occupation for one's integrity or sense of right and wrong.

I got the Doctor, of *Athualpa* to visit me and he is giving me a tonic and says I'll be all right soon.

IQUITOS — SATURDAY, NOVEMBER 26TH

I hope to go and see the Prefect this morning quietly and in a purely unofficial way, and if he wants to have my views on the Putumayo I'll give them frankly. I must take Cazes as interpreter for the Prefect says he does not speak French and my few words of Spanish would not take me far.

Problems of privacy

Bishop has just come to say there are two Barbados men who wish to see me. It is very awkward, as here I have only my bed room (and a tiny table) to write in, and Mrs. Cazes and her servants just outside, and she is a busybody. If I go to Cazes' office, it is worse; there is no privacy — his clerks at the door (two of them speak English) and his peons hammering rubber boxes until one is deafened and all the incomers to the shop &c., to see everyone I speak to. I'll ask Booth & Co., if I can go to their dwelling house and write quietly there in a room of theirs while they are absent at their office. That is the only thing I can think of.

In *El Oriente* of 25th November 1910 (Evening Iquitos paper)

Pasajeros: El Vapor Liberal *procedente del Putumayo, llegado hoy, conduce los siguientes: Roger Casement, Florentino Santillán,*

Jeremias Gusman y hermana, Marcial Sifuentes, Juan Garrido y 12 de tercera.

Interview with Prefect

I went to the Prefect with Cazes as interpreter at 10.15 and stayed until 11.40, a very long interview. I told him much — first of the Barbados men and their ill-treatment — then, at his request, of many of the charges brought by the men against the Agents of the Company by name, and I particularly mentioned Normand, Aguero, Jose Inocente Fonseca, Alfredo Montt and Jimenez. I forgot to give Velarde his due, but that can be repaired. Later, I told him, if he liked, he could question Bishop, and he was delighted, and Bishop is to go at 10 a.m. on Monday morning. He said the Fiscal of the Court, Dr Cavero,[317] is now Prime Minister of Peru and that the Commission of Justice which is about to sail for the Putumayo will be composed of Dr Valcarcel[318] (as Judge), a public officer, troops (public force), officers and a Doctor, that it would leave on a Government Steamer and be absolutely independent of the Company, and that he was only awaiting telegraphic instructions from Lima to despatch this Commission, that he would telegraph at once to Lima to say he had seen me, that I confirmed substantially the worst charges that appeared in *Truth*, that the crimes alleged were revolting, and that justice must be done.

He begged me again and again that there should be no publicity, that I would not write a report for publication, as that would be a "crushing weight" on the "guiltless" shoulders of Peru, that the Company for its "criminal negligence" deserved punishment, that the Indians should be protected in future and all possibility of a recurrence of these things

[317] Dr Cavero was the Prime Minister of Peru during the government of President Leguia and the Peruvian Minister most directly involved with the whole Putumayo. Although Cavero had stated his intent to help the plight of the Indians in Peru, little came of these promises.

[318] Dr Carlos A. Valcárcel was appointed the official Peruvian judge to act on behalf of the Superior Court in Lima and arrived in Iquitos in December to begin investigating the matter. Although he was intimidated over the next two years by Arana and his gang he did eventually publish his findings in a book that records Peru's official side of the whole saga: *El proceso del Putumayo; sus secretos inauditos* (Lima 1915). The book was dedicated to Peru's President Guillermo Billinghurst (1912–14) and to the A.S.A.P.S. in London in a limited edition of a thousand copies. It borrowed heavily from Casement's Blue Book and the Paredes report.

removed. His chief fear was that publicity would follow, that H.M. Government would publish facts, my report, answer questions in Parliament, etc., and that would be international obloquy for Peru. Could that be avoided? Could I withhold from FO the damning evidence of the Barbados men? Could I omit that from my report? I said no, I could not, that I was bound to report fully, that my instructions were to report on the state in which I found the Barbados men and the nature of their relations to the Company, and all the evidence they laid before me would have to be laid before the Secretary of State; but, I said, speaking for myself, I could assure him that there should be no publicity, that as far as I had influence or the humble power to suggest I should beg that the charges involving the welfare of the Peruvian name should in no case be made public, that my idea and wish was, subject, of course, to the permission of the Secretary of State, to write two reports, — one that should deal with the narrower subject of the Barbados men's general treatment by the Company and the causes of complaint they might have against it, that this report should not affront or implicate the Government of Peru, but might — possibly would — be painful reading to the Company. Here he expressed complete satisfaction and interjected, "True, the Company merits all it will get!"

I then went on: "But I must faithfully record all the facts laid before me by British subjects, and here, where my report would of necessity deal with these very damaging charges against Peruvian citizens and implicate many individuals of that nationality, I should make it a separate and confidential report, with the permission of the FO, and I had every hope and every reason to suppose that His Majesty's Government would deal with it as entirely confidential." I said that possibly if the Peruvian Government desired a copy of that confidential report and of the evidence on which I based it, His Majesty's Government of Lima, in a wholly friendly and helpful way might forward a copy. That there could be no question of the British Government wishing to wound or affront in any way a friendly country, and that I felt sure in my heart he need not fear a campaign of publicity directed against Peru. But I said there was one danger, if, for example, this Commission of Justice should fail, through one cause or another, from want of evidence and failure to obtain testimony — a possible contingency. Then there might be fear that from other quarters — not from me — public statements would be made. There were others, beside myself, who now knew the facts. He again and again assured me that the Commission would be a real one, that its object was to avenge the wrongs done, to punish the wrongdoers — he repeated this — and to protect the Indians. That it would be some months at its work, and would be a thorough investigation. That it was taking interpreters too. (This is the crucial point. Will the judge be sincere, and will they get proper interpretation?) He thanked me for talking so frankly, and I said I was saying what I did only to assist him, and his government, to do right. I promised to send Bishop to him at 10 a.m. on Monday, and he was to put any question he pleased to him. The fat is in the fire!

I put in a last word for the Company and against Julio Arana. I said, that admitting the Company had been to blame, and I, for one, thought they had been sincerely to blame, there were two things to bear in mind. First, that it was better for the Indians and the region that a strong Company should be there, working "on another road", on humane and sensible lines, than that the district should be abandoned, or given up to petty traders and isolated "trading" ports. He agreed, and then I said there was a corollary, viz.: that Sr. Julio Arana should not be permitted to be supreme in that region. If the Company had erred, it was he who had founded it, knowing the facts, and in all its statements to H.M. Govt. and in its beliefs, it had acted on his advice by his prompting, so that he was much more to blame than the other members of the Board. Therefore, while saving the Company, to do good I thought there should be a limitation of that paramount influence he had personally exercised in the Putumayo. I hope the Prefect guessed all I meant.

Cazes, I think, translated this faithfully enough, although I more than once found Cazes saying a great deal more than I asked him to say, and once, certainly, he mistranslated what I had said, but it was easy to correct. Several times, I think, Cazes spoke for himself when it should have been for me. However, that is one of the drawbacks of having to try and do through another what I should be able to do myself. Anyhow good only can come from this interview. It will show the Prefect more clearly than he could have realised before the need for making this a real enquiry, and not a sham one, a real Commission of Justice, and not one of white-washing.

I told Cazes of his Captain Zubiaur killing the man by putting him down the hold, and I find he knew it already! And yet, he told the Commission in my hearing in September last that Zubiaur was "such a nice chap", and he knew nothing against him.

He thinks when I mention the name that it was Perez who brought the Indians down from Pensamiento with the flogged backsides and tried to get the enquiry here — and failed. He told the Prefect, by the way, of this when the Prefect asked how it was that no one had ever spoken before. He said people had spoken before, and nothing was done. The Prefect asked where and when, and Cazes said here and in Zapata's time, and that Zapata had hushed it up.

I told him of Aurelio Rodriguez killing hundreds in Santa Catalina, and of the moveable *cepo* made by Crichlow at this brute's order. I told him of Normand killing hundreds and burning them alive, and of Jiménez killing and burning the old woman and the Boras man in June 1908. I did not mention the name of Sealy, Chase or Donald Francis. Poor chaps, I am sorry for them there! — especially for Francis. I told him of Clifford Quintyne brutally flogged by Normand, of A. Walcott hung up by the arms until unconscious, of J. Dyall put in the *cepo* at Ultimo Retiro by Montt, and I assured him that the crimes committed were atrocious, and a disgrace to humanity. He was profoundly impressed, and again and again said that justice should be done. Perhaps the most significant statement he made (apart from his effort to get me to promise that I should not lay all the facts before the FO) was when he said that when the Peruvian Government had consented to allow the Commission of Enquiry to go into the Putumayo, and, above all, to allow me, a foreign Consul, to go there in a public capacity, it was because they believed all the charges brought by Hardenburg and *Truth* were "chantage" inspired, that they had regarded the whole campaign as a calumny and imposture, and, therefore, attached no importance to it. Had they thought there was any foundation for the charges the Peru Government would never have allowed me to go there and investigate, or to have consented to the P. A. Company's Commission. They would themselves have acted — the Government would have sent this Commission of

Justice long ago! Now it was due to the spontaneous act of Dr Cavero, moved thereto by the letter from Barcelona by E. Deschamps. I could not tell him that it was too late in the day to successfully maintain this attitude. They had had all these dreadful charges made here in Iquitos — witnesses on the spot walking about the streets asking to be interrogated, and nothing had been done. I could not say that Arana and Company had bribed Zapata and the local judges, yet we all know it is so. I could not say that I, at any rate, had made no concealment to him, the Prefect, in our first interview on 1st September, when I had so frankly discussed Indian rights and wrongs and had quoted Baron von Nordenskiöld's letter. I did that at the time with deliberation. It was a fair warning given honestly, that I was seriously perturbed, and did not accept all the statements as "fables", as he then assured me they were.

I had thus really shown my hand, and I did it out of honest and sincere motives, so that he could not say I got into the Putumayo on "false pretence". I gave fair warning. Of course, my position now is all the stronger for having been so frank then. He knew quite well I have the whip hand of his and His Government, and he appreciates, I hope, the extreme friendliness of tone, of view, and of personal assurances I have given him today. Also the proof of goodwill I am giving in handing over Bishop, my servant, for him to interrogate.

We did not get away from the Prefect till near 12. His brother came in once or twice. I don't like him. He has a hard, unsympathetic face, and looks as if he hated me, and all foreigners — and others too. The young ADC and other "bloods" in military uniform were outside the door. These people must loathe the sight of me.

Casement doubts effectiveness of the Peruvian enquiry

Cazes says they hate all foreigners, and resent anything like criticism. The position is really a hopeless one, because there is no good in the bulk of the people — only a very small handful have any morality or sense of truth or equity, quite a tiny group I should think. The Indians and Cholos are merely the servile class, the intermediate middle and upper classes, all rogues and blackguards in the main. This Enquiry will be a sham, I think and feel sure, but it will do good. The worst ruffians will either bolt or be turned out, and there will be a change of regime for a time. And that is all we can hope for. It will give the poor Indians breathing space anyhow, and who knows what, later on, if good may not come from it all. Anyhow my coming has forced the Peruvian Government to take definite steps to enquire, "to punish", and, at any rate, to end the worst phases of the "intolerable ill-treatment of the Putumayo Indians."

I cannot record all that passed at our interview, especially as so much of it was in Spanish, between Cazes and the Prefect with me only imperfectly following. However, the Prefect understands a good deal of English, and he must have followed pretty well what I said even before Cazes gave his rendering of it.

Evening

I sent for Bishop in the evening, and told him I wished him to go to the Prefect on Monday morning at 10, explaining that he was to speak to him just as if to me myself. Bishop fully understands, and promised faithfully to tell him all he knows, and to state the truth fully and frankly. I asked Bishop if John Brown and Stanley Lewis would be of any service too; could they be relied on to speak truthfully, and he thinks yes.

We are all to go on a picnic tomorrow, Sunday, given by Booth & Co., on their tug *Manati* up river. They have invited the Prefect and some friends of his, and we start at 9 a.m. I shall perhaps get a chance of further speaking to the Prefect on board, and will then take advantage of it to mention Velarde and the drowning of the Indian on 20th June. Further conversation with Cazes in the evening, who does not impress me. He has practically known all, or a great deal of all, from the first, and has kept his mouth shut like all the rest — for interested motives. He knew it was a British Company, and he never reported one word of these things to the FO in 1907 or 1908, when the charges were made, or when Perez brought the flogged Indians down to Iquitos from near Pensamiento. It is certainly very undesirable that a local trader should be the Consular Officer of a country in a region like this.

The Commissario at Leticia is a young Peruvian named Venegas, Cazes says. He was a junior employé on one of the river steamers! And they make him the Peruvian civil authority at their frontier station with Brazil. No wonder he wanted to raid Brazil for his four Cholo deserters. No wonder the Jiménezes and Normands think nothing of crossing the Caquetá into Colombia, and seizing the Colombians and Indians, and tying them up. No wonder the Prefect is alarmed!

He said he feared the Colombian government would do its utmost to induce H.M. Government to publish my report! I had mentioned the facts that twice this year — in March–May under Jiménez and in September under Normand, expeditions had raided into Colombia across the Caquetá with British subjects employed on the raids, and that Colombians and Indians had been captured, and, in the case of Kodihinka, flogged to death at Andokes. I have not yet mentioned Aquileo Torres, or Ramón Vargas, actually at Atenas when we were there. He had been sent on the road, so that neither the Commission nor myself should actually see him, but he was there right enough. And Aquiléo Torres, after all his crimes, to be sent to Abisinia, the worst section, either to continue killing, or to be killed!

I have not yet told the Prefect of these things, but I shall do so yet. Bishop tells me Viacarra is engaged as interpreter to go with the Commission. This is bad. This is Dublé again! I'll spike that gun.

A Picnic Upriver — Sunday, 27th November

A picnic

Started on *Manati* at 9.40 in heavy rain. The Prefect, his brother, Alejandro Paz Soldan and a Peruvian Naval Lieutenant, named Bravo, were the foreign guests, and then Brown, Harrison and Sibley (?), and others of Booth's people, including Captain Kaas of *Athualpa*. We steamed up river some 25 to 30 miles to a place on right bank called Tarnshiako, where we landed and visited the (mud) Church and were hospitably entertained by the villagers who were delighted to see the Prefect.

I found a good chance on board of telling him more about Putumayo and I told him of Velarde drowning the Indian on 20th June last, of Filomene Vasquez "leaving the road pretty" from Gavilanes, of Joshua Dyall killing the two Indians by smashing their testicles with a club by Normand's directions, and more. I told him that I had heard that Viacarra was going as Interpreter, and that I believed he was not a good choice, that the members of the Peruvian Amazon Company had dismissed him on arriving at Chorrera and were certainly not satisfied with him. I emphasised the supreme importance of faithful and honest interpretation, and of assuring the Indians of every protection if they brought accusations against the Whites. I said a good deal and said it vigorously, and then we dropped the subject and had a pleasant breakfast together. Lt Bravo speaks good English, having been some five years as a Cadet on U.S.A. ship, the *Illinois* for one.

The Prefect's brother told me (in English) that he had been in The Peruvian Corporation[319] and liked the Indians, especially the Campas,[320] very much. He asked me, too, about the Putumayo, and if the charges in *Truth* were true, and I said yes in the main and told him one or two things of what had been declared to me. Also I said that the whole system from top to bottom was undisguised slavery and that the Indians existed only to bring in rubber on the white man's terms. He seemed incredulous, but gave me a much better impression than I had first derived from his appearance.

We returned at 3.15 from Tarnshiaka and raced the *Anastasia* down river. She had a picnic party on board — J. Lilly and Sons[321] — and the race was close and exciting, but *Manati* won.

---

[319] After Peru's humiliating defeat by Chile in the War of the Pacific (1879–83) The Peruvian Corporation a London-registered company was set up in 1885 to lead the initiative to regenerate and reconstruct Peru. The Corporation assumed the responsibility of the republic's external debt of about £50 million and in return acquired most of the country's assets, including all the state-owned railroads, the ferry-boat on lake Titicaca, rights over the bulk of what was left of Peru's guano supplies and around a million acres of land in the Peruvian Amazon. In addition to these generous concessions the Peruvian government pledged to pay the Corporation around £80,000 per annum. Despite the apparent sell-out to British financiers, this package — negotiated between General Andres Cáceres and the British businessman Michael Grace — restored a period of sound fiscal management in Peru and the gradual regeneration of the country. It also led to a very close relationship between British financiers and the Peruvian Government. The Peruvian Corporation continued to manage most of Peru's railway systems until 1972.

[320] The Campa Indians lived along the Ene, Perené and Apurimac rivers and extended through the Gran Pajonal northward between the Pachitea and Ucayali rivers. See H.S.I. Vol III p.537.

[321] John Lilly was another local Iquitos trader who owned a small *aviador* company transporting goods to rubber stations and exchanging them for

Our *Cholo* firemen were all half drunk, and could not keep up steam, otherwise we should have walked away. As it was, we got in well ahead and always with something in hand to spare. Went on board *Athualpa* till near 6 and then home.

I find the lunar rainbow we saw at Chorrera on 6th November was seen here, too, by Mr and Mrs. Cazes, same day and same hour; she says "about 8 p.m.". Very curious thing indeed! Cazes had noted its clear arc, from horizon to horizon, and says it was very vivid. I am thoroughly tired. I offered to send John Brown and S. Lewis also to the Prefect, and he thanked me much. He begged me to give him any hint I could do so that the Commission should not be misled — to put it on the right road.

IQUITOS — MONDAY, 28TH NOVEMBER

Drafting a memorandum

Heavy rain all morning. Up at 6.30 and busy writing out a memorandum to aid the Prefect and the Judge in their work on the Putumayo. I shall make it purely a confidential memorandum of my personal view and suggestions as to where they can best find evidence. I will send a copy to Barnes of the P.A. Company's Commission, and tell them exactly what I have said and done here for their guidance.

Bishop, John Brown and Lewis came only at 10.30 a.m. I was furious and pitched into Bishop as he never expected to be pitched into by me. I sent him at once to Prefect with my card to introduce him.

Brown's accusations

I then told Brown and S. Lewis I might require them to go to Prefect tomorrow and they agreed. Brown confirms dreadful details of James Mapp as against Jiménez and Aguero and Lewis gives further particulars of J.I. Fonseca's crimes in Ultimo Retiro. He too, saw him smashing the testicles of the poor Indian in the *cepo* at Ultimo Retiro. Brown saw Aguero and Jimenez shoot a *muchacho* as a target at Abisinia. Brown

---

rubber which was then sold profitably onto the international market. Lilly became Casement's closest English ally in Iquitos and when Casement returned to Iquitos in 1911 he travelled with Lilly on his launch the *Anastasia*. Lilly's company collapsed at the beginning of 1912 as a result of the slump in the rubber market.

remembers many names of Capitanes and others he saw killed and dates. He accuses Macedo of flogging in the *caucho* store at La Chorrera. It was there it was done chiefly. I told him to be ready for Prefect and also Lewis. Bishop returned at 11.15 or so, saying he had told the Prefect a great deal and the Prefect was grateful and told him he was going to punish the wrongdoers and would send his statement to the Judge. The Prefect wrote me a note of recognition which I attach.

Rio Mar has arrived and I send to find out when she will be going down to Manaos.

Overwhelmed with work

I am overwhelmed with work and no time for more diary. Many Barbadians waiting to see me. They wish to get away by *Athualpa* to Manaos. I promised to take Lewis. Bishop says Gibbs might make a good interpreter for the Prefect — or possibly John Brown himself. I will see before tomorrow.

Have sent round to pay my bill at P.A. Coys. — it comes to £134 odd I fancy, also to get the money of all the Barbados men, some £590 nearly and the passages to Barbados of 8 of them I think.[322] I may send Bishop down in *Rio Mar* tomorrow to try to get the men off by *Clement* on 7th December from Manaos to Barbados.

Bishop says the Prefect asked him to try and get a good Barbados man as interpreter. He says the Prefect assured him he had known nothing of these atrocities on the Putumayo — that he had been here only eleven months and had often asked here in Iquitos and everyone had told him that things were all right there.

He told Bishop that he intended this Commission to be a real one, and that he would be grateful for any help he could get so as to guide the Commission aright.

I sent for John Brown and Lewis and told them I wished them to be fully prepared to see the Prefect in the morning. heavy rain most of the day. I walked towards Punchana late in afternoon, but it was too muddy. Manoel Lomas the pilot

[322] This receipt, signed by Casement, was reproduced in Carlos Rey de Castro, *Los Pobladores del Putumayo* (Barcelona 1914). The Peruvian Amazon Company tried to hold it against Casement that he had consciously misdated the receipt and had written 28 November 1909 instead of 1910. The account was for £87.10/- — the cost of eight passages and was subsequently paid by the Foreign Office.

talked to me — he was "a bit on" — but was very civil and begged me to visit his house.

The Dutch–French Company

Cazes told me something of the Dutch–French Company who have been turned back by the local authorities, and spoke of the disgraceful character of the article in *El Oriente* which attacked them and threatened them with being lynched. The proprietor of *El Oriente* and writer of this disgraceful article is Dr Paredes,[323] a judge of the Superior Court of Iquitos! On the other hand Cazes says that Dr Valcarcel the Judge going to the Putumayo, is well spoken of locally. He has not been here very long and, as the Prefect said, he hopes that he has few local ties or associations, and is not too deeply in with these people. Cazes told me after dinner that round at his lawyer's he had seen a memorial (about a year ago) which had been sent to Lima by one of the local priests, a Spaniard — who had been on the Putumayo.

This memorial begged the Government to take action. The priest stated that he could carry on no evangelising or Christian work on the Putumayo, owing to the condition of the Indians and the inhuman treatment they received. I asked Cazes if he would get me a copy of this Memorial and he said he would — but I'll have to press for it. I'll try Vatan, who is a far more reliable little man than Cazes and has a much better head-piece for anything connected with the country and the people. It is clear to me that as I have got in my hands the most damaging evidence and the witnesses too, this Peruvian judge and the Commission will have to act. They fear exposure above all things. The Prefect confirmed that. He said it would "crush" Peru — so that practically I have the

---

[323] Editor of the main local newspapers *El Oriente* and one of the more respected members of local society, Dr Rómulo Paredes was a supporter of Arana's regime until he was selected instead of Dr Valcarcel by the Peruvian government in early 1911 to compile a report of his own on the Putumayo atrocities. Returning to Iquitos in July 1911, Paredes had accumulated a voluminous number of statements and eye-witness accounts, this time mainly from the Indians, attesting to the horrors committed in the Putumayo. Despite Casement's initial reservations about Paredes, the two men would become close allies the following year on Casement's return to Iquitos when Casement tried to make Paredes into the active figurehead of an anti-Arana party in Iquitos — a scheme that initially worked but then would badly backfire when Paredes began to blame the Putumayo atrocities on British interference in Peru. Paredes's story is told in Valcarcel *op. cit.*

whip hand of these people — or rather the FO has, and it can really, but in a still quite friendly way dictate terms, or at least ensure the cessation of the ill-treatment of the Indians.

IQUITOS — TUESDAY, 29TH NOVEMBER

More Barbados men

A busy enough day. I am overrun with Barbados men. The residuum here in Iquitos — all wish to clear out and , of course, for me to pay their passages down to Manaos. I cannot do this. One of them named Ford actually had the cheek to come up into my bedroom just now to try and steal a march on me. I told him that he and all could earn enough money to get away themselves.

John Brown and S. Lewis came and I sent them to the Prefect. I sent Bishop to find Jeremias Gusmán and he bought him at 9.30 or 10. I told Gusmán he should tell the Prefect all he knew and of all he had done — as a good citizen of Peru — that the Prefect had a right to know everything and that if crimes had been committed on the Putumayo it was his, Gusmán's duty to hide nothing. I asked him if he had flogged and he said yes under orders of my *jefes* — and he would hide nothing — that he would tell all. Brown and Lewis returned to say Prefect was not there and they were told by his orderlies to return at 1 or 2. They and Gusmán did this, but Prefect was too busy then to interrogate them. He merely took the notes of introduction I sent him and told all three men to return at 10 a.m. tomorrow. I gave John Brown a map of the district to explain things and told the Prefect, in my note, to keep it.

A Foreign Office telegram

Got a telegram from FO — in cypher M. sent by post from Pará — it is dated there 22nd Oct. — and it is a warning that I must be very careful how I write of my impressions on the Putumayo to correspondents in England — as I am deputed to report to the Secretary of State. This must be due to my letter to Harris written before I left Iquitos. I presume I deserve the rebuke — altho' I am quite prepared to justify that letter — at least the reasons for my view. Of course from the point of view of discipline I have not a leg to stand on and the FO are quite justified — but I think my motive was a sound one and that the suggestion I made to Harris was a good one. Something of the kind was called for — and may still be called for. These people (the Peruvian authorities) will do nothing unless they are forced to. Publicity is their fear — their haunting dread. Were anything from Hardenburg to be published in America it would do good.

It would not be the "crushing" blow to Peru that an official statement from H.M. Govt. would be — but it would be a sort of gentle reminder that all the eggs were not in one basket and that if they did not reform and quickly reform the state of things I have brought to their notice in the Putumayo then that there were various quarters in the world whence the most serious revelations might be expected. I gave the Prefect a hint of this on Saturday. The Peruvian Amazon Company's Commission (that is to say Barnes, Fox and Bell) will always speak out if the dire need arises. The two first are pledged to me personally.[324]

---

[324] This is the only page of the manuscript of the Putumayo Journal that for some reason was not included in the typescript and it has been crossed out by a single blue line — quite possibly by Casement around the time he sent the manuscript to Charles Roberts. It is nevertheless a highly significant few paragraphs since it clearly touches a secret and delicate matter that would be of great concern to Casement after he returned to London. A copy of the telegram, in Casement's hand, can be found in {N.L.I. MS13,087 (5)}. It says: "You will no doubt use great discretion in communicating with correspondents in England your impression of the Putumayo as you were deputed by Secretary of State to report to him." Casement was clearly offended by this reproof by the Foreign Office and took the issue up when he reached England. In a letter only to be found in copy form in N.L.I. MS 13,087 (6) to Tyrrell dated 12th January he wrote: "I got a telegram from you, that is to say from the FO on 30th Nov at Iquitos which appears to have been sent off on 22 October. It was to warn me to be discreet in correspondence with persons in England as to my impression of the Putumayo etc. — and it puzzled me a good deal until, on reaching Pará on 14th December, I got a batch of home letters, and in several of them press cuttings giving the account of a meeting held in the City Temple on 20th October at which Conan Doyle and others spoke about the Morel Testimonial. So far as I can see, Conan Doyle's speech, which seems to have been reported in several papers must have accounted for your telegram to me. I send you one of the cuttings sent me — as I wish to put right what Conan Doyle has put so wrong." Casement followed the matter up with a further letter to Tyrrell on 19th January {FO 371/968} — there is a draft copy of the same letter dated 17th January 1911 in {N.L.I. MS 13,087(14) }. Casement, however, was wrong to accuse Conan Doyle, and his initial suspicion that it was the result of a letter he had sent to John Harris from Iquitos, was right. The matter was explained in an internal Foreign Office minute to Mr Mallet from Sir Edward Grey {FO 371/968} dated 20 October: "Mr Langley tells me that in the course of an interview which he had a day or two ago with Mr Harris, Secretary of the Anti-Slavery Society, the latter

The *Rio Mar* is to go down to Manaos today. I hope she will pick up the Barbados men at the Javari — and I am writing to Mr Dening or the Vice Consul rather to see that those who are to be repatriated go all by the *Clement*. I got Philip Lawrence his extra passage to Jamaica — the Coy. only paid him to Barbados, so I wrote to say he was entitled to his fare to his home whence he had been brought in 1904 by Juan Vega.

A walk to Punchana

I walked out to Punchana at 3.30. Very hot indeed — stifling. Stopped at the house of Manoel Lomas, the Pilot, at 4.30. He showed me all his children, his wife, his garden &c. &c. Simon Pisango is his brother-in-law — the brother of his wife. He shook my hand again and again and hoped I would return to Iquitos "to the Indians".

Conversation with Vatan

Then back to town and met Vatan and we sat down together. His talk a highly interesting one — first on Putumayo.

He asked if I had found his statement to me made in September was well-founded. I said entirely — that things were as he told me. I would say no more. He quite understood. He said he thought nothing would be done — I said I differed — that I believed now much would be done — that I had a firm confidence in a prompt amelioration.

He said that it was only because I had come in an official character that I was allowed out alive! I laughed. He said:

---

informed him that he had been receiving letters from Mr Casement recounting stories of atrocities which had come under his notice in the course of his investigations with the Peruvian Amazon Company Commission of Enquiry. It seems unfortunate that Mr Casement who has been sent out by the Secretary of State to report to him should at the same time be reporting direct to the Society, and I think it would be well to take what steps we can to put a stop to it, altho' I fear it is too late to hope to do much."

None of Casement's manuscript letters to John Harris is in the Anti-Slavery papers . When Harris came to write his autobiography at the end of his life he did not make a single reference to Casement despite the close association of the two men over both African and South American slavery issues. Casement and Harris fell out in 1912 over the Putumayo Mission Fund. It was Harris who stepped forward in 1916 to "authenticate" the *Black Diaries*. It is worth noting that the 1910 *Black Diary* refers neither to Casement's letter to Harris, the FO reproof of Casement, the news Casement received of Conan Doyle's City Temple speech, or Casement's correspondence with Tyrrell.

"It is true — had you been a mere traveller and had seen things they would have got away with you up there. Your death would have been put down to Indians — I know what I am talking about."

He went on to say that it was not a moment too soon that I had come on the P.A. Coy.'s Commission. My coming, he said, would influence things not only on the Putumayo for good, but right through the Department. They would all benefit from it. Now that the truth had been found out — as he knew it had been — something might be hoped for.

He is a member of the Municipality and he had again and again tried to get street cleaning — even the grass in the square cleaned up — but the Municipality has "no money". All goes to Lima. The lower class here — the Indians, he said were "far better than the whites". I said I knew that — that they were a long way better. He said the best people here wanted to separate. That the Department of Loreto was bled white by Lima — but that they had no educated leaders. They had to appeal always to Lima men to lead them and these were dishonest through and through.

He then told me at some length of the failure of the Dutch–French Colonising Company, and of the disgraceful measures undertaken against them by the Prefect — acting under local excitement. Everyone had been threatened — he himself, the Agent of the Syndicate — had been threatened. I told him I had read the article in *El Oriente* (only today) which referred to them, and it was a disgraceful article.

He gave me many particulars of the syndicate — its aims and wishes and then of the local hostility. I will draw up a separate Memorandum of this all, as it is useful and throws light on the utter unreliability of the Peruvian authorities, and how essential it is for the betterment of things on the Putumayo that they should be impelled by <u>fear</u>. Honour will not move them. Vatan said to me "Are you not sanguine in thinking that anything is going to be <u>really</u> done now? These people promise with no intention to fulfil, and when you are gone ****." I said nothing more than that the <u>facts</u> were known now and to others besides myself and I hoped and believed that real action would be taken.

Vatan is a very intelligent man — I wish Colonel Bertie had come as far as Iquitos even — Vatan would have pleased him. He said, by the way, that the things he had told me when we first met should not have been said to Cazes — Cazes, as a Consul, is useless. He convinces me more and more of his indifference to right. For instance he told me only today of seeing young Burga brutally beating his Indian servant in Hotel Cosmopolita once. He interfered and protected the man. Burga said: "Why, it is my Indian" — and Cazes never hinted at these things to me (or to FO I fancy) when I first came. He knew a very great deal of the Putumayo and kept it quiet — like everyone else in Iquitos.The Arana influence was too strong — and he was a trader and sold to them.

After dinner I went to Booth's house and walked out with Brown[325] round the Square and to the Merry-go-Round where lots of the Indian lads and young men were enjoying themselves. Saw several of the *Liberal* crew there.

IQUITOS — WEDNESDAY, 30TH NOVEMBER

Morning

Wrote down to the Vice Consul at Manaos a list of the Barbados men and sums due to them who may wish to go home to Barbados — asking him to pay them their balances, and if the letter reached him in time to send them off by the *Clement*. Sent John Brown and S. Lewis to Prefect at 10 a.m. and Gusmán, but again he could not see them. He told Brown and Lewis to return in afternoon. This they did and I believe saw him. Asked Vatan privately to give me some "indications" on the Franco–Dutch business which he promised to do. On board *Athualpa* to lunch at 11. They talk now of her not getting away until Monday or Tuesday. It is dreadful. River rising fast since *Athualpa* arrived on 16th, it has risen 6½ feet the Captain says.

Prefect's wife

Called on Mrs. Paz Soldan, the Prefect's wife, and she spoke of Putumayo and the ill-treatment of the Indians — so I told her much, chiefly of the women and children and the disgraceful work put on them. Very heavy rain indeed and it quite spoiled all thought of going out anywhere.

---

[325] In the *Black Diary* entry for 29 November, it was Harrison not Brown who walked with Casement to the square, "Walked after dinner to Booth's House & then with Harrison to Square".

Cazes' hypocrisy — Von Nordenskiöld's letter

Cazes continuing to pretend that the ill-treatment of Indians in the Putumayo was quite exceptional and took place nowhere else in Peru, I said I could not accept his views, that I preferred to believe the evidence of Von Nordenskiöld and of others who all testified as to the slavery (and worse things) of the Indians. I got Von Nordenskiöld's letter to the Anti-Slavery people and let him read it and he then said: "Yes, that is true"! — Amazing — after continually asserting that it was <u>only</u> on the Putumayo, "the sealed book" as he called it, that these things were possible.

He admits that all Von Nordenskiöld asserts is true — that the accounts are falsified — the Indians always "overcharged on what they take and undercredited on what they bring in". I told him Nordenskiöld's letter did not stand alone and that others had and would testify to the same things, and that if this Peruvian judge did not do right on the Putumayo the floodgates would be opened. I find Cazes an exceedingly untrustworthy guide to things here. His first concern is his business, and beyond that he pretends to know nothing.

Casement's photographs

The photographer sent back, after repeated requests, my films developed, but has abstracted No.1 — that of 'Bolivar' in chains that I took at Indostan! He refused to print any saying he had been bothered so much. He has had the roll of film (ten 'postcard' films) since 11th or 12th October and by 30th November this is the result! Of course the Company has stolen 'Bolivar'. Cazes says everyone in town knew we had found him in chains, and that I had photo'd him. Dublé spoke to him of it as "regrettable thing that we should have found this man in chains", but that "satisfactory explanations were given". Were they? David Brown also told me he had heard of it — in the street.

IQUITOS — THURSDAY, 1ST DECEMBER

Brown and Lewis' conversation with Prefect

John Brown and Lewis report that they told the Prefect a great deal. Brown told of Jimenez and Aguero killing Indians wholesale, and of Aurelio Rodriguez at Santa Catalina, and he says the Prefect took it down in writing — also Lewis' statement of Fonseca. The Prefect suggested to Brown that he might need him as an interpreter, he could not say until he had heard from Lima. This is the telegram he told me he expected from the Minister authorising the expenditure on the journey to Putumayo.

He said that if Brown were here when he got the telegram he would send for him. I asked Brown to go to Putumayo as Interpreter if the Prefect asked him to go, and he said he would.[326]

I got up at 5.30, and went to see the Barbados men at 8 a.m., but only two arrived and I sent to Booth & Co., who are willing to engage them and others. I walked out to Morona Cocha at 9–11 with "Wags". the road very dirty, and the lake falling fast.

A visit to the cinematograph

Heavy rain last night and again this afternoon it passed. I walked about a good deal — went to *Athualpa* at 4.30, and saw 'Adolfo' starting for Yurimaguas with many passengers. Invited Brown to dinner at Bella Vista, and afterwards we went to the Alhambra to the Cinematograph,[327] where were lots of Indians — all Indians and a few soldiers. Brown told me two interesting things. First, that he believed, too, the Indians were slaves, and in the rivers even close to Iquitos. He said he was sure of it, and that, when a whiteman was killed or "murdered" by Indians, it was due to his atrocious treatment of them. Within a month, he said, the biggest *cauchero* in Iquitos, Valdimiro Rodriguez had been killed on the Madre de Dios by 8 Indians. The Indians here knew of it before the

[326] See N.L.I. MS 13,087 (10). Casement also paid Brown £10 of the £30 debt that Casement had received from Tizon on Brown's behalf at La Chorrera on 30 October according to a receipt dated Iquitos, 1 December 1910.

[327] The Alhambra was one of two cinemas in Iquitos situated in the main Plaza and was founded by Clemente Alcalá and Francisco de Paula Secunda. After being initially fitted out with a second-hand carousel bought from Manaos it bought its first Lumiere projector in 1902 under the new ownership of Eduardo Fuller — an Englishman. It then began to show early silent films on certain nights of the week. In 1905 a Peruvian, Arnaldo Reategui travelled to France and bought some projection equipment from the Pathé brothers and Gaumont and with and an abundant stock of film set up another cinema, the Jardin Strassbourg. Pará, Manaos and Iquitos were among the first cities in South America to enjoy silent pictures. See Joaquin García, *Rasgos Historicos del Cine en Iquitos y en la Region*. Shupihui No.18 — CETA.

papers published it, and he heard them talking of it among themselves on the Plaza before it became general news. This Valdimiro was one of two brothers, Rodriguez, who "treated" on a big scale in the Ucayali and Marañon and other rivers. He also told me that Lieut. Bravo, the Peruvian naval officer who was with us on Sunday, had told him in strict confidence that the Judge Valcarcel who is going to the Putumayo is not straight, and can be bought. These were Brown's own words. A nice look out. Brown said that the Commission was a sham, sent only because we had already gone to Putumayo and they were trying to save their faces, but that he had few hopes of it doing much. I said nothing, but was glad he told me these things. He tells me there are stocks at Punchana. The Governor there used to be the schoolmistress! She put an Indian in them one day for beating his wife. It was a very hot day and the injured wife came and built a palm screen over her husband to shield him from the sun.

Brown says Cazes cares for nothing but his business, and that he is no use to apply to for information. Got the *Relatorio* of the Priest. It is to the Minister of Justice in 1907, and is a clear indictment of the Putumayo and also of the ill-treatment of the Indians on the Ucayali. It is in the Annual Report to Cayrus of the Minister of Justice — a convincing proof that the government of Peru had long ago been informed. I am copying out all the documents. They are very interesting and convincing, and I see also deal with the Yaguas Indians at Pebas and the *caucheros* then too opposing the Mission, to try and keep the Indians ignorant and in their clutches. Cazes says the Yaguas "may be nice-looking but are very stupid." Evidently he and his compadre Rivez desire they should remain stupid.

Simon Pisango's letter

A letter appeared in last night's *Loreto Comercial* from Simon Pisango, the young pilot of *Liberal*, bringing grave charges against Reigada of the *Liberal*. First rate. I am glad. The truth is coming out. I'll get Simon Pisango to come and see me. I have his photos — two of him — in the films the photographer developed, and I gave them today to a German to print. As soon as I get the copies I'll go and see Simon and give them to him, and then find out about David Serrano and the murder in January 1908.

Huitoto slaves in Iquitos

David Brown says there are heaps of Huitoto slaves here in Iquitos — any number, and they are sold. Mrs. Prefect yesterday spoke of the large number of the "gentle docile" beings here — as servants — and of the duty of the government to protect them. I saw lots tonight at the Alhambra — 'Julio' of the portmaster for one, and another fine big chap and many young ones. They are all through the town — chiefly girls. Wesdin (?) next door have one — a boy who has been to Germany, and speaks Spanish and German. He, of course, is well cared for. Why on earth cannot this Peruvian Commission of Justice begin by asking here in Iquitos these Huitotos how they came to be brought here — what became of their parents, wives, children, etc. also find out how much was paid for them. A very useful preliminary interrogatory could be conducted in this way if there were any desire to find out the truth.

IQUITOS — FRIDAY 2ND DECEMBER

Huambisas kill Peruvians

The *Loreto Comercial* of last night has a letter from Lima about the Putumayo — interesting reading. I sent a copy of it and of Simon Pisango's letter to the Commission at Chorrera. There is the following interesting telegram from Lima in *El Oriente* of 12th November I see:

> *Ha causado aqui gran sensacion la noticia llegada de Chachapoyas, de que los Indios Huambisas, en el Rio Santiago han asesinado a 67 personas.*[328]

This is quite cheerful reading — I am glad to learn that the Huambisas have had another victory — and only regret it is not 6,700 persons! This, I trust, was the expedition that went up with Lores in the *Cosmopolita* and passed the Pongo de Manseriche a few months ago. These gentlemen went to conquistar the Huambisas, but apparently they had found that tribe still a pretty tough nut to crack, and able to do some conquistaring on its own account.

---

[328] A sensation had been caused by the news from Chachapoyas that Huambisas Indians, in the river Santiago, have killed sixty-seven people.

Cazes' untrustworthiness

Cazes knew about Valdemiro Rodriguez Says he was "murdered by Indians," on the upper Ucayali — I said I thought on the Madre de Dios, and he says, yes it was on the main river — but those headwaters are reached from here by the Ucayali. The more I speak with Cazes the less I trust him. He withholds all he can — volunteering nothing, and when he finds one already knows this makes a show of giving information — that is already stale.

I am told there is to be a prize-fight tonight between a Barbados man and a sailor off the *Athualpa* — the latter a sort of white champion. If it comes off there will be a huge gathering.

Arming indians against the Missions

The Frei Pratt who addressed the Minister of Justice about the missions here admits that all the Missionaries were killed by the Huambisas for reasons he could not divine. This must have been the Burga murder. Reigada told me that Burga (the actual Comisario of Putumayo) had armed Huambisas to attack the Mission, and they wiped it out and Burga too! I must find out more about Valcarcel after what Brown told me last night of Lt Bravo's opinion of him. Bravo is the Lieutenant of *America* — the big war launch of the government which is now painted and ready to go — when the Prefect gets the necessary authority for incurring the expenditure required.

Casement confronts Cazes

I sent my camp bed on board *Liberal* today as a present to Tizon with a short note. Cazes says Tizon knew everything — and lied to them in July when he said all the stories were false! But Cazes did practically the same to the FO and yet it is clear he knew just as much or more than Tizon. I told him so at lunch — and he got pretty scarlet. The truth is that there is not an honest truthful man in the public service or in trade in Iquitos — they are all liars when they are not worse. The straightest men here young are Vatan, David Brown and the Indians.

Athualpa *discharges*

It rained a great deal the last three days, and the whole place is soaked through and through. The *Athualpa* is being discharged so slowly there is no question of her going before Tuesday, 6th December. Her date was 27th November, and she arrived in Iquitos on 16th with 2,100 tons of general cargo to discharge. She will load here about 250 tons of rubber (at 90f. freight per ton = £1,125). There is a lot of waste somewhere. It is the outward freight that pays. The two Pará pilots get about £70 a month each at present rate of exchange in Brazil. Nice pay for Mestizo Indian youths who can scarcely read or write.

Brazilian naval mutiny

The *Loreto Comercial* of 1st December has telegrams from Lima saying the ironclads of the Brazilian Navy have mutinied, and, after a futile bombardment of Rio, in which one woman and two children were killed, has put to sea with an unknown destination — This is pleasant news! I wonder how my consulate fared in the bombardment? It seems incredible. A bad beginning for the Presidency of Marshal Hermes da Fonseca![329]

El Oriente of tonight has an article on the constant theft of servant boys and girls (*menores*) who in 9 cases out of 10 are Huitotos from various people in the town, and mentions two quite recent cases in the house; Reigada and Zubiaur (both Putumayo ship captains). What a confession when one comes to think of it. I will keep the article as further proof.

I walked part of the way to Punchana in the afternoon trying to get 'Julio' the Huitoto off the *Liberal* to come with me — but the "road" was too dreadful with mud and water, so I turned back.

Another visit to the cinematograph

In the evening we all went to the Alhambra to the Cinematograph in honour of the Independence of Portugal when the Braganza family freed the country from the Spanish dynasty

[329] A few weeks after the election of the new militaristic and reactionary President of Brazil, Hermes da Fonseca, in 1910, a series of naval revolts startled the nation. On 23 November 1910 the enlisted men of three British-built ironclads and seven warships decided to express their grievances and rebelled, killing a number of officers. They next started firing the guns randomly at Rio de Janeiro but two days later surrendered. A more serious revolt broke out on 9 December when five hundred rebel marines assaulted the Naval Arsenal in Rio. The revolts heralded a new era of violence and social unrest throughout Brazil and Latin America.

in 1640.[330] And the fools celebrating this to-day flaunt their execrable red and green — crude, blood-thirsty colours as one sees them in Iquitos, in vile mercantile cottons — and cheer for the cowardly downfall of a house that led them out of bondage and gave them a historic name and "national flag" — all of which they will hand over to a gang of mercenary "politicos" in Lisbon and Oporto. Portugal is less fit to be a republic than Ireland — an Egyptian republic would beat a Portuguese one — certainly a Turkish republic would give it points for intellectual leadership and firmness of mind and courage of heart. Leading Portuguese are not only robbers but also faineants — the poor people are simple, kind and brave — and as ignorant as the Egyptian fellaheen. An Irish Republic, but better still an Irish state not a republic, if the Protestant and upper classes could be induced to join, would be a fine thing — but with the tenant farmer, the County Councillor and the Dublin Corporation in charge — ahem!

There was not a very big crowd at the Cinematograph. I counted 62 men in uniform — including the band — the so-called military band of Andean *Cholos* — fine chaps to look at, but the devil to play. The row was infernal. It was like the source of the Marañon — in clash and clatter of falling stones and burying cliffs — I had to fly all "overtures" and they began and ended every piece. The things shown were of the usual Latin American type — of the amorous seduction and outraged husband setting — altogether immoral and nasty and the very worst thing to put before an audience mainly composed of young Indians, soldiers and work boys whose natural simplicity can soon be corrupted by what is offered to them thus in the name of the higher civilisation.[331] Higher civilisation! God save the mark.

---

[330] This is perhaps ironic since the Braganza family had been toppled from their throne just a few weeks before by a republican coup in Lisbon after two hundred and seventy years of rule. 1640 is the year in which the Spanish Habsburgs relinquished the Portuguese territories that had been "inherited ... bought ... & conquered" by Philip II as a result of the Braganza's insurrection which restored Portugal to the Portuguese.

[331] Exactly what films were showing at the Cinematograph is not stated, but Casement clearly felt that they were morally unsuitable for an essentially innocent audience. Casement maintained this high, not to say priggish, moral tone throughout this journal while the *Black Diary* entries recording events on his return to Iquitos from the Putumayo would convey a wholly different character.

A forest Indian's village is far finer and more truly civilised than anything in Iquitos I have seen.

Gave Bishop the long Memoria of the Spanish Frei Pratt about the ill-treatment of the Indians to copy out for me. The book belongs to Cazes' lawyer and I must get it back soon.

IQUITOS — SATURDAY, 3RD DECEMBER

John Brown's statement

Took John Brown's statement this morning from 8 to 9.30. He told me many things of Aguero and Aurelio Rodriguez and the hideous murders of these ruffians in Abisinia and Santa Catalina. Bishop says that he saw Gusmán last evening, and he told him the Prefect had had no time to question him much yesterday afternoon but had told him to return today at 8 a.m. He stated that the Prefect wished him to return to the Putumayo — and he assured Bishop he would not be bribed. Alas! there is not one of them will do right, or go straight in this matter by the enslaved Indians. I went out for a walk at 10, and on board the *Athualpa*, which is slowly discharging. There is some talk of her not going until Wednesday now — 7th — a stay of three weeks in Iquitos to discharge 2100 tons!

Cazes is not at all hopeful of the Peruvian Commission. He said last night he had heard in town it might not even start at all! That it was, in any case, only a blind — got up to hoodwink the British Government and to prevent public disclosures — and that he doubted very much if any of the murderers would even be imprisoned.

Gift to Reigada

Captain Reigada of *Liberal* called on me this afternoon at 2.30 p.m. to thank me for a small visiting case I sent him as a *recuerdo* of our voyage. He tells me the *Liberal* will return to Encanto on Wednesday next 7th December. She is taking 15 Cholos or peons — labouring men from this — to fill vacancies. He says Zumaeta is going to recall all the Chiefs of Sections — or all that Gielgud puts on a black list — and that he believes many of them are to come back with him. The *Liberal* will be at Encanto a long time, and does not expect to be back here until early January. He spoke in praise of the Commission (our Commission) and said Mr Zumaeta was very anxious to carry out any suggestions it put forward. What a change!

Victor Israel

I am now going out for a walk to Punchana if possible — if the road is not too wet. The Judge Paredes, editor and leader writer of *El Oriente*, is another of the scoundrels here. This paper is the organ of the Arana gang. I saw Victor Israel yesterday — looking very wretched indeed. Both Cazes and David Brown say he is in fear of prosecution over his famous "Pacaya Rubber Estate" — the Company is an absolute fraud. He is said to have got £70,000 out of it. Incredible.

Letter to Barnes

The weather is very much cooler — and the river rising fast. To-day at 10 a.m. it registered 63'1" at the mole. It is going up from 5" to 6" daily I fancy — but there are often sudden drops too — altho' the upward tendency continues. I shall write to the Prefect tomorrow and give him my memo of the best course for the Commission to follow on the Putumayo — also I shall ask for a list of the personnel of the Commission in writing — and some hint as to the date of its departure. Then I must write Barnes fully and let him know exactly what is being done, so that our Commission may as far as possible keep the other one straight.

I wrote a long letter to Barnes for the information of our Commission, telling him what I knew and pointing out how he and his colleagues could influence things for good on the arrival of Dr Valcarcel. I sent him back the Hardenburg Documents too — annotated and all. They are a great loss to me, but I think it only fair that the Commission should have the use of them under the forthcoming circumstances of this so-called judicial visit to the Putumayo. I also wrote out a very short Memo for the Prefect and sent a copy of it to Barnes for his guidance. In this memo I lay particular stress on the need of good interpretation of what the Indians may say. In the evening dined with David Brown and the Booth people, a very stupid, talkless party — and then I left and walked round the Plaza several times. It was full of the life of Iquitos — all classes.

IQUITOS — SUNDAY 4TH DECEMBER

Out for a walk to the military firing ground with Ignacio Torres as my guide. Took several photos of the ground and trees and a stream beyond. Back at 11 — in great heat — and wrote a little in the afternoon altho' it was stifling. In the evening the Cazes' had a bridge party after dinner which lasted till midnight — and the heat lasted all night. It was really atrocious — not a breath of air and I lay for hours trying to sleep — and then got up and wrote, but the mosquitoes stop that game.

IQUITOS — MONDAY 5TH DECEMBER

A walk with Ignacio Torres

Out for another walk this morning — with the same guide — and first to the firing ground and beyond it to the forest where plenty of people — men, women and children go to cut firewood. Nearly all are Indians and some quite fine types. A lot of soldiers clearing the road and levelling. No officer in charge. All young men from the Andes side — some Ignacio told me from his own home Taropoto. He has been in the army for 8 months and left it in August last. He is now 19½ years old — so he entered it about 18½. He says he is of the *raca Española*, whereas he is almost a pure Indian and speaks Quechua as his native language I find. What a pity that all these people desire to shake off their Indian birthright and pretend to be part of the race of their oppressors of the people who, according to Reigada, have left nothing to Peru but their vices.

Some of these young soldiers are very fine chaps — sturdy, well built and with such cheery brown faces and white teeth — and laughing always. So different from the Brazilian type where every man is so self-conscious, he would not dare to laugh.

I went on with Ignacio to the wireless telegraphy station by the bank of the Itaya and took a photo of it — also of the Cholo soldiers at work.

Tickets for Pará

In the afternoon took my tickets for Pará. John Brown has decided to stay here — and is entering the Electric Light Company's work at £15 per month. He may be available if the Peruvian Judge wants him as interpreter — but I fear this Commission of the Peruvian Government is a fraud.

Gusmán told Bishop today that his second interview with the Prefect had been a longer one and that he had not concealed anything from him. The Prefect wishes him to go back to the Putumayo as an interpreter. He will be better than Viacarra, although I don't expect anything sincere from these people, especially after the revelation of meanness and duplicity displayed in their dealings with the Franco–Dutch Expedition. Two of the Chiefs of this party are going down on the *Athualpa*, and will be able to tell me much privately about it all.

I am convinced the only chance of bringing about a better state of things in the Putumayo is that the Peruvian Government will realise that, if they don't, we will let the world know the truth.

Tonight *El Oriente* contains a paragraph about a gentleman, referred to as an ex-official, who is stated to have been keeping a man in chains here in Iquitos, and grossly ill-treating him. Cazes tells me that the ex-official referred to was once the Commissario of the Napo — nice type of magistrate!

Pablo Zumaeta called on me at 2.30, asking for a list of all the bad people on Putumayo! Said he had been sent by the Prefect. I refused to discuss the matter with him.

[*On 5 December Casement wrote a letter to Sir Edward Grey {FO 371/1200}*

Iquitos,

Sir,

I have the honour to confirm the telegram I caused to be sent by Mr Cazes, on the 28th, ultimo, to the British Minister at Lima, reporting my arrival at Iquitos from the Putumayo on the termination of the mission you had entrusted to me in July last.

I am leaving for Pará by the first steamer and pending my arrival in the United Kingdom I refrain from extended comment upon the state of things found to exist in the Putumayo region.

I left the members of the Peruvian Amazon Company's Commission at La Chorrera.

Throughout my stay in that region I was always with them and I sought, I thought not without success, to carry them with me in the investigations I conducted, strictly on the lines of your letter of instructions.

All the facts that came to my knowledge I communicated fully and at the time to Mr Barnes, the chief of the

Commission, and I have his clear assurance that the evidence thus laid before him and his brother members of the Commission has left no doubt in their minds as to the reality of the charges preferred against the Company's local administration.

On my return to Iquitos, on 26th ultimo, I called on the Prefect, and at his urgent request I placed him confidentially and verbally in possession of some of the evidence that had been laid before me by British subjects, for which assistance he thanked me and, I understand, communicated by telegram an outline of what I had told him to his government at Lima.

I trust that in doing so and in not withholding information sought by the representative of the Peruvian government I have acted in accordance with your wishes.

I may add that my relations with the members of the Peruvian Amazon Company's Commission (as with the Prefect) have been most friendly and that I have every right to think that they individually and collectively share the conclusions I have arrived at, which I hope very shortly to lay before you in full detail.

I have the honour to be Sir,
Your most obedient servant,
Roger Casement.]

IQUITOS — TUESDAY, 6TH DECEMBER

Preparing for departure

Up early, and packed up all for steamer, and at 9.20 called on Prefect to bid him goodbye, and leave my memorandum — Cazes with me. Went to his private house, and found him there and his brother and wife. He said the Commission would start on the 15th or 20th; it would consist of Dr Valcarcel, a Secretary, and a small force of not more than 12 soldiers travelling on a small Government launch. Meantime, Dublé, I understood him to say, was going up tomorrow on the *Liberal* to undertake the dismissal of the worst of the Chiefs of Section — and he mentioned several names, including Normand's, Aguero's, Fonseca's and Montt's. This is indeed cheering news — the idea of allowing the Chiefs of the incriminated Company to go before the Judge, to arrange all the ground, &, if necessary, terrorise Indians and others. What a farce it is going to be! I had not expected anything quite as bad as this. Evidently the Prefect has allowed himself to be talked over by Pablo Zumaeta and Dublé and is practically leaving them control of the cleansing arrangements. It is disgraceful. Well — this will relieve me from all moral obligations of promise — I said if this Commission did its duty there would be no scandal — but it is not going to attempt it even. Went straight on board and found Reigada, Zumaeta, the Prefect's brother and his A.D.C. there to bid me goodbye. Zumaeta told Cazes and myself he was going up to La Chorrera tomorrow! The plot thickens.

He and Dublé together will be a nice house party for Christmas. They are evidently going to try and forestall the "Commission". What a pack of scoundrels all round — the whole gang! The Prefect's weakness is atrocious too. I thought he was really moved to some perception of the need of independent action — independent and firm action quite regardless of how the Company might feel or wish. Here we find him allowing these two men to precede the Commission by a fortnight and to practically get their witnesses ready. If only Barnes were a stronger man! He is weak as water and there is no one at Chorrera with any capacity for dealing with these rascals — and Tizon will join his countrymen. I begin to think the Hardenburg disclosures will not be in it with those I may some day make or call on Barnes, Fox and Co. to make.

Casement's parting decision

The truth will have to come out — the Peruvian Government is more guilty than the Arana Bros. even, and the only thing to do is to try and move the civilised world to action.

Athualpa *casts off*

After lots of handshaking and adieux the *Athualpa* left Iquitos at about 11 a.m. The wharf was lined with people — and the steps and upper mole and bank outside the customs barrier. This is the last view I shall ever have of the Peruvian Amazon — of the Iquitos Indians and their pleasant cheerful faces — of the low line of houses fronting the wide, bold sweep of the Marañon as it comes down from its throne in the Andes — the mightiest river upon earth bathing the meanest shores. If only a good race instead of an evil and corrupt people had first come from Europe with the message of change to these long hidden, gentle people.

There are a lot of cholos going down to Manaos contracted by various *caucheros* to go up the Purus to the Acre Rubber Swamps.[332] All are young boys and men — some almost pure Indians, others *mestizos*. I spoke to several. One, a tall lad of nearly six feet says he has engaged himself to 'Don Mario' as his *patron* for three years — and in any case "he will make plenty of money".

So this senseless rush for money goes on — and when they get it they have no notion of spending it, or making happy homes or pleasant lives. Iquitos is a pigsty and yet it gives the Peruvian government £300,000 a year in Customs dues, and not £2,000 are spent on any public need. One of my latest acts almost was to photograph the thing they are calling a hospital that the Government at Lima has at length voted £30,000 for. I am told, that sum has already been spent on it — and there is not £1,500 worth of work on it so far.

I have fought a stiff fight

The only people I regret at Iquitos or elsewhere on the Peruvian Amazon are the Indians — and those in whom the Indian type prevails. Once the Spanish caste gets uppermost all decency disappears; the Indian still preserves some of his originality, morality of mind and gentleness of demeanour and simplicity of heart. My work is over on the Amazon. I have fought a stiff fight and so far as one man can win it, I have won — but what remains behind no man can see. Anyhow, the party of Englishmen and myself have let daylight in to those dark wastes, and scheme how they may, we have broken the neck of that particular evil. The much bigger

[332] The Acre Rubber Swamps refers to the Brazilian state of Acre which had become the most productive rubber region in all Amazonia by 1910 and continues to this day to have the main concentration of Brazilian *seringueiros*. The region was previously part of Bolivia but the massive migration of Brazilian *nordestinos*, dispossessed by the years of famine and drought in north-east Brazil, began to flock to the area in their tens of thousands in the last decade and a half of the nineteenth century. So many settled in the region that when Bolivia tried to reclaim the area and control the immigrant settlers with taxes the population rebelled, first in 1899 and again in 1902. The dispute was settled by the Treaty of Petrópolis of 17 November 1903. The number of Indians massacred in this process of colonization is not known, as the *seringueiros* were illiterate and the massacres went unrecorded. It was in Acre, in the rubber town of Xapuri, that the leader of the Rubber Tappers Union, Chico Mendes, was gunned down by local *fazendeiros* on 22 December 1988.

question remains — the future of the S. American Indians and Native people generally.

That awaits the challenging of the Monroe Doctrine and the exploring of that fantastic and selfish reservation of a continent — of two continents — for the least capable of mankind. Europe, the mother of nations, must overflow and here is the field of overflow — waiting the stream of fertilising life.

Steamed swiftly down river — and so adieu to the Peruvian Amazon.

PART FOUR

LONDON BOUND

It is not hard to tell the truth; the difficulty is to get it believed.

Sir Edward Grey — British Foreign Secretary 1906–16

Casement travelled with his two Indian boys and the two Barbadian guides, Bishop and Lewis. Also on board were the two directors of the Franco–Dutch syndicate, Julien Fabre and M. Van der Est There is no documentation regarding the downriver journey from Iquitos to Manaos beyond the draft of a short note to the Chief Clerk at the Foreign Office held in N.L.I. MS 13,087 (5) and dated 6 December 1910.

I have the honour to state that I have drawn two bills upon you, Numbers 2 and 3, for the sum respectively of £37.1.0 and £140.18.11 dated 5th and 6th instant to meet expenditure incurred in travelling in the Putumayo region. The first of these bills is in favour of Booth and Coy and the second in favour of D. Cazes esq of the Iquitos Trading Company, and I would beg that they might be met on presentation, pending my early return to the United Kingdom.

Casement arrived in Manaos early in the morning of 10 December. After the civil disturbances of early October the city was under martial law. Large sections of the city were still ruined from the naval bombardment. Casement went to the British Consulate where he saw Douglas Dening, the Booth and Co. representative in Manaos and British Vice-Consul. He discovered that several of the Barbados men had decided that, rather than return home, they would find fresh employment on the Madeira–Mamoré railway, work which Casement helped them secure. To some extent that relieved his responsibilities since now he had far fewer Barbadians to deal with. Casement spent the day organising matters and paid a cheque to the Booth Steamship Company for £100.9.5 for payment of the Barbadian passages. The Athualpa *continued that evening down river and arrived in Pará late in the afternoon of 13 October. The* Fôlha do Norte *recorded the names of the first class passengers to disembark: Julien Fabre, Secorra Villaly, Isabel Canalejas, Roger Casement, Francisco Doet and M.C. Van der Est.*

Casement went straight to the British Consulate. Among his mail was a letter from the Secretary of the Anti-Slavery & Aborigines Protection Society, Rev. John Harris, enclosing a letter from the British and Foreign Bible Society. Harris's letter is lost but the enclosed letter confirmed that atrocities were being carried out elsewhere in the Peruvian montaña.

I have never visited the Putumayo district but I have been in the central forest region of Peru. It is pretty well established that the treatment of the savage Indians of the forest by traders is extremely bad. But what can poor governments, like Peru, Ecuador and Colombia etc do. These vast sparsely populated territories are all in dispute among the various governments. There is no such thing as a police patrol system, without which I maintain it is impossible to protect the Indian.[333]

Casement also received letters telling him of Conan Doyle's speech at the City Temple. In a letter to Tyrrell, written on 12 January when he was back in London, Casement wrote:

On reaching Pará on 14th December I got a batch of home letters, and in several of them press cuttings giving the account of a meeting held in the City Temple on 20th October at which Conan Doyle and others spoke about the Morel Testimonial.[334]

Casement checked into the Hotel do Commercio along with Bishop, Lewis and his two Indian boys. He intended to send them all on to Barbados and wrote some letters to arrange for this.

My own servants (two men) and the two Barbados men I kept at Pará for four days (in my own hotel) were fed and lodged for 6/- a day each.

PRO FO 371/1200 Consul General Casement to Governor of Barbados

c/o British Consulate — Pará

15 December 1910,

Sir,

I have the honour to state that the letter No. 1024 of 20th September last written by your direction reached me by the

[333] MS 13,087 (19) — Letter from British and Foreign Bible Society in Lima to the Rev. John Harris, dated 30 June 1910, and received by Casement at Pará on 14 December 1910.

[334] N.L.I. MS 13,087 (6) Consul General Casement to Sir William Tyrrell — 12 January 1911. It was in Pará that Casement changed his view as to why he had received a reproof from the Foreign Office for "indiscretion". Rather than his initial and correct belief that it was due to his correspondence with John Harris, he felt, in the light of his home mail, that it arose from Conan Doyle's speech at the City Temple.

hands of John Brown just as I was leaving the Putumayo on the termination of my special mission to that region.

I had been informed by telegram from the Foreign Office dated the 16th August last that as John Brown was seriously ill at Montserrat, his services would not be available.

I concluded that this disposed of all possibility of his being able to join me, and did not further communicate with you or Mr Pogson the Consul at Pará, believing the matter to be at an end.

I have to express my thanks for the efforts taken by your Government to secure the services of Brown for my journey.

I note that a sum of £17.12.0 has been expended by the government of Barbados in despatching John Brown to Pará, and on my return to London I shall place the matter before the FO with a view to settlement of the account being made through the Colonial Office.[335]

John Brown has remained at Iquitos at his own request in order to obtain work there, and his whereabouts can always be learned through the British Consulate in that town.

I have the honour to be,

Sir,

Your most obedient, humble servant

Roger Casement

On 16 December he wrote a letter to the Governor of Barbados informing him of his completion of the investigation and that a number of Barbadians would be returning to Barbados.[336]

Sir,

Several men, natives of Barbados, who have been working for some years in the Putumayo district of the Peruvian Amazon are returning to Barbados by the SS *Hubert* due to leave Pará on the 22nd instant. Their names are:

Frederick Bishop
Allan Davis
Evelyn Batson
Edward Crichlow
James Layne

[335] Attached to this letter is an account of the disbursements paid by acting Consul Burnett in connection with John Brown's passage to the Putumayo.
[336] A copy of the original is to be found in FO 371/1200 while the first sheet of a draft copy is held in MS 13,087 (5).

Clifford Quintyne

Allan Davis is accompanied by an indian wife with their child.

The man F. Bishop has been my servant and interpreter during my recent journey in the Putumayo region.

A larger number of men, who also left the Putumayo with me, decided at Manaos, to seek other work in South America rather than return to Barbados.

They were all promised employment on the Madeira–Mamoré railway and were to proceed to Santo Antonio on the Madeira river, I understood on the 13th instant.

The names of these other men are: James Mapp; J. Minggs; A. Hoyte; Sydney Morris; Preston Johnson; Reuben Phillips; Augustus Walcott; Westerman Levine; Joshua Dyall — also a man named Cresset I found at Iquitos.

Two of the men of the party now proceeding to Barbados have made serious complaints to me of ill-treatment sustained by them at the hands of agents of the Peruvian Amazon Company. These men are Clifford Quintyne and Edward Crichlow; the former still bears scars left by the floggings he received. It might be well to have this man medically examined in Barbados as the subject of the treatment received by the employees of the Peruvian Amazon Company is one that occupies the present attention of His Majesty's Government. I have taken down as fully as possible the statements made to me by the Barbados men I found in the Putumayo district which will be laid before the Secretary of State; but as I have no knowledge of shorthand much that they stated has of necessity been passed over. It might be desirable to take more fully than I was able to do, by shorthand, the declarations of these men now going to Barbados for the fuller information of His Majesty's Government. Frederick Bishop, Allan Davis and E. Batson are, I believe, reliable witnesses, so, too, are the other men but their statements to me were obtained with greater difficulty, due possibly to the local circumstances of their situation.

Should you think it well to act upon this suggestion I would request that the shorthand writer employed should be such a person in government service upon whose silence and discretion you can surely count.

The men's statements reveal in some cases the most disgraceful acts committed by agents of the Peruvian Amazon

Company and sometimes by the men themselves (as Clifford Quintyne for instance) acting under orders of the Company's agents; and it would be most undesirable that any publicity should arise in Barbados in connection with what has occurred in the Putumayo region.

I would further suggest that should any of these men leave Barbados in search of employment abroad they should be instructed to leave full particulars of their destination and addresses with some local authority, in the event of it being found later on desirable to communicate with them.

There are still five Barbados men remaining in the Putumayo region. Three of these are still in the service of the Peruvian Amazon Company viz:

Donald Francis
Seifert Greenidge
Armando King

Two others, named Stanley Sealy and James Chase, are acting as servants with the Peruvian Amazon Company's commission now conducting an investigation in that region and they, along with Donald Francis will be returning to Barbados, I believe in a few months.

I may add that I found Frederick Bishop a thoroughly trustworthy man and his statements to me, when tested by other evidence were always found to be true.

In interrogating the other Barbados men his presence might be of assistance.

I have etc. etc.

Roger Casement — Consul General

From Pará Casement sent his two Indian boys with Bishop on to Barbados hoping that the Reverend Frederick Smith S.J. would take them into his care at the Catholic church in Bridgetown. He gave Bishop a cheque for £20 to cover expenses. He hoped that under the care of the Church they would receive a little education and grounding in the ways of civilization before continuing to London.

On 17 December the Fôlha do Norte recorded the departure of R. Casement for Europe on board the Booth liner SS Ambrose. *Among other first class passengers were Capt. H.B. Kearney, M. Van der Est, Antonio Masseira, Roger Malter, Orvard Lorentzen,*[337] *Kraus*

[337] Casement's fellow passenger Orvard Lorentzen is mentioned on four separate occasions in the *Black Diary* although his name is spelt Laurensen.

Johnson, Luis Martins, Joaquin Romariz, Domingos Roths, Joaquin Velhote, Julien Fabre, Raul Perreira, Alfredo Duarte, Antonio Baptiste.

The only fragmentary entry relevant to this last leg of the voyage gives information about the Franco–Dutch trading Company, that Casement had learnt about in Iquitos and whose directors, Julien Fabre and M.C. Van der Est, returned with him to Europe. The fragmentary entry is dated "20 December 1910 while on board SS Ambrose*".[338]

On 30th Nov 1910 Julius Fabre and Macheli Petrus Van der Est wrote to the French consular agent at Iquitos protesting against action of the Peruvian authority of the Department of Loreto.

The letter states the case clearly without going into lengthy details.

The signatories represent an important Franco–Dutch Company which proposed to colonise and exploit the Oriente of Ecuador and Peru. Mons. Fabre had gone to Quito whence, with a special letter to the Prefect of Loreto from the Minister of Peru in Quito dated May 1910 he set out to descend the Amazon. He came by the Morona through savage Indian tribes, but was in no danger until when near the Marañon, at Huachi Yacu he encountered the first Peruvian establishment. This was on Sunday 18th September 1910 and he and his companions on the raft they floated down on met with a sharp fusillade from a concealed party in the forest.

M. Fabre arrived at Iquitos on 29th September on the Peruvian Government launch *Isabelita* commanded by Lt Faura and on 30 Sept he called on the Prefect and told him all his projects.

Nothing was said at all to show that any opposition would be offered — he handed in the letter of the Peruvian Minister at Quito — until SS *Manco* arrived bringing Captain Van der Est, with his steam launch and subordinates on 29 October. Then the trouble began. Capt. Van der Est wrote to the Captain of the port (C.G. Donayre) on 10 Nov — asking permission to put the launch (named *Henrietta* and expressly

---

The *Black Diary* also stressed that he was a "young Norwegian", an effort, no doubt, subliminally to associate his name with Adler Christensen, the shady manservant who accompanied Casement during his activities in Norway and Germany.

[338] N.L.I. MS 13,087 (26/i).

put under Peruvian flag) together on the bank. £787.10/- Gold had been lodged as security for customs duties and all imports brought by Capt. Van der Est had been declared before the Peruvian Consuls abroad at Hamburg and the Consular invoice brought to Iquitos.

The Captain of the port while pretending to give permission never permitted anything to be done — and as a matter of fact every warehouse in Iquitos likely to help the Franco–Dutch company was menaced and obliged to refuse all assistance.

The press started a campaign with threats of violence — and finally in view of the dangerous situation and the impossibility of proceeding or of ever getting their launch put together the two chiefs of the expedition decided to return to Europe and formally lodged their protest with the French Consular agent in Iquitos ...

... Capt Van der Est and Ms. Fabre left Iquitos on *Atahualpa* on 6th Dec — and transshipped onto *Ambrose* at Pará on 17th Dec for Cherbourg. They left their launch in Iquitos and the ten men brought out by Van der Est and Fabre.

Although undated, the only other document that might reasonably be considered to have been written on the homeward voyage is Casement's historical summing up of his investigation. The essay is drafted on the same double-sided foolscap as his Putumayo Journal *and fragmentary diary entries and scribbled in the same pencil. A fuller, although toned-down version of this essay was subsequently submitted with Casement's other reports to the Foreign Office in March 1911 but it was, for perhaps obvious reasons, not included in the Blue Book. The essay demonstrates Casement's deep understanding of South America's long historical tragedy. His comparison of the Amazon and Congo atrocities followed by his analysis of the different colonising methods of Europeans in the Americas was a good summary of the situation granted the tremendous anger he felt as he journeyed back to London with his dossier of evidence detailing the atrocities carried out on behalf of an Anglo–Peruvian rubber company.*[339]

The crimes of the Putumayo, or, as they should be called, the crimes of the Amazon basin, although today less in sum total than the recent crimes of the Congo basin, represent a

[339] Both essays are kept in N.L.I. MS 13,087 (31).

far older, more enduring and more fatal wrong to humanity than that mystery of evil called the Congo Free State. The Congo crime was an effort on the part of a European ruler to put back the clock; the Putumayo crime shows that on one of the Continents occupied for four hundred years by two European races, the clock was stopped four centuries ago.

In immediate cause and in infamy of origin the two crimes are alike, and their product the same — india rubber. But in the Congo case there was always hope, growing to certainty, of civilised intervention; in the Amazon's case there is no such hope.

Behind the exploitation of the Congo people stood only one sinister figure; but behind that figure stood a progressive and vigorous European people who, once the truth was brought home to them and a sense of their national responsibility aroused were sure, in the end, to convert their ruler's perverted conception of personal ownership of men into the juster forms of colonial tutelage.

At worst economic servitude is a great step upward from bodily slavery. Moreover, on the Congo there were from the first treaty rights to be invoked; and on the spot the machinery of civilised administration, efficiently misused to a selfish personal end, could always be turned to the purposes of collective welfare. The machinery was there and a question of its proper direction to the ends of civilisation and not to the fulfilment of one man's greed was certain, sooner or later, to be successfully raised. There were too, on the Congo, many active agencies of humanity — missions directed by able and far-seeing men (both Catholic and Protestant), whose protests could not forever be stilled or stifled; judicial officers and many courageous and dissatisfied administrators who knew that a change must come and who hoped to aid in its coming; foreign Consuls and the influence of neighbouring European States, and finally the certainty that Europe would not tolerate for ever the claim of one of her rulers to set up a vast slave camp where she had decreed that slavery should end and man should be free. (In a word on the Congo the resources of civilisation were not exhausted, and the virility of the Negro, that indestructible virility which has resisted so many and such prolonged assaults was certain to triumph in the twentieth century, over the lash and the chain gang of the sixteenth.)

These elements of hope were some of the factors which gave to Congo reform assurances of success over the heart-rending evils of the central African rubber trade. Alas, none of these guarantees of change can be found in the Amazons. The evil there is deeper and far older; and the remedy nowhere apparent or so remote as to have no bearing on the fate of the enslaved and disappearing Indian.

The failure of Europe and the Monroe Doctrine

Europe is impotent and irresponsible and on the spot there is no civilised people and central authority to be awakened to a sense of duty. There are no treaty rights, there is no public opinion to be invoked; no machinery of executive control to be set working in the right direction; no missions (or missions only in name, just as public officials exist only in name), no pressure of neighbouring states, or, in the end, the hope of European civilisation intervening to insist that the Amazons Indian shall be free. In Africa, Europe in the end counted for more than all the profits of the chain gang, but in South America there is no Europe. European opinion there has no existence, (to the South American states Europe stands only for an overseas banking establishment, useful to finance their development and in return to get large profits from the transaction — she may lend money but she must not give advice) and the United States, desiring not moral headship but commercial supremacy, has no word to speak in South America, for yet a hundred years, that will shock the slavers' susceptibilities. (And in that day the last Indian, the doomed descendant of the Incas, the survival of an earlier civilisation graced with much of the gentleness of soul our own culture has not been able to evoke will have thrown himself, face downwards, to the lash and died in order that some greedy "whiteman" may commit fresh immoralities in Paris or float a respectable Company in London.) Commercial civilisation and its mouthpiece the Monroe Doctrine assure full immunity to the criminal. Under these conditions South America becomes an ideal resort. This Continent, twice the size of Europe but with scarcely the population of one small island of Great Britain is privileged to repeat in the twentieth century the methods of the sixteenth, wherever the latterday "Conquistador" can find fresh native races to exploit.

The conceptions of Cortez and Pizarro are as vigorous today in many parts of the Amazon valley as when the first Iberian stepped on the shores of the New World. The only International understanding that exists (if such the Monroe Docrine can be called) is that the latter day slaver must on no account be interfered with by Europe lest American "freedom" be affronted.

Comparing the colonizing processes of North and South America

The valley of the Amazons covers an area fully two million square miles and the "commercial" product of this vast region has been first (and for centuries) Indians and latterly Indian rubber.

From the Discovery until, say, 1850 the Iberian settlers throughout that vast region went sword, and then gun, in hand in pursuit of Indian slaves. Within little over thirty years of the first coming of the Portuguese "more than two millions of Indians" — we are told by one of the early Jesuit fathers, Vieira[340] — "were slaughtered or killed by bad treatment in the province of Maranham [sic] alone". The intervention of the Portuguese crown and the efforts of the Jesuits to save and civilise the numerous Indian tribes along the course of the mighty river were in vain.

The Portuguese "colonist" wanted slaves, the vice of exploitation was in the Mediterranean blood. Neither Spaniard nor Portuguese went to the New World to colonise as the men and women of northern Europe went to the New England lands and the valley of the Mississippi to dwell. The one went to found a people, the other to find a people.

In both cases, it is true, the Indian suffered. From the English, the Dutch, the French, the Irish, the Redman retreated, defeated in fight and his lands appropriated. The plough drove back the tomahawk. The aboriginal was attacked because his presence was incompatible with the settlement of the European cultivator; and in a conflict of

[340] Antonio Vieira (1608–97), was a Jesuit preacher, orator, writer and defender of the rights of the Indians. Vieira dedicated a large part of his life in Brazil to defending the human rights of Brazilian Indians and speaking out against prevailing attitudes to slavery among the Portuguese colonizers. His sermons and letters are considered some of the great works of Baroque literature and were published in 1908 in fifteen volumes. He also wrote a book of prophecies, *Clavis Prophetarum*, published in 1718 under the title *História do Futuro*.

races, where the soil itself was the prize, the buffalo hunter and the forest warrior vanished before the log cabin and the trapper. The crime of enslaving the conquered had no part in the crime of the conquest. (The inevitable advance of the stronger and settled civilisation swept away the Indian hunting race — the school, the church and the hamlet of the white family replaced the wigwam, the squaw and the dog of the chivalrous savage. Today, where the northern European subdued the forest and broke up the plain one of the greatest nations of the earth has replaced the roving bands of redmen. The tragedy is there: and the generous heart of the white boy, if not the colder mind of the whiteman, throbs still with sympathy for the vanquished.)

But when we turn to the contact of the southern European, the Iberian, with the earlier peoples of the New World we find a wholly different conception of the white man's part and a wholly different end in view, with, it must be admitted, wholly different conditions to be faced.

The true problem for the Spaniard in the New World, and in a less degree for the Portuguese, was to govern the native races he had subdued. There was no question of colonising the conquered territories; the very climate itself forbade this, for the region was, to a great extent, unsuited to the white races. It was, moreover, unlike the northern areas where British and Dutch advanced, thickly peopled and inhabited by numerous races already, in many cases, far advanced in the path of civilisation. Great sovereigns, dwelling in tranquil cities beautified with palaces and temples among the most enduring memorials of human architectural achievement, ruled over vast agglomerations of obedient subjects. The handfuls of white pirates who overthrew their rule and destroyed these ancient states and thrones did not come with wife and child and plough to inhabit and cultivate a new soil. From the first the problem to them was one of government, not of colonisation; differing in detail but primarily the same as that of the English in India or the Dutch in Java.

The Iberian was unequal to the task. While incapable of colonising these vast tropical and sub-tropical regions he was still more incapable of governing the numerous native civilisations he found there. These he could only destroy; and the people who had built them up he could only think of as personal chattels never as fellow subjects or citizens of a common state. Statesmanship, or even rule as such, he never brought to the task. To justify his selfishness, his avarice, the Iberian prostituted his religion itself as a warrant for the exploiting instinct of his blood. The doomed Indian became an "infiele", an infidel, and so was put on a level with the animals, a thing to be personally owned and lashed without a twinge of conscience. In vain the church itself, its most Catholic Sovereign, the Council of the Indies, its fearless and often devoted missionaries protested and worked to save the doomed populations. It was from the first a bloodthirsty scramble of the best fighting men in Europe to get rich quick — a series of personal conflicts to enslave and pillage and make back to Madrid with the plunder. "Conquistador" succeeded "Conquistador", the cross of his sword-handle at once the warrant of his crimes, the surety of his conquest and the crucifix of the conquered. Whole peoples disappeared in a brief hell of slavery and suffering in order that these furious and ferocious filibusters might return to the Peninsula they had left as half-starved peasants with the pillage of the Indies, and wear a cross of gold in memory of a murdered Inca.

The avarice of that Carthaginian blood, so widely blended with the earlier Iberian, — a graft productive of the indifference to suffering and the callousness of pain which distinguish the Spanish from all other European peoples — pushed new Pizarros and new Orellanas further afield in search of an ever retreating El Dorado. Less than two hundred men set out from Cartagena, and pushing up the Magdalena river, scaled the hills and found, on the lofty tableland where now stands the city of Santa Fe de Bogotá a peaceful and exceedingly numerous people. Of a million of Indians estimated as dwelling on this healthy plateau when the boatload of pirates from the Spanish main fell upon them, in less than fifty years not one remained.

And the destruction thus wrought finds its expression after three hundred and fifty years of civilisation, in the impotent stagnation of the capital of the republic of Colombia, a town of perhaps one hundred thousand inert and unproductive human beings.

The great island of Hispaniola that Columbus found possessed by a numerous and gentle race sixty years after his landing showed only two million Indian graves and not one living Indian. But the worst doom of all fell on Peru. Here the

Inca rulers had built up a great state and governed it with a wisdom and humanity far in excess of anything found elsewhere in the New World.

From the time of Pizarro to the present day the Iberian invaders have succeeded in evolving no theory of government that took account of the subject peoples otherwise than as slaves or chattels. One has been accustomed to think that the cruelties and barbarities recorded in the conquest of Peru ceased three hundred years ago with the extermination of the Inca sovereign and nobility, and that, at least, with the coming of the republican form of government the foundation had been laid for a united citizenship, which should embrace Spaniard and Indian in a common bond of citizenship. But this has not been the case. For the first three hundred years it may be said only men landed from each successive squadron, and for centuries the Spanish element in Peru, Bolivia and Ecuador (the territory of the Incas) remained but a white handful. Their object in the great majority of cases, was not to settle in the country and to labour there, but through the labour of the native population, to obtain sufficient wealth to return to Spain. The functions of government began and ended with the enslavement of the native population, whether that enslavement was to take the form of working in the mines or upon the vast haciendas.

The natives were chattels and counted as part of the property that accrued to each free-booter through the strength of his own right arm. Their diminution in numbers was due not to the incoming of white races that, of necessity, had to get rid of incompatible neighbours and to occupy their lands but to the exactions laid upon them and the cruel forms of forced labour imposed to enrich a distant church and state and the present men whose eyes were turned always to Madrid.

Fifty years after Pizarro's conquest, fifty years of crushing exactions which had already slain millions of the Andean population, the Viceroy of Toledo found, by a census he had ordered to be taken, that he had still eight million Indian slaves at his disposal. How many had been already killed or had died under the atrocious regime of himself and his predecessors cannot be said, but it is certain that the Incas ruled an industrious population which must have numbered many millions of human beings.

From the days of Pizarro's conquest, diminution of the Indian population has steadily continued and along with their diminution their equally strong demoralisation. From such a past as this, brought down to the present by successive stages of human degradation, stepped the free-booters who twenty years ago "discovered" the Putumayo.

A docile, defenceless people, termed indeed savages because they went nude, were found by a canoeload of Colombian and Peruvian pirates, inhabiting a forest filled with the Hevea tree of modern commerce — the wild Pará rubber tree. Here the first tragedy of the first coming of the Castillians to the shores of the Pacific repeats itself on a far meaner stage and with far less imposing actors.

In place of the mail clad "crusaders" who stormed Tenochtitlan or laid low the great strongholds of Cuzco, in place of a Guatemoczin or an Atahualpa, we have a Julio Arana and his "chiefs of section" to waylay and entrap, to enslave and massacre the petty forest *caciques* and their child-like clans or families hidden in an underworld of trees. But in both cases it is the same instinct of avarice that propels, working through slavery and employing lawless force to its greedy personal end. Where the earlier Castilian royalist pillaged the Andean Civilisation with his eyes to Madrid, his modern republican prototype — assuredly a meaner type — ransacks the forest in search of slaves with his eyes on Lima.

Who is to blame?

To get rich quick in both cases, and in both cases by the rapid and crushing enslavement of a hapless subject people — this is the explanation of this longest, most sordid and assuredly most appalling tragedy of the contact of Christian civilisation with weaker peoples.

But the crime is not alone that of Spaniard and Peruvian.

Has our Christian civilisation itself no share in the blame? Has our modern commercialism, our latter-day company promoting — whose motto would seem to be that a Director may pocket the proceeds without perceiving the process — no part in this enterprise of horror and shame?

The Aranas "brought their wares (50,000 Indian Slaves) to market" in London. Not, be it observed, to Madrid or to Lima, but to London. And they found English men and English finance prepared without question to accept their

Putumayo "estates" and their numerous native "labourers" at a glance, a glance at the annually increasing output of rubber. Nothing beyond that was needed. The rubber was there. How it was produced, out of what a hell of human suffering no one knew, no one asked, no one suspected. Can it be no one cared?

Rubber clearly drops from thc trees and exudes by its own force, conveys itself down the sodden forest tracks to the river steamer and finally ships itself to Europe and no one is amazed at the prodigy.

Why blame the old Pizarros and the indifferent distant court of Spain? They at least were brave men and shed their own blood, the royal beneficiaries were shining figures on a stage where still the sword was mightier than the pen.

Today the paltry Pizzas of the Amazon woodlands and the Iquitos mart bring their wares to a far more ignoble market, and the product of the shambles becomes by a stroke of the pen, the surest evidence on which a Prospectus can be issued.

Instead of this, he has been from the first enslaved — driven with whips, forced by extortion, oppressed by lawless taxes and varying methods of forced labour to toil not for his own advantage or the advancement of his country but for the sole gain and personal profit of individuals who have ever placed their own desires above the common welfare until death came as sudden penalty for failing strength and non compliance or more quickly overtook them by the way in the form of starvation and disease.

On 31 December the SS Ambrosia *docked in Cherbourg and Casement continued to Paris to visit Herbert Ward for New Year. He explained his reasons for this change in plan in two letters sent to the Foreign Office on his return to England both written on 7th January.*

I left the *Ambrosia* at Cherbourg on 31 December and proceeded to Paris and came on to London on Wednesday 4th January.

Had I stayed on the *Ambrosia* I should not have reached Liverpool until 2nd January and could not have called the Foreign Office before the 3rd.

All expenditure on public account ceased with my landing at Cherbourg on 31st ultimo.

I telegraphed my likely movements from Iquitos on 28 November, indicating the date on which I should probably reach Pará, but I did not think it necessary to seek special sanction by telegraph for leaving the *Ambrosia* at Cherbourg, as at the date of landing there it seemed likely I should reach London quite as speedily as if I were to complete my journey by sea to Liverpool.

As, however, I remained in Paris longer than had been my intention and thus exceeded by two days the actual limit of time in which a journey could be effected, at the quickest, from the Putumayo to London I have the honour to request that special sanction may be given to the course followed for which a separate explanation is being furnished.[341]

FO 371/1200 — Consul-General Casement to Sir Edward Grey

110 Filbert Gardens
Earls Court
London SW

7 January 1911

Sir,

With reference to my immediately preceding letter recording my movements on my recent journey to and from the Putumayo district, I have the honour to state that I disembarked at Cherbourg on my way to London, on 31 ultimo and proceeded to Paris to visit friends for New Year.

I intended to proceed on Monday 2nd instant to London, which would have corresponded in point of time with the date of my arrival here had I continued my journey by sea in the ordinary course. As, however my friends had very special reasons for wishing me to remain over the night of Tuesday the 3rd instant and as His Majesty's Ambassador had invited me for luncheon on that day, I ventured to defer my departure until the morning train of Wednesday, the 4th instant, when I continued my journey to London arriving here in the course of that evening.

[341] Both letters are held in FO 371/1200 and contain information detailing the exact movements of Casement from the moment he left England in July to his return to London on 4 January 1911.

No expenditure of any kind has been incurred by this break in my journey — on the contrary a saving to public funds has been actually effected.

I would beg that sanction may be given to the course I followed, which has involved a loss of two days time in a long journey after several months of somewhat fatiguing travel.[342]

---

[342] The Black *Letts's Desk Diary* for 1911 also has its first entry on 1 January 1911. Comparison between the last entry in the 1910 diary and the first entry in the 1911 once again shows a startling difference in the handwriting. Both ink and style differ noticeably. It is also rather difficult to explain exactly where such a diary might have come into the possession of its supposed author.

BIBLIOGRAPHICAL NOTE

Further information required by the reader can be requested through the publishers' web-sites (http://www.anaconda.win-uk.net/ and http://indigo.ie/~lilliput) where relevant excerpts from the *Black Diary* for 1910 are available for those interested in making their own comparisons with *The Amazon Journal*. The web-sites will also serve as a forum for debate on the subject and will include reviews and articles relevant to Casement and his humanitarian investigations.

*

All references to the collections of papers held at the National Library of Ireland, in the Public Record Office at Kew, Rhodes House Library, the National Archive of Ireland, London School of Economics and at the Franciscan Library at Killiney have been detailed in the text.

Some of the statements collected by Hardenburg and part of Casement's report were published in W.E. Hardenburg, *The Putumayo; The Devil's Paradise – Travels in the Peruvian Amazon Region and an Account of the Atrocities Committed Upon the Indians Therein* (Fisher Unwin 1912). The Company prospectus, allegedly written by Eugenio Robuchon, *En el Putumayo y sus afluentes* (Lima 1907), is a rare book. Casement's annotated copy is in the N.L.I. There is a microfilmed copy at the Bodleian Library, Oxford. The copy at the British Library has disappeared.

Unfortunately there is not enough space within this volume to go into the whole economic and social background of South America and the Amazon rubber boom in the detail it deserves. Those who wish to know more should consult Barbara Weinstein, *The Amazon Rubber Boom 1850–1920* (Stanford 1983) and, for a more botanical and environmental interpretation, Warren Dean, *Brazil and the Struggle for Rubber* (Cambridge University Press 1987). A fine bibliography is to be found in G. Pennano, *La economía del caucho* (Iquitos 1988). Howard and Ralph Wolf, *Rubber: A Story of Glory and Greed* (New York 1936), despite the purple prose, is a good overall account of the rubber industry. More generalized background to the socio-economic history of the period is found in Leslie Bethell (ed.), *The Cambridge History of Latin America*, volumes IV and V. A more accessible recent history on South America is Edwin Williamson, *The Penguin History of Latin America* (The Penguin Press 1992). John Hemming has written the most comprehensive books about the destruction of the Brazilian Indians in his works *Red Gold: The Conquest of the Brazilian Indians* (Macmillan 1978) and *Amazon Frontiers – The Defeat of the Brazilian Indians* (Macmillan 1987).

Britain published a vast number of books on South America during the Edwardian Age and there is a wide choice of relevant travel writing. H.M. Tomlinson, *The Sea and the Jungle* (London 1912), is a well-written account of an Amazon river journey undertaken at the end of 1909; Algot Lange, *The Lower Amazon* (1914) and *In the Amazon Jungle* (1910), are good topographical accounts. An interesting memoir is John Yungjohann, *White Gold: The Diary of a Rubber Cutter in the Amazon 1906–16* (Synergetic Press 1989). Equally informative is *Lizzie: A Victorian Lady's Amazon Adventure*, compiled by Tony Morrison, Ann Brown and Anne Rose (British Broadcasting Corporation 1985). The British Ambassador in Washington, James Bryce, made a journey through South America at the end of 1910 and wrote about it in *South America – Observations and Impressions* (Macmillan 1912). Among the evangelizing missionaries, Geraldine Guinness, *Peru – Its Story, People and Religion* (Morgan and Scott 1909) is the most balanced.

No people on earth have been anthropologized to the same degree as the tribes of the Amazon rainforest. Among accounts contemporary to Casement's investigation is Thomas Whiffen, *The North-West Amazon – Notes of Some Months Spent among Cannibal Tribes* (Constable and Co. 1915). Whiffen edited out his own suspicions of atrocities and despite the book being published in 1915 there is no mention of Casement's investigation or the death of a single Indian. Indicative, perhaps, that there were forces at play trying to cover up Casement's Amazon revelations well in advance of his capture. Whiffen borrowed much from the legendary German anthropologist Theodor Koch-Grunberg, *Zwei Jahre unter den Indianern: Reisen in Nordwest Brasilien, 1903–1905* 2 vols (Berlin 1910). After the First World War Rafael Karsten, *The Civilization of the South American Indians – with special reference to Magic and Religion* (Kegan Paul 1926), gave civilized status to tribal customs and habits; Rafael Girard, *Indios selváticos de la Amazonía peruana* (Mexico 1958) and the seven volumes of *The Handbook of South American Indians* (Smithsonian Institution, Bureau of Ethnology), are all of interest. Claude Lévi-Strauss, *Tristes Tropiques* (Jonathan Cape 1973) is the best place to begin understanding the structural anthropology of the South American tribal world.

More recent anthropological accounts of the region have been led by Michael Taussig, *Shamanism, Colonialism and the Wild Man – A Study in Terror and Healing* (The University of Chicago Press 1987). His work contains an exhaustive bibliography relevant to the period and the Putumayo region. Michael Brown and Eduardo Fernandez, *War of Shadows – The Struggle for Utopia in the Peruvian Amazon* (University of California Press 1992), interprets the millennial issues; Roger Rumrrill, *Vidas mágicas de tunchis y curanderos*, is one of a number of works by the main Peruvian activist. Also of tremendous value is Gerardo Reichel-Dolmatoff's works including *Amazonian Cosmos – The Sexual and Religious Symbolism of the Tukano Indians* (The University of Chicago Press 1971); Stephen Hugh-Jones, *The Palm and the Pleiades: Initiation and Cosmology in Northwest Amazonia* (Cambridge University Press 1979). Of the increasing number of ethnobotanists currently exploring the Amazon in search of miracle cures and medicinal secrets of the tribal shaman none will ever match the stature of Richard Evans Schultes, *Where the Gods Reign – Plants and People of the Colombia Amazon* (Synergetic Press 1988) and Richard Evans Schultes and Robert Raffauf, *Vine of the Soul – Medicine Men, their Plants and Rituals in the Colombian Amazon* (Synergetic Press 1992).

The Putumayo atrocities have been fictionalized in José Eustacio Rivera, *La vorágine* (1924, translated as *The Vortex)*, considered the most important work of Colombian literature until the publication of *Cien años de soledad* by Gabriel García Márquez. In English, Richard Collier fictionalized the story of Hardenburg's adventures in *The River that God Forgot – The*

Story of the Amazon Rubber Boom (Collins 1968). The story of rubber received similar treatment from Vicki Baum, *The Weeping Wood* (Michael Joseph 1945).

My own awareness of this subject was greatly influenced by a number of investigative journalists whose work led me into the whole rubber controversy and our collective need to fight for the preservation of the forested frontiers and tribal lands of the Amazon. Adrian Cowell, *The Decade of Destruction* (A Channel Four Book 1990); Mac Margolis, *The Last New World, The Conquest of the Amazon Frontier* (W.W. Norton 1992); Andrew Revkin, *The Burning Season – The Murder of Chico Mendes and the Fight for the Amazon Rain Forest* (Houghton Mifflin 1990); Alex Shoumatoff, *Murder in the Rain Forest – The Chico Mendes Story* (Fourth Estate 1991); George Monbiot, *Amazon Watershed* (Michael Joseph 1991); Susanna Hecht and Alexander Cockburn, *The Fate of the Forest Developer – Destroyers and Defenders of the Amazon* (Verso 1989).

INDEX

To one I love
I dedicate this song—
That she may know how strong
The bond that binds me is
Where'er I rove.

Time's hand may not untie
One strand that love hath wove,
Nor death can sever
My heart from thine—
For tho' the heart may die
The love that bids it beat shall live for ever.

Roger Casement

Angus Mitchell

was born in Nanyuki, Kenya, in1962 and finished his formal education reading history at Oriel College, Oxford. He is the author of *Spain: Interiors, Gardens, Architecture, Landscape* (1990) and *The Shell Guide to Spain* (1992). In 1992 he moved to South America to investigate the Amazon rubber industry and tribal extermination, resulting in his study of Casement. He also researched and developed the film *Carlota Joaquina, Princess of Brazil* (1995), and now tends a farmstead in the highlands above Rio de Janeiro. A companion volume of Casement's documents, *Roger Casement's Heart of Darkness*, dealing with his second voyage up the Amazon in 1911, will be published in 1998.

The Roger Casement Foundation presents

Casement

Angus Mitchell
will read from "The Amazon Journal of Roger Casement" and talk about the work and Casement's humanitarian achievements.

The Transatlantic Theatre Company
will present an abridged version of Jack Moylett's epic drama "Casement".

The Roger Casement Foundation
621 North Circular Road, Dublin 1
Tel: 01-836 3133   e-mail: transand@indigo.ie
Further Casement info: http://www.anaconda.win-uk.net